GLOBAL MASCULINITIES

SERIES EDITOR Michael S. Kimmel

Men face common issues – the balance between work and family, fatherhood, defining masculinity in a globalizing economy, health and reproduction, sexuality and violence. They are confronting these issues all over the world in very different contexts and are coming up with different priorities and strategies to address them. This new international series provides a vehicle for understanding this diversity, and reflects the growing awareness that analysis of masculinity will be greatly impoverished if it remains dominated by a European/North American/Australian matrix. A number of regional and thematic cross-cultural volumes are planned.

Michael S. Kimmel is a well-known educator on gender issues. His work has appeared in numerous magazines, newspapers and scholarly journals, including the *New York Times Book Review*, *Harvard Business Review*, *The Nation* and *Psychology Today*, where he was a contributing editor and columnist on male–female relationships. His teaching examines men's lives from a pro-feminist perspective. He is national spokesperson for the National Organization for Men Against Sexism (NOMAS) in the United States.

Titles in the series

Robert Morrell (ed.), *Changing Men in Southern Africa*
Bob Pease and Keith Pringle (eds.), *A Man's World? Changing Men's Practices in a Globalized World*
Frances Cleaver (ed.), *Masculinities Matter! Men, Gender and Development*
Lahoucine Ouzgane (ed.), *Islamic Masculinities*
Adam Jones (ed.), *Men of the Global South: A Reader*

About this book

Men of the Global South: A Reader is the most diverse and accessible volume yet published on men and masculinities throughout the developing world. A Reader that also offers a wide range of original contributions, it explores male experience in a uniquely vivid and accessible way. Adam Jones provides a framing introduction that surveys the growing literature on Southern men and masculinities, and links it to the broader study of gender and development. Six main sections portray different aspects of male experience in the global South: "Family and Sexuality," "Ritual and Belief," "Work," "Governance and Conflict," "Migrations," and "Masculinities in Motion." The text, richly complemented by a number of photographs, serves as an ideal introduction to the lives of men and boys from Africa, the Middle East, Asia, and Latin America/ the Caribbean. This book will appeal to students and scholars of gender and development, as well as to general readers interested in gaining a greater understanding and appreciation of men's roles, challenges, and contributions worldwide.

About the editor

Adam Jones, Ph.D., is Associate Research Fellow in the Genocide Studies Program at Yale University. His most recent book is *Genocide: A Comprehensive Introduction.* He has edited two further books on genocide and authored two on mass media and political transition. His writings on gender and international politics have appeared in *Review of International Studies, Ethnic and Racial Studies, Journal of Human Rights* and other publications.

Men of the Global South

A Reader

Edited by Adam Jones

ZED BOOKS
London & New York

Men of the Global South: A Reader
was first published in 2006 by Zed Books Ltd.,
7 Cynthia Street, London N1 9JF, UK
and Room 400, 175 Fifth Avenue, New York, NY 10010, USA

Cover designed by Andrew Corbett
Typeset by Exeter Premedia Services Private Ltd., Chennai, India
Printed and bound in Malta by Gutenberg Press Ltd.

Distributed in the United States exclusively by Palgrave Macmillan,
a division of St. Martin's Press, LLC, 175 Fifth Avenue,
New York 10010, USA

A catalogue record for this book is available from the British Library.
Library of Congress Cataloging-in-Publication Data available.

ISBN 1 84277 512 X Hb
ISBN 1 84277 513 8 Pb

ISBN-13: 978 1 84277 512 7 Hb
ISBN-13: 978 1 84277 513 4 Pb

Contents

Acknowledgments   ix

INTRODUCTION   Worlding Men   xii

PART 1   Family and Sexuality

Hasiba and Qasim   *Muhsin Al-Ramli*   3

Poems of Desire   *N.M. Rashed, translated and introduced by A. Sean Pue*   6

Grandfather Ernesto   *Ana Ruiz-Fodor*   14

Four Lives   *Leslie Lewis*   17

The Men of Bwaise   *Robert Wyrod*   21

Fathers and Children   *Matthew C. Gutmann*   28

Men and Their Children   *Stella Nyanzi*   34

Infertile Men   *Marcia C. Inhorn*   38

Viagra and Changing Masculinities   *Emily Wentzell*   43

Urges and Affairs   *Matthew C. Gutmann*   47

Lovers vs. Wives   *Thomas Michael Walle*   50

Virginity and Masculinity   *Iklim Goksel*   55

The Kurdish Child   *Metin Yüksel*   58

Widow Inheritance   *Stella Nyanzi*   60

The Abusers   *S. Anandhi and J. Jeyaranjan*   64

Revisioning Male Violence   *Juan Carlos Ramírez Rodriguez*   67

Founding Fathers   *Louise Williams*   71

The Home Worker   *Javier Pineda*   72

The Polyandrists   *Rakesh K. Simha*   75

Crossovers   *David D. Gilmore*   77

Out in Africa   *Shuaib Rahim*   78

Gays, AIDS, and Homophobia   *Monica Campbell*   81

The Eunuchs   *Vinod Behl*   84

The Orphans   *Nicole Hallett*   86

The Street Child   *Lutaa Badamkhand*   88

PART 2   Ritual and Belief

The Initiate   *Nelson Mandela*   92

Circumcision: The Victims   *Chris McGreal*   95

The Cattle Thieves   *Solomon Moore*   96

The Hunters   *Niki Kandirikirira*   98

The Wrestlers   *David D. Gilmore*   99
The Fight Clubbers   *Guy Saville*   100
The Room Salon   *Jungbong Choi*   104
The Regulars   *Gary Brana-Shute*   110
The Good Samaritan   *Abel Polese*   113
Abuelita and Lalo   *Tlahtoki Aguirre*   118
The Monk and the Exorcist   *Bhante Wimala*   122
The Key   *Dina Dahbany-Miraglia*   126
The Healer   *Jan Jansen*   129
The Fixer   *Maria del Nevo*   131
The Aboriginal Elder   *Peter Collins*   133
Vodou Magus   *Donald Cosentino*   137

PART 3   Work

The Struggle   *Davan Maharaj*   144
Work Amidst Anarchy   *Mahamut Issa Abdi*   145
The Miners (1)   *Joseph Kahn*   148
The Miners (2)   *Domitila Barrios de Chungara*   151
The Shipbreakers   *William Langewiesche*   153
The Cane Cutters   *Elizabeth Oglesby*   160
The Lobster Divers   *Giovanna Tassi*   162
The Migrants   *Socialistworld.net*   164
The Camel Jockeys   *Phil Reeves*   168
The Slaves   *Osha Gray Davidson*   169
The Sex Worker   *Bangkok Post*   175
The Sewer-Divers   *Marla Dickerson*   177
The Organ Seller   *Larry Rohter*   179
The Shoe-Shine Boy   *Assane Diallo*   183
The Doorkeeper   *Ryszard Kapuscinski*   184
The Entrepreneur   *Abraham McLaughlin*   186
The Bus Driver   *Kevin Sullivan*   187
The Motoboys   *Larry Rohter*   189
The Guitar Maker   *Monica Campbell*   192
The Dancer   *Lynn Maalouf*   193
Okello Kelo Sam: Artist and Activist   *Dixie Beadle*   195

PART 4   Governance and Conflict

The Big Man   *David D. Gilmore*   203
The Mzee   *Amy Berson*   204
The Mossi Chief   *Sabine Luning*   208
The Creole Master   *Douglas Midgett*   211

CONTENTS

The Warlord   *Mark MacKinnon*   215

The Autocrat   *Guy Podoler*   217

"Dear Leader"   *Peter Maass*   220

The Emperor and the Lackey   *Ryszard Kapuscinski*   223

The Criminals   *Heather Hamilton*   225

Manhood and Violence   *Tom Odhiambo*   226

Gangs and Activists   *Suren Pillay*   229

The Lynching Victims *Maria-Victoria Benevides and Rosa-Maria Fischer Ferreira*   233

The Murdered Men of Ciudad Juárez   *Adam Jones*   235

Where Are the Men?   *Marion Birch*   237

The Gay Man   *Josh Hammer*   239

The Targets (1)   *Gary Younge*   242

The Targets (2)   *Jon Jeter*   244

The Targets (3)   *Doug Struck and Keith B. Richburg*   246

"Other Kids Get Killed Too"   *Anna Politkovskaya*   248

The Tortured   *Dinyar Godrej*   250

The Executed   *Mario I. Aguilar*   252

The Prisoners   *Michael Wines*   253

The Brothers   *T. Christian Miller*   257

The Killers   *Jean Hatzfeld*   263

The Soldier-Rapists   *Chris Dolan*   266

Bearing Arms   *Jason E. Strakes*   267

Military Masculinities   *Mona Bhan*   269

The Conscript (1)   *Ewan MacAskill*   272

The Conscript (2)   *Irina Vainovski-Mihai*   273

The Conscript (3)   *Luke Harding*   275

The Conscript (4)   *David Cho*   276

The Conscript (5)   *Kelly Cogswell*   277

The Recruit   *Ashraf Khalil*   279

The Green Card Marine   *Monica Campbell*   281

The Rebel   *Metasebia Woldemariam*   283

The Child Soldiers   *Human Rights Watch*   288

The *Sicario*   *Alonso Salazar*   293

The "Collaborators"   *Justin Huggler and Sa'id Ghazali*   296

The Suicide Bomber   *Ian Fisher*   297

The Guerrilla   *Cameron W. Barr*   299

PART 5   Migrations

Jack-of-All-Trades   *Robert Lacville*   304

Migration and Song   *Smita Tewari Jassal*   306

Migration and Return   *Madia Thomson*   311

The Migrant (1)   *Nargis Nurullo-Khoja*   313

The Migrant (2)   *Naeem Mohaiemen*   319

The Migrant (3)   *Ginger Thompson*   322

The Migrant as "Terrorist"   *Salman Masood*   324

"The Cemetery of the Living"   *Djaffer Ait Aoudia*   326

The Refugee (1)   *Tajudeen Abdulraheem*   329

The Refugee (2)   *Shukria Dini*   331

Pakistanis in Britain   *Ali Nobil Ahmad*   336

Being 49 at Russell Square   *Shyamal Bagchee*   341

Masculine Migrations   *Bob Pease*   343

The Palestinian Israeli   *Magid Shihade*   349

Brooklyn Panyard   *Knolly Moses*   354

The Islamist   *Aje Carlbom*   356

The Music Lover   *Maria del Nevo*   360

Knowing Truth   *Nate Haken*   362

PART 6   Masculinities in Motion

The Pashtun Man   *Abdul-Karim Khan*   368

Right-Wing Men   *Margaret Power*   372

Yorùbá Men, Yorùbá Women   *George Olusola Ajibade*   375

Boys Becoming Men   *Jane Gilbert*   376

The Brothers   *Don Conway-Long*   382

Gender and Generations   *S. Anandhi, J. Jeyaranjan, and Rajan Krishnan*   387

White Masculinities   *Daniel Conway*   393

"A Rebellious Male Youth"   *Sofía Montenegro*   398

A Dialogue with Masculinity   *Mark Clifford and Susan P. Mains*   401

Husbands, Fathers, and AIDS   *Janet Bujra*   405

AIDS, Rape, and Masculine Crisis   *Kerry Cullinan*   407

Working Together   *Alex Doniach and Dean Peacock*   410

Global Man, Southern Star   *Nandi Ayo Bole*   415

About the Original Contributors   418

Table

The discourse of gender: a comparison of hits for search strings
utilizing the Google search engine (3 January 2006)   xiii

Acknowledgments

It is a pleasure to be able to thank those who have contributed to the publication of this work. First, naturally, I owe an enormous debt to the dozens of contributors whose work you will read in these pages – both the authors of original essays, and the many freelance writers and media outlets who have allowed me to reprint previously published materials free of charge. Special thanks to the excellent magazine *New Internationalist*, from which a number of selections are drawn.

For copyright fees I was fortunate to receive a grant from the Ford Foundation, to whom my thanks are due, especially to Dr. Irma McClaurin for the interest she took in the project. Also most generous was Ferrel M. Christensen of the Gender Issues Education Foundation, who first got me interested in issues of men and masculinities, and who made a substantial contribution to production costs aimed at keeping the price of this book in a manageable range. Jo and David Jones also contributed a significant sum to this end, while a number of original contributors to the volume chipped in donations to Book Aid International, which will permit *Men of the Global South* to find a home in libraries of the South that could not otherwise afford to purchase it. For my part, I have declined all cash royalties from the project.

I am deeply grateful to Zed Books for its commitment to *Men of the Global South*, beginning with Robert Molteno, who commissioned it. Anna Hardman, who took over the project, proved as kind and capable an editor as one could hope for. Both she and Anne Rodford in production were supportive as the project evolved to include a far greater number of original contributions than originally planned, with resulting delays in editing and final submission.

I finished the book while on a two-year fellowship to the MacMillan Center at Yale University. I very much appreciate the support extended by Center Director Ian Shapiro and Associate Director Nancy Ruther.

My heartfelt thanks to colleagues and close friends who have accompanied and supported me during some two decades of investigation into the lives of Southern men. A long list of names would be dull to read, so I will limit myself to a bare compendium, with apologies for any oversights: Atenea Acevedo, Carla Bergman, David Buchanan, R. Charli Carpenter, Terrell Carver, Ferrel Christensen, Augusta Del Zotto, Øystein Gullvåg Holter, Tamil Kendall, Michael Kimmel, Evelin Lindner, John Margesson, Fabiola Martínez, Peter Prontzos, Griselda Ramírez, Hamish Telford, and Miriam Tratt.

As always, my deepest debt is to my family, who know me best and love me anyway. My parents, Jo and David, and my brother Craig are perennial inspirations.

It is every author's wish that a publisher will commission a second edition of his or her work. If *Men of the Global South* is so favored, I would hope to prepare an entirely new volume that again combines original and reprinted work. Readers have a vital role to play here. If you know of materials that fit the theme, or wish to propose an original contribution, please write to me at **adamj_jones@hotmail.com**.

Adam Jones

PERMISSIONS

The publisher gratefully acknowledges the permission of the following to reprint materials in this book:

INTRODUCTION

Worlding Men

Adam Jones

In the past three or four decades, an enormous literature – overwhelmingly feminist in orientation – has emerged on the subject of "gender."[1] Originally concentrated upon women of the industrialized West, it gradually expanded to recognize and include the contributions of women of the global South. In this process of "worlding women,"[2] the literature grew increasingly skeptical of generalizations about women as a global class and more attuned to how other variables (notably race and social status) shaped women's experiences worldwide.

This increasing attention to Southern women gave rise, in the early 1970s, to the study of "women in development" (WID), which aimed to counter the perceived inattention to women in development policy and discourse. Proponents of the WID approach called for specific policy initiatives aimed at women and greater female representation in the policy process. Since the early 1990s, the WID framework has gradually given way to the study of gender and development (GAD), which "call[s] for 'gender relations' (rather than women) to be adopted as the primary analytical tenet, and for the integration of a gender perspective in all development activities, and at all levels of the development planning process."[3]

In theory, GAD frameworks provide greater space for the study of "the other side" of the gender coin: that of men and masculinities. But early attempts to broach this theme aroused considerable suspicion and hostility among feminists. Sarah White recalls the response to the first paper she presented on the subject in the early 1990s:

> The first respondent liked it, but as he was the only man in the room, I feared this did not bode well. I was right. The following speakers rained a torrent of accusations on me: my talk was offensive appeasement; I was a sell-out, not a proper feminist; once we started talking about men, women would be crowded out, because men love talking about themselves; what I was suggesting was like fraternising with the bosses rather than holding the line in trades union militancy. Quietly, later, often younger women came to me to say that they had been waiting for someone to speak as I had, that they warmly welcomed this breaking of the silence on men. . . . Those early objections suggested that to talk about men and masculinity was *dangerous*, risking the hard-won gains of feminism and chronically open to co-option, since patriarchal

values and practices remain dominant in both society and development institutions, overdetermining all talk and action.

"That was seven years ago," White writes, "and a lot has changed."[4] Among the changes is the arrival in academia of the generation of "younger women" to whom White refers. The new generation appears less suspicious of, and more sympathetic to, the study of men and masculinities, as indicated by the large number of female and feminist authors represented in these pages. Such scholarship, though, seems far ahead of actual development policy and its implementation, which continues to identify "gender issues" almost exclusively with women and femininities. Even in the field of academic and activist discourse, it is debatable whether much has changed. The study of GAD, along with related subject areas like gender and conflict or gender and human rights, retains an "overwhelming preoccupation with women."[5]

A sense of the disparity in the discourse of gender is conveyed by an Internet search using the Google search engine, which allows the researcher to search for specific strings of words, within quotation marks – for example, *"gender and development"* as opposed to *gender and development*. This ensures that the results include all the words (including common words like "and" that are normally not included in searches), in the desired order.

Table The discourse of gender: a comparison of hits for search strings utilizing the Google search engine (3 January 2006)

Google search string	Hits
"gender and development"	505,000
"women and development"	189,000
"men and development"	734
"women in the developing world"	44,600
"men in the developing world"	453
"women and international development"	12,700
"men and international development"	3 [!]
"Third World women"	109,000
"Third World men"	339
"women and poverty"	72,100
"men and poverty"	175
"underprivileged women"	26,800
"underprivileged men"	314
"women and economic"	32,900
"men and economic"	274
"women and social"	207,000
"men and social"	9,610

continued

Table *continued.*

Google search string	Hits
"women and gender"	1,170,000
"men and gender"	23,100
"women and children"	17,500,000
"men and children"	534,000
"men, women and children"	3,820,000
"women, men and children"	329,000
"women and conflict"	12,100
"gender and conflict"	33,800
"men and conflict"	234
"women and human rights"	82,300
"men and human rights"	157
"women's vulnerability"	28,500
"men's vulnerability"	291

The disparities shown in the Table are striking, sometimes mind-boggling. Note, for example, that a search for "women and international development" generates *over 4,000 times* as many hits as "men and international development."[6] Clearly, the discourse of men and development is at an incipient stage of "thinkability," contrasted with the extensive attention devoted to women (or "womenandchildren").[7] This is true as well for discourses of gender and violence or gender and human rights. With reference to the latter, the hits for "women and human rights" outnumber those for "men and human rights" more than 500-fold.

Following upon feminist framings of gender, and largely derivative of them, a body of literature emerged on men and masculinities. Like the first wave of feminist writing in the 1960s and 1970s, it was overwhelmingly focused on men in the industrialized North.[8] But a few pioneers undertook the task of "worlding men," as this volume also seeks to do. Here, I want to touch briefly on a few milestones along the path to the present work.

An obscure but groundbreaking work is *Men At Risk*, by the Jamaican scholar Errol Miller, published in 1991. This may be the first systematic analysis of Southern men *by* a Southern scholar (and man). It also adopted a global–historical, richly theoretical framework that was, and is, unusual in the literature.[9] Miller offered a radical reappraisal of patriarchy as a form of social organization, an analysis of contemporary social change in the West and the former Soviet bloc, and a stimulating discussion of demographic transformations that were underway in the Caribbean. He also argued for an approach that "located social formations in the Caribbean not just in the mainstream of changes in the world but in the very forefront," and in doing so defied the "chauvinism and arrogance of the current world order." Among the most far-reaching of these changes were those in power relations between Caribbean women and men, exemplified by women's dramatic gains in the areas of income and education. Miller explored the increasingly peripheral presence of men in "matrifocal" families, the rise of gang and random violence, male alcoholism, and Jamaican men's retreat into patriarchal Rastafarianism. "In a real sense," he wrote, "some marginalized men appear to have internalized the forces arrayed against them and have engaged in their own self-destruction, as well as turning their violence outward."

The global–historical dimension of Miller's analysis was also novel. He argued that "from antiquity," patriarchy had "had an inherent problem with men not covered by the bonds of kinship or culture and has traditionally sought to marginalize them through diverse means." He discussed institutions like the "killing [of] all male captives," the castration of men whose lives were spared, and the reduced "opportunities for manumission from slavery" offered to men. All of these, for Miller, "show[ed] that *men's domination of men outside the bonds of kinship and community has been more severe and brutal than men's domination of women within or outside the kin or ethnic group.*"[10] It was not necessary to accept the author's somewhat awkward "marginalization hypothesis" (that women's increasing opportunities were intimately connected to some men's marginalization) to appreciate the scope of his interests and the sweep of his analysis.

It is not surprising that much of the best work on men and masculinities in the developing world in the last decade and a half has been done by anthropologists.[11] These investigators have always placed far greater emphasis on fieldwork and engaged understanding than have sociologists, political scientists, and theorists of international relations. One of the earliest, and still one of the most concise and stimulating, of these ethnographies is Gary Brana-Shute's *On the Corner: Male Social Life in a Paramaribo Creole Neighborhood* (1979), which claimed that studies of the West Indian Creole society had "been biased by an analytical and methodological concentration upon women and their children." Brana-Shute wrote: "Personnel, usually adult males, not regularly appearing within the boundaries of four walls and a roof are overlooked or written off as 'absent participants,' 'street corner men,' and the like."[12] He also adopted a transgressive strategy by studying Surinamese male social interaction in precisely the environment – the neighborhood drinking-spot, or *winkel* – that was much demonized in the feminist activism and scholarship of the 1980s. The result was a sensitive, wide-ranging ethnography that in retrospect seems ahead of its time. *On the Corner* has recently fallen out of print, but I am delighted to be able to reproduce an extended excerpt from the text, with the kind permission of Brana-Shute's widow, Rosemary (see p. 110).

In the mid-1990s, three important developing-world ethnographies joined the literature: T. Dunbar Moodie's *Going for Gold: Men, Mines, and Migration* (1994, focusing on Southern Africa); Roger N. Lancaster's *Life is Hard: Machismo, Danger, and the Intimacy of Power in Nicaragua* (also 1994), which sensitively explored both gender and homosexuality in a Central American context; and Matthew C. Gutmann's *The Meanings of Macho* (1996), about male lives in the working-class suburb of Santo

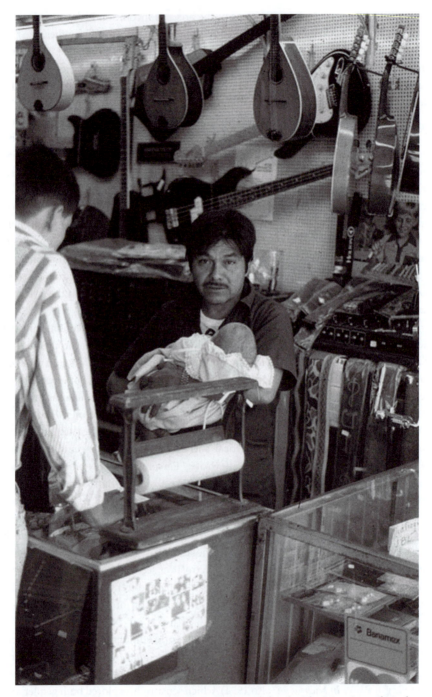

Photo used on the cover of Matthew C. Gutmann's book, *The Meanings of Macho: Being a Man in Mexico City* (Matthew C. Gutmann)

Domingo in Mexico City. All three provided extraordinarily intimate portraits of ordinary men in their roles as fathers, laborers, and lovers. Gutmann in particular has become a central figure in the social–scientific study of men and masculinities; two excerpts from *The Meanings of Macho* appear in this volume. The book's subversive message was conveyed by its cover, a photo depicting one of Gutmann's contacts holding a baby in his arms. Gutmann's research led him to reject "widely accepted generalizations about male gender identities in Mexico [that] often seemed egregious stereotypes about machismo."[13] In a child-positive culture like Mexico's, there were few impediments to the active and multifaceted involvement of men in childrearing: "It is not the case that men are seen as necessarily less tender or caring."[14] Gutmann also devoted considerable space to the darker side of Mexican men and masculinities – domestic violence, drunkenness, promiscuity, and family abandonment. But his book, like those of Moodie and Lancaster, was a welcome tonic: a validation of aspects of male experience that had previously been ignored or derided.

Gutmann went on to co-author one of the first systematic evaluations of men's place in the development process, a 2001 working paper for Oxfam titled *Mainstreaming Men into Gender and Development*.[15] A year earlier, Frances Cleaver had gathered a diverse set of scholars for a seminar at Bradford University on "Men, Masculinities and Gender Relations in Development," papers from which were subsequently published as *Masculinities Matter!*, part of the groundbreaking Global Masculinities series from Zed Books.[16] The series also included Bob Pease and Keith Pringle's edited volume, *A Man's World? Changing Men's Practices in a Globalized World* (2001) and a collection edited by one of the trailblazing men's studies scholars in the South, Robert Morrell (*Changing Men in Southern Africa*, also 2001).[17]

Another significant work is a special issue of *Forced Migration Review* on "Gender and Displacement," edited by Judy El-Bushra and David Turton and published in 2000.[18] This included some thought-provoking meditations on the male refugee experience, with titles like "Vindicating Masculinity: The Fate of Promoting Gender Equality" (Simon Turner) and "Making Young Displaced Men Visible" (Cathrine Brun). In her introduction, El-Bushra explored the shift from the WID framework to GAD and stressed the blind spots of the latter. An aim of the special issue, she wrote, was

> to articulate, more firmly and actively than in the past, the position of men within gender-analytical frameworks. This is a reaction to GAD's almost exclusive preoccupation over the last ten years or more with women's needs, interests and rights. If "gender" [now] implies a web of relationships between women and men, old and young, powerful and powerless, should men not figure, integrally and equally, in the analysis of these relationships? . . . There may be negative consequences for both women and men if they are not. Giving preference to women in assistance programmes may contribute to eroding men's role (as protectors, providers and decision makers, for example) and hence their social position and self-esteem but still not challenge the dominant gender ideology in which men's and women's roles are both viewed as 'natural.' . . . Does the stress on women prevent us from recognizing

discrimination by men against men (older versus younger men, for example, or men from different classes or ethnicities), women against women (when women collude in promoting gender discrimination against each other) and women against men? Can women's rights be supported within a context of broader developmental and humanitarian goals or do men inevitably have to lose when women gain? In short, where do men fit within a gender approach to development?

There can be few more succinct statements of a gender-inclusive agenda for development research.

El-Bushra has also contributed to a broader trend worth citing. Over the past decade or so, scholars of international relations have detailed and problematized the analysis of gender and conflict. Once again, Zed Books has led the way, with its "Women and Violence" series, which in fact casts its net more widely than the title suggests. El-Bushra's chapter on "Transforming Conflict: Some Thoughts on a Gendered Understanding of Conflict Processes" appeared in the 2000 volume *States of Conflict: Gender, Violence and Resistance.*[19] Unfortunately, El-Bushra was one of the few contributors to attend to the male/masculine side of the gender coin. Slightly more open to this subject was a volume published in the following year: *Victims, Perpetrators or Actors? Gender, Armed Conflict and Political Violence,* edited by Caroline Moser and Fiona Clark.[20] This book included Cynthia Cockburn's "Gendered Dynamics of Armed Conflict and Political Violence" and Dubravka Zarkov's "The Body of the Other Man," the latter of which studied Croatian media framings of wartime sexual attacks on detained or imprisoned *men* – one of the first times the subject had been broached in the scholarly literature.[21] However, as R. Charli Carpenter pointed out in an insightful review of the Moser/Clark text, only Zarkov's chapter "chiefly concerns men and masculinity": "although 'gender' is in the title, it seems that women and women's mobilization remain the dependent variable."[22] This is true of a more recent anthology as well: *Sites of Violence,* edited by Wenona Giles and Jennifer Hyndman.[23] Despite its subtitle, "Gender and Conflict Zones," the book actually grew out of meetings of the *Women* in Conflict Zones Network, and no chapter focuses on men and masculinities as such. Perhaps only with my own edited volume, *Gendercide and Genocide* (based on a special issue of the *Journal of Genocide Research* in 2002), have male-specific vulnerabilities and insecurities in a global context begun to receive sustained attention.[24]

The Purpose of *Men of the Global South: A Reader*

Despite the important work on gender, development, and conflict reviewed above, the lives of ordinary (and extraordinary) men in the global South have remained vaguely drawn – or invisible. The tendency has been either to ignore men as gendered subjects, through a straightforward equation of gender with women/femininities; or to consign men to stereotypical gender roles, nearly always negative ones. Men's relationships with females, in particular, are generally depicted as exploitative and aggressive. It is obvious that a more balanced and empathetic portrait of Southern men remains to be drawn.

Men of the Global South aims to help "popularize" the study of men and masculinities in the South. Geared to undergraduate and graduate students, as well as general readers, it emphasizes intimacy, accessibility, and diversity. In choosing and accepting contributions to the volume, I have been guided by one overriding consideration: does the essay or article enable the reader to truly *see* the men and boys in question? The book consists of six thematic sections, addressing major dimensions of male/masculine experience: "Family and Sexuality," "Ritual and Belief," "Work," "Governance and Conflict," "Migrations," and "Masculinities in Motion." For each section, I provide a brief framing introduction that seeks to draw out broader themes and commonalities in the selections. I do not pretend that this is an exhaustive treatment of the subject; merely that it is the most wide-ranging available so far.

Men of the Global South has been in the works for several years, during which time it underwent a significant evolution. At first, I envisaged the book mainly as a forum for previously published materials, with only a few original essays included. Some months before the original deadline, I issued another "call for contributions," to see whether a few more original essays could be found. I was rapidly inundated by an unforeseen flood of proposals, most of which I eagerly accepted. The result is that the book swelled from about half-a-dozen original pieces to over 50. I believe these new materials represent an important and extraordinarily diverse addition to the literature on men and global masculinities.

In selecting previously published work, I have relied heavily on reporting from Western mass media (such as the UK *Guardian* and the *Washington Post*), along with more specialized publications. This reliance on Western sources may surprise some readers. But one thing that distinguishes the Western media tradition is its emphasis on "human-interest" reporting, which seeks to provide deeper insights through firsthand portraits. I believe the reporting gathered here represents some of the most vivid and insightful writing on Southern men in recent years. As to whether a man of the global North like myself has the right or ability to "represent" men of the global South, I leave it to readers to decide if the attempt is valid, and whether it succeeds.

An effort was made to draw materials from all major regions of the South, though inevitably not all are equally prominent. I have been able to sample only English-language sources and, occasionally, sources in English translation. I also chose, after careful consideration, to reject material that focused on what has been called "the Third World at home":[25] that is, the entrenching of poverty and marginalization within Northern societies themselves, particularly among ethnic minorities. With two exceptions (Dina Dahbany-Miraglia and Peter Collins), all the Northern residents in this volume are migrants from the South.[26]

The advocacy dimension of this project should be acknowledged. "Men *need* advocates," an African woman activist told me at a conference in Geneva a couple of years ago. Her words echoed in my head as I worked on the volume. *Men of the Global South* pays ample attention to the violence that men disproportionately commit – against other men and against themselves, as well as against children and women. But I hope readers will also emerge with a lively sense of the challenges, vulnerabilities, and dangers that men confront in the nations of the South. Among other things, the volume devotes considerable attention to men's *positive*, *constructive*, and *honorable* contributions. There is, I think, much to commend and celebrate in this regard.

Advocacy also implies the idea of rights. While a "men's rights" component features in some literature on men and masculinities in the global North[27] – often dubiously, given the privileged status of many of the authors and their subjects – the literature on men and development contains virtually no explicit human-rights dimension. This reflects the unease that scholars and commentators have felt when engaging with feminist perspectives. Most male writers on development and related issues take pains to assert that they are pro-feminist, sometimes hinting that the *main* justification of studying men and masculinities is to bolster's women's status and opportunities.[28] Perhaps these authors accept the view of most feminists (and the wider culture) that the notion of "men's rights" is redundant or a misnomer. It is also possible that they fear a backlash from feminist ranks if they present men's situation and experience in a way that parallels feminist investigations of discrimination and victimization against women. The rights dimension of *Men of the Global South* is mostly implicit. But I hope its attention to contexts in which men are selectively victimized and exploited will prompt discussion – especially among notoriously open-minded university students – about the validity of a gendered framing of human rights for men and boys worldwide.

Notes

[1] The debate over definitions of "gender" seems endless. But for present purposes, "gender" can be defined as "masculine and feminine roles and bodies alike, in all their aspects, including the (biological and cultural) structures, dynamics, roles, and scripts associated with each gender group." Joshua S. Goldstein, *War and Gender: How Gender Shapes the War System and Vice Versa* (Cambridge: Cambridge University Press, 2001), p. 2. This definition rejects the distinction between (biological) sex and (cultural) gender favored by many feminist scholars.

[2] See Jan Jindy Pettman, *Worlding Women: A Feminist International Politics* (London: Routledge, 1996).

[3] Sylvia Chant and Matthew C. Gutmann, *Mainstreaming Men into Gender and Development* (Oxford: Oxfam, 2000), p. 9.

[4] Sarah C. White, " 'Did the Earth Move?': The Hazards of Bringing Men and Masculinities into Gender and Development," *IDS Bulletin*, 31: 2 (2000), pp. 33–41. Despite these comments, White, as the title of her article suggests, is quite skeptical of the turn towards men and masculinities in the GAD literature. She expresses sympathy for the idea that "the limited terrain which has been won for women in development will be eroded: the space itself will narrow and the landmarks subtly shift to accommodate the underlying patriarchal structures of the geomorphology below it" (p. 34). These are common concerns among feminists; I believe they deserve to be taken seriously, but also countered effectively, as Marion Birch does (see pp. 237–39).

5   Bob Pease and Keith Pringle, "Introduction: Studying Men's Practices and Gender Relations in a Global Context," in Pease and Pringle, eds., *A Man's World? Changing Men's Practices in a Globalized World* (London: Zed, 2001), p. 7.

6   When discourse privileges males over females, however – as it often does – the disparities are also notable. Thus, while hits for "women and children" far outweigh those for "men and children," the phrase "men, women and children," with its implicit privileging of men over women and adults over children, is far more prominent than "women, men and children" or "women, children and men."

7   See Cynthia Enloe, " 'Womenandchildren': Propaganda Tools of Patriarchy," in Greg Bates, ed., *Mobilizing Democracy: Changing the US Role in the Middle East* (Monroe, ME: Common Courage Press, 1991).

8   Three emblematic works are Harry Brod, ed., *The Making of Masculinities: The New Men's Studies* (Boston: Allen & Unwin, 1987); Warren Farrell, *The Myth of Male Power: Why Men Are the Disposable Sex* (New York: Simon & Schuster, 1993); and R.W. Connell, *Masculinities* (Berkeley, CA: University of California Press, 1995).

9   Errol Miller, *Men At Risk* (Kingston: Jamaica Publishing House Ltd., 1991). This discussion incorporates passages from my review of Miller's work in *Caribbean Studies*, 25: 1–2 (June–July 1992), pp. 167–72.

10 Miller, *Men At Risk*, pp. 124–5.

11 For an overview, see Matthew C. Gutmann, "Trafficking in Men: The Anthropology of Masculinity," *Annual Review of Anthropology*, 26 (1997), pp. 385–409. A seminal collection is David D. Gilmore, *Manhood in the Making: Cultural Concepts of Masculinity* (New Haven, CT: Yale University Press, 1990; see selections "The Wrestlers" and "The Big Man"). However, as Gutmann notes, despite some powerful work, "insufficient attention has been paid to men-as-men in anthropology . . . and much of what anthropologists have written about masculinity must be inferred from research on women and by extrapolation from studies on other topics" (pp. 386–87).

12 Gary Brana-Shute, *On the Corner: Male Social Life in a Paramaribo Creole Neighborhood* (Prospect Heights, IL: Waveland Press, 1979).

13 Matthew C. Gutmann, *The Meanings of Macho: Being a Man in Mexico City* (Berkeley, CA: University of California Press, 1996), p. 12.

14 Ibid., pp. 75–6.

15 Chant and Gutmann, *Mainstreaming Men into Gender and Development*. See also Caroline Sweetman, ed., *Men's Involvement in Gender and Development Policy and Practice* (Oxford: Oxfam, 2001); Michael Flood, "Men, Gender, and Development," *Development Bulletin*, no. 64 (March 2004), pp. 26–30, available at http://www.xyonline.net/Mengenderdevt.shtml.

16 Francis Cleaver, ed., *Masculinities Matter! Men, Gender and Development* (London: Zed Books, 2003).

17 Pease and Pringle, *A Man's World?*; Robert Morrell, ed., *Changing Men in Southern Africa* (Pietermaritzburg: University of Natal Press and London: Zed Books, 2001). See also Lahoucine Ouzgane, ed., *Islamic Masculinities* (London: Zed Books, 2006); Lisa A. Lindsay and Stephan F. Miescher, *Men and Masculinities in Modern Africa* (Portsmouth, NH: Heinemann, 2003).

[18] The entire issue is available on the Web at http://www.fmreview.org/FMRpdfs/FMR09/ fmr9full.pdf. *FMR* has published similar issues on child and elderly refugees.

[19] Susie Jacobs, Ruth Jacobson, and Jennifer Marchbank, eds., *States of Conflict: Gender, Violence and Resistance* (London: Zed Books, 2000).

[20] Caroline O.N. Moser and Fiona C. Clark, eds., *Victims, Perpetrators or Actors? Gender, Armed Conflict and Political Violence* (London: Zed Books, 2001).

[21] See also Augusta Del Zotto and Adam Jones, "Male-on-Male Sexual Violence in Wartime: Human Rights' Last Taboo?," Paper presented to the Annual Convention of the International Studies Association (ISA), New Orleans, LA, 23–27 March 2002; available at http://adamjones.freeservers.com/malerape.htm.

[22] R. Charli Carpenter, "Gender Theory in World Politics: Contributions of a Non-Feminist Standpoint?," *International Studies Review*, 4: 3 (2002), p. 159.

[23] Wenona Giles and Jennifer Hyndman, eds., *Sites of Violence: Gender and Conflict Zones* (Berkeley, CA: University of California Press, 2004).

[24] Adam Jones, ed., *Gendercide and Genocide* (Nashville, TN: Vanderbilt University Press, 2004). See also the case-studies gathered on the Gendercide Watch website at http://www.gendercide.org.

[25] See, e.g., "The Third World at Home," ch. 11 in Noam Chomsky, *Year 501: The Conquest Continues* (Boston, MA: South End Press, 1993).

[26] The vocabulary of "North" and "South" is inevitably problematic. This book was origi- nally titled *Third World Men*, but I and the publisher (as well as a few contributors) came to feel that the original chronological connotation of "Third World" (i.e., the third region of the world to industrialize) had been displaced by a hierarchical connotation, making the term seem patronizing and out of date. The terminology of "North" and "South" is an imprecise substitute, since not all countries of the so-called Third World are found in the southern hemisphere, nor all "First World" countries in the northern hemisphere. "Southern men" may also be taken as a reference to men of the southern US; hence the adoption of the increasingly common term "global South."

[27] Most rigorously in Farrell, *The Myth of Male Power*; see also Adam Jones, "Of Rights and Men: Towards a Minoritarian Framing of Male Experience," *Journal of Human Rights*, 1 : 3 (September 2002), pp. 387–403, available at http://adamjones.freeservers. com/of_rights_and_men.htm.

[28] See Flood, "Men, Gender, and Development": "Including men in gender and develop- ment work is necessary because gender inequality is intimately tied to men's practices and identities, men's participation in complex and diverse gender relations, and mascu- line discourses and culture. Fostering gender equality requires change in these same arenas, of men's lives and relations. . . . Focusing only on women, in relation to such issues as economic participation, credit, or sexual and reproductive health for example, can leave women with yet more work to do and thus intensify gender inequalities. Women- only projects can mean that women still have to deal with unsympathetic men and patri- archal power relations, and can leave women with sole responsibility for sexual health, family nutrition, and so on." Flood does also acknowledge that "men's suffering (such as men's growing burden of illness or social and economic marginalisation among young, poor men) is worth addressing in its own right . . . ."

PART 1

Family and Sexuality

This opening section seeks to convey something of the diversity and intensity of men's familial and sexual relations. Arguably, nothing is more central to human identity and social roles than the family unit. The family also serves as the major means by which sexualities, and the gender identities bound to them, are produced and reproduced; where conformity and dissidence are sanctioned, in both senses of the word.

From the eroticism of heterosexual longing and romantic courtship, vividly conveyed in Al-Ramli's opening contribution and Sean Pue's translation of N.M. Rashed's mesmerizing poetry, men move to confront new questions and quandaries. Masculine identity is shaped, perhaps above all, by concepts of (hetero)sexual potency and reproductive prowess. Masculine identity and "honor" are traditionally defined by the ability to achieve erection and impregnate women; discipline female sexuality; be a loving and attentive son, father, and grandfather; provide for and protect family members; maintain at least a monogamous "front" in marriage; and pursue diverse sexual liaisons.

These expectations are often burdensome and contradictory, giving rise to some of the tensions evident in these accounts. They also regularly lead to violence – against women, children, and oneself. Male perpetration of domestic abuse is explored here in essays by Metin Yüksel, Anandhi and Jeyaranjan, and Juan Carlos Ramírez. These essays also illuminate the theme of "Governance and Conflict," explored in Part 4. Feminist scholars and activists have effectively destabilized neat distinctions between public patterns of governance on the one hand, and those prevailing in the private sphere on the other. But in examining men's domestic violence, it is important to move beyond black-and-white portraits and Hollywood stereotypes. Anandhi and Jeyaranjan point to the role of class and caste variables in an Indian context, while Ramírez stresses the "need to capture relationships that are constantly in flux, and that are shaped by other linkages – to other men, to one's original family, to the workplace, to sons and daughters, and to institutionalized discourses, whether firmly established or only nascent."

Overt violence is accompanied by subtler forms of control over female (and male) sexualities and family roles. Marcia Inhorn shows how women bear the brunt of Egyptian men's reproductive "failures." Iklim Göksel's essay on masculinity and honor in Turkey describes how "men's lives were embedded in the female: women defined them"; women's "honor" is theirs as well. A similar intertwining of gendered experience is evident in the "decent/indecent dichotomy" examined by Thomas Michael Walle, who argues that "men *need* both decent and indecent women." Male constructions of the "indecent" lover/mistress/prostitute figure also pervade Leslie Lewis's study of Cairo lives and Matthew Gutmann's contribution on "Urges and Affairs." But as Gutmann shows, there may be more mutuality in these actions than is commonly perceived. Women, too, often seek to escape the strictures and contradictions of the traditional sexual unit. This trend can only grow as women's economic and social autonomy expands around the world.

Images of men as violent and controlling fit well with prevailing prejudices. But there is much in evolving family patterns, and men's place in them, that counters these expectations. Matthew Gutmann's classic account of Mexico City men, *The Meanings of Macho* (see the main Introduction), presents a vision of men as fathers and nurturers, which radically unsettles traditional notions of machismo. "Being a dependable and engaged father," he writes in the first excerpt from *The Meanings of Macho* reproduced here, "is as central to *ser hombre*, being a man, as any other component, including sexual potency." Ana Ruiz-Fodor's homage to her "Grandfather Ernesto" depicts a traditional masculinity founded not on abuse or exploitation, but on personal decency and dignity. For her part, Stella Nyanzi, examining the lives and attitudes of Ugandan men, also rejects "homogenizing and 'othering' stereotypes . . . concerning the sexuality and reproductive health of African men." In her second contribution, Nyanzi explores changing attitudes to the Ugandan institution of levirate marriage, which requires a man to marry his dead brother's widow. She points out that standard depictions of levirate marriage, as a mechanism for controlling and disadvantaging women, overlook women's agency and the significant burden that the institution places on men.

Transformations in familial and sexual spheres often reflect more encompassing social change. Louise Williams profiles a man in the new South Africa who seeks to confront his abusive past by pondering "who he wants to be – what sort of husband, what sort of father." Emily Wentzell, researching male erectile dysfunction in Mexico, detects a cultural "shift away from defining the masculine self through erection and penetration," a change that may "facilitate new conceptions of masculinity." Javier Pineda's contribution explores men's frustrations in the face of a sudden and unwanted shift to domestic work – but also their grudging adjustment to the new role. As one respondent tells Pineda: "When it has to be done, it has to be done . . . Today this is the situation."

The discussion so far has tended to present heterosexuality and the patriarchal/patrilineal family as normative. Of course, other social forms exist, such as the polyandrists of Himachal Pradesh, discussed by Rakesh Simha, or those – like orphan boys and street children – denied a "normal" family life by circumstances beyond their control. A wide range of alternative sexual identities is also found, though it can only be hinted at in these pages. David D. Gilmore explores the "sexual indeterminacy" of Tahitian society, in which both men and women "perform most of the same tasks," and "men show no discomfort at assuming a female identity." More darkly, Vinod Behl details the Indian practice of castrating young boys to serve as eunuchs, "trained to dance and sing . . . and then put out on the streets to earn money begging at street corners and in marketplaces."

In a real sense, though, heterosexuality and the patriarchal family *are* normative. This is evident in the discriminatory and repressive measures taken against those who deviate from the norm. A particularly threatening form of sexual dissidence is male homosexuality. (Here, too, there are strong crossovers with the theme of "Governance and Conflict": we will witness the targeting of gay men for state and vigilante violence in Part 4.) Shuaib Rahim explores the evolving situation in South Africa, where gays "have achieved constitutional equality" but find that, in many ways, their daily lives are unchanged. Much the same is true of Mexico's democratization process. But Monica Campbell shows that activism and growing public awareness have led to a more tolerant attitude towards gay men, at least in larger cities.

IRAQ

Hasiba and Qasim

Muhsin Al-Ramli*

Despite Qasim's accustomed serenity, he married his sharp-tongued cousin, who could lay waste to a city with her swearwords. He married her because he could not resist the whiteness of her arm that he saw suddenly one sudden dawn when his bladder, bursting with urine, woke him up. He threw off his blanket and trotted outside to the outhouse dug near the baking oven in the corner of the courtyard. He gazed at the dawn around him as he pressed his hands between his thighs and then saw his cousin from behind the low fence as she too trotted to the outhouse pressing her hands between her thighs, gazing at the dawn around her. So they saw each other and she smiled.

That was the first time Qasim saw Hasiba's smile and the first time he saw the naked arm of a woman, and the whiteness of the flesh struck him. That morning Hasiba had gone out in her sleeveless nightgown. Qasim had only seen the faces and fingers of the

*From Muhsin Al-Ramli, *Scattered Crumbs: A Novel* (trans. Yasmeen S. Hanoosh) (Fayetteville, AK: The University of Arkansas Press, 2003), pp. 21–8. Thanks to Yasmeen Hanoosh for recommending this contribution.

village women because they were usually bundled up in layers of cloth like onions. He stood with his legs spread over the toilet's mouth, aiming the stream of the urine that gushed out with a mechanical pleasure, and gazed over the wall toward his uncle's outhouse into which Hasiba had disappeared. He thought of her urine and imagined the white flesh and the white arm and her feelings of pleasure and comfort, like his own, upon the release of the pent-up urine. He found himself singing, "Your love reminds me of the Euphrates and Tigris every day. Like the meeting of my soul and yours, pure of heart together they lay." Then and there he decided to unite the sources of their urine whatever the cost. And then and there Hasiba rushed out of the toilet toward the door of the house. Her hair fluttered in the wind, her breasts bounced, her white arm glistened, and she slammed the door behind her.

Was it possible that flesh could be this white, this tender? Qasim remained standing, holding his urine hose as the sun rose while he kept repeating the fatal question to himself: Could flesh be this white? Could what flows under her skin be milk or yogurt or poison and not blood? The questions took him to the riverbank alongside the village. He sat on the pebbles, soaking his feet in the water until night fell. He realized that he had not eaten breakfast or lunch. [. . .]

He was not aware of the passing of the morning, but it was a morning white like Hasiba's arm whose image he recalled thousands of times along with the flight of her long hair, flowing behind her head like the tail of a beautiful bird. He saw her bouncing breasts in the waves rippling on the strand. He extended his fingers to the bulges in the sand, feeling the tenderness of her breasts and the yielding softness of her white arm. His palm cupped a rounded stone the size of an orange, sensing in it the roundness of Hasiba's shoulder. "Oh, Hasiba, I didn't know that you hoarded this much womanliness behind your man-eater facade!"

He, like everyone else, feared and avoided her if not to dodge the sharpness of her tongue, then to escape the scratching of her wolfish nails or the lashing of the red tamarisk cane she always carried under her arm to take care of her donkey, cows, and those who accosted her. More than anything else, it was the hardness of her foot that led Qasim to stop playing with her in childhood, or so he imagined it to be when he saw it kick the garbage can from under her brother, who had climbed up to reach the sparrows' nest beneath the roof. Qasim knew they were not her sparrows but that she had claimed them nonetheless. He then asserted in his heart, "The sparrows . . . The sparrows are the sparrows of space, the sparrows of Allah."

Her brother fell to the ground, his arm broken and his broken teeth lying in a puddle of blood beneath his face. Paying him no mind, she steadied the can and climbed upon it as Ali screamed, trying to raise himself, the blood spewing from his nostrils whenever he shrieked in pain. Hasiba reached into the nest, pulled out two eggs, and said, "My eggs!" Qasim said in his heart, "They are the eggs of the sparrows, who are the sparrows of space, which is the space of Allah." Then he withdrew in silence. And even though playing with her had been enjoyable, if scary, like playing with a knife or fire, he never played with her again.

Yet how intense grew his longing to play with her when, from the window of his house, he watched her inventing incredible games, lording it over the rest of the young-sters, and bossing them around with all the ferocity of a tigress! But after he saw her kick that can from under Ali with the explosive violence of a bomb, he resolved to play with her no more. He kept avoiding her as they were growing up, growing until his accumulated longing suddenly exploded on that dawn, that dawn white as the white-ness of her arm.

The words astounded him as he heard the Hajji* his father asking, on Qasim's behalf, the Hajji his uncle for her hand. For the hand stood for the arm, and how did his father know that he wanted Hasiba's arm and not Hasiba herself? Or that what was important was the arm, and after that came the shoulder, the hair, and only then came Hasiba? This matter boggled his mind. Could his father read his mind so precisely? Did his father possess such perspicacity? Or did he, too, see her arm one dawn? Or did his father perhaps hear him raving about the whiteness of her arm to the river or in his sleep? The bewilderment that inspired such questions continued to roil inside Qasim until after they had been married for some time he divulged it to Hasiba herself and made her burst out laughing. She commented sardonically, "All people say that sort of thing when asking for a girl's engagement, you wise man, you Hasiba's idiot, you silly ass."

It was only when they were alone that she slandered him. When they were with others, she feigned submission and addressed him only as "Abu Shaima," father of Shaima, or "Abu Ibrahim," father of Ibrahim. Qasim himself told me all this after nearly twenty-five years of marriage, so I asked him, "And what is it that kept you stuck on her all these years?" He said, "She's gorgeous, cousin. She's always fiery, always fervent, always fighting, always green, and I am an artist. I love adventures and can't relish life except in those regions dangerous because of their beauty – just as a mountaineer or a bullfighter or a circus acrobat does. The joy of the tightrope walker is the keenest of all, because if his concentration is not present in all his senses and his very being, he falls and dies. Like unto him is the tamer of lions and tigers, for he may be devoured at any moment. Herein lies the true worth of his life, consecrated in an instant. And Hasiba is a restless tigress who makes me live all my years like that one instant, in perpetual flame, on the cusp of continuity and separation, permanence and evanescence. Just like that, forever at a bubbling and boiling moment of truth." He revealed something to me that I and every other village son already knew, that Hasiba feared neither him nor any other person or thing in this world at all – save for her father.

"He's the only one I fear in this world," she would say. "I fear him even more than I fear Allah." For her father, when punishing her, would torture her in ways that became notorious among the clans, and not even their delegations could talk him out of such violence. On the contrary, he would threaten to kill her should the mediators persist. One time he turned her face to Mecca and twisted her arms down behind her, and he

---

Editor's note: A Hajji is a Muslim who has made the *haj* (pilgrimage) to Mecca.

stomped on them with his boot. Then he put a knife to her neck and would have slaughtered her like a chicken had not the mediators begged him and fallen on his hand, kissing it, and refusing to leave until he promised not to kill her. Only then did he relent, and then he gave the girl a brutal kick in the head. She rolled over, losing consciousness, while he ordered his terrified, tear-soaked wife to make him strong tea and sat down in the shade on a tin can and smoked a cigarette.

Hasiba was the only sister to seven brothers, all of whom had the nervousness, timidity, terror, and trembling of their mother. Hasiba alone inherited the mad ferocity of their father. When she would scream furiously at her brothers, they could, they swore, see fire blazing from her eyes. Then they would wet their underpants.

PAKISTAN

Poems of Desire

N.M. Rashed
Translated and introduced by A. Sean Pue*

The poems which follow were written by N.M. Rashed (1910–1975), one of the forerunners of modern poetry in Urdu, the national language of Pakistan and a minority language of India.

These three poems outline Rashed's contribution to a larger debate within the Third World about the relationship between colonial oppression, sexuality, and personal emancipation. As a young poet, Rashed followed psychoanalytical models to critique the sexual complications caused by colonialism. He argued that a new relationship with sexuality was necessary for political and psychological emancipation. Drawing upon his experiences as a soldier in Iran during World War II, Rashed expanded his critique of British colonialism to encompass newer imperialisms, both European and Soviet. He likewise expanded his focus from desire to the creation of a new subjectivity – a new man – among the nations of the South. His most mature work, represented here by the last two poems, explores existential humanism as a method for (re)gaining a wholeness of being for men of the global South.

Rashed was born in Gujranwala, a town located in Pakistan after the partition of British India in 1947. He was educated at Government College in Lahore. He later worked for All India Radio in Delhi. During World War II, he served as a non-combat officer in the British Indian Army in Iraq, Iran, Egypt, Palestine, and Ceylon (Sri Lanka). After the partition of India, Rashed moved to Pakistan, where he worked for Radio Pakistan before joining the United Nations in 1952. There he worked as an information officer until 1974

---

*Special to this volume.

in New York, Karachi, Jakarta, and Tehran. He died in England, where he had retired.
Following his instructions, his body was cremated – a controversial act for a Muslim man.

Widely regarded as one of the most important Urdu poets of the twentieth century,
Rashed remains a contentious but alluring literary figure for the Urdu-speaking world in
India, Pakistan, and the diaspora.

In the Howling Wilds of the Boundless Night
("Bekurran Rat Ke Sannate Men," from *Mavara*, 1941)

Sometimes, my love, on your bed
in the howling wilds of the boundless night
My limbs grow intoxicated with passionate emotions,
and from the weight of pleasure
my mind becomes a bog in some wasteland,
and somewhere near it
sleep, like a bird at the start of winter
with fear of some imagined hunter in its heart,
squawks and tests its wings!
In the howling wilds of the boundless night!

Sometimes, my love, on your bed
in the mountains of your breasts, longings
crawl like Africans enduring tyranny!

For a moment, the thought enters my heart that
you are not my love
but a virgin of some coastal city,
and I am a soldier of your country's enemy
who, for a long time, has not had such a night
just to lighten the burden on his soul!
Yearning to excite endless pleasure,
I have escaped from my brigade for a few days!
This thought enters my heart
sometimes, my love, on your bed
in the howling wilds of the boundless night!

Hasan the Potter
("Hasan Kuzahgar," from *La=Insan*, 1969)

Jahanzad, in the alley below in front of your door
It is I, love-struck Hasan the potter
In the bazaar this morning when in the old perfumer Yusif's shop
I saw you
in your glances was that brilliance
in whose yearning I have wandered madly for nine years
Jahanzad, I have wandered madly for nine years!

This was that time during which I
never turned and looked
at my grieving pots –
Those pots, effigies of my deft hands,
lifeless creations of mud and color and varnish,
in whispers they used to say:
"Where is Hasan the potter now?
Through us, through his own work,
he became a god, and like the gods turns away his face!"
Jahanzad, those nine years passed over me
like time would pass over a buried city;
mud in pits
in whose fragrance I used to lose myself
    turned to stone
Flasks and decanters and cups and pitchers and lanterns and flowerpots
my only means of subsistence, of expressing my art
broken
I, Hasan the potter, my feet stuck in mud, dust in my hair, naked,
at the "wheel" with disheveled hair, my head on my knees,
like some grief-stricken god
I used to shape the flow of dreams into pots with the clay and water of imagination –
Jahanzad, nine years ago
You were naive but you knew
that I, Hasan the potter,
saw in your eyes, like Mount Qaf,* illuminating the horizon
that brilliance by which my body and soul had become a pathway
    of clouds and moonlight
Jahanzad, that dream-colored night in Baghdad,
that shore of the Nile,
that boat, those closed eyes of the boatman,
for some worn-out, afflicted potter
that one night was the amber
to which his being is still attached –
    his soul, his body
Yet from that one night's delight that wave of the river emerged
in which Hasan the potter drowned, and from which he has not arisen!
Jahanzad, in that time, every day, every single day
    that ill-fortuned one would come and
see me at the wheel, my feet stuck in mud, my head on my knees

---

*In Islamic cosmology, *Qaf* is a fabulous mountain said to surround the world and bind the horizon on all sides. It rests on the *sakhrat* stone, a giant emerald, which, according to the poets, gives the sky its azure color. It is also the abode of the *devs* (demons), *jinn* (genii), and *paris* (fairies).

She used to shake my by the shoulders –
(that wheel which for years and years had been my only means of living!)
She used to shake me by the shoulders:
"Hasan the potter! Come to your senses
Hasan, look at your ruined house
how will the children's bellies be filled?
Hasan, O victim of love,
love is the game of the rich,
Hasan, look at your house and home"
In my ears this troubled voice was like
cries to a person drowning in a whirlpool!
That heap of tears was, in truth, a heap of flowers
and I, Hasan the potter, was the ecstatic of the ruins
of a city of illusions in which there was not
any sound, any movement
the shadow of any bird in flight
any sign of life!

Jahanzad, today in your alleyway
here in the chilling darkness of the night
I am standing in front of your door
my head and hair disturbed
From the window are those *Qaf*-like enchanting eyes
peering at me again today?
Time, Jahanzad, is that wheel on which, like decanters and cups and pitchers
          and lanterns and flowerpots,
men are being formed and defaced
I am a man, but
one who passed nine years in the mould of grief!
Hasan the potter today is a heap of dust in which
there is not even a trace of moisture
Jahanzad, in the bazaar this morning
in the perfumer Yusif's shop, your eyes
once again have said something
From the brilliant brightness of those eyes
the gentle movement of moisture has risen again in this heap of dust
Perhaps this will turn dust into mud again!

Who knows the extent of longing, Jahanzad, but
if you desire, then I will become again
that potter whose pots
were the delight of every balcony and lane, every city and village
by which the homes of every rich man and beggar were lit
Who knows the extent of longing, Jahanzad, but
if you desire, then I will again turn towards my deserted pots
towards those dried-up pits of mud and water

towards my means of subsistence, of expressing my art
that with that mud and water, with that color and varnish
I would again bring forth those sparks by which
the ruins of hearts would be illumined!

The City of Being and the Tomb
("Shahr-e Vujud O Mazar," from *Guman Ka Mumkin*, 1976)

This tomb,
   on which we've prostrated ourselves
this dark tomb – we do not know:
Is it the glory of a new dawn
   or a buried night?
Was a mirror punished, which from the Beginning
   was prey to an unbreakable knot?
Is it the end of some laughter
   worn out by its desire to last?

This tomb's eyes may be dim,
   this tomb's lips may be sealed
but if a laughing breeze would ever pass, then those doors would open
   which have been closed for a thousand years
If those captive prophecies
   heard this laughing voice, they would arise!

What should we say to those
   who have lost
      the silver and gold of their eyes
         in some sickness, in some accident?
What should we say to those
   who could not bear any ray
      of the dawn of non-existence?
But then there are those who
   once becoming lost
      in the flood of a thousand lanterns
         could not find a trace of themselves!

Sometimes they rode on the dust of the road, sometimes on the sun and moon
   those legendary heroes – how they went past!
They passed, thinking of us as the dust of destitution
   they never heard our voice –
A voice whose melody
   was sometimes a flame, sometimes color
      sometimes a heart, sometimes a soul!
That dampness, that putrid solitude
   which you find in brothels
      at the break of dawn

That long-haired silence, that rustle
which creeps around bank-houses
      all night long
That silence of the tomb
  rules over our present
    laughs at our past!

But desires,
  those shadows of the past age,
sometimes the wings of events
  sometimes the enlivened rays of days to come
They are the winds
  always panting in fire's wild and unbridled dance
Sometimes they wail in the cracks and crevices of a house
sometimes they wail for a twinkle of an eye
  sometimes they wail and the day breaks!

Before me now is that moment
  which my dreams saved
    from the sharp claws of night
In this very moment I would again collect
  those shards of bodies and souls
which by the force of those very winds
  had fallen and scattered
on the road of months and years
which, if the perimeter is within the limit of vision,
are no less in value than a tearful eye!

Of desire –
  which became hope then was lost
    in the desert and vale – I am . . .
Of thirst –
  which was a dream of a shore
    that spilt – I am . . .
Of openness –
  which descended into
    the strait of eyes and hearts – I am . . .
Of one-heartedness –
  which on the roofs of settlements
    became black smoke and scattered – I am . . .
Of the voice of water,
  of the ways of the wind, of the customs of dust, I am the singer!
It is true that life is in a thousand colors
But the one final reality
  is this threshold of death!
It's true
  sometimes death is its own negation,

(that death which you've lived for years)
It's also that lessening of the horror of life –
It was that negation in whose shadow
   you (like my contemplation)
      passed naked –
It is the abundance of that lack
   which you sailed
      across the river of your hunger
Sometimes on the sky and earth (in the season of autumn)
   like the bounties of the scent of saffron and roses
        you were dispersed –
Until now (this is what I beheld)
   around this tomb
from the scent of saffron and roses
   as the fortunes of pilgrims, of travelers
      grew bright
a thousand names, becoming the reverberation of only one name
        sparkled,
from all the faces one eye –
   from all the eyes one glance –
      from all the years one moment poured out
the highways of thousands of centuries to come
   (that had grown tired of watching and waiting)
      became sparks and glittered!

It is true that death is a final reality
but it is a glance, too
buried in a well
like some old woman (steeped in affection)
who peers at us
   from the inevitable moment of the final eternity –
So, O pilgrims,
descend sometime down the peaks of non-being
leap into this one glance
   find the youth of a new life,
      find new dreams of clouds and moon!

No, why should death
      (which is innocent and pure)
need to halt our singing?
At every step of the living
it is with them,
   a partner in the search for wine and bread
As the breeze,
   it is a partner in the hopes and fears of roses
      in their every desire

In our relish of love
   in our desire for union
      in our being, it is a partner
If we are playing
   then it plays against us
      sometimes losing, sometimes winning –
If standing in some city-square we think,
     where should we go?
then, hospitably, it will show us the way –
If we go to a bookstore and pick up a book
then it will unveil the letters to us
   It's a partner in our daily conversation!

So, my city of being,
   wake me up
show me the trees of my longing
that for centuries have been shedding leaves and flowers
   all over the street
Let me see that dawn,
   that undeclining face of day,
that sunlight
   which has darkened our skin from the Beginning
Take me on that wandering road of madness
   With no brush in his hand,
     with no connection to color
with just a piece of stone
   the marvel of the sculptor of madness is seen!

O my city of being
   wake me up!
A crowd is with me
Where I am
   A crowd of pilgrims is with me
For today we
are in the marriage procession
   on the night of a new union of word and meaning!

NICARAGUA

Grandfather Ernesto

Ana Ruiz-Fodor*

My fondest early memories are from the peak of the afternoon. Always, at four o'clock, I walked with my grandfather, Ernesto Pavón. We strolled through connecting parks, from Colón Street to the harbor on the lake. My left hand was loose; my right grew hot in my grandfather's hold.

Ernesto was calm like his Indian mother, but unlike his tempestuous British father. We lived in the large house that he and my grandmother, Angela, built in the 1940s. My mother, Ada Luz, was their only child. Ernesto had practiced medicine since the 1910s. When my mom was a little girl, he was Ilopango's port physician. Though he sometimes appeared feeble, it was a different story when he was preparing medicines for his patients, brazenly smashing and cracking salts and crystals in his mortars. He weighed quantities that he extracted with tiny spatulas. He dropped and mixed them, spreading them onto silver trays. He combined native medicines with the wonders of his time: penicillin, quinine, lithium oxide. He believed these to be arrows in the hands of noble warriors that would assail the heart of evil, in the form of illnesses both ancient and modern.

Most of his patients came from the provinces, and often received advice, medicines, and even their travel expenses from Ernesto's pockets. Every so often, I heard his deep voice calming people in tears. His main words of counsel were: *You can never be broken. Once your body heals, you will again be intact. The illness is there, but it cannot touch you, because there is no space for affliction inside you. Now, be a sport. Smile. Be cheerful. Don't surrender to such a meaningless foe. You know you have the upper hand.*

He was assertive in clinical diagnostics: attentive to guts, eyes, and fingernails. For Easter and Christmas, many of his patients presented him proudly with samples of their fruit – penca guavas, anonas – or their livestock, like the polka-dotted hens and alcarabanes, tall-legged beauties who sang out every hour like nature's alarm clock.

As we approached Darío's park, he would turn fascinatingly talkative. *Did you know that your fingers can make a plant grow millimeters taller, just through the application of their energy? Or: You can actually be dead but still alive, in a way that science is not yet ready to comprehend; so even life is relative. What happens when we die is that our parts are converted to other kinds of life. The same happens to the spirit. It composes a wholeness that comes from virtually everywhere. Even the stones hold living matter and spirit. So it's not madness to show respect to all things, as you expect respect from them.*

---

*Special to this volume.

There was never a subject repeated with him, just broad themes for discussion. Nature was always foremost, but he also debated rituals, usages, protocols, experiments, non-invasive friendships. He loved a calisthenics of the mind. *Think of everything there is, then think of yourself. Behold your wholeness: as everything else is, so are you.* He never emphasized things that were so obviously great that they didn't need to be stated. He talked smoothly, the carved handle of his cane impelling us forward. Sometimes the walking stick would arch up and down with his words, and that was all I wanted to see, block after block, hypnotically attuned to the wondrous worlds that Ernesto's voice unveiled to me.

He was moved to volubility only by unfairness and fear. *Fears?* he told me a number of times. *Have none!* I said, "Yeeeeeees," to cut myself loose; and then listened to his lengthy explanation about why there was no reason to fear the dark, or violence, or punishment. His comments were as daring as my own needs, wants, and endearments; but only with time has his message hit home. I later learned how afraid he must have been when he was taken away from his mother at the age of twelve. His father had taken a mistress in the village, and as a condition of her maintenance, he pressured her to accept Ernesto in her care. She did so, and grew to love him like a son. Petrona, his biological mother, was directly descended from an honorable house: that of an Indian chief, the Cacique Urraca, who was baptized Blas. The chief's son adopted the same first name as surname, as did his descendants, so there were several generations of men named Blas Blas. One of them was Petrona's father, most likely the dominant male figure in Ernesto's early life.

Ernesto always praised womanhood. *As a woman, the mystery of life will become physically yours when you are pregnant. But still that labor surpasses our understanding.* He asked me once to keep a secret with him; it was the kind of "for-when-I-am-gone" secret. It makes me cry each time I think about it. *You know,* he said, *this is a male world. You'll live in submission. But be sure to remember that women are stronger than men by far, in here* – and he drew a circle around himself, with a gesture that I knew meant the soul and the spirit above.

Once, he opened several of his heavy books. They were massive in size; a few had freehand drawings as illustrations. He used them to teach me the art and science of conception, the sexual mechanism, reproductive functions, cells, and all the different substances involved. The event occurred during one long lecture, and under one condition: that we would not refer to the contents of our discussion when we returned to the house, no matter how many times I was asked about our strange absence for the 10 a.m. *refresco* (refreshment), or our late and somewhat uncomposed arrival for lunch. I said only that we had been studying. Later, I mentioned to Ernesto the bean-sprout shape of a woman's sexual organs, but I got no comment from him. I asked again to see the upside-down baby in the uterus, but a curt *Not now* was his only response.

A good man, my grandfather said, is always truthful. *To tell a lie is a violation; it's like a deep wound inflicted first on yourself, then on others. Like an infection, the wound is prone to spread; it can do no good at all.* A decent man, as he demonstrated every day, belongs to his home. He is punctual when called to the table; he comes clean and freshly dressed to his meals. He departs always thankful from a conversation, regardless of its length, subject, or the social station of his interlocutor. Ernesto often used the word "civilized" as a substitute for "educated." He said he knew many indigents who were more civilized than men of society.

A deluge of greetings accompanied us for the better part of our walks due east from our home. Everybody knew him, and had a couple of sentences for him; that made our walks both longer and more relaxed. They all called him "Doctor"; he enjoyed his contact with all of them.

Managua was then a happy place. In my memories of her parks, there is always music playing: Spanish songs telling of love and trust. Bolívar's park first, then Central, and across the street Darío's, ending finally at El Malecón – the harbor walk – at Acahualinca. On the beach there, you could see the steps of prehistoric men and beasts in the petrified volcanic mud. There were the kids of fishermen, defying the lake's pollution, who were always ready to try to talk you out of your extra pocket money.

El Malecón is still my favorite access point to the sunset. There, the waters and heavens dance rhapsodies of blue and silver, their tones ever changing. The world splits into a million colors, then dims at an amazing rate, until it comes back together and you see it as one. This is how I came to divine all souls as infinite: by adding to El Malecón another mile, and another, until all the world was covered with that light. And there were the sounds and aromas: the water lapping at the docks and stones; crickets bleating from the grass; squawking birds flying so high they were out of sight; the smell of fresh tortillas with beans and coffee.

After the sunset was over, the boldest of grays set in. Ernesto and I walked home, watching as little yellow lights shaped the city at night. We stopped a block and a half from a neon sign of lively rose and violet, which read: "The Alameda Theater." For me it was a magical spot. Ernesto had always told me that I should think of my life as a movie, and try to live it in such a way that youngsters like myself would flock to see it. The theater is still there, in the corner of my heart, calling out its movies as life starts rolling.

EGYPT

Four Lives

Leslie Lewis*

Amr

It is 4:30 a.m. As the *azzen al fejra* vibrates through the pre-dawn in Cairo, calling the faithful to prayer, 43-year-old Amr lifts his head from the pillow. His wife is already up, preparing tea and a small meal. They will both pray, then eat before returning to bed for a few final hours of rest. Later, they will rise again and prepare for their respective days. Amr teaches at a local public high school, arriving at 8:30 and departing punctually at 3:30 in the afternoon. Typically, he returns home and relaxes, prays, watches television, and talks with his wife about their day. She is a teacher as well, but upon returning she sets about preparing the evening meal. She is responsible for all the household's cooking, cleaning, and laundry.

The couple has only one son, now in middle school. They tried for years to have more children, but without success. Infertility has become a quiet but growing concern in Egypt, as in many developing countries. There is conjecture that it could be linked to an exponential increase in the levels of pesticide and other toxins in the environment.

Because both Amr and his wife earn an income, and because they have only one child, they have been able to accumulate a number of coveted consumer items. Together, they earn nearly two thousand pounds a month – about $350, well above average. They have air conditioning, a luxury among Cairo's 18 million people; a color TV; a late-model car; even a dated computer. The couple is solidly middle class. They buy nothing extravagant, but there is extra money beyond the household's immediate needs.

Amr prays five times a day, and attends the Friday sermon at the neighborhood mosque. Unlike many men, though, he does not spend much time outside the house, in the company of male friends. Religious, socially conservative, and temperamentally reclusive, Amr stays home most evenings, spending time with his wife and son. He has perfected his skill at making fresh juices and ice cream, and shares his creations with other family members when they gather at the couple's apartment. He does not shake hands or interact in any protracted way with unrelated women. He considers this *haram*, or forbidden by Islam.

There is kindness between Amr and his wife, along with a mutual affection and respect not always seen in Egyptian couples. In public and even private gatherings, neither is demonstrative about these sentiments. Social custom militates against public displays of affection between (heterosexual) couples. Instead, homosocial intimacy is

---

*Special to this volume.

the norm. Women greet women by kissing and embracing; men walk arm in arm with one another in the street.

Because of his strong religious beliefs, Amr remains sexually faithful to his wife. He does not condemn legally sanctioned second (and third and fourth) marriages, since this is permitted under Islam. However, his affection for his wife, and his tendency towards solitude, preclude his taking advantage of this right.

Omar

In the middle of the afternoon, 40-year-old Omar slips out of the office, announcing to no one in particular that he is off to a meeting. Because he is the owner and president of the company, no one challenges his frequent comings and goings. A few employees glance at each other knowingly. He is heading, they suspect, to an afternoon tryst.

Later in the evening, when Omar meets up with his old school chums, all business owners, CEOs, and professionals, he will be discreet about the specifics of his rendezvous. However, they know about his escapades. When the men get together, generally once or twice a week, they often discuss infidelities – the tricky situations and humorous anecdotes related to their clandestine extramarital lives. Politics and society are also conversational fare. They tend not to talk about work; nor, beyond the initial social niceties, do they discuss family.

Every one of the eight men present has committed adultery, but only one finds his activities morally problematic. When pressed about the feelings of their spouses, they protest that they love their wives and families, and provide for them well; consequently, there is no cause for complaint. Women on the side are a separate matter. They are for pleasure, not permanence.

Among these men – in keeping with the broader Egyptian pattern – wives are like mothers to their husbands as much as to their children. Wives know their husbands' likes and dislikes, and reliably tend to their hygiene, physical needs, and creature comforts. They know their husbands' clothes intimately, either washing them regularly or monitoring the maids and ironers who are contracted for such work. Home, for these men, is a haven, and a separate world.

Omar inhabits three distinct lives, and struggles to keep each of them separate and afloat. His schedule of subterfuge both exhausts and enlivens him. He spends many hours at his work, often from eight in the morning until seven or eight at night. There he guides, delegates, dictates, berates, and otherwise manages a staff of forty. His is a moderately successful business, but he faces some financial strain, something that he chooses not to share with his wife.

Omar and his wife have one son, ten years old, whom they have coddled excessively. The child's behavior reflects this, and his parents seem at a loss over how to deal with him. Omar spends a limited amount of time at home. He sleeps there every night, but spends only a few evenings in the company of his wife and child. Fridays are for family. Most men, Omar included, go to the mosque for group prayer at midday; upon their return, the family goes out on an excursion. Families from the lower classes go to parks and the zoo, which charge only a small entrance fee. Middle-class families go to malls and their playgrounds. Omar's family, like others from the upper classes, heads to a private club, where children swim and play while the adults talk and eat. Days spent together often stretch into the evenings.

On Friday nights, families across Cairo gather to socialize and share food. Women congregate in bedrooms and kitchens, talking in low tones, sometimes conspiratorially. Laughter arises periodically from their midst; hands slap in acknowledgement of a particularly good joke or a wry comment. Men occupy the living rooms and balconies, sometimes spilling into outdoor cafes, where they smoke hookahs and drink Turkish coffee. They watch the world from their perch, occasionally reading the paper or discussing local affairs with other men.

The week's remaining evenings are devoted to work, or to social activities with friends. Omar reserves his trysts with other women solely for the daytime hours. Unbeknownst to his wife, he maintains two separate apartments. In spite of his frequent infidelities, however, Omar considers himself a religious man. He prays regularly, including alongside his employees at work. He does not drink alcohol or smoke cigarettes, and professes to live well and honorably. His main concerns are money, his son, his expanding waistline, and the direction of Egyptian politics and society.

Saef

At the end of the working day, 35-year-old Saef crowds into the public bus for his ride home. As the press of the other commuters magnifies the heat, he daydreams about owning his own car. But he realizes with some bitterness that he is unlikely ever to possess such a luxury. Saef has worked for years at the same travel agency, bringing in 750 Egyptian pounds a month – about $130. He lives in a small apartment with his wife, 14-year-old daughter, 12-year-old son, and unmarried brother. The flat is unremarkable, with few luxuries. Particularly bothersome during the sweltering summer months is the absence of air conditioning or fans.

Saef has always felt oppressed by his seemingly endless responsibilities for others. Men's lives and identities in Egypt and the Middle East center on their capacity to provide for dependents. Given the high unemployment rate (some estimate it at 25 per cent) and rising inflation, the financial pressures on men are significant. More and more men are unable to provide for their families; wives must seek work outside the home to make ends meet, or to allow any kind of upward mobility. Economic circumstances, tied to complex international, national, and local factors, have forced a shift in traditional roles. At the same time, growing religious and social–conservative forces make a show of rejecting cultural imports from the West, and glorify the Islamic ideal of separate spheres for women and men. Women should stay at home, runs the rhetoric, while men should occupy the world of work, politics, and civic life. Ordinary men and women thus find themselves caught between contradictory discourses and pressures.

For reasons of pride, Saef will not allow his wife to take work outside the home. But he is miserly in sharing his salary, spending the bulk of it on his own desires and activities. His wife has a small business selling Avon products to neighbors and the women in her extended family, which brings in extra money for household needs.

There is a palpable strain between Saef and his wife. Their relationship is tainted by an incident years earlier, in which a rumor passed from a neighbor to a friend to a cousin that Saef's wife was "going out" while he was at work. The simple suspicion that she might be having assignations with other men was enough to send Saef into a rage. There had been beatings before, but now he hit her with unprecedented severity. She protested her innocence; but once the idea had taken root in Saef's mind – and, as he cringed to acknowledge, in the minds of neighbors and family members – her reputation and his honor were sullied. Their marriage turned bitter and chronically abusive.

Now Saef spends time in the evening with friends, having the occasional affair and returning home late. His wife rarely goes out, obeying his prohibitions in this regard. She has become reclusive, subdued, and more formally religious. Following a trend that has grown over the past 20 years, she wears the Islamic *higab*, and displays a newly intense self-discipline and piety. With this comportment, she has earned a way back into the family fold. But Saef still remains skeptical, distant, and unbending.

Mohammed

The summer sun is setting. The sound of the evening call to prayer rouses Mohammed, 28 years old, from his heat-induced lethargy. If he moves without delay, he will have time to complete his ablutions and prayer. Often, though, he is waylaid by demands from his employer. Mohammed is a *bauwabb* for a small villa in a newer section of Cairo. His duties are to maintain the grounds, clean and protect the property, wash cars, and run errands. His day stretches from the early morning until 1 or 2 a.m. During this span, he does have "down time" for sitting and talking with friends, as well as for a semi-scheduled nap after the *Dohr*, or midday prayer. Otherwise, he is working or on call. For his labor, he is paid 250 Egyptian pounds a month – roughly $43. With this, he supports not just his own family in distant Upper Egypt, but an entire network of extended relations. He is the sole provider for his wife and three small children, along with three widowed sisters and their children: a staggering sixteen people in all.

Mohammed lives simply, spending very little on food or other necessities. He has one day off a week, which he "saves" for months at a time, working every day so that he can make an occasional trek home to wife and family. Given Mohammed's extremely limited means, his opportunities for sexual expression and other pleasures are few. His employer refuses to allow his immediate family to come and live with him, so his contact with his wife is limited to about a week every three or four months. Taking a second wife is unrealistic; nor is it something he desires.

Childrearing is left to Mohammed's wife. He sees and cares for his children during visits; when he can, he brings them small gifts. But this is the extent of his involvement.

Such a sporadic paternal presence is not uncommon in Egypt, and can be seen across all social classes. The collapse of rural economies has forced many farmers to move to Cairo in search of jobs. Men from the upper classes, with education and financial means, often migrate to nearby Gulf countries, Europe, or North America to earn enough to support their families.

Mohammed's class standing is evident in his speech, demeanor, and deference to others. He is quick to help, responding promptly to the calls of "*Ya Ahmed!*" bellowed from windows throughout the day. He is unfailingly polite and solicitous. In spite of this, he is treated poorly by his employers, who openly deride and micromanage him.

Mohammed is religious in an unconscious sort of way. Islam is woven into his life, and he cannot imagine it otherwise. He believes that the greatest struggle for Egyptian men is to find and secure a decent livelihood. The cost of living has increased, and jobs pay little. Survival is hard. He prays regularly, and despite his own difficulties, he regularly thanks God for what he has: "*Il hamdulileh*," he says when asked how he is. He seems to mean it sincerely: "Il hamdulileh."

Four lives

It is late, and as a solstice moon arches across a sweltering sky, four men's days draw to a close. Each of their lives is linked by a culture, a religion, and a shared political, social, and economic climate. Common notions of masculinity, and pressures to provide for dependents, also knit them together. Yet they inhabit disparate worlds. Geographically, only a few miles of Cairo's urban landscape separate them. But they are nonetheless deeply divided by socioeconomic class, rural versus urban roots, and particular interpretations of religious practice. In this respect, they are not dissimilar to men across the global South, and indeed around the world.

UGANDA

The Men of Bwaise

Robert Wyrod*

By late morning, the metal roof was already burning in the equatorial sun, and the small carpentry workshop was stifling. But Rafik was oblivious, just finding his rhythm in the long day's work. At 22, he already had two years of carpentry experience, and was confident in his skills as a maker of beds, chairs, tables, and cabinets.

---

*Special to this volume. All names are pseudonyms.

Rafik's workplace was more a shack than anything else. The walls were half-rotted wood panels, and raw ceiling beams supported the simple tin roof. The dirt floor was covered with lumber, wood scraps, and half-completed projects. The main work area was a blackened table in the rear of the shop, surrounded by a sea of wood shavings that were occasionally gathered up by scavenger boys. Within these ten square meters of space, Rafik and two other men made their living.

The carpentry shop was just one of countless small workshops in Kampala, the Ugandan capital. Like so many others, it was located in Bwaise – a dirty, congested area that is unfortunately best described as a slum.

While Kampala's most attractive feature is its many hills, Bwaise and other flood-prone valleys are home to many of the city's poorest residents. Like all developing-world capitals, Kampala has its exclusive neighborhoods, populated by the Ugandan elite and a large community of expatriates. With a population of over a million, and a national population of 25 million, there is also a tiny Ugandan middle class who have staked out land on the fringes of the city, building more modest versions of the gated compounds of the wealthy.

Yet most city residents subsist on one or two dollars a day, and in densely packed areas like Bwaise, life can be especially bleak. Behind the storefronts that line the main streets, there is a diverse array of housing, from brick and mortar one-storey houses to mud-and-wattle one-room shacks housing entire families. Frequent floods, poor drainage, and makeshift sewers make this housing almost uninhabitable. Life in Bwaise is a perpetual health hazard.

Yet there are good reasons to live in Bwaise. Its proximity to the city center generates bustling business. And while Bwaise has a reputation for seedy nightlife, day-to-day business is its main draw, with dozens of retail outlets, auto-repair shops, markets, butchers, tailors, music stores, furniture showrooms, and carpentry workshops. So while life is harsh in most of Bwaise, there is also opportunity, and a chance for young men to make a living that might lead to a more financially secure adulthood.

This essay provides a glimpse into the lives of three men in their early twenties, all living and working in and around Bwaise. Rafik hopes his skills as a carpenter might be sufficient to navigate the road to manhood. Patrick is frustrated with the difficulties of finding work and has the added burden of being a new father. Michael, for his part, has received a government university scholarship, but is still unsure what his future holds.

*   *   *

Although far from lucrative, carpentry is a respectable profession for men in Kampala. It certainly ranks far below the white collar jobs that well-connected men are able to obtain in government or private companies. But such jobs are minuscule in number, and few men in places like Bwaise even aspire to such work. So across the city, many young men like Rafik hope the craft of carpentry can become their profession.

Barber outside his shop in Bwaise neighborhood, Kampala, Uganda (Robert Wyrod)

In the workshop, it was clear that Rafik took satisfaction in his work. He moved smoothly and steadily, all his motions efficient. His concentration was so intense that he often waited until late in the day to break for lunch. In a week, he could transform huge slabs of hardwood into a simple, but pleasing, king-size bed. Yet, like most workers in Kampala, Rafik never received regular payment for his labor. The owner paid him only after pieces were sold, and fair compensation was left very much to the owner's discretion.

Even a dedicated and hard-working young man like Rafik found this routine exploitation difficult to tolerate. When his girlfriend became ill, he wanted to help pay her medical bills, but the owner wasn't forthcoming. So Rafik quit – which seemed rash, given the precarious labor market and the abundance of carpenters in the area. Yet within a week, he was working in a nearby shop that produced chairs. Most importantly, he arranged payment for each chair upon completion. So while this kind of manual labor was no guarantee of a steady income, the resourceful and motivated could sometimes make it work to their advantage.

But the difficulties Rafik faced in helping his girlfriend with medical bills were only part of deeper problems in the relationship – and money was central to all of them. Rafik was eager to move on to a more adult phase of his life. In Uganda, that means finding a place of your own and having children. Rafik often spoke about how much he wanted to settle down with his girlfriend. When asked if he was faithful, he gave a resounding yes. Part of his trepidation about multiple partners arose from a fear of AIDS, which he mentioned explicitly. Pragmatic concerns about jealousy were also a factor, but for Rafik there was more at stake. As he put it, "I don't want that kind of life. It's better to be in the kind of relationship where both partners are faithful." Manhood, parenthood, and fidelity were all interwoven for Rafik, at least in theory.

Part of what Rafik found alluring about his girlfriend was that she was educated. She had been trained as a nurse, an education significantly beyond Rafik's unfinished secondary school. Employed at the main national hospital, she received a modest but steady income. Rafik didn't find this discrepancy threatening, but rather attractive. She was the kind of woman he could build a future with, as partners. "It's important to have an educated partner, so that you can be a team," Rafik explained. While other men might demand that their wives stay at home, Rafik was interested in a woman with earning potential.

But it was exactly those qualities that proved to be liabilities in the relationship. After being together for over a year, but not yet cohabiting, Rafik's girlfriend stopped taking his calls and refused to meet with him. He was surprised, but he knew exactly why she had left him. As a carpenter working short-term, unsteady jobs, Rafik's financial prospects were limited. A young woman with nursing credentials could do better, and Rafik's girlfriend most likely left him for someone with greater potential. Rafik's vision of a steady partner with whom he could build a home and family had vanished.

The fact that AIDS played some part in Rafik's ideas about relationships is not unusual in the Ugandan context. While Southern African countries have seen HIV infection rates rise alarmingly over the last decade, Uganda's trajectory has been the opposite. Current estimates are that nearly 7 per cent of the adult population is HIV positive: a disturbing statistic, but a dramatic decline from the early 1990s, when infection rates were closer to 20 per cent.

While the government has been credited with addressing the epidemic early on, there is no consensus as to why infection rates dropped so dramatically. Some point to the success of prevention campaigns focused on condom use, partner reduction, and more recently, abstinence – the now-famous Ugandan ABC model (Abstain, Be faithful, use Condoms). Others have highlighted the grim fact that as large numbers of people with AIDS died throughout the 1990s, the number of HIV-positive people declined.

So whether through the tragic loss of life or effective prevention campaigns, AIDS has become part of the cultural fabric of Uganda. This raises a question: has the AIDS epidemic affected what it means to be a man in Uganda? It is no doubt unproductive to think of AIDS changing ideas of manhood in any straightforward way. The AIDS epidemic, relationships, sexuality, and gender are too complex to fit into neat causal formulas. As Rafik's story illuminates, AIDS is just one of many issues that young men contemplate when attempting to become a man in a place like Bwaise.

Yet Rafik's account indicates that AIDS is indeed part of the social calculus that Ugandans employ in making intimate relationship decisions. For some, AIDS has symbolic value, representing a constellation of anxieties about adulthood, family, sexuality, and gender roles. For others, the threat of AIDS may have directly influenced key life decisions. And for those living with AIDS, the disease obviously has an immediate impact on their everyday lives and the lives of their loved ones. Thus, when thinking about what it means to be a man in a place like Bwaise, it is important to recognize that AIDS has shaped Ugandans' lives, but also that AIDS is just one of many issues affecting conceptions of masculinity in Bwaise.

* * *

As Bwaise goes, Patrick's home was not bad. Tucked behind some older houses that were slowing being eroded by floods, Patrick's rented house was relatively new. The owner had built three one-storey spaces that, at first glance, looked more like storage sheds. Each had a large red metal door; the stucco was still cream-colored, not yet burnt orange from the dust of the laterite soil. Most important, the one-room structures were set on concrete foundations that provided some protection from the inevitable spillover of the nearby sewage canal.

Inside, Patrick lived with his wife and newborn daughter. The double bed consumed most of the space, but there was still room for a small desk with a radio. Hanging laundry added some color to the bare walls. Although the space was too small for visitors, Patrick was clearly proud of the home he and his wife had created. It resonated with the feeling of a nest created by a young couple still excited about their independent adulthood.

Yet this sense of domestic harmony rested on shaky foundations. Although Patrick had nearly completed a university program in business administration, he had been unemployed for two years. At 22, his frustration with job hunting had turned to fatalism. "Me, I just give up now. I'm waiting for my time to come," Patrick admitted. While not unwilling to do manual labor, he did not have the right connections to secure such work – or so he said. Ideally, he hoped to open a computer training center in Bwaise. But he knew that such a venture was impossible without start-up capital.

Instead, Patrick filled his days by working as a volunteer for two non-governmental organizations: one focused on family planning, the other addressing domestic violence. While such work provided only a tiny monthly stipend, he found it attractive. It tapped into a genuine desire to do something positive for his community, especially his peers. Such volunteer work also offered regular training that brought him additional respect in the community. In addition, these organizations provided access to the large development industry in Uganda and the possibility that he could network with the right people.

Yet Patrick was a realist. He knew it was unlikely he would get a staff position at the NGOs or that a scholarship would suddenly materialize. But having given up on the job market, he found himself at a standstill. Patrick's wife was luckier when it came to employment. She worked for a while as a gas-station attendant, and then found a position as a teller at a government bank. As the family's sole breadwinner, her small but regular income had to stretch a long way.

Like Rafik, then, Patrick found himself in a relationship with a woman who earned more money than he did. Patrick was well aware of the danger this posed for the relationship, acknowledging that his lack of income might lead his wife to stray. While supportive and grateful for his wife's contribution to the family, he knew her job put her in contact with many men, and it was possible one might seek to woo her. Patrick was as fatalistic about this as about his lack of employment. "I see myself in a fix where I cannot meet some of her basic needs, and then – most people call it temptations, but you never know what might come up, and she could get in trouble. I don't know, that's my worry." AIDS was a concern too, with Patrick stressing the need for safe sex if his wife felt the urge to stray. "I always talk about it [AIDS] with her," he said, "and I always advise her, in case something comes up that is inevitable, to use condoms. I always emphasize condoms, condoms, condoms."

Patrick, however, was adamant that he would stay faithful to his wife. He had seen the consequences of infidelity and polygamy in his childhood. Patrick's father had had three wives, with three families in separate homes. With 21 siblings and half-siblings, his father had nowhere near the resources to support such a large family. As the second wife, Patrick's mother, fell out of favor with her husband, she and her children were left to fend for themselves. Still bitter, Patrick had no interest in a similar fate. "I suffered so much because my father had three women. I don't feel like having any other wife, and I want to have as few children as possible, because I've seen the burden it put on my parents," he confided. The threat of AIDS hardened these attitudes, as Patrick admitted. "Maybe I have a feeling that if HIV was not prevalent, I would have copied my daddy's ways and had more than one girlfriend. But because of HIV/AIDS, I have to stick with one partner."

Given Patrick's precarious financial position, it was surprising to hear that he and his wife were having a baby. As a volunteer for a family-planning organization, Patrick was well versed in birth control, as was his wife. Still, they made a conscious decision to have a child. "At first we used condoms, but we decided to have that kid. Maybe we get some [feelings of] responsibility ... It was after my young sister [had a baby that] we saw there was a need for us to have some responsibility too."

Despite his inability to be a breadwinner, Patrick wanted to move up the ladder of male adulthood and become a father. While some of his NGO colleagues thought that having a child without a good job was irresponsible, for Patrick it was precisely the way he and his wife would prove they could assume fully adult responsibilities. So despite – or perhaps because of – his inability to fulfill the male role of provider, he was ready to become a father.

*   *   *

For Michael, who had lived in Bwaise for all his 22 years, the future seemed more promising. After struggling to find money to complete his secondary education, Michael was about to enter the country's top university on a full government scholarship. No one in his family had ever attended university, and all his peers were on a manual-labor career track like Rafik's.

For a young man from such a poor community, this was quite an accomplishment – the result of focus and determination. Prioritizing his studies, Michael had avoided the daily temptations of an area like Bwaise. Unlike his friends, drinking and clubbing were not part of his regular routine. More significantly, Michael saw relationships with women as detrimental. Not only was he still a virgin at 22, but he had never even had a girlfriend. For Michael, relationships were too fraught with complications that could derail his education. "Girls in Uganda know men should give them money," Michael said. "You can't sustain her. She can get a man who has money. You will not know. You will [only] know later. You are infected [with AIDS] and things like that. That's really what turns me off." Relationships were not only potential distractions and financial drains; they presented serious health risks as well.

Michael's concern about AIDS was hardly unusual, but it was perhaps made more intense by his family's experience with AIDS. He lived with his HIV-positive mother, who was still very healthy and active, and an HIV-positive aunt who was dying of AIDS. While he cared deeply about these female relatives, his home life made relationships seem unpalatable. "You know, when I look at my family home, I look at the patient's home. That really turns me off." It made him realize that "I should be very conscious about whatever I'm doing."

Without the AIDS epidemic, Michael might have still abstained from sex and viewed relationships as problematic. But having experienced the horrors of AIDS, he perceived relationships as burdened with danger. So Michael opted out of them completely. While the effects of AIDS were very real to him, AIDS also came to symbolize all the aspects of life in Bwaise that he wanted to leave behind.

As proud as Michael was of his government scholarship, he knew a degree from the top university was no guarantee of employment. "So now my main goal [is to] study up to my mid-thirties, and then I will look for a family. That is my first [priority], I want to get at least my Master's, and I want to study with my Master's abroad." Relationships, and a family, were low on his list of priorities.

If he waited too long to marry and become a father, Michael knew his community would label him a perpetual youth – someone who had never quite crossed the threshold to manhood. But whatever pressure he felt to become a real man, and show he could take care of a family, was overshadowed by his realistic assessment of his career prospects. Perhaps campus life would change his attitudes. But his mother remained a constant remainder of the hazards posed by relationships in Uganda.

*   *   *

There is no straightforward, guaranteed path to manhood in a place like Bwaise. All routes are beset by complications, compromises, and risks. Consciously or unconsciously, young men in Bwaise weigh risks and responsibilities as they forge their own paths to adulthood. With few successful male role models, many men make poor decisions, unable or unwilling to acknowledge the long-term impact of their actions on themselves and their families. But even more thoughtful and well-intentioned men can feel despair when assessing their options for attaining adulthood. AIDS casts their decisions in stark relief, making them truly matters of life and death. Nearly a quarter century after AIDS was first discovered in Uganda, the disease has been subsumed into the fabric of everyday life. It underlies decisions both mundane and consequential, and is now inextricably bound to conceptions of masculinity.

MEXICO

Fathers and Children

Matthew C. Gutmann*

In earlier studies of families and parents in rural Mexico, anthropologists have emphasized how economic pressures have often influenced couples to have more children. The presence of more children has meant more family members can work at home and

*From Matthew C. Gutmann, *The Meanings of Macho: Being A Man in Mexico City* (Berkeley, CA: University of California Press, 1996), pp. 69–74, 79.

in the fields, and more can be sent to work in the cities. The presence of more children has also served as greater insurance against the uncertainties of old age in a society with meager or nonexistent social-security benefits.

But families throughout Mexico, including Mexico City [where the field research was carried out], are today having fewer children than did previous generations. [Later,] we will examine some of the meanings and goals of *not* having so many children. Here it is worthwhile to briefly consider some of the reasons men and women in Colonia Santo Domingo *do* want to have children. Understanding these reasons is complicated by the fact that for most of my friends in the *colonia*, having children after marriage is a matter of course; few people I know in Santo Domingo have a conscious strategy about having children or, conversely, have decided never to have children. Far more frequent are shotgun marriages prompted by an unwed woman's pregnancy – in other words, marriages brought about to sanctify parenthood. When Angela told me her eldest daughter got married at sixteen, I asked her how old she'd been when she married Juan.

"Seventeen. And my daughter was born when I was eighteen."

"And why are you criticizing your daughter?"

"All right, precisely because of my experience. I never thought my daughter was going to marry. I had so many hopes, so many goals for her. And then she got pregnant and got married."

"You weren't pregnant when you got married?"

"I was too. Finally, the truth!"

Though some men want children in order to demonstrate their procreative abilities and prove their virility, for many more men, and for many women, children provide a way to prove one's worth in other, more important ways. In the manner of vicarious projections, parents in Santo Domingo often talk about the dreams and goals they have for their children, ranging from lucrative incomes to happy and stable marriages. How children turn out is also taken by many as a test of their parents' most significant accomplishments in life.

There is another reason many adults in Santo Domingo want children. At once a most uncomplicated reason and for some readers in the United States – where children are broadly regarded as nuisances much of the time – perhaps the most difficult and naïve explanation to fathom is this: many poor women and men in Mexico City become parents for the fun of it. Finding pleasure in the company of children is considered by people of all generations in Mexico, even childless adults, to be one of the most natural and wonderful things in the world.

In Santo Domingo, some men speak with great pleasure about having jobs that allow them to spend time with their children while they are working, such as those furniture repairmen or cobblers who have little workshops in their houses, or others like car mechanics who work in the street in front of their homes. When the tanker truck arrived at 8 a.m. each Saturday morning to deliver natural gas to the *tortillería* [tortilla shop] across the street, two boys between six and eight years old often accompanied the

Three generations in Havana, Cuba (Adam Jones)

Couple in Trinidad, Cuba (Adam Jones)

men pumping the gas, and sometimes helped them with the hoses. During the summer, when the mailman came putt-putting down the street on his little motorcycle, his young son ran along the opposite side of the street, stuffing letters through mail slots. Other men, of course, talk about staying at work later than they need to because they would rather not go home. More than one man told me that the hardest part of every day was right after work, when he had to decide whether to go home, which meant "returning to my screaming children and wife," or kill time until the rest of the family might have fallen asleep.

Even for men who seem to take little interest, and less pleasure, in their children, most feel some cultural pressures to provide periodic guidance for their sons and daughters. Luciano is a welder who no longer lives in Santo Domingo but whose first family lived near us and who still often works there during the day. While recounting his life one day, Luciano talked to me about the four boys and five girls (including one who had died) in this family: "It makes sense that a boy becomes responsible as a result of the father, of education. And with a girl it's the same, because of education by her mother. Not because of nature, but because it is the obligation of the father to guide his son."

As part of his paternal duties Luciano feels that he has to impart a skill to his sons and then leave them to fend for themselves: "The boys are the ones I am helping. Oscar already knows the *chamba* [job] more or less, so he's going to teach the others. I already told him that I'm going, I'm going to look for work somewhere else so as not to be here. I'm beginning to make myself independent of them so they can teach themselves to be responsible about their house, because if I'm around they don't do anything. They are waiting for me to arrive, or for me to do it all."

This sentiment was echoed by another man who insisted that I not use his name in my book: "If you're a *canijo* [son of a bitch] in your life, your children are going to turn out worse than you. Take women, for instance. If your woman or you is a canijo, then the girls are going to turn out canijas and the boys canijos. If you're *tranquilo* [even-tempered] and the woman is a canija, like in my case, well then, most of the girls are canijas and the boys are tranquilos, because they don't smoke, don't drink – nothing besides *futbol* [soccer]."

What happens if there are no boys? I spoke with Leti, the mother of three girls between ten and fourteen years old. She speculates that the main reason her husband has never taken much responsibility for the children is that they have no sons. She laments that had there been three boys instead, he would have had to live up to (*cumplir*) his obligations as a father, and life would have been very different for her. This situation is felt by neighbors to be rather typical of old-fashioned relations between mothers and fathers, and in this sense more exceptional in a community that has undergone innumerable changes in recent years. Whether she is right is impossible to determine, but she is sure of her perception that with boys her husband would have been at least culturally pressured if not obligated to take on certain accepted male parenting duties.

Leti's husband, Carlos, [a] long-haul truck driver, chooses to emphasize his partici-pation in raising the girls rather than his absence. As with other couples interviewed, Carlos talked of a division of labor he and Leti worked out when the children were young. Leti had them by day, and he got up with the infants at night (he had a different job at the time that permitted him to remain in the Federal District). The first time I met Carlos he told me of his knowledge of world geography. "Test me!" he challenged. I asked him, "What is the capital of Germany?" and he answered, "Bonn and Berlin before; not yet decided today." Over a lunch of rabbit *adobo* that he, with Leti's help, had prepared, Carlos said that when his daughters were very little and he was getting up all the time in the night, he had pinned a map of the world to the ceiling. He would lie on his back, sometimes for hours, rocking a daughter back to sleep and studying the world. "That and being a truck driver is how I know so much about geography," he told me.

Also indicative of how some parents distinguish between their sons and daughters and others do not is the fact that there is great variation in inheritance patterns today in Santo Domingo. Angela and her husband, Juan, will leave all their property to their three girls and one boy, all grown and all married, only the youngest of whom, Norma, still lives in the colonia. The children will have to decide how to divide it among them-selves. Similarly, Marcos and Delia will leave their lot and home to their two girls. However, though he no longer lives there, Luciano, as legal owner of the land and house his first family lives in, has decided that only his four sons will get the property, because, he reasons, his four daughters can find men and move out.

A division of labor, fathers-sons and mothers-daughters, still prevails in some younger families in Colonia Santo Domingo, but many men with small children today like to claim as a point of pride that they treat their boys and girls the same. If they spend more time with the boys outside the home, they sometimes explain, it is because it sim-ply "works out that way," because it is "more convenient" for both the father and mother, or because the boys want to spend time with them more than the girls do. To this must be added the fact that mothers – probably more so than fathers – are often reluctant to have their girls go out with the men. Diego told me that he used to take his girls with him when he went out drinking with his friends, but that he now regrets having done so because such situations are improper for girls – because girls (and women) should not have to hear and witness the vulgarities that are common when men are drinking together. Diego's wife agrees, and so overall it remains the case that from very early on boys are sent off with their fathers by their mothers in a way that girls less often are. [...]

Responses to the survey [I distributed] on parenting indicate the perils of over-simplifying fathering practices in urban Mexico, especially of making generalizations that posit bland homogeneity among lower class men in the form of erratic participa-tion in day-to-day care and little interest in anything more than procreation. In addition, though male identity, especially with regard to Mexican men, is often thought of as equivalent to irresponsibility and violence, for most of the men and women interviewed, at least, being a dependable and engaged father is as central to *ser hombre*, being a man, as any other component, including sexual potency.

Xinjiang, China (Adam Jones)

UGANDA

Men and Their Children

Stella Nyanzi*

Homogenizing and "othering" stereotypes abound concerning the sexuality and reproductive health of "African men." These include their supposedly larger-than-average sexual endowments, their unmatched sexual prowess, their animal-like virility, an affinity for high-risk sexual behavior, their disregard for contraception, and their proneness to HIV/AIDS. Relatively few voices have been raised on the African continent to challenge these assumptions. The most enduring stereotype is that of the African man's desire for children, which turn him into a "baby-manufacturing machine." Images are rife of such men, with their many wives and children.

As an African medical anthropologist, immersed in fieldwork on issues related to reproductive health, my observations and analyses are at odds with notions of "African men" desiring innumerable children and scheming to produce them with multiple sexual partners. Accordingly, family health initiatives, reproductive health campaigns, and male-based sexual-health education calling on men to reduce their number of children are mostly inappropriate and redundant. Many of them are ill-attended, badly received, and scarcely (if at all) implemented. Some of these well-intentioned programs are evidently based on outdated and irrelevant ethnographical accounts of the "reproduction and kinship systems of natives."

This essay summarizes some of the key findings of my research, conducted in diverse settings with men, women, and children in Uganda.

Voices from the ground

My ethnographic participant observation reveals that generation, class, locality, income level, religion, and education all influence the number of children that men desire and actually have. Men from older generations with relatively higher incomes or social status, such as chiefs and professionals, tended to have more wives and children. This was particularly true for Muslim men, who claim that their religion allows them to have as many as four wives. However, even older Christians in these social categories would sometimes quote biblical commands to "go into the world, multiply, and be as fruitful as possible." Similarly, affluent men with separate homes – usually one in an urban center and another in a rural area – tended to have multiple wives, and thus more children. For the older generation, having many children appeared to be a source of pride.

---

*Special to this volume.

But younger men, particularly urban dwellers with education and employment, tended to prefer fewer children.

Kibuuka: I am renting a one-room house in Nnyendo. I live there with my partner. She has one child from another marriage. She did not bring this child to me. My mother really wants me to start having children. But then, when I consider my circumstances, I think it is too early to start having children. I will wait until I get money to marry this woman and build a house. So meanwhile we are using condoms, or I do withdrawal when we forget to get condoms.

Musa: I have two wives now. Their rent is on me. Their food is on me. Their clothes are on me. Their everything is on me. One has two children and the first one has three children. I told them to go to Family Planning so that they can tie their tubes. I do not want more babies. I only make small, small money.

Vincent: Those large families were things that could be afforded by our grandfathers. You would meet one man, and he would still be having children when his eldest children started having children. Those men had large cotton farms, or coffee plantations. And they did not have to send children to school. People would just grow up, eat and marry. But now, heh, things are difficult. Every fee is on you. Even when the government is supposed to provide free education or hospital services, they cannot. So, how do I start having babies with this woman and that one? No . . . only three children with my wife.

Kasozi: When you ask them to fill [in] the question about number of children, they are ashamed to tell you the true number. He has got six children in the village, and four children at home. I went to school with his daughter. I know his family. I think it shames him for researchers like yourself to find out that he is a medical doctor, and yet he has got so many children as if he is uneducated.

Indeed, several motorbike-taxi riders I interviewed in southwestern Uganda reported that they advised their sexual partners to have abortions in the event of an unplanned pregnancy. Some of these men revealed that when a woman insists on having the child, the men make it clear that they do not want any knowledge of, let alone responsibility for, the child:

Antonio: I told her, "My dear, you have to take that thing out." She cried, and told me that she does not want to have the abortion because the child was sown in love. She also said that she feared she might have complications and die during the abortion. "You should have thought about that before you got pregnant," I retorted. "I am willing to give you some money for the abortion. If you do not do it, I do not want to know about the baby. I do not want to get involved. In fact I do not want you to give that child my name."

Interviewer: So what actually happened?

Antonio: I do not know. I saw her around the town for a few more months. She was growing bigger and bigger. After some time, she went to her village. The next time we met, she was married to a shopkeeper in Kampala. I never asked her about the child. I do not want to know.

A study conducted among secondary school students* revealed that such attitudes, values and practice also prevail among adolescents. This suggests that reconceptualizing and renegotiating the value of children begins while these men are still adolescents. Male students often claimed that if they impregnated a girl, they would readily deny responsibility, even changing schools to avoid the girl and unfavorable consequences like early fatherhood, forced marriage, the possibility of having to drop out of school, sanctions from the girl's parents, or imprisonment.† Abortion was a preferred solution for many of these students. Understandably, the opportunity cost of having a child is much greater for a student with much to lose in terms of social standing, whether due to a new reputation as "prematurely sexually active," "sexually loose," or "promiscuous"; or due to a loss of education with its promise of a better future, because school regulations dictate the immediate expulsion of both boy and girl in the event of pregnancy. While faced with peer pressure to be sexually active, adolescents also face intense stigmatization and marginalization the moment they are publicly known to be parents. This stigma is heightened if the adolescents still reside in their parents' home and depend on them for sustenance.

Changing contexts

Unlike earlier times, when a man's father would apportion a plot of his land for his son to move in with his pregnant spouse, parents today will drive the boy out of their household, and even punish him for prematurely "spoiling another's child."‡ In pre-colonial societies, resources such as land, work, and capital were relatively abundant. In Uganda, individuals owned mile upon mile of land for residence, cultivation, animal-rearing, forestry, and in some cases gift-giving. Land was a valuable asset passed down through the generations. As such, men needed cheap labor, supplied in the form of several children. This was made possible by the institution of polygyny, which allowed one man to have concurrent and serial wives. In this era prior to capitalism and intense

---

*J. Kinsman, S. Nyanzi, and R. Pool, "Socialising Influences and the Value of Sex: The Experience of Schoolgirls in Rural Masaka, Uganda," *Culture, Health and Sexuality*, 2 (2000), pp. 151–66.

†S. Nyanzi, R. Pool, and J. Kinsman, "Negotiation of Sexual Relationships Among School-Going Adolescents," *AIDS Care*, 13: 1 (2001), pp. 83–98.

‡The concept of "spoiling" a girl involves the idea of sexually polluting an otherwise innocent girl with acts ranging from talking to her about sex, appealing to her sexual imagination, erotically touching her, having sexual intercourse, and ultimately impregnating her without marrying her.

commercialization, the cost of living was cheap, and men could provide for several wives and children. Children were a highly sought-after resource.

In this postmodern age, by contrast, Africa has undergone myriad transformations. Noteworthy in this context are:

- changing patterns of land ownership and tenure;
- urbanization;
- monetization of economies, consumerism, and commercialism;
- globalization, with its opening-up of previously closed societies to other cultures and ways of life;
- birth control mechanisms;
- women's rights;
- massive unemployment and economic competition.

Individuals lost family land to central governments, thereby losing a valuable revenue source as well as the need for abundant labor to cultivate and process crops. Poverty and privation led many individuals with substantial landholdings to liquidate them, by dividing them and selling them off to different individuals. Massive migration by rural residents seeking better prospects caused extensive urbanization. Conditions in peri-urban and urban settings negated the desire for large families, in part because accommodation is mainly rented, even small houses are unaffordable, the cost of supporting several children is impossible to sustain, and competition is intense for scarce and often unavailable resources. Furthermore, everything now costs money: education, health, accommodation, food, shelter, transport, leisure, and so on. The more dependants, the greater the challenge of providing for them.

Education and exposure to western ideals mean that men are now taught to plan their families, space children appropriately, use condoms, and even secure access to abortion for their partners. Consequently, a man who would once have been hailed for sowing his seed profusely would now be ridiculed, and perhaps given advice about using contraception. While having plenty of children was previously a mark of manhood and a cherished ambition for many African men, it is now often shunned due to social pressure and high levels of unemployment. A common argument seems to be: "If I cannot provide for my children, so that they are continuously hungry, walk around with torn clothes and bare feet, cannot attend school like other children, and become social menaces, how can I call myself a man? What manhood is that?" Today, one's maturity, manhood, and sexual ability can be measured and fulfilled by having only the number of children one can manage.

EGYPT

Infertile Men

Marcia C. Inhorn*

Two cases of male infertility

Madiha and Ahmed

Madiha is a diminutive, attractive, and brave twenty-three-year-old, married to her infertile, twenty-eight-year-old husband, Ahmed, for five years. Both are uneducated and poor, as his carpenter's salary brings them only LE 40 a month [less than $15]. Although Madiha worked in a textile factory before marriage and is willing to work again to improve their economic situation, Ahmed refuses this option, citing the problems of crowded transportation (with men who are "strangers") and Madiha's potential neglect of the housework. Madiha has been seeking treatment for infertility since the third month of her marriage, when her mother- and sister-in-law insisted on taking her to a physician. Since then, she has endured countless "treatments," both ethnomedical and biomedical. Her mother-in-law has brought her vaginal suppositories of black glycerine to "bring out" any infection she might have in her vagina. Traditional healers and neighbors have performed painful "cupping" on her back to draw "humidity" out of her womb. Spiritist healers have said prayers over her and asked her to perform various rituals of circumambulation at religious sites. During one Friday noon prayer, she was asked by a female spiritist healer to urinate on top of an eggplant to "unbind" an infertility-producing condition known as *kabsa* or *mushahara*.

Simultaneously, Madiha has pursued biomedical treatment, at the urging of Ahmed and his relatives, with whom she has lived for most of her marriage. Two of the doctors she has visited have performed a procedure called tubal insufflation, in which carbon dioxide is pumped into the uterus without any anesthesia. One of the doctors told her that her cervix and uterus might be "small" and that "the smallest uterus can't get pregnant"; the procedure might "widen" or "dilate" her. The other physician offered no reason for performing the procedure. In fact, although tubal insufflation is widely practiced as a moneymaking procedure by Egyptian gynaecologists with no specialized training in infertility, this technique, formerly used to diagnose tubal obstruction, has no therapeutic value and may actually produce infertility by forcing pathogenic bacteria from the lower into the upper genital tract.

Madiha also underwent an operation under general anesthesia to correct a "folded" uterus. As she explained, "I didn't want this operation, but my in-laws pushed me and

---

*From Marcia C. Inhorn, "'The Worms Are Weak': Male Infertility and Patriarchal Paradoxes in Egypt," ch. 12 in Lahoucine Ouzgane, ed., *Islamic Masculinities* (London: Zed Books, 2006). Names used here are pseudonyms.

gave me the money." When the operation failed, the doctor asked Ahmed to go to a particular doctor for an "analysis." Ahmed complied, and was asked to repeat the analysis twice and to take treatment.

According to Madiha, it was only then that "I knew I'm alright and something is wrong with my husband." Yet, Ahmed refuses to believe he is the cause of the infertility, and thus rejects treatment. His family, furthermore, refuses to believe that the first son in the family to marry is responsible for the infertility. As Madiha put it, "Even my husband, when I tell him it's his problem, he doesn't answer me. When he went to the doctor for the first time, the doctor told him that he had pus and weakness in his *didan* (literally, 'worms,' i.e., sperm). But he never goes for treatment, even though he knows I want him to. Every time I tell his family that it's 'from him,' they don't answer me. Instead, every time I tell them that I'm going to the doctor, they encourage me to, as if it's my problem. My family won't get involved. They know I'm not the reason and it's something wrong with Ahmed. They're 'relaxed' because they know it's his problem." [. . .]

Shahira, Mohammed, and their ICSI Twins

Shahira is the 25-year-old wife of Mohammed, a 43-year-old lawyer whose father was once a powerful politician. In addition to his legal practice, Mohammed rents a villa to a foreign embassy and owns a business center run by Shahira. She is Mohammed's second wife, married to him now for ten months. Before this, Mohammed was married for 17 years to Hala, a woman now in her forties, whom he divorced two years ago because of their childlessness.

Early in his first marriage, physicians told Mohammed that he suffered from severe male-factor infertility, involving low sperm count and poor motility. He underwent repeated courses of hormonal therapy, none of which improved his sperm profile. Ultimately, he and Hala underwent several cycles of artificial insemination using concentrates of his sperm, and five cycles of in vitro fertilization (IVF), three times in Germany and twice in Egypt. Each trial was unsuccessful.

It was obvious to the Egyptian physicians who undertook one of the trials that Mohammed and Hala's marriage was deteriorating during the course of therapy – a deterioration they implied had something to do with Hala's "strong personality." Shahira seemed to agree: "In Egypt, if a man knows he doesn't get his wife pregnant, he's always upset. And if you're pushing him all the time, and he's the reason for the problem, he feels like giving up [on the marriage], because there are no children to keep in the house. In my husband's case, he preferred to divorce her because their relationship became bad. They had different attitudes and behaviors, and the major reason for the divorce was that he knows he's the reason for no pregnancy. He's kind, and she's nervous and always asking too many questions."

Although Hala has not remarried, Mohammed remarried in little over a year. He chose Shahira, a Christian, after knowing her for five months. Mohammed was less interested in Shahira's "pedigree" (a college degree in tourism, with fluency in French and English) and in her religion (a Muslim man is allowed to marry a Christian woman), than in her youth, potential fecundity, acceptance of his infertility problem, and her willingness to try additional treatments with him. He told her, "I want to marry you, but you are a young lady, and I'm sure you want a baby." Shahira needed a "father figure" and felt that Mohammed could be "both a husband and a father." [. . .] She continued: "I took my decision in two months, without love before marriage, but with my mind. But love has grown – 100%. An important thing in marriage is understanding, feeling secure. That's more important than love. He's kind and when I'm sick, he'll sit beside me and ask how I'm feeling. When I married him, I accepted 100% that I will not have children, and I wouldn't push him. But since I knew his case before marriage, I told him I'd be willing to try [IVF] more than once because he's kind. I was afraid, but I'll try."

A few months into their marriage, Shahira went to a gynaecologist in Maadi, an elite suburb. The physician told her, "You are young and you haven't anything wrong, but the lab report on your husband is bad." She asked the physician about IVF, and he said, "No way, because your husband is a very bad case." Mohammed, meanwhile, underwent five months of drug therapy. His andrologist told him, "Your wife is young. ICSI [intracytoplasmic sperm injection; a variant of IVF] may be successful, because she's young and has no problem. Don't hesitate. You should use any time you have." [. . .]

Shahira suffered uncomfortable side effects from the medications used to stimulate ovulation. Her gastric ulcer symptoms were exacerbated, and she felt abdominal cramping and pain throughout the treatment. "It's too difficult doing this ICSI," Shahira explained. "I take all these injections, I come to the hospital every day, I prepare for the operation, I see the anesthesia, the doctors. It's frightening. My husband – they just take the semen from him."

Once the ICSI procedure was completed, Shahira was still unconvinced of its efficacy. Thus, when she was scheduled for a blood test to determine her pregnancy status, she refused. She was so intransigent that Mohammed finally called the laboratory and had a doctor sent to their home to draw the sample. The next day, Mohammed and Shahira went to the laboratory, where the physician told them: "Congratulations. I wanted to tell you personally." Repeated pregnancy tests, along with three ultrasounds, confirmed that Shahira was pregnant – with twins in separate amniotic sacs.

Now Mohammed is in disbelief. Every day, he looks at Shahira's expanding belly and says, "Now I can't believe I will have children. I will believe it if I touch my son or daughter by myself." Shahira hopes that the birth of his twins will make Mohammed stop smoking three packs of cigarettes a day. Shahira is also concerned about the potential difficulties associated with a twin pregnancy and caesarean childbirth, and the demands of taking care of two infants simultaneously. She hopes that at least one of the infants will be a girl, although Mohammed hopes for a son he can name "Ahmed." If God wills, and the twins are born healthy, Shahira says she won't do ICSI again. "Once is enough. One operation, one delivery. It's too difficult and too frightening."

The cases of Madiha and Ahmed and Shahira and Mohammed illustrate the relationship of male infertility to patriarchy in Egyptian culture. In Egypt, patriarchy involves relations of power and authority of males over females which are (1) learned through gender socialization within the family, where fatherhood gives men power; (2) manifested in inter- and intragender interactions within marriage, the family, and other interpersonal milieus; (3) ingrained in pervasive ideologies of inherent male superiority; and (4) institutionalized on legal, political, economic, educational, and religious levels. Although I do not intend to suggest that Egypt is somehow more patriarchal than other societies, patriarchy operates on many levels in Egyptian society today. Furthermore, patriarchal ideologies cut across social classes, religious boundaries, and household types. However, as seen in the case of Madiha and Ahmed, manifestations of patriarchy are often more pronounced among the rural and urban lower classes living in extended family households. [. . .]

I argue that women suffer over men's infertility because of the nature of Egyptian patriarchy and the kind of patriarchal support Egyptian men receive in their family lives, even when they are infertile. Male infertility in Egypt creates four main "patriarchal paradoxes": (1) who gets blamed for infertility in a marriage; (2) whose gendered identity is diminished by infertility; (3) who suffers in an infertile marriage; and (4) who pays the price for infertility treatment.

The first paradox is seen in the realm of procreative theory, or how Egyptians conceive of the "coming into being" of humans. In contemporary Western reproductive biology, procreation theories are "duogenetic," in that men and women are seen as contributing equally to the hereditary substance of the fetus, formed through the union of a woman's ovum and a man's spermatozoon. However, even with the widespread penetration of Western biomedicine and education around the world in the past half century, the globalization of such a duogenetic model is incomplete. Rather, in Egypt and in other parts of the Middle East, less educated people believe procreation is "monogenetic," assigning men, the "givers of life," primary responsibility for procreation. Specifically, most poor urban Egyptians believe that men are the creators of preformed fetuses, which they carry in their sperm and which are then ejaculated and "caught and carried" by women's waiting wombs. In this scenario, women are not only marginalized as reproducers, but the products of their reproductive bodies, particularly menstrual blood, are seen as polluting to men and the fetuses they create. Although the notion of women's "eggs" is beginning to gain credence, even some educated Egyptians argue that men's sperm are reproductively dominant to women's eggs in terms of biogenetic input into the fetus.

Given this ideology of male procreation, it is a true patriarchal paradox that women, rather than men, are blamed for procreative failure. [. . .] With the advent of semen analysis in Egypt over the past three decades, however, the blame for infertility has shifted slightly. In fact, "worm" pathology is a titillating topic of conversation among poor urban Egyptians. Virtually every Egyptian has now heard of the problem of so-called weak worms. "Weakness" is a common cultural illness idiom in Egypt and is rife in popular reproductive imagery. Most Egyptians now accept the idea that men, too, may be infertile because "the worms" are slow, sluggish, prone to premature death, or absent altogether. [. . .] But accepting male infertility in theory is not the same as accepting it in practice. Although Egyptians are willing to discuss the possibility of weak worms when a couple is childless, they are less willing to accept male infertility as the absolute cause of any given case. [. . .] Rather, women are blamed for the failure to facilitate male procreation. [. . .]

This brings us to the second paradox: whereas infertility always mars a woman's femininity, no matter which partner is the "cause" of the problem, male infertility does not similarly redound on a man's masculinity. There are several reasons for this. First, there is widespread disagreement about the degree to which male infertility can be emasculating. The dominant view is that male infertility is profoundly emasculating, particularly given two major conflations: first, of infertility with virility or sexual potency; and second, of virility with "manhood," the meanings of which are closely linked in North Africa. In Egypt, infertile men are said to "not be good for women," to have their "manhood shaken," or to be "weak" and "incomplete," not "real men." Thus, infertility casts doubt upon a man's sexual and gender identities – that is, whether he is a "real" man with the normal masculine parts, physiological processes, requisite "strength" of body and character, and appropriate sexual orientation. Furthermore, infertility threatens personhood itself or the acceptance of a man as a "whole" human being with a normal adult social identity and self-concept. Indeed, infertility, a condition over which Egyptian men (like men everywhere) have no control, threatens [. . .] those attributes of a man felt to be so ordinary and natural that failure to achieve them leads to feelings of shame, incompleteness, self-hate, and self-derogation. Given the threat of infertility to normative masculinity, it is not surprising that the condition is deeply stigmatizing and the source of profound psychological suffering for Egyptian men who accept their infertile status. Because male infertility is glossed as spermatic "weakness," many infertile Egyptian men seem to take this cultural idiom to heart, feeling that they are somehow weak, defective, and even unworthy as biological progenitors. Many infertile Egyptian men seeking treatment at IVF centers bemoaned their "weakness" and wondered out loud whether they would "pass their weakness" onto their children.

On the other hand, an alternative view voiced by many Egyptians of all social classes is that "a man is always a man," whether or not he is infertile, because having a child doesn't "complete a man as it does a woman." Indeed, whereas a woman's full personhood can be achieved only through attainment of motherhood, a man's sense of achievement has other potential outlets, including employment, education, religious/spiritual pursuits, sports and leisure, friendship groups, and the like. [. . .] Thus, while men and women in Egypt, almost without exception, eventually marry and expect to become parents, the truly mandatory nature of parenthood is experienced much more keenly by women, whose other avenues for self-realization are limited and who are judged harshly when they are unable to achieve motherhood early in their married lives. [. . .] [In addition,] infertility stemming from a husband rarely leads to wife-initiated divorce and may, in fact, strengthen marital bonds. Yet, infertility may lead to husband-initiated divorce or polygynous remarriage, whether or not female infertility can be proven. [. . .]

Other stories could be told of how male infertility plays out in men's and women's lives in Egypt. Such stories must attend to infertile men's perspectives on their marriages, identities, and experiences as members of a society in which men themselves are subject to stressful, competitive, hierarchical forms of hegemonic masculinity. Male infertility presents a crisis of masculinity for Egyptian men, one in which their manhood is shaken to its deepest core. But, as demonstrated in this essay, the effects of such masculine crises do not end there: they redound in multiple, often profoundly detrimental ways in the lives of the women who, by virtue of marriage, must share infertile men's secrets and uphold their masculinity at all costs.

MEXICO

Viagra and Changing Masculinities

Emily Wentzell[*]

Treatments for erectile dysfunction can reinforce or challenge men's ideas of sexuality and masculinity, and men can actively use these treatments either to support or to reframe their understanding of what it means to be manly. The different ways that men use and think about these treatments go hand in hand with their constantly evolving understanding and acting out of masculinity.

Masculinity is, in part, a role men play by referencing different models of manhood and cultural stereotypes. In the 1950s, writer Octavio Paz defined what would become a powerful stereotype of Mexican masculinity: the *macho* man.[†] The macho is violent, tough, and emotionally guarded; most importantly, he has frequent penetrative sex. While the concept of machismo is one widespread idea of how be masculine, it certainly does not characterize all real-life Mexican men. Instead, it is a model that influences, but does not define, men's daily decisions about how to act masculine. Many lower-income men in Mexico City who experience erectile problems, which would presumably be quite damaging to a macho self-image, are employing new ideas about erectile dysfunction to challenge stereotypically macho masculinity.

---

[*]Special to this volume.
[†]Octavio Paz, *The Labyrinth of Solitude: Life and Thought in Mexico* (trans. L. Kemp) (New York: Grove Press, 1961).

In the first half of the twentieth century, when psychoanalysis was popular, persistent erectile problems were called "impotence," and considered to be symptomatic of underlying psychological or emotional problems. In recent decades, doctors have come to view erectile problems as a medical condition called "erectile dysfunction." This shift from understanding erectile problems as psychological or emotional to seeing them as purely medical is an instance of *medicalization*, a process in which an experience is defined as a physical problem treatable only with medical interventions.

The introduction of Viagra cemented this shift in popular understandings of erectile problems from the mind to the body, since Viagra can often produce erections even in men whose erectile dysfunction is known to have psychological roots. Viagra was introduced in Mexico and the US in 1998. It has since become a global force – approved for sale in over 100 countries, and available internationally via the Internet. Researchers have found that about half of men between ages 40 and 70 worldwide suffer from erectile dysfunction. In Mexico, 55 per cent of 40–70-year-olds are found to suffer from some degree of erectile dysfunction, as are 9.7 per cent of men between ages 18 and 40.* (It is important to note, however, that since medical treatment of erectile dysfunction makes money for doctors and drug companies, some researchers may have a financial incentive to discover epidemic levels of erectile dysfunction.)

This change in the understanding of erectile problems occurred simultaneously with major shifts in Mexican masculinity. Anthropologist Matthew C. Gutmann contends that people cope with the gender roles they inherit from the past while simultaneously reshaping them for use in the present.† Mexicans have experienced broad economic, political, and social changes in the past few decades. These have influenced, and in turn been influenced by, individuals' remodeling of gender norms. For example, Gutmann argues that an early 1970s political movement among poor residents of Mexico City created new leadership roles for women, who led seizures of land from the government to build homes. Feminist movements both in Mexico and worldwide have also changed the way people understand gender and masculinity, raising awareness about inequalities between men and women and offering men more egalitarian ideals of masculinity.

Thus, while Mexican men understand machismo as one model for manhood, they often see it as outmoded or harmful. Many men now support behaviors – like tenderly and attentively caring for babies – that do not conform to stereotypical machismo. This does not mean that practices of masculinity have completely changed. For example, Gutmann found that working-class Mexican men were far more likely to say they shared household chores with their wives than actually to do so. It does, however, mean

---

*See S. Glina *et al.*, "Efficacy and Safety of Sildenafil Citrate for the Treatment of Erectile Dysfunction in Latin America," *Brazilian Journal of Urology*, 27: 2 (2001), pp. 148–54.
†Matthew C. Gutmann, *The Meanings of Macho: Being a Man in Mexico City* (Berkeley, CA: University of California Press, 1996). See the two excerpts from Gutmann's work in this section.

that men think critically about machismo, accepting certain aspects of it while rejecting and refashioning others.

To understand how lower-income Mexican men are using the new medical ideas
about erectile problems in their reshapings of masculinity, we must first discuss the
pros and cons of medicalizing the less-than-ideal erection. Medical treatment for erectile dysfunction works extremely well for men whose erectile problems are caused by
diseases, such as diabetes or heart disease. In addition, men are less likely to feel personally responsible for, or feel shame about, a condition that is purely medical.
Pharmacological treatment for erectile dysfunction can also be a quick and easy solution. However, this quick fix may also be a problem, enabling men whose erectile difficulties are caused by psychological or emotional problems to treat the symptom while
ignoring the real problem.

Men in industrialized societies often understand their bodies as functioning like
machines, and their penises as tools for performing sex rather than elements in a complex act that involves both the mind and body.* Viagra use can endorse this understanding of sex as a mechanical act, leading to relationship problems between partners.
For example, researcher Annie Potts and colleagues found that many women in New
Zealand were unhappy with changes in their sex lives that had occurred since their husbands started using Viagra. Their husbands often became focused only on mechanical
performances of penetrative sex, ignoring the emotional and sensual aspects of the act.
Furthermore, when men perceive their bodies as machines, relying on a notion of
masculinity that leaves no room for emotions, the unavoidable occurrence of a less-
than-perfect erection is viewed as a breakdown or failure. Mechanical concepts of masculinity have much in common with the idea of machismo, with its emphasis on
penetrative sexuality.

However, because the medical concept of erectile dysfunction has so many different
meanings and possible consequences, men can use it to support a variety of understandings of masculinity. Since 1989, Dr. Eusebio Rubio, an M.D. with a Ph.D. in
human sexuality, and the founder and director of the Mexican Association for Sexual
Health, has run a Mexico City clinic offering sex therapy, along with medical and psychological services, for low-income individuals. In a telephone interview, he told me
that both before and after the introduction of Viagra, men were deeply concerned with
erectile function, and willing to do anything in order to alleviate erectile problems. The
ability to have penetrative sex, then, has been a consistent criterion for masculinity in
Mexico, as elsewhere. However, both pre- and post-Viagra, Dr. Rubio says that a key
reason men sought treatment for erectile problems was to better satisfy their sexual
partners. Thus, while Dr. Rubio's patients have always been concerned with the ability
to penetrate, and seen this as a key to manliness, they have also badly wanted to satisfy
their partners – a desire that runs counter to the macho stereotype.

---

*See Annie Potts, "Viagra Cyborgs: Creating 'Better Manhood through Chemistry,' " in Potts
et al., eds., Sex and the Body (Palmerston North, New Zealand: Dunmore Press, 2004).

Furthermore, Dr. Rubio states that many of his patients have demonstrated a change in attitude about erectile function over the past two decades. Twenty years ago, most of his patients felt that the ability to have erections was a defining characteristic of masculinity; without erections, they no longer felt manly. Since the popularization of the biomedical model, Dr. Rubio says that his patients are more likely to think, "What's wrong with my penis?" than to wonder what is wrong with their manhood. This shift away from defining the masculine self through erection and penetration can facilitate new conceptions of masculinity.

It is important to remember that individual men understand and act out masculinity differently. The wide array of treatment options available in Mexico City for erectile dysfunction enables men to seek cures that support their particular brand of masculinity. Dr. Rubio says that his urologist colleagues see many erectile dysfunction patients who usually come to the office alone, are unwilling to discuss their problem with their sexual partner, and seek a quick medical solution. Medical intervention in this case may support a more machismo-oriented type of masculinity, in which a mechanical fix is needed to restore sexual function, and in which emotions and interpersonal relationships are removed from the equation. On the other hand, Dr. Rubio's patients are usually happy to bring their partners to the clinic, and think of their erectile problems in the context of their relationships and emotions. Viagra can easily be obtained without a prescription in Mexico City, although it is too expensive for many low-income men to purchase regularly. Some of Dr. Rubio's patients tried Viagra on their own, but could not afford to continue using it, and came to him for a more cost-effective treatment. Thus, it is not only men's understanding of the role of erections in masculinity, but a complex combination of economic, social, and other factors that lead men to seek specific treatments.

In these less traditional models of masculinity, the experience of erection is only part of what it is to be a man, rather than the defining characteristic of manhood. By understanding erectile problems in fresh ways, many lower-income men in Mexico City come to identify their problem as a medical concern, rather than a failure of macho identity. In treating their erectile dysfunction, these men are crafting new forms of masculinity.

MEXICO

Urges and Affairs

Matthew C. Gutmann*

After I had spent several months in Mexico, my research suddenly assumed an explicitly sexual character in a very personal way when my wife and daughter returned to the United States for a couple of weeks. Before leaving, [my wife] Michelle talked casually one day with [our neighbors] Angela and Norma about her planned trip. Angela asked if she was worried about leaving me alone for so long, hinting not so subtly at the opportunity this would present me for *aventuras* (adventures) – in other words, adultery. When Michelle responded that she trusted me and was not concerned, Angela countered, "Well, sure, but do you trust the women?" Michelle had not understood the real threat, Angela counseled: men cannot help themselves when sexual opportunity presents itself.

The day after Michelle and Liliana left, I bumped into Norma and another neighbor, Lupita, at the *sobre ruedas* (open-air market) that is set up on Coyamel Street each Wednesday. After asking if Michelle and Liliana had gotten off all right, Norma turned to me and, forefinger pointed to her eye, said "*¡Te estamos vigilando!* [We're keeping an eye on you!]." Lupita added, with the same gesture, that she too would mount a vigilant lookout. It was mainly a joke by these two married women who had already become like family. But it was also a warning to the husband of one of their absent friends that no fooling around would be tolerated – or go unreported. Implicit, again, was the message that men will try to get away with whatever they can sexually, unless they believe they might get caught.

What is interesting is not that the actual frequency of cheating is that high (or low, for that matter), but the insights all this provided into what many women and men in Santo Domingo [neighborhood] view as an innate core of male sexuality. As Angela told me later when I asked her about her comments to Michelle, "*¿A quién le dan pan que llore?* [Who cries when they're given bread?]" Everyone knows what you do with bread: you eat it. The stereotype of men in Mexico being subject to uncontrollable bodily urges and needs is widely held in Santo Domingo – which just proves that some stereotypes about sexual identities in the region are shared by those living there.

Many men tell of having had affairs with women other than their wives. "*No soy santo*," confides Alfredo, "I'm no saint." The justification for adultery on the part of men is often that men have peculiar "natural desires." Further, men sometimes snickered to me that "*el hombre llega hasta donde la mujer lo diga* [men will get away with whatever

*From Matthew C. Gutmann, *The Meanings of Macho: On Being a Man in Mexico City* (Berkeley, CA: University of California Press, 1996), pp. 129–33.

women let them]." One of the most common expressions for an extramarital affair is *cana al aire* – literally, "a gray hair to the air," the image being that when you find a gray hair you pull it out quickly and fling it away; you do it, and it is over.

Such "flings" are said to be distinguished by their purely sexual as opposed to romantic content. One woman described to me how when her husband was younger he would often disappear on Friday night and not return until Sunday night. She would tell their children that he was working, to protect them, she said. Taxi drivers have an especially wide reputation for casual rendezvous with women fares. After waxing most poetic on the qualities of his wife, one *taxista* told me that he and she have an agreement that *aventuritas* [little adventures] are fine so long as they are not discussed between them later. "Twenty-one years is a long time to be married," he told me, suggesting that the underlying rationale was boredom in the marital bedroom. He also insisted that she has the same freedom to find lovers as he. After all, he reasoned to me, otherwise it would not be fair.

Affairs are discussed and joked about casually by many people in Santo Domingo. On boarding a *combi* [minibus] driven by my friend Rafael, I asked how his infant son was doing. He said the boy of four months was doing great. There was one thing, though, that concerned my friend.

"What's bothering you?" I inquired. It was noisy on the minibus and we had to shout to make ourselves heard.

"Every day the boy looks more like people from the 'other side' [the United States]," he screamed.

"How?"

"He's got bright green eyes. I don't even think he's mine!"

He laughed heartily. The other passengers seemed oblivious to this self-disparaging and semi-lewd commentary. His was not the storybook image of a shamefaced and cuckolded husband.

Marcos told me that his wife, Delia, has been joking for years that Lolo, a neighborhood boy of fourteen, is her second husband. It all started when Delia's sister spread a rumor that Lolo had slept with Delia, Marcos related. "Sometimes I chew Lolo out," he continued, "telling him that I had to go to Tepito [a popular market] to buy my girls shoes when he should be the one doing it."

The documentary record leaves open to question the extent to which such banter is new. For example, the use of the term *cabrón*, which can figuratively refer to a cuckold, is widespread, but by no means necessarily tied to this one meaning or even to a negative quality. Regardless of the history of jokes about infidelity, humorous quips about adultery today take place in a shifting context. Men continue to have affairs; this is nothing new. What has reportedly changed is the number of women who do so, and the fact that some are quite open about having lovers. A particularly promiscuous woman in Santo Domingo has even earned a nickname, La Tasqueña, for her amorous liaisons. La Tasqueña is married to a man who spends ten or eleven months a year in Detroit and returns for only short stays to Santo Domingo to visit her and their two children.

Whenever her legal husband is in the United States, she has a series of men (one at a time) living with her, each of whom moves out temporarily when the legal husband returns to the *colonia*. Her nickname derives from an episode that occurred several years ago during one of her legal husband's infrequent visits. She was very late returning to the house one night, and when she finally arrived she complained that she had missed all the *combis* from the Tasqueña metro stop. The problem was that her neighbors had seen her elsewhere and knew this was a ruse to cover up her date that night.*

Thus one of the creative responses of some women to men's adultery has been to take lovers of their own. Women's activities as varied as community organizing and paid work have led to far greater opportunities to meet other men and to have affairs with them. To whatever extent sexual "needs" were ever associated with men alone, this seems far less the case today in Santo Domingo.

In refutation of the commonplace that many or most Latin American men have their first sexual escapades with prostitutes, none of the men I interviewed from Colonia Santo Domingo save one admitted to ever having been to a prostitute. Nor had any men taken their sons to prostitutes "to become men." Once again, it is possible that my friends and informants were simply covering up sexual escapades from their pasts. More probable, I think, is that paying for sexual services is today more common in some areas of Mexico City – for instance, around the Centro Histórico – than it is in others. Then, too, it is possible that for many of my friends, paying for sex implies an unmanly inability to attract women sexually.

Going to prostitutes may be more of a tradition among young men from the middle and upper classes. In [one] survey on sexuality among high school students [...] 20.5 per cent of the well-to-do boys reported that their first sexual relation was with a prostitute. Men from upper-middle-class homes also speak of the convention whereby the father hires a maid with whom his sons can have their first sexual encounters. Making caustic references to "the excesses of the feminist movement," one lawyer sarcastically told me that young men are often raped by these older and more sexually aggressive *muchachas*, adding, "I know this from personal experience." The lawyer's comments regarding feminism and rape bore witness to a defensive posture assumed by many men in his milieu today. Still, for this man and others of his class background and generation, it was taken for granted that males would lose their virginity prior to marrying whereas females should be virgins until their wedding night.

Female virginity continues to be an important issue for many men, but this double standard is far less an issue among younger men and women, especially as knowledge about and use of birth control by teens becomes more widespread. But the matter is contested – among teens, and between teens and their parents. As part of this gendered and generational confrontation over virginity, a particularly bizarre rumor about

---

Editor's note: I wonder if, in fact, the nickname means that the woman is like a metro station, i.e., with numerous "trains" arriving and leaving.

adolescent sexual behavior in the United States was making its way through the Pedregales* in 1993. Some people had heard, and were convinced, that many girls in the United States have their hymens surgically removed so that the first time they have sexual intercourse they will not experience so much pain. This example, among others, was put forth to my wife, Michelle, to demonstrate that women in the United States have much more sexual freedom and know how better to enjoy themselves sexually.

PAKISTAN

Lovers vs. Wives

Thomas Michael Walle[†]

The cases and argument presented in the following account are based on information gathered during a nine-month stay in Pakistan, mostly in the Punjabi capital, Lahore, in 1996 and 1997.

Largely by chance, I was included in a group of male companions that spent large parts of their time together. They were friends, and some were also relatives or colleagues. With regard to material and social status, the group was very diverse. At its core were three men, Kamran, Shabir and Haider (the latter two were brothers), who became my closest friends and my main informants in understanding the complexities of male gender identity in Lahore. These three men allowed me to join them in most of their daily activities: at home, with family, at work, at restaurants, with friends or with an illicit love relation, at a shrine or a relative's grave, at pool-halls, driving around in cars, purchasing illegal alcohol or smoking hash, or when offering prayers. Shabir was the oldest (aged 34) and was married with two children. Kamran and Haider were in their mid-twenties, and unmarried like me. All three had paid work, but only Shabir was a major contributor to his household's economy. If asked, all three would position themselves as belonging to the upper middle class. Suffice it to say that they were relatively well educated, oriented towards a "modern" way of life, and never really short of money.

When setting out to grasp how male gender identity is constituted, researchers frequently starts with the question: "What are the processes in a society that make a boy into a man?," or "What does it take to be a man?" What I realized during my stay in Lahore was that this "something" constituting male gender identity need not be unitary or consistent. Rather, what it takes to "be a man" changes from one context to another.

Editor's note: Southern neighborhoods of Mexico City, built on volcanic rock.
[†]Special to this volume.

There was a large measure of awareness among the group of men among whom I did my research concerning this fact. Male gender identity is constituted by different, often conflicting values.

The large majority of Pakistanis are Muslims – approximately 95 per cent, according to official numbers. This plays an important role in the structuring of social relations, and is manifested in social and juridical norms. Being regarded as a good Muslim is an important component of social identity for both men and women. What is actually regarded as "proper" Muslim conduct varies among individuals, even though they will generally present it as something fixed and universal, in accordance with the Qur'an and the way of the Prophet.

Included in what my friends regard as proper Muslim conduct is abstinence from alcohol, and from pre- or extra-marital affairs. The qualities connected to this way of life are of a piece with those connected to providing for one's own family and showing respect for elders. Behaving as a good Muslim, confining sexual relations to marriage, providing for the family, and making sure that the family as a whole is regarded as "respectable" are thus all expressions of masculine values.

In some situation, however – mostly in male–male social relations – the behavioral focus shifts away from these prohibitions. Drinking liquor and smoking hash are daily routines, as is boasting of experiences with a girlfriend – preferably one among many. Obviously, such activities conflict with an identity as a good Muslim, and the men sometimes jokingly refer to themselves as "bad Muslims." But they are careful to limit such activities to situations with no direct connection to their families. Some researchers suggest that moral standards apply less to men than to women. My own argument is different. In most situations, it is equally important for the evaluation of both a man's and a woman's character that they restrain from pre- and extramarital affairs, and avoid liquor and hash – that they live according to the moral standards of society. Male companions will frown upon a man who is unable to present himself as a good, respectable Muslim. A man does gain prestige by breaking with certain social, juridical, and religious norms, but this is relevant only in relations among men. Rather than renouncing the value of moral standards altogether – for example, claiming that drinking alcohol is of no significance in judging a person's character – it seems vital to indicate to your male companions where the boundary of publicly accepted behavior is drawn. Masculine prestige lies in crossing that border intentionally, but only temporarily.

* * *

Shabir is planning to throw a party for Kamran – he's celebrating his 26th birthday. A couple of days before the party, Kamran and Shabir were having a quarrel. Nazreen, Kamran's girlfriend for the last five years, whom he wishes to marry, has refused to join him at the party. Shabir argues that it will be ridiculous for him to bring one of his girlfriends if Kamran does not also bring a girl. "Why don't you bring Rubina?" Shabir asks, reminding us that the other day, while peeping through the keyhole, he saw

Kamran kissing Rubina. Kamran claims he is only interested in Nazreen, and that kissing Rubina was a mistake. He puts the blame on her uncontrolled sexuality. Shabir retorts: "You don't love Nazreen more than I love each and every one of my eleven girlfriends. Why don't you give Rubina what she wants – your dick? She's already been married, and cannot become your wife. She's just crazy about your dick!" By urging him to go to bed with Rubina, Shabir is challenging Kamran's manhood. At the same time, he makes a remark about how many girlfriends he himself has – thus making quantity the important factor when it comes to love relations.

In the end, Kamran does bring Rubina to the birthday party, and Shabir takes along his girlfriend Shireen. Shabir is careful to ensure that Shireen does not see him while he is drinking. They have hardly any physical contact at all.

While Shireen is in the kitchen with Rubina, Shabir takes the opportunity to talk with Kamran and me about her. "She's beautiful, isn't she? I can guarantee you that I've never gone to bed with her, and never will. It wouldn't be right, considering her background and all – she's from a very religious family!"

Later that evening, after Shabir has left to drive Shireen home, Kamran says he has problems believing Shabir's statements about protecting Shireen's decency. "Shabir isn't like that! He's so changeable, like a chameleon! Shabir's strength is that he adjusts according to the person sitting before him."

Shabir is trying to leave the impression that he is a responsible man, and Kamran is only questioning the veracity of this responsibility. Earlier, Shabir had mocked Kamran for not parading his manhood when the opportunity presented itself with Rubina. In this situation, then, being responsible and respectable are relevant masculine values. By contrast, Kamran's loyalty and responsibility towards Nazreen are regarded as something unmanly. Both Kamran and Shabir are trying to define the relevant masculine values, but they adopt different strategies in doing so. This suggests that male gender identity is constituted in competition between men over who is best at being a man, based on ideal images of male practice. Obviously, there is not just one way of "being a man," but rather a multitude of male identities being expressed more or less in accordance with cultural ideals.

In the competition between men, a man is judged as being more or less of a man. Masculinity appears to be a continuum. Men evaluate women differently, however. They are classified according to their moral character – as either good or bad. This dichotomization of women leaves little room for "mistakes" on the woman's side. A woman's "decency" is relevant to a man's reputation and masculine status – it's partly his responsibility to ensure that her decency is maintained. The main division in Lahore is between the decent wife, on the one hand, and the indecent lover and prostitute, on the other. But while there is little dispute about the value of a prostitute's moral character, the lover is a more ambiguous category.

All the women I spoke with, and most of the women I heard of who were involved in an illegitimate relationship with a man, had marriage as their ultimate goal. Without exception, her lover had her believing this was his intention, too. When talking with the man in question, though, it frequently became apparent that what he told his girlfriend did not coincide with his real intentions. Very often these men were already married, and had no intention of getting a second wife. For those who were unmarried, the way they spoke about their girlfriend made it plain that they considered her unsuitable as a future wife.

Thus, the man has an interest in (and the possibility of) doing both the "right" and the "wrong" thing regarding prevailing moral standards. When getting married to a woman with whom he has had little or no prior contact – a woman frequently chosen by his family, and thus necessarily regarded by them as decent – a man enhances his masculine status by employing "moral" values. When entertaining a relationship with a woman to whom he has no intention of getting married – a woman whom he therefore regards as indecent – a man enhances his masculine status by employing "immoral" values.

Let us consider two cases that illustrate the ambivalence and transformative aspect of these categories.

The case of Kamran and Nazreen

Shortly after my arrival in Lahore, I encountered Kamran at Shabir's office. He was drunk and depressed, and threatened to commit suicide by jumping off the roof of the four-storey building. The reason, others told me, was the difficulties he was facing in trying to persuade his family to accept Nazreen, his girlfriend, as his future wife. When I met him a few days later, we talked about the incident and his relationship with Nazreen. "I'm not into girls, unlike most other men," he claimed. "I'm sticking with Nazreen. She's the only woman I'll ever want!" But during the following months, several events occurred that changed the way Kamran regarded Nazreen and their future together.

After persistent nagging, Kamran persuaded Nazreen to have sex with him. He told me this was a once-off: Nazreen had "given herself" to him, and they would wait until marriage to have sex again. Despite Kamran's assurances about "not being into girls," he then had a short affair with Rubina – an affair he denied for a long time, until confronted by Shabir, who had seen the two of them kissing.

A second affair, with Benish, proved to have a more serious effect on Kamran's life and his relationship with Nazreen. Kamran never expressed the same feelings towards Benish as he did towards Nazreen; but Benish was madly in love with him, and he never contradicted her when she spoke of their love for each other and future marriage plans. He even reassured her, using the presumably reliable Norwegian researcher as an unwilling witness, that he didn't meet with other women.

Kamran insisted to Nazreen that he was still hoping for marriage, but his efforts to persuade his parents decreased over the months. He told me he no longer enjoyed the weekly meetings with Nazreen – in secrecy, occasionally at my place – as much as he once had. Surely he would get married in the end – to somebody. But for now, he wanted to "live" while he had the chance.

By having sex with Kamran, Nazreen may have crossed the vague, but important, division between "decent" and "indecent" in Kamran's eyes. The sexual act may have altered his intentions. Gradually, Kamran's perceptions of Nazreen may have shifted from a decent potential wife, to an indecent girlfriend. Kamran still wanted to marry a "decent" woman. The question was whether Nazreen fulfilled his expectations or not.

The case of Shabir and Aisha

Aisha became Shabir's girlfriend during my stay in Lahore. Shabir was married, and reputed by his male friends to be a womanizer without equal.

At first, Aisha wasn't any different in Shabir's eyes than any of his previous or present girlfriends. He spoke constantly about her beauty, her slim body and big breasts – emphasizing her sexuality and the sexual aspects of his relationship with her. His intentions towards her undoubtedly focused on sexual pleasure and prestige. He communicated through speech and behavior that he considered her to be "indecent."

During the months that followed, however, Shabir started to prefer Aisha's company to that of his other girlfriends. He began to talk about her in a more respectful way, and expressed concern for her well-being. Gradually, he fell in love with her, to the extent that he started to talk about marriage. As a Muslim man, he argued, he could have as many as four wives – so two couldn't be that bad.

When Shabir's younger brother, Haider, learned about the marriage plans, he was furious. A marriage between Shabir and Aisha was out of the question, he declared. He would personally kill his brother before allowing such an event to take place.

At the beginning of the relationship, Shabir viewed Aisha as a conquest he could boast about, enjoy having sex with, and leave at an opportune moment. His own sexual intentions meant that he regarded her as a girlfriend, hence indecent. Haider, for his part, did not object to the relationship at this early stage. He even envied Shabir for Aisha's beauty; he would have liked to have her as a girlfriend himself. But he could never accept her as Shabir's future wife. So Aisha, at the outset, was indecent in both Shabir's and Haider's eyes. It was the change in Shabir's intentions towards her that had him redefining her moral character – not any dramatic changes in Aisha's behavior.

*   *   *

In light of the foregoing, I suggest that men, or dominant groups of men, have an interest in maintaining a division of women into discrete categories of decent and indecent. Men *need* both decent and indecent women. The decent/indecent dichotomy supplies men with an argument for controlling women that women, too, will support. The continuing emphasis on female virginity should thus be seen as a means of perpetuating male dominance.

If more women, as individuals, are willing to abandon the prerequisite of marital virginity, men can exploit this to achieve their goals of sexual adventures and masculine prestige. They may play along with their girlfriend in maintaining that premarital sex does not affect a woman's decency. But when they have achieved what they want in the relationship, they may come to view the woman as "indecent" – whereupon they will terminate the relationship.

The man is still the one within the relationship who has the power to decide how a woman should be labeled, thus influencing the broader perception of her moral character. One is entitled to hope that, in the longer term, we will see changes in the arbitrariness of this taken-for-granted masculine dominance. The question then is if this will lead to increased gender equality, or if men will find other perceptions and ideas that they can use to maintain their dominant position.

TURKEY

Virginity and Masculinity

Iklim Goksel*

Since the early 1990s, debates concerning female sexuality in Turkey have dominated private and public spaces. Virginity examinations, in particular, have emerged as the central focus of discussions on the status of women, giving virginity precedence over any other social issue on the Turkish agenda. Virginity examinations are performed by physicians on women to determine whether the hymen is either ruptured or intact. An intact hymen confirms a woman's virginity, a ruptured hymen its loss.

The practice of such exams in Turkey surfaced through extensive media coverage in 1992. Four female students at a secondary school for the training of Islamic religious personnel went on a picnic with boys in Simav, a town about 450 kilometers from Ankara, the Turkish capital. Upon returning, they were informed of the school principal's decision to have them undergo virginity exams. To avoid this, two of the girls attempted suicide, and one of them died. In 1997, six adolescent girls attempted suicide by eating rat poison when they found out that they would undergo virginity examinations. They had fled from their dormitory at the Society for the Protection of Children, and had spent the night outside in the city of Istanbul without permission.

These stories point to the weight placed upon virginity as a norm for Turkish women. As media coverage of the virginity exams intensified, both in Turkey and abroad, protests by women's groups, NGOs, and human rights organizations escalated.

---

*Special to this volume.

Reports consistently revealed that the examinations had been conducted on women at the request of family members or state officials.

I conducted twelve months of ethnographic fieldwork between December 2003 and March 2005 within Ankara municipality. I interviewed men from varied social settings in a village, a squatter settlement, and a suburban upper-middle-class neighborhood. My study explored the implications of virginity for masculine identities. In other words, I looked at the preoccupation with virginity and virginity examinations as sites for the production of masculinities. An inquiry into how virginity is articulated and represented in Turkey allowed me to gain insights into the dynamics of men's lives.

One of the themes that recurred in my conversations with men about female virginity and virginity exams was *honor*. Men often told me that to protect their mothers, wives, and sisters was a matter of personal honor. They explained that women were always vulnerable to male sexual advances, especially when men encountered inexperienced teenaged girls whose sexual urges were at their peak. Men's honor would be crushed if they allowed anyone to harm a female family member. It was apparent that these men equated honor with their ability or inability to protect women. They also evinced a deep distrust of fellow men, whom they regarded as preying on women. One man in his late fifties, whom I will call Mehmet, commented as follows:

> Men engage in sexual relations regardless of their feelings. Their physiologies are different from women's. It is my honor to protect the women in my family from the beastly appetite men usually have towards women. It is my duty.

Mehmet was originally from Trabzon, a city in the Eastern Black Sea region, and had migrated to Ankara in the early 1970s. He was an art teacher until he retired in 1990 and began to paint. He was well known and highly respected among artistic circles in Ankara; his paintings sold for $4,000–$7,000 apiece. I spoke with him at his atelier, together with some of his male students. These men had diverse backgrounds. They included a police officer, a restaurant owner, a civil servant working at a bank, a chemical engineer, and an optician. They came once a week to Mehmet's atelier to learn how to paint.

During our conversation about virginity examinations, these men explained to me that they could identify with the school principal who had sought to impose exams on female students back in 1992. While they disagreed with such exams, they explained that it was a difficult situation to handle when teenage girls went off with boys without permission. They expressed fear and concern about the likelihood of girls becoming pregnant in such circumstances. This seemed to them an unbearable situation that could stain male honor. "The principal of any school is responsible for protecting the students; it is a matter of one's honor," said one. They could not imagine a worse scenario than being held accountable for the girls' whereabouts. What would one say to the parents?

I became aware that men's lives were embedded in the female: women defined them. A man was considered honorable and trustworthy only if he were capable of protecting women from harm. Honor and responsibility were used synonymously, and determined a man's reputation, respectability, and dignity in Turkish society. This seemed to me an immense burden to live with.

I also observed men's association of female virginity with purity, cleanliness, and innocence. Their view of virginity was based on the idea that a woman is vulnerable and untouchable, like "a rose that has not been smelled." Sitting with a group of squatter men, I listened as another man in his late fifties declared: "I would not want to step into someone else's pit" – he would not share a woman with another man. He concluded by saying that marriage was sacred, and premarital sexuality was unacceptable, ruining the sanctity of marriage. As he spoke, other men nodded in approval.

I asked this man if premarital sexuality was acceptable for males. He looked at me and responded in a mocking tone:

> Do you think that we got a chance to experience sexuality before marriage? In our village, most of us got married without any sexual experiences whatsoever. Those of us who were fortunate enough were taken to the "you know what I mean" by our fathers or uncles. [Apparently he was referring to a brothel: prostitution is legal in Turkey.] Otherwise, none of the men in my village engaged in premarital sexual relations.

Other men explained that there was no need for such experience. One man objected: "Don't say that! A lot of us were scared to death on our wedding nights." As they shared their stories, I learned that everyone in the group was married by the time they were 20 years old, or upon completion of their military service, which is obligatory for all Turkish men from the age of 18. These men's stories revealed that the value placed upon a woman's virginity, and on marriage at an early age, discouraged premarital sexuality between young girls and boys. They concluded: "We do not approve of sleeping around randomly with anyone one encounters, like they do in the West."

In an upper-class neighborhood, I saw that men considered women who engaged in premarital sexual relations to have been lured away from their sentimental feminine natures, and from essential family values. Premarital sexual conduct categorized women as corrupted by western values. These men operated with strict binary designations of pure/impure, moral/immoral, and honorable/dishonorable. When women were confined to these categories, concepts of purity, morality, and honor were reformulated, and sexual behavior took precedence over any other conduct. The men I interviewed were in their thirties. One, an attorney, commented as follows:

> I currently have a girlfriend with whom I have sexual relations. She lost her virginity to me. I do love her, but I don't know if I will ever want to marry her. She is not the sort of girl I would want to introduce to my mother. After all, she is engaged in premarital sexual relations with me.

His friend, who was pursuing an MBA degree, added:

> Many of us are engaged in sexual relations. Some girls act freely, and are not reluctant to lose their virginity. But I doubt that any one of us will ever consider having a future with them. None of us would want to marry a girl who is not a virgin.

Men mediate notions of modernity and westernization through women's bodies. They associated modernity and westernization with the ability to approve of, or at least tolerate, women who engaged in premarital sex. Thus, all the men I spoke with described a woman's loss of virginity as something that could only be tolerated by modern and westernized men in Turkey. Men often told me they married or would marry a woman "in that condition" because they saw themselves as modern and westernized. A man in his fifties who worked as a financial consultant put it as follows: "I am a modern and tolerant person. A woman's virginity is not an important issue for me. I proved it by marrying my wife, who was not a virgin when we got married."

Finally, for these men, virginity played a role in remodeling ideals of manliness. A woman's virginity amplified masculine strength and power. A man in his forties, who worked as a manager at an insurance company, commented that "to deflower a woman makes me feel manly." Another young man pointed out: "I need to be the first to pick the fruit from the tree."

TURKEY

The Kurdish Child

Metin Yüksel*

Kurds are the world's largest stateless nation, living predominantly in Turkey, Iran, Iraq, and Syria. Kurds are not only divided by state boundaries, but also along linguistic lines, with three main dialects: Kurmanji, Sorani, and Zazaki. Different tribal, religious, and sectarian affiliations also come into play.

Despite these differences, it seems possible to observe a common characteristic. The predominantly rural and traditional Kurdish social structure is accompanied by strict gender divisions, typified by the roles and expectations assigned to males and females. While men are viewed as the bearers and transmitters of the lineage, women and their chastity are considered as symbols of family "honor." An assault on someone's honor, through the violation of a woman's chastity, is one of the most serious crimes one can commit. The compensation for such a crime generally has a very high price: almost always the life of the woman whose "honor" is injured, and sometimes that of the assailant.

One should make two points here. First, a more or less similar conception of "honor" can be found in other Middle Eastern societies and cultures. It is not specifically Kurdish. The second point is that one should avoid simplistic generalizations and stereotypical observations about the position of men and women in Kurdish society.

*Special to this volume. Dedicated to Xanimşo. The author thanks Adam Jones, Mazhar Yüksel, and Hakan Özoğlu for their useful suggestions.

As noted, the Kurds are not a homogeneous mass. There are, for instance, considerable differences in class position and educational level among the Kurds.

In order more effectively to demonstrate gender-based roles and expectations, as well as the deeply rooted understanding of "honor" in Kurdish society, I want to concentrate on a particular incident that occurred in the early 1990s. The family at the heart of this case was living at the time in a village in the Eastern Anatolian region of Turkey. The family had three sons and seven daughters. The two oldest children were daughters, both married. The oldest son, Ali (names are changed throughout this essay), was working as a construction worker in one of the large urban centers in southern Turkey. One day, he ran away with a newly wed Kurdish woman, Zeynep. This was the start of a shocking series of events. We do not know if Zeynep's family had married her off to a cousin contrary to her wishes. What we do know is that she and Ali liked each other, and were willing to run away together. Ali did not force Zeynep to accompany him. After they ran away they were sheltered by one of their fellow countrymen whose house was in the western part of Turkey. All these events took about a week. Zeynep's family threatened the family who sheltered them. So, they had to turn in Ali to his family and Zeynep to her family. It is probable that Ali and Zeynep did not wish to return to their homes, but it seems that they had no practical alternative course of action.

According to witnesses, Zeynep's family decided to kill both her and Ali. Yet negotiations started between the two families, leading to the following result: Ali's family would have to compensate for their son's "dishonorable" deed by paying Zeynep's family a considerable amount of money, buying them a gun, and giving away a daughter in marriage to Zeynep's brother-in-law. On the basis of these three conditions, Ali's life would be spared.

From the outset, it was striking to observe that Zeynep's family was in a much more powerful bargaining position. It was their honor that had been "injured" and "violated," though both Zeynep and Ali were equally responsible for their actions. While Zeynep's family issued demands, Ali's was deeply worried for their son's life. Because Ali's family, too, thought the honor of the woman's family was injured, they could make only weak objections to the other side's demands. They were probably also worried that shedding their son's blood would mean the start of a "blood feud" (*mêr kuştin* in Kurmanji) between the two families.

Note, at this juncture, that both sides were defined according to their patrilineal ties. Thus, for example, Ali's paternal uncles and paternal cousins were every bit as concerned as Ali's direct family. This was not true of the maternal uncles and cousins, who were not considered family members in the same sense.

After the conclusion of negotiations, Ali's family left their village for a city in western Turkey. Two factors explained this forced migration. The first was that Zeynep's paternal relatives were living in a neighboring village. Although the incident ended in agreement, the families were still enemies, and did not wish to encounter each other. The second reason, in all likelihood, was that Ali's family felt uncomfortable living among their fellow villagers, owing to their son's "dishonorable" action. They had acquired a bad reputation, yet they could not resolve this by abandoning their son for his misdeed: as the son, he was also the family heir.

In the end, Ali was married off to another girl, and the family moved to a distant city, where Ali worked as the family's primary breadwinner. Despite declarations from Zeynep's family that she would be killed, this did not occur. She, too, was married off to someone else, while her sister was married off to her ex-husband.

The most tragic aspect concerns Ali's sister, Elif, who was given away as "partial compensation" for her brother's life, with no say in the matter. Her new family cut off all ties with Ali's family, and thus she had no contact with her previous family after she was given away.

A few years after the events described here, Elif's maternal uncle and his wife visited the Mediterranean city where she was living, in order to see her. What her husband's paternal uncle, who is also Zeynep's father, told them is quite striking. He said they considered Elif as someone who had been found "by a bush" (*ber deviya* in Kurmanji) – that is, found in the street. Thus, no one in the world had the right to be concerned with Elif's well-being. Zeynep's father drove this point home by emphasizing to the maternal uncle that Elif was none of his business.* Since they were Elif's maternal relatives, their views and desires did not need to be taken into account.

The case I have described is just one among many that indicates the patriarchal and patrilineal character of traditional Kurdish society and culture. The boy child is valued over the girl. She can be sacrificed to ensure the safety of her father and brothers; they are designated as her protectors, and through them the family lineage is perpetuated.

UGANDA

Widow Inheritance

Stella Nyanzi[†]

Men are usually portrayed as the agents of women's subordination and subjugation, particularly in so-called patriarchal societies. One social evil for which men are standardly blamed, even in academic journals, is levirate marriage. This involves a male

---

*Zeynep's father's attitude here exemplifies the fact that traditional Kurds commonly view male relatives as the "owners" of women (*xwedî* in Kurmanji). This literal translation does not imply a slavery relationship. Rather, it means that men are viewed as the protectors of their sisters, mothers, and wives, as well as the female children of a paternal uncle. In this sense, one comes across Kurdish women referring to *xwedîyê min* (my owner), by which they mean their male relatives from the paternal side.
†Special to this volume.

agnatic relative of the deceased man inheriting – often through remarriage – the widow and her offspring. Widow inheritance is a common practice in certain Asian, South American, and African societies. In Uganda, it is prevalent in several ethnic groups.* It is frequently argued that levirate marriage violates the rights of women who are already disempowered and dislocated by their husband's death. The dangers are allegedly aggravated by increasing rates of HIV/AIDS: according to Bantebya and Konings, even when it is known that a man has died of AIDS, his widow(s) may still be inherited and sexual intercourse may still occur between the widow(s) and the inheritor.†

In an ethnographic study of the effect of HIV/AIDS on death rituals in Masaka District in Uganda, I asked both men and women, including widows, about their personal experiences of widow inheritance. In particular, I asked men why they continued to expose themselves to possible infection or reinfection with HIV by inheriting and having sexual relations with women whose former spouses were publicly known to be HIV positive. If men – the perpetrators of this supposed social evil – are more powerful than women, why would they not abandon a practice that is now potentially dangerous? I sought to understand the varied dimensions and multiple meanings of widow inheritance: how it is socially scripted and negotiated; how it is contested or affirmed by different individuals.

A continuum of experience

Participants from Masaka District revealed that Kiganda culture obliged a male agnatic relative of a deceased man to inherit his widow during the culminating funeral rites. Those who claimed to be devout adherents of tradition insisted it was important to enforce observance of the practice. But other participants argued that "Times have changed, and tradition will also have to change to suit the present." Accordingly, practices varied widely:

> *Kamya, 24 years old:* I was only 22 years old when Sula, my brother, died. I was waiting for my college exam results. Meanwhile, I worked as a minibus conductor. At the burial ceremony of Sula, we discovered that he had left no will. So the clan elders came to me after their meeting. They told me I was going to "take on" Namutebi – Sula's widow – and also her three children. "Ah, me?" I asked them. "I am only a college student. How can I take on the widow?" "It is because you are the oldest brother of the dead man. It is your duty to take care of the widows and orphans. The children are your blood," the old men said. I was shocked. I was angry. Sula was a rich man when he lived. He had his coffee plantation. He never shared his wealth with me. And then I felt fear, because everyone knew that Sula had loved many women. He must have died with AIDS. So his widow had HIV. All these thoughts ran through my

---

*See J.P.M. Ntozi, "Widowhood, Remarriage and Migration during the HIV/AIDS Epidemic in Uganda," *Health Transition Review*, 7 (1997), pp. 125–44.
†G. Bantebya and E. Konings, "HIV Infection in Uganda," *British Medical Journal*, 308 (1994), p. 789.

mind that day, but I could not challenge the clan elders. I went through with the inheritance rites. But since then, I have never gone back to see Namutebi and her children. It is now almost two years.

Makanga, 48 years old: Getrude, my third wife, was my late brother Zziwa's wife. She had two sons and one daughter with him. When he was about to die of cancer, he sent for me. I was shocked to see how sick he looked. We discussed his will. He asked me to become the guardian of his children. I explained that it would be no problem for me, as long as he wrote it in the will and gave copies to different people. He left the property for the heir, but he made me executor to guide how it was managed. When he died, the will was read. Getrude was asked what she wanted to do: return to her people, or to stay with our clan. She chose to stay. The rites were performed. Then I began visiting her and the children, comforting her and buying a few necessities for them. After one year of mourning, I made her pregnant with her fourth child. Later, we had two more children. She remained on Zziwa's land, looking after the banana plantation and the children. I visit her from time to time. She is my third wife. She calls me husband.

Nakawuka, a 68-year-old inherited widow: Look at my wrinkles! I was too old to find another man to marry me. Who would even want me, when I couldn't have children any more? Widow inheritance helps poor, elderly widows to survive. There is someone to provide and protect.

Florence, a 32-year-old remarried widow: I welcomed the suggestion that John's brother inherit me. Then, I only had two small children. The problem is that I was not employed. I was just a farmer. I was growing bananas, cassava and sweet potatoes on John's land. And we had sold some of the land to get money for John's hospital bills. Now I thank God! The brother is paying school fees for my children. He gives us money for our needs. And he gave me some capital to open a stall in the market.
Interviewer: So do you have sex with him?
Florence: Ah, no. I think I have this sickness. See my skin? And I get fevers now and then. Once he tried to touch my body. I sat down with him to explain that I think John died with AIDS. I also have HIV, because we never, ever used condoms. "Think about your own children and wife, not yourself only," I said to him. Now we understand each other. He treats me like his older sister.

Susan, a 36-year-old widow: I have my job, a steady income, and can take care of my children. I refused those backward cultural practices. At the funeral, I ignored the cultural rituals and concentrated on the religious ceremonies. Later, I told the clan elders that I prefer a female inheritor, because she will not pester me for sex. They gave me Lydia, my youngest sister-in-law.

Some widows in our study were forced off their husband's land, or lost family assets like crops, houses, and farming implements to their in-laws. Some of these inheritance wrangles were based on the widow's outright refusal to accept a levirate partner. In an environment of accusations and blame, specifically concerning whether the deceased was suspected to have had AIDS, the widows claimed: "Why should I accept the brother? If he also dies, they will blame me, saying that I came to kill off their whole clan." This runs counter to Ntozi's findings of "malice and reckless behavior among widows and widowers" who knowingly infect their new marital partners with HIV.

On blaming the men

When it comes to the politics of the sexes and gender issues, essentialism often clouds intellectual debate, policy formulation, and program implementation. It is important to unpack general categories of analysis. In the case of levirate marriage, the label "men" is more misleading than illuminating. *Which* men demand widow inheritance? Which men are willing to inherit widows, and which reject the institution outright, or negotiate modifications? And what reasons underpin the various positions?

It is reasonable to blame those men who fail to write a will before they die, or leave wills instructing that their widows be inherited without first discussing the matter with them. Likewise culpable are those men so driven by greed for a deceased's property that they press for widow inheritance as the only means of getting hold of it, or who coerce widows into unwanted sexual activity. But the study turned up many men who certainly did not welcome the idea of inheriting a widow. Their reasons included poverty, migration, fear of AIDS, reluctance to assume responsibility for dependent and unemployed women, and revulsion towards older women (particularly for unmarried men who wanted to choose their own partner). Anti-HIV/AIDS campaigns that lobby against widow inheritance have also had an effect, as have diffuse modernizing influences that undermine tradition on this and other fronts.

Widow inheritance also transcends notions of gender asymmetry – that is, of male dominance and women's lowly status. In part, it is about social interpretations and cultural enactments of responsibility towards the dead. Kinsmen, clan, and society owe a deceased man the care and support of his offspring, widows, and other dependants. Male members of the line are obliged to settle the deceased's property matters, cover his outstanding debts, and propagate the family line so that he "can rest tranquilly." Likewise, a widow does not just owe it to her deceased husband to obey his wishes for her future. She must also act to safeguard the interests of her dependent children, who are deemed to belong to the patrilineal clan. The widow must leave them with her dead husband's heir if she decides to return to her parents or marry into another clan. Maternal attachment, anxiety over children's future welfare, and the social meaning that children bestow on women – increased status, marital security, recognition of maturity, old-age insurance – all inhibit widows from leaving. They instead may *choose* to stay on their late spouse's property, or indeed remarry to one of his agnates.

These unwritten texts are now in a state of flux. Some aspects are being reaffirmed, and others transformed and recreated. The movement to empower women and improve their lot in life means that widows today are more likely to challenge cultural dictates, including inheritance by a man they disapprove of. The women's empowerment process has also influenced legislation in Uganda, so that the constitution now includes stipulations to protect women against abuse and other violations of their rights. In addition, there are legal instruments and procedures in place allowing widows to seek redress if they are unjustly treated by in-laws. Feminist legal bodies like FIDA work at low or no cost to assist the most vulnerable women. Even rural widows are challenging their in-laws, taking them to court, and winning cases where they are deemed to have been disadvantaged in the aftermath of the funeral rites.

In short, it is crucial to acknowledge the agency of women-as-widows in these practices. Some choose to be inherited in order to gain the benefits of remarriage for themselves and their dependents. In such cases, widow inheritance may be an empowering social practice, because it leaves a woman with her husband's property, allows her to continue with sexual activity and reproduction, and so on. Likewise, men may end up as the disadvantaged party – whether by the burdens that new dependents place upon them, or by falling prey to conniving widows who lure them into becoming inheritors.

INDIA

The Abusers

S. Anandhi and J. Jeyaranjan[*]

There are two important aspects of changing norms of masculinity among non-Dalit men [i.e., those not belonging to the "Untouchable" caste] that have direct bearings on reporting of violence against women. One is the linkage between the loss of status of non-Dalit men in the public sphere and the continuity and severity of domestic violence. The second is their inability to be the providers and their powerlessness to "protect" their women from being subjected to sexual harassments of the Dalit youth. The latter aspects seem to have a direct impact on the upper caste men's increased control over the mobility of women, especially in forbidding women going to work.

The non-Dalit men who talked about their loss of power and authority in the public sphere are the ones who reported that they continue to abuse and beat their wives and daughters and also expressed their desire to control women. Nearly 97 per cent of non-Dalit men have identified "no sexual satisfaction" as a conflict area and as a reason

---

*From S. Anandhi and J. Jeyaranjan, "Masculinity and Domestic Violence in a Tamil Nadu Village," in *Men, Masculinity and Domestic Violence in India: Summary Report of Four Studies*, International Center for Research on Women, 2002, pp. 22–6. http://www.icrw.org/docs/DV_India_Report4_52002.pdf.

to use force with their wives. In other words, the elderly upper caste men, unable to contend with their emasculated masculine power in the public sphere, continue to exercise violence within the domestic sphere to compensate for their "lost manhood" and also as [a] reassertion of their masculine power within the families. [. . .] As explained by a 65-year-old Mudaliar [high caste] man:

> In my youth my wife used to be scared of me. I will give her a severe beating. My father used to beat all his daughters-in-law heavily. We never interfered because he would beat us also if we did. Then we also would beat up our wives. . . . People used to be terrified of Mudaliars. Now everybody has run away. My wife still fears me. I do shout at her and at times I beat her up. But I don't quarrel with anyone outside.

Even Mudaliar women report that violence continues unabated. According to a 78-year-old Mudaliar woman, her 85-year-old husband still beats her:

> I gave birth to ten children and none of my sons help me . . . My husband is a bad person. He has no consideration for age. Even now he tries to beat me. I would only shout at him, saying what do you think of yourself even after 50 years of married life? What do you want now? He would not go for any work and would simply eat and sleep. How could we survive? He sold off all the lands that my mother gave me.

The following narration of a 42-year-old Mudaliar woman illustrates how the upper caste men compensate for their undermined masculinity in the public sphere by continuing violence against women in the family:

> . . . Often he [my father-in-law] used to hit her [my mother-in-law] without any reason. The food should be kept ready and hot when he returned from the field. He is more violent in front of his sons and other family members just to show how powerful he is. Even now he continues to exercise his authority by controlling me and other women in the family. He would shout at me and scold me if he sees me talking to someone outside the family. [. . .]

The notion of honor and dignity prevents non-Dalits taking up employment outside the village. Simultaneously, women's employment has directly challenged their male identity as the main income earner of the family. The response of the non-Dalit elders succinctly captures their anxiety and tension resulting from women's employment. Non-Dalit men are anxious about not being able to fulfill the masculine role of being a provider and protector. Their latter role is threatened by Dalit youth who sexually harass their women and by women themselves who are now opting for inter-caste and love marriages. [. . .] As an elder Mudaliar man said, "Did we survive by sending women to work? They used to live timidly. These days they elope and marry. Now in parachery [the Dalit colony] everything happens. We have to keep women in control." [. . .]

For non-Dalit men, violence against women is closely linked to their newfound powerlessness. [. . .] However, for Dalit men, who are gaining new power in the public sphere, violence against women is increasingly practiced in the public sphere. This change is demonstrated most powerfully by the Dalit youth's harassment of upper caste girls in public on their way to work, but it [is] also seen in the youths' control over their mothers and sisters. [...] While most Dalits are not overtly opposed to women going to work, women's employment has considerably eroded the provider role of Dalit men and therefore it is creating new tensions over control of resources and women's sexuality. Dalit men are disturbed by the increasing assertion of Dalit women in both the public and domestic spheres. [...]

Dalit men are unwilling to share domestic labor. Nearly 89 per cent of Dalit men agree that household chores are the exclusive responsibilities of a wife. Providing for all their sexual needs as an exclusive responsibility yielded an agreement level of 94 per cent among Dalit men. Nearly 85 per cent of Dalit men think that childcare is the exclusive responsibility of a wife. They also claim a share in the earnings of women. Dalit youth's new masculine practices include costly attire and other forms of consumption. However, unlike their erstwhile landlords, they lack the material resources to retain masculine power. Instead, they depend on the family resources often earned by their sisters. For instance, an 18-year-old Dalit working girl stated, "On Sundays, we always have to wash their [brothers'] clothes and they would not let us watch the TV. Besides, they take away our money and if we refuse they would complain to our parents who would ultimately support our brothers." At the same time, they are worried about their sisters' sexuality and therefore keep a constant surveillance on them. The following narration of a 22-year-old Dalit working girl illustrates how the Dalit youth control their sisters:

> They [our brothers] always watch our movements and constantly monitor us, whether it is inside the bus or outside. Anywhere and everywhere they keep an eye on us. They follow us even if we go to temple. We are not allowed to talk to other men without their permission and the boys share information among themselves about whose sisters are going where. If we violate their orders they would threaten us with dire consequences; even if they were younger than us they would immediately report us to our elder brothers who would punish us. If you happen to stand near the bus stop you would often hear this remark: "If you cannot keep your sister under control what kind of a man are you?"

Nearly 83 per cent of non-Dalit men and 69 per cent of Dalit men [reported] difficulties or problems with their wives during the past year. Nearly 25 percent of Dalit men and 13 per cent of non-Dalit men had serious fights with their wives. The incidence of restrictions, sanctions and surveillance of their wives is much higher among non-Dalits (12 per cent) as compared to the Dalits (2 per cent). [...] The incidence of emotional violence is also widely prevalent; only the mode of such violence varies. Nearly 76 per cent of non-Dalit men and 53 per cent of Dalit men have done something to instill fear in their wives by their looks, gestures and actions. Both groups of men have shouted [at] and abused their wives, though the incidence is higher among Dalits.

Similarly, men from both the social groups have resorted to physical violence in the domestic sphere. Nearly 43 per cent of non-Dalit men have hit their wives. They have also kicked, beaten, pushed and pulled their wives. Sexual violence does not seem to be as pervasive as emotional and physical violence. But it does occur and more so among the non-Dalits.

Dalit and non-Dalit men cite significant differences in the reasons for violence. As noted earlier, nearly 97 per cent of non-Dalit men identified "no sexual satisfaction" as a conflict area and reason to use force with their wives, while only 40 per cent of Dalit men did so. Similarly, nearly 94 per cent of non-Dalits agreed that it is okay to use force against your wife if she is disrespectful to elders, whereas only 75 per cent of Dalit men did so. However, there were some reasons for force that were more commonly held across the two groups. For example, 97 per cent [of] non-Dalit men and 84 per cent of Dalit men agreed that infidelity was a legitimate reason to use force against their wives.

MEXICO

Revisioning Male Violence

Juan Carlos Ramírez Rodriguez*

When interviewing a man, what is the right moment to speak of violence? How can it be introduced without stigmatizing the male subject? How can it be given the everyday dimension it has in practice? These questions must be addressed if ameliorative actions are to be proposed, without adopting a confrontational approach.

While violence sometimes seems to appear abruptly, out of nowhere, in fact it develops gradually. We tend to approach violence – whether emotional, sexual, physical, economic, or directed against property – as something occasional. Such a perspective focuses on individual acts, depicting violent actions in a kind of photographic way. Think of how many photos, posters, videotapes, films, radio announcements – in short, mass-media products – have been used as evidence of the consummated deed. Such artifacts are a scream that springs from society's pain. Once emitted, it finds its resonance in surreptitious resistance, then as a political banner to rally round.

How to avoid this stereotyped approach, and gain an understanding of what truly underpins domestic violence? How do we distance ourselves from the movie script

*Special to this volume. This essay is part of a larger project titled "Gender and Violence." The author thanks the Carlos Chagas Foundation in Brazil for financial support; the National Council for Science and Technology (CONACyT); the University of Guadalajara; and the doctoral program of the Centre for Research and Advanced Studies of Social Anthropology (CIESAS Occidente).

where an apparently good man falls in love with a beautiful, intelligent woman, and suddenly – because she is pregnant, or because of the food she has prepared, or for one of a thousand other pretexts – she irritates the male to the point where his exasperation becomes uncontrollable, and the violence that all men have within them makes its appearance?

I believe we need to capture relationships that are constantly in flux, and that are shaped by other linkages – to other men, to one's original family, to the workplace, to sons and daughters, and to institutionalized discourses, whether firmly established or only nascent.

The Mexican case presents considerable difficulties in recovering the narratives of males who live in violent relationships with their partners. Having met with male silence, women are resorted to as narrators of the violence that men inflict on them. This strategy only bolsters stereotypes of violence against women, linking it to alcohol, child abuse, and the Mexican *macho* society.

I believe this male silence results from confrontation. Viewing male domestic violence in isolation, ignoring its commonplace character, gives the male subject an impression that one seeks to narrate events with blood, cuffs, kicks, slaps, and bites – the video-clip of masculine violence. What matters, though, is the everyday: the space of family life, with both agreeable and disagreeable elements, likes and dislikes, outbursts of laughter, silences, pain, self-reproach, agitated breathing. The meaning of violence lies in the search for words that cannot be found to express what has never been said; in the images and scenes that appear in the subject's mind as he tells his story.

I sought to apply this methodology in research on domestic violence that I conducted with male residents of Colonia Constitución, located within the metropolitan zone of Guadalajara in Mexico. With over four million inhabitants, the metropolitan zone is the second largest city in the country, and Colonia Constitución has about 30,000 inhabitants. It is one of the popular settlements created in the 1960s, the product of rural–urban migration and of a swelling urban population in dire need of housing. Among its economically active population, one sector is based on wage labor for others, another on providing services, and still another consists of people working for themselves. The neighborhood displays a high degree of social and commercial organization; it possesses recreational and cultural areas, as well as educational and health services. As they say in the *colonia*, "You can live here without leaving, because it's got everything."

Moisés has lived here for nearly all his life. As a boy of five, he came to the city with his family. They hail from a village close to Guadalajara. Moisés now works selling bottled water. He is 36 years old. Ten years after he married Victoria, and after they submitted to various medical treatments, their first daughter was born.

One aspect of his situation that does not inherently "mean" violence, but does imply conflict, is his having had numerous girlfriends at the same time – a constant among many of the males I interviewed. I asked Moisés whether this didn't make for a complicated life. "Yes, it's complicated," he responded, "because my wife caught me once [before they were married] with a real beauty. As a result, since we got married, I've had a lot of problems with her. She might just be bathing me, shaving me, helping me change on my way out, and – 'Ugh! You're going to see Miss So-and-So!'

"It turns into a fight and – bloody hell! – I haven't gotten over it yet. I say: 'You know what? If you don't trust me, I won't go out. I shouldn't go anyway, 'cause I'm whacked from the stress at work. All the pressure from the supervisors, and I come here and just get more pressure from you. Instead of coming home nice and easy and having something to eat and "How are you, dear, and how did it go?," and all that, you start in with your circus. Well, that's no way . . . What's the matter with you? It doesn't feel good to see you. You should calm down and behave yourself, because I can't take much more.'

"I used to hit her before, you know. A lot. I used to hit her for the same reason: because of her being jealous. Great, don't you think? When we first got married, she used to shut me in, lock me up so I couldn't go out. Hmm, that was bad, the way we lived. And then? Things were going badly. So I had to be the strong one, didn't I?

"It was hard. A kick and a cuff and there you are. No, no, it wasn't as bad as that; but I did give her a cuff or two so she would calm down. Then, as you'd expect, she got the message, and then I could talk to her. 'No, my girl, you get this: how do you think it feels? We have to live with what went before. Now we've got over it. So now what? We were [only] going out together then. Now we're married. That's something else, from that point on. From now on we respect each other and all that. I'm not going out with anybody now – no-one here, no-one there. You're the only one.

"'If you're going to live with that on your mind all the time, you'll see our marriage won't work. You'll be upsetting me. Every day the bloody same, when I haven't done anything – it's going to upset me. So if you want our marriage to work, you'd better try and control those nerves. Leave your ridiculous jealousy, 'cause it's not going to work that way.' . . . If there's silly little jealousies sometimes, we control it, you know. 'Cause we're alright together. And it's better now that God has given us this baby girl, and because now there's more understanding between us. We talk more about everything."

Similar is the case of Jaime, who was 28 when I interviewed him. He has spent the whole of his life in the Constitución neighborhood. He is a blacksmith, having learned the trade from his father. His relationship with Adriana, whom he has lived with for seven years and with whom he has two daughters, has changed as a result of vexations, dissatisfaction, and frustrated expectations that have produced dissension and disagreements. While they were still courting, they would get angry enough to push and pull each other; they would stop seeing each other for a day, and then carry on as though nothing had happened. In the first two years of their marriage, their quarreling sometimes rose to the exchange of insults, cuffs and slaps.

When I asked Jaime about physical violence between neighborhood couples, he told me: "No, no, no! We're past that. I also – I didn't hit her with stones or sticks or anything, just a cuff. And she was the same, I mean, when we were really angry, it would come to me giving her a cuff, and she would slap back, and I'd better stop there."

Jaime and Adriana lived with Jaime's parents. When their fights grew too intense, Jaime would leave the room that he and Adriana shared and go to another part of the house to calm down. Although he saw himself as part of the problem, he also thought that most of the difficulties were caused by Adriana's capricious and stubborn manner. Any little thing would turn into "an atom bomb ready to go off."

Jealousies were another constant subject. "From the very start, we had rows and, I can't tell you – I mean, I might see her coming from somewhere and I say [lowers his voice and speaks almost inaudibly] where have you been? Now you're just walking in the street, and some fella . . . and then what? It might be better if I leave or something. But now get this: we'd always fight, but we've never separated. In fact, we haven't separated for a single day; just to show you."

Over the years, Jaime has learned to be more tolerant, and Adriana has adapted to his demands. "It's been quite a long time now since I said: you're not going to have to ask my permission for anything anymore. Because she would say 'Hey, I'm going to see my Mom.' And I'd pick up the thread and say, 'No, you don't need to ask for permission. You're free, you should do what you want. Just don't go off with someone else' – joke like that, right? 'As long as there's nothing left to do here at home – you can't go out with your Mom or go out and about if it means here at home there's nothing to eat, it isn't clean.'"

For Jaime, authority in the household is shared. This translates into what he calls "rules." The most important is to talk things through, and then to give care and attention to the girls; to prepare food and serving his meals; to keep the house and their clothes clean. All the "rules" are activities that Adriana is responsible for. Jaime's commitment is to provide economic resources; this is not a "rule" as such, but something he considers a prerequisite for being able to demand that his spouse fulfill her responsibilities.

He says the confrontations with Adriana have now ceased. "She doesn't really keep up for very long against me, maybe because she knows I'm going to say no. Or perhaps she keeps quiet, doesn't even say it, to stop me saying anything. There's hardly any need now for me to say, 'No! Don't do that! I don't want you to go!'"

"She knows what it is you like and what you don't," I commented. "That's right," Jaime agreed. "We're getting to know each other, and . . . well, there's no point in getting old, and me still telling her off, right?"

We hear, in these accounts, the voices of men telling their stories, reconstructing their lives, adding and subtracting. Men who adjust situations, cope with pain and sadness, revisit their failures and successes. Moisés and Jaime choose particular ways of talking about themselves and their relationships with their wives. They mention personal disagreements and acts of violence in ways that come up "naturally," in conversations that did not specifically mention the subject or referred to it only in general terms. They speak in tones of voice that are sometimes funny, ironical, sad, or annoyed. They also present domestic violence as distant events – as a form of relation that has now been superseded.

SOUTH AFRICA

Founding Fathers

Louise Williams*

While women in impoverished areas have spent the last decades organizing themselves into community groups to improve their lives, it's rare for South African men to participate in community development. But there's an exception to this: the men's group Ebizweni, founded in Graceland, a neighborhood in one of Cape Town's informal settlements.

Ebizweni started out when a small group of men found themselves meeting up regularly on the grass football field near their homes to talk about what was going on in their home lives. As time went on, more men showed an interest in joining the informal discussions, and so it was decided to create a formal organization: Ebizweni Voluntary Men's Association. This, they hoped, would serve as a platform for discussing the problems that have been troubling South Africa's men: poverty, domestic violence, drug and alcohol abuse. Today, three years down the road, Ebizweni has around 80 members and holds weekly meetings in a garage belonging to one of the men.

The two founding members, Xolile and Dumesani, are both in their mid- to late-thirties, but they're very different characters. Even the way they sit while they talk to me is very different. Xolile holds his head in his hands, looking away from me in complete concentration as he talks. Dumesani keeps his glass of beer in one hand, fixes me with his eyes and gestures with the other hand as he tells his story. What comes across very strong[ly] from both of them is their total dedication to the success of the men's group.

"Lots of NGOs are concerned with women," says Xolile, "we feel neglected. We need to recollect men and try to engage them in discussing issues. We're sons of our fathers, they believed that traditionally whoever's in the family is your belongings. We're trying to kill that sort of behavior. We're saying we're sons of our fathers but we're also fathers to our sons, we have to give an example to our sons."

Dumesani and Xolile both told me about the very high levels of domestic violence in Graceland. As we talk about the issues that surface during their meetings I feel I have to ask if they have been violent in their relationships. Xolile says no, but Dumesani takes a deep breath before he talks about his past. I get the impression he doesn't like talking about it, but he does it for me because he knows that he's one of the few men willing to talk about it in public, and it needs to come out in the open.

"I've been in very abusive relationships," he says, "I used to abuse my girlfriend, that was before I got married. I didn't see anything wrong with hitting my girlfriend, to

---

*From Louise Williams, "Founding Fathers," Radio Netherlands, 21 November 2001. http://www.rnw.nl/development/html/fathers011121.html.

instill some discipline or respect. Within surrounding areas there was a lot of domestic violence and it wasn't hidden. What made me move away is to understand the difference between discipline and punishment – I thought when I was punishing them that I was disciplining them. But there is a difference because when it comes to punishing there is pain."

From these words, you can tell that Dumesani still sees himself as the one in the relationship to enforce discipline. I realize that he is no western-style "new man" who goes around hugging trees, getting in touch with his inner child and wanting to have complete equality in his relationship. But from the way Dumesani talks, he shows that he is someone who has thought long and hard about who he wants to be – what sort of husband, what sort of father. With two kids and his wife out at work, he does a lot of the housework as he doesn't have a job at the moment. He's frustrated about being unemployed and I get the impression it's an ongoing struggle for him to fit into his role.

"I was never taught to wash dishes or cook," he laughs. "Those things were done by my sisters. As for me, I thought I was fortunate, that I didn't have to do that, but at my age now, I think something that I was supposed to have been taught, was missing."

They say that converts are always more committed to their faith than those who grew up with it. Dumesani certainly seems to have converted well to being a homemaker.

"I'm very proud to say that today I can look after myself without my wife, ironing, washing my clothes, etc. It's a good thing that we have technology. But I can do that, in fact I think I can do that better than her."

COLOMBIA

The Home Worker

Javier Pineda*

Most of the men interviewed in The District had lost their jobs in the formal sector. They had to face not only the vulnerability of the family given the lack of unemployment benefits, but also their identity problem of not fulfilling their function as providers. Paid employment, as a means both of making money and of getting out of the house, is an important factor for traditional masculine identities here. The absence of such paid employment decreases men's ability to provide for their families and for

*From Javier Pineda, "Partners in Women-Headed Households: Emerging Masculinities?," *The European Journal of Development Research*, 12: 2 (December 2000), pp. 72–92. Editor's note: Pineda's research into men living in woman-headed households was conducted in "The District," a poor working-class area of the city of Cali.

themselves, and is a possible route to challenging traditional masculine identities and behavior. Rising unemployment among poor urban men in The District has pushed most men to find, in the micro-business of their women partner, an alternative means of employment and survival, which has an impact on them both as workers and as men. In the process, not only are traditional masculinities challenged but emerging masculinities, and therefore new relations of power, are created.

[...] Jorge is a 40-year-old man, who is currently working in his wife's home-based business making pottery. He said:

> I worked in a sweets company which went bankrupt four years ago . . . it was closed. When I left it I got sick [. . .] The thirteen years of compensation were lost, thirteen lost years, and then we were unemployed. From then onwards we have supported ourselves with what we are achieving with these pots.

His wife, interviewed separately, said:

> I was dependent on my husband before . . . I liked this [pottery], I always have made a lot of things, cloth painting, decoration of cakes . . . until one day a group of women from here went to learn [pottery] and I began to like this. Suddenly the company in which he was working shut down, everyone was out of work. Then faced with that I said to myself, "if I know an art I am going to put it into practice." This was four years ago. Before, I used simply to go and work with a friend, but to set it up by myself was very difficult. I started from nothing . . . and I was so unlucky that, after he was without a job, he became sick . . . Then it was already clear that I had to do it, I had to look after my children, because they [the workers] were left without any money from compensation, the company threw them out on the street, in bankruptcy. We remained with our little house at least, but I had to face everything alone.

She currently manages the pottery business. She attends to clients, takes orders, does the accounts (informal), paints pottery pieces, manages the cash flow, and goes out to buy materials. She became the head of her household after her husband became unemployed. His illness after a time looking for a job (a logical sequence that I saw in other cases) was certainly a factor that underpinned this process of changing roles and power relations. She also said:

> He was very machista before. Yes! When he was the person that worked and the one who get[s] the money, he wouldn't agree to my going out to work . . . When he was laying down in bed [sick], then he didn't have the chance to reject my going to work. Now, it is so normal that a woman works . . . He didn't like me working. He said "the responsibility is a man's and, as long as the man works, the woman's responsibility is to be at home with the children" . . . and I believe that still is so for many people.

When I asked Jorge what he thought about men at home, he emphasized:

> When it has to be done, it has to be done. I have seen many [men] whose missus has gone to work and they stay at home cooking. Today this is the situation, the woman is getting jobs and men don't. For that reason there are times that men have to stay at home cooking and looking after the children.

Changes in the labor market seem to have broadly shaped gender relations in Colombian society. However, men's acquiescence to women's non-reproductive work is not a big change in a country with one of the highest female participation rates in the labor market in Latin America today, which had already challenged the ideal of man as sole economic provider. What is significant is that men are working at home. Working at home is potentially, but not necessarily, a route to men's everyday participation in reproductive work. Currently, men cooking and taking care of children can be a big change. For most of the men that I interviewed in Cali it is quite normal to work at home, as many micro-enterprise workers do, but to cook and look after children is usually seen as temporary. In the extract above, Jorge talks about housework as a non-male function which men have to perform sometimes, despite the fact that he has shared such a role for some years. The traditional masculine discourses about women's participation in productive work and men sharing in housework are still embedded in this male population, creating contradictions within the realm of daily life. Such contradictions have made new discourses about equity appear among some men. On this subject, I heard a great deal of men's opinions. Wilmar, a man in part-time paid work who shares in some micro-enterprise activities with his partner at home, highlighted an equity view:

> Women's participation is very important for me. We are living a critical situation where there are no sources of work and we are seeing that employment is made easier for a woman than for a man. Then one as man must understand the situation, and not be filled with jealousy or look resentful. We are facing the problem of many households destroyed because of the fact that the man feels undervalued and inhibited, because he must submit to the fact that the woman must occupy places he had never thought of because of *machismo* or rivalry or selfishness. But we must be realistic, we must submit to that situation, to the fact that the woman has the right and that she can also perform public or other jobs that the man previously believed only he could do.

Edgar, one of the men interviewed in the District who was "helping" his partner, points out:

> As it is the economic situation in the country, where many companies all over the place are going bankrupt or are laying off staff, when what happens is, many men become unemployed. At this moment [it] is easier to get a job for a woman than for a man . . . for a man it's very difficult, it's here where woman comes to occupy the place of a man and a man must perform in place of a woman . . .

These extracts illustrate the male job loss described above. In Wilmar's words there is also an implicit recognition of *machismo* as one cause of household "destruction." This recognition is a critique of traditional masculinities and admits the need for men to have a more positive attitude in the face of women's paid work and, therefore, to change masculine attitudes. In Edgar's words, he considers, like Jorge, that there is a right place for women and men in the division of labor, which has been altered, "where a woman comes to occupy the place of a man and a man must perform in place of a woman."

Men's voices speaking about change recognize women's rights as an imposition brought about by economic changes but not as a right to be achieved by itself. Ideals about gender division of labor [are] still seen to be in the traditional model of the man as sole provider, which can no longer exist, but which has not yet found a new paradigm.

INDIA

The Polyandrists

Rakesh K. Simha*

Polyandry, or the custom of a woman having more than one husband, has been practiced in the northern Indian hill state of Himachal Pradesh for the past 5,000 years, but is now recording a decline thanks to swelling male opposition.

The custom is prevalent among some 25,000 designated tribals in the mountainous districts of Kinnaur and Spiti in Himachal Pradesh. Around 20 per cent of the families here practice a unique system of polyandry where a woman is married to more than one husband, all brothers from the same family.

The resistance to polyandry surfaced in the late 1980s when a large number of these tribals – called Kinnauris – started passing the Union Public Service Commission's entrance examination which selects candidates for India's premier civil service, the Indian Administrative Service (IAS).

Moving to metros such as New Delhi and Bombay exposed them to life outside their valley. Not only did they realize that customs such as polyandry were outdated, they had to come to grips with the fact that their wives back home could not switch to an urban mode of life. Many discovered it was simply not possible to share a wife over such distances. For many, discarding their old lives was a matter of necessity. "We would not have been accepted in urban society with an illiterate wife in tow. We had little option other than to look for a life partner outside the valley," says a bureaucrat.

"These young officers asked their parents to relieve them of their wives," says a leader of the Congress [One of India's leading political parties], Ramesh Negi. "Many elders agreed. Where there was resistance, the boys simply went ahead and got married again."

Angsunk (not his real name), who got married at the age of 16, explains why young men like him became so desperate. Angsunk was automatically married along with his eldest brother, then aged 24. When he moved to India's capital, New Delhi, for further studies eight years later, Angsunk had become a father of three children. Two years later,

---

*From Rakesh K. Simha, "Many Husbands Make Woes for Indian Women," OneWorld.net, 24 October 2003, http://www.oneworld.net/article/view/71248/1/?PrintableVersion=enabled.

he cleared the civil service examination. "During training when my colleagues used to ask me about my family, I gave them evasive replies. When people asked me whether I was married under the polyandry system, I had no answer," he shrugs.

The burden of his past proved so heavy that one day Angsunk broke down and narrated his story to a colleague. "She understood my plight and is my wife today," he says, adding that he did not bother to take permission from his family to marry again.

Similarly, Arjun Negi of Kalpa village wasn't too comfortable sharing his wife with his three brothers. So he moved to the state capital Shimla, where he got a job. About three years ago he decided to sever ties with his first wife and marry again. After initial resistance, his family agreed. "I am a relieved man today. I am happy I have a wife and son I can call my own," he says.

Of course, women tied to the system are just as miserable. Take Rajwanti Negi, 35, a housewife in a remote village in Himachal Pradesh. She does all that is expected of a traditional Indian village wife – cooking, cleaning, doing the laundry, and sundry other chores. Except that her daily grind never seems to end. The reason – she has to serve four husbands.

Though she has to manage a complex web of relationships – such as spending time with each of her husbands by rotation – Rajwanti says she has no regrets. "I am happy with the system. I have no complaints about it," she says with a smile. But the system has taken its toll. A little prodding and the veneer of contentment slips. "It's really a grind," she confides. "I have given birth to 12 children of whom five died."

It appears that polyandry was started for reasons of economics. It is mostly practiced in places where land is limited. For instance, in Montong village in Kinnaur only 25 per cent of the land is arable. "Land has long been precious, so keeping it all under one head and controlling the population was necessary," points out the village headman, Rangsing Negi. The solution was marrying all the sons in the family to one woman.

But there is also strong disagreement. "Polyandry is absolutely improper," says 20-year-old Neema Negi, who grew up in a family of three fathers, one mother and five siblings. "It's not good for two or three brothers to share a woman. One will want to dominate and that is not good for the woman."

The chairperson of the Delhi Commission for Women, Anjali Rai, is highly critical of the system. She says its biggest evil is that the wife is treated like a prostitute and often her husbands are not loyal to her. "The mental and physical burden that the woman has to bear is enormous," she insists.

While polyandry has long roots, people like Rai see a ray of hope in the fact that penetration of education and exposure to city life has led to attrition in the system over the past decade or so. But polyandry has its votaries. Ramesh Negi, the Congress leader, wants the tradition to continue. But even he admits, "Girls and boys are becoming more and more educated. They don't want it."

In Montong and in neighboring villages, the custom is on a declining trend. "The younger generation doesn't want to be a wallflower. They want to be different," laments Suraj, a geriatric. "The future of polyandry is bleak."

"The practice may die in the next 20 years. But one can't rule out anything," says Rajender Luthra of Him Yugh, a social welfare organization based in the state capital Shimla.

The practice is protected by law. India's Succession Act of 1956 is not applicable to Kinnaur. This means that daughters do not inherit any property. As only sons inherit property, the land holding remains within the family. Illegitimate children or children born of a widow or an unmarried girl have no property rights. Till about 50 years ago, families employed them as domestic servants. In exchange for their services, a small plot of land was given to them. But now they have legal protection against such exploitation and if they can establish their paternity, they inherit a share of the paternal property.

TAHITI

Crossovers

David D. Gilmore*

In the 1960s, when Robert Levy did fieldwork on Tahiti, he found [...] impressions of sexual indeterminacy [to be] still valid. He writes that sex differences are "not strongly marked" in Tahiti but rather are "blurred" or "blended" (Levy 1973: 234–35). Men are no more aggressive than women; women do not seem "softer" or more "maternal" than the men. As well as having similar personalities, men and women also have roles so similar as to seem almost indistinguishable. Both perform most of the same tasks, and there are no jobs or skills reserved for either sex by cultural dictate. The men routinely do the cooking; women do almost everything that men do outside the house. In addition, there is no stress on proving manhood, no pressure on men to appear in any significant way different from women or children. Men have no fear of acting in ways Westerners would consider effeminate. During dances, for example, adult men will dance together in close bodily contact, rubbing against each other without any anxiety, and most men visit the village homosexual frequently and without shame [...]

Even where minimal sex differences are noted by Tahitians, frequent "crossovers" in role, as Levy calls them (ibid: 235), take place, especially among the men – a situation that he found surprising. Men show no discomfort at assuming a female identity, and a typical male informant would often illustrate a point by saying, "Suppose you are the man and I am the woman, and we have an argument." Sometimes in such an example,

---

*From David D. Gilmore, *Manhood in the Making: Cultural Concepts of Masculinity* (New Haven, CT: Yale University Press, 1990, pp. 203–4).

Levy notes, the informant "would make me the woman and himself the man" (ibid: 235). Levy continues:

> There are many other examples of minute crossovers in role playing by men. Teri'I Tui [a Tahitian informant], for example, demonstrated the traditional method of giving birth to me and to his youngest children by pretending he was pregnant and sitting down on the floor in the proper position. He then asked his oldest sons to pretend to help him with the delivery. Other men, when talking about the nursing of a baby, showed how it was done by holding an imaginary baby to their own breasts. (Ibid.)

Such male crossovers in role playing are not only very frequent but are also accompanied by no evidence of anxiety whatsoever. Levy was struck by this curious nonchalance and continually questioned the men about it. But the men invariably said that there "are no general differences" between male and female in terms of character, thoughts, moral characteristics, or the difficulty of their lives (ibid: 236). [. . .] Indeed, "effeminacy" (Levy's term) is generally accepted as the general and ordinary kind of male personality. Macho types are regarded as foreign and unsavory. [. . .]

This blurring of sex roles is echoed in the Tahitian language, which does not express gender grammatically. Pronouns do not indicate the sex of the subject or the gender of the object, and gender has no role in any other aspect of grammar. It is in fact possible to listen to someone talking about an interaction with another person for a long time without knowing whether the subject or object is male or female. In addition, most of the traditional Tahitian proper names are applied equally well to either a man or a woman.

SOUTH AFRICA

Out in Africa

Shuaib Rahim*

When I was growing up I knew that being a *moffie* [derogatory term in Afrikaans for a male homosexual] meant that I would go to hell. Well, some things have changed since then and some have not.

In South Africa, the country of my birth, sex between men was a crime. Then, in my first year as a university student, my whole world changed. On 27 April 1994, South Africa made a relatively peaceful transition from authoritarian rule to democracy. Suddenly, we had our oppressors and our liberators sitting in the same parliament. Suddenly, we all had rights – *moffies* too. The 1994 constitution introduced an Equality

---

*From Shuaib Rahim, "Out in Africa," *New Internationalist*, 328 (October 2000).

Clause in the Bill of Rights which guaranteed freedom from discrimination on the grounds of sexual orientation.

Yet, at the same time, all the bad laws were still in place. We were not allowed to love whom we wanted to. We were not allowed to be who we were. We were still being called bad names. Perhaps worst of all, we were called un-African. The first of my ancestors came to Africa in the seventeenth century. They came from all over – including Java, Malaysia, Denmark and India. Our family has lived in this country since then. And I am a moffie. Does that make me *un*-African? I must admit that I thought that it did.

I started reading about our history and discovered many interesting facts. Simon Nkoli was a great hero of the liberation struggle. Convicted in the Delmas Treason Trial, along with Nelson Mandela, Nkoli spent more than two decades on Robben Island. While in prison, he "came out" as a moffie to his fellow inmates and was accepted. After his release, he became the face of the struggle for lesbian and gay rights in Africa. I dare anyone to tell me that Simon Nkoli was not an African in every sense of the word.

As for our lesbian sisters, they are of an all-African variety too. The famous Rain Queen of the Northern Provinces of South Africa keeps a harem of more than 20 wives and they do more than bring her tea! In Kenya, it is accepted practice for widowed women to marry each other and recently two such women were legally divorced.

Another argument by the proponents of the "*un*-African" issue is that homosexuality in Africa is a European imperialist import. This is a lie. The actual European imperialist import is the homophobic tradition of British law. In every part of the African continent, there are homosexual practices far predating the colonialist period such as young men having relationships with each other until married. With colonization, European morality, concepts and laws were unilaterally imposed on the African people. Most indigenous cultural practices were classified as depraved, uncivilized or from the devil. The classification of African practices – which in the European context would be considered "homosexual" – as illegal and immoral was a natural consequence of colonialism.

I think many South African leaders realized that this "*un*-African" story was just a red herring, so shortly after 1994, we saw drastic changes to legislation. Most of this work was pioneered through the National Coalition for Gay and Lesbian Equality. This organization was formed in 1994, with founding members like Professor Edwin Cameron, now a Justice of the Constitutional Court, the aforementioned Simon Nkoli and Phumzile Mtwetwa, now Co-Secretary General of the International Lesbian and Gay Association. The Coalition has twice litigated before the Constitutional Court, succeeding in decriminalizing same-sex conduct in 1997 and gaining the equal right to permanent residency for the same-sex partners of South Africans. Other notable achievements of the Coalition include achieving the entitlement of same-sex partners to spousal and other pensions and medical insurance, the right to serve in the military in any role, freedom from discrimination in the workplace and protection from domestic violence.

This legislative reform had a broader impact: it allowed us to claim our identity and take pride in ourselves. Furthermore, South Africa has become a beacon of hope for lesbian and gay people in Africa. On our very borders, we have homophobic regimes. These include the Zimbabwean tyrant Robert Mugabe and others like Sam Nujoma in Namibia and Yoweri Museveni in Uganda. But South African reforms have done more than give hope to gay activists in African countries. Legislative developments in South Africa have a way of permeating through the region, particularly through the Southern African Development Community (SADC) – a regional organization along similar lines to that of the European Union. A very good example of this was the manner in which Namibia reformed its labor legislation. Trade unions in South Africa, together with the Government, achieved significant progressive change in the Labor Relations Act of 1995. This includes the integration of human-rights principles in determining fair and unfair dismissals. Among other things, discrimination against lesbian and gay people is unlawful. At the instigation of trade unions and non-governmental organizations in Namibia, their labor legislation mirrors the South African legislation. In this way, protection for lesbian and gay employees surprisingly found its way into Namibian legislation despite the fact that male homosexuality remains technically illegal in the country.

Back to South Africa. As we said before, many things have changed, but many things are the same. Most South Africans are poor. Many are without formal housing or employment. This creates a harsh dividing line between the "haves" and the "have nots." Sadly, this line also runs between rural and urban; between those who can access their rights and those who cannot. Many lesbian and gay South Africans live in informal settlements. In these areas, crime levels are high and the rights of lesbian and gay people, and human rights in general, are a distant hope. Every day in these townships lesbians are getting raped. Gay men are attacked by gangsters as "soft targets." The only recourse these people have is to public-interest organizations like the National Coalition.

The Gay and Lesbian Legal Advice Centre (GLLAC) deals with some 600 individual cases every year. These range from employment rights to domestic violence. The importance of services like the GLLAC cannot be overstated. When rights live on paper and not in the hearts and lives of people, they amount to nothing. But organizations like the GLLAC are under tremendous strain. As the only service of its kind in Africa, it is comparatively understaffed and suffers from extreme financial pressure. In post-apartheid South Africa, many public-interest funders have diverted their resources to supporting the Government. At the same time, the Government is not making any funds available to services such as the GLLAC. It is in fact quite remarkable that this centre is able to deal with the hundreds of cases it does, in addition to strategic public-interest litigation.

The achievement of constitutional equality for lesbian and gay people marks a remarkable point in the history of every country where it occurs. But it is always a beginning and not an end. In South Africa, we have achieved constitutional equality, but the daily lives of many ordinary lesbians and gay men have not changed. The fight for lesbian and gay equality is always also the struggle for human rights, for social equality and a better life for all. Constitutional equality provides some of the answers, but not all. Many people still have to find answers to questions like "Where will I sleep tonight?"; "What will I eat tomorrow?"; "Will I be raped on my way home?"

I still have to figure out if I am going to hell.

MEXICO

Gays, AIDS, and Homophobia

Monica Campbell*

At a Mexico City public hospital not long ago, Carlos, a thirty-something executive at a US company, tested positive for HIV. It was something he had long feared. "For about a year, I looked gaunt, I'd lost hair, I had sores in my throat – all the classic signs," he said in an interview from his apartment in a well-heeled area of town. But the idea of seeing a doctor, getting diagnosed, and being stigmatized kept Carlos from seeking medication. When he finally got tested, his worst fears were borne out. The general practitioner handed Carlos his results and said brusquely, "I'm sorry. That's all I can tell you right now. I just don't know much about this."

In shock, Carlos left the hospital, without a referral in hand and with no psychologist to cushion the blow. Eventually, a friend of a friend from Carlos's gym referred him to a specialist. Certain that identifying himself as HIV positive would be career suicide – he had seen gay men fired before – Carlos never checked to see if his company's benefits plan covered his illness.

To many in Mexico, Carlos's case – his denial, a flawed medical response, and a culture of discrimination at work – is all too common. On paper, Mexico has outlawed discriminatory practices, and homosexuality is gaining social acceptance. But human rights activists and health groups say that much more must be done to vanquish homophobia at home and work and in hospitals. AIDS treatment is more widely available in Mexico than in most other developing countries, but the stigma of the disease in a macho, Catholic society prevents people from seeking help.

When it comes to fighting discrimination, Mexico's federal government is only now taking action. Most notably, in mid-2005, officials launched their first ever anti-homophobia campaign to encourage people to get tested for the AIDS virus. It began

---

*Special to this volume.

with two radio spots, aired in major cities with the aim of expanding the campaign nationwide. In one spot, a mother, preparing dinner for her son and the date he is bringing home for the first time, says: "You look so in love, my son. So what's your date's name?"

"Oscar," her son replies. A narrator then conveys that equality begins with accepting people's differences.

At first glance the initiative might appear timid, but activists here credit the government for putting aside its conservative ideology and ignoring the Catholic Church leadership in order to address reality. Indeed, AIDS continues to spread in Mexico – and remains heavily concentrated among men who have sex with other men. Destigmatizing homosexuality and bisexuality will enable more people to come forward and get help, argue government officials who worked on the anti-homophobia campaign. Likewise, Raquel Child, an AIDS prevention expert at the United Nations Population Fund, is encouraged by the government's new stance. "Little by little, you're seeing government officials work with civic groups in order to form strategies" to address homophobia. According to Child, these policies put Mexico far ahead of other parts of Latin America – particularly Central America, where governments still back away from any official acknowledgment of homosexuality.

Still, some conservative and Catholic groups are unnerved that Mexico's government is becoming more active in confronting the discrimination that afflicts homosexuals. Catholic bishops have repeated the official Vatican line that homosexual activity is sinful. And the National Union of Parents and Pro-Life – both politically weighty, Mexico City-based groups – oppose the government's anti-homophobia campaign. "We are not saying homosexuals should be discriminated against, disrespected or hurt," says Guillermo Bustamante, the head of National Union. "But this is work for non-governmental groups, not something our taxes should pay for. Why should we fund a mainstream media campaign that validates wayward tendencies and sexual activity that puts people most at risk of getting AIDS?"

At the end of 2004, the government reported 93,979 Mexicans as HIV positive, out of a population of 106 million. The United Nations estimates the number infected at 160,000, counting both reported and unreported cases. Although HIV rates among women is rising, men still account for more than 80 per cent of the 4,000 new AIDS cases reported every year, says Jorge Saavedra, head of Mexico's national AIDS program. Dr. Saavedra credits President Vicente Fox for taking on homophobia and recognizing that "religious issues should not be involved when it comes to a health problem." No effective anti-AIDS campaign can be launched, Saavedra asserts, if society at the same time rejects those most vulnerable to the disease.

Alejandro Brito, a pioneering gay rights activist, edits *Letra S*, a Mexico City-based newspaper supplement about sexual diversity. He says that for the most part, gays in Mexico risk rejection by family and friends. "Mexico still maintains a puritanical mindset toward sexual diversity. We're just beginning to build tolerance – the idea that I publish a supplement that talks about gay issues is still a novelty. But the idea is to continue to wipe away the stigma, get people empowered. Then we can hope that more people will get tested and know their status."

A more open attitude toward homosexuality might have convinced Carlos to seek treatment earlier. Tall, attractive, and articulate, he never lacked for sexual attention. He enjoyed fulfilling his desires in varied ways: from steady relationships to anonymous sex at bathhouses and nightclubs featuring so-called dark rooms, where sex is encouraged. Carlos suspected he had AIDS early on, when his sore throat turned into a fever and a cough. But he remained in denial. Despite seeing ten doctors over the course of a year, "I was pretty full-blown by the time I was diagnosed."

"It takes enough courage just to get an AIDS test," Carlos explains. "By doing so, you're acknowledging your sexuality, that you lead a risky life. If you do eventually get tested, and God forbid you're found positive, you then have an entirely new set of issues to deal with." Carlos's take on the health system did not change until he found a steady doctor, whom he calls an angel. "Let me tell you, the perception here is that if you have AIDS you'll become just another number," he says. "My doctor gives me hope. She tells me I have years to live," he says. "She has told me everything that was left out when I was first diagnosed."

But Carlos is still keeping his illness a secret at work. He is aware that his US-based company may offer some form of medical assistance for employees with HIV. But he has heard upper-level management make enough blatantly homophobic remarks to know that unveiling his condition could be detrimental. What's more, Carlos has little faith that his illness would be kept confidential. With the help of a trusted co-worker, Carlos managed to fudge papers stating that he earned less than his actual salary, so that he could qualify for free medical treatment at a Mexico City AIDS clinic. He felt he had little choice. Even with his executive salary, there was no chance he would be able to shoulder the cost of AIDS treatment without assistance.

On days when he feels sick, Carlos assumes that his co-workers believe he is indeed suffering from some type of long-term illness. "But most people are too polite to ask me about it outright," he says. Carlos said he has made enough comments at his workplace to give the impression that he has cancer. "It's easier that way," he says. "Although AIDS should be looked at as a chronic disease like diabetes, few people here see it that way." He adds: "Now that the worst part of the illness is over, I'm able to work like anybody else."

Ricardo Hernández, of Mexico's National Human Rights Commission, hopes that government efforts – along with an increasingly active network of gay rights organizations – will improve both doctors' treatment of AIDS patients and the health system's image. In early 2005, a report by the Mexican government's human rights commission found that nine of every ten complaints the commission received from people diagnosed with HIV concerned the health sector.

Fighting homophobia might also help confront AIDS on another front – that of the men who have sex with other men while maintaining their heterosexual public identity, and thus risk passing HIV to their wives. "Three years ago, we never saw women come here," says Dr. Octavio Curiel, an AIDS specialist in Mexico City. "Now we're seeing more wives infected by their husbands. If we don't recommend condoms, if we don't recognize that men are hiding their sexual activity from their wives or girlfriends, then the fight against AIDS will be a losing battle."

Curiel, whose medical practice at a public hospital in Mexico City includes 450 HIV-positive patients, adds that health officials in Mexico are still unclear how many husbands are contracting the disease from relationships with other men. It is typical for Curiel's female patients to be unsuspecting of their husband's illicit sexual relations until they test HIV positive. "In much of Mexico," he says, "a homosexual or bisexual man's sexual life is spent in a secret world."

INDIA

The Eunuchs

Vinod Behl*

[Eunuchs] have had enough of life in the twilight zone, and are now ready to make a bid for a visible image of their own. Thus, a petition has been filed in a Chandigarh court, demanding that the People's Representation Act be amended to provide them representation in both Parliament and the state assemblies. The petition goes further, to claim employment reservation in government and semi-government categories, under the sexually handicapped category; and, further, that *suo motu* criminal cases be registered against those who forcibly convert people into eunuchs. Simultaneously, the All India Hijra Kalyan Sabha has sent an SOS to the Atal Bihari Vajpayee government at the Centre, demanding that the government move to ameliorate the miserable conditions under which they exist.

As per a survey done by the Sabha, there are only a few hundred genuine eunuchs countrywide – the rest, numbering around 500,000, are the victims of forcible castration. The petition thus charges that young children are brought to the cities by agents, from villages and towns all over the country, castrated, and then put in charge of a guru at one of the *dhams*, or *hijra* centres. Startlingly, the petition estimates that 100,000 new eunuchs are created by forcible castration.

The petition is pitilessly detailed while describing the ritual of castration. The victim is taken to a deserted spot and sequestered in a hut. For two whole days, he is fed on a diet of opium and milk, maintaining him in a permanent state of intoxication. In the pre-dawn hours of the third day, the boy is held down by five or six eunuchs, while a

---

*From Vinod Behl, "Eunuchs Cry for Justice," *Rediff on the Net*, 20 October 1998.

cord is tied tightly around his testicles to stop the blood flow to the genitals. Thereafter, his penis and testicles are severed with one slash of a sharp knife, and they are then buried. The wound is allowed to bleed, "signifying" the draining of manhood and the onset of womanhood.

Some survive. An unestimated number of young boys, however, die during the process, and are consigned to unmarked graves. The survivor's plight, however, continues. A rounded branch of the pipal tree is inserted into the wound to ensure that the hole is not filled. Heated oil is poured on it, and a lump of *kathha* is used as antiseptic to hasten the healing process. For 48 hours, the new-created eunuch is kept awake to the deafening sounds of drums and music, and maintained on a liquid diet. At the end of this period, the festivities begin – the "gurus" serving *sheera* made in pure *ghee* to all and sundry. Before a eunuch is fully accepted into the clan, however, he is made to sit, with his rectum spread wide, on top of the rounded handle of a grinding stone. Two eunuchs then push the youngster further down onto the handle, till the first drops of anal blood appear. This is taken to signify the first menstruation, and the eunuch is now a "made" member of the clan.

At last count, there are an estimated 450 big, 1600 medium and 35,000 smaller dhams, where the young, castrated children are trained to dance and sing – and clap in that peculiarly recognisable way – and then put out on the streets to earn money begging at street corners and in marketplaces. Alleging that this empire is under the control of a few hijra gurus, the petition says that eunuchs who grow old and whose earning ability is thereby lessened are then dumped, left to die on the streets.

The petition reveals details of the auction of eunuchs in various centres. In Bombay, such auctions allegedly take place in Bhindi Bazar, Pila House, Koliwada, Highway Road, and Andheri. In Delhi, the leading centre is Hare Baba Ki Mazar, near Jama Masjid. At the time of the urs [Sufi festival], eunuchs are auctioned at Ajmer Sharif. Auctions also take place regularly at centres such as Agra, Calcutta, Jalandhar, Baroda, Nagpur and Madras.

Pleading for the liberation of millions of unfortunates, the petition demands that eunuchs be given individual identity cards, that their names be registered in employment exchanges and be considered eligible for Class IV jobs in government, semi-government and private offices, the goal being to enable them to live with dignity. Further, the petition asks the ageing eunuchs be given a state pension of Rs 500 a month. And, finally, that the hijra gurus be booked, and brought to justice, for their heinous crimes. It's a comprehensive charter of demands – the question is whether it will remain yet another of the unheard voices of society's underprivileged.

BANGLADESH

The Orphans

Nicole Hallett*

When Mosleuddin Joy, a slim 19-year-old, tells the story of how he became an orphan, his bright eyes dim. "My father died of a snake bite when I was 11," he explains, "And my mother could no longer support me or my sisters."

His sisters all married young to relieve their mother of the burden. His eldest sister, who was 18, married about a month after their father died. His two other sisters, 16 and 14, were married within two years. But Mosleuddin didn't have this option. So, like many boys in this rural region of Bangladesh, Mosleuddin went to live at the local orphanage.

His story parallels the plight of many boys and young men. The death of a father can be devastating for poor families. It is not considered appropriate for widows to seek employment; nor do they often remarry, especially if they have young children. Sometimes the only option is for mothers to give their children away.

Girls and young women often can aid their families by marrying into wealthier households, who then care for the widowed mother. But this charity often does not extend to sons, who must fend for themselves.

The Charfassion Boys Orphanage is the community's answer to this problem. The drab concrete building, heavily worn from the annual monsoons, houses 100 boys from the surrounding area, who are considered orphans even if their mother is still living. They are fed, clothed, and given access to primary education.

The orphanage was founded in 1971, after a monsoon killed a million people in the province. The rains came so quickly that the riverbanks were breached, causing flash floods that wiped out entire families in mere seconds. Many times, as the waters were rushing in, parents would put their youngest son high up in a date tree, creating thousands of boy orphans in the wake of the storm.

Mizan, 14, can credit the orphanage with saving his life. When he first arrived, tuberculosis had taken over his body, causing a life-threatening infection in his leg. He was close to death when the director of the orphanage, Saluddin, paid for an operation and medication. Now he is still weak, but recovering and attending school again.

But although the orphanage provides a safe haven for many boys, their transition into adulthood is often fraught with difficulty. Noorealam Nirob, 20, explains that while the orphanage helped him as a child, he has conflicting feelings about it now that he has left. "Bengali society is very strict," he explains. "As long as we are orphans, we are fine. But people look down at us. How do we get jobs after we leave the orphanage? Who will hire an orphan?"

---

*Special to this volume.

Noorealam is touching on a very important distinction between men and women in this rural society. Women can often marry out of poverty. Men find it difficult to escape the socioeconomic status of their fathers. In a society that operates almost entirely on social status and personal connections, boy orphans find themselves at the bottom of the scale, and face an uphill battle if they wish to transcend their low social position.

Mosleuddin and Noorealam are lucky. They received high marks on their HSC examinations, and were given scholarships by an international NGO to study in Dhaka. Here, unlike back in the village, people can't identify them immediately as orphans, and they feel like they have a new lease on life. Still, they have received condemnation in Charfassion for "not staying in their place," including from the director of the orphanage, the man who practically raised them from a young age. "He doesn't think that we should be going to school," Mosleuddin says. "He thinks we should be field hands or delivery boys, something more at our level."

Shiraz Redoy, one of the teachers at the orphanage, tries to explain the sentiments of the director. "We care about the boys, but they are orphans." Shiraz was at the orphanage himself as a young boy. His life-defining moment was a romance he had with the daughter of an Australian missionary when he was 17. She taught him English and convinced him to stay in school, despite opposition from his teachers. The romance was short-lived, but Shiraz credits it with convincing him to discount the criticism swirling around him.

He now has a steady job as a teacher, a beautiful wife and two boys of his own. But not every orphan's story has such a happy ending. Secretly, Shiraz is happy for Mosleuddin and Noorealam, but he cannot express such unpopular views in public. "In Bangladesh, orphans are always orphans," he says.

The director, Saluddin, when asked about Mosleuddin and Noorealam, explains it this way: "They don't respect authority. Bengali society is very traditional and we have rules that everyone must follow. They don't follow the rules."

Mosleuddin and Noorealam understand the price they have paid for breaking the rules. They know that they will never be fully accepted in Charfassion, and they worry about the effect it will have on their family.

When Noorealam returned to his home last month, he found another family living there. The landlord had foreclosed and forced his mother onto the street. He has been unable to find her. "I hope that she is with my sister and her husband," he says, "but I am not welcome in their house. So I am just hoping that she is alright."

Back in their room in Dhaka, Mosleuddin and Noorealam study by candlelight for their first university exams. They feel bad about being so far away from their families. "But we have no choice. This is our only chance at a good life," Mosleuddin says. He himself plans to marry and have children someday, but only after he has finished school and has a steady income. "I want to start my own business," he says, and smiles.

MONGOLIA

The Street Child

Interview with Lutaa Badamkhand*

Dolgion, 14, lives in a sewage pit on the fringes of Mongolia's capital, Ulaanbaatar. The air is hot and fetid, with much of the space taken up by two large heating pipes. An all-engulfing stench of rotting garbage and human waste issues from a sewage pipe below.

[Dolgion:] People call us *transheiny* [sewer] kids and shun us. I've been living like this for the last four years. Before we lived in Yarmag District [an Ulaanbaatar suburb] in a *gher* [traditional felt-covered round tent of nomads]. My mother worked as a nurse at hospital. Father had no job. As far as I can remember, he was always unemployed. Once he disappeared for several days and when he returned he gave me a plastic pistol as a gift. I [will] never forget that gift.

Our gher burnt down when I was seven. Me and my classmates were playing after classes when fire started from an electric socket. The two of us tried to suppress it by throwing dirt on it. I had heard that water is no good for electricity. Firefighters arrived only after an hour when our home had already turned to smoking ashes.

A relative of my father took us in. It was difficult to live with another family: too many people, crowded place. Father tried to find another home for us, but he began to drink too much. One day my mum left, and I stayed with Father.

After Mother left us, Father returned home drunk almost every day. At the end, the family we stayed with told us to go away. We did not know where to go and just wandered the streets. Father befriended some bad men and drank with them. Often he would become too drunk to walk and collapse right on the street. I would hang around guarding him. Even if I wanted to carry him away I couldn't because I was too small then. I followed my father like this for more than a month. One day he collapsed again, and I told myself "I cannot take it anymore" and ran away, leaving him behind alone.

Four years have passed since then. I never saw my father again; I don't even know if he is alive or not. After separating from Father, I lived in District 120,000. I wandered the streets, collected food from garbage dumps, begged on the streets. I was small then and people would take pity on me and give good money. There were times I was very hungry. Once I couldn't find anything to eat for two days. At the end I fell unconscious. I learned that it's no good to lie hungry as one may die at the end. It is better to walk and walk.

As winter approached I moved to Narantuul Market [a large food market and flea market]. In the beginning I picked leftovers from a canteen there. Narantuul market is

---

*From Lutaa Badamkhand, "Dolgion: 'Life Is Given Only Once,'" *New Internationalist*, 377 (April 2005).

a dangerous place. If you don't have friends there, children can easily beat you. They usually hang out in gangs. Children who work as market porters are usually older. The younger ones steal, rob other children.

I had a friend there named Cola. Once Cola sold a pair of shoes and it turned out they belonged to his older brother. The brother got mad and beat two of us harshly. Blood was coming out of my ears. I ran away from there and now stay here, in a bunker sitting on the city heating pipes. Already I've been here for two years.

There are six of us living in this pit. Batbaatar is 16. Nyamdorj does not even know his age. He was abandoned by his parents when small. Auntie Uugaana is eldest at 22. Before, kids from the Sharkhad area would come, beat and rob us. But after Auntie joined us they don't come any more.

How do we live? In the morning one of us will go for water. Some wash their faces, some drink water and then we all go out to collect empty bottles. Sometimes it is very cold outside, so we wait until it is noon and gets warmer, then go for lunch at a canteen for the poor. In the evening we sell whatever bottles we've collected during the day. Together we can make 2,000–2,500 tugriks [$2]. Rarely more than that.

A vodka bottle earns 40 tugriks, one soft drink can brings 15 tugriks. With this money we buy food in the evening. Mostly we buy Chinese noodle soup. We put the noodles into a plastic bag, add water and then place them on the heating pipes. There are two large pipes running in the bottom of our bunker. They are so hot that we easily get burnt if we touch them. So in a few minutes the soup gets ready.

If we don't have enough money, on weekends we go to a place giving hot food for free. It's quite far so we take a bus. We don't pay for the bus ride. Many poor people go there on Sunday, so the ticket conductors know.

When we have some spare money, we go to PC game room. It costs 400 tugriks [$0.35] to play for one hour. We have to clean our clothes by rubbing them with snow, wash our faces and hands. Otherwise they won't let us in. They allow us to play only when there are few people there. But with the money we have, we can only play 15–30 minutes each.

Earlier it was much easier to collect bottles. They are becoming rarer now, fewer and fewer every day. People store bottles and cans at home and then sell them themselves. The apartment blocks' concierges collect the remainder. And some adults now own the garbage dumping places. When we go there they chase us away. [. . .]

Why don't we go to a street children's shelter to bathe? True, they don't charge money. But we have no soap and no clothes to change into afterwards. If you hadn't given me a T-shirt [referring to a gift from the interviewer], I would wear the winter jacket alone. Without socks and underwear, it is very easy to get sick in the winter cold.

One of my friends died of pneumonia. He was a year older than me. We hung out together in District 120,000. There was a niche in the wall on the second floor. We would climb there by rope and sleep at night. That day I covered him with my jacket and went out to find food. When I got back he did not wake up. I put my hand on his nostrils; there was no breathing. I immediately called an ambulance, but it never came. It is free to call police and ambulance from [the] public telephone, you know. [Hospitals do not accept children without health insurance.] [. . .]

Shelters? I've been once or twice. Many kids at the shelter learn taekwondo fighting at the nearby sport club. When they hit their feet fly as high as my face. The older ones bully and beat other kids. When New Year gifts were distributed older boys went round the rooms and collected all of them from us. They ate our gifts for days. Older boys are mostly abandoned children brought up in the shelter.

Children's rights? We have nothing. We're just like human garbage. Nobody needs us. Anyone can come and beat us. I want to go to a place where there is no beating. Recently children from that house [points to a residential apartment block nearby] came over and hit us all for no reason. The police come to us only if a theft happens nearby. They take us to the police station where they beat and beat demanding we confess to stealing. They force us to sit on a stool like this [arches his back] and then beat us with batons. Or they tie you tightly on a bench, insert a wooden pole between the legs, right below the crotch and then start rolling it . . . so-o-o painful. [. . .]

All people want to have a good life. I do not know what my life will be like when I grow up. I am afraid that I will die one day with my whole life spent like this, collecting bottles. Life is given only once and I am scared that I will see no good times. [. . .]

When I grow up, I will own a bottle collection point. Most important is to get documents. When I turn 16 I will get a citizen ID card, then work for a while to collect money. With this money I will set up a collecting point.

Other dreams? Well, I will find my parents. I will work all on my own and will find them myself. When I find my parents I will buy a house and we all will live together. [. . .]

PART 2

Ritual and Belief

A common theme in the literature on masculinities is that an adult male identity is not *given*, but must be *won*. To what extent this contrasts with girls' maturation into "women" is open to debate. But it is fair to say that patriarchal society generally has consigned girls to mothering/nurturing roles, in which they are validated by childbearing and childrearing, among other family tasks. Males, though, have been expected to command both private and public spheres. To demonstrate their ability to do so, they must undergo a number of public (as well as private) trials. No one who reads David Gilmore's anthropological study *Manhood in the Making*, with its rich detailing of global masculinity rituals (including "The Wrestlers"), can fail to be struck by the severity and sometimes outright violence of those rites. This is true when we consider Nelson Mandela's vivid account of his trial-by-circumcision, which opens this section (and is followed by a grim coda citing mortality rates from such practices). It is also true when we examine rituals of cattle thievery and woman hunting.

Intra-male conflict and competition are central features of "men's work" (Part 3), and of governance, war making, and state and substate violence (Part 4). But they are also reflected in less formal ways, as with the ritual culture of Rio de Janeiro's "fight clubbers," described by Guy Saville, and in suppressed and tightly channeled contexts like the South Korean "room salon," vividly represented by Jungbong Choi. As with masculine identity more generally (see the introduction to Part 1), women are central to much of this ritual: as targets and victims, as prizes, as spectators and judges.

But if masculinity has traditionally been tied to violence and competitiveness, this no more bounds the possibilities of masculine ritual, and its underlying beliefs and cultural understandings, than mothering inherently defines femininity and womanhood. Nor does it imply that concepts of masculine "honor," so central to male identity, can produce only oppressive and violent behavior. At several points in this book, we meet "honorable" men who appear simultaneously dignified and pacific (see, e.g., "Grandfather Ernesto" in Part 1 and "Global Man, Southern Star" in Part 6). In this section, the reader also encounters masculine rituals that stress solidarity and sociability. These include the institution of the Surinamese *winkel* (corner bar) studied by Gary Brana-Shute, as well as the culinary and medicinal culture, interwoven with a pluralistic view of gender and masculinities, that Tlahtoki Aguirre explores in "Abuelita and Lalo." Even more traditional/patriarchal framings of masculine ritual overlap with elements of hospitality, sustenance, and sharing, as in Abel Polese's essay on "The Good Samaritan."

Ritual often expresses men's underlying spiritual and religious beliefs. These are the subject of the second group of essays in this section. For the most part, the selections depict men who have arrived at positions of social prominence and/or patriarchal dominance through their religious identifications. (The portraits thus serve as something of a bridge for the next section, on masculinities and governance.) Bhante Wimala, a Sri Lankan Buddhist monk, describes growing up under the authority of his father, a village exorcist. Dina Dahbany-Miraglia's evocative representation of the world of Yemenite Jews shows how religion and ritual permeate many aspects of life, buttressing the patriarchal family. The Malian healer and diviner profiled by Jan Jensen serves as a cultural and economic "broker" for his community, as well as a provider of social services. Maria del Nevo's portrait of a Pakistani healer depicts him as an agent of social and generational continuity, similar to the role of "cultural repository" played by Scotty Martin, an Australian aboriginal elder, who also mediates disputes with white society over aboriginal lands and religious sites.

As a means of spiritual expression and cultural preservation, Martin writes and records traditional songs "for everyone to listen to." This link between religious belief and artistic creativity is the focus of the final contribution in this section. Donald Cosentino's profile of Andre Pierre, Haiti's "most cosmopolitan artist of the last half century," shows how Pierre drew on Vodou rituals and spirits to create an "art and philosophy [that] spans not only this world, but planets and constellations beyond."

SOUTH AFRICA

The Initiate

Nelson Mandela*

When I was sixteen, the regent decided that it was time that I became a man. In Xhosa[†] tradition, this is achieved through one means only: circumcision. In my tradition, an uncircumcised male cannot be heir to his father's wealth, cannot marry or officiate in

---

*From Nelson Mandela, *Long Walk to Freedom: The Autobiography of Nelson Mandela* (London: Abacus, 1994), pp. 30–6.
[†]*Editor's note:* One of the principal ethnic groups of South Africa, accounting for about 18 per cent of the total population.

tribal rituals. An uncircumcised Xhosa man is a contradiction in terms, for he is not considered a man at all, but a boy. For the Xhosa people, circumcision represents the formal incorporation of males into society. It is not just a surgical procedure, but a lengthy and elaborate ritual in preparation for manhood. As a Xhosa, I count my years as a man from the date of my circumcision.

The traditional ceremony of the circumcision school was arranged principally for [my friend] Justice. The rest of us, twenty-six in all, were there mainly to keep him company. Early in the new year, we journeyed to two grass huts in a secluded valley on the banks of the Mbashe River, known as Tyhalarha, the traditional place of circumcision for Thembu kings. The huts were seclusion lodges, where we were to live isolated from society. It was a sacred time; I felt happy and fulfilled taking part in my people's customs and ready to make the transition from boyhood to manhood.

We had moved to Tyhalarha by the river a few days before the actual circumcision ceremony. These last few days of boyhood were spent with the other initiates, and I found the camaraderie enjoyable. The lodge was near the home of Banabakhe Blayi, the wealthiest and most popular boy at the circumcision school. He was an engaging fellow, a champion stick-fighter and a glamor boy, whose many girlfriends kept us all supplied with delicacies. Although he could neither read nor write, he was one of the most intelligent among us. He regaled us with stories of his trips to Johannesburg, a place that none of us had ever been to. He so thrilled us with tales of the mines that he almost persuaded me that to be a miner was more alluring than to be a monarch. Miners had a mystique; to be a miner meant to be strong and daring: the ideal of manhood. Much later, I realized that it was the exaggerated tales of boys like Banabakhe that caused so many young men to run away to work in the mines of Johannesburg, where they often lost their health and their lives. In those days, working the mines was almost as much of a rite of passage as circumcision school, a myth that helped the mine-owners more than it helped my people.

A custom of circumcision school is that one must perform a daring exploit before the ceremony. In days of old, this might have involved a cattle raid or even a battle, but in our time the deeds were more mischievous than martial. Two nights before we moved to Tyhalarha, we decided to steal a pig. In Mkhekezweni, there was a tribesman with a typical old pig. To avoid making a noise and alarming the farmer, we arranged for the pig to do our work for us. We took handfuls of sediment from homemade African beer, which has a strong scent much favored by pigs, and placed it upwind of the animal. It was so aroused by the scent that he came out of the kraal [corral], following a trail we had laid and gradually made his way to us, wheezing and snorting, and eating the sediment. When he got near us, we captured the poor pig, slaughtered it, and then built a fire and ate roast pork underneath the stars. No piece of pork has ever tasted as good before or since.

The night before the circumcision, there was a ceremony near our huts with singing and dancing. Women came from nearby villages and we danced to their singing and clapping. As the music became faster and louder, our dance turned more frenzied and we forgot for a moment what lay ahead.

At dawn, when the stars were still in the sky, we began our preparations. We were escorted to the river to bathe in its cold waters, a ritual that signified our purification before the ceremony. The ceremony was at midday, and we were commanded to stand in a row in a clearing some distance from the river where a crowd of parents and relatives, including the regent, as well as a handful of chiefs and counselors, had gathered. We were clad only in our blankets and as the ceremony began, with drums pounding, we were ordered to sit on a blanket on the ground with our legs spread in front of us. I was tense and anxious, uncertain of how I would react when the critical moment came. Flinching or crying out was a sign of weakness and stigmatized one's manhood. I was determined not to disgrace myself, the group or my guardian. Circumcision is a trial of bravery and stoicism; no anaesthetic is used; a man must suffer in silence.

To the right, out of the corner of my eye, I could see a thin, elderly man emerge from a tent and kneel in front of the first boy. There was excitement in the crowd, and I shuddered slightly, knowing that the ritual was about to begin. The old man was a famous ingcibi, a circumcision expert, from Gcalekaland, who would use his assegai [throwing spear] to change us from boys to men with a single blow.

Suddenly I heard the first boy cry out, "Ndiyindoda!" ("I am a man!"), which we had been trained to say at the moment of circumcision. Seconds later, I heard Justice's strangled voice pronounce the same phrase. There were now two boys before the ingcibi reached me, and my mind must have gone blank because, before I knew it, the old man was kneeling in front of me. I looked directly into his eyes. He was pale, and though the day was cold, his face was shining with perspiration. His hands moved so fast they seemed to be controlled by an otherworldly force. Without a word, he took my foreskin, pulled it forward, and then, in a single motion, brought down his assegai. I felt as if fire was shooting through my veins; the pain was so intense that I buried my chin in my chest. Many seconds seemed to pass before I remembered the cry, and then I recovered and called out, "Ndiyindoda!"

I looked down and saw a perfect cut, clean and round like a ring. But I felt ashamed because the other boys seemed much stronger and firmer than I had been; they had called out more promptly than I had. I was distressed that I had been disabled, however briefly, by the pain, and I did my best to hide my agony. A boy may cry; a man conceals his pain.

I had now taken the essential step in the life of every Xhosa man. Now I might marry, set up my own home and plough my own field. I could now be admitted to the councils of the community; my words would be taken seriously. At the ceremony, I was given my circumcision name, Dalibhunga, meaning "Founder of the Bungha," the traditional ruling body of the Transkei. To Xhosa traditionalists, this name is more acceptable than either of my two previous given names, Rolihlahla or Nelson, and I was proud to hear my new name pronounced: Dalibhunga.

Immediately after the blow had been delivered, an assistant who followed the circumcision master took the foreskin that was on the ground and tied it to a corner of our blankets. Our wounds were then dressed with a healing plant, the leaves of which were thorny on the outside but smooth on the inside, which absorbed the blood and other secretions. [. . .]

That first night, at midnight, an attendant, or ikhankatha, crept around the hut, gently waking each of us. We were then instructed to leave the hut and go tramping through the night to bury our foreskins. The traditional reason for this practice was so that our foreskins would be hidden before wizards could use them for evil purposes, but, symbolically, we were also burying our youth. I did not want to leave the warm hut and wander through the bush in the darkness, but I walked into the trees and, after a few minutes, untied my foreskin and buried it in the earth. I felt as though I had now discarded the last remnant of my childhood.

SOUTH AFRICA

Circumcision: The Victims

Chris McGreal*

Four boys have died and about 100 have been admitted to hospital after botched circumcision ceremonies in South Africa. Doctors have blamed "traditional surgeons" who use the same blade to circumcise dozens of teenage boys at a time as part of ancient Xhosa rites of passage in Transkei. The children either bled to death or died from infections. Some of those in hospital are in a critical condition.

Initiates have also complained of traditional surgeons who are drunk or high on cannabis during the cutting ceremony. Health workers have long warned against traditional methods of circumcision, in part because repeated use of the same blade will spread AIDS and hepatitis. Infections are also caused when bandages used to control bleeding are tied too tight. [. . .]

Ten boys died during similar ceremonies in the middle of last year. Families typically pay 200 Rand (£20) for a traditional surgeon and attendants at the ceremony. Most Xhosa are too poor to pay for a hospital circumcision.

Traditional leaders in parts of the Eastern Cape are hoping a tiny clamp imported from Malaysia will put an end to deaths and infections. The "Tara Klamp" does the cutting and then protects the wound, eliminating bandages. And it is used once, eliminating transmitted diseases. [. . .]

---

*From Chris McGreal, "Botched Circumcision Kills Boys," *The Guardian*, 7 January 2000.

UGANDA/KENYA

The Cattle Thieves

Solomon Moore*

The invaders had no ideology to push or grievances to avenge – they just wanted the cows. Hundreds strong, they dashed into this village on tire-track sandals, their beaded collars flapping and red mini-kilts folded high on the thigh – the warrior way. By the end of that afternoon last month [in September 2003], the fighters had taken away scores of sheep, 300 goats and 600 head of cattle. And 30 villagers – mostly women and children – were dead.

In much of the eastern Ugandan and western Kenyan frontiers, people are killing and dying for livestock. In this arid region where seeds often burn in the sand as soon as they're planted, hardy humpbacked cattle are the pivot around which these cultures turn.

Families name their sons after their favorite bulls and stake their prestige on their herds. Cows are doted on and spared hard labor. And when a young man seeks to acquire the sheen of heroism and daring, he goes cattle rustling.

Glory isn't the only thing the young men are after – they're also driven by love. Dowries are paid in beef, so without a phalanx of bovines – the bigger and fatter, the better – a man stands no chance of starting a family.

For most of their history, cattle raids were sanctioned by village elders and carried out by a select cadre of fighters. Tribes usually participated in the raids with sportsman-like respect for rules and procedures: no raiding during drought or famine, no killing unless absolutely necessary, no taking livestock other than cows, no harming women or children, no looting or burning.

But the abundance of casualties during last month's raid by members of the fearsome Karamojong tribe was a sure sign that old conventions are eroding and the fair fight is a thing of the past. When the attack came, most of the village men, members of the more agriculturally based Teso, were fighting the rebel Lord's Resistance Army in the north.

Florence Janet Akello, 36, ran into a hut with five of her children and cowered behind two other women. A Karamojong warrior kicked open the door and fired, killing the women in front of her.

Ten years ago, spears and arrows were the weapons of choice in the border areas. Now it is the assault rifle. Small arms are floating into Kenya and Uganda from Somalia and Ethiopia as well as Sudan, home to one of the world's oldest civil wars. The AK-47 is changing pastoral cultures, increasing the frequency and lethality of cattle raids and destabilizing large swaths of East Africa. Many tribes engage in cross-border raids,

*From Solomon Moore, "No Honor Among Cattle Thieves in Africa," *Los Angeles Times*, 21 October 2003.

lending the clashes a dangerous international dimension. Occasionally, Ugandan and Kenyan troops have pursued the bandits across each other's borders, sparking sharp words in both capitals.

With so much rustling, shepherds are moving cattle to more remote and arid pastures to avoid thieves. The herds' increased mobility is hindering their reproduction and spreading bovine illnesses. Anecdotal reports from the region estimate that cattle stocks in some areas have dropped by half in the past three years.

All of this is straining old tribal customs and hierarchies. In the dusty foothills of western Kenya, the Pokot tribe is entering high season for cattle raids. In August, scores of young women underwent genital excision – a painful and dangerous procedure in which the vulva is scarred and the clitoris removed. Soon, they will be ready for marriage.

But first, young Pokot suitors will need herds. Nameri Komolimo, 20, who lives outside the village of Makutano, has had his eye on a village girl for several years but hasn't married her because he lacks 40 cows for the dowry. There are many young men like Komolimo in the village – ready to wed but with no animals in pasture.

Lately, Komolimo has been tracking some cows across the border in Uganda – they belong to the Karamojong. "When I go on a successful raid and come back with many cows, that is when my father will say that I am grown up," said Komolimo, sporting a hiphop-style Fubu shirt over a traditional kilt. "I am determined. I have been over the mountain and watched their footprints. If I am courageous enough, bullets will not harm me."

But Komolimo has been wrong before. Last year, he and several dozen other suitors raided the Karamojong on the other side of Mt. Elgon, which straddles the border. They brought back scores of cows and goats. "Some days later, they came in large numbers for revenge," Komolimo recalled. "They killed 86 animals, 16 young men and seven mothers. We were displaced from our village. Yes, we made a mistake, but what can we do?

"We wanted the cows. A person without animals has no respect. He is nothing."

Komolimo plans to improve his luck this time by consulting a different *libon*, or oracle. Traditionally, warriors preparing for raids consult these elders to receive their blessings and guidance. "There was a time when raids were limited and elders could intervene," said Etodo Ekwachir, a *libon*. "But the gun gives them the power to go without asking. They say, 'Why should we ask an elder when we have a gun to blow everyone up?'"

NAMIBIA

The Hunters

Niki Kandirikirira*

Boys focusing on defining their masculinity through demonstrable wealth, the number of lovers and the oppression of women and "lesser" ethnic groups, find themselves in competition with older men for the attention of their female peers. The boys, denied access to the multiple relationships that would symbolize their manhood, cannot challenge older men, so blame and victimize the girls. They accuse them of being loose and resort to sexual violence and bullying.

This has led to the establishment of a ritual in the hostels[†] called "hunting." As individuals or in groups [the boys] break into the girls' hostels covered in blankets as disguise, and climb into any bed with any girl. Threatening the girls with sharp implements and sometimes cutting off their underwear with razorblades, they rape them. For boys this is an evening's entertainment, celebrated in their dormitories or back at home by bestowing on the best "hunter" the title "Jagter Nommer Een" (Hunter Number One). For girls it is an evening of humiliation and shame to be endured in silence.

Boys "hunt" and abuse girls in the schools with little or no reaction from adults who, over many years, have come to see it as normal behavior – "boys will be boys." Many teachers and parents themselves were the "hunted" or "hunter" in their school days, and they rarely take the psychological impact on the girls into account. Even if girls report it, they are not counseled; at best they are taken to the nearest clinic. Meanwhile even those boys who are caught are only reprimanded for hanging about and sent back to their hostel or off the school premises. The worst punishment for "hunting" noted during the PRA [Participatory Rural Appraisal] was watering trees, despite the fact that physical punishment is meted out in the case of theft of food, running in the school or even singing at the wrong time in a school event.

In the hostels [. . .] boys disassociated from traditional systems of initiation into adulthood, denied parental care and guidance, bullied by teachers for other misdemeanors but

---

*From Niki Kandirikirira, "Deconstructing Domination: Gender Disempowerment and the Legacy of Colonialism and Apartheid in Omaheke, Namibia," in Frances Cleaver, ed., *Masculinities Matter! Men, Gender and Development* (London: Zed Books, 2002), pp. 125–6.
†*Editor's note:* Subsidized hostels house children between the age of six and matriculation from high schools: "In the hostels, where facilities and supervision are inadequate, the staff underpaid and untrained in childcare and development, children find themselves in a microcosm of the world outside. Hostel staff, having internalized discriminatory ideologies and practices, subject children to physical abuse, humiliation and denial of basic needs in order to victimize and control them. Men seeking opportunities with young girls or wanting to steal from or to bully younger people go in and out of the hostels without challenge as the adults paid to care for the children turn a blind eye" (p. 122).

met with silence on sexual violence, living in squalid conditions with limited food, shelter and care, are learning to act out the societal dysfunction that has been commonplace throughout South Africa and Namibia. Where young black boys daily experience themselves as oppressed and impotent, their frustration about this marginalization is likely to take expression in the domination of girls. [...]

BRAZIL

The Wrestlers

David D. Gilmore*

As is true in many societies that enjoy sports, the Mehinaku [Indians of Brazil] have developed symbolic frames of reference in competitive games and gladiatorial contests by which a man can demonstrate his worth against his fellows. Among the Mehinaku, the main sport is wrestling. All men are expected to wrestle, to play hard, and, if possible, to win. There are matches and exhibitions every day, and challenge duels are constantly being arranged. Every man "wants to be a champion" (Gregor 1985: 95). Because it symbolizes all other skills, wrestling ability is, above all, the measure of a man and a symbolic arena for self-promotion. A powerful wrestler, say the villagers, is impressive, or frightening (*kowkapapai*). Likened to the powerful anaconda in the quickness of his holds and the lightning way he hobbles his opponents, he commands their fear and respect. The women say the wrestling champion is beautiful (*awitsiri*), and he is in demand as a paramour and husband. Triumphant in politics as well as in love, the champion wrestler embodies the "highest qualities of manliness" (ibid.: 145). Not so respected is the loser. A poor wrestler, no matter what his other virtues may be, is regarded as a fool. As he flails about on the wrestling ground, the men shout sarcastic advice from the bench in front of the men's house, urging him to stop eating dirt and to lift his back off the ground before it is broken. The women are less vocal as they watch the matches from the doorways and make muffled jokes, but they too criticize him in private. None of them is satisfied to have a loser or a coward as a husband or lover.

[...] The men engage in these daily combats largely for feminine approval. Success in beating others means success with the opposite sex. Women shout encouragement from the sidelines and coyly make themselves available to the winners. It is interesting here, also, that as successful wrestlers embody the highest qualities of manliness, the losers in wrestling contests are likened to inadequate little boys. The man who loses a wrestling match is said to become "a master of little boys' games" and to resemble a

---

*From David D. Gilmore, *Manhood in the Making: Cultural Concepts of Masculinity* (New Haven & London: Yale University Press, 1990, pp. 89–91).

helpless child (ibid.). Among the Mehinaku, defeat and victory in sports are therefore more than tickets in an inconsequential lottery; nor is wrestling simply a recreation. The contests indicate a man's worth as a functioning adult and are indelible signals of his potential. Avoiding participation in the wrestling matches or losing abjectly are not superficial failings but severe character deficiencies, a betrayal of civic duties. People are not reticent about informing the non-combatant of his obvious deficiencies, showering him with abuse and sending him to the trash heap of society.

Cowardice or incompetence on the mat carries an additional penalty, because it also means being spurned by available females. It is only by playing the game with courage that a Mehinaku man can win and keep a wife, for she will despise him and betray him if he fails to measure up. Mehinaku sexual norms provide for the tacit approval of the wife who cuckolds a poor wrestler; knowing this, most such women carry on adulterous affairs while their husbands sulk helplessly. It is clear that one of the qualities being touted on the public stage is a sense of responsiveness to collective ideals, measured by a willingness to compete forcefully for the culture's highest prizes. A man who fails in the sporting arena, it is assumed, suffers from an inbred character deficiency and will also fail as a farmer and fisherman; he is therefore a poor choice as a husband or lover. This man will have few children to support him later on in life, few sons to revere him and carry on his name, and so he will experience an ever-dwindling status, a progressive social marginalization as irreversible as the physical debilities of old age.

BRAZIL

The Fight Clubbers

Guy Saville*

It's Friday night. In a dusty back street – far from Copacabana's tourist trap [in Rio de Janeiro] – is the satellite settlement of Duque de Caxias. It's a poor, gray town, a world away from Rio's colorful beach life. On its fringes, past the discount shops and street markets stacked high with tropical fruit and rails of cheap clothes, is a squat, dirty-white building. Painted in blue on the side of a wall are the words: "Funk Ball every Saturday."

Two rival groups have already begun to gather outside: Side A and Side B. They are dressed in their best clothes: the girls in tiny hot pants and tight, revealing tops; the boys in Nike and Adidas Bermuda shorts, gold chains hanging from bare chests and bleached white hair cropped to the scalp.

---

*Special to this volume.

By midnight, perhaps 1,000 people are waiting. One of the Side A crowd is Andre, a thin young man with bleached hair and sharp cheekbones. He is awaiting the arrival of a bus – laid on by the funk ball's promoters – bringing his gang from the Dicke da Vila Alizira slum to the club.

When they arrive, Andre greets his people: kissing the girls and giving the boys a reassuring hug. Some proudly bear injuries from previous balls – eye patches, half-healed cuts, arms in slings. Others are ready for the evening's fight with mouth guards and plasters stretched over their noses to stop them from choking on congealed blood.

The crowd joins the disorderly Side A queue at the entrance. After paying their 7.50 reais ($6) to the bottle-blonde sitting in the tiny ticket booth, they file past a pack of bouncers who body-search each person for weapons.

Andre guides his people to the left corner of the club, where the walls are smeared brown with blood from previous fights. Side A and Side B gather at opposite ends of the hangar-sized venue, leaving a gap of around two meters in the center – they call this the Corridor of Death. And it is here that the funk ball turns from being just another nightclub into a place of combat and bloodshed.

The DJ stops playing bad remixes of Dire Straits and the Backstreet Boys, and puts on the first funk record of the evening. The two crowds roar with approval. Underage girls, dancing for groups of guys, simulate sex acts by thrusting their hips and suggestively sucking on their fingers.

This is Brazilian music and sounds nothing like seventies funk, despite sharing the same name. Produced locally and on a limited budget, it lacks the polish of Western music but has a raw, infectious vigor. A mish-mash of influences, it uses the electronic beat of late eighties pop, with bass thuds and slithers of techno. An off-key aggressive rap is often sung live.

Tubarao, whose name means "shark" in Portuguese, says a good funk DJ is able to manipulate the clubbers' feelings of anger. "A DJ gets to know his crowd because we play the same balls every weekend, so we understand the rhythm of their fighting," he explains. "I take great pride in controlling my crowd. If I see they want blood, I'll put on a fast funk tune. But if they need cooling, then I'll soothe them with something for the girls."

The gangs even have their own chants, recorded by their leaders on equipment provided by the funk-ball promoters. Intensely personal, they talk about revenge, poverty, and the deaths of enemies. "The more you listen to funk," says Andre, "the more you . . . love it. It has a hard, intense sound. Great for fighting. It's our own music, about our people, about death and drugs. The things we know."

Funk-ball fights are not free-for-alls. At a DJ's call for mortal kombat – after the notoriously violent computer game – the rival sides try to drag their enemies into the Corridor of Death and back into their own part of the club. Sometimes groups of 10 or 20 funkers cross this central aisle and invade the opposite side's territory. If an enemy – or, as they are known in funk-ball slang, "German" – is captured, they are beaten, often unconscious, unless rescued by a member of their own side.

Even girls fight. Once the sexy dance routines stop they wrestle one-on-one. They punch, snap each other's fingers and use their stiletto heels to mutilate the pretty face of a rival.

Andre has steered his crowd well away from the corridor. "There's no point being exposed right at the beginning," he says. "It's much better to save your energy for later, when things get nasty. Right now people are just playing around."

As he speaks, hundreds of people from Side B put white bandanas on their head and start forming a huge human snake. They begin winding their way around the club, in front of the stage, slowly veering toward Side A. In unison they punch the air and begin their rhythmic, aggressive chanting, demanding just one thing: a fight to the death.

A small group from Side A attempts to invade Side B. They try to break through the line of security men and into the Corridor of Death. One small boy, perhaps no older than 12 or 13, is immediately punched square in the face by a bouncer twice his width and age. He falls back into a web of Side A arms.

Another is less lucky. Three security men, erupting with uncontrolled anger, drag him into the central aisle. They loop an orange plastic cord around his neck and yank him screaming and gasping for breath out of the ball and onto the street.

Andre admits that most funkers are wary of provoking the armed security guards. "You're not allowed to hit back. If you do, they'll kill you. That's the rule."

And then the DJ screams: "Attention Side A. Attention Side B. It's the time you've all been waiting for. Time for the mortal kombat."

Gone is that earlier feeling of celebration from the party in the street. Now Side A and Side B, divided only by the Corridor of Death, are squaring up to fight. A group of young boys starts chanting: "Funk fills us with hate. We will invade. We will . . ." As they bundle across the corridor, the rest of their anthem is swallowed by the music. Bouncers rush, wooden truncheons in hand, to where the fight had erupted. They grab three funkers and drag them, shouting and screaming, out of the club. But the fuse has been lit and pockets of violence explode across the hall.

Nowhere is safe. Young bodies, glistening with sweat and fresh blood, start fighting next to me. One boy, lying on the floor near my feet, has his head stamped on by a rival. A bouncer pushes me toward a small door: "Get in there," he shouts. "You'll be out of the way."

"You've got to understand," Andre bursts out suddenly, "that certain things are important to funkers. First you've got to fight without fear because it's the only way to win respect. I was scared at the beginning but after the first punch in the face I lost my fear.

"Second, you need the right clothes. Then you have to have a girl with a big arse. But most important of all, you need a good crowd, one that'll back you up . . .

"A funker has got to have his trophies. A rival's blood is a trophy and so are his clothes. But if I see my own blood, all I can think about is revenge.

"I remember once stamping on a German's head because he'd made me bleed. His girl was screaming and screaming at me to stop. But that only made me stamp harder."

He continues: "I'm nearly 20 and that's old for a funker. Soon someone else will take over as leader because God gave me a warning to quit. It was 3 o'clock one morning a couple of months ago. I'd been fighting all night but still wanted more. The DJ played our chant and that made me go again.

"I told my friends I was going to fight. It was my day, everything had been going really well and I had the devil inside me. I went alone. I dropped two Germans and then one of Crowd B came and slashed me across my arm with a razor. I could see right through to my bones.

"I was unlucky. Most of the time we leave the weapons in the bus for later because you can't get them inside the ball, but somehow this [guy] managed to get a blade past security. I saw death in front of me that night."

Andre can no longer fully stretch his arm. And some nights, when the city's normally balmy temperature drops, he gets a searing pain around the bones. This is just one of many funk-ball scars he will carry for the rest of his life.

He bristles at the memory and turns to his crowd for reassurance. They start to chant: "We are the terror possessed by hatred. We will invade Side B and take the Germans. We want blood. We want slaughter. We want bodies on the floor."

*　　*　　*

Among the funking crowd, Romulo Costa is an immensely popular man. He owns Rio's largest chain of funk balls, which are run under the brand name Furação 2000 – or Tornado 2000. Each weekend, thousands of young funkers travel to one of his regular nights held in half a dozen clubs across the city. Police insist that if he is imprisoned, the funk-balls phenomenon will cease to exist. He has been hauled into the police station for questioning on several occasions. Once he was detained for over a week, but later released without charge.

In person, Mr. Costa does not live up to his bogeyman image. He comes across as a family man, as someone with an almost benevolent concern for the poor teenagers who inhabit his funk balls. But beyond the bland denials of "I don't promote violence" or "my balls are about peace and music" – which are usually made on the steps of the police station – Mr. Costa says he is rarely given the chance to explain his association with funk.

"People never ask why I promote funk," he says. "They just assume that I enjoy violence. Well, I don't. I'm from the favelas [slums] myself. I've lived in a house without water, in a place where there was nothing to do all day. I've had jobs without prospects which didn't pay me enough to get by on. So I know all about poverty."

This is one of the reasons Costa is so popular among the teenage funkers – he's the boy from the slums made good. He has a family, a beautiful young wife, and the trappings of a middle-class lifestyle.

As a teenager he carried records for the DJs and was eventually employed full-time by a former owner of Furação 2000. He worked his way up the ranks before taking over the business. He even met his wife, Veronica, on the funk-ball dance floor.

Over the years, he has built an empire and now has a stable of DJs who, apart from playing live sets, regularly release funk compilation CDs. He is devoted to funk music, both as a way of making money and, it seems, as a form of self-expression for the poor. And each time he is summoned to the police station, a huge crowd of banner-waving kids accompanies him, pleading: "Don't close our balls."

Mr. Costa has come under increasing fire. His neighbors in the notoriously nouveau-riche district of Barra da Tijuca – about 20 minutes drive from Copacabana Beach – have exerted pressure on his family to leave their condominium. And parents at his two children's private school have successfully petitioned the head teacher to force the family to leave.

"People are scared of me. They think I am dangerous because I come from the favela and because I have money. That's why funk is discriminated against. It is the music of the poor. If you went into any house in the favela you would hear funk playing.

"Of course we get some violence at the balls, but it isn't the organized violence that you read about. Violence is normal when people are repressed and discriminated against. That's why these fights occur. Fighting is an everyday part of our lives."

SOUTH KOREA

The Room Salon

Jungbong Choi*

In his seminal work *The Structural Transformation of the Public Sphere,* Jürgen Habermas identifies the eighteenth-century salons and coffee houses of England, France, and Germany as incubators of the modern public sphere, in which bourgeois individuals came together and engaged with cultural and political affairs. Nearly three centuries later, European salons find their bizarre counterpart in the distant land of South Korea: the "room salon." This is a general designation for drinking places where male customers occupy individually partitioned rooms furnished with dazzling chandeliers, deluxe furniture, and musical equipment. There is some differentiation – among hotel room salons, *dalanjujum, karaoke* bars, *nohraebang,* ticket cafés, and so forth. But these facilities commonly serve as sanctuaries of sensual pleasure, in which adult males luxuriate in the conspicuous consumption of world-class whiskies and cognacs, while indulging in raucous karaoke songs, frenzied dancing, and inane chatter.

Prices for drinks vary according to the status of the bar and the accoutrements of the room. As a rule, a bottle of $30 whisky at market price fetches anywhere between $150

_____

*Special to this volume.

to $500 in a room salon, while a plate of fruit salad or similar side dishes can command $150 to $250.* With service charges added, a party of four ordering two bottles of fine whisky can easily receive a bill in excess of $2,000 for a single night's carousing. This does not include a major extra expense: tips for barmaids. Room-salon revelry is usually attended by beautiful female servers, often referred to as "hostesses," whose primary role is to serve drinks and provide carnal pleasures to male customers. A manager at a room salon in a glitzy area of Seoul says: "Actually, more lavish offers to hostesses are made once the drinking and singing cools off. If girls agree to go for the 'second round', the customers have to pay $200 to $500 for each hostess."† Here, the "second round" is a code-name for sex, which usually takes place in nearby hotel rooms.

One can't help wondering how men on average salaries can afford such exorbitance two or three times a month.‡ Can they maintain their health, work, and family life while frittering away time, energy, and money in the room salon? In what gendered milieu has this practice thrived? In what ways is the libidinal economy of adult males tied to larger socioeconomic formations and organizational structures in South Korea?

I suggest that the ubiquity of the room salon should be viewed as a cultural outgrowth of the male-centered corporate ethos that took shape in South Korea during the era of military dictatorship (1960–1993). Put another way, the room-salon culture expresses the patriarchal norms of Confucianism and feudalism, and shows how these have been reconfigured by South Korean industrialization and modernization.

The political dimension of the room salon

Nearly three decades of military rule indoctrinated South Koreans with an ideology of development as the paramount national objective. Driven by the monolithic imperative of economic growth, businesses and workers alike were thrust into a rat-race of wealth accumulation, with scant regard for procedural legitimacy and fairness. A symbiosis developed between capital and politics. The room salon was indispensable to this symbiosis.

Room salons were the major sites where clandestine deals were struck between parties (usually businessmen) seeking preferential treatment, and those – usually politicians or government officials – who could grant favors. Not only did the room salon serve as a black market for business deals and political bargains, but it was also a breeding ground for scandals based on prostitution, tax evasion, drug dealing, blackmail, and homicide. As is well known, Park Chung-hee, the former president of South Korea, was assassinated by a political aide during a room-salon party in 1979. [See "The Autocrat", p. 217]

---

*As of this writing, the exchange rate for the Korean won is 1008 for one US dollar.

†This quote is based on my personal interview with a room-salon manager, conducted in the summer of 2002. He requested anonymity for fear of being charged with involvement in prostitution.

‡This data is drawn from a survey released by the Korea Women's Association United (KWAU): *The Women's News*, February 2002, p. 3.

Following this farcical tragedy, a joke spread that the country's name had officially been changed to the "Republic of Salon Korea."*

Scandals originating in room salons continue to attract attention, deepening public cynicism towards the economic and political leadership. In 2004, a personal secretary of the South Korean president was found to have accepted a bribe from a local construction company while in a hotel room salon. Video clips of his misconduct, taken with a hidden camera at the salon, were aired by a major TV broadcaster, and stirred fierce debate about the ethical caliber of the administration. In the wake of similar events, some observers ridiculed the nexus between room salons and the South Korean political economy, calling salons the "national parliament and government headquarters in exile."

The room salon, in a nutshell, is a political–economic catacomb where money changes hands, fraudulent deals are consummated amidst music and dancing, and industrialists plot the exploitation of their workers over glasses of exotic whisky. In this sense, it would be a mistake to consider the room salon merely a pleasurable refuge for adult men. In fact, the salon is one of the critical but under-recognized social spheres in which individual and institutional transactions are forged, free of law, ethics, and propriety.

The economic dimension of the room salon

Room salons mushroomed in the urban areas of South Korea during the mid-1970s. This was an era heralded for its miraculous economic growth. Today, room salons are found in virtually every corner of business districts in South Korea. Some draw a correlation between this ubiquity and the prevalence of "hospitality," a central part of Korea's business culture.

It is normal for Korean businessmen to take clients, both foreign and domestic, to these establishments in the hope of sealing a deal. They will gladly overburden their credit cards in Seoul's ritziest entertainment districts to fortify a business relationship with clients. As the head of Nivea Korea commented, "[private] contacts are more important than contracts, global standards, or even laws." He continued: "Never underestimate the power of developing a personal relationship with business partners in Korea that can be accomplished only through 'business socializing.' "†

Owing to the prevalence of such socializing, high-ranking executives and ordinary office workers alike are dragged to room salons to please clients. At first glance, the nature of the "after-hours business" in a room salon might appear obscure, given the sensual atmosphere and entertainment-oriented activity taking place. Nevertheless, it is indisputable that room salonning is an (unpaid) extension of work. Its ambiguity as

---

*The official title of South Korea is Republic of Korea.
†Pyung-Hee Kim, "Korean Business Culture: Ten Rules," *Chosun Daily*, 24 June 2001, http://english.chosun.com/w21data/html/news/200106/200106240143.html.

both a continuation of, and diversion from, official work vanishes when one considers the means and sources of payment for the activities.

As I mentioned, one night of frolic in a room salon may cost roughly 1 million won ($1,000) per person, a sum most commoners could not even dream of spending for a month's entertainment budget. This extravagance is underwritten by a peculiar budgetary arrangement. Both small and large corporations normally budget a considerable sum for "hospitality expenses," which translates into treating business clients to luxury entertainment. In addition, companies issue corporate credit cards to staff who engage in frequent contact with clients. Employees must prove that the meetings are business related, and people on the receiving end of the free entertainment must be identified in the company's spending records. This testifies to the fact that room salonning is a transformed, but still official, form of work.

The excesses of room salons and other similar drinking places are prime culprits of occupational disease and family malfunction. In November 2002, the South Korean Supreme Court ruled in favor of an office worker who had filed a claim against the company where he had worked for 11 years. He claimed that he developed liver cancer as a result of attending business gatherings three days a week on average; this had invariably involved heavy drinking in room salons and similar establishments.

Nonetheless, workplaces are regularly viewed as second homes, and co-workers as family members. Indeed, the conventional role of family as the primary locus of affection and care is shrinking in inverse proportion to the rapidly increasing time and interpersonal attention expended in the workplace. It is men – more accurately, male heads of household – who most acutely experience the decline of family life, as passions and emotions are siphoned towards the workplace. The dutiful breadwinner of South Korea often undergoes a psychological eviction from wives and children. Some years ago, an appalling report was released about how elementary-school children imagined their fathers. Many of the children wrote essays depicting their fathers as drunkards or fatigued couch-dwellers. Children in Korea see their fathers only infrequently on weekdays, for they rarely come home before midnight. On weekends, salarymen fathers are busy catching up on their sleep. They have even earned the nickname "Santa Claus," because they sneak in while kids are sleeping and place some guilt-charged gifts at the bedside.

The ideological dimension of the room salon

Apart from the business meetings to which ordinary office workers are lured, there are numerous functions at which attendance is mandatory. Gatherings and events intended to heighten teamwork and productivity are routinely held: dinners out, picnics, fishing trips, sports events, hiking, and karaoke parties, to name just a few. These seemingly pleasant activities carry controlling implications, imbuing the workers with ideologies and a work ethic conducive to labor management. For instance, major corporations, including Hyundai, Samsung, and LG, emphasize Confucian values like collective consciousness, loyalty, age hierarchy, and harmony. These tenets are rigorously promoted as a recipe for greater work efficiency. In a similar way, room-salon gatherings serve as rituals of labor control, with particular ideological underpinnings: unity, conformity, hierarchy, and manliness.

Of the array of formulaic rites that take place in the room salon, drinking *poktanju* (a type of cocktail, mixing beer with strong whisky) best illustrates the obsession of Korean enterprises with male bonding. Typically, everyone in a room is pressed to drink poktanju "bottoms up," at the same speed and in the same amount. The objective of drinking in such an intimidating manner is to test individual valor and flaunt collective morale. It is strikingly similar to the rites observed by Korean gangsters and Japanese *yakuza*.

Apart from parading collective manhood, the ritual is aimed at getting members drunk as rapidly as possible. This has its own cultural function. Korea is still a vertical society, with a high esteem for age-based hierarchy. The age hierarchy, consistent with the chain of command in corporate and social settings, is both a handy tool for creating solidarity, and a tough barrier to it. Under alcohol's influence, however, the distance between superior and subordinate, older and younger, can be narrowed – or so it is believed. There seems to exist a myth that workplace tensions can be safely defused by rounds of poktanju in a room salon, followed by dancing, singing, and banter. There is no room here for the romantic vision of dignity and drinking etiquette; rather, lewd and exaggeratedly identical mannerisms predominate.

Such laissez-faire behavior is precisely re-enacted with every new visit to a room salon, as if there were a pre-established template to follow. The truth of the matter is that most men in a room salon desperately maintain sobriety beneath their smashed façade, making painstaking efforts to abide by the tacit rule of "going crazy" for the sake of conformity.* Hence, far from being a relaxed and amusing diversion, the lunatic hedonism in the room salon is nothing more than a hollow performance by which a myth of horizontal comradeship is created and recreated. Uniformity is confused with unity, and eradication of individuality is misconceived as harmony. In the end, room salonning is a corporate placebo, used to boost team spirit and labor productivity.

The sociocultural dimension of the room salon

The ritual of promoting workplace camaraderie culminates with semi-obligatory sex with hostesses, i.e., the "second round." Here, patriarchal corporate norms move to the forefront. Buying women together with friends or colleagues is a time-honored practice in many parts of the world, but it is practiced to a truly ghastly extent in Korea. The custom accompanies the long trajectory of male adulthood, from college years, through military service, and into professional careers; it is mediated by institutions that uphold male-centered orthodoxies.

---

*This observation is based on my personal experience during two years of employment on the staff of the South Korean National Congress. I have also drawn on testimony from former colleagues at the National Congress, with whom I had to frequent room salons about three times a week.

Not only does room-salon culture catapult male debauchery into the workplace, but it also fuels the universalization of prostitution. For instance, the *dalanjujum*, a humble drinking place with karaoke machines in an open space, has been gradually transmuted into a second-rate room salon offering "second round" services. So have many other businesses: *nohraebang* (sports massage parlors), motels, public bathhouses, teashops, even barber shops. The younger generation is following in its elders' footsteps in this regard. The so-called Tehran Valley, a mecca of information-technology venture firms populated by aspiring entrepreneurs, is an emerging hub of deluxe room salons, each equipped with more than 100 separate rooms. The room-salon frenzy has even moved into cyberspace. In 2003, one of the nation's largest Internet-based movie providers, Movies Internet Multiplex, premiered a weekly draw for its members, awarding as prizes nights out at a luxurious room salon.* The company announced that the winners would be served fine whisky by girls of their choice, to the accompaniment of a musical group. When the prize announcement was criticized for gender discrimination, the company responded that more than 80 per cent of its 500,000 customers were adult men over 30, with a proclivity for sexually oriented entertainment.

Thanks to the diffusion of room-salon culture, sex has become a gigantic industry in South Korea. According to the Korean Institute of Criminology (2003), it generates 24 trillion won ($23.5 billion) annually, roughly 4.1 per cent of gross domestic product (GDP).† The institute reports that 4.3 per cent of women in their twenties – roughly 330,000 women – are engaged in the trade, while 20 per cent of adult males purchase sex four times a month.‡ The magnitude of the trade has caused a spillover to neighboring countries. Thousands of Chinese women are recruited as hostesses by cheap dalanjujum or nohraebang, and countless female laborers from countries like Russia, Thailand, Vietnam, Philippines, and Indonesia are rushing to Korea (as well as Japan) in the hopes of making a year's salary in a week, simply by selling their bodies.

Despite rising public concern and outrageous social costs, men's desire for these pleasure-jaunts has hardly abated. Recently, the government implemented a new anti-prostitution law, and launched a month-long crackdown on the sex trade.§ Room salons, dalanjujums, and nohraebangs were especially hard-hit by the prohibition of the sex trade and the drastic reduction in alcohol sales (80 per cent of which occur in these establishments). Devastated, room-salon owners and the alcohol industry in October 2004 deployed roughly 2,800 female workers (hostesses and prostitutes) for a demonstration in front of the National Assembly. A powerful interest group,

---

*"Website Offers Room Salon Trip," *Korea Times*, 30 September 2003.
†For details, see David Scofield, "Korea's 'Crackdown Culture': Now It's Brothels," *Asia Times*, 25 September 2004, http://www.atimes.com/atimes/Korea/FI25Dg05.html.
‡Ibid.
§The law was spurred in part by a fire in a red-light district, which claimed the lives of 14 prostitutes. Since then, women's rights groups have called for restrictions on the unbridled expansion of the sex industry.

room-salon owners are vigorously opposed to legal interventions in their "sacrosanct" businesses.

Many foreigners who have visited South Korea are amazed by the country's vibrant and flamboyant nightlife. Underneath the glittering surface, however, lie networks of political corruption, labor exploitation, and male hegemony. To my eyes, the image of South Korean men flocking to the room salon evokes a poignant sense of solitude. The room salon provides only an illusory balm for their personal and socioeconomic misery. Their souls remain hungry; what they need is psychological comfort, not sadistic gratification through abuse of self and others.

SURINAME

The Regulars

Gary Brana-Shute*

Marcell stares out the window, his eye seizing upon every moving object. Last night he worked the night shift outside the city and rode on the dusty, guttered road the 20 kilometers back to Paramaribo to enjoy his day off before returning again that afternoon. The saw-mill that employs him provides food and shelter for the men who work there but, without the excitement of Paramaribo, many men do not like it and prefer the long daily journey back to the foto (city). He arrived in Paramaribo at 2 o'clock in the morning, slept until 9 o'clock, drank a glass of ice water and came to the *winkel* [corner alcohol shop].

At this point Marcell is enjoying the favors of five women, including the one he is currently living with; he has the economic resources to do it. When the women are short of money they can come to him for aid; his periodic disbursals of anything from small change to upwards of Sf 100 [about $50] make him invaluable. They all know where to find him and often in the evenings a whisper through the winkel window will draw him outside. He may call upon them for services (sex, running an errand, house-cleaning) that evening, the next day, or next week. The connection may remain latent, often reactivated first by a woman.

During the last monthly pay period Marcell worked overtime and brought home Sf 435. This is a high salary and by national financial standards would place Marcell solidly in the middle income range. However, Marcell is in debt to the company bank and his paternal aunt, and at the end of every pay period he is penniless.

---

*From Gary Brana-Shute, *On the Corner: Male Social Life in a Paramaribo Creole Neighborhood* (Prospect Heights, IL: Waveland Press, Inc., 1990), pp. 25–7, 34–5, 110–12.

He has Sf 25 left from the Sf 435 check he received a little over a week ago. The money found its way to many people. Chung, the winkel proprietor, got Sf 102 for Marcell's two week alcohol bill. (Some women support themselves and their children on less than Sf 60 per month.) Sf 100 went to the woman with whom he is now living. She uses the money to buy clothes, food, jewelry, household decorations and appliances (for their two-room, worn cottage), and to make contributions to her family who are poor. Because he lived with his paternal aunt off and on for the last 11 years, Marcell gave her Sf 50. To care for her children he gave the aunt's daughter, his cousin, Sf 30. Sf 25 went to Silvia, a woman whom he occasionally visits, as well as Sf 10 for another of his girl friends. The other three young women he visits got nothing this paycheck. His sister looked him up at the winkel yesterday and he gave her Sf 10. House rent at Sf 14 and utilities completed his disbursals.

Asked if he would consider banking portions of his salary, Marcell scoffs at the idea. Much better, he reasons, to be a man of means, indulging pleasures and investing money in persons and possessions, both of which, incidentally, can be converted into cash when need be. Money serves no apparent use in the bank, especially when you need it in a hurry. His women and his friends are many, and a number of people in the neighborhood are beholden to him – for a loan, a gift to an old penniless woman, a bicycle bestowed on a young child. Marcell has a big heart. Besides, he continues, he chooses not to be with just one woman, and through his disbursements has a number at his disposal. One of them, he presumes, will always forsake you in a pinch, so better to increase the odds in your favor. He is also admired by the men for his rather spectacular social and sexual feats. [...]

Marcell will stay at the winkel until about two o'clock today. He will eat later with Sissy, his paternal aunt, because the woman with whom he lives is away. There is no set eating hour. A pot of rice with vegetables and fish is always on the stove and Marcell needs to only take a portion and retire to a meal under the trees in the backyard. If it is not too noisy he may nap at her house, or walk the four blocks to his own house. Most of the men will follow the same pattern, and when they awake at four o'clock in the afternoon they will return to work, stroll downtown, or return to the winkel.

Many men drop in the winkel throughout the day. Most are marginal to the group of about 15 men who frequent the winkel regularly and have good relations with one another. All the men are different, or at least they try to be. Each projects a certain image and supports a particular identity, perhaps as a man of streetcorner letters or through the tilt of a cap perched jauntily on the head or a clever way of turning a phrase or proverb. Their life styles are different too; but similar enough to allow convergence and compatibility in the winkel context. [...]

In all, interaction among the regulars is easy going. A fellow drops by and strolls to the table or counter where his buddies are congregated. Drinks – bottles of beer, rum and whiskey – lie about and the new arrival must merely yell to the barkeep for a glass. The men never share a glass or drink directly from the bottle. He then can sit down, pour a drink and enter into a conversation – or change it – at any point. When the bottle is dispatched he may or may not buy a refill, but has the privilege to take another drink. The exchange of cigarettes and snacks assumes the same arrangement.

When on the corner, the relationships a man has with all the other men present are not of the same intensity. In a sense, within the winkel group each man has his own personal network determined by degree of closeness and compatibility. In the center are those people, one or two, that he considers his good friends – mati – and calls them by that title. These men are usually the same age, economic status and have roughly the same domestic arrangements. They are in daily face to face contact if the situation permits and they alone, of all the men at the winkel, "travel" together. Goods and services are regularly exchanged between them and no tally is kept – assuming of course that a somewhat general balance is maintained in the long run. With good friends one can discuss some more delicate problems without fear of him leaking information to damaging sources, turn to him for aid in a crisis, rely on him for a favor and impose upon him anytime, day or night, at work or off, when he is with a woman or not.

Towards the fringes of a man's winkel network are his acquaintances, persons with whom he is on good terms, drinks and debates with and can expect no attack – verbal or otherwise – no unanticipated blow to his reputation or pocketbook. The relationships are not in-depth but they are genuine, safe and pleasant.

Collectively, all of these personal networks within the winkel, juxtaposing friends and acquaintances, mesh to give temporary form and spirit to the winkel group. [. . .]

The winkel is accessible to men. There are no strict entry requirements, scheduled commitments or rites of passage. A well-behaved man with a good reputation must merely drop by and make his presence known. At the beginning, the winkel group will be cautious, but after observing the stranger over a period of time, discussing his background and finding his qualities acceptable, the porous group boundaries absorb him. Departure is just as easy; one leaves. This type of behavior is replicated in a man's dealings with women. The nature of interaction between men and between men and women is quite similar. Other than agreeable conversation and financial solvency, the winkel places no stringent requirements on the crew members. Many keep erratic schedules and drop in when circumstances permit. However, they are redrawn into the group.

The relationships men form with women, as conjugals and consanguines, are subject to frequent disturbances: departures, prolonged recurrent or non-recurrent absences, shifting, multiple alliances erratically altering the flow of goods and services and so forth. The nature of sexual pairing, tolerating multiple relationships, can breed hostility and jealousy between men and women. For men, whose relationships span many households, the discharge of rights, responsibilities and obligations becomes confusing, conflicting and many times impossible to satisfy. Men are regularly placed in positions of potential discord, and conflict between households often devolves upon them. Interaction between men and women can be erratic and irregular with the relationships themselves brittle, shifting and semi-permanent as men and women work and re-work their uses of time, space and personnel to adapt to immediate circumstances created by either the larger environment or individual choice.

In this potentially turbulent atmosphere the winkel can function as one means whereby men can mediate disturbance in their interaction. The winkel [. . .] is their "association." In this social organization, this clockwork, more goes on at the winkel than merely the consumption of alcohol and lounging around. Social adjustments to changes in domestic and employment status are acted out symbolically and socially in the winkel and are signalled by changes in the structure and content of a man's network transactions. The winkel is their club, their forum. The men did not "flee here" nor are they "failures." Larger society downtown, more prosperous, more European, and the other ethnic groups in Suriname, do not understand the men and muse over their seeming idleness. [...]

These men have adapted to their circumstances and they are quite as aware as anybody else that their winkel-world is not a self-contained, self-generating system or subsystem with clear boundaries. The streetcorner behavior demonstrated by these men is in large part a response to a system that demands little else from them. Given their circumstances, the mating system, household organization and the men's status in the occupational hierarchy – all relationships characterized by loose, shifting and irregular interaction – these men need the compensation that their shop sanctuary provides. Besides, the men enjoy the drinking, camaraderie, ballyhoo and story-telling, and that is reason enough to go "on the corner."

BLACK SEA REGION

The Good Samaritan

Abel Polese*

"Do not be shy or you will stay hungry"

Hello. Where are you going?
We're going to Hala to find a place to sleep. It should be easy, because we're equipped to sleep anywhere.
But you know that if you are hosted here, you won't need anything? (After a brief consultation with an older member of the family) Come on, you will sleep at our place tonight.

There are countries where hospitality rules apply once you enter someone's house. But hospitality in the Black Sea's southern region engulfs the stranger from the first second he[†] enters the country – regardless of whether he is crossing a threshold or simply walking in the street. It guides him in a continuous series of exchange rituals with the locals. Indeed, as Du Boulay has remarked, the stranger somebody is, the more likely he is to

---

*Special to this volume.
†Throughout this essay, the masculine pronoun is used to refer to the stranger/guest.

Breakfast time in Batumi, Georgia (Abel Polese)

be offered hospitality.* This is true whether one is in Ajaria or Turkey, though small differences do exist. This essay draws on fieldwork conducted in Chakva, Batumi and Akcakale to spell out both the commonalities and differences. All these locales are on the Black Sea coast,† and share the religion and cultural legacy of the Ottoman Empire, although Ajaria has been strongly influenced by sovietization in the twentieth century.

When locals perceive somebody to be a stranger to the region, they respond with attention and invitations. These rituals may include smiles and short conversations; the offer of tea, small cakes, or fruit; and invitations to somebody's home for tea, a meal, or even to spend the night. The attitude of the stranger is important as well: whether he is a customer, for example, or a traveler who is willing to interact with the locals. As one informant reported:

> Once, we entered a bar and ordered a small cake. We immediately remarked about been ripped off on the price, but there was little we could do. Having noticed that the owner liked pictures, I took my camera and started a photographic session with the whole family, promising to send the pictures once I got back home. The attitude immediately changed. Although we ended up paying the amount of money requested

---

*Juliet Du Boulay, "Strangers and Gifts: Hostility and Hospitality in Rural Greece," *Journal of Mediterranean Studies*, 1: 1 (1991), pp. 37–53.
†Chakva and Batumi are part of Ajaria, a Georgian Muslim region that used to belong to the Ottoman Empire. Akcakale is a small settlement 20 km from Trabzon, in the eastern part of Turkey.

(around 4 US dollars), we received the attention granted to a guest, not a customer, along with a number of gifts that counterbalanced the feeling of being treated unfairly.

As well, whether the traveler is perceived as rich or poor will determine the kind of help offered:

> After arriving late at night, we asked where it was possible to sleep. He said, "In a hotel," but we explained that we had little money. We were immediately directed to the next police station, where we were offered hospitality for the night and tea with cakes the next morning.

Hospitality rules are described in the Koran, and some authors have stressed the religious motivation of hospitality. While a strong link does exist between the two, religion does not provide a complete explanation. Other factors, according to my observation, are:

(a) *Curiosity.* The fact of coming from a different culture generates curiosity, and the desire to discover something new by interacting with a stranger.

(b) *Human fellow-feeling,* assisted by the relative paucity of strangers who travel to the region. Many people have described Georgia and Eastern Turkey as places where locals are unusually hospitable, in part because these lands are so remote.

(c) *The limits of social welfare.* Solidarity is more developed than in the West, partly because of lower incomes and an absence of government assistance. Sharing what one has with others has a practical dimension.

(d) The idea that hospitality is *honorable behavior.*

(e) The perception that a stranger's visit is a *gift* and produces *trust* and *reciprocity.* Even if people's hospitality is unlikely ever to be repaid in kind, they may still say: "You should not feel obliged to me; I am doing what you would do in my place." Hospitality establishes relations of trust that extend beyond economic convenience.

In the house

Hospitality in the region is strictly gendered. A man is most likely to be offered hospitality by another man, and a male and female couple invited to a house will interact with different family members. Gender distinctions are not as pronounced as one finds in the Uzbeki countryside, for example, where at a wedding, male and female participants are forbidden to set eyes on one another. But while a man will always be invited to sit with male members of the family, the attitude towards female guests is more varied. She is generally expected to interact with female members of the household. In virtue of her status as a guest, however, she may also be allowed among the men, and discouraged from contributing to domestic work. In Ajaria, she may even be admitted to drinking rituals. This demonstrates how the status of stranger may trump that of gender. The female guest occupies a hybrid position: admitted to female activities, but invited to join in male ones within certain limits.

The status of a guest is that of a passive member of the family. Guests will be invited to take part in household activities – drinking coffee, watching TV, and chatting – regardless of their gender. But they will be expected to avoid a more active role, such as helping in the kitchen.

Men will sit in the living room, while women come and go from the kitchen or garden, taking a short break to interact with the guests or rest for a while. A female guest may be invited to view the garden or domestic animals; women of the household may encourage them to learn some of the local habits. The male guest, for his part, may be invited to join men in going down to the river or on other excursions.

Interaction through conversation is subject to certain rules, and these are also gendered. As a general principle, the stranger is supposed to provide news of his country or home. After some time in the household, when he is perceived as less of a novel presence, a male guest may be consulted on more pressing matters. He is relatively free to ask questions, and will be questioned in turn by the locals.

Generally, it is the male guest who is addressed first by male hosts. Stranger status may prompt questions to women as well, but the general rule is that, if a male and female guest are equally able to answer, the man is expected to respond; a woman answers only if the male cannot, or if her own answer differs. For instance, if the male and female come from different places, separate questions may be asked, and separate answers provided.

The stranger will inevitably be questioned on aspects and habits of his native country. Questions tend to be posed quite directly, though they rarely concern intimate matters. General subjects of conversation may include a guest's status; whether he is married; the number of his children; and his occupation. Questions will generally not be asked about personal income; but in Ajaria the guest might be queried about the standard of living in his or her native country. This economic dimension is less likely to be discussed in Turkey.

With men occupying the living room, female-to-female interaction is possible only in some other space, and therefore in another social context. This generally occurs in the kitchen or, when possible, outside. Such interaction is not viewed as compulsory, as it is for men. When it occurs, it may focus on household matters, economic issues, or (in some contexts) the role of men in society. This last subject is more likely to be raised in Ajaria than in Turkey, perhaps because male–female relations were modified by the long period of Soviet rule. Interaction between men and women is rather rare, unless it concerns formal matters such as rituals of offering and receiving, which can be performed by any host toward any guest. In order to be "acceptable," it should occur in the presence of other family members.

As in several southern societies, there is a sense of joy associated with hospitality and with the arrival of a guest who offers the opportunity to establish relations of trust. The role of food is determinant here. Through sharing all that they have, people demonstrate openness towards their guest. Food is a universal language, and is better able to establish relations of trust than conversation, which may be hindered by language barriers, cultural differences, and a stranger's inhibitions.

The dinner

The guest must be fed. A common notion is that he should at all times be free from hunger. Thus, he will be served snacks that allow him to "survive" until dinner.

A major difference between Ajaria and eastern Turkey emerges at dinner-time. In both cultures, the guest is supposed to be passive and merely "receive." But in Ajaria, he will be invited to "not be shy" (ne stesnyajsya), and to ask for anything he needs. In eastern Turkey, such encouragement is not given; it is the host's task to ensure that a guest's needs are satisfied. As one informant reported: "When my father is sitting next to a guest, he barely ever asks whether [the guest] needs anything. He just fills his plate regularly, and the guest is supposed to eat." Accordingly, a guest's request for food displays bad form. It may be perceived as implying a host's failure to fulfill his obligations. As well, it reflects on the host's level of knowledge: there is a common notion that the host knows the local food better than the guest does, and is therefore entitled to choose.

In both cultures, it is common to overfeed a guest in order to honor him. In Batumi one night, we ate a complete dinner, but even when we were full, our hosts continued to serve us. After meat, potatoes, chili peppers, cheese, bread, khachapuri,* salad, and kompot,† we were offered cakes and tea. Finally, fruit arrived, and the male host was still asking: "What else can I offer you?"

Hierarchy at the table varies. The general rule is that the person who cooks only sits at the table after being able to feed all the others. It is usual that the man who returns from physical labor takes priority at the table. However, there are exceptions if the chef changes according to the food prepared. At a barbecue, for instance, the man is in charge of preparation; he is then the last to eat, having prepared food for everyone else. There is some gendered variation in food preparation according to the culture in question. In rural Moldova, for example, the man is active in bread-baking, whereas in Ajaria bread is always baked by female members of the family.

The man – or men, in the case of larger families that include several generations – sits first at the table. The guests eat with him until they are satiated. Female members of the family may also be seated at the table: usually, the woman who cooked the food joins the first sitting, if she is not busy working in the kitchen. In Chakva and Batumi, children were fed last, after everyone else had finished; the fact that female family members did not eat in front of us suggested that they ate elsewhere, while cooking. This is apparently quite common in nearby regions as well. One informant in the Northern Caucasus told me: "Whenever my grandmother made me dinner, I never saw her eating in front of me. I wonder whether she ate at all."

---

*Georgian bread filled with cheese.
†A sweet drink prepared by boiling fruits in water and sugar.

Drinking

Alcohol is much more important in Ajarian society than in eastern Turkey, where we were never offered fermented drinks. In our Ajarian experience, it is worth distinguishing among the roles of different alcoholic beverages: beer, wine and spirits.

The first night we were invited by a family, the father sent the son for draft beer that we drank during the dinner. Little ritual was involved, and we toasted only on the first glass. For the rest of the dinner, beer had the function of a soda. It was often served as alternative to kompot, with the guest allowed to choose according to his preference.

Wine is quite significant in Georgian, and therefore Ajarian, society. Georgian wine has a high reputation in the territories of the former USSR; the local climate favors cultivation. But its price is high, relative to local living standards. Therefore, if the family does not produce its own wine or have neighbors who produce it, it is considered a luxury good, and beer is preferred.

The rituals associated with drinking are centered on spirits like *rakja* and *chacha*, which are normally homemade. The arrival of a guest provides the ideal motivation for beginning the ritual. Again, though this is normally a male activity, female guests are admitted if they come from a different culture – especially if a third person is lacking. (Two men drinking together is permitted, but a company of three is strongly preferred.) Small shotglasses are filled, and one member of the company makes a toast. He may speak and then stop – giving the impression that it is time to drink, even though nobody starts. Then he continues speaking, only to stop again. This may be repeated several times. After drinking, efforts are made to limit the effect of the alcohol, by drinking water and eating something (generally tomatoes, cucumbers, or bread).

Alcohol has the social function of strengthening personal relations and establishing confidence. The guest is much more likely to be perceived as a member of the community if he is willing and able to drink with the men of the family.

MEXICO/UNITED STATES

Abuelita and Lalo

Tlahtoki Aguirre*

One of my most vivid memories of childhood occurred when I was about four years old and came down with chicken pox. I remember thinking hazily that I must have done something wrong to feel like one big mosquito bite. Was I being punished for

---

*Special to this volume.

quarreling with my sisters? Did I get sick because I'd used a swear word? Is this what happens when you don't like eating vegetables?

Everything itched: my legs, my ears, my fingers, even my eyelids. But my mom kept saying, "Don't scratch! If you do, you'll have marks on your skin for the rest of your life!" She added, "Here, this will make you feel better," and softly patted everywhere I pointed to. She kept repeating the routine as she prepared to take me to see *abuelita* (grandma), who lived with her friend Lalo in a house about thirty minutes away.

I loved spending time with abuelita. I would stay with her at least one weekend each month throughout most of my youth – more often if I became ill, or if mom had to pick up extra shifts at work. Abuelita and I would play cards, watch television, go for walks, shop for groceries, or simply talk. The majority of our conversations consisted of me asking questions, and abuelita offering long, detailed answers that demonstrated both her vast knowledge and her attention to detail. While listening, I would sit with my eyes glued to hers, making sure not to miss a word. I wondered: how could she know so much? From whom did she hear such things? Does she have more than one brain?

Abuelita took care of me when I was sick, for two reasons: my mother could not look after me because she could not afford to miss work – she was a single parent raising three children – and abuelita knew which foods to eat, which herbs to use, and which teas to drink when ill. Abuelita would always, whether I was sick or not, tell me about the foods she cooked, and why we should consume them. She insisted on highlighting food qualities in part because of the joy she experienced in working with Mexican foods, and in part because she sensed that I was dying to know.

While cooking *chiles* one day, she beamed with pride: "We [Mexicans] have over two hundred different types of chili peppers! And each one has its own characteristics!" Astonished, and knowing that each pepper has its own preparation method, I asked, "How many can you prepare?" "Almost all of them," she replied.

Abuelita would complement her culinary stories by reciting a list of indigenous Mexican foods, and their benefits. She'd quip: "Eat *caldo de pollo* (chicken soup) for a cold and *nopales* (cactus) to clean your blood, drink *agua de chia* (water with chia seeds) if you have an upset stomach and *agua de jamaica* (water with hibiscus flowers) to help your kidneys, eat *chiles* for your lungs and tortillas for strength." I know she spoke that way to ensure that her dietary knowledge would not be forgotten.

Contrary to what one might expect, given the patriarchy and machismo within many Mexican families, I never encountered ridicule from family members for spending significant time with female relatives or wanting to learn how to cook. My youngest uncle, Carlos, also fixed flavorful Mexican dishes that demonstrated his knack for the culinary arts. Once, during an unannounced visit to his house, he assembled a meal for me in twenty minutes, complete with beans, tortillas, nopales, avocado, chicken, *chiles*, and lemonade. He whirled around the kitchen effortlessly, revealing his expertise and love for all things edible.

And abuelita never seemed to care that I was a boy – later a man – in her kitchen. She made it seem natural when I cooked alongside her, as if a gendered division of labor didn't exist. She couldn't understand why my mother and sisters did not want to learn how to prepare, as she put it, "*nuestra comida y nuestras medicinas*" – our food and our medicines. Once, after lamenting how few people in the family knew how to heal with foods and herbs, she commented: "Well, you will pass these things on to your children and others in the family. You'll probably be a better cook than your wife!"

A few years ago, I asked her if she had taught my youngest uncle how to cook. She laughed: "No, *mijito* [my boy], no. He learned himself, when he was much older."

"Was it weird for you to teach me how to cook when I was younger?" I asked. "No," she responded, shaking her head. She explained that, in her day, women tended to the cooking and the children, and men took care of everything else. "But times change – especially if you live like *los gringos*."

To abuelita, living like the gringos meant living only with one's parents (rather than with the extended family), who worked long hours and had little time to prepare food or spend with their children. Abuelita said the main parent for kids in such families is not human but electronic: the television. She held, by contrast, that parents and other family members – grandparents, aunts, uncles, and cousins – should share responsibility for all aspects of family life. With regard to a couple, she would say: "If they truly love one another, each contributes equally, and both feel appreciated."

Abuelita qualified her statements about her upbringing by noting that she had known a few men who considered childrearing and the kitchen as their central calling in life. Lalo, her housemate, was one of them. He owned the enormous house that he shared with abuelita, and he also possessed one of the largest and most memorable kitchens I have ever seen. Like the rest of his house, the kitchen provided a visual montage of antique fixtures, typical Mexican household items, and assorted pop-culture memorabilia. Bunches of dried garlic and multicolored chili peppers hung from ropes tethered to the ceiling. Mortar and pestle stoneware occupied the countertop alongside baskets of vegetables, ready for use.

The kitchen was more than just eye-candy, however. Like abuelita, Lalo was a culinary master whose brilliance found expression in every snack or meal he made. Not only could he cook Mexican staples, but he knew his way around Chinese, French, Thai, and Louisiana Cajun cuisines. He and abuelita often consulted each other, cooked together, and acted as though they were connected at the hip. They complemented each other: abuelita expanded her food knowledge through Lalo's non-Mexican entrees, while Lalo learned from abuelita's use of Mexican foods and herbs for healing.

Lalo not only loved to cook and decorate his house, but he loved men. He was what my mom called a "*joto*." (She did not use the word offensively – quite the contrary – and indeed, Lalo used it to describe himself.) The way I was told it, he was just like my other uncles who had wives, except that his "wife" was a man. None of this seemed abnormal to me, because although Lalo was not blood-related, he functioned as an uncle for the kids in my generation. We cared for him, and he for us. All the adults treated Lalo as a respected and loved family member, and children almost always follow adults' lead.

I don't recall Lalo letting societal ignorance – that is, homophobia and machismo – repress who he was. Like anyone, he had desires and dreams. I believe if he'd had his wish, he would have been a fashion designer or home decorator, rather than a laundry supervisor at a major hotel. I vividly remember pictures of him dressed up like a female fashion model. These pictures – far from being hidden – covered the walls of the living-room and the Victorian tabletops throughout his house. I thought they captured his true spirit: he exuded charm, style, and vivaciousness.

A few years ago, unfortunately, Lalo decided it was his time to go to the spirit world.

Abuelita always taught me about the inevitability of leaving this world for the next. She would say: "When it's my time, I'll be ready. We all go to the other side someday – why should I be scared?"

We would sometimes ponder what life would be like after we passed. If there really was a spirit world, what was it like? Would we get to see the loved ones who had preceded us? Would our actions affect where we went? What would we do there? Would we remember the lives we had led?

When we arrived at such questions, though, abuelita would often say: "Let's talk about something different. You don't need to think about such things, because you have a long life ahead of you. You're not old like me!"

Abuelita always had a sharp mind, but her body never fully recovered from her migrant work in the US. For years, she had endured intense physical labor and constant exposure to toxic chemicals, working in the fields and factories of the American Midwest. To deal with her health conditions, she believed in drawing from the best of western biomedicine, and complementing it with the best traditional Mexican medicine. Her position, however, changed drastically when many of the drugs she was prescribed for her primary illnesses had severe debilitating effects. Worse, the side effects required their own drugs to treat. Abuelita decided to abandon all the drug regimes she was on, and depend almost completely on Mexican foods and herbs. After the change, she felt better, and looked healthier.

Abuelita was not the only family member to benefit immensely from our foods and medicines. One of my sisters, Xochitl, contacted me a few years ago because her daughter, Ketzalli, kept having sore throats and swollen tonsils. Xochitl told me that my niece had taken so many antibiotics over the past two years that she feared they might not work in the future. Xochitl, her children, and I gathered at her house that evening. We filled our cars with boisterous kids, and set off for the market in search of foods to alleviate my niece's affliction. As we shopped, I helped my sister identify various ingredients that abuelita included in her secret healing recipes, and explained how and why they were used. Xochitl absorbed abuelita's wisdom like a sponge.

Unbeknownst to me, so did Ketzalli. Back at Xochitl's house, I disclosed more of abuelita's confidential instructions while we cooked. Ketzalli asked: "Uncle, how do you remember all the things that great-grandma taught you?" "I tried to always listen real well," I replied. "But she also made me write down everything she told me, so I could pass her knowledge on to you, your brothers and sisters, and your cousins."

Serving as co-pilot in my sister's kitchen marked a turning point for me. Ever since that night, I have realized that one's perception of food cannot be separated from interconnected material conditions. Modern ways of living have profoundly undermined healthy eating practices in Mexico, the US, and around the world.

Understandings of gender and sexuality are similarly shaped by knowledge and material relations. As with many indigenous peoples around the world, several Mexican communities, including mine, recognize and respect more than two genders (male and female). Many also consider non-heterosexuality normal. Such indigenous ways of thinking differ from the oppressive, border-producing ideas that compose most modern knowledge. These tend to produce a belief, and a reality, of uneven polar opposites (such as men/women and heterosexual/homosexual); they accord one side privileges and benefits, and inflict violence on the other.

I have shared this story to highlight the ways in which indigenous Mexican knowledge systems and ways of living have shaped my life, and the lives of those around me. My experiences challenge simplistic notions of Mexican men as hypermasculine (aggressive and dominant) and Mexican women as hyperfeminine (submissive, religiously devout mother-figures). Many of my male relatives, for example, have subverted Mexican masculinities merely by living and understanding the world in indigenous ways. In a similar manner, other family members, such as my abuelita, have circumvented oppressive patriarchy – and its complement, homophobia – simply by dealing with gender and sexual diversity in a nuanced and appreciative way. Through their everyday deeds, my relatives manifest resistance, kindness, and true integrity.

SRI LANKA

The Monk and the Exorcist

Bhante Wimala*

I am Bhante Wimala and, as far as I know, I am the only Buddhist monk in the world who lives as I do. Unlike most monks who wander in their homelands or live ascetically in monasteries, I spend my life traveling over the world to teach and to heal and to bring peace to the people of our planet. I have been traveling now for ten years and have forged friendships across the globe. I like to think that there is a friend of mine who is just waking from a good sleep at every hour of my day. [. . .]

---

*From Bhante Wimala as told to Adam Rostoker, "My Other Life in Serendipity," in Franklin Abbott, ed., *Growing Up Male: A Multicultural Anthology*, 2nd edn. (Madison, WI: University of Wisconsin Press, 1998), pp. 182–98.

As I write this, I am thirty-two years old and have spent more than half my life as a monk. Like many monastic candidates in Sri Lanka, I was sent from my home to live in the temple at the age of thirteen. At fourteen, I took my vows as a novice into the order of monks in the Buddhist temple, and, at twenty-two, I was fully ordained as a monk. I remember that even before I was sent to the temple like other boys of my caste, to fulfill the family's obligation to our faith, I was a very independent and lucky boy. I had known a home. I had a life, a wonderful, magical childhood in the heart of this land called Serendipity [Sri Lanka]. In this world, I knew my place and my future – the last thing I expected was to be selected as a monk. [. . .]

I grew up in the small village of Yatiravana, which means the "lower" Ravana. The village was surrounded by several green mountains, which made us in the valley feel particularly self-contained. All of our lives were held in this emerald navel of the world and I felt at home within those colossal, ancient walls. Growing up, our lives were filled with chores, school, play and worship. Everything we needed or wanted was within our reach. As I consider how snugly the whole universe fit me back then, I can't help but feel sad for the large and confusing world that most children know. We never had the knowledge that something was missing. Everything was at hand. We were content. Most children that I meet today don't have this sense of fullness. [. . .]

While I do not remember my mother ever hitting me or even speaking a harsh word, my father was a cruel and frequent punisher. One of my strongest memories of him involves my fear of his cane. Like many Asians at the time, he considered physical punishment the ideal method of disciplining children. When I went to school nearly all of the teachers had canes for hitting children – especially the principal, who had extra canes in his office. When my mother prevented my father from punishing us, my father accused my mother of interfering with the correct discipline of the children. Sometimes her interference worked; sometimes it didn't, and we could all be beaten very severely. While I recall the beatings as extreme, the sins which earned them seem so innocent to me now. Skipping school, scrapping with other children, and climbing coconut trees were just a few of the many things I remember having done to earn a dose of his civilized punishment. [. . .]

There were other reasons to fear my father. He was the village *gurunance*, a combination of shaman and astrologer. Astrology plays an important part in Sri Lankan culture and it is traditional to consult an astrologer for many reasons. The day after a child is born, a horoscope is cast and astrologers are then consulted on every stage of development. Auspicious times are chosen for the first eating of solid food, the first haircut, the first reading of a book. Parents often take extreme precautions to avoid premature occurrences of these events.

My father was such an astrologer, but unlike most astrologers, my father was also a healer, medium and a psychic for the village. He performed exorcisms, banished curses, and advised people on spiritual, romantic and financial affairs.

One of the most frightening incidents of my life was when I went to see my father at one of his shamanic ceremonies. As I mentioned, I had a strong fear of darkness and this rite took place on a moonless night, lit only by dimly flickering torches and the dull red coals of hot incense. Many villagers I knew were there, but they were dressed strangely in bizarre masks and unfamiliar costumes. All around me was the constant din of drums and horns. Of course, I had often heard the drums and horns at night in the distance and knew something of my cultural heritage, but to be there in the wildly leaping shadows, with masked demons dancing and wailing around me, the reek of incense in my nose, the throbbing of drums and the cacophony of horns – it was almost too much for a little boy to bear.

The rite was an exorcism. They usually were. When demons plague a man or woman they exhibit certain well-known signs. The afflicted person becomes physically ill, shows bad luck or has nightmares. Sometimes there will be signs of dizziness or fainting. At these signs, people become suspicious: it is the nature of demons to conceal themselves as long as possible to avoid the travail of exorcism. As time goes on, people begin to suspect possession. Everything about the person begins to be interpreted in these terms. After a while my father is called in to investigate and, if need be, to begin the rite of exorcism. The purpose of the exorcism is to drive the demon to the surface of the patient so that all persons can see it, then to confront the demon and force it to leave and never return.

The first step is to build a small shrine stocked with food, coconut flowers, incense, certain powerful artifacts, and blood drawn from a living chicken. After a time, lured by the food and the smell of blood, the demon is drawn to the surface. During this time, the participants dance and chant to energize the shrine. Once the demon presents itself, which is normally a horrifying moment, the tests and tortures of exorcism can begin.

My father was the leader in all this. He blew on a conch shell and wore a costume of pure white with a red turban. He directed the building of the shrine, the costuming of the dancers, and led the chanting – some of which came from scriptures that were written in languages that ordinary people never knew. Some chants were fast and would serve to energize the shrine. Other chants were harsh and forceful, calling out the demons and issuing challenges. [...] My father would yell or threaten a demon, force the victim over hot coals, or slice a melon on the victim's belly. Sometimes my father would beat the victim until the demon would leave. [...]

It is interesting that my father's respect for propriety and shamanism led him to a disappointment involving me. In Sri Lanka, as in many countries, there is a tradition of sending one child from each family to the temple. In this way, the family's piety is demonstrated and their community position is stabilized. At first my brother was chosen for the clergy, as he was deemed quieter and more peaceful than I was as a child. But after one year of training, I went to visit my brother and the high priest determined – through horoscopy and palmistry – that I was the family member destined to be a monk, not my brother.

My father was not pleased with the high priest's decision to retain me for the clergy since he had assumed that I would carry on his work as a shaman. As things happened, my brother drifted around law enforcement before eventually becoming a monk, and my father's work ended when he became too ill to continue. Still, it is interesting to think of how I turned out. Had things been just a bit different, I would be leading exorcisms in a red turban and beating the devils out of my neighbors like my father before me. He was, and is, a complex and forceful man.

And yet, there was another side to my father that I saw only rarely, and which surprised me – a part of him that was filled with love. I still remember how my father held me with great tenderness and wept on the day before my ordination. Like most men at that time, he usually did not show his personal emotions beyond anger, so I was quite surprised at his affection. I remember this well because it was one of the few times he ever hugged me.

Also, my father was an honorable man. In Asia, the practice of wife-beating was so common that my father was a notable rarity because he never hit my mother. I was very fortunate not to witness any physical fights between my parents. My father greatly enjoyed the role of family man, provider and protector. He took seriously his responsibilities of feeding, clothing and housing the family.

He was also the spiritual leader of our family and he led a prayer meeting before every evening meal we had at our home. At 7 p.m. every evening, just before dinner, everybody had to stop what they were doing and gather on the front porch of the big house. Attendance was compulsory, and absence without a strong reason resulted in punishment. A few flowers, incense, and a small oil lamp were placed on the altar in front of the picture of Buddha. We sat in a row starting with my father, then my mother and then the children in order of age. Since I had been old enough to sit I had been joining them. We would chant for about ten minutes, meditate for about five minutes, and then worship first the father, then the mother, then all the older brothers and sisters. I thought it must have been terrible to have been the youngest in the family, and I was glad to have had at least my younger sister to worship me. All things considered, however, these prayer meetings were some of the most important and pleasant times in my childhood.

I have considered that these kinds of prayer meetings were a very helpful tradition and had a considerable positive impact on everyone in the family. After this small ritual and meditation, we all felt calmer and more respectful to each other. This created a fine atmosphere for a quiet family dinner, and did much to smooth relations among my eleven family members. I always knew that, no matter the reason, the family would gather for prayer before meals. Perhaps this first taught me the benefits of self-discipline and continuity. [. . .]

UNITED STATES

The Key

Dina Dahbany-Miraglia*

This essay is a first-person representation of the Yemenite Jewish men's world, which is based in the synagogue. All the Orthodox Jewish traditions exclude women and girls from public participation; the first duty of women and girls in every Jewish cultural tradition is to support the Jewish men's world with their labor.

I am 36 years old, happily married with two daughters and a three-and-a-half-year-old son. My wife and I love each other very much; we are very close. Before my son arrived, we shared the housework, the cooking, the shopping, the laundry. We even did windows together. We both work, but overlapping shifts.

I love my wife and daughters, but my son and I share a bond that separates us from his mother and sisters, that excludes all women – our circumcised sameness. This is the single most important key to the Yemenite men's world. It is the key to the world of prayer and scholarship, and in our world, that bond supersedes all others.

*   *   *

I chose the best day of the year to begin my son's training – the first day of Rosh Hashanah, the Jewish New Year, when we begin again the annual reading of the first chapter of the First Five Books of the Torah: Genesis – In the Beginning. On that day, my wife and daughters stayed home. Although the *kanis*, the Yemenite synagogue, was only two short blocks away, I told them not to come. The wind and near-zero temperatures would be too much for them.

When my son and I returned two hours later, we joined his mother and sisters for lunch. We ended our meal with Sabbath songs from the Diwan, the book of poetry attributed to Shalom ash-Shabazi, Jewish Yemen's poet laureate. We then ended our meal with the after-lunch prayer. My wife and daughters cleared the table. My son and I waited until my wife had herded our daughters into the bedroom, gently warning them to be quiet before she closed the door. In the now-silent house, I opened a large-print primer and pulled my son towards me, backwards between my legs. His initiation began.

As I pointed to the letters and called out each one's name, he mimicked me.

Alif - Beth - Jimel - Daleth - Hey - Vav - Zayin - Het - Tet -Yod . . .

We went through the Alif-Beth seven times – in the Yemenite pronunciation. By the sixth time, he was anticipating me. During the seventh go-round, he made only three mistakes. He learned to recognize his first word: Alif-Beth-Alif, ABA: "Father."

---

*Special to this volume.

This most important ritual, the first learning of the letters, was ritually unmarked. There was no audience – no one but the two of us, together, alone. From then on, every evening after dinner we sat together in the silent house, first on the living room couch to learn the vowels, then to combine the consonants with the vowels. I taught him to read as I was taught by my father, as he was taught by his father – to chant the sounds in the boys' *madrassah*, or school, learning tunes.

We moved to the dining-room table when my son was ready to write his first word: "Aba," "Father."

*   *   *

Since he was three months old, my wife and daughters had brought my son to the kanis every Sabbath morning and on most holy days, keeping watch over him while I prayed. They remained behind the *mekhitsah*, the opaque curtain that separates men from women. When he was quiet, they gave him to me. They were always ready to interrupt their own prayers to remove him quickly if he became restless. Our reputation, and his, are clean.

When Passover arrived the following April, my son had just turned four years old. I taught him to read the Mah Nishtanoh, the Four Questions, at both *seders* – ritual feasts. He was so proud of himself! And so were we. His grandparents could not make enough of a fuss over him. Yes, he had memorized it; but by then he could also read it, albeit haltingly. I must admit I had help. My wife and daughters also tutored him on those evenings when I came home late from work. By the time my son was six, he could read and recite the Hebrew blessings. The rabbi of the *yeshiva*, the day-school he attended, placed him in the top first-grade class, even though he was a Yemenite.

His mother and sisters also helped him with his increasingly heavy load of Hebrew and English homework. That reduced the time he and I could spend together in the evenings. But in the winter, Friday evenings and every Saturday afternoon were ours. For Rosh Hashanah, the Jewish New Year, I had already taught him to chant the Haftoroh, the Aramaic supplement to the Hebrew translation that we read during Saturday-morning services. This is a necessary step to prepare my son to take his place in the men's world with honor. He will never be mocked with the jibe, *"Yiqre ma yidhiresh"* – "He reads but he does not understand."

*   *   *

My son was born in March, and circumcised eight days later – on Purim, the day the Jews were saved from annihilation by the Persians about 2,300 years ago. The kanis was packed with friends and relatives for the early morning service. Even more appeared for the *bris*, the circumcision ceremony. My mother and mother-in-law, my sisters and sisters-in-law took care of all the arrangements. Even though they had paying jobs and cared for their children, grandchildren and households, they were the ones who prepared the foods and drinks, and issued phone invitations for the bris. They cleaned the kanis's basement hall, and with help from me and my father, they unfolded the heavy tables. The women and girls set out the chairs. They laid out the tablecloths and napkins, the plastic flatware, the plates, the bowls, the cups (for hot and cold drinks), and the disposable cloths and paper towels.

As always, the men and the women sat at opposite ends of the basement hall, and as always, the women and girls served the men and boys before they broke their own fast. To this day, the members of our congregation who attended recall the wonderful *se'udah*, the post-bris celebratory feast that our women organized. This isn't surprising: my wife, her mother and her sisters are famous for their baking and cooking. We are close keepers of tradition. Although many new mothers attend their sons' *brithim*, circumcisions, when they are held in the kanis, my wife did not: she was still *tomeh*, unclean, from giving birth. We adhered to the letter of the law.

My father-in-law videotaped the circumcision; my father and brothers took numerous pictures, mostly of my son and me.

*　　　*　　　*

My son will be a good husband. He will support and guide his wife and children and, when he can, help his wife and daughters around the house. But his first responsibility is to the perpetuation of the men's world. My son follows in my footsteps – in the footsteps of my father and grandfathers, and of all the men of our *edah*, our cultural community. We follow an unbroken tradition that is over two millennia old. My father and I are not *kohanim*, priests, or *leviyim* – Levites, the priestly assistants. Our hereditary clan is Israel, the lowest of the three. But we are a Yemenite rabbinical family from San'aa with a long tradition of piety and scholarship. My wife also comes from a rabbinical family.

My son will carry our world into the next generation. Soon he will read sections of the Haftoroh in Aramaic, then an entire section of a Sabbath morning *parsha*, the weekly portion of the Old Testament's first Five Books, in the Biblical Hebrew. My heart will be so full of pride when he reads without mistake from the Torah scroll, which does not contain the chanting diacritics or vowel symbols.

When he is 13 years old, he will – like me, my father, my grandfather – direct the reading of the entire parsha, but in the shorter Torah tune. He will read appropriate portions to honor the selected men whom I and my father will choose. He will read passages for those who are less skilled. My son will chant the Biblical Hebrew Haftorah segment in one of the Torah melodies; one of his younger cousins, or I hope a younger brother, will chant the Aramaic portion in the Tarjum tune.

When he is older, when he is married, then he will be ready – and permitted – to chant a segment of the weekly parsha in the elaborate Torah tune. I will prepare him long before then. From that day onward, my son will be a fully participating congregant: a man in our men's world.

MALI

The Healer

Jan Jansen*

"*Namagan bè mi?*" ("Where is Namagan?") is the most often posed question in the village of Farabako, a small village in Mali near the Guinean border. Men and women, old and young, visitors and local inhabitants – everyone seems to be searching for Namagan all the time. Despite his young age – he was born in 1964 – Namagan enjoys a huge renown as a *soma*, a healing/sand divination expert. His renown is not restricted to the Mande Hills, the region of his origin, but extends far beyond. Even people from Conakry (the capital of Guinea, one thousand kilometers from Farabako) visit him. The village of Farabako is a place of ancient renown for the Kanté family, who enjoy prestige as *somaw* (pl.). Their families share a common descent, and live on one large compound. In the last five years, the old generation of healers has died. Namagan is their only successor.

"When I was young," he told me, "I sat next to the old men, and watched how they practised divination. Some people criticized me; they said that divination is bad and would soon disappear, because of Islam and the health care offered by the white people. My age-mates made fun of me, because I often refused to join them in having a good time. Any moment of spare time I passed with the old divination experts. That is how I learned it.

"When I reached the age of twelve, my eyes became sick. They became red and aching every time I went to the millet fields. That is the reason I wear sunglasses so often: because of the millet. Subsequently, I took responsibility for the cows of Farabako. I herded them. In the dry season I wandered with them through the wilderness. During the wet season, too, when food for the cows is abundant, but diseases seriously menace their health, I took care of them. I stayed with them, near the village, and didn't go to the fields with my age-mates. So I learned during the wet season what my fathers did to protect both man and cattle from diseases.

"Only recently have people again come to appreciate sand divination as good and meaningful. Young men, both school kids and illiterate adolescents, visit Farabako and stay for prolonged periods to learn divination from me. Some of them come from far away, since the divination experts of my age are very few. But nowadays the youth wants to learn it. Sand divination has become a big thing!

"I treat my apprentices the way I was treated; I teach them the way I was taught. I feed them the way my parents fed me. They are allowed to attend the divination sessions, and the smarter apprentices are allowed to draw the divination schemes. They wait for me to hear the meaning of the divination schemes. Then I send them into the

---

*Special to this volume.

wilderness to fetch the leaves and the bark necessary for the production of medicaments. An apprentice expresses his respect towards me by working. He will, for instance, fetch a bundle of wood from the forest, or he will work on my fields. I am rewarded by labor, not by cash payment.

"Many of the medicaments we prepare are unknown to you, because the white people don't know our diseases, and they are not vulnerable to them. For instance, we are capable of handling a *kóróte*, a magical poison that is shot at someone from a distance. As a result, part of the victim's body swells, and antibiotics don't work. We have medicaments to protect someone against such a disease – yes, even to cure him. We have many medicaments that protect people from djinns [evil spirits] in the wilderness. We also have much knowledge about manhood, and have medicaments to cope with fertility problems.

"In the rainy season, I spend most of my time in the village. The families of Farabako nowadays have much more cattle than a few decades ago. Every day, I visit the cows and check on their health. In the dry season, I travel a lot; I drive more than eighty kilometers a day on my motorcycle. I am always on the move. People all over the region need to consult with me. I go to Bamako, to Siguiri [Guinea], even to Conakry.

"If strangers pass by the village, they will spend the night on my compound. 'Namagan loves visitors' – everybody knows that. When I am away, my family will take care of the guests. That is the reason why my wife Nasira begged me to marry a second wife. Raising the kids and cooking for all those guests was too much for her. Now, after I married Ntènè last year, things are going more smoothly. Nasira doesn't like the fact that I am away so often. (She is very happy that you are here with us. The respect that a researcher from far away commands, compels me to stay in the village – haha!)

"I don't spend all my time on divination and consultations. The sale of cows and grains is also my responsibility. I sell these to merchants from Bamako [Mali's capital]. I am also responsible for buying goods that the villagers need. Some of them, like fuel and batteries, are sold retail; other things are just donated to people who need them. I am not the compound chief; that is a function held by an old man. I am the *lunyèmogo* [compound manager]. That is why I am also responsible for the orphans and the widows on this compound. I have to feed them, to dress them, and find brides for the male orphans. Since I have a good motorcycle, I can manage all my affairs. We also need the motorcycle to fetch a doctor from Sandama, twenty kilometers away, in case someone is very ill."

The Kanté are blacksmiths, and hence traditionally responsible for health care issues, partially because they conduct circumcisions. However, for me, Namagan is not just a blacksmith, but also a keen cultural broker. He is a Maninka, an ethnic group proud of winning a subsistence from agriculture. A Maninka who refuses to work in the fields is extraordinary indeed – but Namagan is such a Maninka. The Mande hills, where he lives, have in recent decades witnessed an immigration of Fulbe cattle herders. Many came to herd Maninka cattle. These groups distrust each other, and it is thanks to brokers like Namagan that they learn to cohabit. The percentage of Namagan's clients who are Fulbe is large. Namagan established a close relationship with many Fulbe families during his youth, when he herded for more than a decade the cows of Farabako.

Namagan, though, is more than an *ethnic* broker, fabricating new dimensions for Maninka and Fulbe identities. He also is an *economic* broker. The Mande hills are located between Bamako and the Republic of Guinea. In past times, these hills were hardly traversable, and people preferred to take different routes to Guinea. These have been transformed, in the twentieth century, into roads. Over these roads, commercial activities have developed. In the Mande hills, though, there are no roads; only in the 1990s did tracks for trucks come into being. The landscape, however, is so capricious that transport is risky and expensive. Trucks often break down, and the passengers must spend the night on the spot – for example, at Namagan's place. Yet some entrepreneurs do choose to travel through the hills, to smuggle cigarettes and other luxury products from Guinea. As the owner of one of the region's few motorcycles, Namagan is able to participate in these trading networks – not by smuggling, but by "communication management." It doesn't seem that Namagan knows what leisure is. Even the alcoholic drinks consumed during and after a divination session (this is a prerequisite for divination practices; hence somaw are not loved by many Muslims) serve to forge connections and build networks that connect Namagan to the wider world.

In contrast to others in Farabako, Namagan is deeply involved in monetary transactions. He embodies the fact that it is possible to deal with money and, at the same time, remain a Maninka. This is a form of healing, too! Illnesses are not only of the biomedical kind, but may be produced by other evils. "*N mankènè* ['I am in bad health']," says a Maninka, both when he is poor and when he is sick. If Namagan was a "herb doctor" alone, he would be consulted only in case of purely physical complaints. He is, however, a soma – a health expert capable of dealing with all aspects of life that may vex or afflict a person.

PAKISTAN

The Fixer

Maria del Nevo*

While playing in the narrow allies of Gandhi park, one of Lahore's poorer neighborhoods, the children one day witnessed a fight between a monkey and a stray dog. The monkey was owned by a man who visited the area frequently to entertain the children with the animal's skillful tricks. But that day the children stood looking on in horror as the stray dog tore at the monkey's body with its sharp teeth.

---

*From Maria del Nevo, "The Fixer," *New Internationalist*, 232 (June 1992).

"Take him to Babaji," they shouted to the owner, once the dog had been scared off by the stones they threw. "Babaji will cure him."

So the monkey was carried off in the arms of its owner, and when Babaji saved the life of the monkey the children rejoiced. The news of Babaji's healing hands spread like wildfire.

Seventy-nine-year-old Baba Mannah came to Pakistan from Gurdaspur in India at Partition and stayed as a refugee in a village near the border, where he learned to fix dislocated joints from one of the older *pehelwans* (wrestlers) who are famous in Pakistan for their skill at fixing fractures. Baba Mannah learned fast, and when he later reached Lahore he started up a practice which eventually brought him patients from far and wide.

He practises in a small room adjacent to his house where his wife, sons, daughters-in-law, daughters and grandchildren live. The room is filled with huge sacks of rice which he sells to supplement his monthly income. A *charpoy* (string cot) stands up against one wall, and on the floor there is a disused sackcloth where he sits in his traditional *dhoti*, *khurta* and turban. Beside him a collection of jars and bottles is filled with lotions from the bark of the perhwan tree, ground linseed, cloves, *jalatir* (spice) and *rattanjot* (herb).

I crouch down in a corner and watch as Baba Mannah deftly bandages the hand of Khurshid Bibi, a school teacher. She has fallen and fractured her hand. She tells him how she is unable to make chapatti for her husband and finds it difficult to wash out heavy clothes or even write and prepare her classes. As she talks she receives sympathetic murmurs from Baba Mannah, who before finishing the treatment gives her gentle but firm instructions to rest and to try and persuade her husband to assist her by buying chapattis from the bazaar.

All day there is a stream of visitors knocking on his door: villagers from farmlands surrounding Lahore; professors from the city's colleges; business people; locals from his own neighborhood and even women from the palatial houses of Lahore's suburbs, who crouch down in their fine silks on the sackcloth beside Baba Mannah.

They have complete confidence in his method of treatment. Many of them would never even consider going to hospitals, where waiting lists are long, treatment and prescriptions are expensive and the doctors are overworked and impersonal. "Baba Mannah puts me at ease," says Khurshid Bibi, "and I trust him . . . The old styles are better."

"People will always come to people like me," says Baba Mannah with assurance, "because our form of treatment is effective and they have faith in our techniques . . . Our style will never die out because we elders will pass our knowledge on to our offspring. Our treatment doesn't change with experimentation because we don't need to experiment . . . So the people trust us."

As I leave Baba rests one of his strong hands on my head and recites a long blessing for my good health, safety and prosperity. He watches me walk away up the dimly lit alley of Gandhi park. Feeling wonderfully soothed by the old man's company, I understand why people still believe the old styles to be better.

AUSTRALIA

The Aboriginal Elder

Peter Collins*

Scotty Martin is an Australian aboriginal elder of the Ngarinyin and Wunambul tribes, a people who have resided for millennia in the Kimberley region of northwest Australia. The tribes were, as to be expected, greatly affected by colonization in the early twentieth century.

Being a community leader in your sixties, and one of the last members of a historic cultural line, is challenge enough for any man to live up to. Prior to colonization, old people dying might have been cause for serious mourning, but not so much a crisis issue. Nowadays, a death means the irreplaceable loss of a repository of cultural practice, sometimes before a replacement can be found.

Scotty's treasure, if you want to call it that, is that he still remembers his people's ancient ways. Specifically, his "gift" is an ability to access songs and the stories that are bound to the land and life into which he was born – songs and stories passed down from the earliest flickerings of human culture.

He lives today on Mount Elizabeth Station, where he and his parents were rescued from police by the forebears of the current owner, Peter Lacey. Peter's father, Frank, was by all accounts a man with integrity who took up pastoral farming in the area. In the 1940s, he had young Scotty released into his care, instead of being removed from his traditional lands.

From that point on, Scotty took an interest in the cattle-mustering that had occupied his father and grandfather. He and his fellows aborigines mustered at day, and at night the camps became a storehouse of traditional aboriginal culture – at a time when Scotty's relatives and other tribes were being pulled apart and relocated to centralized "projects." For Scotty, this time with his people was invaluable. He learned as his people had always learned – through oral tradition and mysticism.

Scotty's culture is known mostly through the so-called rock art of the Kimberley. As far back as the 1920s, but with renewed vigor in the 1990s, amateurs and professionals alike have descended on that culture from the outside. While many aboriginals have shared their knowledge with the outsiders, few can claim the kind of in-depth instruction that Scotty received during his time with the "old people." And these are things he shares with few people.

The growing interest in aboriginal culture has brought both benefits and drawbacks to Scotty, his family, and the larger tribe of which he is considered a "boss." (In aboriginal English, this means a leader in the knowledge of ancient law and culture.) Most of the bad aspects result from interlopers who circumvent the tribal hierarchy, consulting

---

*Special to this volume.

drunks and people with no real knowledge, who are then presented as "spokespeople" to the often ignorant outside world. When mineral rights, control of flora and fauna, and cultural tourism are up for grabs, it's Scotty's signature that is needed by the interested parties, including some of the world's biggest corporations. So there are many other pressures on Scotty, apart from the day-to-day challenges of living in a bush community.

Scotty derives no income from his land, despite having to sign for it regularly. He has proved in court, as have members of other tribes, that he holds rights as an individual and part of a tribal group to the land that enfolds him. But that is where his rights end, despite the reassurances he receives from unappointed intermediaries who advise him on the progress of "aboriginal affairs" (as they're known). No aboriginal money is allocated – or allowed to be allocated – to the cultural practices of elders within the community. Combined with this scarcity of resources, the fact that aboriginals have been removed from their land, and barred from access to many sacred places, leaves cultural practices vulnerable to erosion and decline.

Scotty is an impressive man. At around 67 years of age, he is physically fit, and can still cross a flooding river or muster a herd if required. After work, he may have to spend a week or two assisting in cultural matters – such as the initiation ceremonies of young aboriginal men – that require considerable physical and mental effort. He is one of the few remaining men with sufficient knowledge to "put boys through Law" – to circumcise them according to the rites predating the colonial era – and to conduct more advanced rites like funerals and sacred ceremonies. The disastrous loss of such knowledge in other indigenous cultures is evident in countries like South Africa, where newspapers report the death or mutilation of dozens of young boys after poorly conducted tribal initiations.

Scotty's income comes from running small tours to sites on the Mount Elizabeth Station property – mostly to the cave site of Murella, which has both Wandjina and Guyon art. It took more than 30 years for Scotty to embark on a path that has led to his recognition as the preeminent living composer in the cosmology of the Ngarinyin, Wunambul, and Worrora tribes, and a source of expertise on the meanings and stories of their ancient art.

Several years ago, Scotty recorded a CD of traditional songs to stimulate his native culture, and to exercise some control over it in a generally lawless and unregulated cultural environment. The songs were accompanied by a booklet of language and explanations, "for everyone to listen to," as he puts it. They were his first major contribution to the body of such artifacts assembled by the elders of his tribe. Sung by a full compliment of Ngarinyin elders, it provided a rare insight into the oral tradition that has been passed on, in Scotty's words, "from father to father, grandfather to grandfather, uncle to uncle, son to son.

"I used to listen to my father and grandfather singing when I was a little boy," Scotty says, "So I knew some songs. My grandfather came to me in a dream and said, 'Here, I have these things for you. I want to give them to you, so they won't be lost and you can carry them on forever'." His songs are the "message stick" that Scotty has produced in an effort to stem the tide of cultural degradation through neglect and misappropriation.

Scotty's traditional name is Nyalgodi. His "dreaming," for purposes of popular explanation, runs from his mother's country near Kalumburu (she is from the Wunambul tribe), and his father's from the Ngarinyin tribe. His father "caught" young Scotty's spirit-child from a sacred water-hole on what is today the Theda Station. This is a natural occurrence in his people's cosmology. Scotty has been to the site where he was "caught," at the Gibb River Road about five hours from where he lives today – but only in his dreams, something members of his tribe can accomplish with sufficient knowledge. Politics had long prevented him returning physically to the place.

In November 2004, Scotty chose to return to the spot where his father "dreamed him up," as part of a film project accompanying his CD. In true aboriginal fashion, the decision was made on the spur of the moment – through inspiration and revelation. He is a heritage-right holder in the area of the "dreaming spot," according to a recent ruling by the Australian Federal Court. The Court has also recognized common-law rights that grant him, in principle, unmolested passage to sacred places of his tribe.

As Scotty's friend and manager of his music project, I was invited to accompany him, together with a filmmaker and sound recordist hired by the Australian Broadcasting Corporation. The idea was to shoot a promotional video and documentary film about Scotty's life and music, and to provide footage that Scotty could use for his own purposes, as part of his personal archive.

We were all aware, however, that pastoralists of the region were unhappy with the Australian government's "native title" court process. Fears of aboriginal claims have led to intense attacks on aboriginal cultural rights, and practitioners of those rights.

Just a couple of years before, the Ngarinyin Aboriginal Corporation, of which Scotty is vice-chairman, had gathered money to buy the station we were going to visit. The purchase would have crowned years of hard work by the tribe, and secured for his people outright occupation rights – not dual title with the owners of the pastoral lease. The sale fell through, however, when a buyer for the current owners outbid the aborigines.

In light of these facts, and the attendant sensitivities, we had tried to forge an accord with the lease owners, notifying them by telephone of our intention to drive up to Theda and visit the site. In what the ever-optimistic Scotty and I both saw as a positive development, the manager said our visit would be fine, though we would have to double-check with the caretaker. We did, and were also told: no problem.

Thus assured of unmolested passage, we left our camp and embarked on the five-hour journey. Scotty was happy – over the moon. Everything was going right for him. He would finally be returning to the place he holds so dear to his heart. The look in his eyes was something to see. It bespoke a man proud in his country, forging a deeper connection through realignment of what he, in his broken English, called a "bent" or "broken-down" relationship with the land.

When we finally arrived at Theda, we were invited in for coffee. Scotty told the caretaker he wanted to look for his dreaming spot in the "blackfella way." Some discussion ensued regarding the rock art carved on walls in the region. Scotty asked if the caretaker had heard rumors of "some more" paintings being taken recently from rock-art walls in the region, which was the rumor going around the "bush telegraph." At this, the caretaker bridled. He responded that he knew only about the rocks that everyone had heard of from the police report several years back. Then, the search for art missing from the site had led to a confrontational scene between Mr. Paddy Neowarra, a senior elder of Scotty's acquaintance, who was chairman of the Ngarinyin Aboriginal Corporation, and a pastoral-company manager who had once managed Theda, but now – we learned for the first time – was restricted to its sister station, Doongan.

The caretaker told us that we should refrain from making the kind of unsubstantiated accusations that Mr. Neowarra had. But we had made no accusations, and didn't intend to. We were merely curious, seeking to confirm or deny the reports we'd heard. Regardless, we explained, we were just here to film. We weren't looking for trouble.

The filmmaker then asked for a location-site release to be signed by the station representative, per ABC-TV protocol. It was a formality, and in many ways a gesture of respect to the station people. But it had the opposite effect. As if on cue, the caretaker grew nervous, and walked away. He returned several minutes later, saying that the principal lease-owner, one of the nation's richest lawyers, had rung up from Melbourne – and had ordered us to leave the property immediately.

Every attempt at mediation foundered. I told the caretaker that, legally, the lease-holders could not refuse Scotty access to the site. Under the Aboriginal Heritage Act and the Native Title Act, as well as common law, this was aboriginal property, and visiting it was an aboriginal right. The caretaker responded that he wasn't denying Scotty permission to visit – but rather, his companions. Now, everyone knew that the caretakers regularly allowed non-aboriginals to film and visit the sacred sites registered to Scotty in his station leases, without first seeking his permission. The fact that these contraventions of the Heritage Act went unpunished made a mockery of the expensive, decades-long process of securing the High Court and Native Title rulings.

The caretakers then told Scotty petulantly that they had been asking him for years to visit; why was he only coming now? Scotty didn't reply. We left the station, a few more hollow-sounding apologies ringing in our ears. Out here, it seemed that if you were black and of few economic means, you couldn't win – even with the backing of the courts. By the time you could ever have your case heard, you would be hung out to dry. We had invested considerable time and cost in the journey, only to encounter a blockade of ignorance and hostility.

Discussing our plight with residents further down the Gibb River Road, it was suggested to us, as if by way of mitigation, that the pastoralists were angry about the native-title handback, and about unfriendly speeches made by the politicized aborigines whom Scotty himself was at odds with. They were looking for ways, we were told, to limit aboriginals to the kind of access that tourists have to seek when they enter aboriginal reserves.

As if on cue, a lightning storm erupted. We arrived back at camp after seven hours on the road. Everything I could say to Scotty seemed meaningless. This was just another of so many instances in his life, when his rights and his just quest had culminated in nothing more than a cold exchange of words. The caretakers had asked why Scotty had never showed up over the years. It was obvious, wasn't it?

Scotty himself said just one thing that day that wasn't in response to a question. It was at the Ngarinyin camp of Muranbabiddi, when we stopped for corned-beef sandwiches. As best as I can recall, he said: "When we got that title, they told us – that land-council woman who represents us – 'Now you should go back to the country. You must all go back to the country.' I'm laughing," he said, recalling this cheery talk about Australian aborigines free to live on their land in their traditional ways. "I gotta go back to the country. Where to? With what? When? How? Who with?"

A big smile erupted on his face, which nonetheless stayed serious. "Do they think I'm stupid or something?"

HAITI

Vodou Magus

By Donald Cosentino*

Although he rarely left his backyard in Croix des Bouquet, Andre Pierre was Haiti's most cosmopolitan artist of the last half century. His paintings and religious objects were avidly sought by museums and wealthy private collectors in America and Europe. He began his career during what art historians now term "the Haitian Renaissance" – those heady years following the Second World War, when a number of Haitian artists, deeply rooted in the visual traditions of Vodou (also known as Voodoo, Vodoun, etc.), began translating their divine visions of the *lwa* (Vodou spirits) into such non-traditional media as oil paintings and steel pan sculptures.

Andre Pierre first expressed his divine visions by painting lwa inside the concave oval of the calabash (*cuit*), a sacred object in the rituals of Vodou. Encouraged by the proprietors of Le Centre d'Art, the Port-au-Prince cooperative which fostered much of the "Haitian Renaissance," Pierre transferred his visions to oil on canvas. All his paintings depict the lwa in apotheosis: Black and Brown gods and kings, often assembled in stately rank around Ogou, military commander of the pantheon, and Ezili Danto, earth goddess and matron of the revolutionary armies that freed Haiti from slavery and French colonial domination. Andre Pierre painted his gods in ball gowns, sashes, epaulettes, and tiaras – costumes appropriated from the slave masters who were killed or driven from Haiti after the Declaration of Haitian Independence in 1804. Vodou's appropriation of these colonial trappings, especially the attributes of the Roman Catholic saints, marks one of the great, and most consistently underrated, transformations in religious history.

---

*Special to this volume.

Andre Pierre, Croix des Mission, Haiti, 1993 (Phyllis Galembo)

Although his reputation grew along with the market for his astonishing paintings, Andre Pierre's artistic motivation and inspiration neither faltered nor changed. As he explained, "I paint to show the entire world what the Vodou religion is. Because three-fourths of the terrestrial globe thinks that Vodou is diabolical, I paint to show them that Vodou is not diabolical. Before I paint, I take this canvas, and I put it on the easel. I wait for an inspiration before describing it on Earth. Then an inspiration comes. I sing a song, and then I describe what I sang. I describe the song on the canvas."

I recorded the artist's words in 1986, during a conversation we had under a great shade tree in his enormous compound. A small, dark man, with a formidable nose and laughing eyes, he was already old and rather grizzled. He wore a cap with a small visor, the kind favored by French workmen. In all the years I have known him, he always wore that cap. His language drifted easily between Kreyol and French, punctuated frequently by cackles of self-delight. His look and style were entirely *sui generis*. Like many Haitians I've met, he was a total original.

During our conversation, he remained in front of his easel, seated on a wooden chair which had been transformed into a work of art. Spattered with dots and sashes of bright paint, it might have been the throne for a Fon *bocio*, a Kongo *nkisi*, or perhaps some intriguing object retrieved from Pollack's garage or Basquiat's garden fence. The compound was a similar conflation of worlds. The buildings were made of mud and daub with pan roofs, just as in West Africa. We sat next to the smallest, which was the artist's living quarters. It consisted of a tiny sitting-room with a cot and a couple of wooden chairs. Hanging on the wall was a portrait of the artist's agent, Issa, painted in an expressionist style more often found on Montparnasse or in Montmartre. Andre Pierre laughingly explained that he had painted the portrait so he could retain something of his agent, since Issa had taken so many things from him.

At the back of the compound were several more substantial buildings, housing altars to the cool and hot lwa whom Andre Pierre served. For in addition to being an artist, he was also *Ganga*, an initiated priest of the pantheons he painted. The altars were heaped with the detritus of modernity preferred by the lwa: bottles of rum and champagne, cigarettes, china dolls, perfume bottles, plaster statues of the saints, rosaries, packets of satin pierced by plastic crucifixes. They were as complexly structured and impossible to classify as the man who made them. Haiti may be the poorest country in the New World, but how could any aspect of this scene be dismissed as "Third World"? What could that term mean, if used to describe such a man or his world? Andre Pierre's art and philosophy spans not only this world, but planets and constellations beyond.

As he spoke of his life, his art and his religion, it all seemed to merge into a seamless whole:

"My life is simple. I've been alone since I was five. I have no father. No mother, no grandfather, nor grandmother. I have been the master of my personality since the age of fourteen. I am the protector of my life. Me, God, the Spirits and the Dead.

"The Vodou religion is before all other religions. It is more ancient than Christ. It is the first religion of the Earth. It is the creation of the world. The world is created by Vodou. The world is created by magic. The first magician is God, who created people with his own hands from the dust of the Earth. People originated by magic in all countries of the world. No one lives of the flesh. Everyone lives of the spirit.

"People who are not aware of this are not profound in their studies. They write and they read, but their study is not profound. It is not sufficient to read from a book. You must study nature. You must study people. You must study your neighbors. You must study that all is dust, and will return to dust. You must study that people possess nothing. One should eat well. Drink well. Sleep well. Enjoy your soul. Wait for the last day."

As Andre Pierre spoke directly of Vodou, he seemed to be describing a way of life more than a religion:

"Vodou is a religion purely Catholic, apostolic, but not Roman. It is not directed by men. It is directed uniquely by God. Since all men are liars, no one is a Catholic. The spirits of Vodou are the limbs of God. God is the body and the spirits are the limbs. To use Vodou, you must be an honest man: one who likes his neighbor. Because it is your neighbor who is God. You receive nothing from God. You receive everything from your neighbor. If you do not know your neighbor, do not put your faith in God who loves you. To love God, you must pass through your neighbor.

"Love, love. Those who do not love are nothing. Love of God. Love of neighbor. Love of work. Love for doing some good. When we have to do something, love of doing it well. You must not judge anyone. One does not know. For God told you, 'You will not see me, but you will see the poor always with you.' When they come to your house to ask for charity, have the courtesy to say, 'I have nothing this morning. Pass by in a few days, and I will leave something for you.' But don't ignore them. Don't deceive them. Why not love the poor? Why do you not have the poor live with you? It's only Vodou which welcomes the poor.

"Vodou allows you to walk with your head held high. Religion makes you walk with your head low. But with Vodou you can fight any war. All men are warriors. But with religion, no. Men are slaves. It is always 'Yes. Yes.' You don't have the right to say anything but 'Yes' to everything they tell you. Slaves of slaves. You don't have a personality. But with Vodou you keep your personality. 'I want,' or 'I don't want.' But in religion there is neither 'I want,' nor 'I don't want.' That's what personality is: the return of the Guinea spirits.

"After Haiti's independence in 1804, they returned. Guided by the star of the Messiah. Guided by the star and the Cross of Christ. Judah's tribe: the roots of David. Ogou returned with a red and blue flag. And [Ezili Danto] the woman saint brought back the Kongo packet. Ogou took the white out of the French flag, and left us a bi-color. He changed the country. He said, 'I am giving this land back to you. I am coming home.'"

For Andre Pierre, none of this was pie in the sky. He had no patience for abstract pieties:

"Hell is on Earth. Paradise is on Earth. Purgatory is on Earth. All is on Earth. Nothing is in the sky. Nothing was made in the sky. No one needs to speak of the sky. Instead of talking about the sky, talk of the Earth. God has said, 'If you don't believe me when I tell you about terrestrial things, how will you believe me when I tell you about celestial things?' God does nothing in the celestial. Even to create the sun and the moon, he put his foot on Earth; all was created on Earth.

"Honor the saints. Honor the relics. Honor the holy Virgin more than the angels and the saints. The Virgin Mary is Ezili Danto. All the saints are lwa. I am married to Ezili Danto. I sleep at her altar on Tuesdays. I have confidence in the spirits. I love the spirits. I live with the spirits. I respect the spirits. I do what I want with the spirits, and they do what they want with me. Because they have confidence that I will never betray them."

I felt privileged to be there, listening to that old man, as if we were talking under a Bodhi tree. I visited Andre Pierre many times after that conversation. One of our last meetings occurring in November 2003. These are the Days of the Dead in Haiti, the annual birthday for the trickster deity Gede, lord of Death and Sexuality. Andre Pierre was now past 90, and looked it. He still smiled impishly, but cataracts filmed his eyes. We talked for an hour about little things like Life! Death! and "What Does It All Mean?" I asked if he was afraid of dying. Through his opaque eyes, he peered into the Heart of

Nothing – which is also Nirvana: "Nothing is nothing to fear," he said. And then added, "The soul is dust," half-closing his eyes. No false hopes: Buddha reclines into sleep. But Buddha cackles, too.

Suddenly, he remembered who we were, and brought out the framed "Lifetime Achievement Award" we had presented to him on behalf of the UCLA Fowler Museum a decade earlier. I gave him a bottle of Five Star Barbancourt Rum, which he asked me to place on his Vodou altar, for Ezili, his mistress.

At the end of our visit, Andre Pierre showed me the canvas he was painting. The lwa are fuzzy and out of focus, like images from a fading Polaroid. The vision remains, though the hand trembles. As we were leaving, he asked for 500 gourdes (about $20). Ninety years old, and still hustling. I was reminded of a favorite cartoon by Gahan Wilson: a little vaudeville comedian in a candy-striped jacket and straw hat is dancing before an audience composed entirely of shrouded skeletons. The dancer looks a great deal like Gede, whom Andre Pierre sometimes painted in a similar costume, clicking his heels before the mirthless cadavers. Wilson subtitled his cartoon: "The sudden realization that, despite our best efforts, all is lost." The dancer is Gede, but he is also Andre Pierre. Death is clutching at him, but he won't stop cracking jokes or dancing.

I saw Andre Pierre most recently on Easter Monday, 2005. Curled on the cot in his sitting room, he couldn't rise or speak. The easel was gone. The paint-box was closed. That wonderful chair he had sat on while painting – the one all covered with painted spots like some Kongo spirit throne – was gone too. The painting of Issa still hung in the sitting room, but he had died the year before. All Andre Pierre's children had disappeared, except his eager son Judson, who showed me a calabash he had just painted in the style of his father. It seemed surreal that such a famous artist would be dying without anyone taking notice.

But there is a coda to this tale. Upon my return to Los Angeles, I posted a message in a Haiti chat-room, bewailing the artist's condition. A month or so later, someone sent a second email, announcing Andre Pierre's death in Croix des Mission. But a third email, circulated in July 2005, provided an ironic postscript. As Mark Twain joked about newspaper accounts of his own demise, reports of Andre Pierre's death turned out to be "greatly exaggerated":

> Le Centre d'Art today in Haiti paid homage to a frail but very living Andre Pierre. While musicians played drums along the veranda, Andre was wheelchaired into the main gallery surrounded by his paintings and facing a bronze sculpture of himself. The homage was organized in part to counteract two circulating emails referring to the death of Andre Pierre.

It seems that in death, as in life, Ganga Andre Pierre, the Vodou Magus, would march to his own drummer.*

Editor's note: Andre Pierre died in October 2005.

PART 3

Work

If asked to describe the gendering of work in the South, many readers would probably think of women working double or triple days, while men live high on the hog from female labor. This standard view contains a good deal of truth. But it is sorely inadequate as a nuanced picture of the challenges, risks, and creative opportunities of men's working lives worldwide. This section attempts to convey something of the difficulties, sacrifices, and rewards involved in "men's work" across the global South.

The most dangerous work in the world is the reproductive labor of Southern women. An estimated 600,000 die annually from complications of childbirth – a silent holocaust, roughly on the scale of the Rwandan genocide, repeated *every year*.[*] When it comes to labor in the public sphere, however, it is men who suffer the overwhelming majority of deaths and injuries on the job, both in the South and in the North. According to the International Labour Organization, "With the exception of agriculture, the world's most hazardous sectors and occupations have predominantly male workforces. Worldwide, the ILO estimates that some 80 per cent of work-related fatalities are suffered by men. In high-income countries, this figure is 86 per cent." [†]

This section begins with an article by Davan Maharaj that sketches the daily struggle for subsistence afflicting hundreds of millions of people in the South. It then presents a range of contributions that explore the diversity and dangers of "men's work" worldwide. We meet Somali men struggling to cope with state breakdown; miners and their families in China and Bolivia; the "shipbreakers" of India, profiled by William Langewiesche; the cane cutters of Guatemala's Pacific Coast plantations;

---

[*]See Gendercide Watch, "Case Study: Maternal Mortality," http://www.gendercide.org/case_maternal.html; and Adam Jones, "Gendercidal Institutions against Women and Girls," in Lea Biason and Marie Vlachová, eds., *Women in an Insecure World: Violence against Women – Facts, Figures and Analysis* (Geneva: Centre for the Democratic Control of Armed Forces, 2005), pp. 15–24.

[†]International Labour Organization, *Safety in Numbers: Pointers for a Global Safety Culture at Work* (Geneva: International Labour Office, 2003), p. 12. Significantly (and typically), the "Gender" section of the report, from which this passage is drawn, is devoted almost entirely to the plight of *female* workers.

Miskito "lobster divers" in Honduras; and South Asian migrant laborers toiling in slave-like conditions in the Middle East. Among the last group are Bangladeshi boys conscripted as camel jockeys in the United Arab Emirates. Semi-slavery is also the fate of the Brazilian agricultural laborers memorably portrayed by Osha Davidson. While the focus on migrant sex work in Thai urban centers has justifiably been on the women swept up in the trade from northern Thailand and surrounding countries, some adolescent and adult males also figure in the flow, as the *Bangkok Post* reminds us.

The remaining contributions to this section flesh out the staggering range of men's work in the global South. An intention here is to counteract stereotypes of a global "male elite," and to arouse empathy for the ordinary men who make extraordinary contributions and sacrifices for their societies, and for more privileged ones as well. Few readers will be able to forget Marla Dickerson's depiction of Mexico City's sewer-divers, "a last line of defense against a threatening tide" in one of the world's biggest cities. Larry Rohter poignantly portrays Brazilian organ-seller Alberty José da Silva, who literally sells his body for a decade's worth of normal wages. Assane Diallo and Ryszard Kapuscinski offer vignettes of life for males in the humble occupations of shoe-shiner and imperial doorkeeper.

It would be equally stereotypical, however, to depict all men's work as dirty, dangerous, and subordinated. Several contributions depict masculine labor in a more positive, sometimes rather amusing light. Abraham McLaughlin profiles a black entrepreneur, William Ngobeni, who drives minibuses on "an unpaved road to South Africa's middle class." Kevin Sullivan's depiction of Mexican bus driver Perez captures the energy and enthusiasm that this voluble man brings to his daily routine. Then there are the offbeat "motoboys" of São Paulo, the subject of *New York Times* reporter Larry Rohter's second contribution to this section. Confronted by the animosity of other drivers on the city's traffic-snarled streets, the motoboys nonetheless "see themselves as free spirits or urban cowboys, defying the conventions of society and envied by stodgy wage-earners stuck in their cars and offices." Monica Campbell returns us to Mexico with her article on Gerónimo Amezcua, a guitar maker whose work, threatened by cheap imports, nonetheless provides a living link to the past. Lynn Maalouf profiles Mosbah Baalbaki, a male belly dancer who captivates Beirut audiences and uses his celebrity to promote "a more homosexual-tolerant society in Lebanon." The section closes with another foray into artistic labor, with Dixie Beadle's essay on Ugandan artist/activist Okello Kelo Sam and his efforts to promote healing and reconciliation through theater and dance.

CONGO

The Struggle

Davan Maharaj[*]

Every day is a fight for pennies.

At sunrise, Adolphe Mulinowa is out hauling 10-gallon cans of sand at a construction site. It takes him an hour to earn 5 cents. Then he hustles to a roadside with a few plastic bottles of pink gasoline, which he hawks alongside dozens of other street vendors.

"Patron! Boss man! Gas! Gas! Gas!" Mulinowa barks as a battered Peugeot shudders past, kicking a spray of loose rocks at his face.

The car does not stop. Mulinowa, a short man in his mid-30s with sad, reddened eyes, squats down again beside his bottles. It is a scene repeated many times in the four hours it takes to sell them. Mulinowa pockets an additional 40 cents. Then, as the sun goes down, he heads to his evening job hawking used shoes and live chickens. A few more pennies.

After a 12-hour day, he returns home to his wife and six children with his earnings: about 70 cents and a bag of cornmeal swinging from his hand.

"We beat the belly pains today," he says in a tired mumble. "Tomorrow, more hard work."

Up and down the teeming streets of Goma [eastern Congo], there is no real work as it is known in the West. There is only what everyone here calls se debrouiller – French for getting by, or scratching a living out of nothing.

Decades of war and disease, followed by a volcanic eruption that entombed nearly half the city beneath a rough crust of lava, have reduced work to a mishmash of odd jobs and scheming. Civil servants survive on bribes. A lawyer moonlights by making pastries. A single mother of four turns to prostitution in her living room, decorated with pictures of Jesus and Mary.

They are among the poorest people on Earth, surviving on less than a dollar a day. In the United States, an individual who makes less than $9,310 a year is considered poor. The World Bank sets its poverty line at $730 a year – $2 a day. Half of sub-Saharan Africa's 600 million people live on about 65 cents a day – less than what an American might spend on a cup of coffee.

It is never enough. In Goma, near the heart of Africa, an average family of seven spends about $63 a month, two-thirds of it on food. With every dollar, they make a choice among competing needs – food, rent, clothes, school and medicine.

Sometimes it is a matter of life and death. Two years ago, Mulinowa's little boy, Dieudonne, or "God's gift," came down with a fever, cold sweats and shakes. Mulinowa knew that it was malaria. He took the 3-year-old to a muganga – Swahili for traditional

---

[*]From Davan Maharaj, "When the Push for Survival is a Full-Time Job," *The Los Angeles Times*, 11 July 2004.

healer – who sprinkled him with water, squeezed the pulp from some herbs into his mouth and sent him home. Two days later, the boy was dead. Mulinowa knows that with 20 cents for medicine to fight the fever and chills, he might have saved his son's life. But he didn't have the money. Neither did the families of three other children in the neighborhood who died about the same time.

"I do not want this to happen to my Annissette," Mulinowa says of his 2-year-old daughter. "That's why we work from dawn to dusk."

In some ways, the Mulinowas are better off than many Congolese. The family's wooden house, resting on an old lava flow, has a tin roof and some wooden furniture. The walls recently were whitewashed with paint from an aid agency. Their neighbors live in mud huts or houses fashioned from rusting galvanized sheets.

In a town of *debrouillards*, Mulinowa has learned to exploit tiny advantages. He has figured out that, because Goma has dozens of gasoline vendors, his chances are better two miles away at the Rwanda–Congo border. There, drivers have to slow down and are more likely to notice him.

His family also improves its odds by spreading out during the day, hoping that at least one member will earn enough to buy food. If Mulinowa doesn't sell enough gas, shoes or chickens, then perhaps his son, 18-year-old Ivan, will have better luck making deliveries with his homemade wooden scooter, called a *chukudu*. For a few cents per trip, Ivan ferries goods through a bazaar of vendors hawking their wares, grilling lake fish on smoky coals and blasting the guitar rhythms of *soukous* stars such as Kanda Bongo Man. Sometimes the merchants also give him small bags of flour or vegetables.

If Mulinowa and his son fail, then daughter Bernadette, 15, might be able to bring in some money selling used clothes, canned sardines or other goods for neighborhood merchants.

The fallback is Mulinowa's wife, Faith, who struggles to feed her family of eight when a 50-pound sack of manioc flour costs $24; a sack of beans, $17; and a dozen salted fish, $7. Occasionally she receives produce from relatives in outlying villages that she can sell for extra money.

SOMALIA

Work Amidst Anarchy*

Mahamut Issa Abdi

I am 18 years old. I am married with three children. I live in a displaced person's camp not far from here. I spend all day smashing the foundations of the wall around what

---

*From "Life in Somalia," BBC Online, 25 November 2004. http://news.bbc.co.uk/2/hi/africa/4040889.stm

Jerash, Jordan (Adam Jones)

was the United States embassy in Mogadishu in order to retrieve the steel rods used to reinforce the concrete.

I sell the rods to people who are building new houses. It's really hard work – and very hot – but it's the only way I can support my family at the moment. I have been doing this for about three years and have gone 3 km around the wall. I earn 1,000 Somali shillings (6.5 US cents) for each rod. I get about 20 rods a day but I have to give half of them to the gunman who controls the area I work. He does not control the whole US embassy – just the wall. The embassy grounds have been divided up between about 70 gunmen and people are working for them all.

I have heard that a new Somali president has been elected in Kenya. I really hope he can come back to Somalia and end this anarchy. If there is a new government, I would like to go to school and learn something. This hammer is very heavy and if I had a choice, I would do something else. But if I could not go to school and had to carry on doing this, at least if there were a government I would not have to give half the rods to the gunman.

Abdidir Ali Hashi

I am 22 years old. I am married but we don't have any children yet. I drive this bus on a 30 km route to Mogadishu. On the way, we go through six check-points run by different militias. At each one, I have to pay 50,000 shillings ($3). This covers the whole day. I cannot do anything about it, if I had armed guards on my bus, there might be a gun-fight and passengers would be killed. Because of those fees, it's really hard to get by and I have to keep the fares for my passengers high. [. . .] The first thing the government must do is to take down the checkpoints, disarm the militias and restore law and order. I also hope that education would be free again. Then I could go to school, get some qualifications and work in an office instead of driving this bus.

Bashir Aden Ibrahim

I have been a gunman for 14 years. I used to be a driver but I was press-ganged into fighting for Somalia's last government, led by Siad Barre. After he was toppled, I started to use my gun to earn the money to support my family.

I live in a former government building with my wife and six children, along with the families of my comrades. I work at a check-point, where we stop passenger buses, taxis and goods trucks but if we see a vehicle with its own security guards, we leave them alone. The amount we charge depends on how much the truck is carrying. If it's fully laden, we can charge up to 1m shillings ($60) but if it's only carrying a half load, we only charge 500,000 sh. For a minibus, we charge 50,000 sh for the full day and then an extra 10,000 in the evening. If the driver doesn't pay, we won't let him through.

This is how we earn the money we need to live. We don't have to give any of our earnings to our faction leader, we keep it all for ourselves. The gun rules Somalia today and my gun is the tool of my trade – it is my pen. If we fight, we fight for our clan. I know this is not a good life but it is the only thing I can do at the moment.

Things were much better during the regime of Siad Barre. Then we were human beings but now we are living like zombies, just surviving, because there is no direction. From time to time, our clan elders have told us to stop fighting but they don't have any money, unlike our faction leaders, so we follow those with the money. [...] Once all the different militias are disarmed, then we will all be equal and we can live together peacefully.

CHINA

The Miners (1)

Joseph Kahn*

Liu Fengtong does not need reminding that it is perilous to dig for coal in Chinese mines. He broke his foot and his shoulder when a tunnel collapsed on him six years ago, and he lost his front teeth when a rock fell on his face a few years later. When he leaves home he walks past the village walnut tree, once the daily meeting place of his two brothers, Liu Fengwu and Liu Fengmin. They worked the same shift at a nearby mine until Oct. 23, when an underground methane gas explosion reduced the family mining fraternity from five men to three. Then there is Mr. Liu's 77-year-old mother, frail and prone to tears, who tells her sons that they must never again go down into the mine shafts.

"I lie to her and tell her I work in a factory now," Mr. Liu said on a recent frigid morning, slipping on his inky canvas overalls and attaching his headlamp. "She could never take it if we told her the truth. But I can't survive without going down."

Becoming a coal miner in China is less a career choice than an act of desperation. It is a job for the poor who calculate that the income, however modest, outweighs the likelihood of injury and the constant specter of death. China began shaft mining at least 1,800 years ago and now produces more coal than any other country, about 1.3 billion metric tons a year. The Chinese coal industry also has few rivals in the number of miners killed and maimed on the job. According to China's official statistics, 6,121 people died in mines last year, 8 per cent more than in 2001. There were an average of 10 fatal accidents a day last year.

Mining is dangerous everywhere, but a Chinese miner is more likely to die on the job than miners in almost any other country. Last year 4.7 Chinese miners were killed for every million metric tons of coal produced. The only higher reported rate was in Ukraine, at 6 miners per million metric tons. A Chinese miner is 117 times more likely to be killed at work than an American miner. Many more miners perish uncounted in prosaic tunnel collapses, explosions, fires, floods and elevator failures that mine owners never report, Chinese coal experts say. Many mine owners keep their records secret.

---

*From Joseph Kahn, "China's Coal Miners Risk Danger for a Better Wage," *The New York Times*, 28 January 2003.

They do not want anyone to scrutinize operations that use manual labor in conditions not much better than those at the dawn of the industrial age in the 19th century.

The miners' days are filled with degradations. They share soiled sheets and hard beds in dormitory rooms. They work without union representation for bosses they never meet. Yet theirs is also a culture of dependency. Though they rarely make more than $150 a month, they do better than peasants who work the surface of the land. If mining kills or injures a family member, the healthy need extra income to pay medical bills and support dependants.

Fang Chunsheng moved to this coal region in Shanxi Province hoping to earn enough to start a business in his native Sichuan. He now uses his savings to help pay medical fees for Fang Jianjun, his little brother and a fellow miner. In November, a loaded coal cart spun out of control and punctured the younger Mr. Fang's body. He broke three ribs and doctors removed his pancreas.

In a place like Zhongyang, nestled in the dun-colored Luliang mountains of western Shanxi Province, coal is by far the most important industry, and the most pressing problem. Dense clouds of smog drift over the arid landscape, the exhaust of coking plants. Smokestacks and elevator towers above mine shafts seem to outnumber trees. Everyone here depends more or less on coal, and nearly everyone knows someone whose life it destroyed.

All six brothers in the Jiang family, ages 32 to 56, work in the same mine, called Hou Wa, in a valley beneath their hilltop village. None had suffered major injuries for years, but that changed last December 30. On that day Jiang Wuchu, 33, was crawling through a 3-foot-high tunnel in a coal seam 400 feet underground when he heard a rumble. He regained consciousness as workers dragged him toward the shaft opening. He had no sensation in his legs. The manager would not let workers use the company car to take Mr. Jiang to the hospital. "They were afraid I would die and cause them problems," Mr. Jiang said. So they bundled him into the back of a taxi. The company agreed to pay for surgery to repair displaced vertebrae in Mr. Jiang's back, but only if it were performed in Zhongyang, where the local clinic resembles a two-storey motel, with concrete floors and black curtains in the doorways to keep out the winter chill.

At least one of Mr. Jiang's brothers skips work each day to help feed, clean and administer therapy to him at the clinic. The mine has so far offered no compensation beyond the initial surgery, and the family has shouldered hospital fees and provided for his wife and three children. Mr. Jiang still cannot move his legs. He often grimaces and complains of intense pains in his back. "We would never tell him this, but our fear is that he is paralyzed," said Jiang Qihu, 56, the senior brother. "I don't want to think about it. We cannot afford even a pack of cigarettes."

The elder Jiang says he has debated whether to press the boss at Hou Wa, a private businessman he has never met, to help his family. But he has heard that the boss tends to retaliate against workers who want compensation. "I'm afraid if we make a big issue he will fire the rest of us," Mr. Jiang says. "The boss has connections with powerful people. We are powerless."

China's government no longer controls mine production as it once did. Local officials supervise the biggest mines and often hire private businessmen to manage them. Tiny mines operating without permits account for a substantial share of production. Many do not follow the most rudimentary safety guidelines, like providing adequate ventilation in mine shafts. Regulators often express outrage over the industry's atrocious safety record, especially after an undiminished spate of accidents in the last several years. Beijing has ordered small, shoddy mines to shut down, and it vows to punish irresponsible mine owners and the local officials who protect them. But China's richest sedimentary rock basins lie beneath its poorest places – its northeast, central and northwestern regions. The incentive to exploit coal has tended to outweigh the penalty for unsafe production. The government also seems inclined to tolerate a high death rate to keep coal, which still supplies about 75 per cent of China's energy needs, abundant and inexpensive.

The situation persists because the people who have the most at stake, the miners, are too uneducated, disorganized or scared to do much about it. "Nobody is going to stick his neck out," said Liu Fengtong. "You open your mouth for nothing." He has been mining for 18 of his 36 years. Although he takes daily detergent baths, the coal clings like a light beard to his face and snuggles into the folds of his skin near his deeply lined eyes.

Mr. Liu skipped work for a week in October to arrange the funeral of his two brothers, who died with 44 other people in a gas explosion at the Zhujiadian mine, just half a mile from his family village. The sprawling mine, one of the few in the area that is state-owned, is visible from his home, as are the tombs of some victims and the walnut tree where his brothers used to meet each day. Now he does his best to forget. He lives and works at a mine in the hills, sharing a dormitory room with miners on his shift. They warm themselves by a coal fire in the early morning before strapping on their equipment. The conversation steers away from safety, as if addressing the topic might invite bad luck.

Mr. Liu's older brother, Liu Fengtai, did give up mining after the accident. He said he could no longer think straight when he was underground. In other words, he is scared. He thinks his little brother should be, too. "I want him to quit," Liu Fengtai said. "I would rather give him what money I have than to see him go down." But Liu Fengtong says mining is his destiny. With two children in school, he depends more than ever on the income. When his shift began, he squeezed on to a capsule-shaped shaft elevator and smiled at a visitor. The sun flashed off his silver front teeth before the elevator was swallowed by darkness.

BOLIVIA

The Miners (2)

Domitila Barrios de Chungara*

In the mine there are two systems of work: one is for the technicians and the other for the miners.

The mine doesn't stop. It works day and night. And that's why they've divided the miners into three shifts. [. . .] When the worker is on the first shift, we women have to get up at four in the morning to prepare our *compañero*'s [companion's] breakfast. At three in the afternoon he gets back from the mine and he hasn't eaten anything yet. There's no way to take any food into the mine. It's not allowed. And anyway, it would get spoiled passing through so many places inside the mine. There's so much dust, so much heat, apart from the exploding dynamite, that even if they were able to eat anything at all, they'd be eating something that was bad for them. [. . .]

So how do they stand the mine? By chewing coca mixed with lye. Coca is a leaf that has a sort of bitter flavor but that makes you forget your hunger. Lye is the ashes from *quinoa* stalks† mixed with rice and aniseed that people chew with coca in order to get rid of its bitter taste. So that's what the miners chew to raise their spirits and so that their stomachs can stand it.

The work in the mine is exhausting. My compañero, for example, gets home and goes to sleep without undressing. He sleeps two or three hours and then he gets up to eat.

The worst, the hardest, is the night shift. The miner works all night long and comes home to sleep during the day. But since the house is small and the houses in the camp are right next to each other, there's no place for the kids to play; they have to stay right there making a racket. And the walls are so thin that when the neighbors talk it seems like they're right there beside us. So the worker can't sleep, and he gets fed up and leaves the house. [. . .] But they're forced to work that shift. They have to obey the company rules, if not, they're fired. [. . .]

The average life expectancy of a miner is barely thirty-five years. By then he's totally sick with mine sickness. Since there are so many explosions in order to get the ore out, these dust particles are breathed into the lungs, through the mouth and nose. This dust consumes and finally destroys the lungs. Their mouths turn black, purple. In the end they vomit pieces of lung and then they die. This is the occupational disease of the mine, called silicosis.

---

*From Domitila Barrios de Chungara with Moema Viezzer, *Let Me Speak! Testimony of Domitila, A Woman of the Bolivian Mines* (New York: Monthly Review Press, 1978), pp. 26–32.
†Grain from the highlands.

Miners in the Cerro Rico mountain, Potosí, Bolivia. The wads in their cheeks are coca leaves, chewed to stave off hunger and fatigue (Adam Jones)

The miners suffer another misfortune: despite the fact that they support the national economy with their sweat and blood, throughout their lives they're despised by everyone, because people are terrified of us and think that we'll give them our disease, even though it isn't true. [...] And also, since the miners chew coca to get them through the day's work, they say that the miners are drug addicts, are *khoya loca*, madmen of the mines. So you can see that our problem is serious. [...]

They pay the miners a pittance. For example, my husband, who works in a special section inside the mine, gets 28 pesos a day now, or about 740 pesos a month. Last year they paid him 17 pesos a day, that is, not even a dollar a day. We have a family subsidy of about 347 pesos, as well as a cost of living allowance the government set because of devaluation, which is a bit more than 135 pesos a month. There's also a wage increase for night work. Adding it all up, my compañero can earn about 1,500 to 1,600 pesos a month. But with what the company discounts for the social security fund, the groceries, school buildings, and other things, we never see all of that money. Sometimes my husband gets 700 pesos, sometimes 500, sometimes we end up owing the company money. And from that my family of nine has to live. But there are workers who are even worse off. [...]

So now I think: if the people came into power and changed this system of life, with the measures we'd take that wouldn't happen. We would even live longer. Because the first thing we'd do would be to straighten things out in the mines, buy new machinery, for example, so that we could work better, make our system of nutrition suit the physical wear and tear our compañeros have to put up with. I especially think that our compañeros shouldn't have to die that way in the mine. You go in there until you literally can't lift a shovel or a pick, and only then do you have the right to retire and receive a little pension. Before that, they don't give you a penny.

On the other hand, if the state looked after its human capital, the first thing it would do – and when one day we're in power I think it will be done – would be to decree that each miner must not work more than five years inside the mine. And at the same time that he's working there, the company itself should have him learn some trade so that when he leaves the mine after five years, he can work at some other job, as a good carpenter, a good shoemaker, for example. But he should have some field where he can earn his living and not spend the rest of his life in the mine.

Because, after all, if we go on the way we are. . . . When will we ever have a healthy society? And if we go on treating people only as human machines that have to produce, produce and then die; and when they die they're exchanged for another force, that is, another person, who is also to be wiped out. . . . Well, this way human capital is just being thrown away, and that's the most important thing a society has, don't you agree?

INDIA

The Shipbreakers

William Langewiesche*

Alang [in the Indian coastal state of Gujarat] [was] a narrow, smoke-choked industrial zone six miles long, where nearly 200 ships stood side by side in progressive stages of dissection, yawning open to expose their cavernous holds, spilling their black innards onto the tidal flats, and submitting to the hands of 40,000 impoverished Indian workers. A narrow, roughly paved frontage road ran along the top of the beach, parallel to the ocean. It was still quiet at dawn, although a few battered trucks had arrived early, and were positioning themselves now for the day's first loads of steel scrap. On the ocean side the frontage road was lined by the metal fences that defined the upper boundaries of the 183 shipbreaking yards at Alang. [. . .]

The workers lived just across the frontage road, in a narrow shantytown with no sanitation, and for the most part with no power. The shantytown did not have a name of its own. It stretched for several miles through the middle of Alang, and had a small central business section, with a few small grocery stalls and stand-up cafés. It was dusty, tough, and crowded. Unemployment there was high. The residents were almost exclusively men, migrants from the distant states of Orissa and Uttar Pradesh. They toiled under shipyard supervisors, typically from their home states or villages, who dispensed the jobs, generally in return for a cut from the workers' already meager pay. The workers chose to work nonetheless, because the alternatives were worse. In the morning light

*From William Langewiesche, "The Shipbreakers," *The Atlantic Monthly*, August 2000.

now, they emerged from their shacks by the thousands and moved across the frontage road like an army of the poor. They trudged through the yards' open gates, donned hard hats, picked up crowbars and sledgehammers, and lit crude cutting torches. By eight o'clock, the official start of the workday, they had sparks showering from all the ships nearby, and new black smoke rising into the distance along the shore. [. . .]

Alang is a wonder of the world. It may be a necessity, too. When ships grow old and expensive to run, after about twenty-five years of use, their owners do not pay to dispose of them, but, rather, the opposite – they sell them on the international scrap market, where a typical vessel [. . .] may bring a million dollars for the weight of its steel. Selling old ships for scrap is considered to be a basic financial requirement by the shipping industry – a business that has long suffered from small profits and cutthroat competition. No one denies that what happens afterward is a dangerous and polluting process.

Shipbreaking was performed with cranes and heavy equipment at salvage docks by the big shipyards of the United States and Europe until the 1970s, when labor costs and environmental regulations drove most of the business to the docksides of Korea and Taiwan. Eventually, however, even these entrepreneurial countries started losing interest in the business and gradually decided they had better uses for their shipyards. This meant that the world's shipbreaking business was again up for grabs. In the 1980s enterprising businessmen in India, Bangladesh, and Pakistan seized the initiative with a simple, transforming idea: to break a ship they did not need expensive docks and tools; they could just wreck the thing – drive the ship up onto a beach as they might a fishing boat, and tear it apart by hand. The scrap metal to be had from such an operation could be profitably sold, because of the growing need in South Asia for low-grade steel, primarily in the form of ribbed reinforcing rods (re-bars) to be used in the construction of concrete walls. These rods, which are generally of a poor quality, could be locally produced from the ships' hull plating by small-scale "re-rolling mills," of which there were soon perhaps a hundred in the vicinity of Alang alone. From start to finish the chain of transactions depended on the extent of the poverty in South Asia. There was a vast and fast-growing population of people living close to starvation, who would work hard for a dollar or two a day, keep the unions out, and accept injuries and deaths without complaint. Neither they nor the government authorities would dream of making an issue of labor or environmental conditions. [. . .]

Today roughly 90 per cent of the world's annual crop of 700 condemned ships now end their lives on the beaches of Pakistan, India, and Bangladesh – and fully half of them die at Alang. With few exceptions, the breakers [i.e., shipbreaking contractors] are not high-born or educated men. They are shrewd traders who have fought their way up, and in some cases have grown rich, but have never lost the poor man's feeling of vulnerability. They have good reason to feel insecure. Even with the most modest of labor costs, shipbreaking is a marginal business that uses borrowed money and generates slim profits. The risk of failure for even the most experienced breakers is real. Some go under every year. For their workers the risks are worse: falls, fires, explosions, and exposure to a variety of poisons from fuel oil, lubricants, paints, wiring, insulation, and cargo slop. Many workers are killed every year.* Nonetheless, by local standards the industry has been a success. Even the lowliest laborers are proud of what they do at Alang. There is no ship too big to be torn apart this way. More important, the economic effects are substantial – Alang and the industries that have sprung from it provide a livelihood, however meager, for perhaps as many as a million Indians. Imagine, therefore, their confusion and anger that among an even greater number of rich and powerful foreigners, primarily in Northern Europe, Alang has also become a rallying cry for reform – a name now synonymous with Western complicity and Third World hell.† [. . .]

The big port city of Bombay has a reputation for being just as dirty [as New Delhi], but on the day I got there, an ocean breeze was blowing, and in relative terms the air was clean. When I mentioned this to Pravin S. Nagarsheth, the shipbreaker I had come to see, he grew excited and said, "Yeah! Yeah!" because relativity was precisely the point he wanted to make to me. Nagarsheth was a nervous little man with a round and splotchy face and some missing teeth. He had been scrapping ships for nearly thirty-five years, first with a small yard here in Bombay, and then in a bigger way at Alang. He was also the president of the Indian shipbreakers' association, and as such he had taken the lead in the industry's defense. He had traveled to the Amsterdam shipbreaking conference to counter the reports of abuses at Alang. In his speech there he said, "All these write-ups, I would say, are biased, full of exaggerations. . . . One, however, wonders whether such reports are deliberately written for public consumption in affluent Western societies only. . . . The environmentalists and Greenpeace talk of future generations, but are least bothered about the plight of the present generation. Have they contributed anything constructive to mitigate the plight of the people living below the poverty line in developing countries? . . . Living conditions of labor in Alang should not be looked at in isolation. It is the crisis of urbanization due to job scarcity. Large-scale slums have mushroomed in all cities. . . . The fact remains that workers at Alang are better paid and are probably safer than their counterparts back in the poor provinces of Orissa, Bihar, and Uttar Pradesh. To provide housing and better living conditions . . . is financially impractical

---

*Editor's note: According to the International Labour Organization (ILO): "Shipbreaking is . . . particularly hazardous, not least in the Asian beachheads where much of the work is now done. Workers' safety is jeopardized by the absence of basic precautions, work planning and training. A number of potential risks are posed by the absence of norms about the condition that a vessel should be in when it arrives for scrapping. These hazards include heavy exposure to toxins and other dangerous substances, notably carcinogens. The workforce, often migrants, usually live in inadequate facilities on or near the site. Noise, poor sanitation and general exposure to pollution from the site have short- and long-term health implications. Low reporting standards mean that the health and safety statistics for this sector are erratic and unreliable." International Labour Organization, *Safety in Numbers: Pointers for a Global Safety Culture at Work* (Geneva: International Labour Office, 2003), p. 11.
†Editor's note: In the mid-1990s, Alang was chosen as the target of an international campaign against toxic and hyper-exploitative shipbreaking by the environmental organization Greenpeace. The campaign continues at the time of writing (see http://www. greenpeace web.org/shipbreak/).

for a developing country like India, where forty-five per cent of the population is living below the poverty line." [. . .]

He was making a valid point about relative levels of misery. I saw another level a few days later in Bhavnagar, the nearest city to Alang, at a re-rolling mill, where hull plates from the ships were being torch cut, heated, and stretched into reinforcing bars. Bhavnagar is an uncrowded city by Indian standards, with a population of perhaps 600,000 in a physical shell that to a Westerner might seem better suited for perhaps a fourth of that. The re-rolling mill I visited was one of many there. It stood on the north edge of town, on a quiet dirt street wandered by cows, at the end of a crumbling brick wall, beyond the dust and din of the city's auto-rickshaws. The mill had a sagging iron gate. A traveler would normally pass it by, perhaps seeing it as a poor but peaceful scene. But I went inside, past an old brick building where clerks sat idle behind bulky type-writers on an outside porch, and on into the dark heart of the mill – a large, open-sided shed where perhaps a hundred emaciated men moved through soot and heavy smoke, feeding scrap to a roaring furnace leaking flames from cracks in the side. The noise in there was deafening. The heat was so intense that in places I thought it might sear my lungs. The workers' clothes were black with carbon, as were their hair and their skin. Their faces were so sooty that their eyes seemed illuminated.

The furnace was long and low. The men working closest to the fire tried to protect themselves by wrapping heavy rags around their mouths and legs. They cut the steel plates into heavy strips, which they heaved into the inferno and dragged through the furnace before wrestling them free, red-hot, at the far end. Using long tongs, they slung the smoking metal, still brightly glowing, through a graduated series of rollers, which squeezed and lengthened it incrementally into the final product – the reinforcing rods, which were piled together and allowed to cool. It was a punishing and dangerous proce-dure, requiring agility, strength, and speed, and also the calculation of risk. The workers were quite obviously exhausted by it. Some, I think, were slowly starving, trapped in that cycle of nutritional deficit all too common in South Asia, by which a man may gradually expend more calories on his job than his wages will allow him to replace.

I traveled from Bhavnagar to Alang, thirty miles to the south, on a narrow road crowded with jitneys and trucks, choked with blue exhaust, and battered by the weight of steel scrap. The road ran like an industrial artery across plains of denuded farmland, on which impoverished villages endured in torpor and peasants scratched at the parched earth. Along the way stood a few open-air cafes, where truck drivers could stop for soft drinks and food, and a few small factories, where oxygen was concentrated into steel bottles to be mixed later with cooking gas for use in the cutting operations farther south. But otherwise the roadside scenery remained agricultural until several miles before Alang. There, next to a small house on the right, a collection of lifeboats listed in the dirt. The lifeboats marked the start of Alang's roadside marketplace, where specialized traders neatly sorted and resold secondary merchandise from the ships. There were yards for generators, motors, transformers, kitchen appliances, beds and other furniture, wires and pipes, cables, ropes, life rings, clothing, industrial fluids, and miscellaneous machinery. The traders lived among their goods. The buyers came from all over India. [...]

My base at the beach was Plot 138. It was a busy patch of ground, bounded at the top by one of the standard sheet-metal fences. I threaded through piles of sorted scrap, past the smoke of cutting crews, past chanting gangs carrying heavy steel plate, past cables and chains and roaring diesel winches, to the water's edge, where the hulk of a 466-foot Japanese-built cargo ship called the Sun Ray, once registered in the Maldives, was being torn apart by an army of the poor. Four hundred men worked there, divided into three distinct groups – a shipboard elite of cutters and their assistants, who were slicing the hull into multi-ton pieces; a ground crew of less experienced men, who winched those pieces partway up the beach and reduced them there to ten-foot sections of steel plate; and, finally, the masses of unskilled porters condemned to the end of the production line, where, piece by piece, they would eventually shoulder the entire weight of the hull, lugging the heavy plates to the upper beach and loading them into trucks – belching monsters painted like Hindu shrines – which would haul the scrap away. And that was just for the steel. Everywhere I looked stood the piles of secondary products awaiting disposal – the barrels of oil and hydraulic fluid and all the assorted equipment destined for the roadside marketplace. In either direction I could look down the coast at a line of torn ships fading into the smoke of burning oil.

Alang at first is a scene of complete visual confusion; it begins to make sense only after about a week, when the visual impact fades, and the process of breaking a ship by hand sorts itself out into a series of simple, brutal activities. The first job is to shackle the ship more firmly to the ground. Using motorized winches and a combination of anchor chains and braided steel cables looped through holes cut into the bow, the workers draw the hull as high onto the beach as the ship's draft and trim allow, so that ideally the bow stands on dry ground even at high tide. The winches are diesel-powered machines each the size of a small bulldozer, staked firmly to the ground about halfway up the beach. The stress on the cables during the winching operation is enormous. They groan and clank under the load, and sometimes they snap dangerously. The workers are ordered to stand clear. Nonetheless, some winch operators sit unprotected by safety cages, and gamble that a broken cable will never recoil directly back at them. It's easy to imagine that sometimes they lose.

After the initial dragging is done, the crews climb aboard with ladders and ropes and begin to empty the ship's fuel tanks: they pump the good oil into barrels for resale, and slop the residual sludge of no commercial value onto dry ground, where it is burned. The empty tanks continue to produce volatile vapors, and pose a risk of explosion until they are aerated – a tricky process that often involves cutting ventilation holes. The most experienced cutters are used for this work, because they are believed to have developed noses for dangerous vapors. Even so, there are explosions and fatalities – though fewer now than before, because of slowly improving safety standards. On some ships the tanks can be sliced off whole, dropped into the water, and winched above the tide line for dissection and disposal. Cutting on hard ground is easier than cutting on the ship, and because the workers are therefore more likely to do the job right, it is also safer. But either way, the yard must demonstrate to Gujarat officials that the fuel tanks have been secured and neutralized before they will give the final authorization to proceed with the scrapping.

With the risk of explosion diminished, the breakers turn their attention to the ship's superstructure, the thin-walled quarters that typically rise five or six levels above the main deck, and in which, because of combustible wiring and wood paneling, the chance of a deadly fire cannot be ignored. The superstructure is like a ghost town, still full of the traces of its former inhabitants. Scattered about lie old books and magazines in various languages, nautical charts from faraway oceans, company manuals, years' worth of ship's logs, newspaper clippings, national flags, signal flags, radio frequency lists, union pamphlets, letters, clothes, posters, and sometimes a much-appreciated stock of liquor, narcotics, or pornography. The scrappers spread through the quarters like hungry scavengers, quickly removing the furniture and galley equipment, tearing into the wood paneling and asbestos insulation to get at the valuable plumbing, stripping out the wires, electronics, and instruments, and making a special effort to save the ship's bell, always in demand for use at Hindu temples. These treasures are roped down the side and hustled to the top of the beach by ground crews.

Then the cutting begins. It is surprising how few men are needed to handle the torches: by working simultaneously on the port and starboard sides, a dozen competent cutters, backed up by a larger number of assistants, can demolish an entire superstructure within two weeks. Gravity helps. Starting with the overhanging wings of the bridge, the cutters slice the superstructure into big sections. There is an art to this, because every ship is different. The decisions about where to cut are made by the yard's owner and the all-important shipboard supervisor. Within the logical demolition sequence (which with variations runs roughly from front to back and from top to bottom) the general idea is to cut off the largest section that can be cleared away from the ship by the shore-based winches. The height and geometry of the superstructure is a crucial consideration, because it affects the way the sections fall. If the work has been done right, when the final cut on a section is made, it falls clear of the hull. It lands on the tidal flat with a dull thump. The ground crew walks out to it, attaches a cable, and winches it higher onto the beach to carve it up. Meanwhile, the shipboard crews may already have dropped another section. At this early stage it can be gratifying work. If the superstructure is flimsy, the crews can make the metal rain.

But the work slows when they come to the hull, where the steel is heavier and harder to cut. At that point, even for veteran workers, there must be a moment of hesitation at the audacity of the business. Using little more than cooking gas and muscle power they will tear apart this immense monolith, which towers above the crowds on the sand. It will take six months or a year to finish the job; men will be injured, and some may die. Almost all will to some degree be poisoned by smoke and toxic substances – and more seriously, no doubt, than they would have been on the streets of India's cities. Nonetheless, the poor cannot afford to be timid.

They go after the hull by cutting off the forward section of the bow, opening the ship's cavernous forward hold to the outside, and making room for an expanded force of shipboard cutting crews. Half of them continue to cut at the forward section, slowly moving aft; the other half burrow directly back through the ship, cutting away the internal bulkheads, until they come to the engine room, near the stern. The ship's engine is not usually saved, because generally it is worn out, and in any case it is often too large to be removed whole. The crews open ventilation holes through the sides of the hull, unbolt the engine, disconnect it from the shafts, and cut it apart crudely on the spot. They drag the pieces forward through the length of the ship with the help of small winches placed aboard for that purpose. [. . .]

Sometimes I wandered across the road, into the crowded shantytown where the workers lived, a place with shacks built of wood and ship's paneling, some on stilts over a malarial marsh that bordered the beach. There were no latrines at Alang, in part because few of the men would have used them. They preferred simply to relieve themselves in nearby bushes, as they had in the farming hamlets from which they came. But of course Alang was much larger than a hamlet, and as a result the air there was filled with fecal odors, which mixed with the waves of smoke and industrial dust to permeate the settlement with a potent stench. People got used to it, as they did to the mosquitoes, and the flies. Discomfort was an accepted part of living in Alang, as was disease. Thousands of workers who were sick, injured, or unemployed lingered in the shantytown during the day, lying on scavenged linoleum floors by open doorways, or sitting outside in the thin shade of the walls. There were almost no wives or children. As in other migrant camps, drunkenness, prostitution, and violence were never far away.

Nonetheless, a semblance of normalcy was maintained. For instance, Alang had a good drinking-water system, a network of communal cisterns supplied by truck [. . .] It also had Hindu shrines, informal cricket fields, and enough spare power for its commercial district to run refrigerators and gay little strings of lights. Each evening when the workday was done, the settlement came to life. The workers cooked outside their shacks in small groups intent on the food, and afterward, feeling renewed, they gathered in the light from the cafes and talked. They laughed. They listened to music. Sometimes they held religious processions. Sometimes they danced. And then on Sundays, when by law all the shipbreaking yards were closed, they washed, dressed up, and strolled among friends, looking fresh and clean-cut.

GUATEMALA

The Cane Cutters

Elizabeth Oglesby*

Last year, at 24, Sebastián Tol was a "champion" cane cutter on the agro-export plantations of Guatemala's Pacific coast, averaging over ten tons a day.[†] At the end of the
harvest season, however, he returned home to the highlands with shoulder pain that
made it difficult to do even routine chores. This year, his place on the plantation work
crew was taken by his 18-year-old brother, Santiago, who also has hopes of becoming
a champion. A month before the start of the harvest, Santiago began buying weekly
vitamin injections for half a day's wage each, which he believes will increase his
endurance in the cane fields.

The Guatemalan sugar industry tripled its production over the last two decades, and
Guatemala is now the third-largest sugar exporter in Latin America. This expansion is
due in large part to a modernization campaign designed to raise the productivity of
cane cutters, most of whom are migrant workers from the indigenous highlands. Long
infamous for using extreme violence to quell worker unrest, the sugar plantations in
Guatemala are now devising alternate means to achieve labor discipline, by combining
new technologies with wage incentives, human capital investments and a refashioning
of workers' identities. Central to this strategy is the creation of a subset of "vanguard"
cane cutters: young men generally between the ages of 18 and 25 who are pushed to
compete with each other to reach productivity goals.

Indeed, productivity has soared across the sector. In 1980, cane workers were paid
by the day and would cut between one and two tons per day; last year they were paid by
the ton and the daily average among workers had risen to six tons. Productivity
increases stem from a combination of technical change and a social re-engineering of
the harvest labor force. Technical changes include heavier, curved machetes, mechanical
cane loading and the Taylorization of cane cutting, that is, the use of time-and-motion
studies to break down the labor process into precise, repeatable movements. Taylorist
methods control how a worker holds and swings the machete, and how many movements are used to cut and lay the cane. But plantation managers stress that, beyond
these techniques, a key component is the effort to transform workers' attitudes toward
cane cutting. The plantations' goal is to create new attitudes that they hope will under-
cut opposition to a labor regime that places increasingly severe demands on the bodies
of workers.

---

*From Elizabeth Oglesby, "Machos and Machetes in Guatemala's Cane Fields," *NACLA
Report on the Americas*, 34: 5 (March–April 2001), pp. 16–17.
[†]Sebastián and Santiago are the pseudonyms of two highlands brothers.

One way this is done is through the masculinization of the harvest labor force. Industrial psychologists recruit and train the cane cutters, who are exclusively male and mostly young. Only men are permitted to live in the migrant camps. Food is prepared in industrial kitchens by male cooks, many of whom learned to cook while serving in the army. The new diets are supposed to provide 3,700 calories daily, and they include a careful balance of proteins and carbohydrates to ensure that workers don't lose weight during the harvest. Cane cutters get oral rehydration drinks and health exams. They are weighed periodically, and their muscles are measured. Their bodies and productivity levels are monitored, and all of this information gets recorded in year-by-year databases.

The masculinization of harvest labor is not only about recruiting men, it's also about reinforcing ideas of masculinity among cane cutters. On the one hand, the mills try to create camaraderie in the work camps and a sense that these are spaces where workers can be free from family pressures. Many of the migrant camps have televisions and VCRs, and there are "entertainment nights" with Mexican *vaquero* [cowboy] films or Rambo movies. Exotic dancers are sometimes hired to perform at the camps, and at the end of the harvest, workers are taken on excursions to the beach or to a local cantina. The absence of older male relatives in the camps creates a sense of heightened freedom, a sort of extended adolescence, for younger workers, especially in a region like the coast that abounds with bars and brothels.

On the other hand, management appeals to machismo in its attempt to foment competition around production quotas. Top cane cutters are awarded prizes ranging from T-shirts to tape recorders, bicycles and a grand prize of a motorcycle. Every week management distributes a computer print-out of the top individual cane cutters and their scores. The "engineers," as workers call them, visit the housing camps regularly. "They tell us how great we are, and that we're ahead of all the other fronts," a 21-year-old worker told me. Another worker elaborated, "We're macho here. It's like a fair, when they put a prize on top of a greased pole. Even though you know you can't reach it, you have to try."

In addition to the seemingly universal belief in the power of vitamin B injections, some cane cutters use amphetamines to extend their endurance. But when drugs are used to dull the effects of exhaustion and dehydration, heatstroke becomes a serious danger for workers in the sweltering cane fields. I asked a crew foreman why he thought many cane cutters were working themselves sick. "If you ask them," he said, "they'll probably tell you it's to get the wages, or maybe the prize. But I can tell you that a part of it has to do with the pure competition." The manipulation of masculinity to boost output doesn't erase workers' awareness of exploitation on the plantations, however. Cane cutters complain about the heat, the grueling hours and the belief that the planta-tions constantly cheat them out of their fair pay. "The prizes and all that, it's a bunch of crap," protested one worker with five years experience. "We're the ones who pay for it, with the money they steal from our pay. They give tape recorders, so what? If they would give out a little bit of land, now that would be worth working for!"

There hasn't been a major labor strike in the sugar sector since 1980, at the height of the civil war, and the sugar unions that existed in the 1970s disappeared with the repression. But temporary work stoppages are fairly common at many plantations, and worker turnover is high. Are cane workers "disciplined" by these practices? Many, like Sebastián Tol, pay a high price with broken bodies, but in general, workers' perceptions of the plantations appear to have changed little. The promotion of masculine work identities on the plantations doesn't make workers dislike cutting cane any less, and it doesn't seem to replace class consciousness. But when this is cross-cut by an emphasis on the recruitment of youth, it does create a separate group of workers for whom labor migration to the coast is a sort of multi-year rite of passage and a stepping stone toward aspirations of future US-bound migration.

Sebastián Tol told me that he wasn't thinking of cutting sugar cane anymore. But he had heard from other workers from the coast that in Alabama there were many jobs "cutting chickens," and that if his shoulder would just heal he was going to try his luck in *el norte* [the North].

HONDURAS

The Lobster Divers

Giovanna Tassi*

Lobster fishing off the Honduran Caribbean is a source of livelihood, but also of death and injury. The lack of safety regulations has left nearly half of the Miskito Indian lobster divers physically disabled. This indigenous community in La Mosquitia lives from the lobster catch. The export of the "Panulirus argus" is also one of the most profitable Honduran exports, especially to the United States. In 2002, according to sources at the Honduran Central Bank, lobster exports brought in 31 million dollars in state revenues. Most are sold to the US restaurant chain Red Lobster, whose spokesman states that the company purchases only trap-caught lobsters, not dive-caught.

During the lobster season, from August to May, most of the adult Miskito men dive, while younger males accompany them in small boats known as *cayucos*, floating alongside the bigger lobster boats. Moving from the cayuco to diving is a rite of passage in the Honduran Miskito culture. A study by the Honduran special ombudsman for ethnic groups and cultural heritage, sponsored by the Inter-American Development Bank (IDB), based in Washington, found that there are 4,200 divers living with injuries, nearly half the total Miskito diving population of 9,000.

---

*From Giovanna Tassi, "Death Looms Over Miskito Lobster Divers," InterPress Service, 3 February 2004.

The working conditions of these lobster fisherman violate the most basic safety regulations of professional diving, say the authors of the study. The Miskito men work 12 to 17 days out at sea, in exhausting five-hour diving sessions at depths of 43 meters, and with equipment of poor quality, says the study. This information was confirmed by Oswaldo Munguía, director of the non-governmental organisation Mopawi (an acronym in the Miskito language for La Mosquitia Development Agency), who has been in charge of issues involving the lobster fishermen since the late 1980s.

For many Miskitos, the fact of being an injured diver is the consequence of breaking a "taboo of the sea," Munguía told Tierramérica. According to this community's traditions, the ocean depths are inhabited by Liwa Mairin, similar to the mermaids of other mythologies, who cares for the marine resources and punishes those who take more than their share by casting a spell that causes them injury. The annual death toll among Miskito lobster divers averages around 50, according to several reports.

Munguía cited a failed attempt to open a mobile diving school as a solution to the terrible situation in which the Miskito divers live. That experience "began with 1,500 divers, and the idea was to create a solid and unique organisation, with branches in other areas of La Mosquitia," whose communities are quite isolated from each other, he said. "But the school failed due to the irresponsibility of the Miskito divers. Some of their leaders illegally appropriated the quotas of their fellow divers, and that undermined morale – and killed the initiative," said the activist.

The ombudsman's report states that each diver receives 2.5 dollars for every pound of lobster caught and weighed. The weigher subtracts five per cent of the total weight because it is assumed that the fresh crustaceans hold excess water. In turn, each diver is to pay around 80 cents per pound to the *cayuquero*, the youth at the helm of the cayuco. Out at sea, the one dictating the rules is the captain of the boat. It is he who decides where each crew member will sleep and who controls the distribution of food (usually biscuits), alcoholic beverages and even illegal drugs, in exchange for snails and fish that the divers catch while they are looking for lobsters.

The "Green Guide for the Professional Diver," published by Mopawi and the Moravian Church (which in a joint effort with a language institute established the written Miskito language and a translation of the Bible), warns that the use of drugs like marijuana and cocaine is extremely dangerous for the divers. These illegal drugs, mixed with the air breathed by the divers, and absorbed into the blood, prevent the adequate elimination of nitrogen, and can thus aggravate decompression syndrome. The syndrome is caused by diving too deep or returning to the surface too quickly, leading to a lack of oxygen in the brain and chronic pain, neurological disorders, partial paralysis or even death.

According to Marcio Castellón, director of fishing at the Honduran Secretariat of Agriculture and Livestock, budget restrictions stand in the way of effectively resolving the problem of the Miskito divers, but the agency is working "on a strategic plan for new fishing policies" and revising the "obsolete" law of 1959 that is in force. The fishing industry has expressed willingness to help train the divers, said Castellón. The report from the ombudsman says there are only two decompression chambers in La Mosquitia, but the cost for such treatment is around 300 dollars – far beyond the means of most Miskito lobster divers.

GULF STATES

The Migrants

Socialistworld.net*

Thousands of immigrant workers have been turned into slaves by Arab capitalists and multinational companies (MNCs) in the oil-rich Gulf States. Millions of poor workers from Pakistan, India, Bangladesh, Nepal, Sri Lanka, Egypt and other countries are working in Saudi Arabia, Kuwait, Qatar, and the United Arab Emirates (UAE). For example, in Kuwait there are 200,000 Bangladeshi immigrant workers. These workers came to these countries for a better future, but instead face a completely different situation. The Arab and multinational companies recruit thousands of workers every year from these countries through respective governments and private recruiting agencies. Starving at home because of poverty and unemployment, these desperate workers want to go to the Gulf States to earn money for their families and to improve their living standards.

Local agents and companies offered them decent wages and conditions, but once these workers have arrived their bosses openly violate contracts and promises. [. . .] In the past these workers were silently facing all these horrible conditions and exploitation, but now they have started to show their anger and fight back. The events in Kuwait and UAE are of significant importance.

More than 1,000 workers employed in a cleaning company in Kuwait held a protest demonstration in front of the Bangladeshi Embassy on Sunday 24 April. They were protesting against non-payment of their salaries for the last six months. The angry workers ransacked the Embassy, broke windows and computers. They were demanding the intervention of the Embassy to ensure they received their back pay. According to the police, 5,000 Bangladeshi workers employed in cleaning firm have not been paid for the last six months. They are left with no money or food, and face starvation and extreme poverty. Police arrested 150 workers who were released after investigation.

According to the police, "This is not the first incident of this nature. Last year, 4,000 angry Egyptian workers took to the streets, burnt tyres and ransacked their employer's office. Labor unrest is on the increase in our country, which we never saw in the past. It has become very difficult for us to use state security forces against these protesters,

---

*From "Oil Rich Arab States Are Heaven for Capitalists, But Hell for Workers," www. socialistworld.net, 27 April 2005.

Egyptian migrant workers on a ferry from Nuweiba, Egypt, to Aqaba, Jordan (Adam Jones)

because it can result in more widespread unrest. The companies should take care of their workers; otherwise they will not accept slave conditions and will come out to show their anger." 392 workers from Pakistan employed in a Kuwaiti company were forced to work in Iraq. When they refused to be transferred the company stopped paying them until they agreed to move. A few workers went to Iraq and three of them were kidnapped and then killed by one of the Islamic groups. The other workers were brought back by the company and kept in a camp without being paid any salaries. One worker was able to make contact with his family in Pakistan, who told the story to the Pakistani media. The Pakistani government was forced to make an intervention on their behalf because of the public outcry. Different Kuwaiti and foreign companies have recruited 16,000 workers from Pakistan, with plans of forcibly sending them to Iraq.

The conditions of migrant workers are worst in Kuwait, a tiny country with a population of only 2.7 million, but which controls one-tenth of global oil reserves, and is completely dependent on immigrant workers. The Kuwaiti regime is one of the most vicious in the Gulf, and many of the rulers of these states spend millions of dollars every year to spread the Wahabi brand of Islam to the poor Muslim countries.

One Pakistani worker describes the situation in the following words: "They treat us like slaves and animals. I was a great supporter of these so-called Islamic regimes, but three years' work in Kuwait has forced me to change my opinion. They treat their pets better than us. My experience shows me that all Muslims are not equal and also not brothers. There is clear division on the basis of rich and poor. As a student I always opposed socialism, but now I think we need ideas like that.

"They teach us about great Islamic values in our countries but they are not implementing it in their country. They spend huge amounts on preaching but not paying salaries to workers."

There are hundreds of workers who want to go back to their own countries, but companies are refusing to pay their back salaries to force them to continue to work in slave wage conditions. There are no trade unions, and workers' rights do not exist. Despite the fears of arrest and deportation, workers of different countries are now coming out against slavery, insults, injustices and super-exploitation. Small sections of the most conscious workers are now talking about the formation of illegal workers' committees to defend themselves against the increased onslaught of bosses. This process is at a very early stage of development and will take some time to overcome the difficulties and problems.

The bosses have used religious and national divisions to divide the workers further. It is important to overcome these divisions to develop strong unity amongst the workers. There is no socialist or left force in the country, but if there was one in existence then it could organise these immigrant workers to become a strong political force. The movement for "democratic reform" is weak and also controlled from the top. While a so-called parliament does exist, the real power in the country is around the king and his family, who holds on to power with the help of US imperialism. Women are denied the right to vote.

The tens of thousands of workers, mostly from South Asia, lured by promises of jobs and better life in oil-rich United Arab Emirates suffer in inhuman conditions. As construction firms cash in on the construction boom in the Gulf's trading and tourism hub, most workers receive meagre salaries and sometimes go without pay for months, sparking occasional protests. They live in overcrowded camps on the outskirts of towns, out of sight of the five-star hotels and luxury resorts which lure millions of tourists from around the world to Dubai. Local newspapers have reported cases of suicide by unpaid workers whose families rely on their remittances.

These immigrant workers are the foundation of a rapid development drive that has turned Dubai from a back-water desert state into a bustling metropolis with a futuristic skyline. Dubai and UAE is a dream land for millions of young people in South Asia. They come to this desert state for a better life and future. But they face super-exploitation and slave wages. They work without wages for months. The situation is worst in the construction industry, which employs the largest numbers of workers. Most of these workers take loans to come to UAE, which they have to repay from the money they will earn here. They cannot go back without sending the money back home to repay the loan. They work for 200 to 300 dirhams per month, which is not enough for them to live on. They live in shacks made up of rows of cement blocks with balconies draped with laundry. On average each housing unit is shared by 12 men, in which they sleep in shifts. The workers say power and water supplies are erratic. They work in very unsafe and dangerous conditions. There are no safety measures or facilities. The non-payment of wages has become so common that even the government has been forced to intervene, after workers started demonstrations to force the employers to pay salaries.

The government Labor Ministry figures show an increase in workers' struggles. According to these figures workers in 24 different companies staged demonstrations and walkouts in the last 16 months. As well as withholding salaries in order to repay loans, the bosses also stop paying wages between different building jobs. According to the ILO regional office in Lebanon, "The UAE is in process of making new labor laws to allow the workers to form unions. We are helping the government to amend the labor laws." These amendments are not being proposed because of a sudden change of heart by the bosses but in order to qualify for a proposed free trade agreement with foreign companies who are scared of the effect of the bad publicity surrounding such barbaric practices.

The ILO office also said that "the country needs to revise its sponsorship system and ensure new regulations are implemented. Gulf countries should look into issues of wages and social and health protection. Workers should be part of a system where their rights are protected. We want to warn all the Gulf states that they should realize the situation and act accordingly, otherwise they will have to face a workers' backlash, which we are trying to avoid. We think the situation is more explosive than the governments realize. If conditions continue like this they will not be able to control the situation very long and there will be more workers' protests." Two years ago workers showed their strength when Pakistani and Indian workers employed in a construction company went on strike for three days; they occupied the construction site and forced the company to accept their demands. In this struggle workers showed their strength and ability to overcome divisions on the basis of religion, nationality and language.

Immigrant workers have had their dreams of a better life and future destroyed. One 37-year-old Egyptian worker, Abdul-Aziz Taha said: "My hopes of a better life have been crushed. We came here to make a living but instead we are in ruins." A Pakistani worker, Hamid, commented: "We toil in scorching heat and high humidity for most of the year. It is very tough to work in this heat, and many workers faint during the work. I am here for nine years and will not be able to go back to my country for many more." One Nepalese worker said: "I paid 5,000 dirham to come here. The agent promised good facilities and wages, but he lied and destroyed my life." An Indian worker described the situation in these words: "I came here fifteen years ago to earn money for my family, but I failed to earn this money and am still living in this hell."

UNITED ARAB EMIRATES

The Camel Jockeys

Phil Reeves*

For one so small, Amir Hossein Rubel knows far more than any child should about the world. He knows about loneliness, hunger, extreme danger and fear. Above all, he knows about betrayal. He, and scores of other little boys like him, have been bought and sold for sport.

Rubel is 12, although he looks seven. He is at the beginning of life but has the hard-bitten air of someone reaching its end. Rubel's ordeal continues now, many months after his rescue. In his damp-blistered safe house in Dhaka there is an iron grille and a padlock on the entrance and a guard on the gate. No one wants him to fall back into the hands of those who preyed on him.

The predators in question are the organised gangs who spirited him away from his family in Bangladesh, smuggled him to the United Arab Emirates (UAE), and set him to work as a camel racing jockey. He was sold into the service of an extremely hazardous sport where the animals who run change hands for 100 times more than the monthly pittance earned by the children who ride them.

Rubel was five when he was abducted. He could not ride a bicycle, let alone an animal four times his height, galloping at a potentially lethal 30 mph. Nor could Mintu Shuel. He was four when he was heaved onto a camel with a whip in his hand and a walkie-talkie strapped to his chest so that his trainers could bellow out orders for him to ride faster. Now 10, Mintu has the wizened air of a professional. His memory of race days suggests that the use of infant jockeys was scarcely a state secret. There were "huge crowds" who "had big cars and video cameras."

What Alom, another survivor who is now 13, recalls best is the hunger. The smaller the jockey, the swifter and more profitable the camel. This is a world where pampered champion animals can fetch $1 m and are trained in their own lap pools. But, God forbid if the boys should put on an extra ounce. The three boys now live in sheltered accommodation, survivors of a trade which human rights organisations say still continues. Yet the authorities involved continue to turn a blind eye.

Rubel unfolds his memories in scraps, a grim little collection from the darkest corners of a child's mind. He answers questions dutifully, but volunteers nothing. He neither flinches nor warms to a pat on the arm and to other attempts to comfort and reassure him. He avoids my gaze. His misery, it seems, cannot easily be shared with an outsider.

---

*From Phil Reeves, "Stolen, Smuggled and Sold: The Frightened Boys Forced to Become Camel Jockeys in a Foreign Land," *The Independent*, 29 October 2003.

But slowly the pieces fall into place. He remembers the day a woman befriended his penniless mother and then moved into a hut in his village. He remembers going to the same woman's house to play with her son and staying the night. The next thing he recalls was waking up to find he and the woman were on an aeroplane. Rubel remembers how, once in Dubai, the same woman pretended she was his real mother. He was handed over to some men and remembers how the soles of his tiny feet burned on the sand when they took him out to the desert to ride the camels. The training was hard and frightening. "If we fell off the camels, the trainers would beat us. Mostly they were rude to us. Only sometimes they were nice."

Rubel once saw another child slip from his perch behind the camel's hump as it was bumping along. The boy fell to the ground and was trampled by the hooves of the other animals. Rubel and his fellow child jockeys slept on the ground in tents, rising before dawn to tend to the camels. Occasionally they were allowed to buy sweets with the tips they were given for winning a race.

Listening to Rubel, or Amir Hossein Rubel as he is formally known, you have to remind yourself he is a child. Nothing about his early childhood in the deserts of the Middle East resembles that of a Western child. There were no toys, no televisions, no books, no computer games, and no love. There was the odd game of cricket in the dust, using an old piece of wood for a bat, with other infant jockeys. But that was it. Meals for his group of jockeys, taken three times a day, were spartan. Rice and bread were strictly rationed by their "masters," the trainers, especially on race day.

The camel jockey issue has been threatening to dent UAE's image as the thriving business nexus of the Persian Gulf, an oasis of five-star beach hotels, shopping malls and golf courses. Yet authorities continue to ignore the scandal. [...] The human rights group Anti-Slavery International insists that boys from Bangladesh, Pakistan and Sudan are still being trafficked. "We continue to receive reports," said Catherine Turner, a spokeswoman. "Children [who have returned] commonly confirm there are other young boys still in these camps, suggesting this is the tip of the iceberg."

BRAZIL

The Slaves

Osha Gray Davidson[*]

On the day of the raid, Guilherme Moreira awakens before dawn in a seedy motel room in the Brazilian town of Palmas and tries not to think about all the people who want

---

[*]From Osha Gray Davidson, "Heart of Darkness," *Rolling Stone*, 8 September 2005.

him dead. It's nothing personal – none of the rich landowners, crooked politicians, dirty cops and hired gunmen who have it in for him have even met him. But that fact provides little comfort. They've killed his kind before, and if they get a chance, they'll do it again.

Moreira gets out of bed and pulls on a gray T-shirt and stonewashed jeans, the same thing he wears on weekends back home in Rio [de Janeiro], 1,500 miles away. A small silver hoop glints from his left ear. No uniforms on a day like this. Uniforms only make you a target. Then he goes outside to check on the weapons.

In the predawn darkness, Moreira can make out the outline of two duffel bags in back of the Ford F-150. The 4x4 is as ordinary-looking as they come: white, unmarked, fitted with local plates for an extra measure of anonymity. The bags are stuffed with 9 mm semi-automatics and .38-caliber revolvers and a stack of bulletproof vests. For insurance, there is a pair of Heckler and Koch MP5K submachine guns, along with enough hollow-point ammo to hold off an entire platoon.

The weapons have been standard issue for Moreira's *grupo movel* – a federal "mobile squad" – ever since four of his colleagues were gunned down on a dirt road in a brutal ambush. The men had stopped to help a motorist who appeared to be having engine trouble; a group of armed thugs suddenly appeared from hiding and opened fire on them, executing the squad leader with two shots to the head. When the gunmen were later captured, they confessed that the "King of Beans" – Norberto Manica, Brazil's largest bean grower – had paid them $17,000 to kill the federal squad. The agents, it turned out, had raided one of Manica's farms. They weren't looking for drugs, or guns, or laundered money. They were looking for evidence that Manica was using forced labor – the official government term for slaves.

Although Brazil outlawed slavery in 1888, landowners like Manica continue to hold thousands of men captive in the vast scrublands of Brasil Profundo – Deep Brazil – a desolate, sun-scorched region that sprawls across a million square miles in the country's vast interior. It's a brutal, lawless land, where drugs and small arms flow north through the "cocaine corridor" and mahogany and other rare woods stripped from the rain forest make their way to American furniture showrooms. Here, on huge cattle ranches and farms known as *fazendas*, enslaved men are forced to work without pay from sunrise to sunset under inhumane conditions. Those who refuse to follow orders are beaten and tortured; those who demand payment or attempt to flee are killed, their bodies mutilated and dumped in unmarked graves. Human-rights advocates in Brazil have documented the murders of more than 1,200 forced laborers, and many more killings are passed off as farming mishaps. One recent "accident" victim, a twenty-year-old named Carlos Dias, was killed by a bullet fired into his eye. "It's like your Wild West," Moreira says. "In the hinterland, the landowner is king." [. . .]

The process from freedom to bondage begins when a contractor known as the *gato* – the cat – enters the slums flashing a big smile and a wad of bills. Hired by the landowners to shield themselves from legal responsibility, the gato promises wealth to any man who'll climb onto his truck – and even a few reais to tide their families over until they return, pockets stuffed with cash. In minutes the flatbed is full and headed out of town. The men travel for hundreds or even thousands of miles. Days pass. Along the way, the gato gives them food and hands out bottles of cheap *cachaça*, a 140-proof liquor nicknamed *mijo de cão* – "dog piss." The men think he's being a good guy, but the gato's plan is to keep them so drunk that they won't remember how they got to their destination, whether it's an isolated fazenda on the *cerrado* or a labor camp in the rain forest.

By the time the hungover men climb off the truck, the gato is shouting at them, telling them that they each owe him a lot of money – for the advances he gave their families, for the ride to the work site, for the sandwiches on the trip, for the "dog piss" they drank. No one can leave, he declares, without paying off their debts – and the debts will continue to grow with every day the men work. If anyone tries to protest, guards with huge revolvers stuck into their belts are present to discourage complaints. The men are now slaves. [...]

It's 1:30, more than an hour behind schedule, when Moreira and his men finally jolt to a stop in front of a large ranch house. Several young cowboys sit on a shaded porch. Moreira and the rest of the squad are out of the trucks in seconds. The cowboys start joking with each other, as if this kind of thing happens all the time, but it's clearly an act. This fazenda has never been raided, and the cops are intimidating as hell in dark sunglasses, ninja-black Kevlar vests with POLICIA FEDERAL in bright yellow on the back, submachine guns slung over their shoulders. Ignoring the cowboys, the squad heads down a path to a smaller house of whitewashed concrete blocks. A man with an enormous gut and the squashed features of a failed boxer is sitting on the porch. He climbs heavily to his feet as the squad surrounds him.

Someone asks his name. "Adail Pereira da Silva," he responds in a gravely voice.

"The gato," Moreira whispers to me. He asks da Silva, "Where are the workers?"

The gato swears he doesn't know. Maybe out in the fields.

"Where?" Moreira insists. The gato makes a show of scratching his head and looking around, as if it might be possible from the porch to spot the workers on the ranch's 22 square miles. The reality is, they could be anywhere. The gato, alerted that the squad was on the way, could have ordered them to leave or had them driven miles from the fazenda.

"Someone tipped him off," Moreira growls under his breath and stalks off.

A high-stakes waiting game begins. Moreira and the gato both know that the clock started ticking the moment the squad arrived. With so much territory to cover, the federal team has only one shot at Santa Tereza. They either find the workers today – and proof that the men are being held as slaves – or they will be forced to move on to other ranches, abandoning the workers to their fate. For now, all the squad can do is wait to see if the workers come back, as the sun slowly sinks toward the horizon.

Two hours later, Moreira sees a sight that makes him smile. The men begin returning from the fields in groups of twos and threes. They are dressed in rags, covered with sweat and grime, and carrying scythes. They stumble down a path in a nearby pasture, heading straight for the gato's house. Now it is the overseer's turn to scowl.

The workers drop their tools and collapse on the porch. Twigs and bits of dried grass crown their heads and seem to sprout from their clothes. Their hands are the stuff of nightmares – palms crisscrossed by cuts, some scarred over, some fresh and raw, others oozing pus. One man is missing a finger. Another man's hands have been recast by work, stiffened like a claw into the shape of the tool handle he clutches all day in the terrific heat.

Moreira identifies himself as a labor inspector and sits down on the porch with a sigh, like a neighbor who has just dropped by to visit. Getting workers to talk is often the hardest part of a raid; the overseer has likely threatened to kill anyone who speaks to the authorities. But Moreira seems genetically engineered for the task. He's average height, with a heavy build and a flicker of sadness in his eyes, his T-shirt untucked and agreeably rumpled – a disheveled Columbo with a Brazilian accent.

Moreira looks at the men slumped around him on the porch. He knows that one of them probably holds the key to the raid's success or failure. At most ranches, one man has earned the trust and respect of his fellow workers and serves as an unofficial leader for the entire camp. "If that guy starts talking," Moreira likes to say, "so will everyone else."

Moreira scans the group. If there is a leader here, it isn't obvious. He turns to a tall, painfully thin man crouched beside him. "It is," Moreira says, drawing out his words, "so . . . fucking . . . hot!"

The man smiles slightly.

Moreira speaks to another man wearing the tattered jersey of a professional soccer team – one that's having a very bad season. "Aren't you ashamed to be seen in that shirt?" he teases. A small ripple of laughter spreads through the group.

A few yards away, one man isn't laughing. He's older than the rest and seems oblivious to the banter. Beneath a mud-splattered STP cap, his face is broad, with startling green eyes and a pencil-thin mustache that has gone white. He leans against the house, his muscular arms folded across his chest in a manner that suggests either self-confidence or defensiveness. Moreira knows there could be lots of explanations for the man's detachment. He could be weary. Or a loner. Or sick. Or simply frightened, feigning indifference to mask his terror. Each explanation has its own logic, but none feels right to Moreira.

Then it strikes him: this is a guy who doesn't make small talk. [. . .]

Moreira immediately stops kidding around. Without a smile or any preamble, he turns to the older man and puts the question to him directly: "What's it like working here?"

The man, whom I'll call Carlos Vilela, glances at Moreira's clipboard and hesitates. On the ranch, everyone in authority works for the landowner. Off the ranch, no one in authority ever exhibited much concern about the fate of enslaved workers. Vilela seems to be weighing the risks. Then, in a voice loud enough for the other men to hear, he says, "It's terrible."

It isn't a complaint. There's no self-pity in his voice or any sign of outrage on his face. He might as easily have said, "The sky is blue." It's a simple statement of fact, and a few of the other men nod in agreement. Moreira asks Vilela if he is willing to give a formal statement about the conditions.

Vilela removes his cap. "Of course," he replies.

The other workers immediately follow Vilela's lead and begin volunteering statements, just as Moreira had hoped.

As the men talk, an ugly picture of life on the fazenda emerges. At sixty-two, Vilela is the most articulate of the 31 slaves in the camp. He has been working on ranches since he was ten. Santa Tereza, he says, is the worst he's seen.

"I've never been on a fazenda where the debts are so high," he tells Moreira. Vilela hasn't received a real in the five months he's been here. When the workers are paid at all, he says, it's in the form of scrip – handwritten IOUs redeemable for goods only at a single store in a distant town. The gato periodically takes all the scrip to the store and returns with the items that the workers requested. But prices have a way of inflating during the drive to the store. The cost of tobacco may double, and then the scrip falls short of the purchase. The difference enters the gato's account book as more debt that the worker must pay off before he's allowed to leave.

The men work the fields at least ten hours a day, six days a week, regardless of the weather. They are fed beans and rice, with a few scraps of meat, which are often spoiled or from diseased animals. Water comes from a well only a few feet from a filthy squat toilet – a hole in the ground – and the men carry the water to the fields in plastic jugs with pesticide labels still on them. By law, the ranch owner must provide safety equipment, but there's nothing like that here. Only a lucky few own shoes, let alone boots. Most go to the fields in the kind of cheap plastic flip-flops that Vilela has on – with predictable results. The second toe on Vilela's right foot curls completely under his other toes. When I ask him about it, he explains that he was cutting down a tall tree during the rainy season, and the axe glanced off the slippery wood, slicing into his foot. The toe was nearly severed, and Vilela wrapped the whole mess in rags. He considers himself lucky because the toe remained attached.

A doctor might have been able to set the toe right, but few of the men here have ever received professional health care of any kind. Forced laborers die from a long list of serious but treatable diseases, including malaria, yellow fever, tuberculosis and dysentery, and all kinds of parasites. Even rest isn't an option for the sick. Vilela recalls the one time he was so ill that he wanted to stay in his hammock. The gato ordered him to the fields. "If you're well enough to eat my food," the gato bellowed at him, "you're well enough to work!" When a slave becomes too sick to work, he's dumped out on the cerrado, where he either gets better or dies.

After taking Vilela's statement, Moreira inspects the unpainted wooden shack where the men sleep. It doesn't look so bad from across the field. Inside, however, the place is an oven. The only windows are holes cut in the wall, and even these are shuttered over. A single bulb dangling from a wire provides just enough light to make out bugs scuttling across the broken concrete floor. There's no furniture, only frayed hammocks, stretched from wall to wall in tiers from the floor to the ceiling. It resembles the hold of a slave ship. I count the hammocks; sixteen men are squeezed into this tiny, airless box.

Moreira paces the room, taking notes for his report. He gets more agitated with each infraction he sees, shaking his head and muttering under his breath. Finally, he reaches some internal breaking point. "You know what pisses me off?" he erupts, his anger landing like a hammer on certain words. "I've been in barns on ranches. They don't look like this. They're clean. Modern. What really pisses me off is when the owners take better care of their animals than their workers." He takes a deep breath, and his sardonic smile quickly returns. "Of course, good cows bring good prices," he says. "Human beings, on the other hand, are very, very cheap." [...]

That night, Moreira and the rest of the squad decide they have enough evidence to prosecute the owner of [the fazenda] on 31 counts of forced labor. The next day, the owner is ordered to show up at the civic building at the center of the closest town. Tubal da Silva Neto arrives with his lawyer, clutching a plastic grocery bag stuffed with tens of thousands of reais – the back pay he owes the workers. He looks like a successful American businessman – mid-fifties, tall, expensive haircut, clothes that are casual but tasteful. He refuses to acknowledge that he has held other men in bondage. "I'm good to my workers," he insists. "If there's a problem, it's the gato's fault." But after hours of negotiations with Moreira, he agrees to pay the workers what he owes them.

What unfolds next is a scene that has happened only a few times in a world in which tens of millions of people continue to be held in slavery. One by one, each worker comes forward to sign a form. Most can't read or write and must place a thumbprint on the signature line. When it's Vilela's turn, he declines the ink pad and picks up a pen. It takes him more than a minute to sign his name, but he does it. Once he has signed, da Silva, seated at a desk, hands him a stack of reais. It's the equivalent of $1,300 – a small fortune here. The slave owner is paying the slave. Da Silva stares intently at a ledger open before him, refusing to look at Vilela. As other workers follow, he does the same thing with each of them: just when it's time to pay up, something in the ledger demands his attention.

Out on the sidewalk, a kind of carnival atmosphere prevails as the workers waiting for their names to be called greet those exiting the building with cheers and thumps on the back. A man in a battered straw hat and no teeth comes out. He's trembling as he shakes hands with every inspector and cop in the mobile squad, thanking them again and again: "*Obrigado, obrigado, obrigado.*"

When Vilela emerges, the workers swarm around him as if he's a member of the squad who freed them. He dutifully shakes hands all around but maintains his poise. I ask Vilela what he plans on doing with all the money he's been paid. He says he'll buy a small farm where he'll live with his wife and children and raise crops.

Vilela searches out Moreira and thanks him. The two men talk briefly and shake hands before parting. Then the former slave walks off down the sidewalk, softly whistling a tune that rises above the barking of stray dogs and the bad music coming from the cafe down the street.

Moreira watches him go. He knows there are countless men like Vilela still enslaved on ranches across Brazil. But despite all he has seen, Moreira doesn't believe in the devil – only in humanity. "Whatever is done by man can be changed by man," he says. "So I do what I can and hope for the best."

BURMA/THAILAND

The Sex Worker

Bangkok Post*

When Myint Tha was quite young, he left his family in a tiny village in Burma's Shan State, and sneaked across the border at Thachilek to find a job in Chiang Rai's Mae Sai district. He dreamed of a secure future in Thailand. He said to himself: "Many teenage Burmese, even girls, have taken a risk to make money in this land. So why shouldn't I . . . as a man . . . try it?" At that time he was still naïve and didn't realise that many of those teenagers, and especially the girls, were not entering into a "respectful [sic] type of job."

Seven years later, at the age of 23, Myint Tha's innocence has long since fled. He now spends most nights at a gay bar in the tourist destination of Chiang Mai, 300 kilometers from Thakhilek. He survives from week to week by having sex with older men.

Miss Duang (her Thai name), a 20-year-old Chinese Burmese, celebrated her third anniversary of working nights at another Chiang Mai beer bar by supplying a customer with drinks and then going to bed with him, much like any other night. Miss Duang observed that in those three years she has seen an increase in the number of men willing to have sex with a stranger for money. "Numerous boys are selling their bodies now. There are many more than I saw back when I first came here," Miss Duang says. She says it is not surprising to hear about another new bar soon to be opened for gays. She adds that many Burmese boys go into prostitution. "Besides Thais and Burmese, I hardly see male sex workers of other nationalities," she said.

A few months ago, a Perspective reporter met another young Burmese, Kyaw Tun, 16, at a small newly opened nightclub with flashing decorations off Ratchadapisek Road in the heart of Bangkok. He was practising dance steps along with dozens of young men, several of whom were presumed to be non-Thai.

Kyaw Tun said, in Thai, "A guy here approached me and offered me a job at this place . . . which is soon to be opened as a nightclub for females." But it is understood by all but perhaps some of the dancers that the new dance arena is expected to receive homosexuals as their main customers, not females as claimed.

"I didn't know any dancing steps before. They (the management) arranged for danc-ing instructors to teach me and the others," the boy said. "Dancing is enjoyable, it isn't a hard job. I was promised three or four hundred baht a night. Working at a food garden (his earlier job in Samut Prakarn) earned me only half of that," the boy said. [. . .]

Educated Burmese have a relatively easy road to start a decent new life in Thailand. For the less educated, and young, there is much less opportunity. The massage parlors and nightclubs offer a greater attraction than the long exhausting hours in the factories

---

*From "Out of the Frying Pan Into the Sleaze," Bangkok Post, 16 December 2001.

and the fields. "That's the best chance for them to earn quick money and survive," a social worker says.

A major question is whether those who enter into prostitution are forced or do so of their own free will. When asked, one Burmese boy at a bar in Chiang Rai answered: "I have never been forced to do it." But he implied that the hardships of his life forced him indirectly. "I think that the boys who come to work here (at the bar) are forced by poverty but not physically." In his view, the beginnings of male prostitution are different than for many women. He thinks many girls are physically forced into prostitution. "For men? I'm quite sure it is rare." [. . .]

The story told over and over to Perspective was that most of the youths voluntarily entered the sex industry when they felt they had no other choices. Said one Burmese boy in Chiang Mai: "My friend and I came here with a small sum of money we had saved together. It was really only enough for transportation. We couldn't get a job right away. Later we borrowed from Thai friends at an interest rate of 10 per cent a month. So, we tried every way possible to make money to pay back the debts. We worked on a farm for a while but didn't make enough to pay back the debt (of several thousand baht).

He continued, "In my case, I met another Thai who knows the (sex) industry. He helped me to get a job at a bar and later persuaded me and several others to earn extra money by sleeping with customers," he says. Since there seemed no other way to pay off the debts, he was persuaded much more easily.

Another boy said that the wages paid by the bars weren't enough to survive on if they didn't go with customers. "The standard 50 baht a night (excluding food) isn't enough," he said. He also said that the bar owner takes a commission from his charge for his services in addition to the bar fee the customer pays him (the owner) for allowing the boy to leave the bar. "If I go out with a client, the owner charges the client a 300 baht bar-fee, and collects another 1,000 baht for my services. When I collect my money from the bar owner the next day I get only 800 baht."

Several of the Burmese boys told Perspective that most of the money they earn goes to paying debts and personal expenses. Only once in a while do they have much spending money in their pocket, if they are lucky enough to have more than a few clients in a week or get extra money from wealthy customers.

One boy said that his clients are mostly foreigners from Japan, Hong Kong, China or the West. "I try to save and send money home to my family. They think I work in a factory."

Illegal foreign workers, be they male or female, have more problems with the police, and are more easily abused because others can always threaten them with going to the police. They face discrimination and abuse in many occupations because they are powerless to complain to authorities. And legal or not, they are allowed to work in some specified jobs, but not in many others.

One Burmese working at a bar in Chiang Rai says: "If you are Burmese, you get lower income and you don't have many rights. We always fear being found by police and arrested." [. . .] Another said, "Sometimes the police arrest us just to get our money."

Others talked about sexual assault and misconduct by clients. "A (Burmese) friend of mine told me that when some clients found out that he was not Thai they abused him and made him do things of a sexual nature he didn't want to do."

Bar owners also take advantage of their vulnerability; they are often paid very low wages, made to work very long hours and do all kinds of extra work at the bar like cleaning and maintenance. "The bar owners can be cruel to us. They know they've got more power over Burmese boys," said another boy in Chiang Rai.

The abuse from so many corners drives them to seek protection from gangsters, or mafia, who sometimes have influence with the police. The "protectors" want something in return, of course. "We have to entertain them with drink and food when we have money," said one young man caught between the police "who enforce the laws" and the mafia "who take care of us." "Thai workers don't have to go through this."

Lack of knowledge of their adopted country is also a problem: "We may learn something about Thailand, but it will never be enough. We're not natives. Some of us don't understand the language. I believe many of us face the same kinds of problems. We don't really know the system here." [. . .]

Past midnight at a smoke-filled gay bar in Chiang Mai, young men in tight swimming suits perform an erotic dance on the stage. With smiles painted on their faces, the dancers await a hoped-for call by a client.

On this Friday night, nearly a hundred customers pack the bar – *farang* [westerners], Hong Kong Chinese, Japanese and Thais drinking and watching. Scanning the young men under the spotlight, the drunken customers don't think of the young men's backgrounds or the hardship of their lives. They're measuring the curve of their bodies and calculating the prices.

Amidst the blasting heavy metal music and the changing color of the smoke in the flashing lights, a boy sips his drink and tells the reporter in a loud and bright voice his hopes for the future: "Even though I have gone to bed with so many men . . . I still want to have a girlfriend. I want to marry . . . to have my own family – a wife and children."

MEXICO

The Sewer-Divers

Marla Dickerson*

The rainy season is fast approaching, when downpours will swamp this region's rickety drainage system. The only thing standing between 20 million residents and streets filled

---

*From Marla Dickerson, "Diving to Keep a City's Sewage on the Move," *The Los Angeles Times*, 17 April 2003. Thanks to David Buchanan for bringing this source to the editor's attention.

with raw sewage may be Julio Cu. Cu is a professional diver, but his domain is neither the rolling Pacific nor the glittering Caribbean. He is part of a small team of frogmen who submerge themselves deep into the bowels of Mexico's City's sewer system to perform some of the filthiest, most frightening plumbing chores imaginable.

Like the Dutch boy who plugged the leaky sea wall with his finger, Mexico City's sewer divers are a last line of defense against a threatening tide. "Too many people and too much waste," said Cu, neatly summarizing the messy task that confronts him daily in one of the world's most densely populated urban zones. Floating in a sea of human waste and industrial chemicals, he and three compatriots unplug pipes, repair pumps and pull the occasional cadaver from canals to keep the *aguas negras*, or black waters, flowing. As if the job weren't difficult enough, they do it completely by feel, groping in liquid so murky that flashlights are useless. The work is dangerous, poorly paid and virtually unknown to millions of Mexicans whose shoes are all the drier for the frogmen's efforts.

To his knowledge, no other dive team works exclusively in the sewers. But then no place can match Mexico City for world-class plumbing problems. Perched 7,350 feet above sea level in a valley surrounded by mountains, the area is essentially a closed basin with poor drainage and a propensity for flooding and earthquakes. Once dotted with shallow lakes and marshes, the valley was siphoned by the conquering Spanish to create more land for their colonial capital. Today, drinking water must be pumped from distant rivers as well as from an underground aquifer whose rapid depletion is causing the city to sink.

Meanwhile, sewage must be pumped up and out of this concave bowl. It adds up to tremendous stress on a fragile drainage system already straining to keep pace with the burgeoning population. "Mexico City is famous for its air pollution, but our water problems are actually worse," said Homero Aridjis, a prominent environmental activist. "You walk the streets, smell the stench of raw sewage and can only imagine what's happening underground." Unlike wealthier cities, which have separate waste and storm water networks, Mexico City has a single collection system that can fill to bursting during heavy summer rains. Spotty enforcement of environmental regulations means that factories and hospitals routinely dump hazardous material down the sewers, where it mingles with human waste, street garbage and other urban runoff.

Most of this effluent isn't treated before disposal. Instead, the raw sewage is channeled north out of the city via open-air canals to be used for crop irrigation in the state of Hidalgo. It's a Faustian bargain for the region's farmers, who desperately need the water, but who have contracted cholera, parasites and other illnesses from using it on their fields. "We're trying to educate people about the risks," said Ana Maria Tavarez, director of health services for the state of Hidalgo.

Mexico City's divers need no such reminders. Gravely aware that each dip into the aguas negras could cause sickness, injury or worse, they encase themselves in waterproof armor to limit their exposure to the poison that surrounds them. Having respect for "the monster" is the key to surviving it, says Cu, 42, who has spent half his life in the sewers. After all these years "I still have fear," Cu said. "We never know what we're going to encounter below." Inside a cluttered storage compound of the municipal water works department, beneath a drawing of a diver kneeling before the Virgin Mary, the frogmen show off the equipment to which they entrust their lives. It starts with a bright red "dry suit," a one-piece, synthetic-rubber garment complete with boots. Waterproof gloves come next, lashed firmly to the wrists with plenty of duct tape. A rubbery turtleneck is pulled over the throat to keep sewage from trickling under the collar. It also serves as a cushion for a steel-titanium alloy helmet that encases the head and locks snugly around the neck. The divers carry no tanks on their backs. Instead, a breathing hose connects them to an air supply on the surface. A two-way radio inside the helmet allows the submerged frogmen to communicate with co-workers up top. Once they resurface, they use gallons of chemical disinfectant to sanitize their bodies and equipment on the spot.

The current four-man team has sustained no injuries beyond a few cuts and eye infections. The work is physically demanding. Yet the divers say the biggest hurdles are psychological – accepting that they are literally swimming in the scatological dregs of society.

"Water is water," said Cu's partner, Carlos Barrios, 47, tapping an index finger on his temple. "The problems are up here in your head." He and the other divers know the inner workings of Mexico City's 6,000-mile labyrinth of pipes and canals more intimately than the engineers who created it. Unable to see in the brackish water, they have memorized the design of pumps, motors, drains and other equipment so they can repair them by feel.

They also remove garbage. Lots of it. Plastic bottles are the most common culprit slowing the sewage flow. But the divers have encountered all manner of junk, including mattresses, furniture, water tanks, trees, even half a Volkswagen that had to be cut up and lifted out in sections. Despite rumors of alligators and sea monsters lurking in the city's entrails, the frogmen swear they have never encountered another living thing. They have, however, run across plenty of dead ones: dogs, cats, birds, goats, pigs, sheep and cows among them. That grim list extends to human beings. Cu estimates his team has recovered more than a dozen bodies for police.

BRAZIL

The Organ Seller

Larry Rohter*

When Alberty José da Silva heard he could make money, lots of money, by selling his kidney, it seemed to him the opportunity of a lifetime. For a desperately ill 48-year-old woman in Brooklyn whose doctors had told her to get a kidney any way she could, it was.

---

*From Larry Rohter, "Tracking the Sale of a Kidney on a Path of Poverty and Hope," *The New York Times*, 23 May 2004.

At 38, Mr. da Silva, one of 23 children of a prostitute, lives in a slum near the airport here [in Recife], in a flimsy two-room shack he shares with a sister and nine other people. "As a child, I can remember seven of us sharing a single egg, or living for day after day on just a bit of manioc meal with salt," Mr. da Silva said in an interview. He recalled his mother as a woman who "sold her flesh" to survive. Last year he decided that he would, too. Now, a long scar across his side marks the place where a kidney and a rib were removed in exchange for $6,000, paid by middlemen in an international organ trafficking ring.

Among poor men like Mr. da Silva and others who have migrated to slums here from Brazil's parched northeastern backlands, word of the market to sell their organs spread quickly. Some who had done so were already buying houses, businesses, cars and refrigerators. The sums being offered seemed a fortune. The minimum wage here is barely $80 a month, and work is hard to find. Many men struggle to exist on odd jobs that pay barely a dollar a day. Initially, the organ brokers paid as much as $10,000 for a kidney – more than a decade's wages. Donors and recipients were not related, in contrast to the usual preference for legal and medical reasons. In fact, they did not even know each other. But they were linked by a trafficking ring that the authorities now say exploited two very different sets of needs – for money and for life itself – at opposite ends of a tangled chain thousands of miles long.

Tracing the journey of Mr. da Silva's kidney through that chain, which spanned four continents and ended in a one-bedroom apartment in Brooklyn, reveals the inner workings of a network that human rights groups say is by no means unique. Rather, they say, it is representative of a global black market for organs, including livers, kidneys and lungs, that touches dozens of countries and generates many millions of dollars a year.

In Alberty da Silva's case, the authorities here say, the organ's odyssey began with two middlemen based in this gritty port city of 1.5 million people: Gedalya Tauber, a former Israeli police officer, and his partner, Ivan Bonifacio da Silva, a retired Brazilian military police officer. The pair, since jailed on organ trafficking charges, not only handed out cash payments [. . .] but also arranged for the medical exams to weed out unqualified donors. They then obtained passports and airline tickets for the donors to travel to South Africa, where the transplants took place. Both countries have laws against commercial trade in organs.

"Six grand is a lot of money, especially when you don't have any," Mr. da Silva said when asked why he had given up his kidney. "No one here warned us that what we were doing was illegal."

The American woman who received Mr. da Silva's kidney initially worried that what she was doing might be illegal. She described herself as deeply religious and concerned with the ethics of transplants. But during an interview [. . .] she also recalled the long years of suffering that made her take the risk of seeking an organ on the international market. The decision to go abroad for a kidney, she said at her third-floor walk-up apartment in Brooklyn, was not an easy one, but necessary nonetheless.

"I had been on dialysis for 15 years and on two transplant lists for 7," said the woman, who asked not to be identified by name, for fear of losing support payments vital to maintaining the health of her transplanted organ. "Nothing was happening, and my health was getting worse and worse." Finally, she said, "my doctors told me to get a kidney any way I could," or expect to die.

She took their warning seriously. The years of dialysis had left her with worsening heart and lung problems. She also suffered from severe osteoporosis. "I had seen four other ladies that I knew pass away" while they waited for kidney donors, she said. More than 3,300 Americans died last year awaiting kidney transplants, and the Brooklyn woman was among 85,000 people on waiting lists in the United States, 60,000 of them in need of kidneys. The average wait can be five years [...].

In the case of the Brooklyn woman, her husband had relatives in Israel who had heard of a syndicate that brokered transplants, and reached out to them. The woman and her husband said that relatives and the brokers reassured them that an operation abroad would be perfectly legal. "I felt helpless, because she was going to die," said the woman's husband, who is in such fragile health himself that he receives disability payments. "Helping her get that kidney was the best thing that I have ever done for anyone in my entire life." [...]

In the mid-1990s, many of the Israeli organ brokers took their patients to Turkey, flying in teams of Israeli surgeons and relying on donors from Moldova, Romania and Russia. But after some patients died [...] the brokers were forced to search for new locations. For both the medical expertise available and its low costs, South Africa emerged as a logical alternative. It was there, in South Africa [...] that [the trafficking ring] brought together Mr. da Silva and the woman who ultimately received his kidney. [...]

While money initially motivated Mr. da Silva to sell his kidney, he said he also came to be moved by the chance to help a stranger. The change, he said, occurred after he, too, arrived in South Africa, his first trip out of Brazil, in what he saw as an adventure that would allow him to see lions, giraffes and elephants. Instead, after 10 hours of flying last August, Mr. da Silva found himself in Durban, a resort city of 1.4 million on the Indian Ocean, where he was shuttled to a safe house. Later, at St. Augustine's Hospital, he met the American woman and learned of her long ordeal.

"It's hard for me to imagine how a person might feel when a relative is about to die, so I don't blame anybody for trying anything to get a new kidney," Mr. da Silva said. He said he also made friends with hospital orderlies and a nurse called Mama Tchuka. Mr. da Silva said hospital employees joked openly about the illegal nature of the transplants and the fact that he and the woman receiving his kidney were of different ethnic backgrounds and could not even speak each other's language.

"It was only when I got to South Africa and was told to sign a document saying that the recipient of my kidney was my cousin that I realized that something was wrong," Mr. da Silva said. "But by then it was too late to turn back." [...]

These days, Mr. da Silva works 44 hours a week as a security guard, but still earns less than $175 a month, money that is the sole support for the 10 other people he lives with.

Even that income was jeopardized when he and other kidney donors were arrested and briefly jailed early this year [2004] on suspicion of violating Brazilian laws against trading in human organs. He and more than a score of other donors still faced criminal charges here.

In the 18 months that ended last November, when the authorities shut down the ring, so many residents from the slums of Recife had volunteered that the middlemen had begun offering just $3,000 for a healthy kidney. All told, the police in Brazil estimate that about 100 men, nearly all poor or unemployed, ages 20 to 40, agreed to sell kidneys. Though some would eventually be rejected for having an unusual blood type, frail health or signs of drug use, more than 60 men are believed to have gone to South Africa.

Recife and its slums had become so lucrative a source for organs, in fact, that Brazilian investigators believe that by late 2003, Israeli brokers, in an effort to swell their earnings further, were considering moving their operations to hospitals here and in other nearby cities. With poverty offering up an unquenchable pool of volunteers, the local authorities say the ring had also begun inquiring about buying other vital organs from poor residents, including lungs, livers and corneas. [. . .]

Among the men who did give up a kidney, some say they have experienced health problems that no one warned them about. "For me, the complications began almost immediately," said José Carlos da Conceição da Silva, 24, a day laborer who hauls produce. He said he required a second operation in South Africa on a lung three days after his kidney was removed. Since returning to Brazil his health has worsened, he said. "I'm tired all the time and can't lift heavy weight, which I have to be able to do if people are going to hire me," he said. "My blood pressure goes up and down, and I feel pain and numbness where the scar from the operation is."

Worse still, after his flight back to Brazil, Mr. da Silva, who is not related to Alberty da Silva, said he was robbed of nearly all of the $6,000 he was paid for his kidney when he went to São Paulo during a layover on his flight home. "I begged and pleaded for them not to take the money, telling them that I had sold my kidney and showing them the scar," he recalled, near tears. Another donor, Rogerio Bezerra da Silva, not related to the others, also lost his kidney and his cash, which South African authorities confiscated after the ring was exposed late last year, and is now the object of mockery in his slum neighborhood.

On occasion, Alberty da Silva says, he shows pictures of his trip to South Africa to the neighborhood children. During the interview, he showed them to a reporter, too, including some of him in Durban with the woman who received his kidney. He also displayed a letter she later wrote, thanking him for "the gift of life." The American woman continues to correspond with him and, though hardly wealthy herself, says she intends to send cash gifts each Christmas and on his birthday.

"They never want you to see the donor," she said of the traffickers. "But I kept insisting that we meet because I know that he is now part of my being. I have a piece of him inside of me, so who wouldn't want that bond?"

SENEGAL

The Shoe-Shine Boy

Assane Diallo*

Assane Diallo is a 10-year-old shoe-shine boy in Ziguinchor, the capital of Senegal's southern region. [...]

I come from the village of Bronkagne in the Futa Toro [region]. I used to work for my Uncle Demba cultivating rice, tilling the soil and sowing rice seeds. But we didn't produce enough and he sent me away.

Uncle Demba told me that it would be hard in the city. But it will be good for me whether or not I bring him back money one day. "With travel you gain experience," he said. It is good for a child to know suffering. Then I will appreciate life when I am older. [...]

Of course I was scared to leave but I also wanted to go. I am proud that he has sent me. I hope I make lots of money. I hope I can come back to my village and give all my relatives presents. And I'll be wearing jeans and sneakers. I already have this nice T-shirt.

In the village I just wore rags. Sometimes there wasn't enough food to eat. We worked very hard but there was never enough rain. And rice needs a lot of rain. Still, we Toucouleur [people] always find a way to survive. If we can't make money from farming then we go out and become traders. That is what my family wants me to do.

I already did it last year. I went to the town of Bakel for three months between the sowing and harvesting seasons. I sold baobab and bissap juice on the street for a market woman. I came back to Brokagne with new clothes and gave my uncle money. He was very happy with me. That's why he wanted me to go again this year.

My aim in life is to be a big trader. As my father died when I was a baby, Uncle Demba inherited his land instead. So now his sons will inherit it from him, not me. That is why I must be a trader. I want to travel to Bangkok and bring back textiles and jewelry to sell here. Then with the profits I will open my own store. That is what we Toucouleur do. If you go to any town in Senegal you will find us with our little stores. My friend's uncle has a big store in New York.

I am now on the third step to my life goal. The first was working for my uncle cultivating rice. The second step was selling drinks on the street. Now the third step is being a shoe-shine boy. It is not easy. You have to find people who look like they have a little extra cash and convince them that they need their shoes shined. And sometimes they won't pay you. They say "Oh, I don't have the change, I'll pay you next time," and you never see them again. They also won't pay if you get any shoe polish on their socks.

That's why I don't want to do this for long. I want to learn how to repair shoes. Then I can work for the older boys who are shoe traders. They go to Dakar [Senegal's capital]

---

*Interview by David Hecht; from *New Internationalist*, 292 (July 1997).

and bring back broken shoes which we younger boys repair for them. I have already begun helping to repair shoes and my friends are impressed at how fast I'm learning.

So my fourth step will be repairing shoes and my fifth step will be to be a shoe trader like the older boys. But when I go to Dakar I won't just bring back broken shoes. I will bring all sorts of things. That is how I will get rich.

I don't need to go to school. What can I learn there? I know children who went to school. Their family paid for the fees and the uniforms and now they are educated. But you see them sitting around. Now they are useless to their families. They don't know anything about farming or trading or making money. Even though I have never been to school, I can count and quickly give the correct change. I also know how to bargain with customers and always make a profit.

The only thing I need to learn is to read and write. But I have started. People from ENDA [a Dakar-based agency] teach me and my friends every Tuesday evening. That's good because it doesn't mess up our work schedule.

My friends told me that a white woman came to talk to them once and told them it is bad that children have to work. She said she would put them all in school but she never came back, and I am glad. If anyone tries to put me in school I will run away. I wouldn't be making any money. Then I would be ashamed ever to go back to my village.

ETHIOPIA

The Doorkeeper

Ryszard Kapuscinski*

A.M.-M. [one of Kapuscinski's informants on life in the imperial palace of Ethiopian Emperor Haile Selassie]:

As the keeper of the third door, I was the most important footman in the Audience Hall [of the imperial palace]. The Hall had three sets of doors, and three frontmen to open and close them, but I held the highest rank because the Emperor passed through my door. When His Most Exalted Majesty left the room, it was I who opened the door. It was an art to open the door at the right moment, the exact instant. To open the door too early would have been reprehensible, as if I were hurrying the Emperor out. If I opened it too late, on the other hand, His Sublime Highness would have to slow down, or perhaps even stop, which would detract from his lordly dignity, a dignity that meant getting around without collisions or obstacles. [. . .]

---

*From Ryszard Kapuscinski, *The Emperor* (New York: Vintage International, 1989), pp. 26–7.

A boy selling mouthpieces for hookah pipes in Cairo, Egypt (Adam Jones)

SOUTH AFRICA

The Entrepreneur

Abraham McLaughlin*

Back in the old South Africa, during the dark days of Nelson Mandela's imprisonment, a gregarious black man named William Khazamula Ngobeni was in his own kind of prison. After working for 17 years as a bank messenger, he earned just $55 a month. One day in 1989, his white boss exploded in rage. "You think because you've worked here for so long you amount to something," he yelled. "Well, you don't, and you never will." With that, he kicked his employee; Mr. Ngobeni decided not to go back the next day. There was no severance, no pension, no recourse.

But this is the new South Africa. Mr. Mandela's African National Congress won nearly 70 per cent of the vote in elections last week. And Ngobeni – "Willy" to his friends – now owns a growing business that shuttles tourists around the country. He marvels at the new opportunities. "We grew up knowing we could only work for a white man," he says. "Owning a business was not for a black man." Until now.

As the nation celebrates its first decade of democracy [April 2004], his rise from expendable messenger boy to budding entrepreneur is emblematic of the millions of blacks who've scrambled into the middle class. But 22 million of the country's 44 million citizens still live below the official poverty line, highlighting how South Africa's struggle is now an economic one – against the oppression of poverty. "We've come this far," Ngobeni says, spreading his thumb and forefinger an inch apart. "We have this far to go," he says, raising his arm above his head.

He – and many others – have made big steps toward economic freedom. This is a man who began life in a grass-roofed hut with his parents and six siblings in rural South Africa. Every night, as the sun went down, they didn't know whether they'd eat dinner.

These days, Ngobeni sports a faux Rolex and an ever-ringing cellphone. Striped polo shirts cover his prosperous belly. On a tour of a suburban house, he shows off the addition to the kitchen and living room he's been building. And he has a favorite keepsake: a tattered plane ticket to London, which made him the first in his family to travel abroad.

Many blacks have seen similar success. Between 1990 and 2000, per capita income among blacks rose 28 per cent, according to Carel van Aardt, a researcher at the University of South Africa. For whites, it rose just 2 per cent. Between 1996 and 2001, the number of black technicians and junior professionals jumped 180 per cent, according to census data. The ranks of black legislators, senior officials, and managers swelled 44 per cent.

---

*From Abraham McLaughlin, "A Black Man's Unpaved Road to S. Africa's Middle Class," *The Christian Science Monitor*, 21 April 2004.

Even for those who've made it, it hasn't been easy. In 1996, Ngobeni was just a Johannesburg taxi driver with a dream. His family was living in a two-bedroom apartment on the edge of the city's worst neighborhood. Razor wire encircled their building's entrance. He scratched to make the $150 monthly rent.

He soon decided there was money to be made from the legions of tourists arriving in Johannesburg. After taking a tour-guide course, he went to a bank for a loan to buy a minivan. The cool response: show us the deed to your house, and we'll give you a loan. Since blacks had only recently been allowed to own property, he figured the white bankers knew he wouldn't have a deed. He was reduced to carting tourists in his ancient blue Opel sedan. On slow days he would even round up his family and take them on tours. "He loves showing people around," says Johanna, Willy's wife.

Soon he saved up enough money to buy a rattletrap minivan. "I missed so many jobs because it broke down on the way there," he remembers, laughing. Busted fan belts. Overheated engine. So many problems. He did finally buy a small house – and marched triumphantly to the bank, deed in hand. But they would only give him a loan for 50 per cent of the price of a new van – at a 25 per cent interest rate. After badgering them every day for two weeks, they finally relented, giving him a loan for 75 per cent of the price.

Even still, he moans, by the time the loan is retired, "I'll pay for the car three times." But now his company – Willy's Tours and Safaris – is growing. He's got three Volkswagen vans and is saving up for a 20-seater bus. [...]

MEXICO

The Bus Driver

Kevin Sullivan*

It's a good combination in Mexico City traffic, prayer and a good sense of humor. So Perez was feeling fine this week as he ground his bus into first gear leaving the Tasqueña bus station, with a crucifix hanging from his windshield and a bug-eyed Bart sticker on his side window.

"Ay, *Guey!*" Perez shouted with a big smile, calling to a buddy in a Miami Dolphins jacket, using the Mexico City slang equivalent of "dude," which sounds like "way" with a soft little g-sound on the front. A minute later, pushing through traffic as thick as glue, Perez picked up a tired-looking woman carrying plastic bags of bananas, limes and a tube of Sesame Street toothpaste. She pressed a two peso coin – about 20 cents – into Perez's hand.

*From Kevin Sullivan, "Two Pesos for a Lift and a Laugh," *The Washington Post*, 3 October 2003.

"*Gracias,*" she grunted. "*Para servirle*" – at your service – he replied with his "it-can't-be-that-bad" smile, practiced over 36 years of moving Mexicans a few blocks, a few miles or a few laughs down the road. He kicked the clutch with his shiny, brown buckled boot, jammed the yard-long stick shift into first, dodged a cement truck and a couple of kids running across the road and looked for his next passenger.

For Perez, it's another day in his office: a lime green 1992 Chevrolet microbus. The windshield is cracked, the seats are ripped, the speedometer and brake lights don't work, there are no seat belts or turn signals. Bus 359 is banged and scraped and dented, held together by the power of Bondo auto-body putty, and decorated with a photo on the crankcase of a bikini-clad woman straddling a Harley. It seats 24 but seems infinitely packable, the way there's always room for one more sock in a duffel bag.

There are 28,000 microbuses on Mexico City's streets. They are an idea from a generation ago – a fleet of half-sized buses that travel down narrow streets and over cobblestones. They stop anywhere they are flagged down, and charge fares from a dime.

But now the city is having second thoughts. Microbuses swarm like big iron yellow jackets on the streets, darting in and out of traffic, often barely slowing down to take on or drop off passengers – anywhere, anytime. They move 4.6 million passengers a day. Streets are clogged and accidents are frequent. They are regularly held up by armed bandits, who sometimes hijack an entire bus, demand ATM cards from all of the passengers, then drive around to several banks to drain everyone's accounts. Now, the city is phasing out microbuses and replacing them with a fleet of new regular-size buses.

Perez can't get too nostalgic about it. At 54, with his salt-and-pepper hair suggesting wisdom won on the streets, he has seen public transportation here go from cars to VW buses to microbuses. He said big new buses are the next logical step; he's already taken the 20-hour course needed to get a license to drive one. "It's a good idea," Perez said, looking in his banana-shaped mirror at a bus full of passengers carrying backpacks and briefcases, toolboxes and diaper bags.

Perez has been driving the same eight-mile, 30-minute route through southern Mexico City for 24 years. He carries about 450 passengers a day and works about 75 hours a week. For that he makes about $1 an hour, all in cash. Like millions of other Mexicans, his wages are under the table and he pays no taxes. Someone else owns the bus, but Perez pays for gas and tire replacements, and he offers bribes regularly to keep police and city inspectors off his back about his cracked windshield, among other problems. He's been robbed at gunpoint three times, so he no longer wears a good watch, gold chains or nice jackets to work. He once spent three days in jail after a car ran into his parked bus, killing the car's driver; Perez said it took the police three days to decide it wasn't his fault. Two weeks ago he got into an accident; it cost him $120 to settle with the other driver. He said he has insurance for the bus, but not enough.

All things considered, Perez likes his job. He earns more than most Mexicans, although it's far less than what his son, an illegal immigrant in California, earns as a roofer. The salary is still plenty for Perez, a widower with six children and eight grand-children, to live comfortably and spend afternoons after his 5 a.m. to 3 p.m. shift relaxing at his neighborhood billiards parlor. "And you meet all kinds of people," he said, taking a coin from a woman hauling a baby and a sippy cup in one hand and her shopping bag in the other. In other parts of the bus, a college student marked up a book with a pink highlighter while a man in a business suit read a magazine about stereo equipment. Two high school girls in the seat right behind Perez giggled as they ate enormous bags of potato chips doused in chili sauce.

His eyes always moving from the road to his mirrors, Perez said the job keeps him laughing – like a while back when a woman got on the bus with two children, and got off with one. Perez arrived back at the bus terminal and found a sleeping toddler in a back seat. The frantic mother arrived a little later. Another day, a woman boarded the bus and found her husband and his mistress sitting there. The two women began punching each other. "The husband didn't know who to protect," Perez said in a fit of laughter.

Perez told his stories weaving in and out of traffic, making change one-handed. He waved at every passing bus. When he saw someone he knew, he pressed a bare copper wire sticking out of his steering column against a bit of metal, sounding his horn. Perez knows how to manipulate the wire to make it produce a sound like a chirping bird or the most salacious of wolf whistles. Near the end of his shift, he made a playful wolf whistle at a friend on the sidewalk, and she laughed and waved back. "There are people out here I've known since I took over this route 24 years ago," Perez said. "We're all getting gray together."

BRAZIL

The Motoboys

Larry Rohter*

This is a city [São Paulo] with nearly 11 million inhabitants and 4.5 million passenger cars, 32,000 taxis and 15,000 buses. Traffic jams more than 100 miles long are not uncommon, and even on an ordinary day, getting from one side of town to the other can take two hours or more.

Only one group in Sao Paulo, South America's largest city, seems immune to those frustrations and delays: the daring army of motorcycle messengers known as "moto-boys." Zigzagging among stopped cars, ignoring lane markers, red lights and stop signs, they regularly menace pedestrians and infuriate motorists as they zoom their way down

---

*From Larry Rohter, "Pedestrians and Drivers Beware! Motoboys Are in a Hurry," *The New York Times*, 30 November 2004.

gridlocked streets and highways, armed with the knowledge that without them business would grind to a halt.

"Nowadays we are so integrated into the economy that São Paulo couldn't function without us," said Ednaldo Silva, a motoboy who owns an agency employing nearly 50 messengers. "People don't like us or respect us, but we are as essential to transport as trucks, and if we were to go on strike the city would collapse."

The bulk of the motoboys' work involves rushing contracts and other legal documents from one business to another, especially for bank loans. But from car parts to architects' plans, human organs for transplant to passports or pizza, there is almost nothing they cannot or will not deliver. [...] Though no one is sure of their exact numbers, estimates start at 120,000 and range as high as 200,000. Many work 12 hours a day or more to earn a salary of $300 a month or less. According to official figures, São Paulo now has 332 motoboy agencies. Competition is strong, and they adopt names, often in English, stressing efficiency: Adrenaline Express, Moto Bullet, Fast Express, Agile Boys, Motojet, Fly Boy, Motoboy Speed, AeroBoy Express, Fast Boys.

With so much emphasis on speed and so much competition with other vehicles, the job is often dangerous. Broken bones and wrecked motorcycles are an occupational hazard, and according to figures compiled by the union, on average, at least one motoboy a day dies in a traffic accident. "The truth is that we're discardable," said Edson Agripino, 38, a veteran of 15 years as a motoboy. "When a colleague gets hurt or killed, the first thing the dispatchers ask is 'Did he deliver the document?'"

Nevertheless, many motoboys, especially the younger ones, see themselves as free spirits or urban cowboys, defying the conventions of society and envied by stodgy wage-earners stuck in their cars and offices. "It's great to be out on the street, on your own, watching the girls, and not in some cubicle with a boss bugging you all the time," said Fabio Cesar Lopes, who at 29 has nine years' experience as a motoboy. "I spent five years at an insurance agency, and believe me, not only do I make better money doing this, but it's a lot more fun."

Ordinary motorists consider motoboys a plague, and hostility between the two groups is fierce and growing. There are at least 17 online chat groups devoted to complaining about motoboys, and conflicts in the street and even fistfights between drivers and motoboys are not unknown. [...] Pedestrians, especially newcomers from small towns in the interior, feel especially vulnerable. In a notorious incident in 2001, Marcelo Fromer, a guitarist in the popular rock group Os Titas, was run over and killed by a motoboy with an expired license, who fled but was apprehended a year later, tried and convicted. [...]

"Everybody hates the motoboys except when they need one themselves," said Caito Ortiz, the director of "Motoboys: Crazy Life," a recent prize-winning documentary. "When he's rushing some document of yours across town, then he becomes your savior, a hero, and you adore the guy."

Farmer, Argentina (Adam Jones)

MEXICO

The Guitar Maker

Monica Campbell*

Adjusting his stocky body on a low stool, Gerónimo Amezcua begins hand sanding a classical guitar in his cool, stone-floored workshop. He works patiently, with tools passed down from his great-grandfather's era, until the instrument meets his standards of perfection.

"I know there are faster and more exact ways to build a guitar, but I like to work *puro ojo, puro pulso*," says Mr. Amezcua, referring to his practice of working by sight and feel rather than with the precise, mechanical devices preferred by his counterparts in Spain and the US.

Like others in Paracho, set high in the mountains of central Mexico, Amezcua prides himself on sticking to a way of life that dates back to the 16th century. Local legend has it that Vasco de Quiorga, a Spanish monk, brought the stringed-instrument trade to Paracho to promote culture and build a self-sufficient economy. The town has evolved into Mexico's guitarmaking capital and today is something of a living museum, where visitors can buy anything from cheap children's guitars to high-end classical models, while peering into old-world workshops.

But remaining loyal to tradition, some warn, may leave craftsmen here unable to compete on the world economic stage, where their products can increasingly be mimicked by foreign hands. China is already building cheaper, factory-made guitars. Mexico's artisans are the latest victims of a wave that's washed tens of thousands of jobs to the Far East.

For years, maquiladoras, or factories that assemble such goods as clothing or electronics, which dot the US–Mexico border, have headed to China, which offers a cheaper workforce and laxer regulations. In all, 500 of Mexico's 3,700 maquiladoras have been shuttered since 2001, costing more than 200,000 jobs, according to the Mexican government. Even traditional Mexican items – from Virgen de Guadalupe figurines and colorful blankets to nativity scenes and marimbas – increasingly carry a "Made in China" label.

Oswaldo Castro, a *mariachi* musician, surveys Amezcua's showroom. "The Chinese guitars are cheaper, but not so great," he says. "They don't know how to make them yet." But customer loyalty is not guaranteed in a country where shoestring budgets can override quality and country of origin. It is said that Paracho – which literally means "guitarmaking" in the Purepécha dialect – houses the world's biggest hive of guitar-makers, churning out about 80,000 guitars a year, priced from $50 to $3,000.

Kenny Hill, an entrepreneur from California, headed to Paracho in the mid-1980s to set up a more export-oriented guitar enterprise. But he pulled out in 2002, frustrated in

---

*From Monica Campbell, "Guitar Makers Play to Tradition in Mexico's Mountains," *The Christian Science Monitor*, 14 April 2004.

part by an apparent resistance from Paracho guitarmakers to adopt his more modern designs and production methods. Mr. Hill now has a guitarmaking business in China. "In Mexico, I ran into few people who really understood the value of capitalizing on something," Hill says. "In China, there is a real serious ambition and will to excel."

Guitarmakers are well aware of the outside competition. Jesus Zalapa, who runs a guitar shop a few doors down from Amezcua's, is petitioning the Mexican government to provide more support to artisans. "Guitarmakers in China can be helped by government subsidies. Here, the producer is on his own. We don't do much for the economy, so there's not much value placed on our work."

Although the Amezcua brand is respected in Mexican guitar circles, family members live modestly. "It's the slow making of the guitar that counts," says Amezcua. "That's how my father taught me."

Meanwhile, the migratory drain in Paracho, mainly consisting of younger men heading to US and Mexican cities in search of better pay, may be a more immediate threat to the instrument-making tradition. "The Amezcuas and other older families will probably plug away for some time. They are content," says Hill. "But it is hard to find any young kids in the business. The best and brightest are leaving town."

LEBANON

The Dancer

Lynn Maalouf*

Every Saturday night, at around three o'clock in the morning, Music Hall's long velvet crimson curtains draw open, leaving way to a slim, tall figure that takes position in a bare setup, standing under a single spotlight. As the first percussion beat rips through the silence of anticipating viewers, the figure's hips take a bold swing left, and then another right, setting off a series of sexually teasing belly dance moves. The now roaring audience is glued to the sight of the dark, dense hair plastered backwards, the toned muscles rippling through tight-fitting jeans, and the heavy gold chains reaching down the navel swaying over a fluid see-through top. The name of the belly dancer is Mosbah Baalbaki, better known simply as Mosbah, the famous male belly dancer act who combines sophisticated dance moves and a playful charisma, and who in the past few years has come to disrupt a long tradition of exclusively female belly dancing in the country.

---

*From Lynn Maalouf, "'Dancing Against the Norms': A Profile of Mosbah Baalbaki," *Al-Raida*, 21: 104–5 (Winter/Spring 2004), pp. 86–7.

In a country dominated by a patriarchal system, where the stereotype masculine figure is characterized by high-gear testosterone-driven personae to the point where the legal system penalizes homosexuality, Mosbah has succeeded, over and above the controversy of his act and image, in dancing his way through the deeply entrenched norms of masculinity. He has imposed himself as a respected public figure on the regional scene: every couple of months at least, he is solicited to perform at private parties for political and financial bigwigs across the globe, from the Seychelles islands, to Milan, Sardinia, Paris, London and Dubai. And when he's in town, he dances before a full house every weekend; even if a few sarcastic boos made by suddenly insecure male voices accompany the cheers, there's no question that a significant number of revelers are ready to wait until that late hour just to see Mosbah's show, which lasts no longer than a mere ten minutes at the most. Mosbah has also attracted considerable international media attention, including a special CNN report in 1999, and interviews with the BBC and the *New York Times*.

Born some 30 years ago and growing up as an only son in Sidon, Mosbah has come a long way indeed, thanks to this "hobby" as he calls it. Belly dancing has allowed him to fulfill his childhood dream, which is stardom: "Ever since I was a kid, I wanted to be a star, a celebrity of my own. I didn't want to be like everyone else. Even when I weighed 120 kilograms, and that is until I was 17, I dressed in daring, eccentric colors. I loved music and adored Egyptian movies. I was always telling my mother that I wanted to go to Egypt to become an actor. But she convinced me to get a college degree first. And she was so right, because when you're educated and have self-respect, you can impose people's respect."

At 20, Mosbah came to the capital to pursue a degree in communication arts at the Lebanese American University. Upon graduation, he traveled to Dubai for a few months where he worked as an assistant director before returning to Beirut to work as a fashion designer for a magazine. During one of his location hunts for the magazine, he met Michel Elefteriades, who at the time owned Amor Y Libertad, a popular nightclub that had just opened. "Michel invited me there one Saturday night. There were around 700 people," recalls Mosbah. "He came up front to me and asked me if I would mind dancing Arabic. He had seen me dancing at another club. He told me to go up to the bar and dance. My first response was: Are you crazy? I can't do something like that! What would my family and my friends say? But I loved the idea. So I made my way through the crowd to the bar. When I tried to get on it, the bartender stopped me. Then Michel cleared it out. I danced to one song. It was crazy and I loved it." This spontaneous episode turned into a weekly gig; two months later, a contract was duly signed with Elefteriades' production company, Elef Records, and Mosbah became officially a male belly dancer, gaining national fame a few months later.

Off the scenes, Mosbah is just as picky with the details of his image as on stage; at the time of the interview with *Al-Raida*, which took place at a beauty institute owned by a friend of his, he was carrying along a checkered red and white Dior purse to go with his red and white tracksuit, a white cap and wide-framed red sunglasses. "Just for the ten minutes of the show, there's a lot of work to do. I have to work out every day to stay in shape; I have to choose the songs, the fabric for my costumes, the setup," he explains. Even the rebellious button of his tight-fitting jeans shirt, which he was clipping back on for the umpteenth time during the interview, seemed to be a deliberate choice serving to expose a perfectly hairless, olive skinned chest.

"I'm not trying to provoke anyone. I don't have anything to prove to anyone," he says. But when he first started out, he did suffer from people's reactions: "Of course, I saw the sarcasm, but didn't pay heed to it. Rumors started circulating and they even reached my family. Luckily, my family and I are very close. They know who I am and what I'm worth. They didn't buy into the talk. But I was hurt. I wanted to quit. It wasn't worth it. But then Michel managed to convince me. I held on because I have faith in what I was doing. I have passion for what I do."

When asked whether he believes he contributed to a more homosexual-tolerant society in Lebanon over the past years, he gives a modest shrug, but then refers to the special report published in 2001 in the French magazine *L'Express*, in which he was identified as one of the 100 Lebanese personalities to follow. In a country and region where deep intolerance of any deviation from the established norms of masculinity runs high, Mosbah has indeed managed to open a breach in these norms by imposing himself as an artist and a cultural icon.

UGANDA

Okello Kelo Sam: Artist and Activist

Dixie Beadle*

I first met Okello Kelo Sam in June 2005. As a theater researcher interested primarily in African performance, I was anxious to see Ndere Troupe's show in Kampala, Uganda. At the center of the performance space was Okello, a tall, thin man dressed lavishly in African costume, with enough charisma to control the audience as well as the 40 or so performers in the outdoor amphitheater. He provided continuity for the night's entertainment, weaving together the presentation of traditional dance and music, interspersing jokes, threads of storytelling, and elements of call-and-response to make the audience a central part of the show.

I was anxious to gain an up-close and experiential understanding of African per-formance, and to get to know the Troupe's members. So I was the first (and only) American to volunteer for a friendly competition in which Okello instructed us how to

---

*Special to this volume.

Okello Kelo Sam (Dixie Beadle)

peel the *matoke* (green banana), walk around the circle, and drink a glass of Mirinda soda – all with clay pots on our heads! Likewise, I eagerly took my calabash and joined the dance circle led by Okello later that evening. I couldn't remember when I'd last had so much fun. But I wasn't interested simply in entertainment: rather, I was looking for performance techniques that aimed to make serious social and political interventions. It didn't look as though I was likely to get that with the Ndere Troupe.

I was wrong. The following week, I stayed at Ndere Center and got an opportunity to discover the serious side of Okello Kelo Sam. Okello was born in Pajule in Uganda's Pader district in December 1969, just seven years after his nation's independence from Great Britain. The region was mostly peaceful, and was home to the Acholi, tradition-ally a pastoral and agricultural people. The pacific environment would not last, how-ever. In 1985, at the age of fifteen, Okello was caught up in the conflict between the government's National Resistance Army and rebel forces. He moved north to Sudan, apparently as a child soldier, though this is an aspect of his past that he chooses not to discuss. On what was supposed to be a return trip to Gulu district in 1986, members of Alice Lakwena's Holy Spirit Movement – an Acholi rebel group that used violence both to challenge President Museveni's heavy-handed measures against the Acholi, and to "cleanse" her people of "witches and sinners" – ambushed Okello and his companions. One of his companions was shot, but Okello managed to escape with a convoy heading to the capital city, Kampala. Understandably, he remains reluctant to elaborate on this time in his life.

In 1987, Okello was living with an uncle who had placed him in a Kampala school. There, he had an opportunity to see a performance by Ndere Troupe. Director Stephen Rwangyezi recruited Okello on the basis of the talents he displayed at a school festival. Thus, at the age of seventeen, Okello had both witnessed political violence and launched his career in the performing arts.

Another war-related event proved formative. In 1996, Okello's younger brother, Omony Godfrey Sam, was abducted from his dormitory in Gulu and later killed by Joseph Kony's Lord's Resistance Army (LRA) – an offshoot of rebels from Alice Lakwena's now-defunct group, which targeted Acholi for rape, mutilation, and slaughter. The loss of his brother was a catalyst in Okello's life, prompting him to use his performance talents to resist the conflict and to aid children abused by the war.

Today, almost twenty years after its inception, the LRA continues to terrorize northern Uganda, abducting and conscripting children as young as eight or nine years old. The kidnapped youths are starved, beaten, raped, and most horrifically of all, forced to kill friends, relatives, and other children. Burnt schools, devastated homes, tattered fields, and the occasional pillaged medical clinic scar the landscapes of Okello's home district of Pader, and neighboring ones like Kitgum and Gulu. The population of displaced people is enormous. An estimated 1.8 million northern Ugandans live in refugee camps, where "crowded conditions and lack of food and sanitation facilities have rendered the population vulnerable to death from malnutrition and disease. Thousands die every month, and despite the nearby military presence, the camps remain targets for rebel attacks."*

Amidst this personal and public ruin, it is difficult to imagine how one man could make a difference. But Okello Kelo Sam chose to fight back – not with violence, but with social activism and performing-arts projects. In 1996, he founded Hope North, a village for displaced children and families in the northwestern corner of Uganda. There, he uses storytelling, dance, and music as tools of trauma intervention. Hope North sits on about fifty acres purchased by Okello. It currently houses 70–80 children and 15 family units headed by adults who have lost their children to the war; the number of residents in the camp, says Okello, "keeps on growing day and night." Some of Hope North's children were abducted by rebels from their former villages; these few were lucky enough to escape the LRA's clutches. Others are orphans. (Sometimes, parents and villagers are reluctant to take children back into their fold when they have been kidnapped and forced to kill: they fear the children might be compelled to kill again.) Projects in the village, which are partially funded by Foundation O 94 in the Netherlands, Hope North USA, and Mirembe Project (USA), include the construction of cottages, classrooms, dormitories, a vocational school, guest-houses, and a bakery as a means of becoming self-sustaining. Towards this end as well, small plots of land are issued for agricultural development.

---

*Human Rights Watch/Africa, *The Scars of Death: Children Abducted by the Lord's Resistance Army in Uganda* (New York: Human Rights Watch, 1997), pp. 4–5. See also "The Mzee" on pp. 205–8.

Judging by the excitement in his voice and demeanor, Hope North is the project that Okello is most passionate about. At least twice a month – more when his harried schedule permits – Okello travels to the village to visit the children. Their emotional trauma runs deep. In an effort to alleviate their pain, he encourages residents to engage in music and dance, part of an art-centered effort to teach them to "survive" and move beyond war and personal suffering. "I try to provide them with instruments so they can make music, and especially drums . . . the drums have so much power to release energy." Okello theorizes that the act of telling or writing personal tragedies can serve to mentally and emotionally "concretize" children's trauma, rather than offering the necessary catharsis. Instead, he encourages the children to pour themselves into the creation of dance, music, and drama, opening up space for rejuvenation. "If they can establish a trust in music and dance," Okello tells me, this serves as "social therapy," allowing children to share their bodily energies and to build trust, both among themselves and in the broader community. It also helps students "to know that now they are back to their roots, their culture." Among the benefits are "increased school performance" for the participating children, and fewer nightmares.

Performance arts therapy at Hope North is not Okello's only creative outlet. He has also made a conscious choice to work in films that deal with social justice issues. He played the role of the antagonist in the 2001 Hallmark production of *War Child: Abduction*, the first in a series of three hour-long movies detailing war atrocities endured by children. Loosely based on the story of Okello's brother, *War Child* focuses on three children abducted from their school by LRA rebels and forced to commit heinous acts in order to survive. He also portrayed a rural clinic worker in *The Last King of Scotland*, a film about Idi Amin that was shot on location in Uganda. Based on Giles Foden's book of the same name, the movie narrates the horrific abuses of Amin's regime against the Ugandan people. American actor Forrest Whitaker plays Amin in the film. After meeting Okello, Whitaker visited Hope North, and is now a vocal supporter of the project.

Okello also serves as secretary-general of the Uganda Developmental Theatre Association (UDTA), overseeing training, programming, project planning, and artistic administration. A Ndere Troupe offshoot, the UDTA comprises more than 1,300 amateur groups engaging in developmental and educational theater. Its focus is on something called "Entertainment Education." According to the UDTA Training Manual, this is "a technique through which vital information is exchanged, analyzed and assimilated in a friendly, entertaining, interesting, familiar, and non-discriminatory way." Governmental and non-governmental organizations, within Uganda and internationally, seek out UDTA members to develop educational scripts revolving around development issues; these are then performed from the county to the national level. As a key member of UDTA, Okello works with satellite groups in performance training and localizing of script content. He also administers theatrical competitions that begin at the local level and eventually receive countrywide exposure. This theater, he tells me, synthesizes entertainment with colloquial languages and practices, encouraging social change in areas such as women's health and education, alcoholism, agricultural development, political education, land privatization, and peace and conflict issues.

In a land where many remain illiterate due to a lack of free public education, developmental theater reaches into areas where television and radio sometimes cannot. Even when "the masses are not conscious of the fact that the theater is providing information," Okello says, the audience is still receiving an education. Outdoor performances in remote areas may attract crowds of up to 6,000 people. At other times, it is necessary to improvise performances in markets and other "found spaces" to generate interest among local people. Watching videos of UDTA performances, I observed how the actors worked to put audiences at ease, and to facilitate post-show discussions between audiences and performers.

Meanwhile, Okello's role as the *griot* (storyteller), artistic director, and program manager of Ndere Troupe provides an ongoing venue for his social activism. To international audiences, the Troupe appears to provide "merely" an entertaining evening of African dance and music in a variety-show format. But a look beneath the façade shows how the performances are rooted in the group's ambitions to effect social change in Uganda through a reclamation of traditional culture. The *Brief of Ndere Troupe*, a collaboratively authored document, spells out the group's goals, noting that the British colonial system "branded . . . African cultural practice as evil, primitive, shameful, and backward." The Troupe reclaims indigenous dance and music as a means of rekindling a "sense of self-esteem, pride, and confidence among Ugandans."

The *Brief* depicts Uganda's ruling class as an "elite" that follows in the footsteps of its colonial predecessors by denigrating the rural population. National and international performances of rural dance and music help to bridge the gap between government and people, and enrich the self-esteem of rural peoples, encouraging their economic and social development. Thus Okello, through Ndere, is able to engage in a mutually beneficial exchange with Uganda's many ethnic groups. They provide performance materials, and Ndere's dancers and musicians showcase their work for broader audiences.

Okello's diverse work has a growing international profile. He is becoming known in American universities and public schools, as well as in several western European, Asian, and African nations. Through lectures, music, dance, and performance workshops, he is educating growing audiences about the war in Uganda, and his country's rich culture. He also uses his travels to raise funds for Hope North. By utilizing a wide network of friends around the world, he is able to cut travel and logistical costs, and donate the bulk of his proceeds directly to the village.

Okello's obligations include extensive trips away from his wife Marian and their three children, but his homeland and its people always call him back. As he told a lecture audience: "In America, you pay allegiance to the flag. In Uganda, I pay allegiance to where my umbilical cord is buried." It is his close ties to Uganda's people and land that shape his constant efforts to fuse humanitarian struggles with artistic creation. "All I want is to be able to use performance arts to advocate for peace and reconciliation, and to help as many African children as possible receive an education," he says. "That is enough for me."

PART 4

Governance and Conflict

In his groundbreaking book *Masculinities*, R.W. Connell proposes a distinction between "hegemonic" and "subordinate" masculinities. "At any given time," writes Connell, "one form of masculinity rather than others is culturally exalted."* This is apparent in the "big man" mode of governance that still pervades so many countries and cultures worldwide. Such men, says Connell, establish a "successful claim to authority" by means that extend well beyond "direct violence . . . though violence often underpins or supports authority."† Violent or not, those who establish social and political hegemony are overwhelmingly male. Only a minority of males achieve such status, however; and the authority they establish is often *authoritative* rather than (or as well as) *authoritarian*.

This mix of legitimate authority and authoritarian coercion is evident in the series of portraits that opens this section. The "big man" of Papua New Guinea, described by David Gilmore; the *mzee* of northern Uganda and the Mossi chief of Burkina Faso profiled by Amy Berson and Sabine Luning; the "big man" who adopts the persona of the "little man" (Edward Leblanc of Dominica) – all combine political acumen and complex mediating roles that usually have little to do with the threat or exercise of violence. Different strategies, including "carrot-and-stick" methods, systematic repression, and outright state terror, are evident in the rule of the Afghan warlord, the South Korean dictator, and the North Korean totalitarian. For every male despot, however, there are literally thousands of underlings. Ryszard Kapuscinski's classic portrait of Ethiopian dictator Haile Selassie vividly captures the relationship between "His Majesty" and his obsequious lackeys: "Let's say that the Imperial gaze just grazes your face – just grazes! You could say that it was really nothing, but on the other hand, how could it really be nothing, when it did graze you?"

Few aspects of masculinity have been so extensively studied as its relationship to patterns and structures of violence. Two essays from Africa examine male involvement

---

*R.W. Connell, *Masculinities* (Berkeley, CA: University of California Press, 1995), p. 77.
†Ibid.

in criminal activity, from that described by the Nigerian writer (and participant) John Kiriamiti to the South African culture of gang violence and petty crime and the measures taken to confront it.

We then turn to explore the violent victimization of men and boys by state and substate agents. In my essay "Gendercide and Genocide," I argued that "the most vulnerable and consistently targeted population group, throughout time and around the world today, is noncombatant men of 'battle age,' roughly fifteen to fifty-five years old. They are nearly universally perceived as the group posing the greatest danger to [a] conquering force, and are the group most likely to have the repressive apparatus of the state directed against them."* The empirical support for these propositions is overwhelming. They are bolstered by the findings of the *Human Security Report 2005*, prepared by the Liu Institute at the University of British Columbia. "Both in uniform and out," write the authors, "men have been, and continue to be, killed, wounded and tortured in far greater numbers than women. . . . Men are also disproportionately victimised by violent state repression."[†]

It is notable, however, that until recently the gender-selective targeting of males for mass killing, state repression, torture, and other atrocities *never* received sustained attention, much less comparative and global–historical study. The phenomenon is mentioned in sources as ancient as the Old Testament and Homer. But while most people might intuitively accept that such targeting occurs, it is so entrenched in diverse cultures as to be almost invisible. The parallel with the phenomenon of violence against women, first denounced and confronted by feminists, is striking. Aspects of social reality must be articulated and persuasively documented in order to be "thinkable." Generations of feminists met this challenge with such vigor and success that, today, "violence against women" is a core theme of human-rights discourse and global policymaking. The massive targeting of males, by contrast, is still widely ignored. More generally, as Marion Birch argues in "Where Are the Men?," "it is clear that the problems faced by men in humanitarian emergencies have received insufficient attention, particularly where conflict is involved."

For one result of the prevailing mindset, consider the subject of murders in the Mexican city of Ciudad Juárez. The emphasis on killings of women ("femicide") has been so intensive that one would hardly think any men at all were killed. Yet a glance at the statistics suggests that about *90 per cent* of those murdered in Ciudad Juárez in recent years were male. In this case and others, could not a legitimate focus on killings of women be combined with a recognition that another side of violent victimization also exists, and merits attention and concern?

---

*Adam Jones, "Gendercide and Genocide," in Jones, ed., *Gendercide and Genocide* (Nashville, TN: Vanderbilt University Press, 2004), p. 10. See also the case studies and other materials compiled on the Gendercide Watch website (www.gendercide.org).

[†]Human Security Center, *Human Security Report 2005*, http://www.humansecurityreport. info/HSR2005/Part3.pdf, pp. 110–11.

The essays in this section cover a broad spectrum of the forms of state and substate violence to which men and boys are disproportionately vulnerable. These include police and death-squad killings and "disappearances"; gender-selective roundups, torture, and "filtration"; vigilante violence; incarceration without trial; and violence against gays. T. Christian Miller's wrenching account of the fate of Colombia's Arias brothers provides an intimate portrait of men and masculinities swept up in pervasive state violence and civil conflict.

By contrast with their targeting for violent victimization, men's *perpetration* of violence – both willing and unwilling – is persistently stressed in the literature on gender and conflict. It is no less prominent in masculine culture and behavior over the millennia. Connell's distinction between "hegemonic" and "subordinate" masculinities can again be cited. It helps us to understand how certain men are lured or coerced into becoming agents of violence. They may be the eager liberation fighters of Ethiopia and Iraq, the soldier-rapists of Uganda, the male *génocidaires* of Rwanda, or the male suicide bombers of Israel/Palestine. They may be arms-dealers who profit from a pervasive climate of violence, or those who otherwise seek to exploit the economic opportunities generated by militarism. Frequently, they are participants in the time-honored institution of gender-selective military "service." The *Guardian* account of Assad, an Iraqi conscript killed during the 2003 Gulf War, serves as a poignant reminder of men's historical role as cannon fodder, as do Ashraf Khalil's and Monica Campbell's accounts of police recruits and Mexican "Green Card Marines" in the same war. Even adolescent boys are liable to be conscripted, as with the Burmese child soldiers described by Human Rights Watch and the Colombian *sicario* (contract killer) profiled by Alonso Salazar in *Born to Die in Medellín*.

These excerpts thus depict males as both governors and governed, both victims and agents of violence. In delving into them, the reader is encouraged to integrate perspectives from earlier sections of the book. The focus here is on public acts of violence. But domestic violence and sexual attacks against children and women (Part 1) also reflect gendered patterns of "Governance and Conflict." The same is true of the violence inflicted disproportionately on male bodies in social–cultural rituals (Part 2) and in the "working world" (Part 3).

PAPUA NEW GUINEA

The Big Man

David D. Gilmore*

There is a vast literature on the Big Men of New Guinea. The magnitude of their achievements is impressive and varied, but a few commonalities stand out. The Highland Big Man is, first, a charismatic local leader who has achieved, not inherited, a leadership role through dramatic actions of personal derring-do that prop up his village or tribe. He earns his position of prominence by a number of practical means, depending upon exigencies of time and place. First, he acts as a leader in war, if warfare is locally a particular concern. If the tribe is threatened, he becomes a military strategist, shielding his group by directing hit-and-run counterattacks to keep the enemy at bay. Like any competent commanding officer, he leads his troops into battle, setting an example by bravely disdaining clouds of arrows and spears. The only difference is that his position is unofficial, without badges or uniforms; but without his "take-charge" management the village would be disorganized and hence vulnerable to deadly sneak attack.

Through this hands-on leadership, the Big Man does something more than fight, fend off enemies, and exemplify a warrior ideal for impressionable boys and aspiring youths: he establishes an artificial social cohesion for the people of his village or territorial unit. This unifying function is necessary because the people who follow him are often of mixed ancestry and diffuse kinship (as is common among Highlands peoples). Weakly tied by bonds of blood, they are drawn together by his protective safety net to form a viable community, establishing a political rather than genealogical unit that otherwise might never gel. Through his example and by the commanding authority of his deeds, he coalesces this community of otherwise unrelated families around his person, counteracting the organic weakness of Highlands genealogy. For example, among the Gururumba (Newman 1965: 44), the power of the Big Men derives from "their ability to attract followers outside the circle of their own immediate kinsmen." There is in fact a conscious awareness of this ingathering magnetism among his vassals. Many local people acknowledge this and openly remark that the local Big Man holds the group together almost single-handedly, giving it the strength and unity it needs but would otherwise lack.

Beyond these crucial military and sociopolitical functions, the Big Man is also an indispensable economic power, an engine of production, motivating and enriching his followers. In farming and herding, he is the unofficial manager for the village, exhorting his people to produce, to work hard, and to save. In return for their loyalty, he accumulates, stores, and later redistributes great quantities of imperishables and foodstuffs,

---

*From David D. Gilmore, *Manhood in the Making: Cultural Concepts of Masculinity* (New Haven, CT: Yale University Press, 1990), pp. 100–2.

acting like a primitive banker or capitalist, rationalizing and centralizing production and extending credit. But unlike his Western counterpart, he is expected to return the goods with interest, enriching his trading partners rather than himself. [...] To capture Big Man status, he may accumulate food and goods, but only to distribute them later in ceremonies and feasts. An expert on the New Guinea Highlands, Paula Brown, summarizes in her book, "The wealth [of Big Men] is dissipated in distribution at feasts; it cannot be accumulated." The Big Man must be above all a capable administrator of goods, enriching his village by amassing capital, cementing exchange networks, diverting group energies away from consumption toward reinvestment. Clearly, he provides the centripetal sources of cohesion and direction that the society needs. All this makes him both charismatic and virile in the eyes of his people.

UGANDA

The Mzee

Amy Berson*

The streak of tight gray curls in his otherwise black hair symbolizes the wisdom that comes with age, and garners him the respect of his fellow Acholi in northern Uganda. This is a culture where the elderly are revered. On many nights, young men and women will come to his village to seek counsel and learn from this wise man, the *mzee*.

In this war-affected region, the wisdom the mzee imparts is treasured. War has been waged here for two decades. During that time, thousands of people have been killed. The youth and children are at greatest risk. They are abducted from their homes and forced to become child soldiers or sex slaves for the rebel group, the Lord's Resistance Army. Over 50,000 children have been abducted, and many have not returned.

The mzee can remember a time when peace prevailed in Acholi-land – when the soil provided plentiful food, and there was not a hungry child in sight. Those years, however, are outnumbered by those of horror and pervasive hardship.

I first met this man in January 2004. I had been working closely with his daughter in Kampala, Uganda's capital, and was invited to stay with her family in their village in Gulu district. I was welcomed into their home like a new daughter, and was privileged to learn from the mzee, whom I affectionately began to call Daddy Gulu.

Everyone has a personal story to tell about the war, and Daddy Gulu is no different. His compound is full of nieces, nephews and cousins who have been orphaned. Most of

---

*Special to this volume. Names have not been used in this essay, to protect the identity of the mzee and his family.

these children lost their parents in a single attack in May 1991, when 24 of the mzee's immediate family were killed. He is one of only two surviving siblings, and has taken on the responsibility of supporting the children and grandchildren of his sisters and brothers.

Through my outsider's eyes, I witnessed a way of life in Gulu that was completely alien to anything I had experienced, or even read about. I observed the phenomenon of "night commuters" – thousands of children who stream into town each night to sleep, fearing abduction by the rebels. I traveled outside the town to the Internally Displaced Peoples (IDP) camps, where people were living "temporarily" while they waited for the war to end. And I fought back tears as I walked through the casualty ward at the local hospital, greeting boys with amputated limbs, child mothers who had been paralyzed, babies with bullet wounds. I felt I was witnessing a living hell.

Through Daddy Gulu's eyes, however, I began to perceive a different situation. As he rode into the village proudly every afternoon on his bicycle, with a broad smile on his face, his joy and love of life were evident. His ability to smile despite such adversity astounded me. I wanted to discover the source of this optimism. And so, on many evenings, sitting around the fire in the middle of the compound or in the comfort of the main hut (which doubled as both the sitting room and the main bedroom), I sat and listened to the stories of Daddy Gulu's life. Listened and learned.

Like many Acholi, the mzee had initially supported the rebel movement that arose among his people. He had witnessed at first hand the atrocities committed by the army of the current Ugandan President, Yoweri Museveni, who seized control of Uganda in a 1986 coup. He told me how he had come across a group of Acholi soldiers who had been buried alive, up to their shoulders, so that they were unable to free themselves. This was not an isolated incident: many Acholi were humiliated and killed after they surrendered their arms to the new government.

Resentment at government atrocities spawned the Acholi rebel movement. Many Acholi soldiers withdrew to Sudan, where they were unified under the leadership of Alice Lakwena. After gathering strength, the movement re-entered Uganda and mounted a campaign to take over the country. To increase their fighting forces, they began to conscript young Acholi, and the mzee reluctantly saw his eldest daughter and son drafted into rebel ranks. There was a bigger cause at stake, though. The pride of the Acholi people had been tarnished, and they needed to win back the respect and power they had lost.

The mzee's son and daughter were primarily employed as "tax collectors" for the rebels. Thus, they remained close enough to visit their family regularly. They would return home, AK-47s slung over their shoulders and grenades strapped around their waists. The mzee would sadly look into the eyes of his children, who would try to avoid his gaze, and wonder how they were coping. He was keenly aware of the way young women were treated by the older, stronger male soldiers, and would try not to let himself imagine what was happening to his beautiful young daughter. It was his son, however, who lost his life among the rebels. In June 1986, he was bitten by a rabid dog, and died three months later.

Following Alice's defeat, a new leader emerged named Joseph Kony. He was a young man from the same village as the mzee, who knew him well. As rumors spread through the village that Joseph and a group of other young men had disappeared in the nearby hills for a few days, Daddy Gulu decided to see for himself what was happening. He found the boys engaged in "strange, witchcraft" practices. For example, they were using calabashes to sprinkle water over themselves, claiming it made them bulletproof.

A few days later, the boys emerged, announcing that the Lakwena spirit had directed them to reignite the Acholi fight. Daddy Gulu, however, still grieved for his son and the lost innocence of his daughter. He was tired of the conflict. Many of his neighbors were also weary and desperate to live in peace. So the boys received little support for their new movement, and were forced to travel further afield to recruit people to their cause.

Months later, a group of rebel soldiers arrived in the mzee's village. They were fatigued after a long journey, and sought a place to rest and set up camp. The mzee opened his compound to them. For the next three days, he sheltered and fed the men, unsure of their intention in his village. On the fourth day, their purpose became clear. The soldiers were members of Alice Lakwena's rebel group, the Holy Spirit Movement, which later merged with Kony's rebels to form the Lord's Resistance Army. They had been sent to the area with a list of people they had been ordered to recruit. If anyone disobeyed, their order was to kill. They presented this list to Daddy Gulu, and asked for his assistance in identifying the people in question. Now that they had rested, they were preparing to carry out their orders.

As Daddy looked through the list, he was shocked to discover his own name at the very top. Halfway down was that of his daughter. He also recognized the names of many others whom he knew; most were teachers and other educated people. He tried to hide his fear as he contemplated his options. After what seemed like an eternity, he looked up, met the leader's gaze, and said:

"Yes. I do know people on this list. That first name is my name. Now, I have sheltered you, I have fed you and I have asked nothing in return. You can either kill me, or repay the kindness I have shown you by letting me go."

The mzee laughs as he tells the story. "Can you imagine? They were so shocked that they were staying in the home of the man on the top of their list that they didn't know what to do. Thankfully, with God's will, they released me."

Early the next morning, the mzee and his daughter fled. By a favorable twist of fate, he was reunited with his wife four months later in Kitgum, a neighboring town to the north. One of their younger daughters had fallen sick, and his wife had brought her to Kitgum hospital. While Daddy cared for their ill daughter, he sent his wife back to their village to collect the others. The family was back together again.

The years the family spent in Kitgum were certainly not free of conflict. The rebel group had gained momentum through its violent abductions of children; it was brainwashing them to become killers. Kony and his child soldiers were inflicting horrors throughout Acholi-land, including in Kitgum. The nights were filled with the sounds of gunshots as battles raged between the rebels and government forces. The mzee told me how these battles had sometimes drawn dangerously close to their new home. He recalled how, on a number of occasions, their house was actually bombed. At such times, the family would have to run from one end to another of the large room they lived in, dodging mortar explosions. Thankfully, all members of his immediate family survived these attacks. Many friends and extended family, however, were not so lucky. They seemed to be constantly attending the burials of loved ones.

After years in exile in Kitgum, the family returned to their home district of Gulu. However, the village still was not safe. They found some land close to town and began to rebuild their lives. They live there to this day, never able to return to their home village, which is farther from town and at high risk of rebel attack.

"One day, when the war has ended, I will take you there," the mzee told me. "It is so close to the Aswa River that you can swim and fish all day. There is so much fertile land and plentiful room for cattle to graze." He glanced around his cramped compound and at the solitary cow enclosed in its pen. Their present home has never been attacked, but the rebels have come dangerously close. As recently as 2004, they abducted children just a couple of hundred meters away. The mzee is still losing family members and other loved ones, and there is no end in sight to the fighting.

Throughout all the years of conflict, the mzee has continued to struggle for both personal and community development. He is a highly intelligent, educated man. With that education comes the knowledge that in other parts of the world, people walk the streets in safety, and children sleep in comfortable beds at night. In northern Uganda, the mzee had worked as a teacher, and his keen thirst for knowledge has led him to seek more information about life in the "developed" world. Early in his teaching career, he lived with a Scottish man and learned what he called "the ways of the white man." He proudly told me how he cooked for himself, and that he had begun to understand the concept of gender equality and women's empowerment. With Daddy Gulu's support and encouragement, his wife has become the chairperson of their village. His daughters have been raised as strong, educated, independent women; they have gone on to gain tertiary qualifications and work for nonprofit organizations.

Adopting western attitudes carries with it certain challenges. One night, I might hear Daddy singing in Acholi and playing a local harp-type instrument. The next night, he would be singing church hymns in English, strumming on the guitar his daughter had brought him from America. While he encouraged his family and neighbors to preserve their traditional culture, I felt that his attempts to reconcile this with outside and modernizing influences had created internal conflicts for him. Cultural clashes are difficult to negotiate at the best of times – the more so when they occur within a single individual.

But the mzee continues on. Each day is a cause for thanks, and the joy he radiates is contagious. His major role in life, as the *Lapwony* (teacher), is more significant than probably even he realizes. It is not just a profession, but a calling; its importance extends far beyond the classroom. How thankful I am that it reached me.

BURKINA FASO

The Mossi Chief

Sabine Luning*

Daily life for *Naaba* Tegre, a Mossi chief, is at once more prosaic and more special than one might expect. Early accounts by French administrators expressed disenchantment with how Mossi chiefs actually lived in their palaces. Captain Binger, who traveled in the region between 1887 and 1889, wrote of his disappointment upon arriving at the palace of the *Moogho Naaba* of Ouagadougou. He had been led to expect a demonstration of great wealth and a beautiful palace. Instead, he found "a series of miserable huts, surrounded by a refuse dump and stables for the horses." He was particularly disturbed by the presence of goats, cattle and donkeys in the royal court.

Likewise, the first time I visited a Mossi chief in the late 1980s, his palace struck me as far too common for a chief. The inner court was used to thresh millet, and cattle were grazing at the back of the palace. Yet the chief's daily life was far from ordinary. A Mossi chief cannot work the land; he cannot visit markets; he cannot have a drink or a meal with just anybody. The daily routine is to a large extent determined by ritual restrictions that keep him from ordinary social events and activities. These aspects of his royal position are viewed as predicaments rather than privileges. In the most literal sense, a chief is less free than other persons.

When I got to know Naaba Tegre, he was well into his sixties, and married to 32 wives. He had come to power in 1963, shortly after Upper Volta (later to be named Burkina Faso) became independent. His daily life in the 1990s was still shaped by a choice he had made when attending to the funeral of his father in 1963. Desperate to succeed to royal office, he had chosen to make changes to the traditional burial rites. He wanted to prove to the new national elite that he was a suitable candidate for succession. The colonial administrators of French West Africa had handed over political power to local Africans who had been educated at Roman Catholic mission schools. The traditional burial rites could hardly be expected to impress this new administrative elite. Naaba Tegre smiled when he asked rhetorically: "We could not embarrass the minister by forcing him to witness a chiefly burial with the deceased wrapped up in the skin of a bull, could we?" Instead, Naaba Tegre chose to perform a Roman Catholic burial in the palace, near the main entrance. After the "modern" guests had left, however, a customary burial was also staged. For this purpose, an imitation corpse had been made from a pillow covered in a straw mat. This "royal corpse" was buried at a site some way away from the palace.

Whether this decision about ritual had actually influenced the choice of the successor was difficult to determine. But Naaba Tegre was indeed chosen, and for a while he

---

*Special to this volume.

settled down in the palace of his father in the village of Silmidougou. However, at a later stage, the village of Maane – not Silmidougou – was selected to serve as administrative center (*Chef de Poste*) for Maane *département*. To be closer to the modern power holders, Naaba Tegre moved from Silmidougou to Maane village. From 1965, the Maane chief resided there, in an ordinary house with nine of his younger wives. The 23 other spouses of the chief remained in the palace in Silmidougou.

Was the chief's move induced by power or personal predicament? I was told that Naaba Tegre had been forced to leave the palace – indeed, that declining to do so would have cost him his life. Reigning in a palace that had been turned into a burial site was simply impossible. The proximity between the living chief and his predecessor's corpse entailed too great a risk. Moving to Maane was the chief's way of solving this dilemma.

After relocating, the chief came only seldom to his palace in Silmidougou, the residence not only of the majority of his wives but also of seven unmarried boys who perform temporary court service. Despite its deplorable state, two residential areas of the palace can be distinguished: the young house (the *yibila*) in the east, and the old house (*yikieemde*) in the western section. In the young house reside the younger wives and the children. The place is usually full of life and noise, and during his visits the chief sleeps in this part of the palace. His preferred wife lives here, and she is the only one allowed to prepare his food. It is said that Naaba Tegre had always to check carefully what he was eating, since he was a permanent target for lethal jealousies.

The rare occasions on which the chief stayed overnight in the palace triggered persistent gossip about his sexual life. The wives in the young house were consistently portrayed as craving sex, and the chief himself was said to be sexually insatiable. Rumor had it that his wives were in fierce competition for their husband's sexual attention: on the way back to his room from his nightly shower, he would be subjected to what some might call sexual harassment by one of his wives, who would literally be trying to drag him into her hut. All these marital ties, and their fertile results, helped to characterize this part of the palace: the young house was crowded with the chief's young children.

The old house, meanwhile, was relatively small and inhabited by the chief's elderly spouses, most of whom had been given to the chief after the death of his predecessor. Central in this part of the palace is the role of the eldest wife, who is ritually responsible for the altar of the royal ancestors. The east–west axis reflects the process of ageing, moving from sexuality and birth to old age and ancestors.

Even in the last decade of the twentieth century, the palace still attested to the chief's importance as a receiver and giver of wives. The chief himself was married to many women, but he also had a large network of (kin)women whom he was allowed to give in marriage to other men. In the past, the court service of young boys had been based on the chief's potential to give wives in this way. Young men who did such service would be rewarded in due course with a wife. The first daughter born from that marriage would return to the palace, and herself be given in marriage at a later date.

In the 1990s, though, this system was in decline and barely functioning. The chief hosted only seven of these boys – four in the palace and three in his house in Maane.

They would have to perform their daily palace tasks as well as attend to the chief's fields. However, men, other than the chief and his kin, are not allowed to enter the palace. The sexuality of the chief's wives has to be invigilated with care. If one of the wives was to have sexual relations with another man, the mixing of this man's sperm with that of the chief would be lethal to the latter.

Restricted access was therefore crucial, and the rule was taken very seriously, as I discovered early in my research. One of the chief's young daughters had fallen ill, and I tried to help out by alerting the male nurse of the *dispensaire* in Silmidougou. Regardless of my appeal, though, the nurse was absolutely forbidden to enter the palace. Despite her vulnerable condition, we had to take the girl to the *dispensaire* for treatment. The chief's absence made male access to the palace even more difficult, it seemed. As a female researcher, I could move freely in and out, but men were on no account permitted entry.

Given this situation, on what terms could boys be allowed to perform service within the palace grounds? Conveniently, men whose court function required access to the palace were symbolically considered to be females. In the past, they had been obliged to wear women's clothes, and their hair in female style. This was forbidden by the state in the 1960s, shortly after independence. But in Silmidougou, the release of these boys from court service is still marked by a ritual in which their "long hair" is cut. In this way, they become ordinary men again, and can marry upon leaving the palace. The boys I knew in the 1990s would laughingly admit that court service had turned them into girls for a few years.

As a consequence, had the chief really resided in his palace, he would have been considered the only man in a palace full of women – and one who was involved in substantial movements of brides to and from the palace. A super-polygynous man was considered super-masculine. This super-masculinity is stressed in the family name of Burkina chiefs and their descendants: *Ouédraogo*, stallion, a term that also celebrates the conquests on horseback that gave rise, historically, to these chiefdoms.

However, as we have seen, Naaba Tegre did not reside in the palace. His daily life was lived in an ordinary house in Maane, the administrative center. His palace visits were limited to ceremonial occasions. He would come to host guests from the national political arena, and to perform rites for his ancestors. For example, in Burkina the 1990s witnessed a return to democracy. President Compaore, who had seized power in a *coup d'état* in 1987, organized presidential elections, for which he depended on the support of the Mossi chiefs. The palace became a center for meetings and rallies.

The atmosphere on these occasions, with the palace full of people, contrasted with the more customary ritual activities. Ironically, the major ritual performed by the chief consisted of his own ritual departure! Near the end of the rainy season, he had to ritually abandon the palace, which is temporarily supposed to become the residence of the royal ancestors. In the past, when the chief left, he would be hosted for a time in another village. However, in the 1990s, people were no longer willing to carry the burden of hosting the chief for days on end. Instead, the abandonment ritual was enacted by moving to the back of the palace on the eastern side, so that the royal ancestors could move in through the front door on the west side. It took me some time to understand this purely symbolic departure. I was told, though, that while changes to the ritual had been forced by shifting social circumstances, abandoning the ritual altogether would invoke the wrath of the royal ancestors, and would almost certainly be fatal for the chief.

In January 1993, Naaba Tegre died peacefully of old age. He left 32 widows, one of whom was pregnant, and over a hundred children, some still being breastfed. His funeral was the occasion for rituals ranging from a Roman Catholic requiem mass to prayers by the *imam*. Representatives from all social circles connected to the chief participated in his funeral rites, from villagers who had taken wives from the palace, to *haut commissaires* (high commissioners). In the interregnum, the chief's eldest daughter was nominated as female chief (*napoko*). She dressed like a male chief, and together with some of her co-wives she filled royal court positions and played host to visitors. Her role was to fill the vacancy until a male successor could be nominated: in between "real" chiefs power could only be entrusted to a woman. It was feared that a man who was given this temporary position would never hand back power. After all, it is in the nature of chiefly masculinity to struggle hard for rulership, and to abandon it only at death.

The life of Naaba Tegre and his daily and ritual activities show how chiefdom in Africa is undergoing rapid change. Yet in the area of ritual, these changes are full of surprises and paradoxes. For Naaba Tegre, juggling different precepts and predicaments was part of the job. He had to live up to traditional images of masculinity – and a menaced masculinity at that. He had to take all sorts of precautions, in particular with his wives, so that his masculinity would not be contaminated by other men. Numerous ritual obligations had to be performed to preserve his life. But these ritual observances took place in a setting in which traditional institutions were crumbling, and new political connections needed to be forged. Loyalties were loosening, and new arenas were developing. But these processes did not lead to the disappearance of traditional rituals. Rather, ritual was adapted to accommodate complex and shifting contemporary realities.

DOMINICA

The Creole Master

Douglas Midgett*

Even before my first visit to Dominica in 1979, one of the stories I heard about the politician Edward O. Leblanc was that his popularity was such that he could run a broomstick as a Dominica Labor Party (DLP) candidate in any constituency on the

---

*Special to this volume.

Edward Leblanc (Douglas Midgett)

island, and be assured of victory. This certainly seemed to apply to his own political career, which extended from his first election to the island's Legislative Council in 1957 to his retirement from active public life in 1974. Leblanc was elected in three different constituencies, including rural villages in the far north of the island and the urban capital of Roseau. Following the 1961 election, which the DLP won, he became Chief Minister of what was still a British colony. When the island attained a new constitutional status in 1966, he became its first premier. In 1970, he survived a palace coup within his own ranks, formed a separate party – the Leblanc Labor Party – and defeated both the breakaway faction and the recently formed Dominica Freedom Party.*

Electoral successes aside, Eddie Leblanc is best remembered for his championing of those he referred to collectively as the "little man": the agricultural smallholders who comprise the majority of rural dwellers in Dominica. In this vein, he was frequently disdainful of the "elites" and "capitalists" – town dwellers from Roseau who had held economic power in the colony, and the political power it brought with it, for decades prior to the rise of the DLP. His feeling for the rural masses was rooted in his own experience

---

*He was also elected in 1958 to the parliament of the short-lived West Indies Federation.

as a village dweller in what was, in his youth, the remote northern region of the island. Vieille Case, like most of the villages on the coast of Dominica, was not linked to others by road. Despite these humble roots, Eddie Leblanc managed to attain an education, including a course at the Imperial College of Tropical Agriculture in Trinidad. He subsequently secured employment as an Agricultural Officer, a post that took him on tours throughout rural Dominica.

Leblanc decried the colonial system that held the island in what he considered a prolonged semi-bondage. The cultural effects of the colonial experience were what most occupied his attention. He championed the use of the Kwéyòl* language, and conducted his campaign meetings in this idiom. His insistence on the validity of indigenous cultural practice led him to initiate National Day celebrations in 1965. Even in his dress he made a statement, eschewing the European coat and tie for the tropical "shirt-jac" style on formal occasions.

In 1985–86, I spoke with Leblanc at length in his home in Vieille Case, to which he had retired after leaving public life at the age of 50. He was reflective about his political career, but apparently not too interested in the present-day machinations of political figures on the island. He had left that life behind, preferring to farm his land in the far north. However, he relished regaling me with his exploits as a politician, especially his struggles with local adversaries and representatives of the British Colonial Office. In these conversations, the personality of the man emerged as the product of his country and heritage.

Leblanc exemplified what I have termed "Anansi politics." By this, I suggest a resemblance, in his actions and storytelling, to the exploits of the West African and West Indian trickster figure ubiquitous in the folklore of these areas. In the mythical tradition, Anansi, the spider-man, surmounts difficult situations and confrontations with more powerful adversaries through guile and trickery. He attains his ends by outwitting those who would otherwise be in a position to control him. For Leblanc, in the preindependence era, the powerful figures were the colonial representatives – those charged with administrative responsibility, and accustomed to unquestioning obedience.

In the Dominica of the early 1960s, infrastructure development was at a very low level. Most of the island had no electricity; few areas had any more than rudimentary phone service; and the villages, mostly situated on the east and west coasts, were not connected by roads to the chief ports of Roseau and Portsmouth. Small farmers growing crops for local consumption and bananas for international markets thus had great difficulties delivering their commodities to markets and ports. It was a situation that Leblanc knew well from his days as an agricultural officer and employee of the Banana Growers' Association. He had an innovation in mind, but the funds were not his to disburse. His country, and his colonized neighbors, were what has been described as "mendicant states" – poor, and dependent on the largesse of a colonial regime that was often inattentive to the needs of these small places.

---

*Orthographic spelling for "Creole."

Thus, as titular head of the colonial state, Eddie Leblanc embarked on a ploy to get roads built by means that epitomize "Anansism." He described the construction of the leeward coastal road to me in these terms:*

> Well, the British had a department in Barbados, and they insisted on building feeder roads, but nothing that they considered as a major road. Because at one time we did a scheme from Layou to Portsmouth so that we could connect all of the (Leeward) coastal villages, and they said that they didn't have this sort of money and they couldn't afford this, but they were prepared to build feeder roads. So I told them that if we had to build feeder roads, there must be a main road to bring the feeder roads to.

Leblanc accordingly arranged for sections of the main road to be built, but disguised. He told his planners to "call it by any name they want to call it, but don't call it a major road." By the time the road neared completion, the colonial authorities would find the main road was nearly finished. The penultimate section was designated to run to a remote location on the west coast. "I told them to prepare another scheme from Colihaut to Pointe Ronde," Leblanc told me. Pointe Ronde is in the middle of nowhere. If the road building had stopped there, there would have been a road with no destination.

> They told me, "No, we have to prepare it from Colihaut to Dublanc. That's the last village before we meet Portsmouth." I said, "No, no, no. I want that scheme prepared from Colihaut to Pointe Ronde." I didn't give them the reasons. But I could foresee things.

He knew that the proposal for the last section would bring British protest, but he was prepared:

> As soon as they saw the word "Portsmouth," six of them [British officials] came down.... [The British representative] told me what they will do, they are going to stop the road right here. I said, "You'll not do that. You cannot do it." He tell me, "Why?" I said, "Because I know the mentality of the Englishman. He has a lot of shame and pride and he doesn't like people to do him things. If he knows that, he is going to make sure that he doesn't allow people to have the upper hand on him to make him ashamed or anything. And I know you don't give me the right to go to United Nations through the front door [i.e., as a colony], but I can enter through the back door, and I can ask them to send a delegation from all Africa and France and other places, come down to see where the Mother Country has stopped a road in no man's land."

The ploy worked. The British gave in. The "little man" had outmaneuvered the holders of the purse strings, and accomplished a task that had seemed impossible. Eddie Leblanc smiled at the memory: "And that is how the coastal road was built."

When we finished speaking, I was about to leave in my rented Volkswagen for the long drive back to Roseau. Eddie asked me to wait for a moment, and then showed up

---

*Interview, 3 December 1985.

with arms full of grapefruit, bananas, and other provisions from his farm. They nearly filled the car's small trunk. My fellow guests at the Cherry Lodge Hotel were the beneficiaries of his generosity.

Edward Oliver Leblanc died on 29 October 2004, at the age of 81, during the week of national cultural celebrations that he had instigated. They included the "Creole Classic Show," the "Night of Belé & Drumming," "Traditional Culture Night," and "Heritage Day." It was a fitting tribute.

AFGHANISTAN

The Warlord

Mark MacKinnon*

The woman in blue fixes her pleading eyes on the governor and tells her tale of woe. Her husband has cancer, she says, and needs more laboratory tests. The family doesn't have the money to pay for his continued treatment.

Like a monarch of old, Ismail Khan [of Herat, Afghanistan] reclines in his chair and considers her case. Once he's heard enough, he beckons for an aide to bring him a telephone. The health department is already on the other end of the line.

"Give this woman free medicine and laboratory work for one year," the self-styled emir of Herat instructs the official. Mr. Khan then turns back to the woman, whose *burqa* is pulled back to reveal a face streaked with tears of gratitude. "We will try to help you. Don't worry any more about the medicine," he says.

"Thank you. Thank you," she breathes.

Hundreds of people have gathered in Herat House on this Thursday morning, each hoping for a fleeting moment of the warlord-turned-provincial-governor's time. They wait for hours beneath two glittering chandeliers, clutching documents to support their cases. Women sit silently to Mr. Khan's right, men to the left. Some have land disputes with their neighbors they want Mr. Khan to resolve. Others are hoping he will give them a job in the civil service. Many come asking for money: Mr. Khan is most commonly asked to help people complete the *haj* – the pilgrimage to Mecca that is the duty of every Muslim physically and financially able to do so.

Many in the room are poor and desperate; they come here knowing Mr. Khan has the power to change their lives with the nod of his bearded head. Just getting in the room today is an accomplishment for them, since it means the emir has deigned to answer their written pleas, which have been dropped off at boxes in the city.

---

*From Mark MacKinnon, "Afghan City Bows Down to a Warlord's Code of Justice," *The Globe and Mail*, 4 August 2003.

Sometimes, he disappoints. An old woman with a wrinkled brown face under her white *hijab* puts her head down on the desk and begs him to help her take the haj. In her hand, she is clutching a picture of herself as a younger woman, fighting for Mr. Khan's *mujahedeen* army against the Soviets. In the photo, she has a Kalashnikov rifle in one hand, Afghan flatbread in the other.

"I was a *mujahed*," she says with a sniffle. "Please help me now. I'm very poor. I have no husband, no sons and no daughters. I want to go on the haj."

Mr. Khan looks for a long time at the photo, then shakes his head. Too many people want him to pay for their pilgrimage. This time, fiscal responsibility must win the day. "The government cannot pay for this," he tells her. Instead, he gives the woman some flour and oil. She seems grateful just to have been allowed in his presence.

If the emir rules by spur-of-the-moment decrees, it seems to be working, at least on the surface.

Compared with Afghanistan's other unruly cities, Herat has a strikingly civilized air about it. In a country where the smell of garbage is often the predominant odor, Herat's wide, tree-lined streets are clean. Traffic flows in an orderly fashion, following the gestures of policemen at every intersection. There's a sense of affluence – perhaps stemming from the absence of beggars and street children – that seems very different from the rest of the country. Strangest of all, ordinary people profess to love their governor.

"Herat is the most progressed city in Afghanistan, and everybody knows that Ismail Khan is the cause of that progress. He is the father of Herat," taxi driver Gholam Rasul said. "Because Ismail Khan is in Herat, Herat is the best city in Afghanistan."

However, beneath the pleasant veneer is what some have described as an apparatus of terror that keeps people in line. Beggars and drug addicts are taken off the streets to "special" prisons. In a report last year, Human Rights Watch accused Mr. Khan of overseeing "a pattern of widespread political intimidation, arrests, beatings, and torture by police and security forces." The report said the governor's security forces arbitrarily pick people off the street, particularly if they happen to be of the minority Pashtun ethnic group. Prisoners are said to have been hung upside down and beaten with electric cables.

In an interview at his refurbished guest house overlooking the whole of his city, Mr. Khan is on the defensive over the Human Rights Watch report. He can't conceive of why so many people have fixated on human-rights issues when so much else in the city is going right.

"Why do you journalists always come here and tell me what a beautiful and safe city this is and then write such terrible things about me?" the legendary guerrilla fighter asked, sounding almost hurt. But he was unable to offer much of a convincing answer.

"Seeing is believing," he says, smiling under his white Santa Claus beard and casting an arm towards the serene city beneath his balcony. "Do you see any human-rights abuses?"

Whatever the truth of the allegations against him, Mr. Khan and his ilk pose a serious threat to President Hamid Karzai's central government. Mr. Khan rules not only Herat, but four surrounding western provinces, giving him control over an estimated

$1 million (US) a day in customs duties – essentially everything that enters Afghanistan from Iran to the west or Turkmenistan to the north.

He keeps a private army of several thousand *jihadis* – blue-turbaned, battle-hardened soldiers who fought with him against the Soviet Union, then against the Taliban. He has yet to merge them with Afghanistan's tiny national army. On the streets, his secret policemen are seemingly everywhere, twice interrupting a short interview with one of Mr. Khan's private soldiers and asking to see the journalist's papers.

The United States believes that Mr. Khan accepts weapons and money from Iran, a country with a long history of involvement in Afghanistan and particularly Herat, which Tehran has historically considered part of its sphere of influence. To counter that, US Defense Secretary Donald Rumsfeld paid a friendly visit to Mr. Khan last year, infuriating critics by describing Mr. Khan as "an appealing person." [. . .]

Back at Herat House, justice is being meted out however Ismail Khan sees fit. A pair of police officers come forward, almost dragging a young man with a fogged-over look in his eyes. The police say the young man had been selling juice spiked with drugs, then robbing his customers after they passed out. He confessed all this, they explain, after they fed him some of the same concoction he'd been selling. Mr. Khan allows himself a delighted giggle at the confused look on the young man's face.

"The punishment should be to give them a little more," he says, laughing heartily at his own suggestion. Then he gets down to business: "This is a very serious crime. People come here to do business, and you have made conditions more difficult," he tells the young man. He orders the youth to give a full confession on television, while still doped up, so that all will know what he tried to do and what happens to criminals in Herat. After that, he's to be turned over to the courts for sentencing, his guilt seemingly in no doubt.

Happy with his ruling, Mr. Khan gives a smile of satisfaction to his aides before turning to the next case: a teacher who has been jobless for nine years. Mr. Khan leans back in his chair again and ponders how to answer. Hundreds more wait silently for their turn, hanging on his every word. Clearly, it's good to be king.

SOUTH KOREA

The Autocrat

Guy Podoler*

Park Chung-hee seized *de facto* power in South Korea in 1961, and was president from 1963 to 1979. He occupies a special place in the collective memory of his nation.

---

*Special to this volume.

On one hand, he is often hailed as "the builder of modern Korea." On the other, he is described as a ruthless dictator who ruled his country with an iron fist. However one judges him, it took a special type of man to bring order to a destitute and chaotic state, and turn it into an important player in the international economy.

Park's lifelong sense of who he was, and what he wanted to achieve personally, shaped his ambitions for the country he would later rule. His early experiences were key to this project. Park was born in the small farm village of Sangmori in North Kyongsang province, near the city of Taegu, in September (or November) 1917. He was the youngest child in a poor family, with four brothers and two sisters. His father, Park Song-bin (1871–1938), was a farmer whom Park later described as brave and honest, but also a heavy drinker.

In one of his early books, *The Country, the Revolution and I* (1963), Park wrote that poverty had been his guide and benefactor. Throughout his adult life, he managed to project an image of honesty and austerity. As president, he wore simple suits and mixed the rice he ate with barley. To save water, he even put bricks in the toilet of his official residence. Widespread corruption resulted from his socioeconomic policies, which emphasized the interdependence of government and business. But Park himself – unlike several other South Korean presidents before and since – seems never to have accumulated illegal capital.

In his heart, Park was above all a pragmatic military man. His pragmatic strain was already apparent as a young boy, growing up in Korea during the period of Japanese colonial rule (1910–45). Park showed a strong determination to succeed and transcend the strictures of his poverty-stricken village life. He excelled in his later primary education, earning admission to the prestigious Taegu teacher's college. After graduating in 1937, he worked as a primary-school teacher in the village of Mungyong for about three years. Those who knew him described him as a strict teacher who imposed exacting demands on his pupils.

In 1940, at the age of 23, Park made an important and controversial decision: he joined the Japanese army. (Koreans were conscripted only later, beginning in 1943, so Park enlisted at a time when the Japanese were recruiting Korean volunteers.) He was sent to Manchuria, at that time the Japanese puppet-state of Manchukuo, and studied for two years at the Manchukuo Military Academy, graduating top of his class. He then enrolled in a two-year training program at the prestigious Japanese Imperial Army Academy in Tokyo, earning the rank of second lieutenant. He saw active service in the Japanese military towards the end of World War II. Park learned a great deal from this stint of service, and it appears to have influenced the governmental and economic measures that he instituted as ruler of South Korea. In 1965, for example, he would normalize relations with the Japanese ex-colonizer – a pragmatic decision that boosted the South Korean economy, but evoked massive popular protests at home.

Park's military career continued after the liberation of 1945. He fought in the Korean War (1950–53), joining the artillery and rising to the rank of brigadier-general. Afterward, he attended a training program at the US Army Artillery School in Fort Still, Oklahoma.

He returned to South Korea to command the army artillery school, and was made major-general in 1958.

In April 1960, a popular uprising ousted the corrupt government of South Korea's first president, Syngman Rhee. This was followed by an experiment with democracy, which Park aborted by leading a military coup – or "military revolution," as he preferred to call it. A civilian regime was established – albeit reluctantly, in the face of US pressure – but the military continued to rule behind the scenes. As the 1960s gave way to the 1970s, Park's rivals and critics came in for increasingly severe treatment. Politicians were banned, jailed, and placed under house arrest. Demonstrations were brutally crushed. Most civil and labor rights were strictly curtailed, and activists were exposed to interrogation and torture.

Just 1.63 metres tall, Park was not a physically impressive man; nor was he a captivating speaker. By contrast with other authoritarian leaders, dictators, and revolutionaries, his speeches to the masses were hardly a mesmerizing one-man show. Instead, as writer Shin Yong-gu once pointed out, Park used silence as a weapon. The silence conveyed a steely, commanding personality, best demonstrated after a 1974 assassination attempt by a Korean resident of Japan, during Liberation Day ceremonies at the National Theater in Seoul. The attacker, who was either a North Korean agent or simply pro-North Korean, missed the president with his shot, but hit his wife, Yuk Young-su. She was taken to a hospital, where she later died. But Park left the theater only after calming the audience by finishing his speech. This sort of emotional restraint was typical of him.

Though constantly seeking to present himself as in control and command, it seems Park suffered from a certain social phobia. When he interacted with people on a personal level, he showed signs of physical unease, even distress. Nonetheless, he managed to nurture some key interpersonal relationships, if only for pragmatic reasons. Two people whom he trusted to carry out important tasks were his nephew by marriage, Kim Jong-pil, and a close aide and leading participant in his military regime, Park Tae-jun. Kim is said to have been the mastermind behind Park's coup, and was delegated to establish and oversee the infamous secret police – the Korean Central Intelligence Agency (KCIA). Park Tae-jun, for his part, was assigned to found and supervise the steel mill that served as spearhead for the country's burgeoning steel industry.

Throughout his rule, Park prided himself on his education and cultural pursuits. He took an interest in literature, poetry, and calligraphy; indeed, calligraphic signs that he wrote are still sprinkled around Seoul's streets. His frugal lifestyle and simple appearance were paralleled by a lack of the kind of personality cult typical of other authoritarian leaders. While his picture often appeared in the media and public places, Park did not have statues and monuments erected in his honor. Instead, he worked to strengthen his image by proxy. For instance, he systematically memorialized Admiral Yi Sun-shin, the great Korean hero who had fended off Japanese invasions in the 16th century. The statue he commissioned of Yi still dominates one of Seoul's busiest traffic arteries. By presenting himself as "a modern-day Yi Sun-shin," Park attempted to bolster the legitimacy of his rule. This was also in keeping with his apparent conviction that, despite his civilian suit, he remained a military man whose task was to defend, discipline, and revitalize the country.

On 26 October 1979, Park was assassinated at the dinner table by KCIA director Kim Chae-kyu, during an argument over how best to confront growing antigovernment demonstrations. It is said that Kim shot Park when the latter persistently criticized and ridiculed him for his inability to put an end to civil unrest. The death of "the builder of the nation" came as a shock to South Koreans, who had grown used to Park's presence as a man and an omnipotent leader.

Park's personal history and character traits were central to the imprint he stamped on South Korea's modern history. As a boy, he had set goals for himself and stubbornly pursued them. As a stern military man, he battled against overt shows of emotion. He demanded no less from those who lived under his authoritarian rule for the better part of two decades.

NORTH KOREA

"Dear Leader"

Peter Maass*

Kim Jong Il, the world's most dangerous dictator, has always been a figure surrounded by mystery and myth. But, from defectors and former aides, a portrait is emerging of family dysfunction, palace intrigue and imperial menace.

The Dear Leader is a workaholic. Kim Jong Il sleeps four hours a night, or if he works through the night, as he sometimes does, he sleeps four hours a day. His office is a hive of activity; reports cross his desk at all hours. Dressed as always in his signature khaki jumpsuit, he reads them all, issuing instructions to aides, dashing off handwritten notes or picking up the phone at 3 a.m. and telling subordinates what should lead the news broadcasts or whom to dispatch to a prison camp. [. . .]

Dictators come in different strains, like poisons. Some are catastrophically toxic; others, less so. Quite often, the harm a dictator will cause is associated with an internal drive to violence or a paranoia that begets violence or a mixture of both. Saddam Hussein is a case in point; his personal viciousness is legendary. Dictators of this sort are easy to read and easy to despise because they are obvious killers.

But what is to be made of a dictator who is charming, as Kim can be, and has never been known personally to raise a weapon or even a hand against anyone? This can be a no-less-dangerous strain of dictator, and in the world today, Kim Jong Il is its most

*From Peter Maass, "The Last Emperor," *The New York Times Magazine*, 19 October 2003.

striking example. Though friendly with important visitors, Kim is vicious to his own people. An estimated two million of them died during a preventable famine in the 1990s, and several hundred thousand are in prison and labor camps; many have been executed.

While I was a reporter in South Korea, from 1987 to 1990, it was common to view Kim as an erratic playboy; tales of his reclusiveness and tastes for women and wine were abundant. He was, it seemed, a nut job, incapable of holding North Korea together once his father died. [. . .] However, since 2000 a flood of information has emerged from South Koreans, Russians and Americans who have met the Dear Leader, and from high-level defectors who have escaped his orbit. What emerges from these sources is a picture of a dictator who is not crazy like Idi Amin or bloodthirsty like Saddam Hussein. Kim can be courteous, he is very intelligent and he doesn't drink nearly as much as he is rumored to. Nor is he the playboy that the popular myth makes him out to be. Instead, his dictatorship mixes high technology with Confucian traditions: a kind of cyberfeudalism. It is an ideology that has been catastrophic for the people of North Korea. [. . .]

According to the official version of his life story, Kim was born on February 16, 1942, in a log cabin on Mount Paektu, the highest mountain on the Korean Peninsula. When he was born, the official version goes, the sky was brightened by a star and a double rainbow.

The truth is that Kim was born a year earlier in the Soviet Union, at an army base near Khabarovsk, in the Soviet far east, not far from the short border shared by the two countries. His father was stationed there as the commander of a Korean battalion in the Soviet Army 88th Brigade, which engaged in reconnaissance missions against Japanese troops. Because it would be inconvenient, for reasons of Korean nationalism, to have Kim born on foreign soil, his place and date of birth have been fabricated in official biographies. [. . .]

[Once in Pyongyang, Kim Jong Il] attended Namsan Senior High School, where the ruling elite's children were educated; he often rode a motorcycle to class. Even then, he was a student of power. According to Hwang Jang Yop, who was a top aide to Kim Il Sung,* the younger Kim showed an early interest in politics. [. . .] In 1964, Kim graduated with a degree in political economy from Kim Il Sung University, an elite institution where, according to a South Korean biographer, he was addressed as "the premier's son." He went to work in the central committee of the Korean Workers Party, first as a ministerial assistant, swiftly becoming a senior official in the propaganda and agitation department, which controlled much of the party's agenda.

Kim was working his way up the system, and working the system, but also looking over his shoulder. Nothing in his rise to power would be easy or preordained. Dynastic succession was far from inevitable, and even if there was to be a dynasty, it was not clear whether Kim would be its beneficiary. [. . .] As he moved to secure his position, Kim needed to remain in the good graces of his father while outmaneuvering his

---

*Kim's father; North Korean dictator from 1948 to his death in 1994.

stepmother, half-brother, uncle, and anyone else – particularly the country's powerful generals – who wished to lead North Korea. [. . .]

It has become clear that Kim Jong Il was running North Korea well before his ailing father died in 1994, at the age of 82, of an apparent heart attack. [. . .] Many North Korea experts believe Kim Jong Il stayed in the background for the sake of appearances: in a Confucian society, a son must defer, publicly, to his father. If Kim Jong Il moved too rashly, he might have engendered resentment from elderly members of the military whose backing or quiescence he needed. [. . .]

Kim's regime is best understood as an imperial court, clouded in intrigue, not unlike the royal households that ruled Japan, China and, throughout most of its existence, Korea itself. Until the 20th century, Korea was led by feudal kings, notably the Yi dynasty. By creating a personal and uncaring regime, Kim Il Sung wasn't stealing a page from only Stalin; he was also stealing it from Korean history, a fact that helps explain its durability. [. . .]

A hallmark of emperors is lavish court entertainment in the face of poverty or distress in their domains. Kim Jong Il appeared to be cut from this imperial cloth. Through the 70s and 80s, stories emerged from North Korea of wild parties Kim Jong Il held, attended by beautiful women and drunken men. [. . .] Accounts of this sort give the impression, outside North Korea, that Kim Jong Il was no more competent to take charge of his homeland than [*Playboy* publisher] Hugh Hefner. Now, however, his bacchanalian ways are being viewed from a different, subtler perspective. As anyone who has spent time with South Korean or Japanese politicians knows, boozing and womanizing are an integral part of their political culture. Your drinking buddy is your political ally. It is the equivalent, in Tokyo and Seoul, of jogging with George W. Bush. Bonds are forged, loyalties rewarded. [. . .]

Kim's hold on power depends not only on his willingness to impose misery upon his people but also on the willingness of the North Korean elite to accept their privileges and say nothing. Many North Koreans are well aware of the repressed and backward state of their homeland and wish it were otherwise; recent visitors say North Koreans quietly express a desire for greater contact with the outside world. The problem is that none of them are prepared to force or even nudge their wishes upon Kim Jong Il. The Dear Leader understands, as smart tyrants do, that perpetual clapping is generated by terror. That is why he works 20 hours a day to make sure the applause of fear does not stop. [. . .]

ETHIOPIA

The Emperor and the Lackey

Ryszard Kapuscinski*

Kapuscinski's classic The Emperor *revolves around the testimonies of various former palace workers under Ethiopian ruler-for-life Haile Selassie. The following is drawn from the comments of "T. K.-B."*

[. . .] The vehicles drove up the ascending avenue and stopped in the Palace courtyard. Here, too, a crowd awaited the Emperor, but a different one from the rabble that had been furiously driven away by the select members of the Imperial Bodyguard. Those waiting in the courtyard to greet the Emperor were from the monarch's own circles. We all gathered early so as not to miss the Emperor's arrival, because that moment had a special significance for us. Everyone wanted very badly to be noticed by the Emperor. No, one didn't dream of special notice, with the Revered Emperor catching sight of you, coming up, and starting a conversation. No, nothing like that, I assure you. One wanted only the smallest, second-rate sort of attention, nothing that burdened the Emperor with any obligations. A passing notice, a fraction of a second, yet the sort of notice that later would make one tremble inside and overwhelm one with the triumphal thought "I have been noticed." What strength it gave afterward! What unlimited possibilities it created! Let's say that the Imperial gaze just grazes your face – just grazes! You could say that it was really nothing, but on the other hand, how could it really be nothing, when it did graze you? Immediately you feel the temperature of your face rise, and the blood rush to your head, and your heart beat harder. These are the best proofs that the eye of the Protector has touched you, but so what? These proofs are of no importance at the moment. More important is the process that might have taken place in His Majesty's memory. You see, it was known that His Majesty, not using his powers of reading and writing, had a phenomenally developed visual memory. On this gift of nature the owner of the face over which the Imperial gaze had passed could build his hopes. Because he could already count on some passing trace, even an indistinct trace, having imprinted itself in His Highness's memory.

Now, you had to maneuver in the crowd with such perseverance and determination, so squeeze yourself and worm through, so push, so jostle, so position your face, dispose and manipulate it in such a way, that the Emperor's glance, unwillingly and unknowingly, would notice, notice, notice. Then you waited for the moment to come when the Emperor would think, "Just a minute. I know that face, but I don't know the name." And let's say he would ask for the name. Only the name, but that's enough! Now the face and the name are joined, and a person comes into being, a ready candidate for

---

*From Ryszard Kapuscinski, *The Emperor* (New York: Vintage International 1989), pp. 13–16.

nomination [to an official post]. Because the face alone – that's anonymous. The name alone – an abstraction. You have to materialize yourself, take on shape and form, gain distinctness.

Oh, that was the good fortune most longed for, but how difficult it was to realize! Because in the courtyard where the Emperor's retinue awaited him, there were tens, no, I say it without exaggeration, hundreds eager to push their faces forward. Face rubbed against face, the taller ones squelching down the shorter ones, the darker ones overshadowing the lighter ones. Face despised face, the older ones moving in front of the younger ones, the weaker ones giving way to the stronger ones. Face hated face, the common ones clashing with the noble ones, the grasping ones against the weaklings. Face crushed face, but even the humiliated ones, the ones pushed away, the third-raters and the defeated ones, even those – from a certain distance imposed by the law of hierarchy, it's true – still moved toward the front, showing here and there from behind the first-rate, titled ones, if only as fragments: an ear, a piece of temple, a cheek or a jaw . . . just to be closer to the Emperor's eye! If His Benevolent Majesty wanted to capture with his glance the whole scene that opened before him when he stepped from his car, he would perceive that not only was a hundred-faced magma, at once humble and frenetic, rolling towards him, but also that, aside from the central, highly titled group, to the right and to the left, in front of him and behind him, far and even farther away, in the doors and the windows and on the paths, whole multitudes of lackeys, kitchen servants, janitors, gardeners, and policemen were pushing their faces forward to be noticed.

And His Majesty takes it all in. Does it surprise or amaze him? I doubt it. His Majesty himself was once a part of the hundred-faced magma. Didn't he have to push his face forward in order to become the heir to the throne at the age of only twenty-four? And he had a hell of a lot of competition! A whole squadron of experienced notables was striving for the crown. But they were in a hurry, one cutting in front of the other, at each other's throats, trembling, impatient. Quickly, quickly, to the throne! His Peerless Majesty knew how to wait. And that is an all-important ability. Without that ability to wait, to realize humbly that the chance may come only after years of waiting, there is no politician. His Distinguished Majesty waited for ten years to become the heir to the throne, and then fourteen more years to become Emperor. In all, close to a quarter of a century of cautious but energetic striving for the crown. I say "cautious" because it was characteristic of His Majesty to be secretive, discreet, and silent. He knew the Palace. He knew that every wall had ears and that from behind every arras gazed eyes attentively scrutinizing him. So he had to be cunning and shrewd. First of all, one can't unmask oneself too early, showing the rapacity for power, because that galvanizes competitors, making them rise to combat. They will strike and destroy the one who has moved to the fore. No, one should walk in step for years, making sure not to spring ahead, waiting attentively for the right moment. In 1930 this game brought His Majesty the crown, which he kept for forty-four years.

SOUTH AFRICA

The Criminals

Heather Hamilton*

While the violent conflict between the Apartheid government and its opponents is over, violence continues to plague the people of South Africa. The annual murder rate is seven times higher than that of the United States, and last year [1997] more than 25,000 people died in acts of armed violence. Rape and domestic violence are rampant, and carjacking – often violent – is notoriously common in urban areas. [...]

South Africa's high crime rates are obviously related to its legacy of apartheid. A recent article by Diana R. Gordon in *The Nation* (November 9, 1998) stated: "Most of the crime problems of South Africa are directly traceable to the old order or the fallout from its collapse . . . Within the brutal context of apartheid, violence was often perceived as a logical and honorable recourse. It addressed perceived threats to the state or, on the other side, countered the repression. The habit of violence born of armed struggle is hard to break . . ."

But there is more to the legacy of apartheid and the struggle against it than just the formation of a "habit of violence." Looking at the conflict in South Africa and the post-apartheid crime problem through gendered lenses can help to expose the role played by conceptions of masculinity in both the political violence and the crime problem.

Jacklyn Cock explores the role of masculinity in the South African conflict in her 1993 book, *Women and War in South Africa* (Cape Town: Oxford University Press). She notes, "There is a connection between masculinity and militarism; the traditional notion of masculinity resonates with militarist ideas. The army is an institutional sphere for the cultivation of masculinity; war provides the social space for its validation" (p. 58).

Men and boys on both sides of the conflict were socialized into seeking validation of their masculinity within the context of the war and violence. Boys became men through the rituals of violent conflict. But today the conflict is over, and violent crime is on the rise – is there a connection? A study released in September 1998 by the Johannesburg-based Centre for the Study of Violence and Reconciliation indicates that there may be. The study was conducted among 13 to 25-year-olds who were serving jail terms or already involved in crime. According to an Africa News Serve article ("South Africa: Youths Expect to Have Life of Luxury," September 22, 1998), a complex mix of masculinity and consumerism has given rise to an attitude among young men by which they believe that they deserve a "range of possessions, like smart cars, designer clothes, and good looking women, at any price." The study found that for those who did not

---

*From Heather Hamilton, "Gender and Crime," http://www.pressroom.com/~hbhamilton/crime.htm.

come from poverty-stricken or broken homes, peer pressure and a desire to prove themselves as "men" led to their indulgence in violent crime.

> My friends in the township enjoy talking about stealing cars and because I'm from the white school they think that I won't do it. They think that I am not strong, that I'm not man enough. I want to prove to them that I can do it even if I'm in a multiracial school. I want to show them that I'm a man too. – Jabu, from Durban

The youths interviewed also indicated that one reason for a life of crime was to satisfy the demands of their girlfriends:

> . . . We use our money for useless things like clothes, alcohol, drugs and the groove life. Ladies also demand a lot. They don't want boyfriends who don't have money. – Steve

And while the young men claimed that they broke the law to provide for the demands of their girlfriends, they also claimed that since they paid for the women when they went out, they were automatically entitled to sex, and, if refused, to physically abuse their girlfriend: "If I pay for her, she's my woman [said one informant]. Tell me what I would have paid for if she does not want to have sex with me? I speak, she listens. I'm the man."

Whereas during the conflict young men could prove their masculinity in the context of the political conflict, today they are increasingly turning to crime to prove that they are men. For some young men, crime has replaced war as the boy's rite of passage to manhood. The official war in South Africa has ended, but young men are continuing a war of their own, with tragic results for both the greater South African society and the individual women in their lives.

KENYA

Manhood and Violence

Tom Odhiambo*

John Kiriamiti is best known in Kenya for his semi-autobiographical novel, *My Life in Crime*, published in 1984. He subsequently wrote *My Life with a Criminal: Milly's Story* (1989), which reads like a sequel to the first novel. Two other books appeared in the 1990s, *Son of Fate* (1994) and *The Sinister Trophy* (1999). His latest novel, which is also supposedly semi-autobiographical, is entitled *My Life in Prison* (2004), and offers readers an inside account of life in Kenyan jails.

---

*Special to this volume.

Kiriamiti's writings provide an overview of the life of a Kenyan criminal in the 1970s and '80s. Personal details about Kiriamiti are scant, and he has mainly been known to the public and scholarly community through his books. Kiriamiti's fiction provides readers within a critical insight into Kenya's world of crime and urban life in the first and second decades of postcolonial rule. From the petty criminality of pick-pocketing in the streets of Nairobi, bag-snatching, and mugging, to hardened bank-robbers, Kiriamiti's novels recount mostly the experiences of male criminals – although, naturally, with some women involved – and the resulting violence when they are confronted by the police, in Kenya's cities and towns.

Kiriamiti's criminal life begins as some form of juvenile protest and rebellion against parental and school control. He comes from a more or less stable family: both his parents were teachers, and he claims to have been "well provided for." It seems, therefore, that his rebellion is natural for a youth of his age. But Kiriamiti is sucked into another world altogether when he deserts school and home, and heads to Nairobi, the economic and political capital city of Kenya. Once there, he realizes that life is tough for those without a regular source of income. He turns to criminality, joining gangs of youths who snatch bags from unsuspecting women and pick men's pockets in order to survive. This social transformation for Kiriamiti is inevitable because formal employment is hard to come by in Nairobi, the more so for a person without proper skills. He succinctly summarizes his situation: "So, now here I was back in Nairobi and on my own, but this time with a different occupation. I was now a pickpocket under instructions. I had so far managed to pick the pockets of about six people and had got away with about Shs. 1,500.00 which I had shared with Wanjau. He himself was, of course, a professional, and I only an amateur."

Both in the foreword and the conclusion to *My Life in Crime*, Kiriamiti implicitly condemns or warns the reader against crime. "I am a reformed person. I am wholly decided on the right side of the law for as long as I live. The main reason is that I have learnt that crime does not pay." But much of what he recounts in these novels involves his personal journey into a criminal world that provides him with material things – money, cars, a good house, expensive clothes, access to high-class hotels – and with a life better than that of many from his social class. In *My Life in Crime*, Kiriamiti evolves from a youthful street criminal into a cunning and intelligent organizer with a reputation for ruthlessness in dealing with those who double-cross him. From a pickpocket using minimal violence, he matures into a gunslinger for hire, robbing banks and eluding arrest for long periods. He writes: "Within two years, that is between 1965 and 1967, I had become known to many criminals, from robbers, car breakers, shop breakers to car thieves and racketeers. I had also come to be known by the name of Jack Zollo. I left the risky job of picking pockets and joined car breakers. This was risky too but not half as risky as picking pockets."

The money from the bank robberies is spent mostly on drinking, buying female companions for brief sexual liaisons, and purchasing expensive goods. For instance, on one occasion after he and his gang had robbed someone and he had received his share

amounting to Shs. 6,000.00, several thoughts run through his mind: "I thought of buying a second hand car but I realized that I would have to employ a driver. I thought of
buying a plot [piece of land], then I remembered that they cost over Shs. 30,000.00. I
realized that the money had confused me completely. So, I decided to buy furniture the
following day. I would also buy a radio and a record player. 'A tape recorder too would
do, if all goes well,' I said to myself." But even these possessions do not last long, as they
are liable to be sold off when there are no jobs. As well, whenever he has money, the
man known as Jack Zollo spends most of his time in one of the bars that litter Nairobi.
This leads him to complain at one point: "The problem with me was that with all the
cash I had, I did not buy a thing I could live to remember. Instead, I spent it on beer
from this bar to the other, making sure that every prostitute looked my way." These bars
are his second home, serving both as hiding places from the law, and as sources of
information about the latest happenings in the Nairobi underworld, and as places to
meet women and fellow criminals.

He lives with a female partner, Milly, whom he describes as his "Helen of Troy": "I
really enjoyed living with that girl. She is one of the rare type in any country." But
Kiriamiti/Zollo has no moral qualms about spending his time with other women. He
runs to Milly whenever he is wounded in a shootout with police, or when he has to
"cool off." But women serve as mere accessories in his life. They do not feature in any of
his key decisions, and he is as likely to betray or lie to them as he is to speak with them.
He shares hardly any secrets with Milly, and she does not attempt to intervene to reform
him. Women are simply appendages to his male character and identity: comforters,
companions, and nurses. They allow him to demonstrate his manhood through sexual
prowess (which explains his promiscuity even when married), and through providing
them with the material things they need. It is instructive, though, that throughout the
time that Zollo is involved in crime, he hardly ever victimizes or violates women
directly.

Zollo's fellow criminals, on the other hand, are like his brothers. They protect him,
and in return he safeguards their interests. By recounting the stories of his adventures
and great escapes, these men contribute to his fame as a daring, violent, but successful
criminal. Confrontation with the police, car chases, arrests, tortures, convictions and
jail – these provide only thrilling moments for Zollo, enabling him to pit his wits and
energies against those of other men. Zollo sees the police not just as representatives of
the law, but as fellow males against whom he can test himself: outrunning them, best-
ing them in a shootout, or surviving their intensive interrogations. When he is eventually arrested and interrogated by a police officer, Zollo quotes a Kikuyu proverb that
underlines his experiences with the police: "I knew for sure I was beaten but I was not
going to sing a chorus to everything he [the interrogator] said. The Kikuyu elders say
that 'Ona igikua ni iikagia thari.' The proverb means, for instance, that if you are fighting with a person you are sure is stronger than you, you can't stand and let him beat you
just because he is stronger than you. You must at least try to give him a punch. You may
surprise yourself and find yourself actually beating him."

Kiriamiti returns to his core themes in *Son of Fate* and *The Sinister Trophy*, both of which he characterizes as "proper fiction," compared to the two earlier books. Again, his protagonist is a man who struggles to earn a living legitimately, and is eventually drawn into the world of crime. At the end of *The Sinister Trophy*, the protagonist seems to suggest that his criminal life is too hectic and demanding. By refusing payment for the (criminal) work that he had been hired to do, and which he had completed successfully, he seeks his freedom. "It has been a long dark night since I accepted the assignment. I have achieved what I did. I feel that the best thing do is to leave things at that point and try my best to forget them. When I leave this room I'll not turn round to face you, that is as long as you'll be here. Nothing is going to change my mind because this is the only way to gain personal freedom. Freedom from within, freedom that cannot be questioned by anybody because it is self-made – that is what I'll work towards from now on." It is as if the protagonist – and by extension the author – is recanting the raw and violent masculinity that typified his life, and now seeks solace in one of his many women: "If there was anybody who could console me right now it was Catherine Malowe."

Kiriamiti's stories of crime and violence reproduce a discourse of Kenyan men in struggle and competition among themselves for the spoils of a postcolonial state – whether as members of the underclass, the propertied class, or the government and its agents. In the cities and towns, men fight for the limited resources available, and it is those who are the most manly – or the most violent – who end up with the spoils.

SOUTH AFRICA

Gangs and Activists

Suren Pillay*

A few years ago, I found myself among some youths who were familiar to me. I did not recognize them at first, because their faces were covered by the checkered scarves that we associate now with the Palestinians. It was in a community called Rylands, one of the two group areas designated by the apartheid state for so-called Indians in Cape Town. It was also the neighborhood I grew up in. The last time I had seen youths covering their faces in this manner in the neighborhood was about ten years earlier. And at that time I happened to be one of them. It was during the school boycotts of 1985. We used the scarves to protect our faces from identification by the police as we set up barricades of burning car-tires in the street, and when we hurled petrol bombs at the ubiquitous canary-yellow police vehicles that surrounded our schools.

---

*Special to this volume.

This time the youths I met were participating in a march organized by a newly-formed group called PAGAD – People Against Gangsterism and Drugs. It was formed by local community leaders, particularly teachers, who were fed up with the prolifera-tion of gang violence and the drug trade on the Cape Flats. Their unhappiness was framed within a particular religious–moral discourse. They were overwhelmingly Muslim, and it was to Islamic scripture and symbolism that they turned to articulate their desire to, in their words, "rid the community" of gangs and drugs. The strategy was to call public meetings, at the end of which a march would proceed to the house of a drug dealer. He or she would be given a 24-hour ultimatum to cease selling drugs, or face the consequences. Most people covered their faces during these marches for fear of retribution from the drug dealers and the gangs they were part of. Some did it, no doubt, because the drug dealers might recognize them as former clients.

The movement grew rapidly, but largely unnoticed by the mainstream press in Cape Town. That is, until one of these marches, to the house of Cape Town's most feared and powerful gang leaders, became a spectacle. The Staggie twins, Rashied and Rashaad, were leaders of the Hard Living Kids – the HL's, as they are known on the Cape Flats. By the mid-nineties, a turf war was unfolding between the Hard Livings and the other big gang on the Cape Flats, the "Americans." As the marchers stood outside the house, one of the twins, Rashaad, arrived in his SUV. He drove into the thick of the crowd, jumped out of the vehicle, and started mocking those assembled. A scuffle broke out, and in the darkness, shots rang out. When the crowd surrounding Rashaad moved back in panic, he remained standing, shocked, with blood oozing from a gunshot wound. Within second, more shots penetrated his body, and he fell into the gutter. A petrol-bomb was flung at this limp body, bursting into flames upon impact. In a surreal moment, Staggie then stood erect and briefly walked, arms flailing, shrouded in flames, before finally collapsing on the tarred road. I can describe this event in detail, because it was recorded and photographed by the press contingent present. The image of the flame-shrouded Rashaad Staggie's final steps were played over and over on the local news in the following days, and the pictures were similarly ubiquitous. Pagad was no longer just an organization that those of us from the Cape Flats knew about. It was now a national security concern – more so than the issues its members sought to address.

My concern at that time was with the representation of Pagad in academia and the media. Even though this was long before the hysteria post-9/11, all kinds of Orientalist phobias about Pagad were circulating, such as that it was instigated by the Iranians. In the months that followed, I went to Pagad marches, spoke with members, and attended their meetings. That's when I realized that I knew some of the youths involved. They were part of what was called the G-Force – a group whose identity was closely guarded, because they were armed, and were most likely involved in a spate of pipe-bombings that ensued during this time. I had been to school with some of them; I knew others from around the neighborhood. A number of key gang leaders were killed in drive-by shootings, all after having been warned by a Pagad march. When I asked some of them why they were resorting to violence, they said they felt that the new South Africa was not protecting them sufficiently, and they had to take the law into their own hands. Of course, the state could not allow its monopoly over the legitimate use of force to be threatened, and Pagad itself was quickly criminalized.

*   *   *

I had grown up in Rylands – a mostly middle-class, so-called Indian neighborhood. It is more homogeneous in class than in ethnic terms, however; and in racial and religious terms as well. Rylands is bordered by working-class communities, then designated for "colored" people. Silvertown, Bridgetown, Mannenberg, Bonteheuewel, Heideveld: these neighborhoods were also the product of the Group Areas Act, which dumped people into strictly racialized neighborhoods. They were also places where some of the most powerful gangs on the Cape Flats flourished. Our neighborhoods were not sealed off; people moved among them, and many kids from surrounding areas attended the local schools in Rylands.

Between 1983 and 1984, when I was around twelve, my friends and I were passing through a painful process of male puberty and its attendant horrors. Some of this involved the opposite sex, of course, as well as cars. But we were also deeply fascinated and fearful of those older boys at school who belonged to the gangs. One character in particular, Youssy Eagle, filled us with awe. He was a member of a gang called the Five-Bob Kids, and was a few years older than us. He would challenge anyone to a fight, and was known to carry a knife longer than the palm of your hand in the inner pocket of his school blazer. We had all clamored to see him beat the daylights out of some poor contender at the back of the school where the fights usually took place.

We found ourselves talking the gangster talk and walking the gangster walk. This meant using the colloquial phrases of gang language, which were unavoidable on the Cape Flats. It also involved wearing American-style clothing – not the hip-hop influences of today, but the zoot-suit look of button-down shirts, pleated slacks, Jack Purcell sneakers, or the really prized Florsheim shoes. And your pants had to hang down really low at the back, indicating that you were a veteran Mandrax smoker – because one of the side effects of Mandrax was that your butt disappeared. Mandrax at that time was the most widely used drug on the Cape Flats. You crushed up the tablet and smoked it with marijuana out of a bottleneck. And you had to carry a three-star Okappi, a pocket knife which you could buy at most corner shops, and which, after hours of practice, you could flick open in one single-handed rhythmic maneuver.

Like myself, most of my friends did not, strictly speaking, come from working-class families. Most of us did not have any traumatic family history. We mostly went to bed with a full stomach, slept on a comfortable bed, and had mothers intensely concerned with our well-being – a teenage boy's nightmare, of course. Yet there we were, talking like gangsters, hanging out with gangsters, dressing like gangsters. If there was a hero at that time, other than the iconic Bruce Lee or Rambo, it was the local gang leader, whose recognition we craved. We were, in retrospect, wannabe's. We didn't aspire to a life of crime; rather, we dabbled in stealing apples from the local shop in order to establish our criminal credentials.

My own future as a gangster – not that, by all indications, it would have been a particularly successful one anyway – was disrupted by the intrusion of student politics in 1985. I grew attracted to a different vision of personhood, and a different vision of society. But it was also a vision that glorified the figure with a gun. This time, it wasn't the gangster who was idolized, but the AK-47-wielding guerrilla fighter, operating in secret, striking at the state, and landing a blow for justice. This was violence that needed no justification: it was on the right side of history.

I became a member of the student representative council, chairing it for two years during the state of emergency. SRCs were banned under the state of emergency, so it was rough going. Some of the activities we organized were mass rallies, which brought together diverse schools on the Cape Flats. We would often walk to the neighboring schools, and sometimes students would get robbed by gangsters along the way. I would have to negotiate with the gangsters to return what they had stolen. Perhaps I'm prone to nostalgia, but the gangsters would often return the goods. After all, we wielded greater violence than they did, and our form was condoned by large sections of the community. Some gangsters would tell us they thought we were crazy – they spent all their time evading the police, and we were fighting them in the streets. But they also grudgingly respected us.

There were schoolmates, or rather comrades, who were in charge of organizing this violence. At our school we called them the A-Team – the action team. Their faces were always covered when they went out to stone or petrol-bomb a police or army vehicle. By 1986, the army had been permanently installed in our areas, and there was an abundance of targets and battles to plan. Successfully blocking off a road for a few hours became a huge cause for celebration. For a few hours, it was a liberated zone. Without psychologizing, I do think some were better disposed than others towards these kinds of activities. And some would probably have joined criminal gangs if they hadn't been in our political gang. In fact, some gangsters, like the much-feared Johnny Laughing Boy, renounced their gang membership and became some of the bravest of the street-battlers. Skipping the country to become a guerrilla fighter was the ultimate status symbol for many. It was widely aspired to, but few of us summoned the courage to progress from stones, petrol-bombs, and militarist posturing to "taking to the bush," as we called it. At the end of the day, I suspect that many of us found mother's cooking and the girl we had a crush on more captivating!

Some of my school-friends did graduate from wannabe's to hardened criminals; some are still in gangs, and some are drug-dealers. One is in jail for rape. The last time I heard, our lead gangster at school, Youssy Eagle, was in jail for murder. But others do more socially accepted things, like being lawyers. Youssy's brother is now a member of the ANC.

The violence of the gangs, and of the young students, had one thing in common. And it was not their common relation to the means of production, as Don Pinnock, for example, has argued in the most well-known text on the Cape Flats gangs.* It was the image of heroic grandeur that was most captivating, and that provided something to aspire to. It is that grandeur that provides the ethical sensibility governing the self's conduct in the everyday existence of the gangster, or the young political soldier who moves from the wannabe's to the veteran, to – in the words of the criminologist – the "hardened." A profound sense of one's own conduct is required to be a gangster; it is not a condition of lawlessness. The "skollie," as the gangster is derogatively called on the Cape Flats, is intensely governed by law. But it is not a law whose founding violence is legitimated by invocations of "the nation," or "the community," or of "national security." The skollie is anti-social, if you view him as a member of one form of the social. But to the aunties, mothers, and supporters who lined the streets at recent trials of notorious gang leaders in Cape Town, who have spoken glowingly about the positive roles they play in the community, about how they pay rents, take care of school fees, resolve disputes – this is another account of the social. It is an account that sublimates its own founding violence, and the violence which keeps its own laws in place, to its own sublime objects of desire.

BRAZIL

The Lynching Victims

Maria-Victoria Benevides and Rosa-Maria Fischer Ferreira[†]

"Catch him!" "Kill him!" "Lynch him!" The young man – a thin, dark mulatto no more than twenty years old – runs frantically down the street. Shoppers have taken off after him because he appeared "suspicious." As the young man is chased down the street, he drops the few things he has taken. The pursuers' shouts attract neighbors and passersby. At that moment, peaceful citizens are transformed into a "community of lynchers." They have become implacable "justice makers." The young man is pummeled, kicked,

---

*Don Pinnock, *The Brotherhood: Street Gangs and State Control* (Cape Town: David Philip, 1984). For my critique of this work, see Suren Pillay, "Experts, Terrorists, Gangsters: Problematizing Public Discourse on a Post-Apartheid Showdown," in Herman Wasserman and Sean Jacobs, eds., *Shifting Selves: Post-Apartheid Essays on Media, Culture and Identity* (Cape Town: Kwela Books, 2003).
†From Maria-Victoria Benevides and Rosa-Maria Fischer Ferreira, "Popular Responses and Urban Violence: Lynching in Brazil," in Martha K. Huggins, ed., *Vigilantism and the State in Modern Latin America: Essays on Extralegal Violence* (New York: Praeger, 1991), pp. 33–4, 40–41.

clubbed, stoned – even women and children take part. The man's pursuers tear off his clothes and tie one end of a rope to his neck; the other end is attached to a horse's tail. The horse gallops off, dragging the hapless victim along the ground. The young boy's body is torn to shreds; he is a victim of "people's justice." The police who finally arrive to take away the body are not able to identify the mutilated lynch victim: "Bandits must do more than merely die, they must [physically] suffer."

The punitive fury of lynching is far removed from any real desire for "justice." Lynch violence goes far beyond rehabilitative action, as illustrated by the countless lynchings in Brazil in which the victim's body is assaulted with extreme brutality even after death. Many lynch victims are castrated (particularly in cases of suspected rape) and mutilated; others are tortured beyond recognition, the skull often crushed by paving stones.

The above example of lynching illustrates [. . .] "anonymous lynch action." These lynchings are usually carried out on the streets of large Brazilian cities by people who are strangers to one another. In contrast with such "anonymous lynchings" are "communal lynchings," which involve participation by a large part of the population of a *bairro* or small city. The crime allegedly committed by the lynch victim generates very broad popular mobilization. Communal lynchings are highly ritualized; there is a degree of coordination, with leadership and a certain degree of planning.

In one communal lynching, in the small Brazilian city of Matão, a large number of residents pulled their young lynch victim from the court and strung him up in the public plaza. The lynchers are said not to have shown the slightest vestige of remorse or pity. For the townpeople – even those who did not take part in the lynching – "the young man's death represented no less than an act of justice." The naturalness with which residents witnessed the lynchers' violence was so disturbing that it frightened even the police commissioner. [. . .]

In another example of communal lynching, a fifteen-year-old boy, a former ward of the Brazilian State Foundation for the Well-Being of Minors (FEBEM), was accused of several assaults, armed robberies, and the murder of a bar owner. The boy was lynched by outraged members of the community, who declared: "It [is] the best thing we have done here." "God should help those folks who kill bandits." "We did a good job of cleaning up." The young boy's lynching was preceded by a symbolic punitive ritual: relatives of the murdered bar owner forced the accused killer to attend the bar owner's funeral service, after which they lynched him. The lynchers then chartered a bus and delivered the victim's body to the police station, where it was presented to the police. [. . .]

MEXICO

The Murdered Men of Ciudad Juárez

Adam Jones*

The corpses have piled up in their hundreds in and around the Mexican border city of Ciudad Juárez. Often, the victims are found in the desert, buried in shallow graves or with their bleaching bones scattered around the landscape. Most are young. Many were tortured before being murdered. Gender plays a decisive role in the killings; there is evidence of official complicity.

In the past decade, around 90 young women in Ciudad Juárez have been abducted, brutally raped and tortured, and serially murdered. Their fate has recently, and belatedly, prompted sharp criticism of Mexican authorities' failure to adequately investigate the killings and bring the perpetrators to justice. But this essay is not about those cruelly murdered women. It focuses, instead, on the overwhelming majority of victims. It is about the murdered *men* of Ciudad Juárez.

As Debbie Nathan wrote in an article for the *Texas Observer*: "Slaughtered, butchered and scorched male corpses are found far more frequently than women's bodies are. [But] few seem surprised, much less outraged, by this male-on-male carnage." For a clearer idea of murder patterns in Ciudad Juárez, consider statistics cited in the 2002 annual report of the Inter-American Commission on Human Rights (see http://www. cidh.oas.org/annualrep/2002eng/chap.vi.Juárez.2.htm). According to the IACHR, "1993 marked the first year of a notable increase in the killing of women" in Ciudad Juárez. "While 37 women had been killed between 1985 and 1992, approximately 269 were killed between 1993 and 2001. . . . One analysis based on death certificates and other data concluded that 249 men were killed between 1990–1993, while 942 men were killed between 1994–1997 – a 300% increase," partly reflecting the explosive growth of the cocaine trade across northern Mexico. "According to the same study, 20 women were killed between 1990 and 1993, and 143 women were killed between 1994–1997, a 600% increase." (See http://www.cidh.oas.org/annualrep/2002eng/chap.vi.Juárez.2.htm)

The concern of the IACHR is to emphasize the sharp increase in murdered women. There is no doubt that this merits serious concern and attention. Despite the grisly rumors of satanic rituals, "snuff" films, and serial-killer cartels, the key factors are probably more quotidian, though no less atrocious. Hundreds of thousands of young women have flooded into Ciudad Juárez and the surrounding *maquiladora* zone since the onset of the "Free Trade" era in relations with the United States. The independent roles and assertive public behavior of these young women run counter to Mexican tradition, and seem to have aroused a murderous backlash among some men. Tradition-minded men and women alike contend that these women are "asking for it"

---

*Published in Spanish in *Letras Libres* (Mexico), April 2004.

by dressing provocatively or walking the streets at night without a male escort. One can only lament the persistence of such mindsets, and the violent pathologies that they fuel.

But we can also examine the IACHR statistics from another angle. They give a total of 942 men murdered from 1994–1997, as the homicide rate for women was also skyrocketing – accounting for 143 murdered women during the same period. Thus, men accounted for 87 per cent of murder victims; women, 13 per cent. This indeed represented a notable change from the 1990–93 period. Back then, the gender gulf was even more yawning, with men constituting 92.5 per cent of victims.

It is worth noting that the IACHR's figure of 269 women killed between 1993 and 2001 includes *all* murdered women, not just the roughly one-third of victims apparently targeted by the serial killer or killers. It includes numerous female victims of domestic violence, for example. Note also that in 2000, the most recent year for which I was able to find statistics, 215 men were killed, along with 27 women. This represented a slight increase in the proportion of male victims over 1994–97, to just under 89 per cent. Running somewhat counter to gender stereotypes, only 51 killings were classified as drug-related, including five of the murdered women.

What might explain the shunting aside of the overwhelming majority of Juárez's murder victims? In part, it attests to the status of the murdered women in feminist discourse and activism. Usually conflated with other violent female deaths, the serial killings are presented as an example of "femicide" – sex-selective killing. Again, such a strategy has merit. Serial killings of women are an enduring feature of male criminal activity (the killers are nearly always men, except when the murders occur in "caring" environments like hospitals and nursing homes). Emphasizing the murders of women also provides an important launching pad for discussions of themes such as exploitation of female labor in the *maquiladora* zone, the violent reaction of many men to modernizing trends in gender relations, and the brutal domestic violence against women that frequently results.

But there are also more dubious reasons for this marginalizing of male victims. A standard operating procedure in feminist scholarship and activism dictates that when a complex social phenomenon like murder is addressed, certain rules must be followed. Briefly put, trends that evoke concern and sympathy for women – in this case, the sharp rise in women's murder rates in Ciudad Juárez – must be carefully separated out and presented in isolation. Data that threaten to offset or contextualize the portrait, perhaps to the detriment of an emphasis on female victims, must be ignored or suppressed. Hence the invisibility of the nine-tenths of Juárez's murder victims who are male. This ensures that the relevant data are available only to those prepared to dig for it. (The statistics in the IACHR report are buried in footnotes; Debbie Nathan's article, cited earlier, is the only one I have seen that actually casts a critical and skeptical eye over prevailing framings of the Juárez killings.)

This feminist strategy reflects, and exploits, cultural convictions about men that are nearly universal. Men are seen as the "natural" victims of homicidal killing, for two main reasons. First, in most cases, men's killers are other men – and we all know that "boys will be boys." Second, men are viewed as implicated victims. As some people believe that young women are "asking for" victimization when they violate social norms of clothing and comportment, so prevailing mindsets depict men as "asking for" the deaths that come their way when they involve themselves in informal or criminal activities – even though (as in Ciudad Juárez) there may be precious few other employment opportunities, particularly when women workers are favored in the *maquiladora* sector. One could argue that the "asking-for-it" framework is objectively more valid in the case of men. However, the bias against male victims might also be more pervasive and unquestioned, especially given feminist successes in alerting us to patterns of discrimination and violence against women.

This is terrain for analysts and activists that cries out for exploration. Surely, it is the moment for a human rights lobby group like Amnesty International to step in and stretch our minds a little. But Amnesty's only interest in the Ciudad Juárez murders lies in the relatively small minority of female murder victims – as reflected in its detailed August 2003 report, "Intolerable Killings." Everyone should read and ponder this report; it has much to say about women's patterns of violent victimization, and the entrenched sexism that underlies it. Can one hope that soon, Amnesty or some other influential actor will also devote attention to the other nine-tenths of victims – Juárez's murdered men?

HUMANITARIAN WORK

Where Are the Men?

Marion Birch*

Seventy per cent of those living in refugee or displaced persons camps are women and children. Where are the men? The usual answer is that they are dead, fighting or seeking employment elsewhere. How many of them really want to be doing these things? It is likely that many have been forced to take up arms to feed their families, others to protect their communities or their principles, out of fear, a lack of alternatives or because of peer pressure.

I recently helped run a course called Gender in Humanitarian Assistance. The course was suggested and sponsored by Oxfam, who have a long history of involvement in gender issues. It has now been run twice by International Health Exchange (http://www.ihe.org.uk), who recently merged with Engineers for Disaster Relief (http://www.redr.org), reflecting the broad scope of skills and people involved in

---

*Special to this volume.

humanitarian action. The evaluations from the course participants were very positive, but one request stood out: can we have more about the men?

The problems faced by women in humanitarian emergencies, from the Balkans to southern Sudan, are beyond imagining. It would be pointless to try and create some sort of scale to measure them against those faced by men, with which they are anyway inextricably intertwined. But it is clear that the problems faced by men in humanitarian emergencies have received insufficient attention, particularly where conflict is involved.

In emergency-type situations, it is frequently the men who are expected to move away to seek work or join a militia. The traditional caring role of the mother and girl child will continue and sometimes be reinforced, as the family tries to adapt to its rapidly changing circumstances. The man's role of caring-through-providing is likely to be severely disrupted, and he may resort to perilous survival strategies to try and provide for his family. If conflict, or the search for work or pastures for his livestock, take him far away from his family, he is adrift, not knowing how they are faring and open to risky lifestyles that are commonly adopted by men away from home.

The dilemmas faced by men are evident in the detail. The soldier at the checkpoint who, having made it clear that it wasn't his idea that you should be searched so thoroughly, is keen to assure you that he writes poetry. The young soldier who trades in part of his ration to sleep with a prostitute because the warmth of her body reminds him of his mother. The student in a far-off place who abandons his higher education to step into the shoes of his brother who has been killed in one of the world's most violent conflicts. The child soldier who felt he was expected to be an adult one day and a child the next, and who would have much preferred to have received the same demobilization package as the adults so he would have more to offer his family. These are the real people behind the generalizations conflict so often produces.

Although many people can identify with these individuals, mass them together in rebel armies and militia groups and they suddenly become less understandable. Meanwhile, it is likely that their own convictions are becoming hardened, and any room for maneuver they might have had in their lives drastically reduced.

There are many groups and organizations that focus on the needs of women and children and empathize across vast distances with their needs and concerns, but there are few such organizations for men. Solidarity is a word not often used in this context. Yet is there really that much difference between the young man desperate to escape the poverty trap and get an education in Mississippi, and the young man desperate to preserve his respect, earn for his family and make some sort of sense of his country in Fallujah [Iraq]?

More understanding between men who are in superficially very different, but fundamentally alarmingly similar, situations could help prevent the unthinking assumptions about "the other" that are all too easy to make in conflict situations. This is far from a new idea. Men from both sides in the First World War emerged from the trenches to celebrate Christmas together, despite orders to the contrary.

More understanding of the issues faced by men in conflict situations is a challenge for everyone, including those working in humanitarian assistance. Trying to improve our course [on Gender in Humanitarian Assistance] in this way feels like a drop in the ocean, but is an effort we are keen to make. This is far from detracting from the problems faced by women. In the balance, women can only benefit from a closer look and a greater recognition of the problems faced by men.

EGYPT

The Gay Man

Josh Hammer*

He was standing in the lobby of the Marriott Hotel in Cairo, just in front of the reception desk, when I first laid eyes on him. A chubby, pleasant-looking man in his mid thirties, he wore a fashionable black turtleneck and a pony tail that set him apart from the conservative-looking Arab businessmen congregated in the opulent lobby. I nodded at him and flashed him a copy of *Newsweek*, as we'd agreed on the telephone; he gave me a little smile of acknowledgment and followed me out the glass door and onto the banks of the Nile. As we stepped into a taxi for a trip across town to Cairo's bustling bazaar district, Horus, as he called himself, admitted that his pony tail was a risqué statement in today's conservative Egypt. "People give me looks," he said, in near perfect English. "I'm now considered a 'suspect.'"

These are perilous times to be gay in Egypt. During the past 12 months, a massive police crackdown against homosexual men has terrified the country's deeply closeted gay community and raised a chorus of criticism from human rights groups in Europe and America. Nobody knows how many gays are languishing in Egyptian jails – the number is certainly in the hundreds – or what prompted the massive dragnet. But because of the strict societal taboos against homosexuality, Egyptian human-rights groups have shunned such cases, leaving it to a handful of local gay activists to raise legal fees and provide other support. The work can be hazardous. Gay activists in Egypt risk ostracism, arrest and even violence. But for crusaders like Horus, one of perhaps a dozen Egyptians who has "come out" to friends and family, heightening the world's awareness of human rights abuses takes priority over personal safety.

Born into an upper-middle-class Cairo family, Horus came out eight years ago, he told me, following a traumatic breakup with a longtime lover. The man had been a fellow performer in Horus's theater group in Cairo; but he was so ashamed of the

*From Josh Hammer, "One Man's Tale," *Newsweek*, 16 February 2002.

relationship that he kept it a deep secret, refusing to let them be seen together in public. Eventually he left Horus, claiming that homosexuality was a "sin." At first, Horus felt betrayed and angry. "Then I thought to myself, 'How can I blame him when I'm doing the same thing he's doing?'" he says, sipping thick Arabic coffee in an outdoor stall. "I also was hiding who I really am."

He first revealed his sexual identity to his theater colleagues, most of whom proved to be supportive. His immediate family was far less so. "My brother was very homophobic. He accused me of being sick, called me a faggot and told me I had to be treated by a psychiatrist." His father, a chemist at a Cairo university, responded by walking out of the room and refusing to discuss the subject further. (His mother had died years earlier.) Even sympathetic relatives responded with a measure of denial: a favorite aunt still invites him to her house for social engagements – to meet available women. "She still believes that I just haven't met the right girl," he said with a resigned smile.

Gradually, his activism deepened. In 1999 Horus wrote and directed an experimental play for a Cairo theater called "Harem" – a pun on the Arabic word "Haram," meaning forbidden – a semi-autobiographical work dealing with homosexuality and other taboos. The play was praised by many Cairo critics and selected as an entry into an international theater competition in Europe. But some members of the Egyptian nomination committee called the work "immoral" and, after a heated debate, the play was withdrawn. Since then, Horus says, he has had difficulty finding financial support or a stage for his plays.

Even as his work in the theater dried up, he was finding a new identity. In 1998 Horus became the "moderator" of an Internet mailing list and chat room for homosexuals that caught on in the Cairo underground; within a year more than 800 subscribers had signed on. The Internet brought Horus into contact with other Egyptian gays who had similar stories of shame, self-loathing and deeply closeted lives. He encountered young men who had been locked out of their homes by their parents and forced to sleep on the streets, others whose fathers had savagely beaten them, some whose parents had forced them to seek psychiatric help so they could be "cured" of their "disease." At the same time, he discovered that his chat room was providing a desperately needed service: it was allowing gay men to be candid about their identities, to discuss their frustrations, and develop a support network of fellow gays. "There were three optimistic years when people were finding their way to us and other Web sites, and we started to have hope that maybe one day people will understand that we exist, that we are visible," he says.

Then came the crackdown. Apparently worried about spreading gay activism and anxious to placate its fundamentalist Muslim constituency, the increasingly conservative regime of President Hosni Mubarak tightened the screws on Egypt's homosexuals. In 2000, Horus says "we started to hear about an Internet crimes department – set up mainly to trap gray men on the Internet." That year, two men who ran a gay Web site were arrested, convicted of various crimes and sentenced to lengthy jail terms. The government also intensified its harassment and prosecution of gay men gathering in public places.

In 2000 eighteen homosexuals were convicted and jailed for two years following a dragnet of Cairo nightclubs and discotheques. Then in the spring of 2001, came the case that made headlines around the world and became a symbol of Egyptian intolerance: the arrest of 53 gay men at the Queen Boat floating discotheque on the Nile in Cairo, and their highly publicized trial last November before a special State Security Court normally used to prosecute suspected Islamic terrorists.

The Queen Boat case had a personal impact on Horus. Although he rarely attended parties on the boat, three of his closest friends were amongst those arrested that night. Within days, the Queen Boat case "took over my life," he says. He pressured reluctant attorneys to defend the arrested men, contacted their families, raised funds abroad via the Internet, followed the trial and wrote lengthy reports for international human-rights groups. He even took the dramatic step of appearing undisguised on CNN International to talk about the case. In the end, 22 of the defendants were convicted on charges ranging from defiling religion to debauchery; one was sentenced to five years in jail, while the others drew prison terms of between one and three years.

The last few months have left Horus feeling increasingly pessimistic. His Internet chat room has all but disbanded. Most of the gay men he knows are frightened and have stopped going out at night. Every day brings new stories of roundups of homosexuals in Cairo and other cities; several friends have been held for as long as sixty days without charges and beaten badly in prison.

Horus is now trying to arrange attorneys for eight suspected gays picked up in the Nile Delta city of Damanhur and charged, like the Queen Boat 52, with defiling religion and debauchery; last week police refused to allow the lawyers entrance into the prison where the suspects are being detained. "Egypt was one of the most open-minded countries in the area, but now we are more conservative than any other," Horus said, leading me through the labyrinthine alleys of the bazaar. He flinches at the sight of a half dozen Egyptian security policemen making their rounds past souvenir stalls and coffee shops. "I get paranoid whenever I see the police these days," he admits.

He points to a cluster of burqa-wearing women gathered outside a mosque: "Look at that. A few years ago those women would have raised eyebrows in Cairo. Now, nobody pays attention. The fundamentalists are taking over this country."

Horus's increasingly high profile as a gay activist in Egypt has begun to earn him invitations abroad even as he finds himself at growing risk at home. Next week, he is flying to the United States to attend a human rights conference, after which he plans to tour the country for the first time. He says he has often contemplated leaving Egypt for good. "I'm going through ups and downs," he says. "One day I feel the country isn't safe for people like me. Other days I think I should stay and fight." At a taxi stand on the edge of Cairo's old city, Horus bids me farewell. "I try to stay hopeful," he tells me, shaking my hand. "But it's a very dark time right now."

JAMAICA

The Targets (1)

Gary Younge*

Jamaican police officers fired 16 bullets into Reagon Beckford before they left him for dead: one for each year of his life and one for good measure. He was one of seven young men killed in Braeton, on the outskirts of Kingston, shortly before dawn on March 14, 2001. The police say they were killed in response to shots fired from a house, but neighbors in this densely packed alleyway recall things differently; they heard gunfire, a commotion as the police entered the house, then beatings and pleas for mercy. "They were screaming for help and shouting 'murder,' 'dem murdering us,'" said one, asking not to be named. Some witnesses said that after a brief pause, police told the men to say their prayers, and then the area echoed with gunfire: 46 shots in all. One victim, Andre Virgo, was shot four times in the head.

The police say the men were responsible for killing a retired customs officer and a school principal earlier that month. There will never be a trial, so the facts will never be known. But there is little evidence of a gun battle, no bullet holes in any of the neighbors' houses.

"It would not be possible to achieve the pattern of gunshot wounds on each of the young men's heads in the manner described by the police in their statements," a British firearms expert, Inspector Jon Vogel, said in a report on the killings. "I suspect that their heads were made temporarily immobile while the shots were fired at relatively close proximity."

When Reagon's mother, Valdine, asked a policeman why her son – who had never been wanted for any crime, she says – had been killed, he said: "He was in the wrong place at the wrong time." When it comes to police shootings there have been a lot of Jamaicans in the wrong place at the wrong time. Two weeks ago Renee Lyons, 10, was shot in Majesty Gardens when a policeman was chasing a man smoking marijuana. Two men and two women were killed in the Crawle district in May. In 2001, between July 7 and 10, 27 people ranging in age from 16 to 83 were killed in West Kingston.

According to Amnesty International, Jamaica has the highest number of police killings per capita in the world: an annual average of 140 civilians over the past 10 years in a population of 2.6m. But as far as anyone can recall – the police refuse to release the figures – only one policeman has been convicted of unlawful killing in the past four years. Dennis Daly, a lawyer and human rights activist, said: "Special police squads have had a licence to kill, and to do so with impunity. There has been a tacit understanding that those taking action against criminality would be immune from prosecution."

---

*From Gary Younge, "We Don't Have Police, We Have Gunmen," *The Guardian*, 28 August 2003.

Andre Virgo's mother, Dorothy Lawrence, said: "They're not fighting crime, they're making more crime. We don't have police, we have gunmen."

Despite the lack of action against individual police officers, there is some evidence that pressure from human rights organizations and foreign governments is forcing the government to respond. It invited Scotland Yard, the Canadian Mounties and US law enforcers to help investigate the killings in Crawle. In June the crime management unit, which was responsible for many of the killings, was disbanded and its head, Renato Adams, given a desk job. But given the scale of the problem and the extent of the institutional resistance to solving it, most regard the recent progress as limited at best.

"The rhetoric and the atmosphere around human rights is getting better," Piers Bannister of Amnesty International said. "But the real test will be when the number of killings falls and the number of convictions of police responsible rises." In a country beset by crime, poverty, inept government, a violent political culture and a huge foreign debt, few believe that the conditions exist for that day to come soon.

Far from Montego Bay and Ocho Rios, where tourists bask in secure communities, murals of Bob Marley and Marcus Garvey, often pock-marked with bullet holes, look out over intense urban deprivation. Activists accuse the police of failing to protect crime scenes, threatening witnesses and manipulating jury selections to prevent the conviction of those responsible for shooting unarmed civilians. [. . .] Yet despite the killings, public support for the harsh police tactics is high and the political will to address them is weak. Mr. Adams remains a national folk hero, hailed for dispensing summary justice by gun where the judicial system had failed.

"Many people don't have faith in the justice system," said Susan Goffe, the vice-chairwoman of the human rights group Jamaicans for Justice. "So that's why you get this vigilante justice. It is reflected in the wider society."

In areas where unemployment is high and social security virtually non-existent, the gun is more than just a criminal appendage for young men. Yvonne Sobers, head of Families against State Terrorism, which supports relatives of those killed, said: "In a community without a safety net the gun represents the safety net. The gun is power, money and manhood." [. . .]

In December the government endorsed a paramilitary style of policing. Scores of young men were rounded up for questioning, 24-hour curfews were imposed, and derelict buildings were demolished. The aim was to cut crime by 20 percent, but murders are slightly up this year.

Last week the police commissioner, Francis Forbes, admitted: "I think we have to go back to the drawing board."

BRAZIL

The Targets (2)

Jon Jeter*

Carlos Magno de Oliveira Nascimento died where he fell, mercifully quickly. Carlos Alberto da Silva Ferreira's efforts to fend off the fusillade with his forearms were futile; he also died of a gunshot wound to the head. Returning home from work, Everson Gonçalves Silote stumbled into the ambush and found himself immediately surrounded by police officers. Witnesses said they saw police shoot him execution-style when he reached for his ID.

Tiago da Costa Correia was the last to die. The gangly 19-year-old ran when he heard the first shots but was struck six times in the chest and abdomen. When the police caught up to him, he was lying fatally wounded on the sidewalk, gasping for air and pleading with them to save his life. "I am a worker," the witnesses recalled him saying again and again. "I have a child."

But the four police officers simply hovered over him, talking among themselves and ignoring him, the witnesses said. It took 20 minutes for him to die.

"There was no rage," said Leandro de Paula, who saw the shooting spree unfold in April from a distance of about 75 feet. "There was no remorse. There was no shame at what they had just done in plain sight. The police weren't even curious that a man was dying beneath their feet. They were just indifferent, completely indifferent, like they were waiting for a bus. They didn't even bother to look down at him."

The killing of four unarmed young men – a student, a mechanic, a cab driver and a construction worker – outside a barbershop in this shantytown [Morro do Borel] in northern Rio de Janeiro was part of a growing campaign of terror waged by the police and police-sanctioned death squads, marauding through poor sections of Brazil's cities or attacking street children and in sweeps through drug trafficking areas. The deaths of these innocent victims were uncommon only because witnesses spoke publicly about what they saw. [. . .]

Across Latin America's largest country – in shantytowns, or *favelas*, such as Morro do Borel – a shadowy network of uniformed, off-duty and retired police officers team with civilians to mete out vigilante justice to drug dealers, petty thieves and other young men, most of whom are black and poor. A government study this year [2003] concluded that death squads operate in 15 of Brazil's 26 states. In São Paulo, Brazil's largest city, 435 civilians were killed by police in the first five months of the year, a 51 per cent increase over the same period a year ago, according to statistics compiled by Global Justice, an independent Brazilian human rights group.

---

*From Jon Jeter, "Brazil's Polarizing Police," *Washington Post*, 26 October 2003.

But it is here in the squalid brick-and-tin favelas that ring the jarringly beautiful coastal city of Rio de Janeiro where the violence is most acute. With more than two months left in the year and a Southern Hemisphere summer approaching, Rio de Janeiro has already equaled last year's record number of police killings. Nine hundred civilians have been killed by police, according to statistics from human rights organizations. [. . .]

Brazil's militarized state police and local civilian police forces account for more than one in every 10 killings in Rio de Janeiro, according to human rights organizations. Human rights workers and government officials said the problem is likely far worse since official statistics do not include killings by secretive death squads, often staffed and always sanctioned by police to help keep the streets clear of drug dealers. [. . .]

The two most infamous examples of summary executions by police occurred within days of each other in 1993. In July of that year, six police officers jumped from two cars and opened fire on a group of about 40 street children sleeping in front of the Candelaria Catholic church in central Rio, killing 11 people [males] between the ages of 11 and 22. The following month, 40 hooded police officers armed with machine guns raided a favela on the outskirts of town known as Vigario Geral in retaliation for the slaying of four police officers. When they finished, 21 people had been killed. [. . .]

A statistical analysis of forensic reports on police killings by Global Justice and Amnesty International indicates that 40 per cent of people slain by police last year were shot at close range, 61 per cent received at least one shot in the head and for every civilian wounded in confrontations with police, three were killed. A third of all people killed by police showed signs of having been beaten.

"These are executions," said Rubem Cesar Fernandes, director of Viva Rio, a non-profit organization that campaigns against guns and violence. "These numbers cannot be explained by running gun battles between drug dealers and police and the police come out on top. These numbers can only be explained by torture and summary executions by the police."

In January, a uniformed police officer shot 11-year-old Wallace da Costa Pereira in the back at close range. A 19-year-old police officer on the job for less than a year has been charged with shooting Pereira, who was homeless and bought food with the money he stole picking pockets and committing other petty thefts. Street children who knew him said the police officer had been trying to extort money from him. In June, residents of Mangueira on the outskirts of Rio said police officers had arrested and handcuffed five suspected drug dealers, then killed each of them with a single gunshot to the head.

Incidents like these horrify residents of poor neighborhoods but comfort them as well, said Fernandes and others. Polls repeatedly show that 15 to 20 per cent of Brazilians, weary of crime, support death squads as a way to keep their neighborhoods safe from drug traffickers. "They only kill the criminals," said Joaquim de Souza, who lives in Rio das Pedras, a poor neighborhood of ramshackle brick homes, open sewers and a death squad that is an open secret. "We don't want the drug traffickers in our neighborhood, selling drugs to our kids. We have poverty, but our streets are safe. Who cares if the rights of some scum are violated?" [...]

Residents of Morro do Borel said the four young men killed by police in April were anything but menacing. None had a criminal record and all either had jobs or were enrolled in school at the time of the shooting. Nascimento, an 18-year-old exchange student in Switzerland, was visiting his grandmother during a school break. His friend, Correia, 19, left home after working all day to get a haircut and buy chocolate candy for his year-old daughter. "These young men were as far removed from drug dealers as anyone you could find," said Correia's mother. [...]

Witnesses said the officers piled the bodies into police cars and took them to the hospital after the shootings even though it was clear that all four men were dead. Residents said that is common. Police officers disturb the crime scene and often dump the bodies in another location, claiming that the suspects died in a shootout with one another, not police, residents said.

"This was a textbook police killing," said Jonas Consalves, president of the Morro do Borel Residents Association. "The only thing different is that this time people had enough and spoke up. These young men were citizens, not criminals. Usually, the only thing that matters is what the police say. This time, we broke the silence."

Five police officers have been charged in connection with the slayings and are awaiting trial.

"The police have terrorized poor people for so long," said Correia's mother, "and people are tired of being afraid. We're not going to allow the police to simply murder people with impunity." [...]

EAST TIMOR

The Targets (3)

Doug Struck and Keith B. Richburg*

Jani thought he was safe on the ferry. After three days of terror in East Timor, the boat would take him and two college friends to safety, he thought. Then the militiamen boarded. No young men may leave East Timor, they announced as the boat prepared to depart. Jani, 27, tried to hide; the militiamen caught his friends. "Are there any others?" they demanded, Jani recalls. "No, no other young men," his friends replied in a last gift of kindness.

---

*From Doug Struck and Keith B. Richburg, "Refugees Describe Method to Murderous Rampage in E. Timor," *Washington Post*, 14 September 1999.

They marched Armando Gomez, 29, and Armando DiSilva, 30, to the front of the boat and killed them as 200 refugees watched. Gomez's body was dumped into the sea, DiSilva's on the ground by the dock.

Jani raced through the boat. "Please help me," he whispered to the other refugees. A woman motioned to him to hide between her and her children. The searching militiamen walked by.

The account of Jani, now a fearful refugee in western Timor, adds to the mounting evidence that victims of the murderous rampage by militia gangs in East Timor following the territory's overwhelming vote for independence from Indonesia were systematically culled from the population at large.

Young men, political opponents of the Jakarta government, Roman Catholic clergy and anyone else suspected of favoring the independence opposed by the militias were targeted, in a chilling echo of the techniques of systematic killing seen in Kosovo.

In Jakarta today, the top UN official for human rights said she had gathered consistent and credible evidence that members of the Indonesian armed forces and police had engaged along with the militias in a "well-planned and systematic policy of killings, displacement, destruction of property and intimidation" that could lead to prosecutions before an international tribunal. [. . .]

Here in Kupang, in western Timor, the militias "had names of all of the [pro-independence] party members, and they were killing them one by one," a refugee said. "The militias had names, pictures, addresses. They had lists," Jani said. "They went to the houses and to the port and to the police headquarters, and they took people who were pro-independence."

"At night, the militias would come to the houses" in Dili, the capital of East Timor, a third refugee said. "They were looking for young men. The militias knew that most of the young people there were for independence. If they found us, they would kill us."

The refugees spoke in secret with a reporter, and all pleaded that their full names not be used. The militias that terrorized them in East Timor reign over the refugee camps here in western Timor and move freely around the town of Kupang. Accounts from the camps say the militias are searching for opponents.

The fear is pervasive, even though western Timor was supposed to be a place of safety. Refugees here shun foreigners, and several stopped talking in mid-interview because they said they were scared. Foreigners and local journalists are not allowed inside the camps. Foreign aid workers do not enter; Indonesian officials who make tours of the camps insist that no foreign reporters accompany them.

But in clandestine conversations, refugees described the campaign of terror that followed the announcement of East Timor's vote on independence: 98 per cent of eligible voters had cast ballots, 78.5 per cent of them for independence from Indonesia. The fires that soon engulfed so many homes in Dili were not set randomly, but were used to drive people from their homes, a 23-year-old student said. "They threatened us with guns and machetes, and we heard all the men were going to be killed and the houses burned. They came at night to our house, but I ran out and hid in an empty Red Cross house," he said. The next night, his home was burned. His family fled, and he does not know where they are.

CHECHNYA

"Other Kids Get Killed Too"

Anna Politkovskaya*

"I was glad when they took us to be shot." Mohammed Idigov, a sixteen-year-old tenth-grader at the village's High School No. 2, has the eyes of a grown-up man. Combined with his teenage angular build and awkwardness, this looks strange. As does the calm way in which he is talking about what happened. During the twentieth purge, they tortured him with electric shocks at the "temporary filtration point" set up at the edge of the village, along with adult men. On the morning of February 1 [2002], the worst day of the purge in terms of its consequences, Mohammed was arrested at his home on Nagornaya Street, thrown into a military KAMAZ truck like a log, and then tortured while the commanding generals watched. General Moltensky himself seemed to loom nearby – at least, that's what Mohammed thought.

"How come you were glad? What about your parents? Did you think about them?"

He furrows his eyebrows like a child, fighting back his tears:

"Other kids get killed too."

A pause. The boy's father, a retired Soviet Army officer, stands nearby. He spreads his hands the whole time, repeating, "How can this be? I myself – I was in the army. How can they do this?"

"It was cold," Mohammed continues. "They made us stand facing the wall for several hours, with our hands raised and our legs apart. They unbuttoned my coat, pulled up my sweater and started to cut my clothes with a knife from behind, down to my body."

"Why?"

"So that I'd be even colder. They beat us all the time. Whoever passed by would hit us with anything he had. Then they separated me from the others, put me on the ground and dragged me around in the dirt by my throat."

"Why?"

"No reason. Then they brought sheep dogs and started siccing them on me."

"Why?"

---

*From Anna Politkovskaya, *A Small Corner of Hell: Dispatches from Chechnya* (Chicago: University of Chicago Press, 2003), pp. 97–9.

"To humiliate me, I think. Then they took me to be interrogated. There were three men asking questions. They didn't introduce themselves. They showed me a list and asked, 'Do you know which of these are militants? Who's treating them? Who's the doctor? Where are they staying for the night?'"

"And what did you say?"

"I said I didn't know."

"And what did they do?"

"They asked, 'Do you need some help?' And they started to torture me with electric shock – that's what they meant by 'help.' They attach the wires to you and turn the handle. They probably made this device themselves, from a telephone. The more they turn it, the stronger the shock. During the torture they asked me where my Wahhabi brother was." ["Wahhabi" is a derogatory nickname for a Muslim militant.]

"Is he really a Wahhabi?"

"No. He's just my older brother. He's eighteen, and my father sent him away so they wouldn't kill him the way they kill a lot of young guys in the village."

"And what did you tell them?"

"I kept silent."

"And what did they do?"

"They gave me more shocks."

"Did it hurt?"

His head on his thin neck slumps below his shoulders, down to his angular knees, as he crouches on the floor. He doesn't want to answer. But I need his answer, so I insist:

"Did it really hurt?"

"Yes." Mohammed doesn't raise his head, speaking almost in [a] whisper. His father is nearby, and the boy doesn't want to appear weak in front of him.

"That's why you were happy when they took you to be shot?"

He shudders as if he had a high fever. Behind his back I can see a bunch of medicine bottles with droppers, syringes, cotton swabs, and tubes.

"Whose are those things?"

"Mine. They beat me so hard, they damaged my kidneys and lungs."

Mohammed's father Isa, a thin man with a face all plowed with deep wrinkles, joins the conversation:

"In the previous purges they took my older son, beat him, and let him go. So I decided to send him away, to stay with friends. In this purge, they crippled my middle son. My youngest one is eleven. Will they take him next? None of my sons shoots, smokes, or drinks. How can we go on living?"

I don't know. Nor do I know why our country [Russia], along with Europe and America, has allowed children to be tortured in the beginning of the twenty-first century in one of the modern European ghettos, mistakenly called "an antiterrorist operation zone." The children of this ghetto will never forget.

IRAN

The Tortured

Dinyar Godrej*

Babek, were he not flesh and blood, might be a mirage [. . .] He is careful not to use his name when I introduce myself and, in the story he recounts, all the names of his family members are similarly suppressed. [. . .] When we finish and he leaves, there is a sense that we will never see each other again. He has come to treasure anonymity.

[. . .] "I used to be a teacher of literature in Iran. The reason why I was arrested was because I was trying to stop children going to war and dying for nothing. I was also like other people trying to talk about our rights and asking the government to deliver on its promises. So that's why I became suddenly, overnight, a communist. They have to find a label to stick on you." It was 1980 and [Ayatollah] Khomeini's reign of terror was taking hold. The dreaded Revolutionary Guard were becoming a law unto themselves and, with the advent of war with Iraq, people found themselves imprisoned and awaiting execution for the vaguest of charges, sentenced in secret without access to defence lawyers or a jury. Khomeini believed "criminals should not be tried; they should be killed." [. . .]

Babek knew it was only a matter of time before they came for him. It first happened at three in the morning. He had taken a sedative to help him sleep and suddenly the door was kicked open, breaking it to pieces. "There were these four Revolutionary Guards in my room. They just pushed me and said: 'We are going to search the house.' And when I said: 'You have no right to search my house; where is your warrant?,' one of them pulled a gun and said, 'This is our warrant; don't talk so much.'" He was kicked in the stomach and dragged to jail without being allowed to dress. He was released a few weeks later. "That time it wasn't very difficult because they weren't a very established regime, so there was a fear that they might lose their control of the people." By the time of his last arrest things were very different. Babek had already seen one of his brothers destroyed both body and soul after 48 hours of continuous torture. He died of his injuries.

The Guards came for Babek at a relative's house, saying: "We just want to talk with him for a minute, then we will bring him back." "They dragged me out, blindfolded me, put a hood on my head, tied my hands and put me into a van. The Revolutionary Guards were insulting and kicking me, saying: 'You fell into the trap like a mouse.'" They drove to another city where he was herded into a yard with other prisoners. When the hood and blindfold came off, he saw that his 14-year-old brother had also been picked up. They were immediately separated and Babek was taken for questioning.

A gun's barrel pointed at his head, he was commanded to remain stock still. The slightest movement and one of the guards suggested chopping off a finger. They found

---

*From Dinyar Godrej, "Torture – Never Forget," *New Internationalist*, 327 (September 2000).

his salary in his pocket and accused him of receiving money from a communist organization to fight against religion and the regime. When Babek tried telling them it was
his salary he was put in a narrow, long-ceilinged room that had formerly been a toilet.
"There was dirt on the floor and blood stains on the wall. Later on I was told a prisoner
who had been shouting anti-regime slogans had been shot in the head there.

"For five days they didn't open the door for me or give me any food or drink. My
stomach felt like it was bleeding. I was bursting to go to the toilet. There was a cup, a
milk cup with the name of a city on it. That's when I knew where I was. I urinated in it."
On the fifth day when a guard finally opened the door, he was made to drink it.

He was then taken to a place they called "the basement," a word which has forever
been sullied in his mind. "They tied my hands and feet and I was on the floor. They
attacked me. I was thinking, 'Oh God, they are going to do the same thing to my
brother. He cannot survive, I cannot survive.' I thought they would kill me."

He regained consciousness to find a guard leaning over him giving him water. "He
said, 'Drink it, my son.' And I remember the words I said: 'I'm not your son, I'm just a
prisoner.' He said, 'Drink it. Don't let them torture you. Tell them the truth.' I said,
'What truth? There's no truth. The truth is I am just a teacher and I haven't done anything, I haven't taken arms against the regime, I haven't killed anybody. I'm a human
being. If that's a crime, you have to kill the entire country, kill everybody.'" [...]

He was called to write down answers to a list of questions. The torturers, suffering
from delusions of omniscience that often plague the power-crazed, decided what was
truth and what a lie and demanded alternative answers. Eventually, "one of them said:
'Take him downstairs and kill him. Empty 20 bullets into his headstrong communist
head.' I was back in the basement and they asked me if I wanted to write something to
my family. So I said I wanted to write to my mother. I wrote: 'Sorry I haven't been a good
son and gave you a lot of pain.' And I gave her my love. I was blindfolded and my hands
and legs were tied together. Then they started firing, they were shouting: 'God is great.'"
Babek listened to the shots ringing out, thinking his life would end at any minute.

In the interview room he asks me to stop the tape for a minute. It is now nearly
20 years since the event, but he feels he is in a time machine, reliving the experience. "It
is always fresh. You cannot say that it stops, it doesn't matter if one is tortured physically
or mentally. The physical pain you suffer for a while and it disappears, but the mental
scar in your mind and in your heart – it doesn't leave." [...]

[Babek now lives in London, but his] own family is left behind in Iran, out of touch.
His mother is a shadow of her former self; his father, a once proud man who never
bowed his head to anybody, aged almost overnight when catastrophe befell his sons –
he died four months after Babek's flight from the country. [...] Babek knows that the
situation in Iran still prevents justice being served against the men who ripped apart his
family. He has come to view justice differently. "I managed to achieve what I wanted,
studying, having a job, marrying and having a family of my own and also thinking
positively. My torturers took so much away from me, but I managed to take the smile
away from them. They lost, they missed me.

"I will be the messenger for the lost blood. I am going to talk about it. I will never let people forget – what happened and what is still happening. People have to be reminded all the time."

CHILE

The Executed

Mario I. Aguilar*

After the 1973 military coup in Chile, led by General Augusto Pinochet, thousands of supporters of Socialist President Salvador Allende were arrested. Many of them remain "disappeared" to this day; others were executed without trial, and without the know-ledge of their families.

In most instances, families filed legal suits against the military government, or reported their cases to international bodies. The case of Leopoldo Benítez was more complex, and it did not appear in the legal files of the Vicariate of Solidarity until Chile's return to democracy in 1990.

Leopoldo Benítez, also called Polo, was born into a middle class family in 1936 in the southern Chilean city of Concepción. His father worked for the Banco del Estado (National Bank), and the family relocated to many towns and cities of Chile. Leopoldo finished secondary school in Santiago and studied at the Catholic University, graduat-ing as an architect. Later, he pursued postgraduate studies at Rice University in Houston, Texas. On his return to Chile, he became professor and director of the School of Architecture at the Catholic University.

Leopoldo Benítez was a warm character with an intensely caring personality. He was a chain-smoker who liked to play the piano. Though well-to-do as an architect, he decided, following his political convictions, to build homes for the poor on weekends. He also did manual work in shantytowns, repairing roofs and painting houses. He returned from his weekend labors happily covered in mud.

Part of the complexity of Leopoldo's tale lies in his family life. He had four children with two different wives, and took care of many university students and young political activists who worked in the shantytowns. Even after divorcing his first wife, he spent considerable amounts of time with his children. I was part of a wonderful month-long summer holiday with him and his children in Tongoy, northern Chile. His daughter, Katia, who was six months old when Leopoldo disappeared, today is an accomplished graphic designer who studied at her father's own university faculty.

---

*Special to this volume.

He eventually severed relations with his father, who supported the right-wing political alliance, and he also ceased his involvement with the Catholic Church, accusing it of being an instrument of the well-to-do. His second wife, Myriam Bessone, agrees that he was not always an easy man to live with. But he was a joyful character, always on the move, always painting, always working alongside others.

Leopoldo was arrested on 17 September 1973. Even today, it is not possible to say precisely why. It's said the police were looking for a certain "Polo" who had fired on them. Leopoldo was at the home of his parents-in-law at the time of his arrest; he hadn't been involved in any confrontations. The police entered the house, confiscated some rifles used for hunting, and took him away, claiming that they had found Polo along with a cache of arms. The family heard shots a few minutes later, but it's not clear whether Leopoldo was killed then or shortly after. (On the same day, the flat of Leopoldo's sister, Gabriela, was searched – the strongest indication that the military did not target Leopoldo on the basis of mistaken identity.)

The following day, 18 September 1973, Leopoldo's family received a tip from a friend in the military. His body was found in the Santiago morgue, with several bullet wounds from a submachine gun. His wife did not file a criminal case against the police, because she herself was working for the Civil Service, and had a small daughter to worry about – Katia. The case was finally filed on 25 June 1990, but has yet to produce any result.

Leopoldo Benítez was an ordinary man. He married, he fathered children, he went through a divorce. But he was also an extraordinary man. Despite his privileged upbringing, and the educational and financial possibilities that life brought him, he showed solidarity with others less fortunate. And he lost his life because of his own belief in a more just society.

MALAWI

The Prisoners

Michael Wines*

Since November 10, 1999, Lackson Sikayenera has been incarcerated in Maula Prison, a dozen iron-roofed barracks set on yellow dirt and hemmed by barbed wire just outside Malawi's capital city. He eats one meal of porridge daily. He spends 14 hours each day in a cell with 160 other men, packed on the concrete floor like sliced bacon, unable even to move. The water is dirty; the toilets foul. Disease is rife.

---

*From Michael Wines, "The Forgotten of Africa, Rotting Without Trial in Vile Jails," *The New York Times*, 5 November 2005.

But the worst part may be that in the case of Mr. Sikayenera, who is accused of killing his brother, the charges against him have not yet even reached a court. Almost certainly, they never will. For some time after November 1999, justice officials lost his case file. His guards know where he is. But for all Malawi's courts know, he does not exist. "Why is it that my file is missing?" he asked, his voice a mix of rage and despera-tion. "Who took my file? Why do I suffer like this? Should I keep on staying in prison just because my file is not found? For how long should I stay in prison? For how long?"

This is life in Malawi's high-security prisons, Dickens in the tropics, places of cruel, but hardly unusual punishment. Prosecutors, judges, even prison wardens agree that conditions are unbearable, confinements intolerably long, justice scandalously uneven. But by African standards, Malawi is not the worst place to do time. For many of Africa's one million prison inmates, conditions are equally unspeakable – or more so.

The inhumanity of African prisons is a shame that hides in plain sight. Black Beach Prison in Equatorial Guinea is notorious for torture. Food is so scarce in Zambia's jails that gangs wield it as an instrument of power. Congo's prisons have housed children as young as 8. Kenyan prisoners perish from easily curable diseases like gastroenteritis. When the African Commission on Human and Peoples' Rights last visited the Central African Republic's prisons in 2000, it heard that officers had deemed 50 prisoners incorrigible. Then, dispensing with trials, they executed them. Even the African Commission's special rapporteur for inmates has not visited an African prison in 18 months. There is no money, says the rapporteur, Vera Chirwa, a democracy activist who herself spent 12 years in Malawi jails under a dictatorship.

"The conditions are almost the same," Ms. Chirwa said. "In Malawi, in South Africa, in Mozambique, in almost every country I have visited. I've been to France, and I've seen the prisons there. In Africa, they would be hotels."

Most African governments spend little on justice, and what little is spent goes mostly to the police and courts, said Marie-Dominique Parent, the Malawi-based regional director of Penal Reform International, a British advocacy group. Prisons, she said, "are at the bottom of the heap." With so much misery among law-abiding citizens, the world's poorest nations have little incentive to improve convicts' lives. But, then, not everyone in African prisons is a convict. Two-thirds of Uganda's 18,000 prison inmates have not been tried. The same is true of three-fourths of Mozambique's prisoners, and four-fifths of Cameroon's. Even in South Africa, Africa's most advanced nation, inmates in Johannesburg Prison have waited seven years to see a judge.

Some of Africa's one million or so prisoners – nobody knows how many – are not lawbreakers, but victims of incompetence or corruption or justice systems that are sim-ply understaffed, underfinanced and overwhelmed. Kenya's former prisons commis-sioner suggested last year that with proper legal representation, a fifth of his nation's 55,000 prisoners might be declared innocent. The most immediate and apparent inhu-manity is the overcrowding that Africa's broken systems breed, compounded by disease, filth, abuse, and a lack of food, soap, beds, clothes or recreation. A survey of 27 African governments by Penal Reform International found that national prison systems operated, on average, at 141 per cent of capacity. Individual prisons were even more jammed: Luzira Prison, Uganda's largest, holds 5,000 in a 1950s facility built for 600. Babati Prison in Tanzania, built for 50 inmates, housed 589 as of March.

Malawi's 9,800 inmates, living in effectively the same cells that were too crowded when they housed 4,500 a decade ago, are luckier than many. Three years ago, half the prisoners had yet to go before a judge. Under a pioneering program run by Penal Reform International and financed in part by the British government, paralegals have winnowed that to fewer than one in four – among the lowest rates in sub-Saharan Africa. Yet the flood of newly accused still outstrips Malawi's ability to deliver justice. [. . .]

Paradoxically, democracy's advent has catalyzed the problems of Africa's prisons. Freedom has permitted lawlessness, newly empowered citizens have demanded order – and governments have delivered. Malawi's prison population has more than doubled since the dictatorship ended in 1994. But its justice system is so badly broken that it is hard to know where to begin repairs. Malawi's 12 million citizens have 28 legal aid attorneys and eight prosecutors with law degrees. There are jobs for 32 prosecutors, but salaries are so low that the vacancies go unfilled. So except in exceptional cases like murder and manslaughter, almost all accused go to trial without lawyers. The police prosecutors who try them have only basic legal training. And the lay magistrates who sit in judgment are largely unschooled in the law. [. . .] Malawi's police officers can take two years merely to send prosecutors their report on a homicide. Prosecutors need months more to decide whether the case should be taken to a lower court, the start of a legal process that lasts years. [. . .]

Shortages of judges, prosecutors and lawyers ensure that justice is both sluggish and mean. Many inmates sit in cells for lack of bail that can total less than $10 or $20. The interminable wait between arrest and courtroom torments the innocent and lets the guilty escape justice. Evidence in police stations is misplaced or discarded. Witnesses die or move away. Mr. Kayira, the prosecutor, encounters such cases far too often, after much life has been wasted and long terms already served, by both the innocent and the guilty. "There have been many times when I have used the discretion granted me as a prosecutor to tell the police to release a person who has been there five, six years," he said. "I look at their file and say to myself, 'There isn't the evidence here to convict this person.' " For prisoners like Lackson Sikayenera, their cases lost in a system that only sporadically works, the only alternative is to hope someone hears their pleas for help – and to make a new life.

The Road to Prison

Built 40 years ago to house 800 inmates, Maula Prison, on a recent visit, held 1,805 inmates, all but 24 of them men. Mr. Sikayenera lives in Maula's Cell 3, one of 160 in a pen as big as a two-car garage. Once a farmer near Dowa, a dirt-road village 25 miles north of Lilongwe, Mr. Sikayenera was sent here after he killed his elder brother Jonas. Their father, he said, gave him a choice tobacco plot that Jonas claimed was rightfully his.

Jonas threatened to kill him if he did not surrender it. Lackson refused, he said, and Jonas attacked. "To protect myself, I took a hoe handle and hit my brother on the forehead, and he fainted," he said. "Then I went to the police to report that I had harmed my brother." The police jailed him, then moved him to Maula Prison a week later.

That was 2,100 days ago. "I have not seen my family since 1999," he said. "I was the only productive person in my home, and now there is too much poverty for them to afford transport to see me. The only communication I have gotten is from my first wife, who informed me, 'I am tired of staying alone here, and I am going to get married.'"

"Life is very hard here," he said. He and the other men spend daytimes in the prison yard, a field of thick yellow dust with an outdoor privy, a communal shower and one water spigot. At 4 p.m., they are herded into a dozen concrete cells. Fourteen hours later, at 6 a.m., they are let out again. Their cells have iron-barred windows and thick walls to discourage escape attempts. A sporadically working shower and toilet are crammed in each cell's corner. One cell wall is painted glossy black – a blackboard where inmates scrawl trivia like the cell's head count, prisoners' faiths and works of chalk art, like drawings of autos and dream homes. Prisoners sleep on blankets on the floor, too tightly packed to reach the toilet – too packed, in fact, even to turn in their sleep. One inmate awakens the rest each night for mass turnovers. The most privileged inmates sleep on their backs, ringing the walls of the cell. Everyone else sleeps on his side.

"It is so unhygienic here," Mr. Sikayenera said. "Basically, if you need any source of water, you have to get it from the toilet. The showers, most of them are broken. There is a lot of dysentery. A lot of the time, the water isn't running." Maula Prison's commanding officer, an expansive man named Gibson Singo, disputes none of that. "They were designed for 50 or 60 people in one cell," he said. "But now it's 150, 155. If you talk of human rights, there is no way you can put 150 people in one room."

Maula and four nearby prisons split a monthly state allotment of $12,500, from which Mr. Singo must pay Maula's 124 employees and meet inmates' needs. Maula's share is laughably small. There are no prison uniforms, no blankets, no soap, save what charities provide. The only food is *nsima*, corn mush leavened with beans or meat from the prison rabbit hutch. The only drink is water. The mush is boiled in massive tubs outside the prison, where wardens moved the kitchen after hungry inmates began fighting over the food. The old kitchen is now a rudimentary school, its lessons scrawled in chalk on the walls.

These conditions exact a cruel toll. Maula Prison lost an average of 30 prisoners a year in 2003 and 2004 – about one death per 60 inmates. The average for American prisons is one death per 330 inmates. It could be worse: Zomba Prison, 100 miles south, loses one in 20 inmates annually. But it is bad enough.

"It's just unbearable," said Frances Daka, 32, jailed on an unresolved murder charge since 2002. "We make ourselves live, just to survive." Survive they do, in ingenious fashion. On each cell's wall, beside the chalk artwork, is a list of rules, laws that are both prosaic and telling: "Do not make noise when the lights are off"; "Do not smoke during prayers." Prisoners must be clothed, lest a bare body excite sex-starved men.

"Sodomy is not allowed in this house," one rule states. A cell hierarchy maintains order. A minister of health checks daily for sick prisoners and arranges medical care.

If justice outside the prison is slow to come, inside it is swift, lest unrest ensue. Cell policemen "arrest" rule breakers, and cell magistrates hear evidence and pronounce sentences. "Let's say someone was helping himself while the others are eating," Mr. Sikayenera said. "This person might be given 500 days of cleaning the cell." After 20 or so, the offender might be taken again to a cell judge, who can grant a reprieve. "The reason why there is all this hierarchy is to find conflict resolution," Mr. Sikayenera said. "So there is no chaos. And it's effective. In most of the cells, you find there is no fighting. People don't break the rules."

Mr. Sikayenera is the magistrate of Cell 3. For six years, no one in Malawi's justice system has decided whether he should be punished or freed. But in prison, elevated by seniority and fellow inmates' respect, he metes out mercy and retribution with an even hand. And without delay. "When a case comes up," he said, utterly without irony, "it is dealt with. Right there."

COLOMBIA

The Brothers

T. Christian Miller*

The five Arias brothers grew up here [in Arenal, Colombia] in this land of sorghum and gold. They played soccer together on the town's dusty field. They made cards for their teachers in the four-room schoolhouse. They said their prayers in the whitewashed Catholic church.

Then, on a day burned in their minds like a brand, leftist guerrillas killed their father. The rebels tied Plutarco Arias to a tree and shot him twice in the chest and once in the head, punishment for what they called collaboration with the Colombian army.

Their father's execution on that day 16 years ago ended the Arias boys' childhood, tore the brothers apart and hurled their lives down different paths. One joined the guerrillas. A second became a right-wing paramilitary fighter bent on vengeance. A third won election as president of the town council. A fourth began dealing drugs to escape the poverty that engulfed the family. And the fifth was bludgeoned by paramilitary fighters and buried alive.

The Arias story is Colombia's tragedy in microcosm, chronicling how a spasm of violence turned children into soldiers, pitted brother against brother and destroyed

---

*From T. Christian Miller, "A Family Undone By War," *The Los Angeles Times*, 4 October 2003.

a family. Amid nearly 40 years of internal conflict, tens of thousands of Colombians have grown up in a world saturated by violence.* Like a family business, generation after generation inherits the work of killing. Each death produces a new crop of recruits, many of them young like the Arias brothers, who ranged in age from 6 to 16 when their father was killed. About 11,000 children fight for Colombia's guerrilla or paramilitary groups – one of the highest totals of child soldiers in the world, according to a recent Human Rights Watch report.†

The story of the Arias brothers – William, Yubin, Herman, Jimmy and Elias – also helps explain the savagery of the Colombian conflict, in which ideology has all but disappeared from the battlefield, replaced by motives such as profit, power and revenge. The fighting flares in forgotten towns like Arenal, where guerrilla and paramilitary fighters clash over control of the lucrative drug crops that fund the war. The battles are small, brief and cruel, waged with AK-47s and homemade bombs, chainsaws and machetes. Frequently, they are personal: the Arias brother who joined the paramilitary fighters once nearly assassinated his rebel brother. Now the two have deserted their respective groups and entered a government program that they hope will lead to new lives. They want to reunite one day with their brother the town council president. "The only thing that violence brought us was more violence," said Elias Arias, now 22, the youngest of the brothers. "It ruined us."

Yubin Arias was 15 when he buried his father. He remembers the day, May 6, 1987, clearly. A neighbor came to the family's palm-thatched hut and whispered to his mother. She collapsed on her knees on the dirt floor and began sobbing. "Now I have no one," he remembers her crying. "Now I have no one."

At the time, guerrillas from the National Liberation Army, a rebel group known as the ELN for its initials in Spanish, freely wandered the towns around Arenal, a remote region of central Colombia known as Sur de Bolívar. Plutarco Arias had been hauling lumber with his mules when an army officer commandeered the animals to transport supplies for his troops fighting guerrillas in the hills. Soon after, the guerrillas captured Plutarco, tried him and sentenced him to death for cooperating with their enemies – even though Plutarco insisted that the mules had been stolen from him. They left him dead by the road as an example to other villagers. [. . .] Upon learning of his father's death, Yubin and his mother borrowed a horse to retrieve the body, in a small town about four hours away. There, villagers refused to help with the burial. In a country where people are afraid to do anything that will attract the attention of the men with guns, they thought that aiding the dead man's family would make them targets. The local mortician refused to sell Yubin and his mother a coffin.

---

*For an analysis of the gendering of Colombia's violence, see Gendercide Watch, "Case Study: Colombia," at <http://www.gendercide.org/case_colombia.html>.
†Human Rights Watch, *"You'll Learn Not to Cry": Child Soldiers in Colombia* (New York: Human Rights Watch, 2003). Available at http://www.hrw.org/reports/2003/colombia0903/.

In the end, Yubin moved his father by himself. He found one of his father's mules and tied the body behind it. The trip to the town cemetery stripped the skin from his father's back. The boy and his mother dug a 3-foot-deep hole in the cemetery, then lined the sides with three boards they had scavenged. Because they could not find a cover for the makeshift coffin, they had to fling the dirt on Plutarco's face. Yubin remembers muttering to himself over and over: "Damn the guerrillas. Damn this world."

He spent the next few years twisted in fury. His father's death plunged the family into poverty. His mother took to getting up early in the morning to scrape the intestines of butchered cows with boiling water to make a local dish called *mondongo*, work that burned her hands and made her sick. The younger children sold the soup in the street. The older ones decided to abandon school and move to a nearby city to find jobs. It was the beginning of the end of the family. A year after Plutarco's death, Colombia's paramilitary fighters came looking for recruits. They took Yubin and three other boys whose fathers had been killed by guerrillas to a jungle camp. There, the paramilitary members had captured a rebel. They had cut off his hands and feet and mutilated his genitals. The guerrilla was moaning, barely alive. One of the fighters handed Yubin a knife. "Cut him. The vengeance starts now."

Yubin vomited. "I was terrified. I said I wanted to fight the guerrillas, but not in this way," he said.

Yubin credits the experience and his conversion to evangelical Christianity a few years later with convincing him that violence was not the way to seek revenge. Instead, he became involved in politics. He ran for a seat on the town council and won.

Now 31, Yubin is a man with a somber face and skin the color of a caramel. He is the president of Arenal's council, the father of three, a man who seems to know everyone in town. He takes pride in showing visitors Arenal, population 3,000, which lies three hours and two ferry crossings from the nearest paved road. Many of the mud-and-wattle homes have new zinc roofs. A US program has installed septic toilets in some homes. Brilliant pink bougainvillea plants blossom on the dirt streets.

Still, the town has no phones or sewer system. The river is contaminated with runoff from nearly exhausted gold mines, whose trickle of wealth is extracted with ever greater quantities of chemicals. Worse, the town is still in the middle of a conflict zone. Fields of bright green coca, the base for cocaine, blossom nearby. Paramilitary members shake down local merchants. The guerrillas control surrounding towns. Both groups tax the coca farmers, and have crops of their own.

Yubin's family has been torn apart by the conflict. He doesn't want his town to suffer the same fate. "It's very difficult to explain our story to anyone," he said. "Sometimes life doesn't let you live like you want to. We were put in the middle of conflict. We took different paths. It's not only us, a lot of people have done the same thing. It's what happens in Colombia."

*   *   *

Elias Arias doesn't remember his father's face. He was 6 when Plutarco was murdered. Yubin told him the details when he was older. Like all the Arias boys, he habitually ran errands for the guerrillas for money. But after hearing Yubin's story, he walked up to a local guerrilla. "You're the ones who killed my father!" he screamed.

Elias' mother, Fulvia, never fully recovered from the slaying. She wore black for much of the rest of her life. She wept frequently. She took to bed for long stretches of time. When she died of cancer in 1998, her hands scarred by the early mornings of boiling water, Elias blamed the guerrillas. "When I saw my mother die," he said, "I decided that somebody had to pay." At 16, he tried to enlist in the local army unit but was told he was too young. Instead, he ran off to join the circus – a paramilitary circus. The troupe traveled through rebel-held areas in Colombia. While putting on shows, the members would quiz locals about the location of guerrilla hide-outs and roadblocks, pretending to be concerned for their safety. Then they would relay the information back to commanders, who would plan and carry out massacres, which Elias says he never participated in. "Who's going to suspect a circus?" he said, smiling at the ruse. [. . .]

After two years in the circus, Elias was sent back to his home region to join the local paramilitary unit, known as the Central Bolívar Bloc. He made his name as a daring fighter, once leading a raid to rescue a commander's girlfriend who had been kidnapped by rebels. Even now he recounts those adventures with relish. Slender and boyish, he takes on the air of an excited teenager playing a video game. He flings out his arms, jumps in his chair and twists his baseball cap around and around on his head. "I called the commander and said: 'Poom! We cut their heads off. Poom! We filled them full of lead, and now I have your woman,'" Elias said. "He said, 'Kid, no way, I don't believe it.'"

In November 2000, the fighters handed Elias another mission: kill his brother William. A nurse who had joined the guerrillas long ago, William was known throughout the region as a skilled medic. Elias said he had no problem with the request. His brother was a guerrilla, and guerrillas were the enemy: "He was their doctor. If we killed him, it'd be a huge blow to the guerrillas," he said. So Elias planned to meet William in the town where his father had been slain years before, a hamlet called Micoahumada. William was organizing local coca farmers to protest a US-backed aerial fumigation campaign that was wiping out the guerrillas' primary source of income – the taxes on coca leaves.

When Elias got to town, he arranged to meet William outside a local hotel. The idea was to shoot him when he arrived, then flee. But at the last moment, William canceled, saying he was too busy organizing the protest.

Until a few weeks ago, William thought the visit was an intelligence-sharing meeting to make sure the two brothers' units did not accidentally clash. But when he and his brother were describing their days as combatants, he learned the true nature of Elias' mission. "You tried to kill me?" he asked incredulously, tears welling in his eyes. Elias looked to the floor and said, "I know that if I had killed you, it would have been a terrible mistake."

*   *   *

A year later, another Arias brother paid the price for having a guerrilla brother. Jimmy Arias was 20 when he left Arenal to pick coca in Mejia, a nearby town dominated by the paramilitary groups. The wife of a paramilitary commander accused him of stealing her gold chain. When troops investigated the charge, they discovered that Jimmy's brother was a guerrilla. They declared him a collaborator and sentenced him to death. Jimmy dug his own grave, then stood in front of it. A fighter smashed in the back of his head with a shovel. Jimmy fell in the hole, unconscious but still breathing. The fighters buried him alive. A villager from Arenal who was working in Mejia at the time later told the family the details.

Elias, the paramilitary fighter, decided he now had two scores to settle: he must kill the guerrillas who killed his father, and the paramilitary fighters who killed his brother. He spent two fruitless years chasing the man he believed was responsible for his brother's death before deciding to leave the paramilitary force this winter [2002–03]. His wife gave birth to their first child, and urged him to leave before he was killed. It has not been an easy decision. Before, he had been paid about $400 a month, a good salary by Colombian standards. Now he makes nothing. He had power and respect as a fighter. Now he must take a bus three hours from his home for government classes to train him to manage a corner drugstore. The paramilitary fighters have called him several times, he said, and offered him his job back. So far, he has steadfastly refused. He said he has left behind his life and wants to start over. [...]

*   *   *

William Arias had a dream a few days before his father was killed. He was in Brazil, his parents having sent him to live with family friends when he was 10. In the dream, his father was in a soccer field, doubled over. "My children," he moaned. "My children."

When William, the oldest of the brothers, got the news that his father had died, he immediately returned to Arenal. He was 16 and suddenly the head of the family. He went with Yubin and their two sisters to find work in a nearby city on the border with Venezuela. There, he held down three jobs while he struggled to continue his studies as a nurse. Not long after he earned his degree in 1991, an ELN guerrilla commander who knew him from Arenal asked him to examine several sick rebels. William resisted. But the commander was insistent. "The commander suggested that it would be better for me to join them," said William, now 32. "If not, they wouldn't take it well."

Faced with the threat, William became a guerrilla. He justified his choice by deciding that he would act as a sort of double-agent, treating those in need while searching for his father's killer. Eventually, however, he grew attracted to the rank-and-file guerrillas, often teenage peasants who believed that the rebels offered a way out of a life stooped in a field, picking beans and corn.

Even when he learned that the guerrilla who shot his father had been killed in a brawl with another rebel, he remained with the ELN, eventually moving up to become a regional commander in charge of social and health programs. He lived in guerrilla camps in the high reaches of the San Lucas Mountains. He amputated limbs and extracted bullets from wounded rebels. He helped poor women deliver children. He set up youth soccer leagues where the children would sing the rebels' revolutionary anthem before games.

"I discovered that there were some innocent kids, some of them illiterate, manipulated by revolutionary politics and convinced that they were going to see a social transformation, that they were going to see a change for their families and the future of their kids," William said. "But the commanders were a bunch of businessmen, out for money, not political triumph."

In 2001, faced with an offensive by Elias' paramilitary group that nearly wiped out the ELN in the region, William fled and wound up joining the Revolutionary Armed Forces of Colombia, or FARC, Colombia's largest and most powerful rebel group. He was shocked when the local FARC commander ordered the execution of two teenage rebels, one 13 and one 14, for trying to desert with their weapons. The two were shot point blank in the head after a revolutionary trial. But his decision to leave came only this spring [2003], after FARC guerrillas in another part of Colombia killed a former peace negotiator during a botched rescue operation. The peace commissioner's killing "snuffed out the little light that I had shared with the guerrillas, this hope I had had, and revived the memory of the murder of my father," he said.

William, an articulate, educated man with a round, gentle face, is now enrolled in the same government demobilization program as his brother, though the two are housed separately. [. . .] William lives in a dormitory-style house in Bogotá, the capital. He hopes to have his nursing degree – obtained in neighboring Venezuela – recognized. "I realized that what I had done was wrong," he said of his decision to join the guerrillas. "I realized that I had always been wrong."

He spends his days worrying about his son, a 14-year-old who lives in a small town in central Colombia. During his years with the guerrillas, William had little to do with the boy, who now has an alcohol problem. The boy has been threatened by local paramilitary fighters, who conduct "social cleansings" in which they kill prostitutes, alcoholics and others they deem undesirable. William fears for the boy.

The cycle threatens to continue.

*   *   *

The Arias brothers had been planning to reunite this fall in a town near Arenal. But the fate of their brother Herman led them to cancel those plans. Herman Arias avoided joining either the paramilitary or the guerrilla fighters. The third-oldest brother, he vowed to make enough money to lift him and the rest of the family from poverty. He became a "mule," transporting cocaine processed in Sur de Bolívar to a nearby city, where it was flown out of the country toward the United States. He would stack bricks of cocaine in a cooler hidden under stacks of fish.

In September 2001, he was caught with several pounds of cocaine in his home and sentenced to three years in prison. He was released in May [2003] and spoke with his brothers several times about a reunion. Last month, he disappeared. William's contacts told him the guerrillas had kidnapped Herman as punishment for William's desertion. Elias' friends said the paramilitary fighters seized him to settle an old drug debt.

For the Arias brothers, the mystery surrounding their brother's fate is just another chapter in the chaos of their upbringing. It is just one more link in the same chain of events that long ago shattered their lives.

For the wider conflict in Colombia, Herman's disappearance means little. The war will grind on undiminished and indifferent. Another life has vanished into violence. Another Arias brother has been swept away.

RWANDA

The Killers

Jean Hatzfeld*

Pancrace: Some began the hunts with nerve and finished them with nerve, while others never showed nerve and killed from obligation. For others, in time, nerve replaced fear.

Many displayed nerve while they were working, and fear as soon as the killing stopped. They simply fired themselves up during the melee.

Some avoided the corpses, and others did not give a spit. The sight of those corpses spreading through the marshes, it could put courage into you or weigh on you and slow you down. But most often it hardened you.

Killing is very discouraging if you yourself must decide to do it, even to an animal. But if you must obey the orders of the authorities, if you have been properly prepared, if you feel yourself pushed and pulled, if you see that the killing will be total and without disastrous consequences for yourself, you feel soothed and reassured. You go off to it with no more worry.

---

*From Jean Hatzfeld (trans. Linda Coverdale), *Machete Season: The Killers in Rwanda Speak* (New York: Farrar, Straus and Giroux, 2005), pp. 48–9, 190–1, 193, 226–7, 233.
Editor's note: The testimonies describe mass killings of the Tutsi minority in the Nyamata district of Rwanda during the 1994 genocide, in which about a million Tutsis and moderate Hutus were slaughtered in just twelve weeks, mostly by machetes and hoes. It was the fastest, most intensive genocide in recorded history. Much of the killing in Nyamata district involved tracking down Tutsis hiding in swamps and marshes. Although the Rwandan genocide is notorious for the participation of women (and even children) in the killing and other atrocities, men carried out the majority of the murders, and were the only ones forced by the genocidal regime to "work" as killers. The interviews for Hatzfeld's volume were conducted with men imprisoned for their participation in the genocide.

Jean-Baptiste: The more we killed, the more greediness urged us on. Greediness – if left unpunished, it never lets you go. You could see it in our eyes bugged out by the killings. It was even dangersome [*sic*]. There were those who came back in bloodstained shirts, brandishing their machetes, shrieking like madmen, saying they wanted to grab everything. We had to calm them with drinks and soothing words. Because they could turn ugly for those around them.

Alphonse: We slogged through the marshes with a crowd of people to kill. The mud came up to our ankles, sometimes to our knees. The sun hammered our skulls. The papyrus tore our shirts and the skin beneath. Colleagues were watching us. If they saw trembling, they sneered and called us cowards. If they saw hesitation, they grew angry and accused us of treachery. If they saw generosity, they scolded and called us old women. They were quick to abuse us.

In that situation, the jeering of colleagues is awful to overcome if it gets around your neighborhood. [. . .] This taunting is a poison in life. You try to protect yourself from it, of course. So you join the camp of the ones doing it. When the killings begin, you find it easier to ply the machete than to be stabbed by ridicule and contempt. This truth is impossible to understand for anyone who was not there beside us. [. . .]

Man can get used to killing, if he kills on and on. He can even become a beast without noticing it. Some threatened one another when they had no more Tutsis under the machete. In their faces, you could see the need to kill. [. . .]

But for others, on the contrary, killing a person drove a share of fear into their hearts. They did not feel it at first, but later it tormented them. They felt frightened or sickened. Some felt cowardly for not killing enough, some felt cowardly for being forced to kill, so some drank overmuch to stop thinking about their cowardice. Later on they got used to the drink and the cowardice.

Me, I was not scared of death. In a way, I forgot I was killing live people. I no longer thought about either life or death. But the blood struck terror into me. It stank and dripped. At night I'd tell myself, after all, I am a man full of blood; all this spurting blood will bring catastrophe, a curse. Death did not alarm me, but that overflow of blood, that – yes, a lot.

Pio: Killing Tutsis . . . I never even thought about it when we lived in neighborly harmony. Even pushing and shoving or trading harsh words didn't seem right to me. But when everyone began getting out their machetes at the same time, I did so too, without delay. I had only to do as my colleagues did and think of the advantages. Especially since we knew they [the victims] were going to leave the world of the living for all time.

When you receive firm orders, promises of long-term benefits, and you feel well backed up by colleagues, the wickedness of killing until your arm falls off is all one to you. I mean, you naturally feel pulled along by all those opinions and their fine words.

A genocide – that seems extraordinary to someone who arrives afterward, like you [the interviewer], but for someone who got himself muddled up by the intimidators' big words and the joyful shouts of his colleagues, it seemed like a normal activity.

Élie: In the camps* many came to feel intimidated by what they had done, and others changed in prison, like me. I wrote short notes of apology to some families of victims I knew and had them delivered by visitors. I denounced myself and I spoke of my guilt to the families of people I killed. When I get out, I will take gifts, food and drink; I will offer enough Primus beer and brochettes for proper reconciliation gatherings.

After that, I'm going to take up ordinary life again, but this time with a good will. I'm going to turn a kind eye on my neighbors bright and early every morning. I want to sow my plot of land, or weld, or saw wood, or do masonry; I'll eagerly accept odd jobs. Or be a soldier if necessary in patriotic and dangerous situations, except without aiming or shooting a gun. From now on, I don't want to kill even a highway robber anymore.

Pio: I think that if Providence helps me get out of prison, I won't waste my days as I do now. I'll go back to my hill and look for a good wife; because of the events, I am still a single man. I see nothing to keep me from a proper life. Anyway, I find no satisfaction in going somewhere so as to hide from angry looks. A stained life is better than one that isn't mine anymore.

If forgetting is merciful, I shall be grateful. If the opportunity arises, I shall express my regrets; if the opportunity returns, I shall apologize again. I shall make patience and shyness my companions. I am truly finished with playing the tough guy. If life in good company was possible before, it still ought to be, in spite of those stupid killings.

In any case, we must all get used to the evil we experienced, even if this wickedness took different forms for different people. Because we all had to bear it in our own way.

Ignace: I am a good farmer, and I no longer own even one basic tool. My children have scattered far and wide without sending me comforting words. I receive no news about the soundness of my house. I haven't walked upon my hill since the killings. I am discouraged. Sometimes I feel terrified by the look in the eyes of the survivors who wait for me. I feel disappointed by all I have lost.

When I get out, I think I will manage for food. But comfort and respect, as before – I can tell already these are gone for good. My life zigzags in prison, always banging into things, and the only goal I can find for it is my field back home. I yearn to hold the hoe firmly in my own two hands, to bend to my work without hearing another word, except talk about crops.

Editor's note: At the end of the Rwandan genocide, as Tutsi rebel forces closed in, hundreds of thousands of Hutu streamed across the border to eastern Zaire (now the Democratic Republic of Congo). Their ranks included numerous genocidal killers like Élie.

UGANDA

The Soldier-Rapists

Chris Dolan*

Fieldworker's testimony about sexual attacks by Uganda People's Defence Force (UPDF) soldiers on 7 February 2000:

[Soldiers entered a village] where displaced had gone to collect foodstuff [*sic* throughout]. At 8:30 p.m. one of the forces (UPDF) raped a very old mother of 70 years. She was at her home . . . According to information I collected from her she complains of pain in the lower part of her stomach. She says the soldier played sex with her for many hours (2 hours). She could not make an alarm and he had a gun. According to her statement she is worried about being affected with AIDS (HIV). When I opened the cloth from her stomach, I found that it was swollen badly. This woman has got 50 grandsons and granddaughters. And she has 8 children who are now very matured. Her husband was the late Mr. O.

On the 8/02/2000 at 8.00 p.m. another mother in the same village was also with another soldier raping her. She is called S.D., she is 29 years old and she has one child. The woman is now very worried about being infected with AIDS. She was [forced] to accept sex for 1 hour. Now the woman is crying all the time [. . .]

Another woman on the 9/02/2000 was also raped, she is Mrs. A.M., 43 years old and she has 3 children. This soldier took 2 hours intercoursing this old mother. At the moment she complains of the stomach pains, cervix pain and constant malaria. She is from the same village [. . .]

The case of rape became common within this area because UPDF had settled for 2 days. And at night they scatter to operate.

Another case also happened to a wife of Mr. O.O. who is called A.N. She is 30 years old with 6 children. It was 7.30 p.m. that this soldier came and sent away the husband . . . from his home and forced the wife to enter the house to play sex. This soldier took 10 hours to play sex with the wife of O.O. Now the woman complains of stomach pain and with a lot of worries of being infected with AIDS. She also complains of cervix pain due to over playing sex with her [. . .]

The husband tried to boycott the wife [i.e. not have intercourse with her – *Dolan's interpolation*] but his parents advised him not to beat the wife because it wasn't her need (wish) to meet the soldier.

In conclusion, people in the camp and the few who go to collect food are really very worried and not happy because these [soldiers] are more harmful than rebels.

---

*From Chris Dolan, "Collapsing Masculinities and Weak States – a Case Study of Northern Uganda," in Frances Cleaver, ed., *Masculinities Matter! Men, Gender and Development* (London: Zed Books, 2002), pp. 73–4.

THE PHILIPPINES

Bearing Arms

Jason E. Strakes*

The proliferation of small arms – handguns, rifles, grenades, and automatic weapons – in war-torn Third World environments is intimately related to the social roles of those who manufacture, sell, purchase, and use them. Though often regarded as minuscule in the realm of global politics, small arms are significant for their capacity to inflict massive casualties and structural damage, with minimal expense or technical knowledge. The number of casualties inflicted annually around the globe by various types of weapons is actually inversely proportionate to their size and power.[†]

It has been demonstrated statistically that men are both the predominant users and the principal victims of small arms worldwide.[‡] The conditions of acute instability, violence and poverty that typically prevail in crisis settings provide a strong motivation to be armed – not only for personal security, but as a symbol of social status associated with being able to wield influence and defend one's property. This situation drastically increases the incentives for participation in the arms trade, either by purchasing weapons for personal use, or by producing and distributing them for profit.

Nowhere is this truer than in the low-intensity war that persists on the island of Mindanao in the southern Philippines. This complex, multifaceted struggle is one of the world's oldest unresolved conflicts. While its origins have been traced to numerous ethnic, socioeconomic, and religious factors, the central dynamic of the Mindanao conflict is the disenfranchisement of the Muslim minority, or Moro, in relation to the dominant Filipino Christian culture. Yet, while religious differences have conditioned rather than driven these tensions, the definition of personal roles in a Muslim social system also motivates men to engage in or acquire the means of violence.

How do traditional social roles in a stratified developing society – and gender relations in particular – influence the acquisition and use of firearms? Who enables and facilitates weapons proliferation, and for what reasons? Jarah "Jerry" Hamja, Mindanao political activist and president of the Public Services Labor Independent Confederation (PSLINK), has remarked: "It's a joke among the Muslims that they love their firearms more than their wives."[§] In a situation in which males are expected to demonstrate

---

*Special to this volume.
[†]See David Kinsella, "The Black Market in Small Arms: Examining a Social Network," paper presented at the 45th Annual Convention of the International Studies Association, March 2005, p. 1. <http://web.pdx.edu/~kinsella/papers.html>
[‡]"Conflict, Peace-Building, Disarmament, Security: e) Gender Perspectives on Small Arms," United Nations Department of Disarmament Affairs, March 2001, p. 1.
[§]Quoted in Christopher Johnson, "In the Philippines, an Enemy with Three Faces," *Asia Times*, 22 February 2002.

their competence as leaders and breadwinners, gun ownership becomes a currency of acceptance and esteem. This standard is similar to Muslim communities in other parts of the world, such as Bosnia and Afghanistan, in which the traditional status of the elder male as provider and protector creates a close personal identification with firearms and other material goods. Thus, an individual's desire to own a weapon is not simply based on a rational motive of self-preservation. Value may also be attached to firearms according to ingrained customs and beliefs that are reinforced by common practice.

The dangers of everyday life in Mindanao provide further explanation for the abundance of small arms among the populace. In addition to the various groups engaged in armed revolt – including ethnic secessionists, Islamic radicals, and communist-rebel holdovers – additional threats range from organized crime to recurrent feuds between opposing clans that often erupt into gunfights. It has been estimated that roughly 70 per cent of the Mindanao adult male population possesses one or more firearms, and pistols and machine guns alike are highly affordable for the average man.[*]

But in a frequently cited study of the local arms trade, none of the interviewees referred to self-defense as a primary concern or reason for owning guns. Rather, the most common factor mentioned was the prestige commonly attached to ownership, and the power, both real and imagined, that one enjoys as a result. In this context, gun ownership is associated with all manner of interpersonal capital. The more arms one possesses, the braver, the more politically influential, the more successful, and the more attractive to women one may become.[†]

Black-market weapons have entered the southern Philippines from various sources. These include both national governments and private traffickers in neighboring countries. Yet one of the primary sources of supply for small arms in Mindanao today is found inside the country itself, in the Visayas Islands in the north of the archipelago. In the city of Danao in the central province of Cebu, a cottage industry has developed to manufacture homemade weapons, or *paltik*, which provides effective, if slightly less efficient, replicas of firearms from the world's leading arsenals.

Local arms dealer "Ronberto Garcia," 53, former farmer and gunsmith Boy Dalmasin, 40, and enterprising weapons-maker Jose, 35, have one thing in common: they are all participants in a burgeoning clandestine economy that is tacitly accepted and patronized by many in their community.[‡] Their clientele is drawn from a wide range of occupations and income levels – including business owners and politicians – who do not carry the stigma of involvement in organized crime or affiliation with insurgent groups. All three men assert that they are simply providing services for which

---

[*]Marco Garrido, "Small Arms Availability in the Philippines," December 2002.
[†]Merliza M. Makinanao and Alfred Lubang, "Disarmament, Demobilization and Reintegration; The Mindanao Experience" (Ottawa: Department of Foreign Affairs and International Trade, 2001), p. 14.
[‡]"Gunsmiths Making A Killing in Philippines' Boomtown for Illegal Arms," Agence France Presse, 6 May 2005.

there is a steady public demand. "We are just plain businessmen who sell something people want," says Garcia. Most importantly, each justifies his involvement in an illegal trade by the absence of viable alternative employment. Arms manufacturing allows them to provide food, shelter, and education for their families, and to live comfortably in a way that might otherwise be beyond their reach. "The money is better than what I would earn being a fisherman or a farmer," Dalmasin says. "This is just for us to get by and be able to eat every day."

And yet the proliferation of small arms in the Philippines is not simply a matter of economics. Infusions of weapons from US military aid to the national armed forces may also contribute to the abundance of guns that are lost, stolen, smuggled and resold on the black market. These often wind up in the hands of criminals and armed groups, as well as average citizens seeking to defend themselves in the ongoing struggle between insurgents and the central government in Manila. In this context, the situation of the common man comes to the fore. "Civilians are the usual victims of this war," said Kahlid Sali, a 35-year-old father of two. "We might as well die defending ourselves."*

INDIA

Military Masculinities

Mona Bhan[†]

Yuntan has been fighting for the Indian military since he was 21. He was posted to the Siachen glacier as a military recruit two years ago. It is challenging even to survive at 21,000 feet above sea level, he muses, while relishing the dried apricots from the village – a delicacy he has missed terribly since his last vacation.

"I had never thought of joining the military before the India–Pakistan war in 1999," Yuntan says. He was in high school when the war started. Since his village was consistently being bombed by artillery shells from Pakistan, he decided to leave for Leh, a safer district in the Ladakh province of the disputed state of Jammu and Kashmir. But he joined the military soon after the war. He is now fighting the Pakistani army on the world's highest battlefield.

As I listen to Yuntan, on a cold January morning in the village of Garkon, the street outside bustles with unusual activity. Military preparations are underway to celebrate India's Republic Day in the village. Yuntan tells me that Republic Day was never a festive occasion prior to the war of 1999. "It is only after the war that the Indian military

---

*Mars W. Mosqueda Jr., "In Self-defense," *The Irawaddy*, 1 July 2003.
†Special to this volume.

realized how strategic this village was." Now, a steady stream of army jeeps and trucks rumbles past on the dusty road that runs near the village.

Yuntan tells me how he used to be scared of the *fauji* (military) as a child. "Years back, when Garkon was not a border, we would only spot *fauji mush* (army men) once in a while. Those moments were scary. We would see an army vehicle on the road and hide behind big boulders." Those childhood nightmares are now distant memories, as Yuntan readies himself to assist soldiers in preparing for the ceremony.

The Brogpa community, to which Yuntan belongs, lives in villages situated along the contested line of control (LOC) between India and Pakistan in Ladakh. Soon after Indian independence in 1947, India and Pakistan fought their first war over Jammu and Kashmir, the northernmost state of India. The state was divided into two halves, and demarcated with the line of control that snakes close to the Brogpa village of Garkon.

Although Garkon has been a border village for over fifty years, Brogpas assert that the frontier has moved closer since India and Pakistan fought their most recent war in 1999. Their cultivable fields were transformed into battle-zones; they could see and hear the shells exploding daily. As well, military-style governance dramatically reshaped the social and political life of Brogpa men and women. Given their familiarity with the area and its peculiar terrain, an increasing number of local men were incorporated into the military. Ladakh Scouts, which was only a unit before 1999, has been upgraded into a fully-fledged regiment of the Indian Army.

Yuntan decided to join the Army as a result of the recruitment drives by the Indian army in Garkon and its adjacent villages. He recalls that his parents were reluctant to allow him to join up. But he was fascinated by the military uniform, and made up his mind to wear one. "*Fauji* look so different, don't they?" he asked me.

Employment pressures have also played a role. Given the paucity of government jobs in Ladakh, and the dearth of opportunities for higher education, Brogpa men find it hard to secure coveted jobs with the state government. Military recruitment provides them with a decent monthly salary and pension benefits.

Yuntan's first military role, however, was not as a soldier. During the war, he worked as a porter. He had been kitted out in nearly full military uniform, and imagined he would be doing real military work. But for three months, he lugged supplies for the military to their recently established high-altitude border posts. In addition to carrying ammunition for the army, he would carry dead and desiccated bodies down from the icy peaks of Kargil.

To become an official recruit, Yantun had to take a written test and a physical exam. Here, he considers himself fortunate. He passed on his first attempt – unlike his friend Lamchung, who failed the recruiting exam five times.

Like Yuntan, Lamchung had helped the military during the war, and says he gave up school to "fight for the country." But after repeatedly failing the test, he feels dejected. "My shoulders don't measure up to the standards set up by the military," he says.

With most of his peers successfully joining the military, Lamchung feels left behind in the village. He tells me with utmost seriousness that he is working hard to expand his chest size. He has been exercising a lot, and tries to eat good food, but nothing seems to help. In the meantime, Lamchung continues to perform porter duties for the military. Like most households in Garkon, Lamchung now owns a couple of donkeys. Porting has become the most lucrative occupation for majority of Brogpa men: they can earn up to 20,000 Indian rupees in the season that lasts from April until November.

Brogpa elders often reminisce about the old days, when each household in Garkon owned a minimum of a hundred goats. They tell stories of young boys and men leaving for their high pastures with a flock of *nor* (cattle) at the onset of summer, and returning with *gan* (yoghurt), *phlem* (clarified butter), and *mos* (goat meat). Men would come back and then celebrate *ya-tra* (festival) in the village. *Phlem* was an indicator of wealth and prosperity. Men were proud to be *pajlus* (herders). Most of the men would also hunt for wild goats.

Social and political transformations over the years have redefined categories of wealth, status, morality, and masculinity. The Indian army has occupied most of the high pasture grounds. The number of goats has decreased in Garkon, and as a result, herding has become an occasional activity only. Villagers distribute the responsibility of herding among different households (*bari*), with only one or two villagers taking the entire stock of animals out for grazing. "Times have changed now," an older man told me. "The maximum number of goats any household owns now is 15 or 20. However, the number of donkeys has grown steadily." Porting has therefore replaced herding as an everyday occupation. Hunting, meanwhile, has become an illegal and a dangerous activity. In 1999, Brogpas were so alarmed about possibly being misrepresented as "Pakistani terrorists" that they threw their guns into the Indus river.

Gender roles have undergone tremendous transformations, and a clear-cut division of labor now prevails in Garkon. Men derive their prestige and status from non-agricultural jobs outside the village. Some years ago, women were not allowed even to touch the *zho* (a hybrid between a yak and a cow) during *bahispa*, the ploughing of the fields. But this taboo has eroded as women have increasingly taken on all aspects of agricultural work. Moreover, even the category of *pajlu*, "herder," and the meanings Brogpas associate with it, have undergone changes. People often use pajlu to connote a lack of a wider world-view and a formal education, and the inability to earn cash through government or military jobs. The word evokes everything that is *not* modern. For Yuntan, this difference is not just conceptual but physical. It is the difference between wearing one's hair long and braiding it, as Brogpa men did as pajlus; or cropping it short, as army recruits have to do. It is also the difference between wearing a *gumboot* (a locally made shoe of goat hide), in contrast to heavy black leather boots. It is also the difference between wearing sunglasses and not wearing them.

Whether they are able to join the military as formal recruits or must make do with porting, Brogpa masculinity has become connected with the ability to access high-altitude army posts that Brogpa women are rarely allowed to visit. The meanings that Brogpas ascribe to being male are therefore far from fixed, as wider political events have transformed men's self-conceptions along with their lives and livelihoods.

Ministerial guards in Damascus, Syria (Adam Jones)

IRAQ

The Conscript (1)

Ewan MacAskill*

Many of the dead in the Iraqi army [in the war of 2003] were like Assad, from poor Shia Muslim families, unwilling conscripts in Saddam Hussein's army. His family said he was too poor to pay the bribes to his officers that might have secured him a safer posting and avoided him being sent up to Iraq's northern frontline, where he eventually died.

He lived in one of the poorest parts of Baghdad, the sprawling district formerly known as Saddam City, now renamed Sader City, which is home to about two million Shia Muslims. He lived with his uncle, Najim Adan Shahim, in a home packed with his extended family, sharing a small room with seven others. He left behind few possessions: a jacket and a pair of trousers. The family do not even have a picture of him.

Najim, who lost a brother in the Iran–Iraq war, said that before Assad was conscripted he had been working as a navvy, doing odd jobs in the construction industry. "Even if he had survived the war, he would not have been able to achieve anything in this country, coming from the background that he did. He would have just ended up doing the same job."

---

*From Ewan MacAskill, "Assad Abdul Hussein, 20," *The Guardian*, 16 May 2003.

His family came from Amarra in the south, moving because of the famine that came when Saddam persecuted the Shia after the Gulf War in 1991. The middle-class of Baghdad look with horror at conditions in Sader City but Assad's family, arriving without proper registration papers in Baghdad, ended up in an even worse area, living under corrugated iron in the Shishan district. He had three brothers and two sisters. His family eventually sent him to stay with his uncle, which was seen as a step up.

Shy and quiet, he liked reading and football, and sitting down with the family to chat and gossip. His family said they thought it was unlikely that he would have married because he would have had trouble getting the necessary money together. At the age of 18, he was conscripted into the army, [and] sent to an infantry training centre in Amarra. He had to buy his own uniform and was paid only 5,000 Iraqi dinars (about $2.50) a month.

Many Shia did not want to fight in Saddam's army but had no choice: the alternative was to be shot. "The officers in charge were all corrupt," Najim recalls. "You had to bribe them with money or alcohol – and if you did not, your life was hell." In November Assad was sent to the oil city of Kirkuk. He was killed when a cluster bomb was dropped on his unit.

IRAQ

The Conscript (2)

Irina Vainovski-Mihai*

Karim brings two mats into the garden. It seems rather odd to me. I follow his gait and gestures: slow, controlled. He spreads the mats, then brings the blue plastic sheet used for outdoor dinners. He is preparing for something; but lunchtime is still hours away.

Suddenly Karim turns his head and stares, unblinking, at a man who has just appeared at the end of the garden. He is followed with tiny steps by a woman.

Karim and the other man kiss each other on the cheek three times, hug each other energetically, pat each other on the shoulder. Their *dishdasha* tremble in what seems to be a scuffle, transformed into a tender bodily contact. Finally they separate in silence and crouch on a mat, Karim carefully smoothes the hem of the dishdasha over his feet, and places a hand on the guest's knee. The women, including me, sit on the other mat. Stillness. A slight "tap-tap" as Karim drums with his hand on the other man's knee. Karim takes out a cigarette and gives it to the guest. And then the first words, addressed to me – the foreigner – while looking through me: "This is my brother Akram. He just came for a leave from the frontline."

---

*Special to this volume.

I nod to him, I smile, I say: "*Hala bik, ya hala bik.*" Welcome.

I hear the sound of tea-sipping, the "tap-tap" on Akram's knee, the rustle of the match with which the woman to my right side – surely Akram's wife – lights her cigarette.

I sink into gray images:

One night I was driving on the highway from Basra to Baghdad. The empty and monotonous scenery was summoning me to speed, until I was tempered by truck headlights. They passed by me: the first, the second. I stopped the car at the roadside, unable to drive further. I was suffocating; my palms were damp with perspiration.

The trucks were literally piled with soldiers, one upon the other. In the moonlight and the headlights, I distinguished arms, legs, heads, jumbled together in disorderly fashion. At first I thought the bodies were those of Iraqi soldiers who had died in a recent Iranian attack. Then a soldier waved to me. Under him in the truck, someone else's arm and leg moved.

I told myself it was a nightmare, a flashback to Goya's drawings, a hallucination provoked by the solitary drive in a country at war. The next day, I found the explanation: a massive relocation of troops. Soldiers moving from one frontline to another, sleeping in a hustle-bustle on the way from one fight to another. Dreaming, perhaps, of their return home, or at least a brief leave when the family would rush to meet them, and their entire village would vibrate to women's joyful cries.

But here sits Akram, as speechless as his brother.

"When did you come?" I ask him.

"Don't you understand that he just arrived?" answers Karim. "He only took off his uniform and had a shower. Now he will go to have a sleep. It's so hot here, outside, and I see he's tired."

The brief return of one of those many soldiers whom others have chosen to be the enlisted man of the family. One whose kin had decided they could do without him for a while. One obliged to help his brothers avoid conscription by declaring themselves, in accordance with the law, family sustainers.

A soldier's return, with no children running excitedly in the street, no women raising their voices in joy, no uncle listening to the accounts of battle and bravery. Just a shower, a clean dishdasha, a cigarette, a glass of tea. His brother tapping him incessantly to confirm that he is here, safe and sound, and that he will return to the fight – one of them *has* to go to fight. And his wife following him like a shadow.

AFGHANISTAN

The Conscript (3)

Luke Harding*

The Taliban have forcibly conscripted tens of thousands of men over the past two weeks in a desperate attempt to bolster their 45,000-strong regular army against an imminent American attack. [. . .] Gangs of Taliban soldiers have implemented the edict by dragging men at gunpoint out of their homes. They have also seized them in the streets or pulled them out of cars as they attempt to flee the country. These recruits are now being sent to vulnerable positions in the frontline – and are likely to be the first, innocent casualties of any large-scale American military onslaught.

One mother from Kabul, Faheema, yesterday described how her son, a second-year medical student, was seized by a Taliban press gang. [. . .] "A Datsun pick-up full of Taliban arrived outside our house. Two Taliban with guns stood at the door and one of them came in. They dragged Farhad off. I cried and pleaded with them not to take him away. They said 'You will see him later,'" Faheema recalled.

Across Afghanistan, Farhad's story is being repeated. The Taliban have warned that they will shoot any new recruit who tries to escape. To minimize desertion they are also transporting recruits to provinces far away from where they were originally seized.

The heads of local mosques have been instructed to draw up lists of all men of fighting age, which means anyone over 18. There is no upper age limit.

"My husband disappeared two or three days ago," Gul Pari, who reached Pakistan after a six-hour trek through the mountains, said last night. "He had gone shopping in the bazaar with my children when the Taliban caught him. The Taliban have taken most of the males in my village. A few of them escaped when they became aware of what was happening. I have got no idea where my husband is now. The Taliban may have killed him or he may be in jail." [. . .]

Malika, who fled from the remote drought-ruined northern province of Faryab, lost one of her brothers to the Taliban two weeks ago.

"My brother was searching for wood for turning into fire. He didn't come back. A neighbor told us the Taliban had taken him," she said. "They take girls too. If the Taliban get to know a beautiful girl is living somewhere they will take her."

Malika, who belongs to Afghanistan's minority Uzbek community, said the Pashtun-dominated Taliban had taken away 2,000 Uzbek women from her area for use as concubines. The women were often sold to other Taliban fighters from southern provinces for around £500 each, she said.

---

*From Luke Harding, "Taliban Forcing Thousands into Army," *The Guardian*, 4 October 2001.

Local men could avoid being conscripted by paying a bribe, she added. The minimum rate was £300 – a fortune by Afghan standards – anything less and the man would be beaten to death. [. . .]

Faheema, whose husband was killed during the Soviet invasion, said she fled Kabul to prevent her younger son from also being conscripted. On her way out, she passed truckloads of unwilling recruits being driven to the front. "I saw a lot of people who had been arrested. They were shouting: 'Tell my house, tell my father and mother, that they have taken me.' The Taliban are blocking all the roads out of Afghanistan and are taking away the young boys."

SOUTH KOREA

The Conscript (4)

David Cho*

There was nothing Paul Yoo wanted more this summer than to be a bellowing, flag-waving, crazed spectator at what he considers the greatest sporting event on the planet: the 2002 World Cup. [. . .] Now, though, he's punting the once-in-a-lifetime opportunity, spooked by news reports and talk of a government crackdown on men aged 18 to 35 who have not completed their required 30-month army tour of duty and return to South Korea.

Indeed, the World Cup poses a dilemma for thousands of native South Koreans who [like Yoo] live elsewhere – caught between their distaste for the draft and their desire to see their country compete, at home, for soccer's biggest prize. [. . .] There are tens of thousands of draft-eligible South Koreans living in this country [the US] – on student or other visas, or as permanent residents – at least in part to avoid military service back home, according to the South Korean Embassy.

Leaving their homeland might free them from army duty, but it carries a price: these men cannot live or hold a job in South Korea until they are beyond draft age. If they attempt to return for a long period, they risk expulsion or the very thing they might have tried to escape: the draft. South Korea even posts military officials at its international airports to catch draft evaders.

Yoo [. . .] decided "it wasn't worth the risk." [. . .] "People lose sleep over this issue," he said of the draft. "Part of the discomfort is, you never know what the Korean government is going to do once you are there."

---

*From David Cho, "Korean Fans Torn By World Cup, Risk of Draft," *Washington Post*, 13 May 2002.

SOUTH AFRICA

The Conscript (5)

Kelly Cogswell*

In 1948 white Afrikaners of the National Party came to power claiming God had ordained them to rule South Africa. The National Party then consolidated power by stripping black South Africans of whatever human rights they had left. They built up their army and used it liberally, merging patriotic duty with fundamentalist Christian zeal until there was no difference between them.

While this era is well known for its black victims, little information is available about how the apartheid army also abused its white gay conscripts. In June 1997 South Africa's post-apartheid Truth and Reconciliation Commission acknowledged that human rights violations against gays had occurred on a scale much larger than anyone had thought.

Effects of militarization

The militarization of apartheid South Africa increased as resistance to apartheid grew at home, and liberation movements sprang up in other African countries. The National Party quickly came to see itself as facing, in the 1977 words of Defense Minister Magnus Malan, a "'total onslaught' against the country and its inhabitants . . . involving so many different fronts . . . that it has gained the telling, but horrifying name of the total war."

To fight the total war, the South African Defence Force (SADF) needed cannon fodder. After 1957, conscription by ballot was introduced. In 1967, the government instituted universal conscription for all white males over the age of 16. Duration of service was gradually increased from nine months to two years. Despite incredible homophobia and penalties against homosexual activity, even gay men were not exempted. Women, mixed race, black, and Indian people were eventually allowed or recruited into the military, but the military remained predominantly white male.

The growing militarization was reflected not only by the increase in bodies holding guns, but in an increasing rigidity on the ideological front. White had to be ultra-white. Men had to be supermen, women superwomen. Drugs were evil because they created bonds across what had seemed like insurmountable barriers of race. And sinful, criminal, diseased homosexuals, despite the fact that they were required to serve, were as much enemy as the African National Congress. [. . .]

---

*From Kelly Cogswell, "Property of the State: The Torture of Queer Soldiers in the Apartheid Military," *theGully.com*, 25 August 2000. http://www.thegully.com/essays/africa/000825aversion.html.

The conscript

In the movies, the stereotyped sergeant always says ominously to his fresh, crewcut recruits, "you're mine, now." In South Africa, in the decades of apartheid conscription, they meant it. Young men, mere teenagers, were sold into slavery by their society. They couldn't quit, walk away, or object to anything unless they wanted to face beatings, rape, jail, electroshocks, or worse.

Conscripts as young as 16 were taught to be fierce, brutal, and insular. Hazing was ferocious, especially of the least masculine or gung-ho conscripts. Some were tied to trees, had shoe polish rubbed around their genitals, then were displayed to the whole regiment or platoon. Others were beaten "to make men of them," or raped.

In another violent bonding ritual, groups of conscripts would arrange to go into white civilian bars, pick fights, beat up civilians, and gang-rape women. Sometimes they were actually ordered to do this by their commanders, so the young men could learn the vital difference between "them" and "us."

On occasion, commanders ordered circle jerks [group masturbation] as part of bonding efforts. At least once, according to *The Resister* publication, an NCO at the Maritzkop camp forced conscripts to drop their trousers "and 'commit indecent sexual acts' with each other." Rape was an all-purpose tool used for everything from persecuting gays to torturing captive soldiers. Conscripts who objected to any of this sometimes found themselves in military psychiatric hospitals being treated for abnormalities.

Faced with that environment, and no way out, some conscripts seriously abused alcohol or drugs, or attempted to commit suicide. Many of those succeeded. No one knows how many of these were gay.

The homosexual flash point in the apartheid army

As if the military weren't bad enough already, a confluence of nasty elements made the torture of many gay and transgender conscripts almost inevitable. The first factor was that South Africa's military (and civil) law labeled male homosexuals criminals and threatened them with punishment. Add to this the army's complete control over its conscripts, the South African Dutch Reformed Church and [its leader] Gereformeerde Kerk's view that homosexuals were sinners, the medical profession['s] pathologizing of them as diseased, the white Christian National Party's perception of itself as attacked from without, which heightened their already vicious intolerance of dissent or difference within, and you've got a lot of [Josef] Mengeles on your hands.

Given this, the official practice of reporting suspected homosexuals to both the military's South African Medical Services (SAMS), and also to chaplains, was simply a preliminary to torture.

Treatment

When forced to choose between the public shame of being handed over to the South African Police and prosecuted in a criminal court, or being treated in a psychiatric hospital, thousands of conscripts "consented" to be treated by SAMS, especially if they themselves had internalized homophobia.

Some may have chosen differently if they'd known career military doctors in SAMS would be implicated in the torture of captives, including the use of electric shock treatments and drugs banned by international treaties. [. . .] Or maybe they wouldn't have. These homosexuals, white gay or effeminate boys of 17 or 18, may have expected to be treated better than black enemy captives. They weren't. They were shuttled off to psychiatric wards along with white military objectors, drug users, liberals, and the truly distressed, all of whom were considered disturbed and abnormal, and were given heavy doses of Valium.

None of them had it easy, but gay conscripts suffered the worst. The "treatments" these young homosexuals endured included *Clockwork Orange*-type aversion therapy with plenty of electric shocks – also done to drug users. Some homosexuals were chemically castrated without their knowledge. Others were physically castrated. That process was sometimes followed by the implantation of testicular tissue from a straight man. There were lobotomies, hormone injections, and complete sex changes. Few, if any, were truly consensual.

IRAQ

The Recruit

Ashraf Khalil*

Two weeks ago, 25-year-old Maysan was heading to a police recruiting station on Haifa Street [in Baghdad, Iraq] when a suicide bomber detonated his explosives-laden car near a long line of aspiring officers. The blast killed 47 people and wounded 114. Maysan, who arrived after the blast, recalled scraping the remains of some would-be recruits into banana crates. The next day, he returned to the police academy – to apply again, he said.

"Why should I worry?" he asked with a shrug last week, standing in the shade outside another recruiting center in the Dora district of the capital. "God will protect us."

Hundreds of potential recruits have been killed in attack after attack by insurgents, but the spiraling body count has failed to scare away large numbers of young men, who still line up to join Iraq's nascent security forces. On Monday morning, a car bomb

*From Ashraf Khalil, "Lining Up for Dangerous Work," *Los Angeles Times*, 5 October 2004.

outside a recruiting center in Baghdad killed at least 15 Iraqis and wounded 80. Most of them were aspiring officers.

Iraqi officials boast that applicants for positions with the police and national guard far exceed vacancies. A Western diplomat in Baghdad marveled at the "high societal threshold for pain" that keeps the recruits coming back. But many young Iraqis say they flock to recruiting stations not because they're brave or patriotic. Applying to the police and guard merely offers them a chance to join one of the few paid occupations in the country.

"It's either the army or the police, or you become a thief," said Jaafar, a 31-year-old applicant who, like Maysan and others, declined to give his full name.

Survivors of Monday's attack said high unemployment left them little choice but to line up for police work. "We have become stuck between the hammer of unemployment and the anvil of terrorism," said Riyadh Mehdi Salman, who traveled from the southern town of Nasiriya to apply. "We all know that several explosions targeted these centers, and even when we join our posts, we will be targeted as well, but we have no other choice." [...]

Recruits acknowledge that working as police officers carries risks, but they are quick to point out that ordinary Iraqis endure a steady wave of kidnappings, suicide bombings and intense clashes between guerrillas and US-led forces. "All of Iraq is dangerous. Life is dangerous. What's the difference?" said Uday, 27, one of several men gathered outside a recruiting center [...].

Uday and his companions arrived after recruiters had selected 120 applicants and then slammed the doors shut. They were lured by the prospect of earning $220 a month, a living wage in Iraq. Despite the locked doors, the other hopefuls waited outside, clutching pink folders that contained their applications. "Maybe they'll need another person or two," Uday said.

Before the US-led invasion, Uday worked as a commercial photographer in a Baghdad studio. Maysan, balding and with a droopy mustache, was in nursing school. Another applicant said he was a vegetable farmer who was driven to the recruitment line after his business failed amid a lack of seed and pesticide subsidies after Hussein's regime fell. The young men said they had never previously thought of joining the police and planned to return to their former professions "after the situation calms down," as Uday put it. [...]

Successful applicants are not guaranteed a lengthy tenure, for various reasons. Standing outside the Dora recruiting center, Qassim Mohammed grimaced as he tasted an MRE [meal-ready-to-eat] of salsa cheese spread, tossing the package behind him. He recounted that he was a member of the national guard's first class of recruits. But shortly after joining, the 22-year-old said, he began receiving death threats. A letter slipped under his door urged him to quit. "We know you," it read. "You're a son of the area. We know your family."

He kept the job until several men stopped him on his way home from work, pointed an assault rifle at him and offered him a last chance to quit. "I walked straight back to the base and turned in my ID," he said. The men who threatened his life "drove me home from the base." Asked what he would do if the same thing happened after he joined the police, Mohammed said, "I'd quit again."

MEXICO/UNITED STATES

The Green Card Marine

Monica Campbell[*]

Fernando Suarez del Solar feels a sense of urgency about the war in Iraq – and not just because he lost his only son there two years ago. It is his duty, he says, to warn young Latinos about the perils of joining the US military and becoming, like his son, a "green card Marine," lured by promises of a college education, post-service career and fast-track citizenship.

Three years ago, President Bush offered accelerated citizenship to any green card holder who has served in the military since September 11, 2001. Instead, the bereaved father tells would-be recruits, they could wind up like Marine Lance Cpl. Jesus Suarez, killed at age 20 after he stepped on an unexploded cluster bomb in March 2003, during the first week of the war.

"Immigrants are generally the first on the front lines," Suarez said. "They should know where they'll end up."

While there is no way to confirm the truth of that assertion, Latinos comprise more than a third of the 41,000 foreign citizens in the US fighting force, according to the Defense Department, with the largest number – 8,539 – from California. Immigrant troops are most visible in the Army and Marines, the services with the highest casualty rates in Iraq, but barely present in the Navy and Air Force, Pentagon records show. From March 19, 2003, when the Iraq war began, through April 9, 2005, of the more than 1,500 US service members who had died in Iraq, 171 were Latinos, said Bryan Driver, public affairs officer for the Marines' Casualty Assistance Branch in Quantico, Va. The largest number – 103 – were in the Army, followed by 69 in the Marines, 3 in the Air Force and 2 in the Navy.

Neither the Pentagon nor the immigration division of the Homeland Security Department counts green card military personnel by country of origin. But anti-war groups such as San Diego-based Aztec Warrior, which Suarez founded after the death of his son, estimate that almost half the Latino troops killed in Iraq were noncitizens, with Mexicans comprising the majority of that group.

---

[*]From Monica Campbell, "Dead Recruit's Father Wages Campaign Against 'Green Card Marines,'" *San Francisco Chronicle*, 22 May 2005.

Suarez, a short man with thinning black hair and tired eyes, has barnstormed across the United States to discourage immigrant recruits, providing them with information about noncitizens' rights and lists of organizations that offer college scholarships as an alternative to joining the military. He reaches "new immigrant families who don't understand the military system yet," said Jorge Mariscal, a literature professor who specializes in Chicano studies at UC San Diego. "It's only in the last year or so that other Latino groups have recognized the dilemma of green card soldiers, and Fernando has played a key part in making that public."

In past months, Suarez has made several visits to San Francisco, Oakland and Berkeley. "I think he's had a big impact, at least in the Bay Area," said Susan Quinlan of the Oakland office of the Central Committee for Conscientious Objectors. "An awful lot of anti-war activists and certainly counter-recruiters know of him and admire his work."

It's hard to measure whether counter-recruiters such as Suarez are having an effect on the declining rates of military signups. But Flora Ortiz, a 17-year-old high school senior from El Monte, in the low-income outskirts of eastern Los Angeles, said she was hit hard by his presentation. Ortiz, a US legal resident born in Guadalajara, Mexico, said that for years she had planned to join the Marines. She was drawn to the discipline of boot camp and the chance to "make my parents proud," she said in a phone interview. The death of a cousin in Iraq in 2003 didn't discourage her, and she already had started the paperwork. But in February, while she was researching a paper about Latinos in the military, Ortiz heard Suarez speak. Afterward, she told him about her enlistment plans, and they talked about alternatives. "But you know what really got me?" she said. "I just saw his eyes – they were so watery. I realized I never wanted my mom's to look like that." Ortiz is now planning on community college and wants to be a kindergarten teacher, although she's still uncertain whether she made the right choice.

Late last month, Suarez took his personal campaign to Mexico, where he told audiences of prospective immigrants that they could lose their Mexican citizenship by serving in a foreign army, according to Mexican law. Although the military deducts education costs from their monthly paychecks, Suarez told them US recruiters fail to explain that. And he warned them that noncitizens are barred from becoming officers or serving in posts requiring access to classified information – an assertion confirmed by Douglas Smith, a spokesman for the Army Recruiting Command at Fort Knox, Ky. "If we build awareness here, it'll spark more conversations across the border about the realities of the war," Suarez said during his Mexico City swing.

On a recent evening at Mexico City's National Autonomous University, the nation's largest public college, Suarez addressed about 100 students with his standard warnings. Hugo Oscar Ramirez, 21, an international relations student who attended the event, said he has discussed joining the US military with a cousin who lives in San Bernardino County. "We talked a lot about whether he should join the Army to earn money for college," Ramirez said. "None of this noncitizen stuff came up. In any case, I don't think he'll join. It's too dangerous."

Suarez, who is a Mexican citizen, owned a laundry business in Tijuana. He moved to Escondido (San Diego County) in 1997 with his wife, son and three daughters so Jesus could establish residency, join the Marines and then pursue his goal of becoming a Drug Enforcement Administration agent. In his native Tijuana, Jesus had mourned the loss of too many friends from drug-related deaths and pledged to do something about it, his father recalled.

Most recruits sign up for four years of active duty and four years in the reserves, said David Griesmer, a spokesman for Marine Corps Recruiting Command based in Quantico. But Suarez said a Marine recruiter in San Diego lied to Jesus by saying he could become a DEA agent after serving for just a year. "Of course it doesn't work that way. He couldn't join the DEA after a year. But we didn't know that when Jesus signed up," Suarez said. "We didn't know which questions to ask. And I don't think ours is an isolated case." [. . .]

Since his son's death on March 27, 2003, Suarez has swapped his quiet life as a cashier at a 7-Eleven store in Escondido for that of a full-time activist. Sponsored by San Francisco's Global Exchange and the American Friends Service Committee, a Quaker anti-war organization, Suarez has already spoken at 150 schools across the United States. He has traveled to Iraq twice to speak with Latino troops. "Some people tell me, 'Those anti-war activists are using you,'" Suarez said. "But it's the reverse: I'm using them."

His wife, Rosa, refuses to meet with the mothers of other dead US soldiers, saying it's too painful to talk about. His daughters wish he would stop his campaign. "They think that the things I say about Bush and the war will get me into trouble," Suarez said. David Rodriguez, national commander of the American GI Forum, an organization of Latino veterans, said most Latinos are unlikely to join an anti-war campaign. "I feel for the guy. It's pretty painful to lose a son," said Rodriguez, a Vietnam veteran who lives in San Jose. "But when you join the military, you go in to fight for the United States."

At every stop he makes, Suarez carries a Marine-issued laminated photo of his son and a sign that reads: "Bush lied, my son died." He says he will continue to speak out as a way of honoring his son's memory. "This photo keeps me going," he said. "I take it out before I speak and say, 'OK, *hijo* [son], help me out here. What should I say?' And he advises me."

ETHIOPIA

The Rebel

Metasebia Woldemariam*

In May 1991, the Ethiopian People's Revolutionary Democratic Front (EPRDF), a coalition of rebel forces, toppled the government headed by the dictator Mengistu

*Special to this volume.

Haile Mariam. The largest group in the coalition was the Tigray People's Liberation Front (TPLF), which was formed in the northern province of Tigray in 1975.

Fitsum was a Tigrayan youth when he joined the TPLF at the end of 1977. He was, and still is, known as "Tagai Fitsum" – literally, "the fighter Fitsum"; the "Tagai" moniker is used by most TPLF members, and conveys how their experiences as rebel fighters shaped and defined their identity. Fitsum was among the fighters who seized Addis Ababa, Ethiopia's capital, in May 1991.

Fitsum described two life experiences that profoundly shaped him: the death of his older brother in 1977, at the hands of cadres of Ethiopian dictator Mengistu Haile Mariam, and entering Addis Ababa to overthrow Mengistu's government. This is his story in his own words.

The Beginning: Mekele, August 1977

I am from the town of Mekele, in the province of Tigray. We often heard about Derg* atrocities in our province. In the town of Axum, Derg cadres herded students and teachers into the compound of the National Telecommunication office, where they shot them. The cadres announced that the students and teachers were killed because they supported the *Weyane* [Tigrayan rebels]. I believe this was near the beginning of the "Red Terror" campaign [of political repression] in Tigray. We heard rumors that Axum was red that day as blood mingled with the rainwater. It is said this red mixture seeped out of the compound and stained the streets.

Shortly afterwards, the Derg cadres brought the Red Terror to Mekele, my town. They rounded up thirty-five students and teachers. They were tied together and forced to walk on the busiest road in town, to make sure as many people as possible saw them. Then they were shot. On their corpses were placed placards reading, "This is a TPLF-supporting dog," or "This is an enemy of the people," things like that.

Within the month, about twenty youths from my neighborhood were killed in a *kebele* compound.[†] It was said that dogs were allowed to lick their blood. The most shocking thing for us was that the killers were also from Mekele.

I was still very young at the time, about 16. While these murders shocked me, what led me to become a rebel fighter was the killing of my older brother, Mahari. He was a university graduate and the primary provider for our family. Mahari got a job in the Ministry of Agriculture in Addis Ababa, but he would often visit us.

On 29 August 1977, shortly after midnight, six cadres from our kebele knocked on our door. They asked whether Mahari was home, but it was clear that at least two of them knew he was working in Addis: they were his friends, Tesfaye and Negussie. My mother said "Tesfaye, you should know Mahari is in Addis Ababa," to which he replied: "I heard he's returned."

---

*"Derg" is the acronym for Mengistu's military junta government.
[†]Kebele is a neighborhood association or administrative division.

Fitsum (Metasebia Woldemariam)

Tesfaye then said, "Never mind, good night," and the cadres left. A week or so later, Mahari and around 15 others were brought to Mekele from Addis Ababa as prisoners. At six in the morning of the following Sunday, we heard shots outside our house. We thought there was trouble at the neighbors'. I went to investigate about an hour later, and I saw a body on the road. I did not immediately recognize it as my brother's, as there was so much blood on the face. But there was a placard on the body: "Mahari, a puppet of the Tigrayan and Eritrean rebels." And then I knew.

My mother made such a scene on the street, crying, yelling, and pulling at her hair, that local cadres put her in prison. Later that day, my father went to collect Mahari's body. He was told to pay 100 ETB for each bullet used. Since Mahari was shot once in the back of the head and once in his back, my father paid 200 ETB. We buried him at the Medhan Alem Church.

A few days after Mahari's death, I left home. I spent some months in Kuha trying to find out how to join the TPLF rebels. When I finally met up with some fighters in a place called Gugur, they interrogated me to make sure I wasn't a Derg spy. They asked about my education, my neighborhood, and my family. I told them I had studied only up to the fourth grade. I described my neighborhood and my brother's killing. I was told to return the next day. I was again asked about my neighborhood, and as I answered, one of the rebels started laughing. I had not noticed him, but it was Hailu, a man from my area. I later found out that they looked for someone from my area to verify my identity. That is how suspicious they were.

At the time, I was deemed too young to fight, so I was placed on propaganda detail. We would go from town to town, singing patriotic songs to encourage people to join. About a year later, when I was 17 or 18, I started the six-month training to be a fighter. My first battle was on the Sudan border. We started in Tigray province and made our way to Addis Ababa on foot. If we were wounded, we would be treated at our medical centers in the countryside, and then rejoin the rebellion. I twice sustained serious injuries, and spent six months in the medical center.

The End: Addis Ababa, May 1991

Four rebel divisions were closing in on Addis Ababa. The first was to remain in the Nazret area. The second was to seize the airport at Debre Zeit.* The last two divisions were to enter Addis Ababa – one to be stationed in the Entoto area, and my division to surround the Bole [International] Airport and the palace.

At 2 a.m., my division arrived at Sendafa, about 40 km northeast of Addis Ababa. We were on foot, as usual. Early in the evening of the third day, we were told to start moving towards Addis Ababa. We arrived at the outskirts of the city at about 8 p.m. that night.

---

*Nazret, also known as Adaama, is about 75 km southeast of Addis Ababa. Debre Zeit is approximately 40 km southeast of the capital.

My group leader received a radio order that we should take our positions by the palace; we were told the United Nations building would be close by. None of us had been to Addis Ababa before, but some local students guided us. Residents also gave other fighters directions to the location. We had expected the residents to be hostile, but that was not my experience.

We had spies in Addis Ababa, and our leaders also listened to the radio. We knew that Mengistu had left Ethiopia a few days before, so we really did not anticipate heavy fighting. But soon after we reached the palace area, we received another radio call ordering us to withdraw, as Mengistu's soldiers were indeed ready to engage us in battle.

It turned out that the Derg had deployed new soldiers from the southern regions of Ethiopia to guard the palace. They did not speak Amharic or Tigrinya,* and we wondered whether they had heard that the Derg had virtually collapsed.

So we withdrew for the night. Early in the morning, the fighting started. We had been ordered to use only light weapons, so as not to damage buildings, but the enemy was using heavy artillery and rockets. At around noon, we also turned to heavy weaponry. Many, many died, but the result was that the palace fell under our control.

You cannot imagine our joy. A small group of rebels was left to guard the palace, but the rest of us started celebrating. It was an incredible moment for us. I personally had spent at least twelve years as a Tagai. And while I would continue to fight in smaller campaigns, this was the most important victory for me.

My small group was sent to guard the rear entrance to the United Nations building. We noticed a very large three-storey house right across the street from the UN. We debated whether we should ask the owners to let us use their roof, which was an ideal location to place our artillery and guard the UN. If the owners declined, our directive was to accept their decision. We were told to have as little contact with Addis Ababa's residents as possible, and not to inconvenience them in any way.

The owner, an older woman named Mimi, readily acceded to our request. Indeed, Mimi was very motherly towards us. She was especially touched to see the women fighters, and she invited them in to bathe. Despite Mimi's kindness, we were a little suspicious at first. We had heard that many of Addis Ababa's residents were hostile to us. We were told not to accept food or drink, as these might be poisoned. So on that first day, when Mimi invited us to dine, we declined to do so.

The next day, Mimi served food on a large common platter. When she noticed that none of us would touch it, she took a bite, as though to prove it was not tampered with. We were satisfied and ate. It continued like this for a few weeks, with Mimi offering us lunch, until our mission at the UN ended. But to this day, I consider Mimi a very close friend, and I visit her regularly.

---

*At the time, Amharic was the official language of Ethiopia. According to the latest (1994) Constitution, it is "the working language of the federal government." Tigrinya is another Ethiopian language.

In those early days in Addis Ababa, our hair was still long, and we were dressed in German shorts and shirts, fatigue-style. We wore sandals, and were very skinny, but muscular. All the men and women in my group* had spent years fighting.

During all those years, I never forgot what I was fighting for. I never forgot my brother, and the cruelty of the Derg. Although sometimes it seemed impossible to remove the Derg, I believed I was better off dying in the effort than not fighting them. That is why seizing Addis Ababa was so important to me. That was the happiest battle of my life.

BURMA

The Child Soldiers

Human Rights Watch[†]

When Myo Chit was first captured by a recruiting team at age twelve, he says he already had a vague foresight that "if I joined the army life would change for me. When I was with my parents I never knew about smoking, drinking, gambling . . . now I know all of these things." Though he may have foreseen that life as a soldier would drag down his character, he certainly did not realize that after three months of Ye Nyunt training,[‡] five months of military training, and a year in the army, he would be beating villagers with rifle butts and threatening to shoot them as he tried to force them onto a truck to take them as porters for the army. But by his own testimony, this is what he was doing. "At night we went into town and captured them everywhere, or we took a truck to a village and captured them. Sometimes they refused so we beat them. I didn't beat them with my fists, I used my rifle butt. I hit a man 27 or 28 years old one time. I felt unhappy about it, but I had my commander's order. We were ordered to get as many as we could. We could get 50 or 60 a night." When Myo Chit was reliving this he was particularly animated and excited, and he admitted that he felt proud when his unit returned to camp with a particularly large number of porters. Only when directly asked how he felt about treating villagers this way did he express any remorse. In May 2001 he fled the

---

*Sixteen men and four women.
[†]From Human Rights Watch, " 'My Gun Was as Tall as Me': Child Soldiers in Burma."
[‡]*Editor's note:* Ye Nyunt means "Brave Sprouts." "Often referred to as a youth organization, in reality Ye Nyunt is a network of camps for orphans and other boys, run by the army. . . . It appears that now street children and other boys who are rounded up for recruitment but are too small to be soldiers are sometimes sent to a Ye Nyunt camp to be held and trained until they are large enough to be enlisted in the army." (From the report.)

Demobilized child soldiers, Democratic Republic of Congo (Dimitri Falk)

army, but later joined an opposition army because "I like fighting." Now 15 years old, he clearly has yet to fully confront or resolve the conflict in his own mind about what he did as a Burma army soldier.

The effect on Myo Chit reflects the dehumanizing effect of his training and his time in the army. From their first day at the Su Saun Yay recruit holding camps the recruits are pushed to forget their identity and their humanity. Deliberately cut off from contact with their families, they are treated brutally by their superiors and often prevented from fraternizing even among themselves. After the training they are separated from those they were recruited with and sent off to distant battalions, where they are further brutalized by their commanders and encouraged to view the local population as their enemy. They are threatened against forming friendships with local civilians, and forced to commit abuses against those civilians under threat of severe punishments if they do not obey.

Such experiences can have particular consequences for children, who are more impressionable than their adult counterparts. [. . .] It is surprising how quickly the youngest soldiers say they adapted to combat. While openly admitting that their first time in battle they closed their eyes and cried, several of them found that by their second or third time in combat they had lost almost all fear, and eventually some said they almost enjoyed it.

Repeated exposure to violence and degrading treatment affects child soldiers' relationships with other soldiers as well as civilians. Moe Shwe was forced into the army at age thirteen, and at age seventeen, "When I was drunk I forced a girl to marry me. A Burmese girl. Her father is a sergeant. She was staying in the camp." In the Burmese context, particularly among soldiers, "forcing" a girl to marry usually means raping her and then either offering or demanding to marry her. At approximately the same time he was promoted to lance corporal, but some junior officers and NCOs who had a grudge against him beat him up so badly that he was hospitalized for a week and had to have his spleen removed. On his return from hospital, he shot dead one of his officers and ran away from the army, leaving his wife and their five-month-old daughter behind. He now assumes he will never see them again, and wants to be a Karen [rebel] soldier; if he saw his father-in-law during combat, he said, "No problem. I'll shoot."

Though the child soldiers are gradually drawn into the web of inhumanity within the army and human rights abuses against civilians, most of them never quite lose the underlying sense that something is wrong. This leads some to run away and others to suicide, but for most it leads to attempts to rationalize their behavior or to distance themselves from things they have done. When asked about things their units did, they openly admit that their entire unit committed abuses but add that they themselves were somehow never part of it.

The testimonies of Nyunt Swe and Khin Maung Than regarding the massacre they witnessed in Shan State reflect the confusion of many child soldiers about their experiences. When Nyunt Swe, who was 15 when the massacre happened in early 2001, first mentioned the massacre in answer to a question on a different subject, it was to say, "I saw one time when we attacked a Shan camp and we captured some Shan soldiers and killed them. I was afraid to kill them, but the others did it." In answer to the very next question, how many were executed, he suddenly stated, "They were not Shan soldiers, they were the Shan soldiers' families." After answering the next question regarding when it happened, he immediately added, "They were all women and children." In a second interview a month later, Nyunt Swe described the massacre more openly and ended by saying, "I felt sad, because they had done nothing wrong and knew nothing. I would have refused to kill them like that. . . . I was kind to the villagers and I didn't want to kill them. I hated the soldiers when they did these things."

The testimony of Khin Maung Than, who was 13 when the massacre happened, is more troubling. The first time he was interviewed he openly brought up the subject of the massacre: "We captured about ten women and children after some fighting with the Shan. The captain with us asked [by radio] for orders from the battalion commander, and the order was to kill them. This is not right, these were women and children. I have a mother, sisters, brothers, and they were like them. They knew nothing about the fighting." Toward the end of this interview he became quite emotional as he worried that "maybe my mother and sister are crying because they don't know where I am or what is happening to me." When interviewed again a month later he described the massacre in much greater detail and quite openly, but appeared to have dissociated himself from it. When the women were raped, "I didn't see it, I was in the shop eating the biscuits." Though he said that he "felt very bad" when he saw the women gunned down with automatic fire, when asked his feelings in looking back on the massacre as a whole he only remarked, "I feel nothing." He claimed that the subject was never discussed afterward within his unit and that he suffered no nightmares as a result; "I felt nothing against my friends because they were just obeying orders. We didn't talk about it." When asked if he would have obeyed if ordered to kill one of the children, he responded, "If you don't follow orders that means you are against your country. . . . If ordered to kill a baby and I don't, I'll be sentenced to death and someone else would still kill the baby. So I would kill the baby." He stated that if he were to meet a relative of one of the women who was killed, "I'd ask him the question, 'Why was your relative in that area? Are you a rebel?' We only killed the relatives of the Shan rebels." At the same time, however, he admitted "I feel sad for those who are dead. I don't feel angry with the soldiers who killed them but I feel angry with the person who gave the order to do that." If he could dictate the punishment for that person, "I would give the order to kill him." Later, when asked if he felt regret about the things that his unit did, he said "no."

After reviewing the transcripts of both interviews with Khin Maung Than and Nyunt Swe a mental health professional experienced in counseling refugees noted the difference in Khin Maung Than from the first interview to the second. In the second interview,

> The subject spoke of the massacre in a calm and sober manner, which contrasts sharply with the information he is relating. . . . Often people suffering from Post Traumatic Stress Disorder (PTSD) portray a detached manner when relating stories of gross violence. There is also a numbing of affect or mood that most patients with PTSD exhibit. Both of these symptoms were shown by the subject, in fact a number of times he said that he felt "nothing." Given the subject's age at conscription and the events that he has witnessed and been a part of since then, i.e. beatings, killings, rape and massacre, there is little doubt that he has been and continues to be traumatized. The manner in which he answers the questions in the second interview is that of a soldier, not a 14-year-old boy . . . Though he understands that many things that he is a part of are wrong, he is unable to perceive himself as belonging to those incidents and so sees them with an observer's eye. As is generally the case with survivors of violence and ex-soldiers who may be suffering from PTSD, the ability to appoint emotion to violent events is too stressful.

At present neither Khin Maung Than, Nyunt Swe, nor any other of the former soldiers interviewed by Human Rights Watch have any access to counseling to help them overcome the traumas they have suffered through. Instead they must focus all of their energy simply on survival. They and thousands of others forced into the army at an early age will most likely have to live with the after-effects of their time as soldiers for the rest of their lives. [. . .]

Many soldiers eventually find life in the army unbearable. For some it is the constant abuse and exploitation by their commanders. For others, it is witnessing the brutal treatment of villagers who remind them of their own families, or simply missing their own homes and parents. When asked why they fled the army, most deserters cite a combination of these reasons. As Than Aung expressed it, "How could I be happy? I never wanted to become a soldier. Firstly, I didn't want to be a soldier anymore. Secondly, I saw things like soldiers taking the villagers' belongings, and that made me upset. I didn't want to eat from the villagers' belongings." [. . .] Though many want to flee, they feel trapped. Officers routinely tell the soldiers that if they are caught by resistance forces they will be killed in a brutal fashion. If they flee in areas where there is no resistance, there are army checkpoints everywhere. They also fear that if they flee the army their families will be put under surveillance, and may be interrogated and otherwise harassed. The soldiers also fear what will happen to them if they are recaptured. [. . .] According to Salaing Toe Aung, "Before killing me they'd send me to prison. They'd kill me or send me to prison." Moe Shwe added, "If you just ran away you're sent to prison for three to five years. If you ran with a gun and joined the KNLA [Karen rebels] you're killed. Whether or not you ran with a gun, if you've joined the KNLA you're killed." [. . .]

Some soldiers, however, are beyond the point of running away. Their officers may have crushed their self-image beyond repair, they may have lost all hope in the future, or their fear for themselves or their families should they run away may be too great. The reasons can never completely be known, but these soldiers choose to kill themselves. In most of the cases which were related to Human Rights Watch, those who chose to do so were child soldiers. Moe Shwe, now aged twenty: "Three from my group. They put a gun barrel in their mouths and fired. They were 14 or 15. Three killed themselves altogether, all children. When we were on operations they couldn't climb the hills and their NCOs beat them, so later they killed themselves. It was three separate occasions." Others also reported two or three suicides in their units, usually among younger soldiers. Even in Htun Htun's unit, where the punishment for desertion was not very severe, "[s]ix soldiers killed themselves, all at separate times, in Lwin Ba Pa, in the jungle. It was while I was based at Min Done. They were about 15 or 16. They wanted to leave the army but couldn't get permission, so they pointed their guns at themselves and killed themselves. I didn't want to stay there anymore because I was upset by this. But I didn't want to kill myself, I wanted to run away."

COLOMBIA

The *Sicario*

Alonso Salazar*

Testimony of Antonio, a gang member in Medellín

I'd like to be out on the streets of my neighbourhood again, that's my territory. I love walking down them. I've always got my wits about me of course, my eyes wide open and my gun in my pocket, because I've got as many enemies as friends. You never know where you might get shot from. A lot of people are after me, I've got a lot of admirers in other gangs. The law is also on my tail. If I get out of here [prison], I'm going to be real careful.

There've always been gangs in our neighbourhood: the Nachos, the Montañeros, Loco Uribe's gang, the Calvos . . . and as the song says: "this bed ain't big enough for everyone." You have to be on the look-out, if you're not careful one of the other gangs muscles in and people start leaving you. You have to make sure of your territory, that's the main thing. The biggest war we ever had was with the Nachos, who were hired killers like us. When they first showed up we did nothing, but then they started throwing their weight around, upsetting people. Until one day Martín, one of our gang, told them where to get off, and they shot him. That same night we went up to their place and taught them a lesson. Six of us went up there in groups of two: we met up on the street corner where they hung out, and took them completely by surprise. We shot two of them. They thought they were such tough guys [that] they never even imagined anyone would come for them.

A few days later they came for us. We were waiting for them. I put a handkerchief over my face, put on a baseball cap, and went out with my submachine gun. Others from the gang were covering me, watching what would happen.

"We want peace, not war," one of the Nachos shouted.

"We don't want peace, what we want is war," Lunar shouted back, and fired off a volley into the air.

Of course they didn't really want peace, what they were trying to do was to see all our faces so they could pick us off. In the end, they retreated back up the gully. "Get them to start making your coffins," they shouted from up top.

From then on it was war. They would come down into the gully, we'd go and raid them, both sides would try to ambush each other . . . it was a real shootin' war that left a lot of people dead.

The Nachos went to pieces after the police got their leader in a raid. Even I have to admit that the guy was a real man: he and this other guy were fighting it out with the

---

*From Alonso Salazar, *Born to Die in Medellín* (New York: Monthly Review Press, 1992), pp. 27–32.

pigs for hours. They say that when Nacho had only one bullet left he shut himself in the bathroom of the house they were holed up in and shot himself in the head. After that his gang was nothing, they had no stomach for a fight. A few days later the law arrested about twenty of them, and now they're all in Bellavista [jail] for a good long while.

The gang wars have been tough: whole families have been wiped out in vendettas. What happens is if one of the gang or one of your relatives gets killed, you go out and get the bastard who did it, or one of his family; but we never touch women. If you don't react, they walk all over you.

We also fight the police, but it's easier with them. They're shit scared when they come up here, and we know our own territory. Of course they've caught me twice, and I ended up in Bellavista as well.

The first time was the hardest. I'd been holed up in a house in a nearby neighbourhood. About midnight I woke up to hear them knocking the door down.

"Open up, this is the police," they shouted.

I tried to escape out the back, but the place was surrounded. Before I could do a thing, the police were everywhere. They put me into the patrol car without even letting me get dressed, and took me off to the F-2 [police] headquarters. All they found in the house were three guns we had stashed there.

At the station they put me in a tub with water up to my neck. They left me there all night freezing my balls off, and ran electric current through me too. They kept asking me about the others in the gang, who the leaders were, but I didn't say a word.

"Think you're a real tough guy, don't you, you fairy," they shouted, kicking me as hard as they could in the stomach.

I didn't think I was tough at all, but to grass [snitch] on people is the lowest you can go. They asked me about enemies of mine, but I didn't even give them away, although I knew where they hung out. It's like Cruz Medina sings in the tango: "Don't anyone ask who wounded me so, you're wasting your time, you'll never know. Let me die here in peace, and don't be surprised at that, when a man is a man, he won't squeal like a rat."

I was sent to Bellavista prison for illegal possession of firearms. I didn't have a record, and they couldn't get anything out of me, so they got mad. They even tried to get people from the neighborhood to testify against me, but nobody would. There may be people who hate your guts, but they know that if they start blabbing, they're signing their own death warrants. Either you get them once you're out, or one of the gang does it for you.

I was three months in the slammer. That was only about long enough to get over the beating the pigs had given me. I met several of the gang in the jail. I was lucky that the boss man on our block was an old guy I'd done a job for, who liked me. If you end up in Bellavista with no one to look after you, you're done for. You get kicked from block to block until you end up in the worst hole, where they steal everything you've got, even your sex.

That's why I was lucky, because I had someone to look out for me. Of course I met up with a few of my old enemies too, some of the Nachos and others. But the worst was a guy called Pepe, whose brother I had shot. I told the boss man about him, and he said: "Tell him to get out of here, and if he cuts up rough about it, send him to the funeral parlour."

I sent the message to Pepe, and a few days later he changed blocks. Whatever the boss man says goes. Nobody in there can do anything without his permission. [. . .]

I paid my way out of Bellavista. There are people who act as go-betweens with the judges. My case was easy, because it wasn't a serious charge and nobody came forward to accuse me of anything else. I paid around 250,000 pesos. Or rather, some associates of the gang who'd just done a job paid it for me.

After that I went back to my patch, to my normal life. Half the time I'm happy, the other half I'm worked up. When I haven't got anything to do, I get up late, it's almost dark by the time I hit the streets. I hang round the street corners listening to rock music with the gang or I go to a bar with my girl to listen to love songs or country music.

My girl is called Claudia. I know I can trust her, she knows what I do, and backs me up, but she doesn't want to get involved at all. She works in a dress factory and comes home early every day. She's got expensive tastes: she likes new clothes, jewels, all the fancy stuff, and I give her everything she wants. At the weekend either we go out to bars in Bello [neighborhood], or dance salsa, or go down into Manrique to listen to some smoochy music. She's a good-looker, but what I most like about her is that she's serious. Because there's a lot of girls who make your eyes pop, but most of them are just good for a quick lay, a one night stand. Sometimes we like to party at the houses we hide up in, and we get girls in. Fabulous women, but they're only out for what they can get from you. The only real girlfriend I've had is Claudia. [. . .]

Things have got very difficult. This gang's appeared called the Capuchos, they're killing people all over the place. It was them who shot me. I knew they were after me, that's why I split from home. But then I got it into my head to go up and say hello to the old woman and Claudia. I thought everything was quiet because the police were snooping around the neighbourhood a lot at the time. I didn't want any trouble, so I went up there without a weapon. Ma soon told me that they were out looking for me. I wasn't worried, I knew they wouldn't dare come up to the house. It's in a narrow gully, so long as you're under cover you can take on anyone.

I was waiting for some of the gang to arrive with the guns so we could get rid of those guys. By the time night fell and they hadn't arrived, I realised things were getting serious. So I climbed out of the back of the house and made for the road up top. I walked about a block, and saw a bus coming down, so I waved it to stop. Just as I was getting on, I saw a kid about two meters from me with a shotgun. Then I felt this heat spreading all through my body, and that was the last I knew. I was out for four days before I came round. What got me most was that a lot of people in the neighborhood knew what was going on but didn't warn me. The Capuchos had every exit staked. I guess it's everyone's turn sometime, and that day it was mine.

What I wish is that they had killed me there and then, without time for me to let out a sigh or feel any pain, or even to say "they've got me." I'd have preferred that to this feeling that my body and my mind are being torn apart. Having to stare death in the face all day long, grinning and beckoning at me, but not daring to come any closer. Better to die straight off, so you don't get to see how all your so-called friends abandon you. In here you realize that people are only with you in the good times. As Don Olimpo sings: "When you're on top of the world, you can have friends galore, but when fate trips you up, you'll see it's all lies, they won't want you any more." I don't care about dying, we were all born to die. But I want to die quickly, without all this pain and loneliness.

PALESTINE

The "Collaborators"

Justin Huggler and Sa'id Ghazali*

At dawn in the Tulkarem refugee camp yesterday, two Palestinians were led out into a side alley where the executioners, their faces covered with hoods, shot them at point-blank range. Then their bullet-filled bodies were dragged into the main square, where they were propped up and displayed to the crowd for 15 minutes. The alleged crime of the two men was collaborating with Israeli intelligence. Eighty-six Palestinians have now been lynched or summarily executed by militants for collaborating with Israeli security forces since the start of the *intifada* three years ago, including the two men killed yesterday.

Israeli security forces frequently use Palestinian informers, who tell them the whereabouts of wanted militants or warn of planned attacks. The two men killed yesterday, Suleiman Faraj, 23, and Samer Goma Ofeh, 19, had allegedly confessed to betraying Sirhan Sirhan, a local leader of the militant group Islamic Jihad, who was shot dead by the Israeli army earlier this month [October 2003].

A videotape of the two men confessing was shown in the refugee camp's main square the night before they were killed. About 2,000 people watched as Faraj and Ofeh, visibly scared, listed the names of the militants who were assassinated by Israel after they had informed on them. In return, they said on the tape, the Israeli authorities made payments to their bank accounts after each successful assassination. Faraj and Ofeh admitted on the tape they had been linked with the Israeli intelligence for more than two years. The crowd reacted angrily, calling for the militants to execute them, according to sources in Tulkarem.

---

*From Justin Huggler and Sa'id Ghazali, "Palestinians Cheer Militant Executions of 'Collaborators,'" *The Independent*, 24 October 2003.

Only 10 members of their families took part in the two men's funeral. Some people shouted during the burial that their bodies should not be allowed to rest in the refugee camp's cemetery. Anguished family members of the two victims hurled stones at the house of one of the militants they believe was involved in their execution.

The two men disappeared three weeks ago. Their families went to the Palestinian police but nothing was done about it, according to sources in Tulkarem. It now transpires they were kidnapped by Islamic Jihad, who interrogated them and then filmed their "confessions." Al-Aqsa Martyrs' Brigades, another militant faction, said that Islamic Jihad had kidnapped them but that both groups had taken part in the executions "to share in the honour."

In past cases in which Palestinians have confessed to collaborating with Israel, they have told how they were blackmailed by Israeli intelligence officers. Even so, there is widespread support for the killing of collaborators among Palestinians. [. . .] Several Palestinians have been tried and sentenced to death by Palestinian courts for collaboration with Israel but only two of those executions have ever taken place. Others have been lynched after crowds "mysteriously" got into the jails where they were being held.

The official claimed that Palestinian police were unable to prevent the killings because the local police headquarters had been destroyed by the Israeli army. But the source in Tulkarem disagreed. "There is a security apparatus in Tulkarem," he said. "They receive salaries. But they do nothing."

PALESTINE

The Suicide Bomber

Ian Fisher*

After the horror of a suicide bombing, the parents of the bombers almost always say that they were shocked, that they had no clue their child was prepared to do such a thing. But Yousef Iktaishat [of Nablus] admitted today that he saw the signs as long as a year ago in his teenage son, Islam. He says he even tried to talk him out of it.

"I told him, 'Look, you need to get an education – you can['t?] be involved in politics,'" Mr. Iktaishat said. "And we agreed on that."

---

*From Ian Fisher, "2 Suicide Bombers Fulfilled Their Fathers' Worst Fears," *The New York Times*, 14 August 2003.

Ghazi Jarwan, who lives just a few hundred yards away, was so concerned that his own son, Khamis, might have volunteered for a suicide bombing that he called the Palestinian police on Monday, the day after his son disappeared from work.

These two fathers never met until Tuesday, when word spread through Nablus that their sons – both 17, who knew each other slightly but were apparently working separately – had carried out suicide attacks that morning. They killed one Israeli man who was grocery shopping and an 18-year-old army recruit at a bus stop.

Today the fathers met again, at a memorial service here for their sons, where their mourning mixed with pride that the boys had died as martyrs, as Palestinians call suicide bombers, and anger in their belief that Israel was to blame.

"I can't control my kids," said Mr. Iktaishat, a grocer. "The Israelis come to provoke us. Even if I accept that provocation, my kids don't." [. . .]

Even before their similar attacks only 40 minutes and a few miles apart, Islam Iktaishat and Khamis Jarwan had much in common. They lived a few minutes walk apart, Mr. Jarwan in a new house – dynamited to rubble today by Israeli soldiers – in the Askar refugee camp at the outer fringes of Nablus. Mr. Iktaishat lived in an apartment complex just outside the camp. Both lived with their large families and tried to make money selling small items on the streets, where Mr. Jarwan made less than $2 a day.

Of the two, Mr. Jarwan seemed to have a more typical profile for a militant, though his family said they were not aware of any formal ties. He often threw stones at Israeli soldiers, and while confronting soldiers last August was hit by a rubber bullet and, later the same day, a live round in his leg. Five of his friends were killed in the last three years of fighting, his family said. In a diary now buried under rubble, his family said he once wrote, "After you lose a friend, death will be easy."

On Sunday he did not return from his job on time and called an older brother to say he had gone to see his boss. The family later called the boss's house, and the boss's wife told them that her husband was in Jordan and that Mr. Jarwan had left early, saying his mother was ill. The next day his father called the Palestinian police to warn them of his suspicions, given his son's anger after the Friday raid. An Israeli security official said tonight that the Palestinian Authority had not shared that information with them.

"I had a feeling my son might do something," Mr. Jarwan said.

That same day, Islam Iktaishat disappeared too. The family said he had never been involved in stone throwing and was not, despite his name, especially religious. His immediate ambition was to join a friend to study in Russia. "He wanted to get away from this miserable life," his brother said.

But a year ago he expressed, in a way his father did not specify, a desire to become a suicide bomber, and he often flashed anger during Israeli military operations in Nablus.

"When the Israeli military attacked, he would say: 'What kind of life is this? How is this life?'" his brother said.

Fayez al-Sadr, the Jarwans' next-door neighbor, said he wondered how the bombings, and Israel's usual response of destroying the houses of suicide bombers, would reverberate in the next generation of Palestinians in Nablus. At 3 this morning, he said,

Israeli soldiers banged on the front door of the Jarwans' house with a stone and gave them 10 minutes to leave. Worried about collateral damage, Mr. Sadr woke his four young children, all sleeping in one bedroom, and hurried them out just before the blast tore a huge hole in the room. With the blasted-out window framed surreally with orange curtains, the view is now of their neighbors' toppled house.

"Of course now my kids will be full of hatred toward anything called Israeli soldiers," Mr. Sadr said. "They will grow up with these memories."

IRAQ

The Guerrilla

Cameron W. Barr*

One night [in Baghdad] at the end of June, a young Iraqi man goes out to ambush an American convoy near the central Iraqi town of Fallujah. He is wearing his favorite blue tracksuit. He is a small guy, solid and compact, with cropped dark hair and a chin that juts out slightly. He likes tough sports, especially handball. He can stub out a cigarette on the calluses of his left palm. It will be his first time in combat.

Although he has trained only fleetingly for what he is about to do, he is not afraid. "If I die for a reason, that's a nice thing," he says later.

Since President Bush declared major hostilities in Iraq over on May 1, a rising tide of ambushes, explosions, and small-arms attacks has killed 60 Americans.

The man's motivations for attacking the convoy are simple: to resist the American "insult to Iraqi and Arab tradition." His remarks, during a two-hour interview at a Baghdad hotel, convey a sense of betrayal and trampled dignity. "They might have helped, but they destroyed things," he says of the Americans in Iraq. "They provoked." He mentions the "unfulfilled promises" of the Americans (to bring democracy, to make things better), their mistreatment of Iraqis (especially when male US soldiers encounter Iraqi women in raids or at checkpoints), their unwillingness to stop looting, help Iraqis in need, maintain stability. "Now nothing is under control," he says.

Beyond individual accounts, the origins of the anti-American guerrilla war are obscure. US officials and officers have long blamed the remnants of Saddam Hussein's Baathist regime. They have also begun speculating about the possibility that "foreign fighters" or even Al Qaeda are participating in the Iraqi resistance. But the man in the blue tracksuit is no Baathist; he complains about the old regime's corruption and

*From Cameron W. Barr, "The Making of an Iraqi Guerrilla: One Man's Tale," *The Christian Science Monitor*, 15 August 2003.

other failings. He cites his two years as an Army conscript. For enlisted men, he says, military service was like living in a jungle full of lions – the rapacious, bribe-soliciting senior officers. His career as a handball player stalled because he wouldn't or couldn't pay a bribe to get on the national team.

He does not deny that he is part of an armed group fighting the Americans. But he seems to know – or is able to say – very little about it. The group is nameless, he says, and so decentralized that he is not certain who is behind it. He says he doesn't think foreigners are involved, but he admits he might not know it if they were. His experience is impossible to corroborate independently, but the details of his account offer some reassurance that it is genuine.

That night in June, the man and five like-minded Iraqis arrive separately at a prearranged spot along a country road. He has never met three of the others. The organization is divided into cells for the sake of security. Between them, they have three rocket-propelled-grenade (RPG) launchers and two mortars. The men with the shoulder-fired RPGs spread out along the road, hiding in the scrub. The mortar men pull back to gain some distance on the road and calibrate how far they will have to lob their shells. This is their plan: the man wearing the tracksuit will hit the convoy's rear vehicle with an RPG. Then one of the others will do the same to the lead vehicle, boxing in the Americans and making them vulnerable to repeated strikes from RPGs and mortars. It will be a bloodbath.

At about 11 p.m., the US convoy rolls into view: five Humvees and three or four Bradley Fighting Vehicles. The man has seen a Humvee up close, thanks to the three days he spent in early June as an interpreter for a US military unit in Habaniya, not far from Fallujah. Although he studies English literature at university, his language skills are weak, so it is no surprise that he did not last long in this work. But he says he was the one who decided not to return to the American base. He applied for the job "so that I would be close to them and know about their vehicles and see whether [the Americans] have good intentions." They do not, he concluded. "American soldiers have a lot of hatred for the Iraqi people," he says.

At the base, he helped US soldiers question Iraqis who had come to tell the Americans about those organizing attacks. The man says he passed the names of these informers to his underground organization, but adds that he doesn't know whether any action was taken against them. The man says the experience of being among the Americans turned him against them.

Crouching in the bushes by the side of the road, gripping the handle of the RPG launcher, the man in the blue tracksuit hesitates, unsure whether he can hit his target. He has only used the weapon twice before, at secret trainings conducted by his organization just four or five days earlier.

This is his moment. He fires.

The grenade shoots past the target and explodes against some rocks. The Americans don't stop their vehicles, but they begin firing their weapons. The Iraqis abort the attack, fleeing separately into the darkness. The man says two of them were wounded by US fire.

The man in the tracksuit is disappointed by the experience. He says he was not well trained. He has risked his life in the attack, and he has failed. He remains part of the underground group, but its leaders have not asked him to take part in another mission.

Later he hears that the Americans came to the scene the next day and interrogated everyone who lives in the area, looking for weapons and those who carried out the ambush. For these Iraqis, the attack only worsened the US occupation's imposition on their lives. Failed missions such as these, he says, have caused his group to pause in their attacks. Perhaps the Americans, he says, "might fix something." In case they do not, the group is recruiting more members.

PART 5

Migrations

In the opening contribution to this section, Robert Lacville's "Jack-of-All-Trades," lie the origins of this volume. I remember reading Lacville's affectionate profile of Fafo – a Ghanaian whose roamings over the African continent included stints as seaman, diamond miner, taxi driver, and guerrilla fighter – and marveling at the cosmopolitan and daring character of this "ordinary" man's life. I clipped Lacville's article, and added it to a freshly created file titled "Men – Third World." That was 15 years ago. Much later, in conversation with editor Robert Molteno at the London offices of Zed Books, I proposed the idea of a collection of writings about the lives of men in the global South. A formal outline followed, along with Robert's response: "We should do this."

Originally, I had slotted Fafo's portrait into the "Work" section of this volume. Reviewing the contributions, however, I realized that many involved themes of international mobility and migration. Was there ever a time when this was not an integral part of adult male experience? While some cultures were migratory and others sedentary, it seems that for their male component, there was usually an added spur to movement, often across great distances. The motives were diverse: above all, economic need, even desperation; often coercion (e.g., through military conscription and "press-ganging," or exile as dissidents and criminals); frequently a desire for adventure, new horizons, and fresh opportunities.

Smita Jassal's study of "Migration and Song" in India shows how entrenched is the phenomenon of male migration for labor purposes, and how a folkloric subculture – here expressed in popular song – arose around men's prolonged absences and occasional returns. Madia Thomson sketches a similar push and pull in the life of Moroccan migrant Lahcen. Alienated by his work in the city, Lahcen returns to the village where he is known and respected; but economic necessity again draws him away. Nargis Nurullo-Khoja conveys the diversity and dangers of life for Tajik male migrants in Russia.

Considerable risk is involved in many of these male migrations, as Naeem Mohaiemen conveys in his examination of South Asian men swept up in the Iraq war. Then there is the pervasive global institution of human smuggling.

In recent years, we have heard a great deal about *trafficking* in human beings – notably the deceitful luring of women for sexual exploitation in foreign lands. By contrast, *smuggling*, in which would-be migrants and refugees pay middlemen to transport them across international boundaries, has been largely overlooked, except to the extent that it poses a security "threat" to recipient countries. But smuggling seems to be more widespread than trafficking, and much more destructive of human lives – predominantly male lives. Ginger Thompson's account describes Mexican men waiting to place their lives in the hands of "coyotes" who promise to deliver them safely to work opportunities in the United States. Two subsequent essays, by Salman Masood and Djaffer Ait Aoudia, explore other links in the global smuggling chain.

As with human trafficking, refugees from the South are normally depicted as "womenandchildren." An often-cited statistic is that 70–80 per cent of all refugees are drawn from these groups. But this is deeply misleading. A moment's thought establishes that "womenandchildren" – that is, adult women together with girls and boys – constitute roughly 70–80 per cent of Southern, and indeed most, populations *as a whole*. Nothing suggests that women and girls are overrepresented in refugee flows, compared with men and boys. In fact, recent UNHCR data suggest that a small majority (51 per cent) of refugees are male.* Two contributions, by Tajudeen Abdulraheem and Shukria Dini, convey the stresses and strains of the male refugee experience.

Other aspects of masculine migrations are explored in the essays by Ali Nobil Ahmad, Shyamal Bagchee, and Bob Pease. Here, we witness men striving to adapt to radically different cultures, whether it be the Pakistani men in Britain described by Ahmad and (poetically) by Bagchee, or the men of varied geographical origins, studied by Pease, who have migrated to Australia and struggle to preserve their masculine identities in a new land. Magid Shihade recounts a somewhat similar quest: growing up as a Palestinian man under Israeli control, and grappling with questions of selfhood and racial discrimination during his subsequent sojourns in Germany and the United States. Knolly Moses portrays Trinidadian migrants in New York City who find solidarity and self-expression sharing the vibrant music of their homeland.

Another Palestinian, Isaac, is the subject of Aje Carlbom's contribution. The essay could as easily have been placed in the "Ritual and Belief" section, since for Isaac, Islam serves as "a cognitive map" providing him with "social status and symbolic capital, and with a sense of existential meaning." What interests me in the present context, though, is the tension between Isaac's role in a Muslim "society-within-a-society" in Sweden; his efforts to "show that Islam is compatible with life in Europe"; and his "inserti[on] . . . in a transnational network that extends across Europe, the Middle East, and parts of Southeast Asia." It seems from this and other selections that

---

*UN High Commissioner for Refugees, *2003 Global Refugee Trends* (Geneva: UNHCR, 2004), www.unhcr.se/se/pdf/Global_trend_2003.pdf.

migrations are both physical–geographical and spiritual–existential. Indeed, in this globalized world, "migration" may take place without ever leaving home. The final two contributions, by Maria del Nevo and Nate Haken, touch impressionistically on this theme. They explore the impact of western mores and popular culture on young men in Pakistan and Cameroon, and the sometimes uneasy hybrid identities that result.

WEST AFRICA

Jack-of-All-Trades

Robert Lacville*

One of the most striking aspects of West African life is its mobility. There are few men I know who have not traveled widely in the region. Many of the women also travel, often for commerce. They are not just limited to the West African sub-region, either: they may easily fly off to Zaire [present-day Democratic Republic of Congo], or even to Saudi Arabia, or to Thailand to bring back cloth, jewelry, precious stones . . . Others travel with their husbands to find work on the coast. In years like this after a poor rainy season in 1990, the men travel to find work, forced to seek money for grain to feed their families because the harvest failed. In a good year, plenty of the wealthier villagers will spend a fortune on the pilgrimage to Mecca. For sure, West Africans are great travelers. Sometimes they travel just for adventure. [. . .]

I met a Ghanaian the other week, whose story illustrates West African mobility. Fafo's story is more unusual than the typical laborer or truck driver. But it is not untypical of the adventuresome nature of the region.

After five years in the army at home, Fafo became a seaman. He joined a cargo ship with a crew of 38 (half of them Americans, the rest Greek), and he became an oiler. This is a filthy job, and fairly dangerous, and means spending long hours in the heat and stench of the engine room on dirty tramp steamers around Africa and the Mediterranean. Fafo worked for a German-Greek company out of Stockholm. He is a tough cookie, and they liked him. He even learned a bit of Greek, and some unpleasant German words as well. And he was satisfied with poor non-unionized wages: after all, on board a ship you can spend nothing. Back home he bought four taxis (which later were all smashed in various *coups d'état*), and he became a substantial person in his community. As a Muslim, he also took three wives, on the strength of his shipboard wealth. They and their 17 children represent a pretty heavy charge nowadays, now that he is just a salaried driver without any second income.

---

*From Robert Lacville, "From Egypt to Angola," *Manchester Guardian Weekly*, 30 June 1991.

Around 1975, Fafo decided to seek his fortune on the grand scale. Arriving at the Egyptian port of Alexandria, he took his pay and set off with a friend for the diamond mines. "There are no diamonds in Egypt" I hear you object. Right enough. Believe it or not, Fafo set off from Alexandria for the diamond mines of Angola in southern Africa. The distance from Alexandria to northern Angola is about 3,700 miles. To give you an idea, it is like travelling from Lisbon to the Urals, or from Mexico City up to Anchorage, Alaska. There are no tarmac roads and no frontier posts where Fafo went. And they did not take a car or bus. Fafo and his shipmates traveled 3,700 miles on desert trails and forest tracks along frontiers where no customs men travel, riding petrol lorries and cassava trucks, river canoes and smugglers' wagons wherever they appeared. And they reached Angola.

This was pre-independence Angola. There were MPLA [guerrilla] troops fighting in the north, UNITA [guerrilla] troops in the south, and the common enemy was colonial Portugal. Later the enemies became each other. Fafo and his friend didn't care about all that. They settled down to dig and pan for diamonds. But while Fafo was ignoring the war, the war did not ignore him. Firing was heard, it grew nearer, and our Ghanaian friends decided to take cover. Firing passed overhead, and fighting passed them by. When Fafo crept up into the diamond panning area he had staked out, there was a soldier lying wounded. "Dis soldier he get bullet in de side so we go take him to de camp for doctoring." The camp was not far away, and it belonged to the MPLA liberation army of Aghostinho Neto, which was about to win the war for Luanda and for power [. . .]. The MPLA took in the wounded soldier; and they took in Fafo as well! To his annoyance and dismay, he found himself enrolled by force in the MPLA.

This was no chocolate soldier affair, but a dirty guerrilla war. The army was a motley composition of Africans of all nationalities led by Cubans, the whole hotch-potch communicating in broken English. Fafo drove a Land Rover with a mounted sub-machine gun. Once when scouting ahead for the main body of 1,000 men, he drove straight into a government ambush and escaped by crawling back through the forest. But finally the MPLA and their Cuban allies won.

So Fafo said he would take his wages, thank you, and go home now. The Cuban captain didn't have a budget for wages. He had Fafo bound and gagged and blindfolded so that he wouldn't know where they were, and put him in a box. This box they put into a canoe. And then they paddled the canoe two days downstream through the dripping heat (with Fafo cramped in his stifling box) until they put him ashore in Zaire.

The Zairian police put Fafo in prison until a compatriot took pity on him and paid his fare to Kinshasa. There his sister was living, and she borrowed the fare to Nigeria. From Nigeria Fafo hitch-hiked as far as Mali . . . where he spent a year as a taxi-driver . . . and then went home. Later that year Fafo returned to Sweden to become a seaman once again. Now he is getting tired, and he has become a lorry driver at home.

"I once see my Cuba captain again. Now he is become very big man, dis Captain Saya. Now he become Cuban Ambassador in Sierra Leone. He very strong man. He like me too much, and he come wid me to my house to see me. Dat make some two years back. But you know somesing, Meester Roberts: dey still not get no independence in Angola!" [...]

Your travels have not made you wealthy, Fafo, but they have given you some rich understanding of Africa.

INDIA

Migration and Song

Smita Tewari Jassal*

In the 18th and 19th centuries, eastern Uttar Pradesh and Bihar witnessed male out-migration on an unprecedented scale. Beginning in 1834, when liberated slaves refused to work on sugar plantations, a labor shortage fuelled large-scale colonial recruitment drives for indentured workers in Mauritius, British Guiana, Trinidad, and Jamaica. The peak of labor importation came in the 1870s and 1880s, and most of the recruits in the prime age group of twenty to thirty were drawn from the United Provinces and western Bihar. Only 23 per cent of the emigrants were women.[†] Hence, for over two centuries, the absence of older male siblings, who either left Calcutta [now Kolkata] to seek their fortunes in the sugar colonies or were absorbed into the city's emerging industrial centers, meant the countryside was systematically depleted of young, able-bodied males.

This essay explores through folk songs, especially those sung at the festival of Holi, the construction of masculinity in a region of male migration from the Bhojpuri-speaking belt. As masculinity is best understood in relation to women, I explore two contrasting motifs that predominate in the songs. One is the jaunty, heroic figure, carefree and oblivious to the suffering of the wives and lovers who wait for him. He sends no letters home, and when he returns it is with a *bengalin* (woman from Bengal) or *kubri* (hunchbacked) – euphemisms for the "other" woman. He is the eternal wanderer, even a foreigner: on a quest for adventure and money, and neglectful of his ties back home.

This motif of the wanderer stands in stark contrast to another qualitatively different figure: that of the younger brother who stays behind. The figure emerges almost as a substitute for the former. Frolicsome and playful, he is a tease, but also a source of

---

*Special to this volume.
†See Prabhu Mohaptra, "Restoring the Family: Wife Murders and the Making of a Sexual Contract for Indian Immigrant Labour in the British Caribbean Colonies, 1860–1920," *Studies in History*, 11: 2 (1995), p. 231; and Arun Kumar, *Rewriting the Language of Politics: Kisans in Colonial Bihar* (New Delhi: Manohar, 2001), chapter 2.

support and comfort to those whom the wanderer has abandoned. The motif of separation in these folk songs evokes the epic *Ramayana*, where the hero, Rama, is always
linked to his brother Laxmana; or the *Mahabharata*, in which Krishna's fortunes lead
him to abandon his childhood sweetheart, Radha.

> *Tuhun to jaiba raur muniya*
> *Se hamra ke ka le aiya re muniya . . .* *
> When you go away on your journey
> Pray, what will you bring for me?
> For you, I'll get a form-fitting blouse
> For myself, an eastern Bengalin

Calcutta, the home of the Bengalin (the "other" woman from Bengal) in this song,
was the favored destination of migrant workers from the Bhojpuri-speaking belt. Since
the days of the British East India Company, and continuing through the period of
industrialization, the region had drawn its workforce from eastern Uttar Pradesh and
Bihar. The literature of migration records this outflux; the folklore documents the
breaking up and atomizing of family life, and the absence of male family members from
their rural roots, sometimes for years at a stretch. During this time, they invariably
entered into second marriages and alliances with local women. Folksongs recount how
they succumbed to the charms of the local women from Bengal and, in the process, lost
any urge to return to the village. The folksongs provide a rich source to understand the
trauma of separation, and how migration shaped the consciousness of the region.

> *Babariya jhaar ke na*
> *Ghoomte ho nagariya . . .*
> Wandering he must be
> Through exotic towns
> With hair groomed, jauntily
> A striped stole over his shoulder
> Oh! for a glimpse of him
> The wanderer!

This song reverses the male gaze to look at the man instead, reveling in his heroic
glory: remote, unapproachable, and thus even more attractive. It is to the woman left
behind that this particular jaunty appeal is directed. The song, composed by Bhikhari
Thakur from the folk musical *Bidesiya* (Foreigner), is the best known of the genre
(Thakur).

Today, Bihar continues to provide seasonal migrant labor to agrarian Punjab, and
both eastern Uttar Pradesh and Bihar feed the industrial workforce and service economy in the metropolises of Delhi, Mumbai, and Calcutta. As such, the songs we are
examining here do not merely evoke a historical reality, but reflect contemporary social

---

*For longer songs, only the first two lines of the vernacular are given.

conditions – which surely accounts for their pervasiveness. The songs can be read as a record of the social history of migration, and a society's coping strategies in the face of the monumental social changes that the upheavals triggered.

While the history and process of continuous migration from the region is documented in these outgrowths of the poetic imagination, it is the Holi festival that appears to have provided space for the jocular element and liberty-taking to receive full-blown expression. Holi represents a liminal state in time rather than space, and the application of new, more fluid rules allows for breathing space, offering a release from corrosive and destructive aspects of society. The festival is reminiscent of the role of collective sacrifice in ancient civilizations, the integral violence of which served a functional purpose, allowing the social body to be reborn and rejuvenated.

Phagun mein Baba devar laage
In the month of Phagun, even an old man may seem like one's younger brother-in-law

Are holiyo mein aaja baur bhail ba tamanwa sajanwa ho
Kab le khepi hoi baiganawa sajanwa ho
Oh! Return in the Holi season, crazy one; that's my wish
How long will you stay this time, my uncaring love?

Are' kaute phaguna biti gauile re, porodesiya na auilen
Are' desiya na auilen, porodesiya na auilen . . .
Oh, how many Phagun seasons have passed, since the dweller in foreign lands returned?
Oh, the traveler never returned
My jewelry remained locked within the cupboard, and the traveler didn't return
Deep inside by breast, I nurse a huge wound
My heart desires to frolic with my husband in Holi
Oh, he spoilt all the fun, the traveler he didn't return
Oh, how many seasons since he returned
Oh, elder brother-in-law did return
Seeing this, my heart is pained
Have mercy on me, sinner, my husband did not return
Sometimes I think, just out of spite I'll send off a letter
That Moti's son is pressing his attentions on me
If he has a new mistress, who is she? The traveler did not return
For the sake of Gudu, I've been in waiting for a whole year
Shielding my modesty from the gaze of Vipin
Tell me, for whom did I guard all this? The traveler never came.

In rural contexts, there is a startlingly easy transition between imagery and symbols common to both agricultural and human fertility. D.D. Kosambi's insight, that Holi rites were designed to encourage procreation,* is borne out in the following song. The song

---

*D.D. Kosambi, *An Introduction to the Study of Indian History*, 2nd edn. (Bombay: Popular Prakashan, 1975).

also evokes a mood of regeneration: of going back to the womb, to the seed, to creation in its pristine stage. And it exemplifies the spirit of the season, capturing the yearning that is central to it:

Kohiya aibo Bhaiya ho, agutaail biya bhauji
Laagol haawa phagun ke, paniyaeel biya bhauji . . .
When will brother return? The seed has ripened, sister-in-law
With the winds of the Phagun season, the seed is laden with sap
At first, just a touch was a big deal
Now the ripened seed tumbles with its own weight
Shall I say I made it even juicier, sister-in law
With the winds of Phagun, the seed is laden with sap
First there's marriage, only then milk and grain in the home
But this time, the bounty within the blouse drips!
This time the seed has ripened within the body
With the winds of Phagun, the seed laden with sap
Maybe a baby boy, the warmed-up seed, sister-in-law
With the winds of Phagun, the seed is laden with sap
When will brother return? The seed has ripened, sister-in law.

One of the themes that the folk musical *Bidesiya* explores is the woman's dependence on her younger brother-in-law, or *devar*. In the absence of a migratory husband, sometimes for years, there were considerable obligations for the *devar* to fulfill.

Hamra ke Bhauji kaheli behaya
Brother's wife thinks I'm shameless!

Gori jobanawa hilaawe parapaari
Devara bhataar mein karave maara maari
The fair one shakes her fulsome breasts
Igniting a war between husband and his younger brother

The bond between men and their elder brother's wives traditionally contained all the ingredients of a typical "joking relationship."* In the north Indian context, the defining features of the bond between these two kin have been teasing and a spirit of alliance, combined with a woman's expectations of support from her younger brother-in-law in times of need. All this took place in an otherwise hierarchical, sometimes hostile environment – the woman's new marital home. A man's younger brother could expect to receive favors from his elder brother's wife in return for the support he provided. The element of teasing and jesting disguised a mutually advantageous bond, easing the

---

*On joking relationships, see A. Radcliffe-Brown, *Structure and Function in Primitive Society* (Glencoe, IL: The Free Press, 1959).

often difficult transition for a woman to her marital home, and bestowing affection and "indulgences" on the husband's younger brother.*

In accordance with patriarchal tradition, the *Jeth* (the husband's elder brother) had to be avoided as the senior member of the particlan; he was second only to the father-in-law in degrees of avoidance. The relationship with the devar or younger brother was much less restrictive, more congenial and familiar. It required no symbolic avoidance, such as veiling. The suggestive overtones of today's songs, the hints of sexual favors and familiarity, obscure from view the pragmatism involved in a woman's cultivating an ally within the husband's clan. This is precisely the dimension that contributed to the joking, teasing, and sexual undercurrents that characterized the bond:

> *Holi mein loote da lahaar, bhauji rang dale dau*
> *Pore pore bhauji tohaar charhal ba jawaani* . . .
> Let me abandon myself to the Holi mood, sister-in law, let me color you[†]
> Every bit of you, bursting with the abundance and glow of youth
> Just to look at you is mouth-watering
> Youth is so kind to you, sister-in-law, let me color you
> Let me abandon myself to the Holi revelry, let me color you
> Your blouse and knees, leaving no part
> Today, consider me your husband, let me color you.

A preoccupation with women's sexual transgressions in parodying, jocular, and lighthearted tones is reflected in the songs. The possibility of women's sexual transgressions being granted legitimacy, even for the brief duration of the festival, hints at underlying male anxieties. The humorous twists seen here reflect a need to manage these anxieties in ways that channel threats to the established gender hierarchy. By parodying the unease, and identifying it with the "ritual" subversion inherent in Holi, patriarchy actually ensures that potentially threatening transgressions will not occur in reality.

---

*In parts of north India, and among certain intermediate and agriculturist castes that permitted widow remarriage, the bond extended to an unstated understanding that should the woman face early widowhood, the younger brother-in-law would marry her. Among non-Brahmanical castes, this practice provided an alternative to *sati*, the self-immolation of widows on the husband's funeral pyre. See Prem Chowdhry, "An Alternative to the Sati Model: Perceptions of a Social Reality in Folklore," *Asian Folklore Studies*, 49: 2 (1990), pp. 259–74.

†Holi, the spring festival characterized by a temporary suspension of gender and caste hierarchies, is celebrated all over India on the harvest full moon. The mood is carnivalesque, and the revelry aims at subverting social norms so that after every such release, order may be restored and society may return to its original functioning. Over the month of Phagun, the mood builds, reaching a climax on the morning of the festival, when the drenching of everyone in sight with colored water and colorful powder is the norm.

Occasionally the songs have a more ambivalent tinge:

Jaldi se chhutti leke aaja more raja
Holi mein jobana garam bhail ba . . .
Hurry up, take leave and come my love
In Holi my breast is warmed up
Hurry up take leave and come, my love
Younger brother-in-law is acting shamelessly.

Devara ki chaal hamra laage bara boora ho baalam
Daale rang uthaake phurhoora ho baalam . . .
Brother-in-law's ways I find most annoying, beloved
He tosses handfuls of color and then disappears, beloved
Sometimes he puts his hand right into my blouse
Tosses handfuls of color and just disappears, beloved.

Given the temptations presented by the elder brother's absence, improper advances by devars must surely have occurred. But it is more tempting to view these verses as another way of managing the insecurities of migrant men about the women they left behind.

We can conclude this brief account by pointing out that this folksong genre represents an assertion of lower-caste masculinities. This is in defiance of sanskritization norms, which typically involve the adoption of upper-caste practices, especially where restrictions on women are concerned. That the song genre continues to thrive, in spite of sanskritization and the efforts of reformers who dismissed the genre as corrupt, attests to its resilience and cultural logic.

MOROCCO

Migration and Return

Madia Thomson*

I met Lahcen while conducting fieldwork in southwestern Morocco. He was one of many people in the region who sat with me to chat about their lives and villages.

Lahcen was born into a family of former slaves who, in Tashelhit Berber, the language of the southwest, are referred to as *isemgan*. He is keenly aware of this aspect of his identity. It once determined his family's status in the village: until 2000, they managed the annual slave festival that all villagers looked forward to, and consequently they were

---

*Special to this volume.

held in high esteem by many in the village. Even now, his origins allow villagers to situate him in community life.

Lahcen's life has evolved in a way that is in keeping with other southwestern Berber migrants. Born in the late sixties, he attended the local elementary school. He also studied in a neighboring village that housed the communal Koranic school. But even those in the countryside, like Lahcen, could feel and see the effects of independence and the new opportunities it brought. Lahcen decided he could not stay in the village. His status as a descendant of slaves was not much of a factor in this decision. Rather, migrating in search of employment and self-betterment had long been commonplace among Berber men, and some married women. Even in the 1980s, when Lahcen made these decisions, the village provided little more to the economy than human labor.

Lahcen went first to Tetouan, where he served as an aide to a local *caid* (government official). Seeking something else, perhaps better pay, he left Tetouan for Casablanca, where he worked as a *garçon* (waiter) in a café. For someone like him, with little schooling and no training in city work, this was the least offensive job available to him, though not necessarily the cleanest.

Lahcen eventually tired of this too. He decided to return to Iligh. The motivation for his move, shared by other migrants who made it, revolved around a feeling of belonging. This was expressed best in his reference to another member of the village, his friend Bihi, who had also lived in the city and subsequently returned to the village. Detailing his friend's plans to build a new house, Lahcen explained: "He is a native of the region, so he can do what he wants. No one can stop him; he is at home. He can leave, but nowhere else will they accept him." The same, he suggested, was true of me: "No one will accept you here [in Iligh] because you are American. In the States, no one will accept you, because you are from 'Senegal' [i.e., sub-Saharan Africa]."

Clearly, Lahcen believes that living anywhere other than one's place of birth, around those who know you well, leads to unease and lack of acceptance. This idea is indicative of a particular mentality, not easily identified as rural or urban, but perhaps one inherent to people who live in social groups with a keen sense of the personal relations binding them – what I call "relationality." Home, in Iligh, is where Lahcen is known, and where he is sure to be recognized. When one links this need for belonging to expedients of relationality, the "normal" one-way trajectory of migration from village to city becomes a less assured, predictable occurrence. One realizes that urbanization is not a "given," and need not be a permanent choice for people living in the countryside. The possibility of a migrant's return to his rural roots becomes, therefore, a necessary part of any development scenario.

During his return to the village, Lahcen decided to get married. Again, as someone virtually unknown in Tetouan or Casablanca, young and without much income, his marriage prospects there were slim. Returning to Iligh to choose his bride ensured him the consideration due to someone from a well-known family, someone respected for his diligence and his desire to improve his prospects. His future in-laws were people around whom he had grown up; they knew his family; he had little explaining to do.

Though young in comparison with some white-collar city dwellers, he proposed to a young woman in the village whose father was an Iligh native of *isemgan* origin, and whose mother was *issouqi*, that is, of free black origin.

Lahcen stayed in the village for most of the time it took for three of his children to be born. Both he and his new family resided in the family compound with his mother, father, and siblings. Together with other men who had chosen not to live and work elsewhere in Morocco, Lahcen worked in the fields, farming a bit, and took odd jobs to ensure his and his family's well-being. The annual *moussem* (festival) in August brought a period of concentrated work, relatively close to the village. His desire to stay in Iligh, with its isolation and lack of non-governmental economic opportunities, meant that he had to settle for little in the way of monetary gain. Longer-term employment and a better salary would have required leaving the douar.

After the birth of his third child, Lahcen went to Laayoune in Western Sahara, where he found a job in a fish-canning plant. Though it required him to live away from his family, paying them only occasional visits, it provided him with a better income to support them. One imagines that having stayed at home for the birth of his three children, Lahcen did not like the idea of leaving again for employment; but the need to provide for the basic needs of his family, such as food and clothing, quickly overrode any desire to stay put in his comfortable surroundings. When we last spoke, he seemed content with his new job in Laayoune.

TAJIKISTAN

The Migrant (1)

Nargis Nurullo-Khoja*

Tajikistan is a tiny country squeezed between Afghanistan, Uzbekistan, and China. The strategic position of the state, and its past as a Soviet republic, have brought increasing pressure from diverse actors, following in the footsteps of the intrigue-laden "Great Game" of the nineteenth century.[†]

Starting in 1991, Tajikistan witnessed one of the great migrations of recent times. The Soviet Union disintegrated, and Tajikistan slid into civil war until 1995. Thereafter, in just three years (1996–99), a mass flight of perhaps 200,000 Tajiks occurred. Most sought work and refuge in Russia, becoming by some margin the largest migrant group

---

*Special to this volume.
[†]The "Great Game" was a struggle between Russia and Britain for control of the Central Asian region.

in that country. By the end of the twentieth century, there were thought to be a million Tajiks living abroad, 800,000 of them in Russia. Perhaps no country of the former Soviet Union has been so deeply affected by out-migration as Tajikistan.

The launch phase of the Tajik migration to Russia was heavily dominated by men. But by the end of the 1990s, women were crossing borders in large numbers as well, usually to enter segregated labor markets. Women from northern districts of the country began to migrate for service-oriented jobs. Domestic work is the usual destiny of Tajik women in Russia, particularly in large cities like Moscow and St. Petersburg. Some local authorities have even argued that female migration has increased so dramatically that women now constitute half of all migrants.

Migration and poverty

Poverty provides the main spur to migration, and is also the setting in which migrants deploy their remittances to relatives at home. With a per capita GDP of US$180, Tajikistan remains one of the poorest countries in the world, ranking 112th out of 173 countries in the 2002 Human Development Index. However, poverty reflects not only absolute living standards, but also a perception of *deteriorating* conditions. Tajiks' multi-dimensional view of poverty encompasses aspects such as a lack of hope; feelings of exclusion from social and commercial life; the trauma associated with failing to feed, clothe, and house one's family members; and the difficulties of perpetuating traditions that are seen as vital to the permanence of the family unit, such as male circumcision, marriage, and funerals.

According to the World Bank, 83 percent of Tajiks live below the poverty line. Most of the national wealth and personal property built up before 1991 was destroyed in the civil war, which claimed 50,000 lives and caused some US$7 billion-worth of damage. The ensuing outflow of migrants left huge gaps in the Tajik economy and administration, particularly since at least 40 percent of them were qualified professionals.

Gender and Tajik migration

One of the key creeds of Tajik masculinity is the *mardigari*, which means "to act as a man." There are some correlations between this ideology and Mexican machismo. Both are characterized by cults of virility, with exaggerated aggressiveness and intransigence in male-to-male interpersonal relationships, and arrogance and sexual aggression in male–female relationships.

To get a better idea of how *mardigari* has influenced migration patterns, and been shaped and reshaped by them, I undertook ethnographic and qualitative research that included both formal and informal interviews, as well as participant observation. I interviewed 23 Tajik migrants living and working in Moscow and Dushanbe (the Tajik capital). Seventeen of the migrants were men and six women. Eight were in the 16–25 age group, ten were aged 25–35, and five were from 40 to 63. Twenty of them were married, and of those all had children. All were Muslims; 15 were ethnic Tajiks and eight were Uzbeks. Our conversations covered a diverse range of issues, including the legal status and medical care afforded to migrants, their economic integration, social networks, and so on. Being Tajik allowed me to penetrate deeper into the reality of these subjects' lives. Detailed portraits would consume more space than is available, so instead I briefly present seven personal stories, and try to draw some insights from them.

Story 1

Boboi Murtazo's family is considered well-off. Six of his sons, out of twelve children alto-gether, work in different Russian cities. Only four of them are married. They are originally from the Rasht Valley, which is particularly known for its culture of mutual aid and support. They have spent the last ten years in Russia, developing considerable skill in maneuvering through the Russian bureaucracy and negotiating encounters with militia. They earn about US$900–$1000 per month, and send about half of it to their parents and their families, who all live together as one large family.

This story is quite typical, and also exemplifies how the formation of new masculini-ties may be tied to migration. In the modern Tajik community, migration is *equated* with masculinity. If he is equipped to go to Russia and support his family back in Tajikistan, he is *mard* – a real man. Conversely, Tajik men who do not migrate may seek to bolster their masculinity by increasing pressure on women or other community members.

Migration theorists have also emphasized the importance of social networks, in this case communities from the Rasht Valley (other Tajik regions, such as Kuliab, Kurgan-Tubi, Khojand, and so on, could also be cited). Over time, ties between origin and destination become a source of social capital – defined as the wealth of informal family, kin, and community ties between migrants and many others, built up through the cumulative migrations between two given countries. For households, such capital decreases migration risks by providing better information to migrants before they set out, as well as facilitating border crossings, job connections, and economic assistance.

Among members of the "residual family," and especially the parents of migrants, there is often an expectation that the sons will return, generally upon marriage, and with the anticipation that they will rejoin the extended family. There is a strong relationship between migrants' remittances and subsequent house-building, and thus between migrations and a migrant's subsequent trajectory in life. The investment of migration is intimately related to key rites of passage to adulthood and social status. However, as Tajik migrations mature, and processes of family reunion and settlement occur in the destination societies, the realization dawns that return might never take place. Though hard statistics are lacking, the trend for migrants not to return is definitely on the increase. Gradually, then, we are observing a new tendency towards reorienting migrants' savings and investments, and a consequent falling-off of remittances. If houses are still built or enlarged in the region, they are for the use of family members, or as bases for returns on holiday. They become symbolic markers for a final return that may eventually – or increasingly may not – take place.

Story 2

Saidkul was the only hope of his mother and six younger sisters. His father was killed during the period of civil conflict (1991–95) that followed the fall of the Soviet Union. His mother gathered up all the family's valuables, borrowed money from relatives, and arranged for Saidkul, aged just 16, to go to Russia to work. She was anxious for Saidkul to start helping the family through remittances. But Saidkul could not fulfill these expectations: he was robbed and killed on the Uzbek–Tajik border. The message all but destroyed his mother, and it was unfortunately not a rare occurrence: in 2004 alone, 442 Tajik families received official death notices from Russia.

Story 3

Said was 18 years old when he decided to leave his village in a remote mountain area along with his uncle. "For the first few months, I could not talk to people, because of the language block," he explained. "For four years, from 1994 to '98, my uncle and I were hiding from the militia. Without papers, it's so complicated to go outside, so I preferred to be at home rather than walking around." His uncle was deported back to Tajikistan in 1999. Fortunately, though, Said found a job as a waiter. Now he has sufficient money to send to his elderly parents, his brother, who was injured doing construction work in the Russian Siberian town of Tumen, and other members of his large family. His parents have amassed sufficient funds to marry him and his brother to girls from a neighboring village.

When men from a remote village (*kishlok*) migrate to Russia or other former Soviet countries, they usually find employment in the service sector – as waiters, or as cooks preparing Tajik and Uzbek national food, or dishwashing in restaurants, or working in the construction center. This is a major occupational shift for men coming from the countryside. In Tajikistan, they worked for families, managing agricultural properties. The Tajik family is a typical patriarchal unit with a strictly gendered division of labor. Migrating men discover there is no division anymore: they must agree to take whatever work they can find, even traditional "women's work."

Police harassment and abuse was a common theme in the interviews conducted for this essay (see also the following story). It is notable that all 14 of the men interviewed in Moscow had been arrested or stopped at least once by Russian militia. Five of them had been deported to Tajikistan, though all had subsequently returned to Russia. One has the strong impression that women's illegal status does not provoke such a severe response from the authorities, though there are as yet no hard statistics on deported women.

Story 4

Suraiyo (a 35-year-old woman): "Our family has been working in Moscow for three years. I sell fruits and vegetables in the Cherkizov market in Moscow. My husband takes care of the children: we have three daughters and one son. He has to take care of them because I work until late. He cannot work in the market because of the Russian militia . . ."

Men like Suraiyo's husband must confront not only the economic vulnerability of their families (given the lack of unemployment benefits), but also the challenge to their identity that comes with not fulfilling their function as providers. Paid employment, as a means of making money and getting out of the house, is vital to the traditional masculine identity of Tajik men. At the same time, these men must reckon with women's new economic empowerment and transformed gendered identity. The resulting feelings of powerlessness may lead to conflict, aggravating male violence and causing the breakup of couples. In this context, it is worth recalling Matthew Gutmann's comment that masculinity and femininity "are not original, natural, or embalmed states of being; they are gender categories whose precise meanings constantly shift, transform into each other, and ultimately make themselves into whole new entities."*

Story 5

Safar is a 17-year-old from Rudaki district. He is standing on a street outside the Shoh-Mansur bazaar in Dushanbe, the Tajik capital, where males from schoolchildren to elderly gather, waiting to be hired for basic manual work. "There was a drought for two years, and the crop wasn't good," Safar says. "We weren't paid by the kolkhoz [collective farm]. My family was close to starvation. As the oldest son, I had to leave to look for work." Safar does not find work every day, but when he does, he is paid as much as 10–15 somoni (about $3–5). This is equal to his entire monthly wage in his village's cotton fields.

Poverty is far more widespread in the country's remote and rural areas. Poverty indicators in rural areas are nearly double those in urban zones, at every educational level; while the chances of being poor are about six times greater for employed individuals in rural areas than for urban employed. However, data are often not available for peri-urban areas, most widespread around Dushanbe and Khojand, where economic circumstances tend to be more difficult and unstable, and where the interlocking of internal and international out-migration is most visible. Indeed, some of the rapidly growing peri-urban areas are even more impoverished than remote rural areas.

For *mardikors* (workers) like Safar, as for Tajiks in Russia, police harassment is commonplace. They are routinely driven away, have their passports confiscated, or are pressured for bribes. Yet this seems preferable to life at home. It is the luckier migrants who end up in Russia, where unskilled workers can earn $200–250 a month. The exodus of hundreds of thousands of otherwise unemployed men to Russia acts as a stabilizing factor, a kind of social safety-valve. Yet there is no guarantee this avenue will always be open: Russian authorities are placing increasing pressure on immigration.

---

*Matthew C. Gutmann, *The Meanings of Macho: Being a Man in Mexico City* (Berkeley, CA: University of California Press, 1996), p. 223.

Story 6

Shokir once served in a Russian military unit in Tajikistan, and has a Russian passport. He was the first among his relatives to gain legal immigration status, and so is de facto patriarch of his family. His wife and children have passports as well – but as a man, his social status is much higher. Shokir is in charge of assisting friends and relatives coming to Russia; he is able both to accommodate family and friends and help them find employment.

Story 7

Karim had six children when he decided to leave for Russia. In his final days at home, his wife invited a local religious woman leader and other female neighbors to pray as a group, in order to increase his chances of finding work in Russia. Karim did get a job – but then he married a Russian woman. He did not call for his Tajik family to reunite with him. His oldest son, who is 16 years old, is thinking of going to Russia as well. But he does not want to ask for his father's assistance.

Family is a powerful institutional structure in Tajik society, and occupies an important place in the migration process. The socially integrated, supportive family structures may have advantages in terms of shared hardship and a common household strategy of migration. But they are generally predicated on a strongly patriarchal authority. In almost all cases, the person receiving remittances and administering the family budget is the male head of the family. Women usually have an important function in managing the material life of the household, but they do not take part in decision-making.

Traditionally, before the Soviet period, Tajik communities had a classical Muslim structure, in which the men went out to work and provided economically for the family, while the women stayed at home, did the housework, and looked after children. Women were not permitted to participate in paid work. However, with the introduction of a cotton monoculture during the Soviet era, young women between the ages of 17 and 25 became the preferred cheap-labor force for Soviet collective farms. Men were reluctant to work for miserable wages in the cotton fields. As a result, some shifting and renegotiation of gender roles took place in rural Tajikistan during the Soviet period. But women were still stuck doing the housework and caring for children. Greater participation in labor markets and access to personal income did not yield greater influence or control for women in the household, and did little to revolutionize structures of patriarchal authority.

The strength of family structures has endured through the long transformation from pre- to post-communism, and the patriarchal family unit has remained a fundamental social institution in all rural and most urban parts of Tajikistan. Inevitably, though, some dismemberment has taken place through large-scale migration, as with Karim's family (above). As well, the patriarchal mindset has reemerged in new forms since the Soviet collapse in 1991. Young men, in particular, have reinvented some strategic aspects of traditional Tajik patriarchy to serve their own needs. These include a new form of exploitation of young Tajik women: trafficking them abroad for sex work.

SOUTH ASIA/MIDDLE EAST

The Migrant (2)

Naeem Mohaiemen*

I have a ritual when I arrive in the hotel in a new city. After a quick shower, I immediately go looking for a spot to get Internet access. In Beirut to present my work at an arts festival, I discovered that the best location to receive wireless internet signals was the hallway outside my hotel room. Sitting on the stairs to check email every morning, I soon became a familiar sight to the maids cleaning the hotel. On the third day, an Asian maid finally worked up the courage to ask me in English: "Are you Indian?"

Forsaking my usual sarcastic response, I simply replied, "No, I'm Bangladeshi." Her face immediately lit up. "I'm from Bangladesh too!" Switching from halting English to rapid-fire Bengali, she started asking me which district I was from, where my home village was, when I had arrived, what I was doing there, and more. Farzana[†] was from Comilla. She was one of two Bangladeshi employees in the hotel. The other was Anis, a downstairs guard I had noticed earlier.

Farzana said something which made me realize why she was so excited: "Allah, you know, I have been in Beirut for seven years, been at this hotel for five years. You are the first Bangladeshi guest I have seen. We see Indians all the time, but Bangladeshis, never!" Here was a very uncomfortable contradiction. While I presented at the conference, Farzana would be cleaning my room. Even within the flattening conditions of diaspora life, class privilege had reasserted itself.

During the two weeks that followed, Farzana and I fell into a routine of morning conversations. From these *alaap*s I learnt that Bangladeshis were relatively new arrivals here, but had already become one of the big groups of migrant workers, after Ethiopians and Filipinos. Sri Lankan maids were of course the Lebanese archetype (their horrific conditions are documented in Carole Mansour's recent film *Maid In Lebanon*); but Bangladeshis were starting to replace them in some jobs.

Although the community was recent, almost everyone had been here for at least seven years. Seven years is roughly the amount of time that new visas had been blocked under the previous Syrian regime, so that was the marker for migration. Although the Bangladeshis had established a strong community, they mixed freely with other migrant groups. A day after I visited the Sabra–Shatila Palestinian refugee camps, I learnt from Farzana that it was also the site for the very popular Sunday "Bangla market." That was when roving Bengali sellers would set up temporary shops next to the camps and sell Bengali food, trinkets, music, and films. "Not just Bangladeshi," she said proudly, "but others also buy our items!"

---

*Special to this volume.
[†]Names were changed to protect identities.

After the festival ended, Farzana invited me to have lunch at her home. There, I met several other members of her community, mostly working as maids and building guards. The man who interested me most was Hamid, a garrulous nightguard who became my guide through Beirut. To start things off, I asked Hamid why he had two massive posters of assassinated Lebanese Prime Minister Rafiq Hariri. This seemed an odd juxtaposition with progressive Lebanese who mourned Hariri's death while maintaining a healthy skepticism about his ties with big business. But Hamid very enthusiastically told me that Hariri was the man who could claim credit for rebuilding war-torn Beirut. "If only Bangladesh could have a Hariri," he added wistfully. Though some Lebanese artists had warned me that there was a lot of racism in Lebanon, Hamid and his friends seemed to have absolutely no complaints. Rather, he kept insisting that the Lebanese treated them "fairly," and certainly better than other Arab countries.

The only time Hamid became tentative was when he started talking about his family. Like many other migrants, he had managed to return home only once during his twelve years. During that trip, he married, and brought his wife back to Beirut. Soon afterwards, his wife gave birth to their first son, Rubayat. But the pressures of providing for both wife and son were too much, and he was forced to send them back to Bangladesh. When I asked how he was coping without his new family, Hamid gave a slightly embarrassed smile. Then he stood up straight and said: "This is what's written in our fate. Allah gives some a lot, so he has to give others little. This is the path written for us, so we just have to manage."

As if to change the topic, he started showing me pictures of his son. In one photo, Rubayat was standing in front of a silver Porsche. "I asked them to do that on the computer," he explained, pointing to the car. Looking again at the sports car, I wondered if it was meant to give the family back home an illusion of wealth, or whether it was simply there as a nice backdrop. Hamid started handing the photo over to me, and I protested that I couldn't take his copy. "No, no, take it, I have many more copies"; then, with a quiet insistence: "Please. I want you to take it."

As I walked back to the hotel after lunch, holding the envelope with the photo in my hand, I thought about this paradox: global migrants have very little in terms of stature, rights or earnings, but somehow they still manage to find dignity and happiness in their transient lives. I had glimpsed a fragment of this in Hamid's stories.

*   *   *

I was reminded of the Beirut episode by television footage of a recent hostage crisis in Iraq. Unlike previous kidnappings of westerners, morally problematic in themselves, the hostages this time were migrant truck-drivers. Looking at the scared faces of Tilak Raj, Sukhdev Singh, and Antaryami, I wanted to ask the kidnappers: are these really the "agents of Empire"? Desperately poor men, who went to Iraq for their Kuwaiti employer, were now hostages and pawns in the power struggle between the occupation forces and the insurgents.

Speaking to the Indian press, one hostage's father, Sher Singh, said: "With great hopes we had sent our son abroad in April this year by selling a piece of land. Little did we know that we [would] have to face this." His wife Jaspal Kaur added: "What can we do? We are very poor people." It is poverty like this that forces millions of Indians, Pakistanis, and Bangladeshis to work in sub-human conditions in the Middle East and Gulf region. That same cycle had trapped these men in a terrifying ordeal. The fate of seven hostages – three Indians, three Kenyans, and an Egyptian truck driver – also demonstrated that the Iraqi insurgency was no heroic rebel army or genuine alternative to empire. Rather, it was a nihilistic group with a program to drive out the occupation "at any cost." That "any cost" included the complete erasure of any class-based politics within an anti-imperialist critique.

Thinking of the Indian hostages, Himangshu Datta, my old barber in Dhaka, also came to mind. One day, while cutting my hair, he calmly announced that he was changing his religion to Islam. Apparently, for would-be Bangladeshi migrant workers to Dubai, being Muslim could provide an advantage. In the hope of getting a job as a driver for a Dubai government office, Himangshu was going to get a certificate with a Muslim name. I asked him what he would do about his nether regions, and he sadly answered: "Listen brother, I need to make money to send back to my family in the village. I will do anything. What is one little *khothna*?"

For a man to abandon his religion for migrant work in the Middle East, with its nightmarish work standards, speaks of the poverty people seek to escape. Human Rights Watch (HRW) recently issued a report on the condition of foreign workers in Saudi Arabia. The revelation that "Guest Workers" are systematically abused should come as no surprise to anyone familiar with the kingdom's history and its relatively recent abolition of slavery. Sarah Whitson from HRW reported that the organization "found men and women in conditions resembling slavery." The report described "the abysmal and exploitative labor conditions many workers face, and the utter failure of the justice system to provide redress." Based on interviews taken in Bangladesh, India and the Philippines, HRW found evidence of exploitative labor practices, rape of women workers, and the beheading of guest workers accused of crimes without proper legal process. Visitors to Saudi Arabia have witnessed the racism that brown- and black-skinned pilgrims face in Mecca. Like hundreds of Bangladeshis every year, my parents endured these indignities during their pilgrimage. When he returned from Mecca, my father told me: "To them, we will always be *miskeen* (beggars). It doesn't matter what we do, or where we come from."

Reports of terrible conditions for migrant workers do eventually filter back. Dead bodies are also flown home. But the flow of migrants continues and grows. Pundits talk about fanatical hordes in the "Third World," willing to die for religion. But the experience of migrant workers shows that poverty trumps ideology and religion as a driving force for the vast, working-class populations of these nations. In this respect, they share something even with the American soldiers in Iraq, many of whom are from the economic and racial underclass and joined the army for economic opportunities.

By kidnapping these laborers, and using them to punish the occupation, the Iraqi insurgents display a willful ignorance of the position of migrant labor in global power equations. During Vietnam, anti-war activists saw the Vietcong as a people's liberation army because they stood up to the crushing power of the United States. The conflict was framed in the popular imagination as capitalism versus communism. But in the present crisis, viewers would be hard-pressed to find any heroes among the insurgents. In the end, it will be poor people everywhere – in dusty Iraqi towns, desperate Indian villages, and army recruiting centers in Michigan – who will pay the price.

MEXICO/UNITED STATES

The Migrant (3)

Ginger Thompson*

Wire fences are all that mark the border here [in Sásabe, Mexico] between the United States and Mexico. Still, Juan Flores, a 31-year-old Mexican farmer tired of living on $5 a day, said that sneaking north would be anything but easy.

The land, he said, is a death trap.

Standing on the southern side of the fence recently, Mr. Flores stared out at the end-less desert that stretched into Arizona. If all went well, he figured, it would take him two days to cross the rattlesnake haven and reach the nearest Arizona highway. Thanks to a few days of rain, the afternoon temperatures had dropped to a bearable 88 degrees, but at night, he worried, they could fall into the low 60s.

To keep his load light, Mr. Flores carried only two apples, a bag of tortilla chips and a gallon jug of water. But after viewing the mountainous terrain ahead, he wondered whether he would have enough to drink. "I am not worried that the *migra* will catch me," he said, using the migrants' word for the United States Border Patrol. "I am worried that if I get lost the migra will not catch me."

Once as barren of people as it is of rainfall, the desert here is one of the newest and fastest-growing gateways to the United States for illegal Mexican immigrants. But it is also one of the most inhospitable regions of North America, known for fierce winter storms and 110-degree summer temperatures that turn the ground into a human grill. As the flow of immigrants here thickens, the area Mexicans call the Altar Desert has become a place of ultimate sacrifice.

---

*From Ginger Thompson, "The Desperate Risk Death in a Desert," *The New York Times*, 31 October 2000.

According to the Immigration and Naturalization Service, 369 immigrants have died trying to cross the border since last October [1999].* Some 100 of those deaths occurred along the Arizona–Mexico border, up from 19 deaths in 1998. A majority of the Sonora–Arizona deaths were caused by hypothermia, dehydration and drowning.

Mr. Flores, a stout man with the coarse and stubby fingers of someone who works the land, said he had heard dozens of stories about immigrants who had died from exposure to the heat and cold this year crossing the Altar Desert. He acknowledged that the journey ahead might seem foolhardy.

But then he talked about the needs of his wife, and of their dreams for their three children, especially his newest son, born just two weeks earlier. He said he was determined to try. "Of course I am scared," Mr. Flores said. "But it's better to be scared and try to make a better life for my family than to stay and watch them go hungry."

Mexican government officials and human rights advocates say the soaring desert death toll is evidence of the failures, and some say cruelty, of recent United States border enforcement operations. Those operations have doubled the number of agents along the border, concentrating them in major urban areas like El Paso, San Diego, Brownsville and, most recently, the Arizona cities of Douglas and Nogales.

But from Sásabe, population 3,000, it is clear that the increase in agents along the United States side of the border has not stopped immigrants from their illegal crossings. It has caused them to cut new channels through more perilous areas. [. . .]

Officials of Grupo Beta, a Mexican agency created several years ago to protect the rights and security of immigrants, carry rehydration kits and antivenom medicines in their vehicles for emergencies. They said they had rescued more than 1,000 immigrants this year. Specially trained units of the United States Border Patrol have made close to 2,400 rescues.

In the town of Altar, the last stop in civilization for most migrants headed into the Arizona desert, churches have begun offering them free meals and residents have opened boarding houses where they can get a bit of rest before moving on.

It is a dust bowl of a town off the highway to Tijuana. The tallest building is the church, where an altar is decorated with banners that read, "This is a place where migrants are recognized and treated as brothers." Surrounding the plaza are rows of check-cashing counters and taco stands that have opened in the last few years to serve the migrants.

Residents of Altar said the downtrodden strangers began passing through a few years ago, arriving in twos and threes. Today they come in busloads, from 300 to 800 each day. They fill the plaza and wait for paid guides, called coyotes, who promise them safe passage across the desert for fees ranging from $100 to $1,000.

---

*According to the *Houston Chronicle* (19 November 2005), "A record 473 migrants died in the last year while crossing the US–Mexico border, the most since the US Border Patrol began tracking such deaths in 1999."

Many do not get their money's worth. Officials on both sides of the border say the coyotes often tell migrants that the journey takes hours, rather than days. And once paid, the coyotes often abandon those who run out of water and feel too weak to keep going.

"We try to tell the people not to cross in the desert," said the Rev. Rene Luis Castañeda, the priest who serves the small ranching communities around Sásabe. "They can make more money over there, but no amount of money is worth their lives." With a shrug, he added, "Most don't listen."

Librado, 50, a father of three who would not give his last name, said he had come to the desert from the lush, tropical state of Veracruz.

"Everything looks the same," he said. "I hope I will be able to tell whether I am walking forward and not backward." The landscape here looked to him like the surface of the full moon that shone above.

And from where he stood, he said, the United States seemed just as far away. Turning to a new acquaintance before setting off on his journey, he sought some reassurance.

"You think we will make it?"

PAKISTAN/MACEDONIA

The Migrant as "Terrorist"

Salman Masood*

Sitting in the compound of her mud house in this dusty farming village [Rirka Bala] in eastern Pakistan, Bibi Bakhtan, 61, wiped dust from a framed photograph of her dead son and posed a universal question.

"Can mothers forget their sons?" she sighed.

Surrounded by grandchildren and a few ambling goats, her voice quivered with grief as she talked about her son, Muhammad Riaz. Just over two years ago, Mr. Riaz, then 30, and five other Pakistani men and an Indian, were shot dead in Macedonia by the local police. At the time, the police said the men were Al Qaeda-linked terrorists plotting to attack Western embassies in the capital, Skopje.

This month, the Macedonian government disclosed that a police inquiry had found the slain men innocent of those charges. They were not terrorists, but rather illegal immigrants seeking a better life in Europe. And their killing, the inquiry found, was an effort to advance Macedonia's status in the campaign against terrorism.

"It was staged, a monstrous killing of seven economic migrants," said Mirjana Kontevska, a spokewoman for Macedonia's Interior Ministry. The March 2002 killings,

---

*From Salman Masood, "A Dream Dies in Macedonia," *The New York Times*, 10 May 2004.

she said, were part of an attempt by the interior minister at that time, Ljube Boskovski, and four police officers to "present themselves as participants in the war against terrorism and demonstrate Macedonia's commitment to the war on terrorism."

Interviews with the families of the slain men reveal one common wish: to earn a better living by going abroad. All had found illegal passage to Europe before falling prey to what Macedonian authorities called a "meticulous plan to promote Macedonia as a player in the fight against global terrorism."

Life moves slowly here in Rirka Bala. Trucks and tractors move ploddingly on patchy roads that pierce fields of wheat and sugar cane and link small mud and brown brick houses scattered among the fields. The inhabitants are small farmers who toil under the scorching sun. Villagers say few here can afford an education.

But among the mud houses every now and then stands a grand multistoreyed house with huge front pillars and marble finishing. Local residents say these towering houses have been built with money sent back by Pakistanis working in the United States or in Europe as laborers, cab drivers or technicians. The affluence of some, it seems, has aroused envy in the hearts of many.

Muhammad Riaz belonged to a caste known as Mussalis, Hindu converts to Islam who do menial jobs in the villages of Punjab. He, too, dreamed of having a big house, like the ones he saw in his village and neighboring towns, relatives said. He thought going to Europe was the only way he could fulfill this dream. And so his family borrowed $1,550 from a local landlord, paid $850 to a travel agent to arrange a fake visa and passport, and gave the rest to Mr. Riaz for travel expenses.

Trying to get into Europe illegally is common here. "There are so many people who have gone abroad on fake documents and are earning now," said Mr. Riaz's mother, Bibi Bakhtan. "We didn't think it was wrong. Everybody was doing it."

During the late 1970s and early 1980s, it was relatively easy to get a visa for the United States and parts of Europe, village residents said. But as Western countries toughened their immigration policies, the human trafficking business flourished in this district, Mandi Bahauddin, and in neighboring Gujrat.

Gujrat, in particular, is notorious as a human trafficking hub. Over the past decade, Pakistani news media reports suggest, Gujrat's traffickers have sent at least 200,000 Pakistanis to Greece, Italy, Spain and other countries. One popular route has been through Iran, Turkey and Greece into other European countries, according to local news media reports.

In November 2001, Mr. Riaz went to Turkey via Iran, according to his family. "Riaz called us from Turkey in early 2002 and told us that he was fine," said Mehr Din, his father. That was the last word his family received from him. "We didn't hear anything else until one day his body came in a coffin," said Mr. Din, 70, his wrinkled, sun-bronzed face contorting with pain. Having placed all their hopes and borrowed money on Mr. Riaz's journey abroad, the family expects to be in debt for the next seven years.

According to Macedonian authorities, the six Pakistani men – Mr. Riaz, Omar Farooq, Syed Bilal Hussein Shah, Asif Javed, Khalid Iqbal and Ijaz Ahmed – were in

Bulgaria hoping to make their way to Western Europe when they were lured across the border into Macedonia and housed by Macedonian police who then shot them. After the killings, Macedonian officials displayed uniforms and badges bearing the insignia of the National Liberation Army, an ethnic Albanian rebel force that fought government troops. Ethnic Albanian politicians denied any links to the slain men. The Indian killed with the Pakistani men was a Sikh whose identity is still being sought by Ansar Burney, a Pakistani civil rights activist.

Among the victims was Ijaz Ahmed, 21, who according to his brother, Azhar Javed, a 33-year-old cab driver from the village of Silvia, wanted to go to Europe to help his family. Mr. Ahmed hoped to help the family escape from the poverty that had ensnared it for generations.

Sitting glumly with his 66-year-old mother, Ghulam Fatima, who sobbed at each mention of her son, Mr. Javed said that many people from Sivia were working abroad. "He wanted to earn money like them, so he could arrange for the weddings of his four sisters," Mr. Javed said. "He wasn't a terrorist."

In the nearby village of Sohawa Diloana, Muhammed Mehdi, 47, a retired army wireless radio operator, said he thought sending his 18-year-old son abroad would improve the family's living conditions. His son, Asif Javed, left Pakistan in August 2001. His father last heard from him when he telephoned from Turkey in early 2002. Eight weeks later, news of his death [reached] his father.

"Now I tell people, 'Eat dirt but never send your children abroad,'" he said, sitting in the village cemetery. He adjusted a garland on his son's grave, and prayed.

FRANCE

"The Cemetery of the Living"

Djaffer Ait Aoudia*

The camp, the size of about four football pitches, lies beneath an immense corrugated steel roof. A long queue forms for the showers. Washbasins, blackened with streaks of human bristle, overflow with used water. The toilets are collective, with no taps or paper. Children play with disposable razors as if with toy cars or planes. A smell of dead dog pervades the camp.

From the canteen a queue stretches to the end of the camp. Refugees are allocated to makeshift tents according to their country of origin. More than 1,300 refugees live here,

---

*From Djaffer Ait Aoudia, "We Are Already Dead. This is the Cemetery of the Living," *The Observer*, 26 May 2002.

cut off from the world. They have only one ambition – to get aboard a lorry on the Calais–Dover ferry. For this they need the services of the *passeurs* or smugglers.

Socially, Sangatte is organized like a pyramid. At its base are the refugees, suffering and submissive. At its top are the passeurs who promise El Dorado in Britain for a fee of between $500 and $800. The passeurs are mostly Kurds and they are the kings of Sangatte. In theory the heated cubicles are reserved for women and children. But the refugees have nicknamed them "travel agencies" because in practice nearly all are occupied by the passeurs, who negotiate the terms for clandestine crossings. [...]

Mohamed, a Kurd of about 30, wearing a leather jacket, is one of the "guides" in charge of leading the refugees to a lorry park where drivers stop before embarking on the ferries. He speaks Arabic, English, Kurdish. In his blue tent he receives Afghans, Palestinians or Albanians in a thoroughly business-like way.

"For $800 you get through as a matter of course. What's more, you travel in the windbreak on the roof of the cabin or in the ventilated compartment beneath the trailer. It's better than under the tarpaulin."

After six months in the camp, Mohamed has saved a good deal. "The passeurs make much more than I," he says. How much? He brings out a wallet and counts the contents: $3,000 and a bit more. "And this, these are my takings from yesterday. I've only $100 out of the $600 which go to the passeur." He adds: "These are wicked people, capable of the worst. But they pay. And in this business it's like drugs. You're married for better or for worse."

For those wanting to make the crossing things have got worse. Only about 50 manage to make it to England each day. The others are brought back by the police into the overflowing camp where meals are rationed and blankets are given out in dribs and drabs. The Red Cross, it is clear, is seeking to deter new arrivals by offering only minimal comfort. But the effort is in vain. Even sleeping on the ground, in temperatures as cold as 3°C, does nothing to discourage the desperate and the destitute.

Ahmed the Afghan is 30. His face is lined with wrinkles. He lost his father in the war with the Red Army, his mother in the civil war and two brothers in the American bombardments of Kabul. "There's nothing left for me there." In mid-November [2001] he fled his country, enduring three freezing months in the mountains. In Iran, a Kurdish smuggler led him to Turkey. From there a boat set him down on the Greek coast. Then Italy, then France. "This has cost me nearly $8,000, the money I inherited from my grandparents, which my mother kept even through the wars." Like the others, he's not going to give up when he is only 22 miles from England.

Some try to break into the Eurotunnel site and travel on the train. Others try to bypass the passeurs and get on to lorries. The first group risks electrocution. The second can get into bloody confrontations with Kurdish heavies who rule over embarkation areas. It's because of these "independent" runs that Sangatte has seen knife fights between Afghan refugees and Kurds.

Tonight a little group, myself among them, has decided to make an attempt on the lorries. It's 5:30 p.m. and we're at Sangatte-Calais bus station. The guide stands at the bus entrance to check his clients. The other passengers, including local people, are aggressively thrown off. The bus driver has no control over his vehicle and the guide has forced him to play a cassette of Middle Eastern music at high volume.

The camp's tensions have entrenched local hostility. "A few days ago," recalls a taxi driver, "a refugee sheltered in a restaurant up the road was found with a knife in his back. He had been attacked by a smuggler. But now the local residents no longer seek to distinguish between the little refugees and the passeurs. They lump them all together."

Three-quarters of an hour. Four kilometers on the highway. Calais. Early evening mist. The lights of boats in port. Beyond lies Dover, England, that Eden where the police don't have the right to check the identities of illegal entrants! Here police checks are feared, above all by Algerians who, if their situation is "irregular," risk expulsion. The passeurs, on the other hand, are considered stateless and therefore cannot be expelled.

Suddenly we slip into the bushes to get round the port by way of passeurs' paths which run along the beach. In a depot yard stand the fateful lorries. There is general delight. "Look at this lorry with a right-hand drive," exults one of us. "If we manage to take it, tomorrow I'll buy the whole world a breakfast."

Towards midnight, jumping over rocks, we approach. Then Chakhwan, the smuggler who controls this zone, bursts in on us, followed by his henchmen. He kicks a Palestinian refugee in the head. Other blows rain down. One of his heavies starts throttling one of the Algerians. When he defends himself, one of the passeur's gang pulls out a knife.

Chakhwan and his men consider their "business" threatened. They hesitate at nothing. "We are already dead. Sangatte is the cemetery of the living," they tell me.

We flee towards another parking area. Other passeurs are there, brandishing wine bottles, their faces bloodied. They still pursue us. Four kilometers further on we find another service area. There are lorries, and not a living soul in sight. But there's no time to celebrate. Two men, armed with heavy sticks, run towards us. They're Egyptians, bodyguards and interpreters of the smuggler who controls this patch.

Lukman, known as Luciano, was once a pimp in Belgium. He is an Egyptian aged about 35, wearing a three-quarter-length Italian coat with his head closely cropped. He has escaped a recent wave of arrests. All the refugees know him. He's not going to let us hang about on his patch. Our threats to call the police have no effect. "Go ahead," he says. "You're all going to be expelled from France. So get lost."

It's time to give up. Tomorrow, maybe, we'll start again. A few sighs, or murmured prayers. In Indian file the little column returns to the miserable antechamber of Sangatte.

GHANA

The Refugee (1)

Tajudeen Abdulraheem*

"My name is Kofi Amega. I am a Ghanaian and I arrived in Britain in December 1984 with a visiting visa to seek political asylum. My application is still pending. I came from Lomé, Republic of Togo, West Africa, where I escaped to in 1983 after evading security agents in Ghana who would have imprisoned or killed me. The Government of Togo and that of Ghana have not seen eye to eye for years. But there has been periodic rapprochement between them, using refugees as pawns. It works on the basis of 'you return my enemies and I will return yours.'

"Ghanaian refugees – especially soldiers and occasionally politically active civilians – became hostages of the Togolese Government. So although there is a United Nations Commission for Refugees in Lomé I was reluctant to register because the Togolese authorities had ways of finding out who is who, and could use anyone in an exchange with the Ghanaian Government. Instead, like many refugees, I traveled around the West African Coast to avoid the Togolese police. No state would accept us for fear our Government would accuse them of 'interfering in its internal affairs.' And so we just kept moving, like rolling stones, never staying long in one place.

"Finally sheer desperation made me seek an escape from this helter-skelter life. I managed, through the help of friends, to secure somebody else's passport and traveled to the UK as a visitor. I arrived in London in December 1984 full of hope. Having gone through a British educational system and served in the colonial army, I expected certain standards of British justice. Indeed my fellow exiles in Africa, while fearing that my false passport would be discovered and I be returned to Ghana, had otherwise envied me. They assumed my difficulties would be over.

"Well, my passport was not detected and after the usual accusatorial probing at the airport I was let in on a visitor's visa. Straightaway I inquired about organizations or individuals who could help me. That was when my problems began. I got passed from one solicitor to another because I had no money to pay for their services. And because I had not claimed asylum on arrival at the airport many refugee organizations were reluctant to handle my case. Moreover, no sooner had I arrived than I had to start working to keep myself and get accommodation.

"Since my visa was only for six months I was anxious to quickly get my application to the Home Office. But being penniless I had to make the application myself without realizing the processes involved. I wrote down my experiences as I recollected them.

---

*From Tajudeen Abdulraheem, "Refugee in Orbit," *New Internationalist*, no. 233 (September 1991).

But when I was eventually able to afford a solicitor I had to re-write the statement, so the two accounts were slightly at odds with each other.

"By then I was getting £33 a week from the State for my upkeep (excluding accommodation). It was hardly enough for food, let alone travel in London. Yet by law I had to wait six months after my application for asylum to apply for a work permit.

"All this time, my predominant feeling was of guilt. I had not seen my family for almost two years by the time I reached London. My wife had had a second baby while I was on the run. My first child had only been four years old when I left. By the time I got here, the economic situation in Ghana – bad when I left – was worse. Yet I could not send them money because I was barely surviving myself.

"I had become an irresponsible father, an absentee husband and a lost son. I had hardly even maintained regular correspondence when I was wandering. What could I say? It was unfair to increase my family's emotional load with my stories of woe. I just kept hoping things would get better so I could write. Weeks became months, months became years. I postponed letter-writing to Christmas. But it was miserable – and so I further postponed writing until Easter. Time went by – and I often felt my whole life was a waste.

"It was over a year before I got a notification to appear before the Home Office Committee investigating my case. I was told that there were many contradictions in my story. Therefore I was not being granted full asylum. Instead I had 'limited leave to remain' pending an appeal. It meant I could stay – but for how long?

"By this time I had the right to work. But few employers would take me knowing that I could leave at any time. So I remained in the underworld of casual jobs; low pay, high risk, unprotected labor. And still I had my immediate family to think about. How could I ask them to come when my own feet were not firmly on the ground? Anyway under my 'limited leave to remain' I was only legally entitled to ask one member of my family to visit after I had been here four years. I received letters from home with joy, but I often ended up sobbing after reading them. Finally I could not wait any longer for the slow, grinding wheels of the immigration office. My wife and children came to Britain in 1988, four years after I had arrived, and started asylum procedures when they entered the country. By then I was something of an expert in asylum applications. Even so their cases are still being dragged through the bureaucracy. But then, so is mine.

"I attended my last appeal at the Home Office a few months ago. No decisions have been reached on my case. So it's seven years now that I have been living in uncertainty and hope . . ."

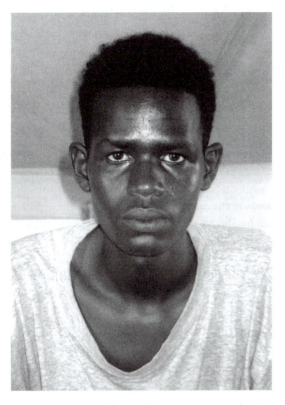

Darfurese man in a refugee camp along the Chad–Sudan border (Eric Markusen)

SOMALIA/KENYA

The Refugee (2)

Shukria Dini*

In this short essay, the focus is on Somali men who became refugees owing to the collapse of the Somali state and the resulting anarchy and violence in the 1990s. These refugees fled to neighboring Kenya to seek refuge, ending up in the Dadaab camps.[†] Here, I will

*Special to this volume. The author wishes to thank the refugee men in the Dadaab camps who shared their experiences and stories with her so generously. Thanks also to Adam Jones for helpful critiques of this essay.
[†]In the Somali – or any – context, male refugees are not a homogeneous group, nor do they experience displacement and camp life in the same way. They differ by age, class, ethnicity, education, marital status, and urban versus rural backgrounds.

examine the impact of forced displacement on Somali men, particularly those residing in the Dadaab refugee camps run by international humanitarian organizations. How does forced displacement and life in camps affect male refugees' confidence, self-image, and identity? The essay is based on field research carried out in the Dadaab camps in Summer 1999.* I interviewed ten men who live in three camps. They shared with me aspects of their lives, ranging from the isolation of daily life in a refugee camp to alienation, the loss of identity and country, and the absence of loved ones.

The Dadaab camps were established to offer temporary accommodation for Somali refugees, but in reality they have become permanent closed "homes" with no opportunities for refugees. Once in camps, refugees lose access to opportunities such as higher education, employment, and other chances to improve their situation. When refugees arrived in these camps in the early 1990s, they believed that within months – at most a year – they would be able to return to Somalia. When temporary refuge became an extended reality, men stated that they had lost their livelihoods, status, dignity, and manhood. They felt they lived like prisoners, with their status established and defined by others in the relief organizations. When asked how displacement and a long period in the camps affected their previous masculine roles, they replied, for example:

> In pre-war Somalia, men were responsible for providing their families with food, money, shelter, protection. However, this is no longer the case. As a result of our displacement from Somalia, we male folks in the camps have become dependent on the charities of relief organizations. UNHCR and CARE have been our heads of household, the main providers and decision makers.

Refugee men, despite their losses, are able to theorize and analyze their positions as refugees, and the ramifications of that status. Their displacement and encampment have reversed traditional gender roles, not only between the two sexes but between men and relief organizations. A new kind of masculinity inevitably becomes prominent, as relief agencies become sole providers to the families and children who were once under the care and control of these men. Relief organizations feed them and attend to basic needs – determining who will receive support, when, how, and where. These men lamented the loss of their traditional roles as fathers, husbands and brothers. They are now unable to fulfill or carry out their "defined and entitled" roles as main providers and decision-makers.

When asked what they are currently doing in response to this loss of traditional roles, some men stated that they had adopted coping mechanisms by participating in income-generating activities. Suleiman, a tailor in the Ifo camp, noted: "I may make 100 shillings for the entire day by doing some sewing. This amount of money makes a huge difference in supplementing the meager aid basket we get." Although little income was generated from such entrepreneurial activities, some of the refugee men said the work

---

*The Dadaab camps are located in the northeastern province of Kenya, close to the Somali border. They have been home to Somali refugees since 1991.

brings with it a kind of dignity, and provides them with a meaningful role within their families. By such contributions they measure their roles as men, fathers, and husbands.

Other men had joined voluntary camp associations – such as Water and Sanitation, the Community Health Group, and Conflict Resolution and Education – encouraged by the relief organizations to promote community self-management among refugees. These men indicated the importance of such a space in helping them cope with the disempowerment caused by a prolonged period in the camps:

> Participating in these community associations has given us some sort of personhood. We can have a say in these community consultations, meetings, and strategizings aimed at promoting community self-management. It has given us a space where we can interact with other male or female refugees, share ideas and exchange information, and work together for the betterment of our exiled community in these camps.

However, the male refugees involved in these programs were critical about the "current push" for community self-management by relief organizations, particularly when accompanied by numerous budget cuts in services for refugees. "What is to manage when there are no funds for these programs?" asked one man. "Relief organizations see us as partners when their financial pots are empty and [they] want us to play active roles in certain programs without any financial support." As well, male refugees with skills and education were more likely to be involved with such camp management activities than those with lesser qualifications. Male refugees who were neither involved in income-generating activities nor participants in camp associates stated, for example, that

> As long as we are *Qaxooti** in these camps, we cannot earn an income, feed our families, make choices or plans for our life. We are no longer the masters of our lives and plans. Someone else has control over our lives – when to collect the food basket, the water and basic medicine.

One of the refugee men interviewed was Hassan, who was 48 years old but appeared older, apparently due to the hardships of exile. In prewar Somalia, he was a primary teacher in the Somali capital of Mogadishu. He had been living in the camp known as Ifo for almost ten years with his wife and four children. In describing the experience, he said:

> We are no longer persons anymore in the eyes of the humanitarian organizations. No-one asks us, nor is interested, about our story – what we have done in our lives back home, what skills and potential we have. Here, we are simply treated as hungry bodies which need to be fed. . . . We are seen as numbers of beans and blankets.

---

*The term "Qaxooti" – pronounced "Kahooti" – is a Somali word referring to a refugee. The men despised this term, considering it demeaning and implying a destitute, helpless, and forsaken status. They felt the new identity reduced them from a full being to a number, through the issuing of ration cards and block and section designations designed to facilitate the distribution of relief "hand-outs."

Another refugee, Hussein, living in Hagadhere camp, summed up the feeling of depersonalization and the impossibility of being recognized as someone who was once self-reliant and an active member of society. "It is terrible, because you are not seen as a productive person who is capable of doing anything valuable for himself or for his family." When asked how they deal with the depersonalization imposed by the aid agencies, the men said they can do nothing. "Even if we try to resist it, we still depend on the 'hand-outs' which these organizations provide."

What disturbed these male refugees most was the equating of refugeehood with being lazy, a non-person, and dependent. Relief agencies depicted refugees as inactive, dependent victims to justify their non-participatory, top-down form of humanitarian operation and secure funds for its continuance.

Despite the hardships of refugee life, and the challenges of everyday survival in the camps, these male refugees indicated they were proud of themselves as Somali men who had fled the civil war and avoided taking part in the clan warfare ravaging their homelands. Ibrahim, who was in his 50s and part of the Hagadhere camp management, stated:

> The existence and presence of male refugees in these camps in fact says a lot about our [men's] decisions not to participate in the clan violence. I refused to kill, loot and maim any human beings. I fled from the chaos and simply did not want to be associated with the misdeeds of my clan, its militias and warlords.

This quote casts doubt on the stereotypical image of men in war zones, particularly those portrayed in the media. Somali men and boys who were armed to the teeth with various military weaponry regularly appeared on international television. But there are many men like these, who refused to participate in killings and looting. Should this decision not be recognized and rewarded by relief organizations? Should they not be used as peacemakers in their community?

Another important subject is the link between these male refugees' confidence and self-image – or lack of the same – and sexual violence against women in the camps. The Dadaab refugee camps are considered to be among the worst on the African continent. Among other things, they are not secure, in part because of their proximity to the Somali border and resulting proneness to gun-running. This affects both the refugee population and the relief organizations' operations. A particular issue is the rape of women and young girls, especially when they go out to collect firewood for cooking, and during the night in their tents. Most of these women and children fled the lawlessness and violence in Somalia, but now find themselves confronted with violence in their supposed "refuge." The men were asked about their views on this specific form of violence toward women and girls. Farah, a former civil servant, stated:

> Every time I hear that a woman or a young girl is raped, my heart aches. We menfolk get nervous and feel uncomfortable hearing about such incidents. We become the prime suspects as "the rapists." It is very common to blame all men when rape occurs in the camp. I am not denying that women and girls are raped here, but there are a few sick men who do such despicable things to their womenfolk. It is much easier and

safer to blame the poor refugee men than the male local inhabitants who rape our women and girls.

Farah and his fellow male refugees stated that when such incidents occurred, their image and reputation were tarnished. When asked why they do not go out and collect firewood themselves, to save their women and girls from potential rape, some stated that they preferred not to interfere with women's work, while others suggested it was not appropriate – "manly" – for a male to collect firewood for his family. While female refugees adjusted to changes in gender roles and responsibilities, many men clearly still adhered to their strictly defined place in Somali society, even while in exile. Others acknowledged they had a role to play in averting the possibility that women and girls could be raped while carrying out these tasks. However, Ahmed noted his own experience when he went on one occasion to collect firewood:

> I was beaten very badly by armed men. They told me that if I ever come back, they will not spare me next time. So it is obvious to me that these men deliberately want to sexually violate our women and girls. The men are the local men (ethnic-Somali Kenyans), armed, who have freedom of movement and are familiar with the locale. The rapists are these men and not the male refugees.

It is hard to tell who the real culprits are here. What is known is that women and girls are raped by men in and near these camps. But there is no evidence that most or all refugee men are rapists, and it is important to avoid sweeping generalizations, as these men themselves caution.

Some of the male refugees in these camps have been supportive of their families and their "temporary" community. They have been the peacemakers, and have offered guidance; they are the elders, supporters of women and children, decision-makers. Sheikh Ali, a well-respected man in his refugee community, was active in conflict resolution and played a pivotal role in maintaining peace among members of diverse clans. He provided guidance and advice to all who came to him. In one incident, a market of the Hagadhere camp was burned down. This led to tension between various clans, as one clan member was assumed to be the arsonist. Sheikh Ali and other elders and religious figures carried out *Maslaxa* meetings to avert bloodshed.* The outcome was successful; the destroyed market was rebuilt, and life went on.

To depict refugee men as inactive, dependent, and non-supportive of their families thus ignores their capabilities and their importance to the well-being of the Dadaab refugee community as a whole.

Maslaxa (pronounced Maslaha) is a traditional form of conflict resolution often performed by male community leaders.

UNITED KINGDOM

Pakistanis in Britain

Ali Nobil Ahmad*

One of the potential pitfalls inherent in any project about Third World men lies in the danger of reifying the boundaries of their existence by isolating their experiences from those against whom they are frequently defined as "different" – white people, women, Westerners, and the middle classes. With this in mind, the question of how Southern men relate to alterity (otherness) is analyzed here, within the specific context of urban, middle-class migration from Pakistan to Britain in the 1950s and early 1960s. It is based on material from an oral history project built around the life stories of five Pakistani students and professionals who arrived in the UK already, in a sense, Europeanized. The interviews were conducted with a number of individuals I know personally: my father, Nobil Ahmad; three of his close friends (Nasir Ahmed, Amanullah Khan, and Ajmal Malik); and his uncle, Merghoob. The smallness of the sample was deliberate: what follows is less a conventional sociology than a micro-study or series of portraits exploring individual motivation and experience.

Back in 1999, the first time I interviewed my father, I asked him about his earliest memories relating to the idea of Englishness. He replied without hesitation:

> I think one of the odd things about the idea of Englishness – not Englishness but being slightly different, was that where I was living in an inner city area [in Lahore] – I remember, I was the only one who used to go to school in shorts instead of a *shalwar kurta*, being made fun of by the people who were living there. And having a solar hat – you know these thick hats English people used to wear in films in summer, in safaris. . . . I used to have one of those.

Englishness, it seems, was by no means distant or alien to my father as a young boy in Lahore. Indeed it appears, here, internal to the subject; embodied in his social skin, his clothes and hat, which personify the Anglo-Indian colonial sensibility fostered by the British policy of co-opting rural and aristocratic elites. Colonial civil servants and low-level administrators such as my grandfather, who often spoke limited English themselves, sent their sons to English-language boarding schools where nineteenth-century English discourses of class and masculinity predominated.

The resulting generation of doctors, dentists, engineers, and lawyers, to which my subjects belong, was in a sense already Anglicized. A steady trickle of them began to arrive in British universities from the mid-nineteenth century, following the inauguration of Western education in India with Lord Macaulay's 1835 Minute, to study Law,

---

*Special to this volume. This article draws upon material gathered in an MA thesis completed at UCL History department in 2001, supervised by Catherine Hall.

Medicine, Engineering, and to take Civil Service exams. By the 1930s, Indians were the largest group of overseas students in England. Some settled in Britain to work after completing their studies. Others, most famously Gandhi, Muhammad Ali Jinnah, and Jawaharlal Nehru, returned home.

Standard explanations of why Pakistanis left for Britain during this period frequently take the "traditional" Asian family household or income-pooling unit as the driving force of migration and unit of analysis. Yet for Indian and Pakistani migrants of the type studied here, Asian social structures did not exist in any pure sense. The imposition of British culture and values meant that colonialism penetrated the very inner dynamics of Indian society, and was lived out at the level of the family. This fact had profound implications for gendered constructions of subjectivity: men were increasingly assimilated into an Anglicized bureaucracy. Women, in contrast, found themselves confined to domesticity as bearers of indigenous "tradition," beyond the reach of Western "modernity." My father's mother "didn't speak any English at all." Nor, indeed, did Aman's or any of the others'.

Though Anglophilia was generally male, it was not uncommon amongst the lower-middle classes. Nasir, whose father was an Urdu and Pharsee teacher, was born, like Aman, in a small town called Jhung near Rawalpindi, "where buffaloes roamed around freely." His family lived in a *kacha* house, not brick-built but made of mud. His father was a religious man, suspicious of British culture, who would not let his children have breakfast until they had read a few pages of the Koran. Nonetheless, Nasir says,

> I knew quite a lot about England and about London, actually. I even knew all the streets, most big streets like Piccadilly, long before I decided to come over – from the British library and books. Even before I came, I was watching the films in Lahore. There were three or four cinemas which showed non-stop American and British pictures.

Where did Nasir's interest in England come from? "I don't know. I suppose I generally wanted to see places and travel and things like that." His thirst for knowledge about England was such that he appears to have felt very little sense of cultural displacement either in London or in Edinburgh, where he sat his dentistry exams:

> Even before I came I was quite familiar with the British character and I quite liked the way of life and the British culture. I didn't feel a complete stranger when I came over. . . . I know Scotland's not my country, but I felt quite at home in every situation – at work, with friends.

Most of my subjects, on the whole, deny being "overwhelmed" or "excited" upon arrival. They had already lived through the upheaval of a partition that created 12 million refugees. Coming to England paled by comparison with that experience. They tended not to privilege it as the central moment in their lives, which were characterized by constant movement before and after migration.

Nor did they experience great difficulty adjusting to being in a "different" culture. Aman "didn't drink in those days," but began after joining doctors in Derby with a glass of wine late one evening in 1954. Nasir was similarly comfortable adapting to British pub culture. He began "gradually" in Scotland, "particularly during the New Year and Christmas period." Nasir and Aman's experiences, in this respect, deviate considerably from the clichéd picture, painted in sociological accounts, of rural Pakistani labor migrants driven solely by the will to accumulate capital and return "home," preserving their culture by "erecting social boundaries" that "effectively insulate certain areas of their life and protect them from modification" in the meantime.*

And yet, their testimony gives clues as to how these men experienced cultural newness in the metropolis – as exposure not to something so monolithic as "English culture," but rather to a certain *kind* of popular, domestic Englishness, different from the upper-class English culture that had attracted them on the periphery. Nasir says:

> I think while I was in Edinburgh in the hospital I used to listen to the radio there – I used to listen to BBC Radio Three, and they used to play classical music, and I used to quite enjoy that. And then the Beatles came on the scene and I just couldn't understand what all the fuss was about! Girls screaming and all – it wouldn't have been bad if their music was good, but as far I was concerned it was totally rubbish.

The interest in classical music which Nasir developed in Pakistan thus underwent a kind of subtle reconfiguration through contact with the mundane realities of lived experience in Britain. He soon learned that the exported Englishness he was accustomed to in the colonies was by no means reducible to English culture in England.

Of all the men I interviewed, only Ajmal admits to experiencing a real sense of dis-placement, following his arrival in England in 1953 on a cricket scholarship. His life as a professional cricketer in Staffordshire began in difficult circumstances. He spoke English, but "not so well." Life in England "was totally different," with "different values" which took "a long time" to adjust to:

> ... There was some general election when I came, and my landlady, her husband and their daughter, they each voted – but they voted differently, for three different people. And I thought, how could that be possible? I thought the man of the house was the master of the house, and what he says goes! . . . Over here people had their own freedom . . . total independence. They could do what they felt they wanted to do and not rely on parents so much.

The profoundly different gender relations in Britain were experienced as strange, and took some getting used to. The others, too, found gender and sexual relations "slightly different" and more "liberal," even "strange," but none so much as Ajmal, whose early years were characterized by the kind of "homesickness" that so often features in discussions of migration.

Yet Ajmal rapidly relinquished the "orthodox Muslim" lifestyle he was accustomed to: "I had forgotten everything. Life in Staffordshire was a very different way of

---

*Patricia Jeffery, *Migrants and Refugees: Muslim and Christian Families in Bristol* (Cambridge: Cambridge University Press, 1976), p. 82.

living – and when there were so many attractions – [laughs] you know how it is: being a cricketer, my options were more than some . . ." He is alluding to opportunities for relationships with English women, a theme that was often emphasized by the interview subjects. "The freedom to pick and choose," Ajmal remembers, meant "some of them were having the time of their lives." They had, after all, arrived at the height of the so-called sexual liberation that characterized the 1960s; it is hardly surprising that some Pakistanis enthusiastically embraced the new "freedoms" that life in the West offered. "Coming from a very closed society where you have no contact with the other sex – here it was total freedom," Ajmal recalled. "Go where you like, *do* whatever you like – that was quite an eye-opener. So I signed on the dotted line."

Having ignored his father's wishes and gone to London, Ajmal continued to take what he called the "selfish view." "I didn't write so much as he did. He used to write every second day, telling me off and saying what an ungrateful son I had been." Often invoked as the principal embodiment of the migrant's unbreakable link to the "homeland," the family connection that supposedly spans continents is, upon closer examination, far from the unchanging umbilical cord it is often depicted as. Aman, for example, didn't return to Pakistan until 1986, after 25 years in England. He had continually ignored the pleas of his family to visit. Upon finally arriving, he was scolded by his brothers and sisters, who demanded to know why he hadn't come earlier. He was greeted with the news that his mother, who had died while he had been away, was heartbroken that her son "went away and never came back." "England," she apparently had decided, "is a bad place." Ajmal, too, returned soon after his mother died to the news that she had been "very upset. She remained upset. That's one thing I'll never forget or forgive myself for. She said, 'I let him go. He hasn't returned. And now I've forgotten his face.' "

Some of my subjects had British teachers in the English medium colleges and universities they attended in Pakistan. But overall, the British "were very aloof," in Aman's words. Because of this social buffer, it was in Britain that middle-class Pakistanis often first experienced whiteness at an interpersonal level. My father described an early encounter with a white woman who ran the hostel he stayed at in Edinburgh:

> I said, "Hello. I'm Nobil Ahmad. I'm coming to stay." She said she didn't know anything about it, but that "It doesn't matter . . . In this house, we don't mind if you're colored." I didn't know what she was talking about. I'd never heard the word ["colored"] before.

The white gaze asserts itself here as an imposing homogenizer of non-whiteness. Asked how he saw himself before he came to learn he was "colored," my father replied: "I just saw myself as very socially acceptable and coming from a very good family – a well-off family able to send kids to England." This class-based self-image was soon displaced by that of race, as he entered a white society that ascribed racialized meanings of Otherness. The Other, unsurprisingly, often remembers vividly key moments in this process.

But moments such as these do *not* constitute the totality of my subjects' experiences. They were able to advance considerably in a racist English society, and to some extent benefited from systems of social domination that excluded working-class whites.

My father was able to secure a job in a practice where eight or nine white nurses worked under him. He and two other Australian dentists sat separately from them at lunch, in an important display of hierarchy.

More generally, the presence of working-class white women in the narratives, as acquaintances and friends as well as romantic and sexual partners, is striking. Nasir met his wife, Rosemary, in 1966 at the dental practice in Brixton where she was working as a nurse. Aman, too, casually mentioned that "socially, you took the nurses out – to a restaurant or cinema or something." Asked if "difference" ever got in the way of such relationships, he exclaimed: "No!" Nurses were more interested in the fact that men like himself were "handsome young doctors." "Hospitals," he joked, "were like harems for doctors in those days."

The increasing prominence of white women in some of these narratives is accompanied by a growing sense of estrangement from Asian femininity. Perhaps the most profound expression of this is the strain on the intimate relationships these men had, above all on the maternal bond. Their mothers, more than anyone else, interpreted the presence of white women in their sons' lives as disastrous and to be avoided at all costs. Ajmal's mother was "upset . . . when she came to know I'd married an English woman. . . . She said, 'Oh, he's become a Christian, what's the point in talking about him?'" The white woman appears here as alluring, almost predatory.

A few of my subjects sought to resist this gradual process of "whitening." Merghoob's marriage to a Pakistani woman, soon after his father died, was arranged by his family as part of a conscious effort to maintain his distance from white women. ("They were afraid probably that I'll get married to an English girl.") Merghoob admits he "had quite a few girlfriends," but claims he "never got serious with them." He "preferred Pakistani girls to get married and settle down." He describes growing repulsed by white women after initially being attracted to their "difference": "Their habits and that sort of thing didn't exactly fit into my feelings – like their wives mixing up with other friends and sort of things – it felt very odd. . . . I thought they were substandard, these people."

On the surface, these comments are about culture. But they are also about how whiteness is racialized in the Pakistani imagination. Just as Pakistanis and other immigrant groups are stereotyped and labeled in the white mind, whites are represented and imagined by Pakistanis through cultural practices perceived as different, sometimes inferior. And just as the white imagination fixes Pakistani-ness within a discourse of *purdah* – arranged marriages and rigid codes of socio-sexual behavior – Pakistani tropes of whiteness focus on the organization of the family, sexual conduct, and woman as the bearer and embodiment of group identity.

Some men, then, consciously placed distance between themselves and whiteness in a bid to resist assimilation into a "different" culture, reified and fixed to white femininity. Others embraced it unquestioningly, arguably at the cost of their relationships with their families and, in particular, with Asian women.

Whatever their relationship with alterity, though, it is clear that each man, in different ways, "signed on the dotted line" (to use Ajmal's words). Migration and its aftermath set in motion processes which irreversibly changed them. Sometimes these choices were conscious; often they were not. The cultural syncretism which made "here" become "home," experienced through encounters with English culture and whiteness, was "a gradual process, rather than a sudden break," Nasir points out. An example is his own growing affection for the Beatles' music. Only a few years earlier, it had sounded like "rubbish." But "I became quite fond of the Beatles with their later albums. I think with *Abbey Road* – when that came out, I thought it was quite good."

INDIA/UNITED KINGDOM

Being 49 at Russell Square

Shyamal Bagchee*

i have been here before
sometimes alone
or my wife with me
or we with our children;
but never before at age forty-nine
this unremarkable cuspy year
and all by myself
the place hasn't changed much
a scattering of oversized pigeons
abundant roses, degenerate
on straggly bushes
unkempt overall like my thoughts
this june mid-morning

time on my hand i wonder
what could this place mean
to a teenager growing up in new delhi –
plenty, when recalled by his
father on winter evenings
the family gathered in the warm kitchen
closeness spurring vulnerable memories:

at forty-nine he went to distant london
to round out an education
stubbornly acquired in orphaned youth
and with dry sandwich in hand

_____

*Special to this volume.

he sat often on a bench like this one
among the many roses
missing wife, two sons
a daughter barely five
– no telephone in his
shared mezzanine flat
nor among the modest furnishings
of his faraway home,
cut off
seeking hard to fare well
in his self-made career
(i call alberta twice a day
and they even faxed me once
in these four days of absence)

brushing ghee on hot chapattis
low voiced but trying to sound
casual, even self-mocking,
speaking of unspeakable loneliness
of a middle-aged man taken from
his home
(and i too was lonely then
scared of growing up relentlessly
with no one to check things out)

and as children play around me
today in russell square
my daughter's bright face
ringed by curls, my son's eyes
deep and tentative
come back to me
terribly clear, terribly dear
and i think i know
what children mean, and father too

the place hasn't changed much
or so i imagine,
that it had been the same place
some thirty-five years back

i fly back in two days;
three years ago
on the bank of the yamuna
i cremated my father,
who once sat in this park

AUSTRALIA

Masculine Migrations

Bob Pease*

This essay discusses the early stages of an Australian Research Council-funded research project on Migrant Masculinities. The project involves a comparative inquiry into the subjectivities of men who have migrated to Australia from four culturally diverse regions of the world: Southern and East Africa, the Middle East, Southern Asia, and Latin America. The focus is on the voices of 22 of the men drawn from 12 countries in these regions. All of the men interviewed were over 18 years at the time of their migration; they had resided in Australia for at least three years and no longer than ten years at the time of the interviews.

The research on structurally marginalized and subordinated men explores the contribution such men can make in changing dominant masculinities. My argument is that a critical analysis of masculinities in Australia must begin by analyzing the ways in which marginalized and subordinated masculinities are changing. Immigrant men are in contradictory positions in relation to dominance and subordination. By taking the standpoints of structurally marginalized groups of men as points of departure, the research removes hegemonic masculinity from the center of the analysis. By doing so, it not only contributes to the reorientation of masculinity studies but to the rethinking of the concept of masculinity itself.

Furthermore, a number of feminists have argued that some forms of feminism have paid insufficient attention to racial and ethnic differences within genders.[†] Given that research evidence demonstrates that migration influences the relations between men and women,[‡] a critical examination of immigrant men's masculinities contributes to knowledge about gender-based inequalities in immigrant communities in Australia.

Many writers argue that migration provides women *and* men with the opportunity to transcend traditional sex roles. Boyle and Hiffance, for example, argue that it can "act as an escape route from oppressive patriarchal societies."[⁵] Willis and Yeoh emphasize

---

*Special to this volume.

[†]See, for example, Floya Anthias and Nira Yuval-Davis, eds., *Racialized Boundaries: Race, Nation, Color and Class and the Anti-Racist Struggle* (London: Routledge, 1992); Paul Boyle and Keith Hiffance, eds., *Migration and Gender in the Developed World* (London: Routledge, 1999); and Harriet Bradley, *Fractured Identities: Changing Patterns of Inequality* (Cambridge: Polity Press, 1996).

[‡]Hammed Shahidian, "Gender and Sexuality among Immigrant Iranians in Canada," *Sexualities*, 2 (1999), pp. 189–222.

[⁵]Boyle and Hiffance, eds., *Migration and Gender*, p. 9.

how "a new location provides a space in which gender relations can be renegotiated."*
In this view, domestic patriarchy is reliant upon support from its environment. Is
patriarchal authority eroded by migration? Or is the "patriarchal bargain" simply
renegotiated?

It is important to avoid the stereotyping of non-Western men as patriarchal and
backward in gender terms, in contrast to more egalitarian white men. I do not assume
that immigrant men are "stuck in sexist traditional male roles while white educated
middle-class men are forging a more egalitarian role."† Rather, I want to understand
how gendered power operates in different immigrant communities. I look in particular
at four main themes: the importance of the provider role; the division of domestic
labor; the impact of migration on men's status and authority in the home; and consi-
derations about whether men's gender roles have changed as a result of migration.

The importance of the provider role

Masculinity has been associated with the provider role in all of the countries in these
world regions. The issue of being sole provider was thus central to all of these men.
Being a man was based on providing for a family and being a "family man," as the
following comments illustrate:

Men from Southern and East Africa

"To be a man is to be someone who works hard to earn a living."

"Being a man is being a provider. That's one of the most basic and significant roles
of the man. It is to be head of the family, even in the absence of the family, you have
to have shown the ability to be able to provide, not only for yourself, but also for your
siblings and your brothers and your sisters."

"Where I come from, to be a man is to be able to support your family."

"The role of men in society is to provide for their families."

Men from the Middle East

"The feeling of myself as a man will be improved if my wages improved . . . I am a man
and I am responsible."

"The man has got the responsibility to support the woman and the family."

---

*Katie Willis and Brenda Yeoh, eds., Gender and Migration (Cheltingham: Edward Elgar,
2000), p. xv.
†Pierrette Hondagneu-Sotelo and Michael Messner, "Gender Displays and Men's Power:
The 'New Man' and the Mexican Immigrant Man," in Harry Brod and Michael Kaufman,
eds., Theorizing Masculinities (Thousand Oaks, CA: Sage, 1994), p. 200.

Men from Southern Asia

"A man in Vietnamese society is like a foreign minister. The man usually works outside the family. . . . The woman in the family is like an interior minister."

"I think that the man goes out working, to bring home the bacon like they say and the woman does the home work."

"Traditionally, the man will have to go out, find a job, bring home the food and the women will stay home and do the housewife thing . . . Those are the main objectives of Vietnamese society."

"The main thing is to be a provider, to be the one who looks after the family."

Men from Latin America

"I always wanted to be the man who. . . supported a family."

"We're talking about South America. You have to be married and have kids and work and maintain the family and your wife has to be at home."

"Work is the fundamental basis . . . for any man."

Division of domestic labor

The flip side of the dominance of paid work in men's lives is the expectation that men will be the head of the household and women will do all the domestic work. The men's focus on work was thus contrasted by their sense that men from their culture did not help out with the raising of children or the care of the household.

Men from Southern and East Africa

"A perfect partner is someone who . . . is willing to make it possible for me to be head of the family. As I always say, you can't have two lions in the same den. It doesn't work. I mean you come home from work, where somebody is your boss, so you get harassed the whole day. You don't want to come home where there is another boss to boss you around the whole day. I mean, you will never win."

"I think that the woman should be the custodian of the home. I mean, they should be able to manage the home to the best of their ability, to make sure the life of others is actually quite easier."

"The girls spend their time in the kitchen, because they get their story from the mother's side."

"[The role of the female] was cooking, fetching firewood, looking after the babies."

"There was no time women should be equal. . . . The man is the head of the house. . . . That's very un-Kenyan . . . I don't really think men should stay home and look after the baby."

"The man is the head of the house. . . . There are things that the men are entitled to say and do; African women . . . respect that. When you come to this country, I think you find it doesn't [work]."

"A man should be able to be head of the house. It's like a country. You have to have a leader. You can't just have everybody standing there and saying what they have to say."

"Men are the head of the families . . . Whereas women's . . . main job is to look after the family, the children, the house and do house duties. In our culture, if you're a married man, you will never cook really. Cooking is a woman's job. Cleaning is a woman's job."

Men from the Middle East

"I think that the responsibility in the house is the father, is the man . . . Man is the roof of the house."

"The roles are very different between the man and the woman in my culture."

"If you ask all those women . . . She says I like it. I stay home. I look after my husband. I look after my kids."

"Man is measured by his ability to perform some tasks, and also these tasks are those that a woman cannot do . . . A woman will never be a man and a man cannot be a woman. Man is man and woman is woman."

"We are leaving woman to do according to her nature and the best of her ability. She has housework and looking after the children."

Men from Latin America

"The woman is the owner of the kids and the men just make kids."

"If you are . . . growing up as a boy, they don't let you into the kitchen. The idea is that the women should work at home and the men outside the house."

The impact of migration on men's status and authority

The process of migrating to Australia upsets this division of labor in some ways. Men's authority is undermined because of a change in their public status, with men being forced to take employment well below their qualifications. At the same time, though, this reinforces the importance of employment in their sense of self, as the following comments illustrate:

Men from Southern and East Africa

"I prefer to be in Kenya. That's for sure. . . . There are many things that I can do back at home that I can't do here. There's respect back at home . . . There's that respect in society because you know your place within the society."

[On going back to Kenya] "It's coming from a place where you don't have authority to a place where you have absolute authority. It takes time to get used to it [in Australia] . . . I completely lost the authority in my home. . . . I think you're best to live in Kenya. . . . I was highly respected where I come from . . . and to drop from there to where I was [as an immigrant], was a very big shock."

"Back in Kenya, I get more respected, treated like [the] head of the home."

Men from the Middle East

"In Iraq I was working, but here I could not find work. This means that there is no recognition even of my humanity . . . Those who do not work are like dead people."

Men from Southern Asia

"It was quite hard for me . . . as a male and as a Vietnamese doctor. I feel shame because I've been on unemployment benefits for a long time."

"It's hard for them [Vietnamese men who live in Australia]. They have to be head of the family, and now they have to cook. They have to feed the children."

Men from Latin America

"I had my own chauffeur in Mexico. I had power . . . coming to Australia I was known by no one."

"So overnight from gallivanting around Havana, I had to be stuck in my house 24 hours a day, mowing the lawn, and cleaning the dishes and cooking . . . I had to change my whole background, my whole identity."

"It would be better to be a man in Bolivia . . . There's a saying in Bolivia: that it's better to be the head of a mouse than the tail of a lion. In Bolivia, at least, I would be the head of a mouse. Here, I am pretty close to being the tail of a lion."

Changing Gender Roles?

The discussion about what was involved in being a man often reflected the sense of an unchanging masculine identity. Many of the core elements that the men based their masculinity upon were felt to be identical both "here" and "there." That is, most of the men said very little had changed in their own sense of masculinity and manliness as a result of migration – even when some of their practices had changed. This did not mean that there weren't changes involved in migration, but that these were managed and dealt with from an already strongly developed sense of what it means to be a man. And this sense was often founded on an essentialized vision of manhood, as the following comments attest:

Men from Southern and East Africa

"I think that there are certain gender universal issues that still exist between African and Australian men, if you like . . . things like being the head of a family and being a father . . . There are certain things that are universal for all men."

"The roles of men and women [in Africa and Australia] are similar in a way, really . . . The roles are the same but are performed differently."

Men from the Middle East

"Masculinity is masculinity anywhere you go. The meaning of masculinity is with me. It didn't change . . . A man is a man and a woman is a woman."

"Actually a man is a man wherever he goes, whether in Australia, in Iraq, in London, anywhere. I prefer to be a man anywhere I go."

"The man everywhere is a man. In every country it's the same. . . . You experience some difficulty in terms of language and education, but it does not affect yourself as a man."

"I adhere to my concept of masculinity. I leave Australians to do what they want to do. If they want to leave their women just to go, freedom without limits, they're free [to do so]. . . . If man becomes a woman and woman becomes a man, we are against our nature, and we will be punished by the nature too."

Men from Latin America

"Ahhh, it's the same. I listen to a lot of talk-back radio, and there's a lot of macho people. . . . Men hate women and women hate men. . . . They are men everywhere, here, there, on the moon. . . . You're a man no matter where you are."

Concluding comments

We can see from these responses that some experiences of manhood and masculinity transcend cultures, although they may be experienced by the men as culture-bound. Manhood is measured by the ability to provide for families, and men feel they are entitled to respect and service from their female partners.

When they migrate, they experience a threat to their ability to maintain the provider role, and their authority in the family is challenged. The men experience marginalization in this culture, and they have to contend with an increase in women's status. At the same time, they endeavor to hang on to their traditional conceptions of masculinity and manhood in the face of these new challenges.

While one of the aims of this research is to chart the ways in which immigrant men are changing, it would appear on the surface that there is a strong sense of continuity in these men's sense of masculinity as they settle in Australia. However, while many of the men expressed the view that little had changed in their experience of masculinity, it is also clear that they have had to adapt in practice to the changing roles of women and a decline in their status as men. Although the men interviewed are endeavoring to hold on to an essentialized view of their masculinity, it is apparent that this strategy is becoming increasingly difficult to maintain in the face of the challenges to their manhood that they encounter.

The research so far confirms that race relations and culture play an important part in how masculinity is constructed and expressed. We need to understand that the influences on masculinity are broad, and constituted by macro-factors such as class, race, culture and social hierarchy. We can make sense of what these changes mean for men through researching their life histories in the context of the global forces that shape their lives.

ISRAEL

The Palestinian Israeli

Magid Shihade*

I grew up in Kafr-Yassif in northwestern Galilee among a Palestinian community that remained in Palestine after the 1948 war and the creation of the state of Israel. Palestinians had to become Israeli citizens if they wished to remain in their homeland. Having nowhere to go, they became Israeli citizens in a state that was built on the ruins of their country and their people.

My family was relatively poor. Not having access to education, the only thing they could do was to offer their labor, and so they worked mainly in farming and as hired labor on Israeli farms. I was one of twelve children; six boys and six girls. My family was also socially conservative, and my father did not allow either his boy or girl children to date. Father was tough on all of us as far as school performance went. His view was that if we did not get good grades, we had to get out of school and work on the farm to help the family out. The threat of taking me out of school if I did not get excellent grades in all subjects was my major motivation for performing well.

I was educated within the Israeli Zionist educational system. We were taught many positive things about the state of Israel and about Zionism, such as that Israel was created by the will of God and the Jewish people, and that Israel is a democratic country that allows people to live in peace, happiness and prosperity. I learned later that the reality was very different from what we had learned in school.

My parents always warned us about getting involved in politics. They said that our family had been very involved politically, and had got nothing but troubles and disappointment. I remember the days when father and uncles, like so many Palestinian citizens in Israel, were involved with the Israeli Communist Party – the only party at the time that allowed Arab membership – and hearing about my father or an uncle being detained, placed under house arrest, deported to other cities, or forbidden to move out of the village without the local military governor's permission. These reprisals were part of the price they paid for opposing Israeli policies. So this is something I was not encouraged to explore for myself.

My friends in high school also generally avoided politics. We were young, and wanted to enjoy our youth, if that was possible. We didn't think much about political issues unless there was a big event that forced itself on us. Thus, in 1982, while we were in high school, we heard about the Israeli invasion of Lebanon to bring "peace for Galilee" and to destroy the PLO hold on Lebanon. We also heard about the massacres of Palestinians that occurred in Lebanon, about the killings in Sabra and Shatila camps. The images on TV were gruesome. Students and some teachers in my high school

---

*Special to this volume.

decided to demonstrate against the killing and massacring of Palestinians in Lebanon. Despite my parents' warnings, I went along to the demonstration. I didn't understand why the Israeli security forces massed all around us were trying to intimidate us from marching on the streets of the village. They were also arresting some people. Why would they do that? Was it so wrong to protest against the massacres of Palestinians in Lebanon that the Israelis said they had nothing to do with (it was supposedly only the work of some fanatic Lebanese Phalangists)? These were questions that came to my 16-year-old mind.

One evening, when I was in eleventh grade, another incident sparked some political afterthoughts. I was walking around the streets of my hometown when my friends passed by me unexpectedly, driving in a nice car. They asked me if I'd like to go with them to the city for a drink. I agreed to join them, even though I was afraid my father might find out that I was doing something that he did not approve of. After a couple of hours of hanging out in the city, we drove back late at night to Kafr-Yassif. We were listening to Arabic music, driving relatively slowly on the winding highway. Suddenly, an Israeli border security jeep turned on its siren and followed us. We didn't know why. When we stopped, the soldiers came up to us and asked for our identity cards. When they found out that I didn't have my identity card with me, they started pulling me toward the jeep to arrest me. To be honest, though I was very angry, I was more afraid of my father than the soldiers. Three Israeli soldiers, all tall and muscular men, surrounded me. But I refused to go with them. I pulled myself out of their grip by pushing my leg against the jeep, and I insisted they release me. I told the soldiers that I would come within three days to the police station and show my ID, as the law stipulates. In the end, after much pushing and threatening motions with guns, the soldiers realized that I was not going to give in. Finally, they let me go. I was so relieved. Now my father did not have to know about this incident, and he also wouldn't know that I was off with friends having fun in the city.

Later, I talked about the episode with my friends, and we discussed why the Israeli border patrol had stopped us. We agreed it must have been the sound of Arabic music that had attracted their attention, and we didn't feel safe doing that again. We could survive without Arabic music in the car during our trips to and from the city. We started to see how the cultural oppression of Palestinian citizens in Israel is part and parcel of daily political oppression. Even Arabic music could be a threat to state security!

After completing high school and taking the matriculation exams, I applied to Hebrew University in Jerusalem to study law. A few weeks after graduation, with college about to open, none of my Palestinian Israeli classmates or myself had received a response. We decided to take a trip together to the university to make inquiries at the admission office. Our group consisted of three male and three female students. We each had a small bag with snacks and documents that we needed for the trip. On the way to Jerusalem, the bus stopped at the airport bus station. Three Israeli soldiers boarded the bus, female and male, and ordered me and my two Palestinian male classmates out. I was shocked. Why didn't they pick on the three female classmates? And how did they pick us out from the rest of the passengers? Was it our look, our clothes, our smell?

We got out of the bus, which left to pass through the airport. The three soldiers asked us all kind of questions: "Where are you from? Where are you going?" But they didn't ask our names. They told us to throw everything in our bags onto the floor. After some arguing and hesitation and threats from them, we complied. Then, without really searching them, the soldiers told us to pick up our belongings. They started making fun of us for applying to the university, joking about the fact that we wanted to study. It was a humiliating experience. The last time it had been Arabic music. What next?

These incidents were also lessons to me about how the violent masculinity embodied by the Israeli system of oppression is inflicted not just by males but also by females. As with the American soldiers, both male and female, who are today abusing Iraqis, such incidents are part of a system of masculinized aggression designed to humiliate, harass, persecute, and collectively punish Palestinians and Arabs more generally. It is also strange to see persecuted minorities in Israel, such as Moroccan and Ethiopian Jews, being employed as agents of violence against other minorities – as with the Latino, African, and Asian-American soldiers in the US army. Why would minorities assist in inflicting on other minority groups the kind of violence they themselves have suffered?

*   *   *

Later, after finding out that I had been turned down by Hebrew University, I decided to follow some of my Palestinian classmates abroad, to the University of Cologne in West Germany. I prepared everything to leave the country; three of my brothers accompanied me to the airport. There, at the entrance, I was searched by Israeli airport security, as were my brothers. When we entered the airport, there was yet another round of searches and interrogations. I was taken aside and searched "in detail." The Israelis searched both my belongings and my body. Then one of the security personnel, a woman, asked me to follow her. I said I needed to say goodbye to my brothers first. She said not to worry about it. I was individually escorted by Israeli security to the airplane.

When I arrived in Germany, I called my family to let them know that I had made it safely, and asked about my brothers. My mother told me that they were still at the airport! Later, I learned they were arrested there by Israeli security, because it was considered suspicious for them to have accompanied me!

I was eager finally to embark on my studies. I registered to study German first, in order to be able to study law later. During the first few weeks of the German class, when we were able to converse a bit, the teacher asked us the basic questions people ask when they first meet you: "What's your name? How old are you? Where are you from?" The last question was confusing. What should I say? Was I Israeli? Not really. Palestinian? Maybe. My classmates told me to be aware of a Jewish Israeli man who sat in every language class and did not talk, but simply listened carefully to what we said in the class and with whom we talked. So I felt trapped. I said to the teacher: I am from Israel. She asked me: Are you Jewish? No, I said. "Then you should say, 'I am a Palestinian from Israel.'" She did not know that in Israel, to utter the word 'Palestinian' was a risky business at that time. So, I simply replied, "Okay," without repeating what she had instructed me to say.

Despite my desire to study, my wallet was not responding well to my wishes. After I'd completed the German course in ten months and studied law for a year, I had no money left to support myself. I decided to return to Israel. But there, I felt trapped. I wanted to study, but in Israel I had no chance to go to university. So I thought of going to Bir Zeit University in the West Bank. But the first Intifada [Palestinian uprising] had just begun, and the university had been closed by the Israelis. I was advised not to wait around for the university to reopen, because the situation could continue for some time. In that sense, the Intifada was a curse. But it also marked a political reawakening for me, as for other Palestinian youth. I learned how the state's policies can crush one's hopes and aspirations, and how a system of oppression can control and dictate one's life. I saw in the Intifada how Israeli occupation, supported by American power, controls, humiliates, and crushes Palestinians just for wanting to live in freedom.

I decided to check on the option of studying in Egypt. After a few visits to the Egyptian embassy, I was told to forget it. One embassy worker told me they wouldn't give me a student visa because I had an Israeli passport. I said, "But I am Palestinian." I was told that the Egyptian government could not say they did not want Israeli Jews coming to Egypt, out of fear being branded racist. So they made it difficult for anyone with an Israeli passport to get a student visa. They were afraid of Israelis going as students but engaging in espionage. Why couldn't the Egyptians understand that they were harming someone like me, who had no bad feelings toward Egypt, and no intention of working for Israel? I learned that the Arab states repressed the Palestinians too, in certain ways.

Time was running out for me, with no school and no decent prospects in sight. Then, in 1990, the Gulf War began. I was among many Palestinian Israelis who cheered for Iraq whenever an Iraqi missile hit Israel. Why shouldn't I? This was a racist state, pushing me down. Israeli Zionists claim they came to Palestine to escape persecution and discrimination in Europe, yet they do the same thing to the Palestinians. They have just replaced old victims with new ones.

After the first Gulf War ended, I went back to Germany, hoping things would work out financially this time. They did: I managed to stay in school by doing illegal work. A few years later, personal and family circumstances led me to leave Germany for the USA. American students in Germany had told me that the people in the US were nice, not like the American government. They said my opposition to the US, and my suspicion of everything American, was based on personal feelings about what the US had been doing in the Middle East – supporting Israel and its brutal policies against the Palestinians and other Arabs. I wanted to be hopeful and open-minded, and in any case, I had little choice. In 1994, I landed in Pennsylvania.

Once there, I decided to look for a school to continue my studies. I learned that my German course credits could not be transferred to American universities, and I would have to start my schooling all over again. This I did. But it was another step back, another source of frustration. And it was boring for me to sit around with 18-year-old students, so I decided to keep busy by studying more subjects.

One of the first classes I took at the University of Pittsburgh was on Middle East politics. I learned that it was not just the US government that represents the situation in the Middle East inaccurately, but also professors at American universities. My reaction was to pursue Middle Eastern Studies. I completed a Master's degree in International Studies, and continued in an interdisciplinary Ph.D. program in Middle Eastern Studies at the University of Washington. Now I am writing my dissertation on the causes of violence between two Palestinian communities in Israel.

After over 10 years of living in the US, I saw and experienced myself the problems that many Palestinians and Arabs face in America. In certain circles, there is sympathy for the plight of Palestinians and (currently) Iraqis. Some segments of US society have a certain sympathy for Arab women. Yet the Arab man is never really welcome. Sometimes he is fetishized or desired, but as a body, not as a mind. As in Europe, the Arab man is the object of political, cultural, and social contempt – at work, at leisure, at school, and in media and popular representations.

This contempt arises from the racist stereotypes and propaganda that imbue all aspects of people's lives in the US, from media to politics and the education system. American movies and TV have always portrayed negative images of Palestinians, Arabs and Muslims in general, and Arab males in particular. Now, after September 11, many American television shows are increasingly geared toward issues of "security" and "terrorism." The Arab male is always represented in these shows as the target, the enemy, the suspect. He never fits in, never belongs. The Arab man is never "cool." He can legally become an American, but he never belongs politically or culturally.

I realized after living in the US for a little over a decade that the problems of choosing from available categories of self-definition are similar to those that I had always encountered in Israel. The identity categories I grappled with in Israel were: Israeli Arab, or Palestinian-from-Israel. Here they were: American Arab or Arab American. Are these categories necessarily in conflict? They bring so much contradiction with them. How can an Arab man identify with a system that oppresses him, discriminates against him, holds him in contempt, even kills him? How can one belong if one is despised, hated, and humiliated?

I have learned that education can mislead. My schooling in Israel taught me that that country is noble and egalitarian, and the US is a good friend of Israel because they share common values. What values? That both countries are melting pots of immigrants? The notion of the melting pot is problematic, because it implies a homogeneous culture that everyone should be absorbed into. This obscures the fact that the white man remains the dominant one – the definer of the imperialist structure. I would say, rather, that both Israel and the US are melting pots of genocides against the natives, and melting pots of lies. Both countries are also good example of how colonialism is complicated by race and by the co-opting of minorities, including females, who parti-cipate in the oppression of Arabs and in imperialism more generally. In Israel there was

Golda Meir and David Levi – a Moroccan Jew; and in the US, there is Condoleezza Rice and Alberto Gonzales.

I cannot belong in such a melting pot, even if I wanted to. The Palestinian poet from Galilee, Samih Al-Qassim, has a poem titled: "Persona non grata." An undesired person. For me, that is what the Palestinian or Arab male is, wherever he lives: undesired.

UNITED STATES

Brooklyn Panyard

Knolly Moses*

By subway it is an hour away from my Madison Avenue job, though in many ways it is much further removed. A nearby mosque blares the call of the muezzin at sundown. Crack sells briskly nearby, although Muslims once sent dealers scampering before television cameras from a local news program. One night, in front of several dozen witnesses, an unwilling victim blasted a mugger with a .357 magnum. Even the police stay in their cars in the Bedford-Stuyvesant section of Brooklyn where the Metro Steel Orchestra once rehearsed.

When I first arrived to learn to "play pan," most members of the steel band seemed bemused. In that milieu, a white collar is more disruptive than a ghetto blaster. To survive two sweltering summer months, I had to win hearts and minds. My determination to learn the instrument bred an unaccustomed humility: those who have mastered what was once a crude and folksy instrument from the ghettoes of Trinidad tend toward arrogance. Some saw my presence as an anthropological intrusion. I quickly restored the lilt to my accent, and began taking off my tie a block away. Sometimes, I would buy someone a Guinness Stout, the preferred drink in the panyard. But that soon became a costly concession. So I began to depend on my generally pleasant nature and skill at repartee to reconnect with some fellow West Indians.

I had emigrated from Trinidad, the home of the steel band, 18 years before. Somehow, college and graduate school, marriage, and a journalism career had all gotten in the way of the one thing that I had dreamed of doing since I was about four years old – playing an instrument made from a 55-gallon drum. Growing up when the steel band was a centerpiece for gangs, I was discouraged from associating with it. But many nights in my youth, steel-band music lulled me to sleep. Finally, recognizing my mortality in a sober moment, I decided I could put it off no longer.

I picked Metro because of its brilliant arranger, Clive Bradley. A lover of big-band music, Bradley gave to the terribly dissonant steel instruments some of their

---

*Special to this volume.

finest orchestration. He caresses a calypso melody with the warmth of a Caribbean sun. He structures a tune with such fluid logic that you almost guess his next note.

One night I came upon several members of Metro encircling someone who was playing. When I squeezed my way through the group, I found they were listening to a Bradley arrangement that was ten years old. Though it's not written down anywhere, like most steel-band music, this band member had retained all its beauty and complexity.

Among the mostly unemployed immigrants who are Metro's members, uncounted in this year's census, I found a treasure trove of human values. I discovered a camaraderie and community that was absent from the Madison Avenue jungle where I worked. Most of all, I uncovered parts of myself that assimilation had so rudely rejected.

One band member regularly brought his son to rehearsals, so that mine would have a playmate while I labored to distinguish a sharp from a flat note. An unspoken bond developed the day I took both boys to the Brooklyn Museum. Eventually, the band member began to teach my son to play the pans, as a way to get a permanent playpal for his son. And I noticed that I was the only person in the band he never begged from.

The dreadlocked leader of my section displayed Job-like patience with my inability to master the phrasing of the *soca* music that we rendered. Though often amused by the way I phrased questions, and the questions themselves, he became a teacher and a friend. He put me on an emotional high the night he handed me a Metro band shirt. Both underclass challenge and immigrant hope, it proudly proclaimed: "I was born a Desperado."

Vincent Yip Young, an experienced pianist, gave me his rubber-tipped sticks to coax mellow tones from the harshly percussive steel. Later, he loaned me one of his instruments, so I could practice at home. He was playing the pans again after a five-year lapse, because his doctor thought it would ease the stress that had nearly crippled him when he began a career as a recording executive. He confessed that playing the pans was the only activity that allowed him to relax.

One hot evening, a man who appeared homeless apart from our rehearsal building, and whose breath stank from inebriation, pulled me aside conspiratorially. He told me the band needed people like myself "to steer the fellas right." "They are some good boys," he said, "they just need a break." He seemed to have gone astray a very long time ago, but he was utterly respectful around me after that.

The talent in Metro is immeasurable. No one called Con Edison to turn on the lights. The burned-out building was made structurally safe without the help of an architect or engineer. The steel frames that house the pans were designed and built almost overnight. Band members made some of the instruments themselves. And while no one reads music, they can play to precision anything they hear. Members would drop delicate hints whenever I played the wrong phrasing.

Band membership rekindled roots, and erased our collective memory of how we were lured to the metropolis. Among these young men, the betrayal of their dream once they arrived in New York is tangible. Very few of them can keep alive the kind of hope that Jesse Jackson so often exhorts. In some ways, this explains why they wanted so badly for Trinidad to win the soccer game that sent the United States to Italy for the 1990 World Cup. Randy Harvey, a sports writer for the *Los Angeles Times*, told me in Trinidad on game day that he had never seen people come together so strongly over sport. He would have been more surprised by the response in the West Indian communities in Brooklyn.

Despite the Madison Avenue influences on my speech and style, I forged a strong bond with these young men. A friend of mine, at whose home Nobel laureate V.S. Naipaul has been a visitor, likes to say that the author's early work was easy. Vidia, as this friend and I refer to him in our conversations, only had to record the riches he found in these characters. He simply brought to his writing the same talent that is abundant in the activities of the immigrants. Unfortunately, opportunities were not always forthcoming for them, and those that came along were not as lucrative as Naipaul found in the world of letters. Few of them have been able to turn their talents, and their human values, into currency for the competition they encountered in America.

SWEDEN

The Islamist

Aje Carlbom*

Isaac is a Palestinian man who moved to Sweden in the late 1980s. He is well-educated, with a university degree in architecture. A married father of three, he lives in a middle-class neighborhood just outside the central part of the city of Malmö, in southern Sweden. We met for the first time in the early 1990s, when, together with my wife and colleague Sara Johnsdotter, I carried out anthropological fieldwork in a neighborhood called Rosengård, famous in Sweden for the large number of Muslims who reside there.[†]

Over the years, Isaac and I have met several times, in various locations, for discussions about politics and religion. These formal interviews and informal talks have shown me how Islam can be used to organize an individual life-project. For Isaac, Islam is a symbolic system that frames his activities, and gives him direction in diverse social spheres.

In recent decades, integration has been a topic in Europe. Successful integration is often defined by holding a job and being a taxpayer. The example of Isaac indicates,

---

*Special to this volume.
[†]The fieldwork is discussed in my Ph.D. thesis, *The Imagined versus the Real Other: Multiculturalism and the Representation of Muslims in Sweden* (2003).

however, that an individual may be well-integrated politically and socially without formal employment. In fact, it is possible to argue an opposite hypothesis: that it would be hard for Isaac (and others like him) to be integrated into an Islamist project if he had to make a career as an ordinary worker.

Isaac defines himself as an Islamist, and has done so since his university studies in the Middle East in the 1970s. Back then, the Islamists were mainly involved in a struggle with communists. He is a former member of the Muslim Brotherhood who, like some other European Islamists, now belongs to a loose grouping of Muslim intellectuals who are trying to construct a European vision of Islam. Ideologically, he is close to the activist and researcher Tariq Ramadan. Some of the code words of this project are "renovation" and "liberalism" – a liberalism, however, that is firmly anchored in the fundamentals of Islam.

Describing the project, Isaac says: "Some aspects are open for change in Islam, but others are not. You can never change the fundamental belief in one God and such things. Methodologically, Islam is open to various interpretations. For example, *jihad* and *dawa* are duties for a practicing Muslim,* but this struggle may be conducted in various ways. As I see it, the best way to spread Islam is to act in a humble and mild way, in order to provide a good example for others." His is a common stance among Islamists who reject violence as a means of effecting political change, but who nevertheless regards the Islamization of public space as an important political goal.

Isaac is active in both local and global politics. Locally, in the city of Malmö, he is engaged in the Muslim public sphere, where different actors compete for ideological hegemony. He is often invited as an *imam* to various mosques – both the large, transnational mosque, and the smaller mosques administered by activists of the Muslim Brotherhood and the Saudi-inspired Wahhabi movement. At times, he has had conflicts with Muslims in the latter group. They have accused him of being too liberal in his approach, and of holding what they regard as profane ideals. He has also, in his role as a marriage counselor, received several death threats from Muslim men who think that he is too "soft" on women. On a regular basis, he consults with Muslim couples who have relationship problems. Since Isaac often sides with the women, he annoys the men. His marriage-counseling work has led him to the conclusion that it would benefit both Muslim women and society in general if Sweden officially legitimized *sharia* laws. "As it is now," he points out, "Muslim couples can divorce according to secular law, but

---

*In the West, it is common to associate *jihad* ("effort") with militant activities. However, the term has a more general meaning: that true believers should make an effort for Islam. This effort should be understood in a social context. Isaac and Islamists like him believe that in the European setting the effort should be peaceful: for example, partaking in the democratic system, praying five times a day, and helping neighbors. *Dawa*, which is part of jihad, has the more specific meaning of an invitation or call to Islam. This can be accomplished in various ways. To write an article, to be interviewed, to call to prayer, to act as a good example for others – all can be understood in terms of dawa.

stay married according to sharia. This means they can benefit from social welfare. When it comes to Muslim women, it is complicated for them to divorce 'bad' men. Since most Muslims are married according to sharia, a court in their former home country has to break the contract. This may be difficult, because of the patriarchal structure in the Middle East and elsewhere." Isaac argues that if well-educated and liberal imams were employed in Sweden to handle family matters according to sharia, this would benefit Muslim women in the country.

For some years, Isaac has also organized a Koranic school in the 20-year-old mosque situated in the south of Rosengård and financed by Libyan and Saudi capital. This school teaches between 10 and 20 Muslim teenagers with varied ethnic backgrounds. In order to compete with commercial (and criminal) activities in the surrounding urban landscape, Isaac works hard to teach the Koran in a positive atmosphere, including convening quiz games and other fun activities. His teaching of the words of God is far from the media stereotype that depicts young men bent over the Koran, memorizing its contents. Here, boys and girls learn together; laughter echoes in the mosque along with the instruction. The course is often held on weekends, when regular visitors are few. This also has the advantage of making it possible to spend the night in the mosque. I slept very well there, having received the Koran, newly translated into Swedish, after a brief public ceremony.

Locally, in the neighborhood of Rosengård, Isaac is deeply involved in the struggle for Muslim minds. In this respect, his Islamic political work is congenial to the Swedish public. But Isaac is also engaged in Swedish politics. For Islamists such as he, no obstacle exists to participation in secular political life. On the contrary, this is almost a religious duty. According to Isaac's Islamist logic, only through participation can Islam influence matters of relevance to Muslims and Islamic teaching; only in this way is it possible to establish connections and network with Swedish policymakers.

Many Islamists have joined the ruling Social Democratic Party in Sweden; but Isaac is a member of the right-wing Moderates. He represents the party in the local parliament, which involves a great deal of work. He has to learn how Swedish society operates, and develop opinions on matters as detailed as how neighborhood playgrounds should be renovated.

Muslims in Europe are sometimes the target of Islamophobia from the majority population. Nationalists of the Swedish Democratic Party frequently warn against Islam, and spin scenarios of an Islamist takeover of the nation. In the city of Malmö, a regional grouping, the Scania Party, is particularly Islamophobic. One of its main political goals is to get rid of public displays of Islamic identity. Thus, Muslim women should be forbidden to wear the *hijab*, and *halal* food in school should be banned. The party is obviously one of the main political enemies of Islamists like Isaac, and he is aware of this. But instead of using confrontational tactics, he has tried to build social relationships with Scania members, based on dialogue and trust. In discussions with them, he tries to explain fundamental aspects of Islam, seeking always to provide a good religious example.

During the last 30 years, the city of Malmö has undergone changes that have had profound consequences for the economic survival of its immigrant population. Transformations in the global and domestic capitalist order have reshaped the social context for immigrants. Some have responded by starting up their own businesses, such as small shops and other service facilities. In some, though not all, of these activities there is a clear link between economy and religion. Isaac, for example, is a member of an Islamist economic network in the city whose members put aside two or three thousand Swedish crowns every month. They meet regularly to decide which local Muslim will be granted the money to invest in a business, such as opening a kebab kiosk or a grocery store. While this is done with the best of Islamic intentions, one consequence is arguably to entrench Muslim enclaves and promote marginalization. When combined with the establishment of cultural and religious institutions, such as Muslim daycare centers, Islamic schools, and mosques, Islamists like Isaac seem to be working to create a society-within-a-society. This is common in other countries, but a new phenomenon for Scandinavian nations like Sweden.

Isaac does not, of course, perceive the creation of such enclaves as problematic. For him, segregation will exist independently of whether Islamists act to promote it. From his perspective, a greater problem is that Muslims in general are not sufficiently Islamized, or practice Islam in a faulty way. "It is of great importance," Isaac contends, "to take power over the education of Muslims, and show that Islam is compatible with life in Europe. If we do not establish Islamic institutions that teach a sound and correct knowledge of Islam, a space will be opened for extremists or terrorists to make inroads in Muslim minds." He is worried that ideologically conservative or radical actors will establish local hegemony. This has been a theme of discussion between us for many years: long before 11 September 2001, he had pointed to such problematic tendencies in Islam.

While Isaac involves himself in various local projects, he also participates in activities with a more global character. Through the years, he has inserted himself in a transnational network that extends across Europe, the Middle East, and parts of Southeast Asia. Accordingly, he travels all over the world – mainly for Islamic conferences, but also to visit family and friends in the Middle East. Although he is socially anchored in the city of Malmö, he leads a transnational life.

An important project for him these days is to try to alter the stereotypical conceptions of the West that prevail in the Muslim world. Whenever he has the opportunity, he defends Europe to his fellow Muslims and the wider community. Isaac often repeats his favorite slogan: "In the Muslim world there are many Muslims, but very few who follow Islamic values. In Sweden, there are few Muslims, but society is organized according to 'Islamic' ideals." The Scandinavian social and political system, for him, reflects many core Islamic values.

For the last couple of years, Isaac has worked to establish a European branch of the Organization of the Islamic Conference (OIC). The European offshoot is called the European Islamic Conference, and is an umbrella organization designed to represent

Muslim populations and interests to various European authorities. Regularly, Islamic imams and other leaders meet to discuss matters of integration for European Muslims. During a conference in Graz, Austria, the participants declared their support for "the theological instruments of *ijtihad*: the principle of a free formation of opinion within the framework of Islam, the freedom to apply different schools' knowledge creatively and in dialogue, and, in general, [to promote] the central role of the intellect." Participants also denied the existence of a "European" Islam. "Only the term 'Islam in Europe,'" they stated, "offers an adequate definition for the development of a European-style Islam on the basis of a dynamic image of one all-encompassing Islamic belief."* That Islam is a universal, rather than specifically "European," religion is a common view among Islamists in Europe and elsewhere. The term "Euro-Islam" is mostly used by European academics.

It is possible to view Isaac's Islamist activities as an alternative way of building a career in a context where formal work is hard to come by. But I know him to be a firm believer in God – one recognized as such by other Muslims. Islam provides him with a cognitive map, with social status and symbolic capital, and with a sense of existential meaning.

PAKISTAN

The Music Lover

Maria del Nevo[†]

Hussain sits at a desk in the corner of the library. He gazes with admiration at a magazine which he has propped up against the wall, his eyes shining, his mind far away.

"Baji?" (older sister) he whispers to me when he realizes that I am watching him, "Have you heard of Ozzy Osbourne?" "The name sounds only slightly familiar," I whisper back.

Undeterred by my ignorance he throws name after name at me, song after song, but I've heard of very few. He looks disdainful for a moment before his eyes are irresistibly drawn back to the picture in front of him.

At noon he comes to share the contents of his tiffin box with me. He talks of his studies and his internship at the local newspaper where he goes every day after lunch. "Reporting," he says with great seriousness, "is my passion."

---

*Taken from the program for the EIC conference, Malmö, Sweden, 5–7 December 2003.
[†]From Maria del Nevo, "Ozzy and Hussain," *New Internationalist*, 238 (December 1992).

Talking of passions reminds him again of Ozzy Osbourne. "I had over 20 posters of him and other rock stars all over my bedroom wall," he says. "But my father ripped them down in a fit of rage and threw them away. He said that I shouldn't idolize drunks and drug addicts . . . I should be indulging in something more suitable. But what else is there?"

Hussain isn't unusual for a boy of his 19 years and urban middle-class background. Like many of his peers he doesn't know what to do with his spare time. "Most evenings," he says, "I just go to my bedroom with a friend and we listen to music or have a boxing match."

There is no shortage of other forms of entertainment; theater groups and cinemas abound, although Western films are usually censored to the point of obscurity and local films, according to Hussain, are "obscene." But there are very few neutral meeting points where young people can relax and share their interests; only parks and a few sports clubs. "And what's the point of going on picnics and outings when they are all-male affairs?" Hussain asks. "Even if a college girl did come she would end up constantly looking over her shoulder, afraid a family friend might see her."

On public holidays, parks, zoos and funfairs are dominated by boys and men who cannot conceal their inner frustration. These places are out of bounds for girls, whose parents won't permit them to be exposed to possible danger or harassment. The sexes have to find more devious ways to meet. "There is always *poondi*," says Hussain with a cheeky grin. "For that we usually go to Liberty Market."

Poondi roughly translates as "harmless flirtation" and is a strongly rooted cultural pastime in Pakistan. Traditionally it took place between boy and girl neighbors on the roofs of houses in old cities. But today it is conducted in plazas and bazaars and consists of eye contact or pursuing a girl by moped to relay some romantic message.

"Some boys who do telephone *poondi* might even get a date with a girl," says Hussain. But such triumphs are rare. When they occur the date has to be carried out like an undercover operation and often the girl backs out after a few meetings for fear of getting a bad reputation.

"In the West a boy of my age can make his own choices," he explains. "He can talk to girls, drink, listen to any type of music. We don't necessarily want to indulge in these things. But we do want the freedom to choose. And our parents don't understand – they feel threatened."

The harmonious appearance of Pakistan's close-knit extended families often masks tension between young and old. While the older generation remains steeped in cultural customs, young people experience fashions and crazes swept over from the West via the satellite TV revolution. They are discarding their traditional baggy trousers and long shirts for jeans and joggers. And instead of listening to ancient poetic verses, they are headbanging to Black Sabbath and blaring out rap from their car stereos.

"My father says I am free to express myself to him. But I can't because our culture dictates that young people do not assert themselves before their elders," says Hussain. "Heavy Metal is my only outlet. All my pent-up energy is released when I listen to it."

Having aired his frustrations he gathers up his tiffin box. And tucking the picture of Ozzy back into his bag, he prepares to leave for his afternoon job.

CAMEROON

Knowing Truth

Nate Haken*

Techno bass pounding music in time with my heart; I stepped outside to breathe the cool air by the swimming pool. The dark waters sloshed quietly against the tile. I stood there, breathing heavily. Outside, the pulsing music was muffled and the vague silhouetted images of people danced in the flashing windows. I dipped my finger deep into the dark waters and drew a little circle.

"Barry," declared a voice.

I looked up and saw Mbende standing next to the owl cage in the yard. All around were cages: monkeys, butterflies, tropical birds of many kinds and colors. This party was at my classmate Sonya's house. Her father was a banker here in Cameroon, and before that in Kenya. Sometimes she had parties at her house.

"Mbende," I said.

"Barry," he said again. Mbende's father worked for the Ministry of Foreign Affairs. As such Mbende had spent the early years of his childhood in Washington, DC. "You," he said. "You do not know the truth. I say that you do not know truth."

"Hello, Mbende," I said.

"Do ya not hello me. I am trying to enlighten you."

"So enlighten me," I said.

"Well, you and all your foreign friends – Wait." Mbende leaned over a bush and vomited. Then: "As I was saying, you and all those inside dancing, I say, fuck y'all." He shouted, waving his hand towards the party. "Fuck y'all! Dat's right, you heard me. I say fuck y'all."

Inside, there were Americans dancing. Also there were some Brits and a Polish girl. And several Germans, one who used his arm stub, from which his hand was severed, to the utmost aesthetic advantage. He danced in the manner of a martial artist with his stub as his leading arm. He was a good dancer in the flashing black lights and the sound of techno rhythms.

"All right, then," I said.

"Listen. Although you probably do not believe in magic, me, I do. And so last week, I went to the house of a man I know that reads shells. I asked him one question."

---

*Special to this volume.

Dominican Republic (Adam Jones)

He paused for a moment, looking at his raised index finger thoughtfully. "The question is unimportant. It was personal. Incidentally, the answer was yes. That's what the spirits said. But the point is this. I then asked a second question. I asked if I would ever know God. The man threw the shells onto his mat and the answer was no. To confirm, I asked him that question three times. And every time, the answer was no."

"There you have it," I said.

The door opened and for a moment the music became suddenly clear. It was a song about a dove. The door shut again. Peter came stumbling out. "Mbende," he shouted. "I know you're out here. Where you be, man?"

"Yo, Peter," Mbende said.

Like Mbende, Peter spent his middle school years in the United States. His father was the chief of a small village northwest of Yaoundé. Peter was going to be chief when his father died. Peter did not want to be the chief of a small village in Cameroon.

"Is the *petit magasin* open now, or is it closed for repairs, ya know what I mean?" Peter asked.

"Twenty-four seven," Mbende said. "How much you want?"

Peter bought 4,000 francs worth of the marijuana. "How comes your poetry?" Peter asked.

Mbende sat in bars most nights composing gangster raps in notebooks. He liked it when people asked him about his poetry. Most days he snuck into the American Club. Both Peter and Mbende were looking for a job. Or a visa.

"Not bad. Not bad," Mbende said. "I think I've got a good one in the works this time."

*   *   *

The next day after school, I went out to the road. People called to one another in the sun, shook hands with a finger snap. Everywhere were people shaking hands and laughing, playing cards, slaughtering pigs and drinking beer, moving to the hip-wiggling *makossa* music that played in every house and car and corner store. I bought myself some street meat and a baguette on the shoulder of the road. "*C'est bien cuit?*" I asked.

"*Bien bien,*" said the salesman.

"*Ajoute de piment,*" I said, and the salesman sprinkled hot pepper on my meat. Munching on my sandwich, I stuck out my index finger and waited for a taxi. A taxi pulled over. "*L'école militaire,*" I said. The military school was across the street from the American club.

"*Combien?*" he asked.

"*Cinq cent.*"

The driver nodded. "*Devant,*" he ordered. So I sat in the front seat, in another man's lap. There were already four in the back. One of those in back was Mbende.

"Barry," Mbende said.

"Mbende," I replied.

"Did you know that the greatest early civilizations were built by black people?" he asked.

"Yes," I said.

We drove past the brewery and then through the market place. People selling fabric and toothbrushes bustled, pushing carts and shouting at their friends and calling to potential customers. They shouted in many languages. We passed people washing cars with buckets of muddy water sloshing, and a crazy naked man walking, weaving his way through the streets yelling something about apocalypse.

"Police," explained the driver as he whipped a u-turn and went down a different road. Eventually we came to the military school, which was right across the street from the American club. Mbende and I got out of the taxi and paid the driver.

"See ya soon," said Mbende and he walked around to a low place in the wall behind the tennis courts. I walked in the gate and showed my ID to the guard.

Once inside I ordered a Coke to wash the spicy from my throat. Then I borrowed a basketball and went onto the court. Shooting free throws, I made my third basket when Mbende appeared and challenged me to a game.

"Barry," he said.

"Mbende," I said.

"Ya feel lucky?" he said.

"All right," I said.

"Do ya?"

We played one-on-one and he kicked my ass. He was a good basketball player.

"Your mama," Mbende said, as he scored another jump shot.

Anyway, so he got a lot of points on me that day. But then the guard noticed him, and asked for his ID. Mbende tried to talk his way out of it, but the guard was resolute. Then the guard asked him questions about marijuana and threatened to search his bag. Mbende became as docile as a lamb.

Before kicking him out onto the street, the guard took a picture of Mbende and put it in the guard shack so all the guards would know that this man wasn't wanted around here, either.

PART 6

Masculinities in Motion

In preparing the introductions to the different sections of this book, I have been struck by how much of the commentary about men and masculinities has a truly global resonance. Whether in the South or the North, globalizing trends – notably Western-style liberal democracy and neoliberal economics – have eroded traditional masculinities. Partly as a result, generational changes also seem more dramatic and sweeping than ever before. The nature of these transformations, and their implications for men of the global South, are the main theme of this closing section.

The section begins, though, with three essays that convey how traditional masculinities continue to be influential across much of the South. Abdul-Karim Khan, Margaret Power, and George Olusola Ajibade describe deeply entrenched gender identities and socialization patterns, from Africa to West Asia and South America. Concepts of masculine honor and dominance still hold sway in these societies, with women drawn into the "patriarchal bargain" on varying terms.

Such visions of men and masculinity are now being radically undermined, often for the better (by encouraging a more expansive vision of human freedom and equality), sometimes for the worse (as positive and constructive visions of masculinity are replaced by alienated and destructive ones). The remainder of the section explores the sources and consequences of gender transformations across the global South.

Jane Gilbert's essay on "Boys Becoming Men" in Uganda and Don Conway-Long's anthropological study of Morocco describe worlds in which traditional masculine ideals are still influential. But individual variation, generational shifts, economic upheavals, and the advent of a more "democratic age" produce different visions and negotiations of gender roles and relations. S. Anandhi, J. Jeyaranjan, and Rajan Krishnan also explore generational tensions and the influence of changing patterns of production and consumption, this time among men of dominant and subordinate Indian castes. Daniel Conway's essay on "White Masculinities" appraises the impact of revolutionary political change in South Africa, and shows how sociopolitical and economic reconfigurations have challenged the hegemony that white males enjoyed under apartheid – even those who were otherwise marginalized, such as draft resisters. Despite their difficulties in adjusting to the new order, Conway argues that millions of white men "have continued to contribute to the country that they once brutally controlled, and in the process are creating new meanings of what it means to be both a man and South African." Much the same tack is taken by Nicaraguan feminist Sofía Montenegro in excerpts from my 1991 interviews with her. Montenegro examines how Nicaraguan men's roles and identities were shaped by economic upheavals, notably the capitalist modernization of agriculture after World War II. The social changes of the Sandinista Revolution, and the *contra* war that followed, further encouraged a questioning and reformulation of traditional gender patterns.

In their "A Dialogue with Masculinity," Mark Clifford and Susan P. Mains describe deeply alienated masculinities in contemporary Jamaica. Masculine crisis there is fuelled by "prevailing social conditions – often including contexts of poverty, violence, and gun and gang culture . . . [that force] many young males to adopt hyper-masculine values and behaviors as a survival strategy." Mass media similarly proffer the panacea of "hyper-heterosexuality and hyper-masculinity." But alternative ways "to be and 'big up' a man" are available, thanks to the efforts of diverse civil-society organizations.

In other contexts – notably African ones – masculine crisis is intimately connected to the worsening AIDS epidemic. Janet Bujra cites evidence that Tanzanian men's "mode of self-definition . . . is linked to the spread of AIDS, directly or indirectly," with generational change again playing an important role. Kerry Cullinan shows how traditional *isoka* masculinity in South Africa, based on multiple sexual partners, is "being challenged by AIDS," and is increasingly associated with "dirt and irresponsibility." While Bujra emphasizes that transformed gender relations have spawned a new respect for women's roles and rights, Cullinan notes that they have also exacerbated violence against women. But various projects and organizations in South Africa are working both to stanch expressions of violent masculinity and to confront the threat of AIDS. They include not only the Men for Change group cited by Cullinan, but also the South African Men as Partners Network, the focus of Alex Doniach and Dean Peacock's contribution. Doniach and Peacock relate the experiences of refugee men from Burundi and Rwanda living in the Hillbrow neighborhood of Johannesburg. In discussing both their own predicament and that of their female partners, these men receive and transmit new "messages about HIV, violence and gender equality."

The volume closes with Nandi Ayo Bole's essay for her father, "Global Man, Southern Star." After this section's thoughtful analyses and refined commentaries on men and masculinity, I take pleasure in presenting an intimate portrait of perhaps the most "complete" man I have met in the course of preparing this book. Bole's "daddy" is simultaneously a man of tradition, of his age, and of the future. His life seems imbued with core human values – dignity, integrity, constancy; a nurturing and forgiving spirit – that are filtered through gender, but ultimately transcend it.

PAKISTAN/AFGHANISTAN

The Pashtun Man

Abdul-Karim Khan*

Pashtuns are the world's largest tribal group, some 35 million strong. The majority (22 million) lives in Pakistan, with the remainder in Afghanistan. Their common core is a cultural code, *Pashtunwali*, that defines their sense of Pashtun-ness. Pashtunwali combines the chivalry of knights with the *bushido* of the samurai. It defines the Pashtun as a man of honor (*ghairath*), and holds him to a certain standard in conducting his affairs, whether tribal, social, or national. His life is spent guarding his family's name and honor, even amidst extreme adversity. Indeed, the very term "Pashtun" means "man of honor."

No matter where he is, a Pashtun must obey the first "law" of the code of Pashtunwali: hospitality (*melmastya*), which must be extended even to strangers. Most Pashtuns, especially western Pashtuns, live in arid lands and depend on subsistence agriculture. Yet their hospitality attests to their generous character. Pashtunwali holds the guest, too, to certain standards: to refrain from stretching his host's hospitality to the limits, and avoid shameful acts.

Manliness is an ideal in Pashtunwali, but a more complex one than is usually credited. To be a man means to stand up to the bully in the tribe, and to protect society's weaker members. Ordinarily, the Pashtun must protect anyone seeking shelter – even his enemies running from their enemies. Often even a person fleeing from law enforcement agencies will receive shelter. But if the absconder has committed a crime that causes shame, such as raping or killing a woman, he surrenders his right to shelter, along with any claim to a Pashtun's hospitality.

Pashtunwali guarantees the protection of "three Z's": *Zan* (woman), *Zar* (gold or property), and *Zamin* (land). A Pashtun's womenfolk, property, and land are his inviolable assets – especially women. Insulting, sexually harassing, or touching someone's wife, sister, or daughter can mean ruin for the culprit and his family. Even during the fury and frenzy of Pashtun tribal warfare, women and children are never touched. Molesting an enemy's womenfolk is the most un-Pashtun act a warrior can commit.

Violation of any of the three Z's constitutes a major crime that can be redressed only by obligatory revenge-taking (*badlaa*). Given this culture of revenge, it is not surprising that armed hostilities and murderous feuds are common among Pashtuns. A son may be killed for his father's crime, and vice versa. In this way, a single crime or act of revenge can spiral into a family feud that lasts for generations. As a young officer in the

---

*Special to this volume.

British colonial army stationed in Pashtun country, Winston Churchill had this to say about the Pashtuns (Pathans):

> The Pathan tribes are always engaged in public or private war. Every man is a warrior, a politician and a theologian. Every large house is a real feudal fortress made, it is true, only of sunbaked clay, but with battlements, turrets, loopholes, flanking towers, drawbridges, etc., complete. Every village has its defence. Every family cultivates its vendetta; every clan its feud. The numerous tribes and combinations all have their accounts to settle with one another. Nothing is ever forgotten, and very few debts are left unpaid. For the purpose of social life . . . a most elaborate code of honor has been established and is on the whole faithfully observed. A man who knew it and observed it faultlessly might pass unharmed from one end of the frontier to another. The slightest technical slip would, however, be fatal.*

As the colonial authority discovered, a Pashtun's loyalty to his social superior depends on how he is treated. Even a slight act of disrespect can transform him into a killer. Many British officers in India never understood why a Pashtun *sepoy* (soldier) had emptied his gun into a haughty officer. The British called it treachery. The Pashtun called it vengeance.

It is the duty of a Pashtun son to avenge the murder of his father or any loved one. Until he does, his honor will remain in question, and people will whisper behind his back about his cowardice and excessive love of life. Revenge satisfies a collective psychological need for justice. The whole village knows what was done, and to whom; the whole village takes pleasure in an act of revenge successfully performed.

In taking revenge, however, a Pashtun must never hurry. Effective vengeance may involve decades of patience. According to a popular story, a village elder chided a fellow Pashtun for his impatience and haste when he killed the murderer of his father – after fifty years. But when the opportunity arises, a Pashtun must not miss it.

A Pashtun is more dangerous still when weakness precludes him taking revenge promptly. He will never forget what an enemy did to him or his family or tribe. He perseveres, keeping his enemy guessing and constantly on guard. In a strange way, weakness makes the Pashtun man stronger. It gives him time to reflect patiently on the past, and plan in a clearheaded way for the future.

Even though a Pashtun never forgets, he may still forgive – even his worst enemy. The obligation of revenge is counterbalanced by another commandment of Pashtunwali: *nanawatay*, or entering for entreaty. When his enemy enters a Pashtun man's neighborhood, places his life in his hands, and begs for his forgiveness, a Pashtun is under a heavy obligation to grant it. Usually, this involves an enemy begging the village *jirga*, or council, to intercede on his behalf. If the Pashtun accepts the jirga's request, his enemy will enter the *hujra*, or men's assembly place, and slaughter a sheep or goat, denoting his surrender and contrition.

The jirga is a powerful Pashtun social institution, and it may impose its own terms of reconciliation. For example, the aggressor may give a piece of land to the widow or

---

*Winston Churchill, *My Early Life* (New York: Scribner, 1996 [1930]), p. 134.

children of a murdered man. The aggrieved family, of their own free will, may choose to reject the offer of compensation – yet forgive the enemy anyway. Pashtuns pride themselves on being large-hearted persons, and they like to forgive their enemies in commensurate fashion.

Xinjiang, China (Adam Jones)

Baracoa, Cuba (Adam Jones)

CHILE

Right-Wing Men

Margaret Power*

> When [Chilean] women felt that their fundamental values were threatened by the
> Allende government, they reacted. Men never organized a march of men to protest
> the Allende government, but women did organize a women's march against Allende.
> Women dared to go into the streets and they weren't afraid. Men were afraid.
>
> – Hermogenes Pérez de Arce[†]

Hermogenes Pérez de Arce is a journalist and important figure of the Chilean Right. He
actively opposed the Popular Unity government of Salvador Allende (1970–73) and
supported the military coup that overthrew it (11 September 1973). By presenting
women as the bold, aggressive gender and men as the more timid, cowering one, his
comments, which many right-wing men echo, appear to reverse the gendered roles of
men and women in politics and society. Did right-wing men in Chile relinquish their gendered identities as dominant figures and accept the political preeminence of belligerent
Chilean women?

This essay argues that they did not. Right-wing men in Chile were quite willing to let
women assume the visible, public roles in the movement against Allende while they
stepped to the sidelines and, ostensibly, played secondary roles. However, their acceptance of women's prominence was predicated on their perception that far from
challenging their patriarchal power in Chilean families, society, and politics, women's
anti-Allende activism ultimately served to confirm it. I draw the information used in
this essay from the interviews I conducted with thirty Chilean men between 1993 and
2003. Most of the men I interviewed were upper- or middle-class public figures who
were recognized representatives of political parties.

In general, right-wing Chilean men understood women's opposition to Allende as
an expression of their gendered identities as wives and mothers. They attributed their
political sentiments and public activities to their domestic duties and affective relationships. As right-wing politician Francisco Prat noted, "In Chile women have always been
the responsible element in the family. A woman is a mother and during [the Allende
government], she felt anguish because she did not know if her children would return
home or not. Chilean women are responsible for the domestic economy. They buy what
[their family] needs. When there are shortages or lines, when they can't buy what they

---

*Special to this volume.
[†]Hermogenes Pérez de Arce, interview by the author, Santiago, 9 June 1994. In December
1971, women organized the March of the Empty Pots to protest against the Allende government. They subsequently organized a variety of anti-government activities and became the
public symbol of the opposition to Allende.

need for their home, women feel this lack most directly. That is why women spontaneously organized themselves and were the protagonists in the massive citizens movement that clamored for a change in government [the *coup d'état*]."*

Prat's words reflect sentiments expressed by many right-wing men. Since they ascribed women's political activity to their socially designated roles as wives and mothers, they did not perceive women's demonstrations or demands as threats to men's dominant position within the home, the political parties, or society in general. These men understood the political value of supposedly apolitical women protesting the Allende government, which is why the men consistently supported the women's actions.

All the right-wing men I interviewed held binary definitions of gender. If they depicted women as courageous, then they described men as cowards, as the opening quote illustrates. A number of men extolled women's virtues, while criticizing men's vices. Women, they claimed, were a product of their "solid roles within the family";[†] men, on the other hand, were "irresponsible." Many of the men I interviewed would agree with Pérez de Arce's comment that "men like to drink more and work less [than women]." However, Pérez de Arce was not describing highly successful men like himself; instead, his comments reflected the extent to which class-based stereotypes permeate Chilean discourse. When these men spoke of male irresponsibility and alcoholism (as they frequently did), they referred to lower- or working-class men, their male Other. Pérez de Arce's comments reflected his and his class counterparts' own image of themselves as responsible, vice-free upper-class men whose personality and lifestyle justified their powerful positions within Chilean society and politics.

Across the board, all the men I interviewed believed that women were more conservative than men, as indeed voting results over the last half-century have shown.[‡] Miguel Angel Poduje, a lawyer who served in the cabinet of Chilean dictator Augusto Pinochet for seven years, stated that women are conservative because they "want tranquility." Poduje considered men (who vote for the left more than women do) "more volatile, restless, dissatisfied, and adventurous." Offering a different perspective, Prat stated that women acted "because they are less inhibited. Men could lose their jobs [if they demonstrated against Allende]."

General Medina Lois, a Pinochet stalwart, explains Chilean men as a product of their racialized history. "Chile is born as a result of the Spaniards who came to America to conquer land for the King and souls for Christ. Little by little the natural fusion of the races takes place when the Spanish soldier unites with the Araucanian aborigine [the massive rape of indigenous women]. It was natural for these soldiers to have 40 or 50 women at their disposal; this was not deliberately produced, it was the fruit of

---

*Francisco Prat, interview by the author, Valparaiso, 12 April 1994. At the time of the interview, Prat was a Senator from the right-wing Renovación Nacional Party, a landowner, and the father of nine children.

†Miguel Angel Poduje, interview by the author, Santiago, 5 April 1994.

‡In Chile, men and women vote separately, so it is possible to tabulate votes by gender.

natural eroticism. This produced a *mestizaje* (racial mixing), which strongly influenced the Chilean sensibility. This sociological definition [?] has an impact on Chilean men. The Chilean man likes war, soccer, those types of things."*

Yet, despite their praise for women, these men's affirmation of biologically defined and socially constructed gender roles meant that right-wing women (who equally accepted these ideas) never seriously threatened male power; and right-wing men never really considered surrendering it. Their apparent but insincere self-effacement was, instead, the result of a strategic decision that the mobilization of women would significantly advance their plans to remove the Allende government.† However, right-wing men neither manipulated the anti-Allende women nor passively observed their attempts to undermine the government. The anti-Allende women consciously acted to oppose a government they held responsible for the economic hardships they suffered, and the men both supported the women's efforts and carried out their own work as well. Gender complementarity, in the service of a right-wing movement!

Comments made to me by several of these men contradict their own statements about women's politics and courage, and betray the men's attitudes towards women. For example, when I asked Pérez de Arce how he fared with women in his successful run for Deputy in 1973, he replied that "more women [than men] voted for me when I was younger because I was so good-looking." Sergio Onofre Jarpa was president of the rightist National Party, which spearheaded opposition to Allende. He, too, lauded women's ability to organize the pivotal December 1971 March of the Empty Pots, and graciously acknowledged their contribution to the anti-Allende cause, "especially in terms of publicity." He recognized that women were both the symbol of the opposition to Allende and some of his most public enemies; he credits women's "more passionate" nature with making them more visible. However, when push came to shove, it was "men's actions that made the change in government possible."‡

Even though they verbally attribute much of the success of the anti-Allende movement to the actions of women, right-wing men stepped to the forefront of the struggle and resumed their gender-defined roles on numerous occasions. When the anti-Allende women protested in the March of the Empty Pots, brigades of men from the opposition parties escorted them to protect them from attack. The Chilean armed forces, that quintessentially male organization, overthrew Allende and imposed the military dictatorship that ruled Chile for seventeen years.

---

*General Medina Lois, interview by the author, Santiago, 24 December 1998.

†For further discussion, see Margaret Power, *Right-Wing Women in Chile: Feminine Power and the Struggle Against Allende, 1964–73* (University Park, PA: Pennsylvania State University Press, 2002).

‡Sergio Onofre Jarpa, interview by the author, Santiago, 4 August 1999. This depiction of the role of right-wing men conflicts sharply with that of right-wing women, who credit themselves with creating and leading the movement that both undermined the Allende government and encouraged the Chilean military to intervene against it

Reflecting his definition of the Chilean armed forces as the savior of the nation and the protector of women, General Medina Lois offers his explanation as to why the military intervened against Allende. "There was mass pressure from two thirds of the population, of which women [constituted] the majority, who were desperate and believed they had no future. That is why there was a military coup in Chile; well, we call it a 'pro-nouncement,' not a coup. We responded to the natural feminine sensitivity of women." Thus, the Chilean military acted like true gentlemen and answered the pleas of women – medieval knights to the rescue of the damsel in distress. Their action simultaneously removed the Allende government and asserted proper, patriarchal gender roles.

NIGERIA

Yorùbá Men, Yorùbá Women

George Olusola Ajibade*

The image of men and women in Yorùbá culture determines the rituals associated with every stage in their lives, and also their roles in the society. Right from birth, girls are perceived in the light of their future roles as mothers, and boys as prospective fathers. The notion of masculinity and femininity is evident even during the stage of delivery. If a pregnant woman's labor is short, the Yorùbá believe that the baby is likely to be a male child who is keen to come into the world with the male's few encumbrances. If the labor is prolonged, they think the child is likely to be a female, who will have to carry many things with her in order to be a fulfilled mother (*Abiyamọ*).

Both male and female newborns are referred to as *Ìkókó/Aròbó/Àlejò*. The name assigned to the child may be gender-neutral, feminine, or masculine: gender is not the main principle governing naming practices. Personal names in Yorùbá society serve instead as a "a reflection of the social order for it is those events, values, and belief systems which have psychological and socio-cultural reality for its family, clan, or community that provide the cultural information and rules for the construction of the baby's name."[†] But there is one respect in which Yorùbá philosophy about gender differentiation is enacted in the naming process. A male child is christened on the ninth day, a female child on the seventh day, while twins are named on the eighth day. The governing belief is that the male child has nine bones in his skeleton, the female child seven bones, while twins are considered to possess eight bones. This traditional practice conveys the patriarchal structure of the Yorùbá people, implying the supremacy of males over females.

---

*Special to this volume.
[†]F.N. Akinnaso, "The Socio-linguistic Basis of Yorùbá Personal Names," *Anthropological Linguistics*, 22: 7 (1980), p. 279.

Many other aspects of the traditional society point to this patriarchal structure. The Yorùbá Oríkì àbísọ – praise names given to children at birth – differ, with those given to female children attesting to tenderness and elegance, while those given to male children demonstrate strength and manliness. This carries over to objects in the natural environment. For example, hard and tough yams, stone, and trees are called male/tough yam (*Akọ isu*), male/tough stone (*Akọ òkúta*), and male/tough tree (*Akọ igi*), respectively. The male is considered hard and durable, while the female is seen as fragile, soft, and flexible.

The culture allows men to marry more than one wife, but polyandry is not acceptable to the Yorùbá. Once a woman marries, she becomes a lifetime resident of that house, with all her belongings. In the past, men saw their wives as property, regularly beating and harassing them. They even cited with pride the proverb that "*Ọré tí a mú na ìyálé ó ń bẹ lájà fún ìyàwó* – the rod that is used to beat the senior wife is kept in reserve for the junior wife."

Despite these patriarchal features of Yorùbá society, men and women are regarded as complements. This is reinforced in a proverb: "*Bí ọkùnrin réjò tí obínrin sì pa á kí ejò sá ti má lọ ni*" – if a man sees a snake, it does not matter if a woman kills it, so long as it is killed. This emphasis on complementarity means that it is strictly forbidden for any man or woman to remain single among the Yorùbá. Such a person is considered irresponsible. The relatives of Catholic clergy, for example, are not too happy with their decision to remain celibate.

In the religious lives of the Yorùbá, males and females are priests of certain Deities, such as *Èlúkú, Òsun, Sànpònná,* and *Sángó*. The initiation of men into these religious cults symbolically converts them into females, in order to enhance the manifestation of the Deity during possession. The initiated man automatically becomes the wife (*ìyàwó*) of that Deity, though this carries no sexual implications. The men therefore dress like females, including their hairdo. The intimacy that exists between husband and wife in normal life is transferred to the male priest who has married the Deity. He therefore possesses the power to know the secrets, the do's and don'ts of the Deity, by this spiritual transfer of femininity. Cross-dressing taps the spiritual virtues and powers in male–female complementarities, according to Yorùbá cosmological understanding.

UGANDA

Boys Becoming Men

Jane Gilbert*

Almost all gender work on "development" has focused on women. Only recently has it been recognized that men also have been profoundly affected by societal and cultural

---

*Special to this volume.

change, and that changes in men's traditional roles contribute to instability within societies. In the West, there is increasing concern about the lack of appropriate role models for boys and their underachievement in school, along with public debate about what constitutes masculinity in western society. But for *any* society, it is crucial to understand what stories are told to a boy about becoming a man. What roles are possible for him? How is he to define his masculinity?

Whether a baby is born male or female is the most important "fact" in all cultures. Gender remains the core of one's identity, affecting all aspects of life, both individually and socially. The concept of "hegemonic" masculinity recognizes that in each community, particular forms of masculinity will be considered desirable and particularly valued. This hegemonic masculinity determines which men are considered "successful" by their own society, and strongly influences how boys and men judge themselves in turn. This essay is based on the personal accounts given by participants attending a workshop on "Masculinity and Conflict" in Gulu, Uganda, and supplemented by personal testimonies from men in that region.

Hegemonic masculinity in traditional Acholi culture

The workshop group was mixed in terms of sex and age, but there was almost universal agreement about the "ideal" man, that is, the model of hegemonic masculinity in traditional Acholi culture. A man was considered successful if he married, had a home, provided for his family, could solve problems, "controlled his temper," and was respected by the community. Women participants also stressed the need for a man to be a good provider, and not be "harsh or rough" with his wife. All participants considered it essential for a man to be able to provide security, protection, and food for his family, and to earn his own living by working the land and hunting. He should defend the family and provide education, medical care and clothing for his children.

Certain aspects of the division of labor between the sexes were held to be non-negotiable. For example, the idea of a man cooking provoked laughter from both male and female participants; the idea was considered demeaning and ridiculous. All participants stated that women should not construct houses or dig graves, and men must not grind meal or collect water. In extreme circumstances, men *could* collect water – but only on their bicycles, not on their heads as women do. If a woman had paid work outside the home, she would employ another woman to help, but would not expect domestic help from her husband.

Thus, the "ideal" man was seen by both sexes predominantly as a successful breadwinner who was respected by his community. Men's valued attributes were almost completely instrumental. Very little comment was made about any aspect of "personality," or of nurturing characteristics, and most participants viewed the fundamental role-changes brought about by conflict in Uganda as a cause for despair and regret.

Growing up as an Acholi boy

The identity of each child, whether male or female, is formed in part by the cultural messages received in childhood. Children of both sexes are controlled and punished, often very subtly, to make them conform to their society's image of how men and women should be.

To consider what these "messages" are in traditional Acholi culture, workshop participants were divided into male and female groups. The women were asked to compare their own upbringing with that of their brothers, and to consider how they were bringing up their own sons compared with their daughters. The men were asked to consider their experiences of boyhood. Unsurprisingly, the differences in upbringing between boys and girls were profound and specific, beginning at an early age.

The women stated that boys were expected to be involved in community decision-making, while women were not. Girls' education was also considered less important. "Being a girl" involved not running about, not arguing or playing, but doing housework. Girls were mocked if they ran around the compound (the Luo equivalent of "tomboy" is a pejorative term). They were expected to be "humble" and to accept the authority of elders. Because girls were expected to marry and bring in a dowry for the family, the women felt that girls were fed and dressed better than boys, and protected by boys when groups of youths went out together. However, the women commented that boys were encouraged to "own" women; many of the female participants described being brought up in families where their brothers had been allowed to physically beat them. All the women felt that boys were more "free." After the age of twelve, boys could sleep outside and go where they wished, while girls could not.

The men's descriptions of how they had been expected to behave as boys was clear and detailed. Many tasks, such as cooking, fetching water, grinding, babysitting, and serving food, were off-limits to them. Boys and men were expected to hunt, care for domestic animals, clean the compound, make the fire (girls were never allowed to do this), learn traditional dancing, and travel to far-off places for messages, even if they were afraid to do so. (Girls, by contrast, were always kept at home.) The men admitted they had sometimes felt isolated and lonely, particularly as they had to sleep apart from their mother from the age of three or four. But they were expected not to cry or protest. It seemed as if the provision of physical closeness and comfort to boys stopped abruptly at the age when they began sleeping separately. A number of the men stated that they had envied younger children, and had often cried alone.

Masculinity through "doing"

A boy's traditional socialization included specific training: to hunt, throw a spear, and learn the origins of his clan; to receive bracelets from girls who liked him; to learn traditional rituals and dances; to build a hut and respect his elders. He was also expected to be brave enough to defend his family, control his sisters, delegate responsibilities to younger boys, and help when someone died. Almost all of these are public duties, exposed to community surveillance. Boys pay a price for this focus on the outside world and greater freedom: comfort and sustenance for their vulnerabilities are denied them. They must learn rapidly how to be brave, or pretend to be, and to deal with their emotional needs alone.

Traditional socialization by fathers and uncles was held to have many advantages. A boy would have clear role models, and know what was expected of him. He would be aware of his role in passing on traditional knowledge to the younger generation. As a child's identity is based on his father's clan, so the father is the basis for that identity. Participants felt that if a boy-child was illegitimate or lacked a father, he was likely to be mocked at puberty, as he had no family history. Also, a male who failed to conform to what was expected of him would lose the respect of others, become an object of fun, and in extreme circumstances have to leave the village. None of the participants mentioned any disadvantages for boys who grew up in traditional ways.

Childhood experiences of violence

The second day of the workshop focused specifically on participants' experiences of violence, both as children and adults. Some of the interview questions designed to collect testimony from other men in Gulu also concentrated on the role of violence in traditional Acholi society, and the impact of the ongoing conflict in Uganda.

Initial discussion confirmed what has been found in all cultures: that Acholi boys and girls play very differently. Participants described Acholi girls' play as primarily domestic and cooperative in nature, whereas boys' play involved strength, physical prowess, and "harassing" girls. Participants thought that boys needed to prove themselves in front of other boys, and to maintain their pride in front of girls. However, it was also asserted that, while boys were naturally more aggressive, they could be "guided" and disciplined, and their need to compete against each other could be expressed in non-violent ways.

Almost all of the women had grown up frightened of men and boys. As children, most had direct experiences of both physical and verbal abuse from the opposite sex. They had witnessed direct acts of violence by their father against their mother, and been frightened of domestic arguments. Many said they had come to "hate" their father because of what they had seen; their childhood experiences had taught them to fear all men.

Men also described witnessing and participating in violence during their childhood. They described how older boys had encouraged violence at school, and said that violence-as-revenge in inter-clan fighting had once been common. All described being encouraged to fight, if necessary, when looking after cattle; they felt they would be mocked if they failed to retaliate, or lost the cattle to another clan. It was also recognized that not all boys wished to be violent, and that violence was abhorred by some men; but peer pressure made deviation from the norm difficult.

The fundamental place of violence in the boys' traditional socialization was also a theme of the testimonies. In past times, Acholi boys had been trained for inter-tribal warfare (mostly disputes over cattle), and for hunting. "*Acholi in the past had pride, they did not accept defeat or surrender."* Some described socialization into violence as having intensified during the colonial era, when the British specifically recruited Acholi men for the army, based on their reputation as warriors. But all recognized that the current conflict in Uganda was different from anything that had occurred in the past.

Social disintegration, violence, and poverty

There are elements common to both social disintegration and boys' marginalization in present-day Acholi society. These include population movements due to political instability; poverty; the weakening of traditional authority structures; the global growth of "youth culture," and society's failure to provide educational and socioeconomic opportunities. Both workshop participants and interview respondents drew links between poverty, the dissolution of families, and the likelihood that boys would join military units to survive. With property and wealth destroyed, there was *"no alternative but to fight for survival,"* as one man said. Others commented: *"Without a home, life becomes impossible." "What one looks for is life, just to see one's self the next day." "Poverty can lead to frustration and can make a person do what he or she is not meant to do." "People are cruel now, not because it is in their culture or nature, but because of their poverty." "A poor man is an angry man."*

The breakdown of agriculture, loss of cattle, and the ensuing poverty has meant that, even if schools were still functioning, parents could not afford to send their children to them. These factors, in conjunction with the absence of the informal education once provided by elders (who now have been killed or lost their authority), and combined with the undermining of cultural values, make boys far more susceptible to antisocial influences.

Both workshop participants and interview respondents thought that young people had suffered more than any other group from violence and the breakdown of Acholi society. Comments included: *"The war was not started by the youth, they were misled and have been forced to commit violent acts to survive." "The children are not actually bad, but when their parents are killed, there is no one to take care of them."* Joining military units was a means of survival, and violence could become a means of empowering men when socially acceptable ways of proving themselves were absent.

Workshop participants made clear distinctions between boys brought up in the town and those raised in the villages. Boys from town generally had much less knowledge of traditional culture. The absence of fireplaces in urban dwellings was considered highly significant, as it meant there was little time or opportunity for boys to learn traditional ways. Participants felt that greater knowledge of western culture had made boys despise their own traditions: there was now a much greater gap between older and younger generations. Some methods of traditional socialization still remained in towns: for example, men still hunted, albeit for smaller animals, and, even in towns, it was also still considered essential for a man to be able to build his own hut. Some of those interviewed commented that not being able to build a hut in protected villages and camps had a profoundly negative effect on men's self-esteem, reducing men to "*the status of dogs.*"

Men interviewed in Gulu despaired at their powerlessness to end the conflict without government or international intervention. They were grief-stricken by the fact that, because of societal breakdown and the long duration of the conflict, a generation of boys was growing up with little knowledge of cultural traditions, and having witnessed – sometimes perpetrated – violent acts. Comments included: "*When other means of survival have gone, violence has become a way of life.*" "*What can a person without a gun do to rescue himself?*" "*To me this war is not going to end soon, because it looks like it has become a song; whenever [a man] listens to such a song, he is reminded of the past, and finds it difficult to forgive.*"

By implication, respondents felt gloomy about the possibility of finding other means to define manhood except through bearing arms and inflicting violence. When certain ways of being a man are valued by others, boys and men cannot simply abandon them without the provision of alternative narratives that enable them to conceptualize manhood in more positive and constructive ways.

It is beyond the scope of this essay to consider the complex political situation in Northern Uganda, and how it might be brought to an end. Thousands of people have died, and the way of life of tens of thousands of others has been obliterated. People grieve not only for the deaths of loved ones, but for the loss of traditional customs, traditions, and ways of life – which in the past had included the traditional socialization of Acholi boys.

Normal psychological reactions to catastrophic loss include anxiety, despair, and anger. These are all evident in the comments of participants and respondents. The ability to find meaning in life has been fundamentally disrupted. Adaptation to loss requires psychological reintegration at both individual and societal levels. If the stability and predictability of life has been invalidated by catastrophic loss, new frames of meaning have to be created, and threads of continuity between past, present and future have to be found. What components of boys' traditional socialization still make sense, and can be used to construct positive role models? What new visions of Acholi manhood can be generated? What positive and life-affirming stories about boys becoming men can be told to the next generation? Confronting these questions means engaging not just with the absence of traditional socialization patterns, but with the global impact of western cultural models. Any "development" work needs to address these fundamental issues. Men's voices, experiences and knowledge must be heard; their contribution as culture-bearers for the next generation must be explicitly valued and actively supported.

MOROCCO

The Brothers

Don Conway-Long*

The Bennis family of Meknes, a lovely old city in the Moroccan heartland, became the family I grew to know best over the year I lived in Morocco. The two older brothers became friends to my wife Carol and me, and eventually we were taken to Meknes to meet their family. I met the first of these brothers in September 1992 at an English language bookstore run by a Moroccan man who had spent several years in England. The shop served the needs of Moroccan students of English as well as the English speaking community in Rabat. Housni was then a third cycle (Master's level) student of English literature in Rabat's Mohammed V University.

One afternoon, I asked Housni to tell me the history of his family. I wanted him to go as far back as he could, telling me details of the men in particular, but also about the women in relation to the men. He knew stories about his parents' parents. But he did not know anything about relatives before that. So we began with the two grandfathers: Hussain (paternal) and Ahmed (maternal). These two men married sisters, producing Housni's parents (Mohammed and Rashida) as cousins who actually grew up in the same household.

Hussain was an illiterate man, who sold mint in the central market in Meknes. There were family stories about him once owning land outside Meknes, upon which he may have grown the mint, but Housni did not know for certain. He may have purchased it from farmers. Somehow, the family lost the land after the death of Hussain; again, Housni did not know how. Housni is named after this man in Arab style, transforming the name but retaining the triliteral root – *hsn* – victory.

Ahmed, the maternal grandfather, was a soldier in the Moroccan army serving under the French in World War II. He apparently also fought in France for the Free French against Vichy and the Germans, after which he stayed in France for a while. On his return, he had multiple jobs that he failed to keep for long because of drinking problems; during the time he also was known for beating his wife. Housni's mother tells stories of being a little girl, and, after a night of drinking and beatings, she would tell her mother they didn't need this man who provided no money, drank, and committed violence against her. She would urge her mother to divorce him, which she did have the right to do because of the well-known violence, but she did not do so, out of moral peer pressure – "a good woman did not do that to her husband." However, at some point he turned himself around, ceased the drinking and became the religious Muslim that Housni knew as a child. He was, in Housni's memory, an educated religious man who read often, usually the classic epic narratives of Arab literature. Ahmed lived in

---

*Special to this volume.

Casablanca with his son, Housni's uncle, a well-off and generous engineer who has been called upon to assist the family in times of need. (For example, this uncle provided a loan for Housni to travel to the United States for his graduate training.)

When Ahmed's wife, Khadija, died in her forties, Rashida, Housni's future mother, then in her twenties, took over as the senior female of the household. She worked to raise her sisters and her youngest brother (a year old when his real mother died), who to this day, Housni says, still calls his sister "mother." Rashida was already married herself; Driss was born about two years after the death of Khadija. Four other children followed. Rashida, essentially, raised two successive families. She is a model of fortitude and dedication to family.

Rashida's husband had died years before I met the family, in 1982, when Housni was 16. Mohammed had been a butcher, and had made a good living. He was, in Housni's memory, an intense worker, regularly spending sixteen hours or more to make the shop successful. His day began at 4:00 a.m., when he would go to the slaughterhouse to select the meats for the day. He would return home to awaken the family, have some coffee and go off to the butchers shop. Meat selling would begin at about 9:00 a.m., but first there was the preparation of the new day's meat after it was delivered from the slaughterhouse. He worked through noontime, when the rush of sales began to die down, after which he would return home. He ate his dinner at 2:30 or 3:00 p.m., followed by a nap. He returned to work at about 4:00 p.m., staying at the shop until about 8:30 p.m. or so. Summer hours were a bit different; he would take a longer break in the heat of the day, only returning to the shop at about 5:00 p.m., returning home at about 10:00 p.m. At home, he had his own special chair, where he would smoke his *kif* [marijuana] in his little *sibsi* pipe, which was accompanied by tea or coffee. When Housni was recalling this, he asked if I knew "how fathers in Morocco like to act manly." Sometimes, he said, "they don't act, but it's just there." When the kids came home, everyone would be sitting together in the large area, and all the kids had to keep quiet for him. When dad was there, he was strict about silence and peace. He would sometimes tolerate play with a soccer ball, but even that would not last long. Even so, he was not the physical disciplinarian; Housni said he could count the number of times he was beaten by Mohammed. In Housni's retrospective estimation, he had been a "nasty boy," and his mother was the one who responded with the frequent beatings. Mohammed talked to Housni, which somehow was more persuasive in changing Housni's misbehaving than his mother's physical punishments.

Following Mohammed's death, the family had to sell the butchers shop, and let out their larger home, moving to a smaller one in another district. Rashida made money by doing embroidery, the craft she had learned in her youth from the nuns with whom she had studied. Driss had wanted to take over his father's shop, but was deterred by the family in favor of the study of computers. He later got a job with a company in Rabat, where he lived when I arrived. Housni, having decided to learn English, did well enough to flourish in his studies, being the only member of his cohort of friends in college to receive a scholarship to third cycle studies. His sister Khadija worked in a pharmacy.

The younger two siblings, Umm Kultoum and Abdel Haq, were both still in school. Rashida had succeeded in ways that most Moroccan working class people were unable to; all her children were educated well above the Moroccan average. The fact that she did this as a widowed mother with five living children (her first child had died in infancy) was a clear demonstration of her forthright determination and strength of character.

*   *   *

Housni seemed to me to be a clear thinking, scholarly young man of principle, kind and thoughtful of others. As I grew to know him better, my first impressions were borne out. Driss was interviewed a bit later. He seemed very much to be the elder brother of the family, somewhat forceful, a bit impatient, with an independent, rebellious streak. The interview with Abdel Haq came after the Meknes visit. He was definitely the quietest of the three brothers, the "little" brother (though the tallest of the three) who remained uncertain of himself, and who looked up with respect to his two older male siblings. He was the only one of the three men whom I saw doing housework of any kind; he served us often (along with his mothers and sisters) for the frequent coffee and pastry breaks. He also seemed quite dedicated to his studies.

In answer to the first of my questions – the meaning of masculinity – Driss gave the most traditional answers, speaking of bravery, responsibility, ambition, and of maintaining reason over emotion. The first part of his answer is a good reflection of Driss's personality. He averred that "Masculinity is not a little thing, it is a great thing – very complex." The statement is a good indication of his bluster, of his aggressive approach to the world and his sense of his masculine self. He also was the only one to define his masculinity by being different from women, saying "one must distinguish oneself from the woman in how one looks and the way one dresses." He also claimed that a man should not stay at home; "it is natural to go out – because of physical strength." But he also recognized that education was essential in the development of a man, being the "only way for a man to suit his position in his society and to be respected. Education prevents him from being an outcast and a burden on society." He used a local proverb to describe this: "*Bla hdma bla qraaya kilkalb bla khraya*" (Without a job, without education, like an untamed dog).

As the eldest brother, Driss's personality was the most domineering and stubborn of the three men. He seemed to pride himself on his abilities to get things done, to get others to act, and to function well as the oldest male in the family (at times, to the irritation of his siblings). He was very assertive, even aggressive at times, a man firmly in charge of his surroundings.

Housni gave a more religiously inflected answer. For him, masculinity was to "first be a human being," after which responsibility was essential – to oneself, to one's family, as well as to one's future wife and children. The man must be religious, educating his children in the principles of Islam. "What a man does reflects what he is. Being a man is showing how you are a man." Housni was also concerned with virility, which he defined as the ability to sexually satisfy his wife. "From the Qur'an, it says a man should practice sex enough with [his wife]; [otherwise,] maybe she needs more and will look for it elsewhere. If he is not virile, she has the right to get a divorce." Finally, "a man must seek employment; it is shameful to do nothing."

Responsibility is central here as much as it was in Driss's answer. However, many of the other, more typical masculine definitions detailed by Driss are missing. This fits Housni's character. He is, as I have said, the most religious of the three brothers, the most dedicated to education, and much more thoughtful than the others. Discipline, responsibility and religiosity are at the core of Housni's identity.

Abdel Haq, the quietest and youngest, gave a short definition of masculinity: "Faithfulness, trust, self-confidence, and belief in God." Such preciseness was his style throughout the interview.

These three young men were sons of an exceptionally strong and capable woman. What influence did that have on their sense of gender differences? All three retained some sense of its importance. Housni said the following:

> I think there are differences, but these are according to individuals. One important thing is that we are obviously different, men and women; what is of great importance to the man is the femininity of the woman – [it's] part of the woman's nature to be loving, caring, tender. It doesn't mean these are not qualities of men also, but that they are characteristics of women. It gives her a personality of her own, different from men. I think that men and women are complementary, they complement each other; the man has to do something and the woman has to do another thing. I don't think women think differently from men.

Housni additionally recognized the social power of men that extends into many, but not all, families. But he also saw the rise of a cooperative, egalitarian ethic in families that is the result of a decline in the absolute power men once had. Driss denied any difference in levels of power; "we live in a democratic age" in which everything has changed. Abdel Haq gave the most interesting answer here, stating:

> About 70 percent of Moroccan men are suppressed – they are the lower and working classes; as for the upper class, they have the power of public opinion, they agree or disagree on political matters that shape the nation's destiny. Money allows them to buy or determine everyone else's future. They have good positions in society. As to women, they have the power of their bodies which is determined by age (the older, the less power). Apart from that, their fate is like that of men.

He also decried the reduction in propriety, the rise of immorality and materialist pursuits.

A clear demonstration of Driss's pragmatic way of thinking about gender behaviors is this response to the question of whether a man was the head of the household in Morocco:

> Yes, he is head of the household and should be. It is not a paradox; being the head vis-à-vis the outside world is culturally built and culturally bound, to insure the

respectability of the family in the eyes of others. But inside the home he is not the head; there should be a cooperative "heading" by the husband and wife.

Driss demonstrates here a mature sense of the interaction between public conservatism concerning established gender structures and relationships, and the private processes internal to a given relationship that are often a vanguard for the changes that the wider public will eventually accept as the new norm. While not exactly a progressive assertion of women's rights, his view does recognize the difference between peer pressures for conservatism and the more open negotiations of a real day-to-day relationship, within which live desires, dreams and urges to freedom and equality. Perhaps Abdel Haq, who expresses the far more conservative view that a woman needs a man to "guide her and be a good example for her," will follow his brother's lead as he grows older and gains more social experience. Then again, perhaps not.

On issues of authority and discipline, the three brothers were rather close in their opinions. None expressed any support for the use of physical discipline against one's wife, though they differed slightly on how conflicts were to be solved. "I hate violence, prefer cooperation and peacefulness, and would like to be flexible about everything, except things related to religion, of course," said Housni. Driss believed the husband should play the role of the "corrector (maslah)" for his wife, not as an imposition on her, but rather based on discussion and agreement. He disliked the concept of discipline used in the question. His belief was that "once you beat a woman you lose much – especially and first, frankness and openness is gone for good." Again, his opinion shows maturity and good sense. Abdel Haq, on the other hand, did feel discipline of the wife was sometimes necessary, "when she beats the children, doesn't know how to discipline, spoils the children or behaves with bad manners," but yet again "one should never beat one's wife."

In the end, these three brothers exemplify one of the consistent characteristics in the development of masculinities – variability. All three, as far as I knew, were good men, brought up well through a circumstance – the death of their father – that could have had extremely negative consequences for the entire family. But they persist, they study, they work hard, they care about each other. The point is not the predictability of their futures, but the fact that masculine identity, like culture itself, is shared and individual simultaneously, with no standard pattern for what aspects of a culture's gender ideologies will fit each man.

INDIA

Gender and Generations

S. Anandhi, J. Jeyaranjan, and Rajan Krishnan*

The mainstay of economic activities in Thirunur, a *zamindari* village [in Tamil Nadu state], had traditionally been agriculture. The zamindars lived far from the village and controlled it by proxy through the upper caste Mudaliars. The Mudaliars were the rent-paying direct tenants of the zamindars while all other lower caste men were their sub-tenants. The Dalits were the agricultural workers. The abolition of the zamindari system in the 1950 put an end to this traditional agrarian regime. The erstwhile direct tenants, viz. Mudaliars, became landowners either by paying a paltry sum to the zamin-dars as a token price for the land they cultivated or by claiming occupancy rights. However, other caste men continued to remain as tenants or agricultural laborers of Mudaliars. Once dominated by the Mudaliars who controlled the landed resources, Thirunur is undergoing discernible change. [. . .]

The expansion of the Chennai [formerly Madras] urban agglomeration has had noticeable impact on its border areas. Thirunur is located about 35 kilometers to the south of the city and is very close to Mahabalipuram, a township subsisting basically on tourism. The proximity and contiguity to the metropolitan city and its dynamics has drawn this hinterland into its orbit. The hinterland, in which Thirunur is located, pro-vides labor and land to the expanding city. Many workers commute daily to the city. The industrial expansion has reoriented the land use pattern in the region. Agricultural activity is on the decline, with land acquiring new functions and increasing value. [. . .]

For the Dalit elders, the past is a picture of men wearing loincloths going very early in the morning to the fields to labor the whole day, under the supervision of their Mudaliar masters. They had to take their young sons also to run errands for the Mudaliars, collect cow dung and graze the cattle. They used to be fed by the Mudaliar women in the morning and at noon. It is in the act of handing out food that untouch-ability was reiterated most powerfully and on a day-to-day basis. As a 49-year-old Dalit puts it, "They used to pour gruel from a distance into the palm-leaf cups we held. Even after pouring the gruel without touching the cups held by us, they would not take the vessels straight away inside. They would keep it outside, rinse it with cow dung, purify it; and only then the vessels would be taken inside."

The owners were tough taskmasters. Any imperfection in the work like failing to plough the land in straight lines would invite the wrath of and physical violence from

*From S. Anandhi, J. Jeyaranjan, and Rajan Krishnan, "Work, Caste and Competing Masculinities: Notes from a Tamil Village," *Economic and Political Weekly*, 37: 43 (26 October 2002). The study from which this excerpt is drawn was funded by the International Center for Research on Women, Washington, DC.

the Mudaliar employers. As Elumalai, an elderly Dalit man, remembered, "There would be a lot of work during cultivation. If the plowing was not done properly, the Mudaliar would come running and beat us below the hip." [. . .]

Out of the 50 to 60 Dalit families in the village, only four or five families owned any land. Poverty forced them to steal from the fields of the landlords in the night. This would usually happen with the connivance of a fellow Dalit who had been retained by the landlord to guard the fields. As a 67-year-old Dalit man, like many other Dalit elders, claimed: "Thieving was very common among the Scheduled Castes as there was poverty and they had no land to cultivate. Even when Mudaliars used to guard the four corners of the field, the 'colony people' [Dalits] used to sneak in and harvest rice grains with bare-hands. Some even used to take baskets and collect rice with bare hands." [. . .]

The above description, which has been gleaned from interviews and focus group discussions with Dalit elders in Thirunur, points to the total denial of masculine identity to Dalit men in the non-household domain, because of the logic of land relations and caste. If the right to exercise power, employ aggression, and dispense justice shape masculine identity in a semi-feudal agrarian setting, none of these attributes were available to Dalit men. The public violence on Dalit men deployed by Mudaliar landholders, the institutionalized corporeal practices that ensured that Dalit men supplicated before the Mudaliars, and acute forms of untouchability signify this. On another count, Mudaliar women carried out the act of provisioning food in the most humiliating way to Dalit men on an everyday basis. Provisioning the household being a conventional pivot on which masculine identity revolves, the act of Mudaliar women provisioning Dalit men was an act of refusing masculinity to Dalit men. [. . .]

The dominant response to this emasculation of Dalit men by the Mudaliars and other forms of humiliation and violence seems to be staging acts of symbolic wish-fulfillment in safer locations. As a 47-year-old Dalit man recounted, "even if the Dalits could not beat up the Mudaliars in person, they dismembered the bodies of Mudaliars after their death – when the bodies were left in the burning *ghat* for cremation. When they cut the dead bodies or beat them [into the fire], they used to abuse the body saying, 'You have beaten us and tortured our forefathers, and you deserve more than this.'" These symbolic acts are simultaneously inscribed by the Dalit men's desire to be masculine enough, and an acknowledgement of their inability to be so.

The Dalit men's inability to protect "their" women against the sexual domination of Mudaliar men was again an important plank on which their lack of masculinity was enacted. For instance, an elderly Dalit man recollects, "In those days, when SC women worked in the fields folding up their *sarees*, many Mudaliar men would look at their exposed thighs and pass some lewd comments like 'the land shows up well and needs to be ploughed.' Some of them of course had illicit affairs with SC women, which is a well-known fact in the village." This is a view that was endorsed by several of the elderly Dalit respondents. What we see here is a straightforward story of upper caste male privilege over lower caste women's bodies, which in turn, constructs the lower caste men as effete.

However, the sexual encounters between Mudaliar women and Dalit men were a terrain of more complex negotiations with serious consequences for the masculinity of Dalit men. Let us take the following two accounts given by Dalit elders as instances to explore this. The respondent cited above notes, "many Mudaliar women expressed their sexual desires for Scheduled Caste men and forced them to have to sex with them." Similarly, Krishnan, a 72-year-old Dalit, recounts,

> The affairs of those living in *pucca* houses would be silenced and the affairs of those living in huts would be broadcast all over. Many Scheduled Caste men going to work in farms and houses have had sex with Mudaliar women; but it would be silenced and the woman would be married off to someone else. At the same time, if a lower caste woman talks to someone, the onlooker would spread the news that he saw them naked.
>
> Women in Mudaliar households would be voluptuous because of eating well, drinking milk and curds. Eating beef and working hard, the laborers would have well-built bodies. So those women invite these men to bed. But no one would come to know of it. The man would not talk of it fearing reprisal from the landowners.

Both the accounts allude to the fact that within the caste–class matrix of power, the sexual encounters between Mudaliar women and Dalit men were initiated by Mudaliar women and not by Dalit men. They talk about how Dalit men were forced into or invited to have sex by Mudaliar women. If "sexual conquest" of women by men is a conventional sign of masculine identity, the very act of women initiating sexual encounter denies these encounters the quality of sexual "conquest" by men. Dalit men emerge as mere bodies without will, "conquered" by Mudaliar women for their own pleasures. Equally important is the regime of silence imposed on these encounters by Mudaliar men. This silence enforced by the caste–class power of upper-caste men, denies the possibility of any "verbal display" of these encounters by Dalit men and represents them as "sexual conquests." Without display, masculinity, which is always in a state of insecurity and requires constant demonstration, is rendered unavailable to Dalit men. [...]

Dalit youths

Even while their parents consider owning and cultivating land as an important indicator of their social status, the Dalit youths take special pride in stating that they do not know how to till the land. This is so even in the face of poverty. As Anjalakshi, a 45-year-old Dalit woman, notes, "Both my younger sons are not going to work. It would be good at least if they work in the field at least. But they say they will never do agricultural work. We are not able to admonish them."

This act of withdrawal from agricultural work and instead looking for non-agricultural work outside the village is a move by the Dalit youths to break away from the history of subordination of their fathers and grandfathers, which is closely tied to agricultural work. For instance, a middle-aged Dalit man remarked, "Nowadays men do not work for landowners [upper caste]. They also don't allow their parents to work [in the fields]. They go to work in the government or in factories in Aalathur, and do sculpting, construction work, laying roads, etc. Because of this, they are no longer slaves and live free." [. . .]

However, the freedom from agriculture comes with an enormous economic cost for the Dalit youngsters. Work in the non-agricultural sector is sporadic with long stretches of unemployment. The employment history of most of the Dalit youngsters is marked by a great degree of footloose-ness. In order to keep themselves employed, they move across different jobs. Lawrence, a 20-year-old Dalit, recounts, "After studies I worked in a mechanic shed in Chennai. I stopped working there because of a small problem. Then I was working in sculpture-making in Mahabalipuram. I did not like that work also. Then I worked as a painter. After that I joined the rowdies in Kodambakkam in Chennai. We will collect *mamool*, create trouble, etc. . . . I am [now] doing painting work in Paiyanur itself." Similarly, a 22-year-old Dalit youth notes, "I worked in a hotel in Mahabalipuram for a week. I did not like it and came back here. I worked in an Alathur company for one and a half months. I did not like it because of the night shift and I left the job. I now undertake piecework in this village." Despite switching across different jobs as a strategy of survival, unemployment among the Dalit youngsters is quite acute. [. . .]

Another way in which the Dalit youth assert their new masculinity and also separate themselves from the past Dalit subordination is by consciously recasting their appearance. Dress is the most noted and talked about feature of their appearance. If the old Dalit men can be recognized by their loincloth and a towel, the second generation by their *dhoti/lungi* and shirts, the current generation of Dalit youths can be identified by their jeans, tee-shirts and shoes. Sporting a cap, wearing chains, bracelets and wrist-watches are added embellishments. Even the non-Dalits have to acknowledge the new appearance of the Dalit youths. As a non-Dalit youth commented, "Today they [Dalit youths] are the ones who dress very well and eat well. They have a jolly good time. They appear to be upper-caste people." In other words, if appearance encoded caste distinctions, the Dalit youths, in the process of redefining their masculine identity through consumption, are unsettling such distinctions.

Apart from their dress, they are also conscious of their physique, and take every care to maintain their bodies trim and proper. They keep their appearances smart by taking care of their hairstyles, moustache, etc. They also do quite regularly body-building exercises like weight lifting and take keen interest in sports. According to them, an ideal man is someone who should have a well-built body and a good physique. As an 18-year-old Dalit youth states, "A woman without a loud mouth and a man without a good physique cannot live in this village. Because every day there would be some quarrel."

As part of constituting their identity through consumption, Dalit youths also indulge in tobacco and liquor. Though drinking has never been uncommon, the present day youths are accused of indiscriminate consumption. Also, even while the Dalit elders did drink liquor and smoked, these habits were not employed to display manliness. This is evident from the fact that the older Dalit men always chose a discreet secluded place for drinking – a space that is completely marginal to the public space dominated by the upper-caste men. Elderly Dalit women too enjoyed the same space as men in the consuming of liquor. Thus, in earlier times drinking had to be a discreet activity and not displayed in public, as it could be construed as disrespect shown to upper-caste men. However, drinking by the Dalit youths is to affirm their masculine identity in the public and to challenge restrictions imposed by upper castes, as evident in the drunken brawls they engage in. Referring to the Dalit youths' smoking in public, for instance, Krishnan notes, "I would use betel leaves even now only out of the sight of Mudaliars . . . But youngsters of the day borrow money, buy cigarettes and smoke anywhere with no consideration for elders." His invocation of both Mudaliars and elders in general points to the fact that the activities of the Dalit youths emasculate not only the Mudaliars, but Dalit elders as well. [. . .]

This refashioning of the masculine self by Dalit youths through acts of consumption comes at an enormous cost. Not based on adequate earnings, it places tremendous pressure on the thin resource base of the Dalit households and leads to varying degrees of violence within the domestic space. Commenting on the appearances of the Dalit youngsters, a 65-year-old Dalit man, in exasperation, remarked, "They [Dalit youths] borrow money and buy pants, shirts and shoes and go after some woman and bring her home. That's all about their life. They don't think in terms of making money, buying land or building a house." [. . .]

With the increase in the spatial mobility of young men and women and the proliferation of sites of encounter between them such as bus stand and factory shop floor, Thirunur has witnessed during the past ten years a number of elopements and inter-caste marriages. In this context of new sexual possibilities, love plays a central role in defining the masculine identity of the Dalit youths. As a prelude to love, their major pastime is to tease the girls who go to study or work. For instance, a Dalit youth of 16 years who travels by bus regularly says, "In the bus there would be much of fun and frolic. Singing, dancing and ridiculing, etc. '*Agarathi pesuthal*' is the term used by us to describe a certain kind of wit and humor. Some laugh, some get angry. After two years, one Suganya studying in eighth standard started laughing at my *agarathi*. I started pulling her half-*saree* and hair. That's how we began to love each other."

Enticing upper-caste girls is considered a major challenge to the masculine identity of the Dalit youths, and they consider it a victory if they can fall in love and marry the upper-caste girls. When asked why the Dalit boys show specific interest in upper-caste girls, a 17-year-old Dalit working girl said, "Most of our boys fall in love only with the upper-caste girls. The reason is, those girls try to ignore these boys and they take it as challenge to entice them and make them fall in love with them. The girls behave in that way because they think they belong to superior caste. That's why these boys consider it a conquest to win the love of a Mudaliar girl. Very few love our own caste girls."

Though such inter-caste marriages involve invariably upper-caste women who are poor and go to work, they, being presented as instances of upper-caste men's lack of control over "their" women, stand as a challenge to the masculinity of the upper castes as such. For example, a middle-aged man belonging to the Vettai Naicker community laments, "In those days we couldn't even stand in front of the Mudaliars' house. We had to go to the rear entrance to run errands. If the Mudaliars happen to touch us, they will immediately take a bath. But now everything has changed. The Dalit boys take on everybody. They even elope with Mudaliar girls. Nobody can question them." Equally important, these marriages place enormous stress on the masculine identity of the upper-caste youngsters. [. . .]

Unemployed or casually employed, but in need of extra money to meet the demands placed on them by the new norms of masculinity, the Dalit youths strain the limited family resources to which their contribution is sporadic and meager. This in turn leads to conflicts between them and Dalit elders. One of the major complaints by Dalit elders is that the youngsters refuse to work in the field and also refuse to work elsewhere, but expect the family to meet their expenses. A 48-year-old Dalit man states that his son used to do some sculpting work and earn Rs. 700/- a month. But all of a sudden he stopped working and also retorts saying that it is for the father to earn and provide for the son. He feels that even if his son doesn't provide for the family, if he goes for work he could at least relieve them from meeting his expenses for dress, cosmetics, etc. One of the Dalit elders, summing up the situation, came out with a limerick, which translates as follows:

> They look very stylish – boldness in excess
> They all the time stare at young women around
> Sorrow in the house – they put up big airs
> A shame to tell the truth –
> Their fine clothes are borrowed.

In domestic conflicts between the Dalit youths and Dalit elders over resources, it is the youths who seem to have an upper hand through violence. This subverts the traditional authority of the elders within the household based on age. This is accompanied by a devaluing of their authority in the public domain as well. As already noted, the Dalit youths light a cigarette wherever they please. They don't stop talking to a girl when elders approach. Interestingly, while almost none of the Dalit elders complained about the challenge posed by the Dalit youths to the caste-based hierarchy, their anguish is invariably about the irreverence shown by the Dalit youths towards the authority within the household and community.

SOUTH AFRICA

White Masculinities

Daniel Conway*

> There is . . . in the new South Africa, a chance for the remaking of masculinities, along with the reconstruction of the system.
>
> – Debbie Epstein

White men in South Africa were once among the most privileged individuals on earth. They benefited not only from an authoritarian, Calvinist, and patriarchal ideology, but also from an economic and political system designed entirely for their benefit. White men in contemporary South Africa, by contrast, inhabit a dynamic and contested social, economic, and political space.

Post-apartheid South Africa is based on a constitution that embodies non-racial individual rights and, in particular, designates women and sexual minorities for special protection and advancement. Indeed, South Africa has one of the most advanced legal regimes for sexual and gender rights anywhere in the world. Furthermore, "affirmative action" policies have specifically sought to bolster the economic position of societal groups other than white men. It is hardly surprising, therefore, that white heterosexual men have deeply felt the impact of democratization, and the loss of their once supreme status. Steyn writes that for white people generally in post-apartheid South Africa, "there is an acute sense of loss of the familiar, loss of certainty, loss of comfort, loss of privilege, loss of well known roles"; their "delusional home [has] now collapsed."[†]

The perceived impact of employment policies, combined with high levels of crime and the net emigration of whites to Europe, Australia, and elsewhere, have been interpreted as signs that white masculinity is in profound crisis. This essay focuses on the contemporary self-narratives of white men who challenged hegemonic masculine norms in the 1980s by refusing to serve in the apartheid-era South African Defence Force (SADF), and who now must renegotiate their gendered and racial identities in a multiracial, democratic state.

Apartheid was premised on control, authority, and dominance. These qualities also infused constructions of hegemonic white male identity. The consolidation of Afrikaner political dominion over English-speaking whites, along with the black population, rested on the articulation of a particular Afrikaner masculinity. Nationalism and masculine identity were thus a mutually constitutive process.

As white South Africa's predominance became contested from the mid-1970s onwards, militarization and violence were increasingly tied to white male identity. By the 1980s, compulsory military service for all white men had become an essential component of

---

*Special to this volume.
†Melissa Steyn, *Whiteness Just Isn't What It Used to Be: White Identity in a Changing South Africa* (Albany, NY: State University of New York Press, 2001), p. 150.

apartheid governance. It was an accepted ritual and rite of passage by which white men could be judged and affirmed by the wider white society. Furthermore, conscription was celebrated as a symbol of white unity in the face of a common threat: a means by which intra-white cleavages could be moderated and a new white South African identity forged.

Although the majority of white men complied with their military duties, this should not be conflated with universal enthusiasm for duty. Crisis tendencies in white masculinity were bound to surface long before South Africa's first democratic elections in 1994. The final two decades of apartheid witnessed a dramatic rise in white male levels of suicide, alcoholism, gun and sexual violence, road deaths, and "family murder" (whereby white men killed their families and then themselves). There was a direct link between attempted suicide and militarization: indeed, in 1988, one white South African soldier attempted suicide every day.

Net emigration of whites from South Africa was evident from 1986 onwards. The majority of emigrés were white men following the so called "chicken run" to Australia and Europe. By the late 1980s, the Nationalist regime's ability to manage consent in its constituency was quickly evaporating. The government confronted a small but assertive white anti-apartheid activist community, with significant support from the press and English-speaking community; and, more ominously, a large neo-fascist movement on the right, which appealed to a sense of Boer heroism and militancy that rejected the supposedly "treacherous" and "weak" National Party and its dilution of grand apartheid.

The resounding endorsement of negotiations leading to democracy in a whites-only referendum (1992) testified to the white population's exhaustion, and a recognition that previous strategies to maintain minority rule had failed. Nevertheless, the disintegration of white rule and the discourse of forgiveness and reconciliation in contemporary South Africa has not made it easy for many whites, especially white men, to renegotiate their racial and gender identities. The apartheid past still holds a considerable part of white society in its thrall. Books celebrating apartheid South Africa's military prowess still abound in mainstream South African bookshops. A Google search for "apartheid and military" turns up a plethora of nostalgic internet sites maintained by former troops and their supporters.

White South Africa has clearly struggled to come to terms with its complicity in the apartheid past. The revelations contained in the hearings of the Truth and Reconciliation Commission (TRC) from 1996 to 1998 shocked many whites, hitherto shielded from apartheid's realities. An Afrikaans-speaking student of Denise Ackerman's summed up the feelings of many when he lamented that the TRC made him realize that "My parents lied to me, my school lied to me, our leaders lied to me, the church lied to me. I don't even know about God anymore. I have put him outside my house. I don't know anything anymore."*

---

*Quoted in Denise Ackerman, "On Hearing and Lamenting: Faith and Truth Telling," in H. Russel Botman and Robin Petersen, eds., *To Remember and to Heal: Theological and Psychological Reflections on Truth and Reconciliation* (Johannesburg: Human and Rousseau, 1999), p. 47.

Many whites openly rejected the evidence of atrocity and inhumanity conducted in their name, branding the TRC as the "Cry and Lie Commission."*

Adapting to a multi-racial democracy in which black men and women dominate has also posed numerous challenges. On the extreme right, the Afrikaner Weerstandsbeweging (AWB) refused to participate in what it branded "the most bizarre democracy in the world – a democracy in which the unemployed have finally taken charge of those who work, the uneducable now rule the productive and squatters govern the suburbs."† This rejection of multi-racial democracy culminated in a foiled 2003 plot by the right-wing "Boeremag" group to overthrow the government. White-liberal political interests have also confronted a dramatically new environment. The parliamentary caucuses of the previous "white" parties of the New National Party and the Democratic Alliance gained a respectable representation in the first post-apartheid parliament, and joined forces in 2000. Their alliance was short-lived, however; and in 2003, the New National Party joined their erstwhile political enemies in the African National Congress. The rigid parameters of apartheid had given way to a sociopolitical environment in rapid flux.

The TRC recognized the commitment that anti-apartheid whites had shown to the liberation struggle, and also that white men were victimized as conscripts. Indeed, a special hearing was held on conscription, documenting the experience and sacrifices of conscientious objectors. It concluded that compulsory military service was a crime against humanity. White men who had objected to conscription were branded traitors, cowards and homosexuals by the apartheid regime and its supporters.

Many of the former objectors I interviewed are now part of South Africa's business, governing, and academic elites, their new hegemonic status an acknowledgement of the role they played in the liberation struggle. However, some individuals acutely feel the contested nature of their racial and gendered identity – precisely because of their awareness of the sacrifices they made in the 1980s. For example, Dr. Ivan Toms, an objector who was sentenced to 18 months in jail in 1988, is now Director of Health in the Municipality of Cape Town. I asked him, "Did you ever regret choosing to go to prison?" After a pause, he replied:

> No, [but] sometimes I've been hit when "affirmative action" and things at work have also hammered me. There's still a case going through the Labor Court: a person, a colored female who didn't get my job, is claiming that she should have got it because I am a white male and she is a colored female. My frustration there is saying, well, I didn't . . . all right, maybe I benefited by being able to go to 'varsity [university], although the joke is I probably struggled much more than her to get through 'varsity: she comes from a very wealthy background, [while] I came from a very poor white family. And you feel you've been hit, it's a double whammy. You've been hit by the apartheid system, and you've been hammered because when it comes to the crunch,

---

*The TRC report itself noted that the "white community often seemed either indifferent or plainly hostile to the work of the Commission." *Truth and Reconciliation Commission of South Africa Report, Volume 5* (Cape Town: Juta & Co., 1998), p. 196.
†Cited in Antjie Krog, *Country of My Skull* (London: Vintage, 1999), p. 154.

you're a white male in the number-crunching. But overall . . . people respect me, and they know me in the community.

Toms is a white man who has done more than most to demonstrate commitment to the new South Africa. Yet he, like his ECC contemporaries, remains inevitably part of the white milieu, and struggles to adapt to changed circumstances.

On another occasion, I listened to a narrative that seemed to mirror a much wider white discourse of disillusionment. One of my interviewees talked about how, at school, he would have heated arguments with his dormitory mates about South African politics, with him advancing a much more liberal viewpoint. After explaining the standard points of contention, such as the right of black people to vote, he added:

> I think the counter side to it is that they [his classmates] might say, well, the type of thing you were calling for – that schools should be integrated and everyone should have a vote – well, look what's happened in the rest of Africa, and now take a look at our country . . . Are *you* happy? Has not the prophecy of what we said, about things to the north of us being bad, come true in our own country? I think one could have a very interesting conversation about that, because I do concede that whatever is good about our country since '94, there's a lot that I am very critical of.

I was struck by how this echoed some of the apartheid state's attacks on the viewpoint of objectors, and its claims about what could happen if apartheid ended. Another former objector termed President Mbeki a man "not worthy [to be] president," while still another remarked that "Black rule in South Africa has started to mirror some of the system of propaganda which is the legacy of apartheid." Identity in South Africa continues to be heavily informed by racial subjectivities, and white men who contributed to the liberation struggle in the 1980s in defiance of the norms of their community have found that these previous sacrifices are rarely relevant to contemporary economic and political imperatives.

One group of white men *has* unambiguously benefited from the new South Africa: gay white men. The gay-rights movement has been well organized and assertive, and the South African Constitutional Court (which also has an openly gay judge, Edwin Cameron, on the bench) has consistently advanced gay-rights legislation. As Oliver Phillips reflects, for many gay men, "the constitution has lent a new level of esteem to being South African, and a new level of self-esteem to being gay."* Gay culture in white South Africa has flourished since 1994, with significant and trendy "gay areas" in metropolitan Johannesburg and Cape Town (the latter proving to be a popular international holiday destination for gay men).

The significance of the Constitution and its emphasis on gender and sexual minority rights has not been lost on conservatives of the old order. The Reverend Peter Hammond, a notable pro-apartheid and pro-military activist in the 1980s, had his book, *Homo-Fascism*

---

*Oliver Philips, "Ten White Men Thirteen Years Later: The Changing Constitution of Masculinities in South Africa, 1987–2000," unpublished paper, 2002, p. 14.

in South Africa, censored by the Constitutional Court, and raged that "The Constitution thus laid the basis for what has essentially been the frightening advance of special privileges for those engaging in sodomy in SA . . . Essentially what the Constitution has done is grant privileges for perverts."* Other conservative forces, surprisingly, have been less resistant to this change in the order of South African masculinities. A recent study of the integration of gays and lesbians into the South African National Defence Force found universal political acceptance of the changes to the military, and high-level institutional commitment, with no discernible problems among the rank and file.† White South Africa has moved rapidly from profound homophobia to tolerance and open celebration of sexual minority rights; it is homophobic forces that are now ghettoized.

The rapid changes in the first ten years of South African democracy have posed many challenges for white men, even those who campaigned and sacrificed for that democracy to come to fruition. However, as one exiled military objector who returned to South Africa in the early 1990s reflected:

> I think in South Africa, as a society that is transforming, it is possible to do something that has meaning, and that for me is one of the things that has been really interesting about being back: the opportunity to be involved in a society that is changing very quickly.

The 1996 Constitution directly challenges the supremacy of white, heterosexual men. But it has opened spaces for previously subordinated white masculinities to be liberated and affirmed. Employment policies discriminate against white men; yet a recent study of white emigration concludes that white men continue to dominate the productive market, despite widespread perceptions of disadvantage.‡ Indeed, the neoliberal macro-economic policies of the ANC have ensured that white-controlled South African multinationals, such as Anglo-American, Old Mutual and South African Breweries, dominate their respective fields.

Despite its flaws, South Africa as a society of the global South provides a remarkable example of how a post-conflict society can forgive and offer a degree of acceptance to former oppressors. The extent to which individual white men have been able to negotiate the new terrain varies considerably. But it is undeniable that millions have continued to contribute to the country that they once brutally controlled, and in the process are creating new meanings of what it means to be both a man and South African.

---

*Africa Christian Action, "Homo-Fascism in South Africa," http://www.christianaction.org.za/articles/homofascism.htm.

†Margot Canaday, "A Study of the Integration of Gays and Lesbians in the South African National Defence Force (SANDF)," Center for the Study of Sexual Minorities in the Military, University of California, 2002.

‡M. Ackerman *et al.*, "A Survey of Rhodes University Postgraduate Students' Perception on the 'Brain Drain' from South Africa," unpublished MA thesis, Rhodes University, 2004.

NICARAGUA

"A Rebellious Male Youth"

Sofía Montenegro*

[Sofía:] I look on our men with compassion. Particularly because Nicaragua is a very young country, with very young males. They are malleable. Everything depends on your approach. You can push them into a corner, or you can make a bridge for them to cross. I prefer to build a bridge. My sense is that men have reacted defensively, not only because we feminists are attacking their privileges and denouncing inequalities, but also because we pointed to the problem without offering any alternative. That only leads to a dead-end.

This comes from guerrilla tactics, you know. If you push someone into a corner, but don't want to eliminate or kill him, you have to leave him a way out. In the first wave of feminism, there was no way out for men. If you, as a woman, denounced men and applied your views consistently, you wouldn't want to live with *one* of these guys. One the other hand, the prevailing norm makes most people heterosexual. So you sort of have to be with one guy at a given moment. The question then becomes, how to build the bridge, and get the other guy to cross it – not all the way, but at least to a meeting-point in the middle.

There was an experiment made here during the war [against counter-revolutionary *contra* forces in the 1980s] that began as kind of a joke, but turned out to be very reveal-ing. The Army was very worried about the rate of desertions, and they found that most of the deserters were not running from the enemy, but were sneaking back to the cities because of their profound fear of what was happening with "their" women while they were away. To address the problem, the Army put together a seminar and gathered some chosen troops, a representative mixture. The soldiers were complaining that the Revolution and its *comandantes* [top leaders] should stop talking about women's rights. [. . .] The soldiers argued they could fight with more peace of mind if they could be sure the women weren't off screwing around somewhere.

The sociologist-psychologist that the Army brought in explained to the young soldiers why women couldn't and shouldn't return to their traditional patterns of behavior. At the end, the soldiers in this seminar came to understand women's pro-blems better, and their reaction was very interesting. They said, "Fine, we understand, we can make the effort to adjust. But if you don't like us the way we are, you have to tell us what are the new rules of the game. Because the problem is, now there are no rules! The behavior we grew up with is no good anymore." And this was creating a lot of anguish and disruption.

---

*From Adam Jones, ed., *"A Woman and a Rebel": Sofía Montenegro and the Sandinista Revolution* (unpublished manuscript, 1992).

What really touched my heart was the plight of the young men, saying: "Help us. What should we do?" But their attitude was one of openness, not rejection. It's a positive attitude. You couldn't just tell them to go to hell. Obviously, the women's movement wasn't prepared for this. It still has to resolve this problem in order to provide a positive platform that men can learn to live with. Women have to be taught how to argue with and persuade the particular male they're living with. Because the easy answer is just to leave him, but that doesn't really solve anything.

For one reason or another, the men here – the [Sandinista] Revolution has made them open to the possibility of change, not only socially but on a *personal* level. Because they've observed, themselves, how they've changed over the years, and they *believe* in change. They know they're stuck in patterns that don't really belong to them – that belong to their parents, or to rock culture, or to the past. They're in a process of seeking and finding themselves. Obviously, they've done less thinking on this subject than women have, but they have the will, they can see how the different projects can coincide. That's the importance of mixed-group spaces and debates, in addition to the private spaces women need.

One thing you must bear in mind is that many men, during their time [fighting] in the mountains, discovered the experience of love for other men. I don't mean sexual love, because when you're huddled up close to your *compañero* [companion] in the middle of a freezing night, the last thing you can think of is being horny. But they've discovered affection, loyalty, commitment. They're coming back to the cities and to the universities as men, no longer boys – but still young. They have hundreds of questions! Even the turmoil and chaos of the election loss [the Sandinista defeat in 1990] has had the effect of creating a cauldron in which new ideas can develop. This is a *rebellious* male youth, not a reactionary one. It's full of empowering experiences – they've passed through their rites of passage into manhood, and this new manhood they are seeking with open eyes, whether it's in the way they look at women, or politics, or whatever. This opportunity comes once in a generation, you know. We mustn't miss it.

*   *   *

Machismo exists in Nicaragua, but it has deep economic roots that need to be understood. If you don't grasp the deep structure that sustains social phenomena, whatever you do will be superficial – or wishful thinking, at any rate. [. . .]

To make a sex-education campaign in Nicaragua, for example, you have to understand the character of Nicaraguan men. It's not that everywhere they're polygamous, but in general, each man has at least two or three women besides his wife. That's the reason it doesn't work to appeal on moral grounds to loyalty or fidelity. That might work for a society that's founded on the nuclear family. Nicaragua isn't. The family structure imported by the Spanish had a nuclear element, but was also a classic extended family, a clan-type structure. As for the peasant family – well, it was destroyed when capitalism established itself here in the 1950s. The plantation economy shattered it. Capitalism needed labor for its coffee and sugar and cotton, and that meant two things were necessary. First, peasant lands had to be expropriated, in order to force the peasantry to become a proletariat on the plantations. Second, the labor supply had to be adjusted to the needs of seasonal production. Before, the peasant family had a piece of land, its cow, its means of subsistence. When they were expropriated, the men were forced to work different crops all over the national territory, according to the season. A massive pool of male migrant laborers was created.

Men became "sailors of the land." They might have a job working a particular crop for only three months a year. When they finished with the coffee harvest, they'd move from the mountains down to the coast to harvest the sugar. That was the only way they could earn a salary year-round, assuming the work was there to be had. That pattern prevented anything like the formation of a stable family nucleus, of course. So what the poor men did – this idiosyncrasy of the Nicaraguan male – is that in each place they went to work, they tried to create bonds, tried to forge the nucleus of a family. This is the *drama* of Nicaraguan men: trying to create a sense of personal stability, never finding fulfillment. They could never say, *This* is my home, *this* is my wife and children. Instead, they spread children wherever they went.

Maybe now you understand my compassion for males here. Theirs is a never-ending story of trying to build a home of their own where they can feel even that small amount of security, that bit of soil in which the roots of affection and a sense of belonging can grow. This fragmentation of their lives has had an impact on men that we can hardly begin to measure. That's why we must not see the males of this country as the enemy. They are victims. They have been denied the possibility of building a transcendent relationship with a single person; instead, they go jumping from one woman to another, they fall into a woman's arms as someone would fall into the embrace of a drug, into oblivion.

This stereotype of the Central American male as shiftless, rootless, irresponsible, a drunkard – it's *true* in large part, but it's terribly short-sighted. All these phenomena are the result of the factors I've outlined for you. If you fail to understand the social fabric which produces such a man, you don't understand a damn thing. That's the reason we [Nicaraguan feminists] are working to avoid a direct confrontation with men, as far as possible. It's too easy to forget that you're in the same boat in many ways, and the answer you come up with had better be a universal one.

JAMAICA

A Dialogue with Masculinity

Mark Clifford and Susan P. Mains*

Frequently represented as an idyllic space to "get away from it all," or to rekindle past love affairs and nurture new ones, the Caribbean island of Jamaica has also come to symbolize contested spaces in relation to gender relations and sexuality. These subtexts are rarely discussed in international mainstream media, unless a specific dramatic event has recently taken place (such as the cancellation of overseas tours promoting homophobic Dancehall musicians). However, a closer examination of ongoing tensions around gender, and specifically masculinity, point to the need to interrogate these conflicts further. In this dialogue, we illustrate the ways in which narratives of masculinity, space, and fear have become embedded in the island's cultural landscape. The format of a dialogue was chosen to begin what we hope will be a broader discussion about prescriptive and repressive notions of gender and sexuality, and to think through the possibilities for encouraging more progressive spaces and forms of masculinity.

We begin this dialogue by addressing homophobia and depictions of morality in Jamaican popular culture. This is followed by a discussion of gender-related violence and media representations. We expand on these themes with an examination of positive role models, education, and community activism.

The public face (and space) of homophobia

SM: In November 2004, Human Rights Watch launched a Report, *Hated to Death*, which examined the forms and depth of homophobia in Jamaica. In doing so, it shone a spotlight on some of the ongoing debates about sexuality and gender in the island.[†] One of the more telling, and controversial, findings was that police and government organizations were complicit in these discriminatory practices, and facilitated a climate of violence and fear – for gay men in particular. The report moved beyond stating that homophobia was an individual concern, to illustrate the ways in which narrowly defined gender and sexual roles are policed and punished through broader frameworks, such as state institutions. I was wondering: to what extent does this report help us to draw connections between the private and public understandings of gender and sexuality, and the ways in which the "public good" can also be profoundly negative for specific individuals?

---

*Special to this volume.
[†]Human Rights Watch, *Hated to Death: Homophobia, Violence, and Jamaica's HIV/AIDS Epidemic* (Human Rights Watch, 2004), http://hrw.org/reports/2004/jamaica1104/.

MC: I recently read a column in the *Jamaica Observer*, in which black British MP
Diane Abbott compares British and Jamaican approaches to public morality.*
She suggests that in Britain, the essence of public morality is how society treats its
fellow beings, whereas in Jamaica, public morality consists more of standing in
judgment of others, which she terms "a voyeuristic morality." Jamaican legislation
against homosexuality is a relic of the British colonial penal code, and is centered
around the criminalization of an essentially private act – that of penile anal penetration. The law makes no distinction between public and private: all acts of anal
penetration are equally illegal. This exposure of private consensual interactions
to public scrutiny and sanction has serious implications. To actually police what
happens in people's bedrooms, you first have to breach the fundamental human
right to privacy, not to mention rights to family life, self-determination, and freedom of expression. The state essentially denies homosexuals, and men in particular, these rights – leaving them open to abuse by private individuals and agents of
the state. Homosexuals are in effect second-class citizens under the law. The current trial of the musical artist Buju Banton, for forced entry into the home of four
allegedly homosexual men and subsequent violent assault on them, is a good
example of this. Much of the public discussion of this trial has revolved not
around the criminal assault on these men, but around a perceived attack on Buju
Banton, and Jamaican artists in general, by gay-rights groups. This focus suggests
that maintaining public morality, as defined by strict norms of masculinity, takes
priority in many people's minds over protecting the human rights of individuals.

Violence and public images

SM: I think this issue of human rights and their marginalization is an important point
for thinking about Jamaican masculinity in general. The problems of reinforcing
narrowly defined patriarchal expectations of what it means to be "a real man" are
most obvious in the context of violence. This is so not only with regard to homophobic violent crimes, or male-on-male gang violence, but in relation to the
growing incidence of violence against women and children on the island. Just in
recent weeks, there has been a series of highly publicized abductions, rapes, and
murders of young girls and women. These have been described in the *Jamaica
Observer* and *Jamaica Gleaner* as a way for male-dominated criminal gangs to exact
revenge on easier or "softer" targets by going after female relatives or associates of
their intended victims. Newspaper commentators have noted that the general
assumption in the past, that women and children were spared this sort of violence,
has been shown to be far removed from the lived experience of many Jamaicans.
That this assumption existed at all is problematic. It points to a certain level of

---

*Diane Abbott, "A Voyeuristic Morality," *Jamaica Observer*, 23 October 2005. http:// www.
jamaicaobserver.com/columns/html/20051022t200000-0500_90862_obs_a_voyeuristic_
morality.asp.

denial, combined with a marginalization of women's concerns for safety – given the high rates of sexual assault, abuse, and domestic violence that women and children have been experiencing for years. In a UNDP report, Barbara Bailey notes that there is a direct link between increasing homicide rates and rates of other violent crimes.* This is a cause for real concern, given that Jamaica now has the highest murder rate in the world. A significant number of these violent crimes are inflicted by men against women, often against someone they are familiar with: "Data provided by the Emergency Unit of the Kingston Public Hospital indicates that every day approximately 20 women are treated on an outpatient basis for wounds requiring stitches, and that 90% of these situations are the result of domestic violence."† The fact that, despite such adversity, many women have managed to support their households (officially, almost half of all Jamaican household heads are female) suggests that rather than fitting the image of a softer, dependent gender, women have developed a range of resistance strategies to ensure survival. Unfortunately, these strategies exist in tandem with enduring images of hyper-heterosexual masculinity, which often plays out contests for control on bodies that are represented as "feminized" in the public imagination, whether women's, children's, or gay men's bodies.

Learning to be men

MC: Indeed, the promotion of hyper-heterosexuality and hyper-masculinity can be viewed as both a symptom of, and a contribution to, a crisis of masculinity, involving the marginalization of a significant sector of the Jamaican male population. This particularly affects those at the lower end of the social spectrum. Socio-economic and historical factors combine to foster low self-esteem, which contributes to poor performance in education, and subsequent difficulties in finding employment or career advancement. Percentage-wise, males perform consistently worse than females at all levels of the education system. Also, partly as a result of better education, women are more easily able to adapt to today's changing labor market, and have made quite significant gains. By contrast, men, especially those working in manual professions such as agriculture, have experienced a decline in their employment possibilities. Much of our population is situated in the inner cities, where prevailing social conditions – often including contexts of poverty, violence, and gun and gang culture – combine to create a harsh environment that forces many young males to adopt hyper-masculine values and behaviors as a survival strategy. With limited opportunities for personal development, many fall into criminal activities. It's popularly assumed that

---

*Barbara Bailey/UNDP, *National Reports on the Situation of Gender Violence Against Women: National Report Jamaica* (United Nations Development Program, 1999), http://www.undp.org/rblac/gender/jamaicabigfile.pdf.
†Ibid., *Executive Summary*, http://www.undp.org/rblac/gender/jamaica.htm.

a breakdown in traditional values is partially to blame, and that what is needed is a return to so-called family values, as well as more positive male role models that disenfranchised youth can emulate. In this context, we can consider the current promotion of musical artist Jah Cure and his number one song *Reflection*, a mournful lament of life in prison. Singing about his incarceration and its deprivations, Jah Cure, a convicted rapist, works the theme of rehabilitation with lines such as "I swear, I can be a better man." Perhaps to garner public support for his early release from prison, these sentiments – laudable in themselves – have been used to justify the hype surrounding this singer. At face value, his story of redemption and success through adversity provides a positive role model in the face of the growing disenfranchisement of many young lower-class men in our society. What is downplayed, though, is that at no time during this recent round of publicity has Jah Cure acknowledged his violent rape of a woman. In fact, he has criticized her for publicly recounting her ordeal, suggesting that in doing so she is somehow hindering his progress. This lends a rather empty ring to his emotive lyrics about rehabilitation. In spite of this, the male-dominated music industry and media, by disregarding the ordeal of the rape victim, perpetuate her ordeal every time Jah Cure's music or interviews are given airplay. By this means, they reinforce a patriarchal value system based on control, where regardless of status, "man run tings."

SM: The Jah Cure case seems to highlight a lack of accountability for past actions, which also points to the ways in which powerful forms of masculinity rarely emphasize responsibility as a central component. Visibility, whether positive or negative, is far more desirable than accountability. In Jamaica, this is seen as holding true for musicians, politicians, gangsters, and business-owners alike. For many people, this lack of ethics and transparency in day-to-day life has led to a sense of frustration and disenfranchisement from formal political processes, leaving few constructive alternatives.

At the same time, I think the issue of education and role models is an important one. Both young boys and girls face substantial challenges as they pass through their educational programs, such as violence, teen pregnancy, and residential instability. In an assessment of the school system in Jamaica, Carlston and Quello note that there is "a very positive attitude to schooling by households-families and government."* But the experiences of this system and its outcomes vary substantially among boys and girls, different income groups, and rural and urban populations. While girls tend to do better in terms of literacy and general achievement – despite the patriarchal culture they have to negotiate – ironically, upon graduation, they find that managerial and executive positions are still largely male-dominated. A return to traditional gender roles may appeal, but it fails to

---

*Beverley Carlson and Janet Quello, "Rose II: Social Assessment" (Projects and Programmes, Ministry of Education, Youth, and Culture, 2002),
http://www.moec.gov.jm/projects/rose/socialassessment.htm.

recognize that those same traditional ideals are reflected in the adoption (and encouragement) of "macho" personas for boys in schools, and the reluctance to hire and promote qualified females in political institutions and the workplace.

The above discussion points to the many hurdles that Jamaicans face in critically engaging and promoting concepts of masculinity – and more expansive gender roles – while offering a positive alternative to the dominant social and political climate. Progressive masculinities need to be framed and understood not only as idealistic, but as identities that are socially, culturally, politically, and economically desirable and profitable. If narrow and oppressive depictions of masculinity continue to be presented as the most expedient and convenient route to wealth and power – without a discussion of the diverse benefits to be gleaned from other conceptualizations of gender and sexuality – then hyper-masculinity will win, and lose, the day.

In terms of education, there is already substantial interest in school activities – academic competitions, fundraisers, and sports activities receive significant parental and media support. This could help to build more interactive decision-making among parents, students, teachers, and policymakers, and to support networks that challenge what we think boys and girls can and should be. Such networking requires ongoing collaboration that meaningfully engages all participants in the decision-making process. Organizations such as Women's Media Watch, Jamaica Forum for Lesbians, All-Sexuals and Gays, Jamaica AIDS Support, Families Against State Terrorism, Jamaicans for Justice, Women's Inc., the Bureau of Women's Affairs, and school alumni associations have worked to challenge negative images of Jamaican masculinity, and to promote more diverse progressive identities through workshops, educational training, advocacy, publicity campaigns, and protests. Such organizing and activism provide positive examples of masculinity, and offer an important entry-point to understanding how we learn what it is to be and to "big up" a man.

TANZANIA

Husbands, Fathers, and AIDS

Janet Bujra*

I want to illustrate how another masculine identity, that of husband and father, is held up to question in response to the AIDS threat. We organized a group of male and female

---

*From Janet Bujra, "Targeting Men for a Change: AIDS Discourse and Activism in Africa," in Frances Cleaver, ed., *Masculinities Matter! Men, Gender and Development* (London: Zed Books, 2002), pp. 222–4.

coordinators [in Tanzania] whose twelve members were chosen in village workshops. Men chose half their own number from among male village office-holders. This group brought together men and women in a community where women were normally silent in mixed groups. We organized the first meeting with some trepidation.

Strikingly, a discussion of sexuality and health turned into a charged debate about domestic labor. One of the men blamed mothers for the bad behaviour (sexual immorality) of young people. The women were incensed and pointed out that men gave very little support to their wives. As fathers they did little to ensure that children were under control. The debate now took a surprising turn, with two men taking the side of the women. In so doing, however, they displayed two very different versions of masculinity, one more conventional, the other subversive.

The "subversive" was a young man in his mid-twenties. His sister had died of AIDS and, in the absence of his mother, he had been the one to care for her, performing intimate tasks and tending her *in extremis*. This man had spoken out courageously in an earlier workshop: "My sister had this illness and she lasted for three years or more, and her needs were great. All her money was finished and she got worse. She had nothing left. But I did get the right food for her, milk, eggs and so on." At the time I noted that his brave statement was received in silence; few publicly claim AIDS victims as relatives. Whether it was the experience of nursing his sister, or for some other reason, this man had a very different view of women's lot. In this earlier workshop he had also boldly asserted: "You know, there are many women here who, even after they have a child, they don't get good food. She is swollen with hunger. She has to look after herself, while the man who created the problem by giving her the child has disappeared into thin air!"

I observed one of the village leaders quietly reprimanding him, perhaps because he had made this statement in front of "outsiders" (the workshop facilitators). At the coordinators' meeting he immediately endorsed the women's perspective. After detailing women's work burdens, he described husbands rolling home drunk and demanding food: "Do you, the man, have a right to that food? But you eat it! . . . I'm not saying all men are like this. But many leave everything to their wives."

This was challenging talk in mixed company and the other men looked angry or uncomfortable. The situation was rescued by the elderly treasurer of the mosque committee who assumed a more conventional masculine role, that of elder statesman. He assuaged the women's anger by conceding men's shortcomings as fathers and husbands. It was true men left women to do all the work, taking no responsibility: "We are dictators in our own homes." Details of how domestic tasks should be shared now emerged:

> Let's say it reaches Saturday – it should be my responsibility to buy the soap for washing the clothes. Am I there? Or am I out? And maybe at the end of the week there are clothes to repair, the child's uniform is torn and so on – but do we involve ourselves? We don't. Saturday we say – "it's the weekend" and we come rolling home at ten or eleven at night. Do we ask for a report on what is going on at home? No! . . . Fathers don't even know their own children and have to call them "You! what's-your-name!"

[. . .] The government puts no restrictions on men's freedom. It doesn't insist upon their responsibilities, so it is not surprising that young men are found roaming about at night, spreading AIDS.

The women were delighted, cheering him on. The rhetorical flourishes were deceptive, however, as the elderly man again deflected blame on to "young men." His continuous reiteration of the word "we" is also deceptive, for he does not mean himself. This was most apparent when he spoke of how fathers did not take an interest in their children's schooling and how they had no idea when children had failed exams. Everyone knew that his own son was completing high school, and a daughter followed the next year – one of less than a handful from this village. What he was doing was to relate biological fatherhood with a variety of ways of playing that masculine role, and implying that fathers had to change if there was to be any hope of combating AIDS.

Here, then, is some evidence of men's growing awareness that their gendered identity is in question, and that their mode of self-definition as men is linked to the spread of AIDS, directly or indirectly. More than one definition of "masculinity" also emerges, with the key differences being defined by age/generation and by marital and reproductive status. These are not antithetical positions; it is evident that young unmarried men are simply apprentices who will eventually adopt the *gravitas* of older men. Older men play to a script of authoritative and wise leadership, young men are permitted to sow their wild oats; both modes are seen as legitimate ways of expressing manhood. But herein lies the rub, as one elderly man put it: "If we look at the people who are dying of this illness it is young people – it is not the old (*wazee*). They go to Tanga, Dar and other places [large cities] and then we are shocked to find them coming home to die." They are shocked as fathers and as men to find that sowing wild oats reaps death. And with all their masculine and parental authority, they cannot save the young men who "don't listen."

SOUTH AFRICA

AIDS, Rape, and Masculine Crisis

Kerry Cullinan*

As South African men struggle to define their identity, researchers grapple with what has made this country's men into what they are.

---

*From Kerry Cullinan, "Men in Crisis," *Health-E News Service*, 8 July 2003. http://archives. healthdev.net/gender-aids/msg00605.html. The research cited in this excerpt was presented at a conference on "Sex and Secrecy" held at Witwatersrand University in July 2003.

The South African man's reputation is in crisis. He is held responsible for one of the world's highest rape rates, including the rape of children and babies. He perpetrates domestic violence, which is commonplace. And womanizers who prefer condom-less sex are driving the HIV/AIDS epidemic, experts tell us.

A range of researchers grappling with what has, and is, framing this male identity have identified economic circumstances, the new political order and HIV/AIDS as important factors. How the word "isoka" has evolved is an important indicator of how masculinity has changed, says Mark Hunter, a doctoral student from the University of California at Berkeley.

In the early 1900s, the word was associated with coming of sexual age and referred to young men who were popular with women. Generally, an *isoka* had two or three girlfriends, with whom he often practiced thigh sex (*ukusoma*) rather than penetrative sex, says Hunter who has been conducting research in Mandeni in KwaZulu-Natal.

This was seen as a youthful phase and he was expected to marry one of his girl-friends. A playboy who didn't marry was denigrated as *isoka lamanyala* (dirty), or a man who had gone too far. Marriage and the maintenance of a homestead were seen as the ultimate expression of manhood. But by the end of the 20th century, high unem-ployment and the high price of *ilobolo* (bridewealth) made marriage unaffordable to many men. Hunter says all but one of the men over 60 he interviewed were married, whereas virtually none of those under 35 were.

With few prospects of marriage, *isoka* manhood was now characterized simply by having penetrative sex with multiple partners. Thus, what was once a youthful phase had become an end in itself. But, says Hunter, the association between successful man-hood and many partners is currently being challenged by AIDS and *isoka* is coming again to be associated with dirt and irresponsibility.

"Unlike funerals, weddings in Sumdumbili are a rare event. Day by day, funeral by funeral, AIDS bears harder down on the *isoka* masculinity," says Hunter. "The symp-toms couldn't be more emasculating and demasculinizing: some of the most virile, popular and independent bodies are steadily transformed into diseased and dependent skeletons, shunned by friends and neighbors.

"Indeed, it is at the many funerals, as mourners walk in a slow circle around the cof-fin, taking a shock[ed] glance at the deceased's diminutive body, where the contradic-tions of *isoka* are most tragically played out. Consequently, men and masculinities are under huge scrutiny and critique."

While AIDS may be curbing multiple sex partners in Mandeni, many residents of Bushbuckridge believe that democracy has led to the escalation of rape in their area. In interviews with Isak Niehaus of the University of Pretoria, residents argued that the increase in rape could be blamed on a loss of control by the apartheid regime, chiefs and parents, all of whom meted out harsh punishments.

"There are no more rules. The original chiefs are dead and their sons are powerless," said one, while another remarked: "Now everyone is doing it." [. . .]

In examining the circumstances of 45 rapes, Niehaus concludes that "the clear majority of rapists were disadvantaged men who raped women to mimic masculine domination. They were sexually inexperienced youngsters, unemployed men who failed at being providers and senior men who perceived their dominant position within the household as being under threat." Seventeen of the rapes were by gangs, and Niehaus concludes the motives were "male bonding and sexual socialization."

To demonstrate this, Niehaus tells the story of a gang rape witnessed by one of his informants at his cousin's house. A youngster arrived with his girlfriend. She was plied with alcohol, and raped by seven boys. "When I got into the room, I saw the guys. They were busy screwing her – the one after the other," said the informant. "The boys were drunk and lay next to the bed. They would say 'my turn.' She was unconscious when they screwed her. It was all night long. One man said that he wanted to screw her for the fourth time. I wanted to join them and I had already taken my pants off. But my cousin discouraged me. He said this could land me into trouble." Niehaus says his informant told him that the young man had offered his girlfriend to his friends because "he was the youngest member of the group and wished to win their friendship."

While Bushbuckridge residents may blame the rise in rape on democracy, Wits [Witwatersrand] University's Liz Walker has found that the post-1994 political changes have had a positive impact on a small group of men in Alexandra township. Faced with a sense of individual crisis over their role as men, often as a result of being involved in domestic violence, they had been inspired to join an organization called Men For Change and try to find a new role for themselves.

The 1996 Constitution, and the policies and laws that followed it, have introduced a "constitutional sexuality" which promotes gender equality, recognizes gays and lesbians, and has allowed citizens access to previously unavailable books, films and magazines and adult sex shops, says Walker. But this "very liberal version of constitutional sexuality does not speak to many masculinities of the past" that are "steeped in violence and authoritarianism." Instead, it promotes the ideal man as one "who is non-violent, a good father and husband, employed and able to provide for his family," says Walker. While the "old masculinity" was destabilized, men were unsure how to construct a new one or to relate to women as equals.

"You know, the biggest problem facing men today is women," 28-year-old Tumi tells Walker. "Women are emancipated now. They are much more self-sufficient, they are able to do things for themselves. They don't need us men to survive."

Mandla (33) joined Men For Change after being charged with beating his pregnant girlfriend. He admitted that "I abuse her still" even though "I want to change."

Of the 17 men interviewed, Walker says one striking common feature was the violence they had witnessed or experienced, often from their fathers, while growing up. But the men attracted to MFC wanted a different destiny to that of their fathers, and were often motivated by wanting to be good fathers to their children.

"Confusion and uncertainty around the nature of masculinity and male sexuality, and the expectations men have of themselves, each other and women are contested and in crisis, giving rise to new notions of manhood," concludes Walker. Time will tell whether these new notions of manhood – mitigated by AIDS, gender equality and economic hardship – enable South African men to relate to women as equals.

SOUTH AFRICA

Working Together

Alex Doniach and Dean Peacock*

In Johannesburg's notoriously rough inner-city community of Hillbrow, refugee men have come together despite ethnic differences that have elsewhere led to genocide, to provide each other with support and to challenge the gender stereotypes that threaten men's and women's well-being.

Pascal Akimana shivers when he thinks of the atrocities he witnessed in the Burundian civil war. The women who were forced to murder their own children by soldiers. The men who beat him with stones until he cried in pain. Today, he is a refugee living safely in Johannesburg, but he is still haunted by the nightmares of his past.

Akimana, 24 years old, is a small man with high cheekbones, a focused stare and a soft voice. He comes from a Hutu family, and was almost killed three times by the Tutsi rebel army. Although he was trained to hate and kill Tutsis in Burundi, he is one of almost 2,000 Burundian refugees who, on South African soil, have learned to forgive. "In South Africa we are all brothers. What tribe you were born into is irrelevant here," Akimana said. But not all refugees who flee safely to Johannesburg are as optimistic as Akimana. Many are angry and traumatized, he said.

According to the United Nations refugee agency (UNHCR), Akimana is one of more than 500,000 Burundian refugees who fled war and death in their home country and poured across African borders, including South Africa's. When Akimana reached South Africa, his feet were swollen and bloody. He had no money, and slept on the streets until he found odd jobs and was able to buy food and rent a room in the suburb of Yeoville. But like many others, Akimana was thankful to have finally reached safety. In South Africa, he qualified for refugee status, and though he struggles to survive, he no longer lives in constant fear of torture or death.

Bonaventure Kageruka tells a similar story. He, too, experienced the horrors of war and ethnic hatred. As a Rwandan Tutsi, only he and his sister of his entire family survived the 1994 genocide; she was raped and is now living with HIV. "We used to be called cockroaches and snakes," he says. "I was deprived of all fundamental rights. We could

---

*Special to this volume.

Pascal Akimana and Bonaventure Kageruka participate in a Men as Partners workshop with other refugees from Rwanda, Burundi, and the Democratic Republic of Congo; Hillbrow neighborhood, Johannesburg, South Africa (Oscar Gutierrez)

not have a say because we were a minority. This situation resulted in many civil wars and eventually the genocide in 1994, where around one million Tutsis and some Hutus lost their lives in 100 days at the hands of the Hutu majority."* Kageruka traveled to South Africa nearly two years ago. Here, his experiences have been decidedly mixed. On the one hand, he has received support from various refugee groups and faith-based organizations. But has also been held up at gunpoint on multiple occasions.

Like Kageruka and Akimana, Desire Masabarakrza, 34, has worked hard to make South Africa home. He sees himself as one of the refugees who have thrived since crossing the border into this country. He was forced to flee Burundi after the start of war because he came from a mixed home. His father was a Hutu and his mother a Tutsi, leaving him with no safe side to take. "I couldn't run to the Hutu side or the Tutsi side so I decided to run away," Masabarakrza said. "I ran for eight years as I wanted to get far, far from Burundi. People with money ran to Europe. People without money walked south.

Masabarakrza is a tall man with a wide grin and gregarious demeanor. Sitting in the well-decorated living room of his Yeoville apartment, he smiles as he talks candidly about the harrowing years he struggled to start a new life in Johannesburg. "When I finally made it into Johannesburg I only had one rand," Masabarakrza said. "I spent 50 cents to buy a carton of eggs and 50 cents to make a phone call. When I put the change

---

*See also selection "The Killers."

in the phone, the machine ate my money." Masabarakrza's spirit wasn't deterred. He had a contact in South Africa, another Burundian, who he was told could help him. Masabarakrza's didn't eat for the first three days in the country, but eventually he connected with other refugees and found a bed to sleep on. Home Affairs granted him refugee status, and he worked hard. "I did anything to make money without stealing," he said. "I sold tomatoes on the street, I worked as a security guard." Eventually he worked his way into a stable job as an electrician, his trained profession in Burundi. Today, he lives a good life in a well-furnished home with his wife and three-year-old daughter. "Life is good," he says.

Not all refugees are so lucky. Deo Hakizimana, 41, sits on a fold-out chair in his one-room home. His two small children lie on the king-sized bed that stretches almost the entire length of the room. They chew on apples and giggle while the voices of an Afrikaans sitcom softly hums on the family's small television.

With pained eyes, he explains that finding work is almost impossible. He struggles to pay rent and feed his family. He holds a piece of white paper protected by a plastic slipcover. This document, creased from years of use, is one of his most valued possessions. It is the only proof of his identity, and a key to his new life in South Africa. "Once the rebellion started, I decided to leave the country because I feared my family would be killed," Hakizimana said. He snuck out of Burundi on foot and eventually wound up in South Africa where he declared himself a refugee and was granted asylum.

Hakizimana has lived in Johannesburg for five years, and still has not received the little red book that grants him refugee status and proves his legal right to get a job in South Africa. The only document he can show employers is the slip of paper he received from Home Affairs granting him asylum from Burundi. "This isn't identification," Hakizimana said, shaking the paper. "How do you expect to get a job with this? Employers take one look at it and turn me away." He is one of thousands of refugees who face innumerable daily challenges.

Since 1993, the Department of Home Affairs has maintained an open-door policy that grants asylum and refugee status to many who apply. Theoretically, refugees are guaranteed the same rights and privileges as any South African – and even more, because they are also granted international protection, said Nkosana Sibuyi, spokesperson for the department.

But life in South Africa has not been easy for refugees, where the quality of life is often poor. Over two-thirds of refugees had experience in skilled and semi-skilled jobs upon arrival in South Africa, but here most of them are unable to find work, according to the UNHCR. Nonetheless, many would rather struggle here than return to a country ravaged by decades of brutal tensions and civil war.

Malita Sunjic, the UNHCR spokesperson for South Africa, said UN policy in South Africa does not give additional money or aid to refugees, because instead they are given the right to live in the country and enjoy the benefits of the national constitution. This means they have access to healthcare and education for their children. "Once they come here, they get the freedom of not living in a refugee camp, but they also get the responsibility of fending for themselves," Sunjic said.

With little support from the South African government or the United Nations, refugees like Pascal Akimana, Bonaventure Kageruka, Desire Masabarakrza, and Deo Hakizimana have found support, a sense of purpose and greater optimism through their participation in the South African Men as Partners Network, an initiative coordinated by EngenderHealth in collaboration with dozens of other organizations across the country.

Invited to attend MAP workshops at the Esselen Street Clinic in Hillbrow, Akimana and Kageruka spent four days in intense reflection with other refugee men from Francophone Africa, talking about their experiences of male socialization. Led by a mixed team of South African and refugee facilitators, they explored their understandings of masculinity and manhood. Akimana remembers, "it didn't matter which country we were from, we had all been taught that being a "real man" meant that we should always be in charge, never back down, have the final word, drink alcohol, and have multiple sexual partners to prove our manliness." The facilitators then asked the group to consider the implications of these messages for men and women's health. Kageruka says, "as the facilitators pushed us to think about what it meant to us to be a man, I realized that our socialization as men contributes to all sorts of problems – war, rape, domestic violence, and HIV/AIDS."

Reflecting on his own past as a war survivor and a refugee, Akimana quickly saw the parallels between his own experiences of violence and the violence that women face on a daily basis. "I saw that every day women are forced to live with the same sort of fear I experienced in Burundi and on my journey to South Africa. Like us refugees, it is difficult for them to exercise their rights. Like us, they are always wondering whether they are safe."

Both said they had been looking for a way to make a difference in their new country. Akimana says, "I realized at that workshop that I could work with other refugee men to address violence and HIV/AIDS." He quickly signed up as a volunteer with Engender-Health, and now runs MAP workshops and organizes community education events in Johannesburg's inner city.

Kageruka says there is a clear need to work with refugee men. Thousands of refugees flow into Johannesburg each year, and they comprise some of the poorest of the city's residents. The high levels of trauma among the fledgling communities that reside mostly in Hillbrow, Berea and Yeoville can lead to high levels of gender-based violence. Similarly, the high concentration of single men living in isolated communities far from their families has supported the emergence of many brothels and numerous commercial sex workers, a situation often associated with both HIV transmission and violence against sex workers. "We put so much focus on South Africans, but someone needs to help the refugees," Kageruka said. "I feel that within a supportive group, we can help make a change."

On a Tuesday morning in Hillbrow, Kageruka and Akimana are at work together, Hutu and Tutsi standing on either side of a flipchart at the front of the room, talking about violence, gender equality, and human rights. Twenty-nine men and women gather in a brick room in the Esselen Clinic for a MAP workshop. Under fluorescent lighting, the two men lead the group of refugees in activities and discussions that invite men and women to speak about the challenges and rewards of living in their new city. The group also discusses male role models, and the participants testify about the qualities they admire in men. Kageruka shares his experiences with the group, saying that sexism and gender roles are ingrained in Rwandans at a young age. "If you look at equity in homes, women work like donkeys, but what about the men who claim to be physically and morally strong? Do they use their power positively? In my home, my mother worked like a machine, looking after six children, three boys and girls and helping throughout the house. I never saw my father helping my mother. I witnessed this situation myself and I wondered, what has my mother done to undergo this diabolical situation?"

The messages that Kageruka and Akimana seek to convey are heard by the group's participants. "Before I attended the workshop, I never thought of any of these things," said Laurence Kasadi, a refugee from DRC Congo. "In our country we often see women as machines, as objects. Now I have started to analyze a woman's role in society. It isn't something I took the time to do before." Informed by his own background, Kageruka says, "I understand how freedom costs an arm and a leg, but with my voice I will raise it to set women free and stop HIV and AIDS."

In an effort to provide continuity and follow up to those men who have participated in a MAP workshop and want to do something about gender inequality and HIV/AIDS, Akimana, Kageruka and colleagues from EngenderHealth started a MAP Community Action Team, or MAP CAT, which meets every other Saturday. CATs were introduced by EngenderHealth to emphasize community action and promote community owner-ship. These groups now reach out to men in *shebeens* [bars], on the street, at work, or in taxis.

What makes the inner-city MAP CAT initiative unique is its focus on supporting refugee men who work to end violence against women and address HIV and AIDS. One of the Hillbrow CAT members, Albert Paye from the DRC Congo, is a skilled artist, and has developed a series of posters depicting scenes of domestic and sexual violence or risky sexual behavior. These posters are hung around public places such as shopping centers; a MAP CAT volunteer stands near and asks passers-by their reaction to the images, in an effort to spark dialogue about gender and HIV/AIDS.

Nhlanhla Mabizela, a 32-year-old MAP project coordinator and facilitator for the Hillbrow MAP CAT, said CATs have helped in Hillbrow by targeting men who might not otherwise receive messages about HIV, violence and gender equality. "The Hillbrow program reaches men who are otherwise often neglected or ostracized, but who have a critical role to play in addressing HIV and AIDS," he says. "We hope the MAP CAT men will become more involved in a range of activities, including home-based care for people ill with AIDS and broader community education. And as they do this, we hope that South Africans will recognize their contribution to the country we share."

AFRICA

Global Man, Southern Star

Nandi Ayo Bole*

Remember daddy, when I was tiny and read the world in your voice and eyes and you pointed to a place beyond that only you could see (but I believed you). I do not remember the words you used, but the feeling of what you said was: *Inside the star is the heart of God, and inside that heart is where home was. That the earth held us to herself, and if she did not, we being creatures of endless spaces, would float dreamless around the entire cosmos.*

*   *   *

Dear Daddy:

(I know writing from the locus of the "third world" – wherever that is – it is not expected to call one's daddy, daddy. But being your daughter means that I am a mistress escape artist gleefully slipping out of whatever limiting, delineating categories the world might try to squash me into.) I am at the cusp of 40, still calling you daddy and happily peering through a window into the heart of you, invoking insights for an anthology of men from "our" world. But in thinking of you I find that world difficult to locate. It keeps blurring its boundaries and stretching into the furthest black hole in the soul of the universe. A million stories of you sneak into this window, each one proclaiming "the-who-you-are" "thing." Who are you, daddy?

You are "retired," but not from life. You are currently nurturing your new "foundry": Sulwe Incorporated, something of your own. But you were Chief Executive Officer of a high-profile, internationally recognized organization. I used to laugh at the listings of boards in which you were director and Chairman. You needed two business cards to list 40 – the ones you wanted known. Board member, leader of numerous committees in as many organizations of the world as there ever could be (I exaggerate but a little). Patriot, African, humanist, human being, husband and daddy.

The "daddiness" of you: An image of me, six years old and home from that first awful venture into life – school. Ah! The feeling of being vanquished by the strangeness of it all. I forced tears back until you came home. Then a torrential weep storm launched itself at you, burrowing into your heart, hiding from the world.

I used to think all fathers sang: "Big girl, don't cry. Big girl, don't cry." (You should now know that I did not want to be a big girl that evening. It meant drifting into eerie currents on a cold sea, away from the harbor of home – home is where you snore!) You laughed a big all-is-right-with-the-world laugh. But, tell me daddy, when you laughed – I always did wonder why there were already tears in your eyes.

---

*Special to this volume.

Fast forward, 22 years later and I am dashing off somewhere to "seek meaning," to "understand life" (bankrolled by you – was there a father ever so resigned to embracing such a peripatetic offspring?). You said, remember – you said: "Baby" (all nine of us are baby to you – the variation is in tone), "Baby, your daddy is as constant as the Southern Star. You *will* find me if you ever get lost." (Worn are the paths – in sky, sea, heart and life that have taken me back to the safe den of your presence, you know.) I race through life certain of only one thing, the Southern Star – come bomb, tracer fire, terrorists called John and Armageddon – stands firm.

It has taken a long, long time to comprehend that not many Daddy-Men make a detour after a tiring conference to deliver a winter coat to penurious daughters half a world away. Few Leaders-of-Delegations tell bemused deans: "She gets very cold." (Resigned glee when class was interrupted and the tutor reading a note said, baffled: "Your daddy is here.")

I know. I know he is here.

Daddy, you are an eclectic mix of realist-voyager-dreamer-seeker. I think you are an artist of life. The canvas is the whole cloth of your being. You are not afraid of what is drawn on you, but you mind very much that what your children shall see in their life is beauty. You have quietly thrown yourself before that which might horrify us – including the ghastly partners-to-be some of us have paraded before you – and you allowed yourself to be terrorized for us. You are the voice who tells his children, even when there are new hurt lines etched into your face, that "Life is beautiful. Life is good . . . Imagine . . . and love its immense possibilities."

Possibilities.

You are Africa for me because your life tells me – even when sometimes I shudder in disgust – of the possibility of Africa. I never understood why you would not skip our crumbling capitals and go to New York, Geneva, Vienna . . . go and live the life of a well-taken-care-of UN worker. You "set your face" and chose to stay close to the hearth, the land in which you have relentlessly believed. When a wave of debilitating, puerile national rhetoric assails you, when I see you analyze the news and your face is craggy with . . . worry . . . sorrow . . . do you regret your choice to stay? Most likely not.

If experience refines the soul, then the best of this landscape lives in your heart. And it is profoundly glorious, eternally true and therefore beautiful. You are a handsome man – but life has chiseled its longing into your face and used a palette filled with your sweat, broken hopes, and blood and secret tears. (I have seen your tears, daddy, even though you have hidden them from us your children – I saw them once and became afraid, because I knew that if you could cry then the world was not perfect.) You are a man of humor with the wickedest belly-laugh I know of, infecting all who hear it. You recognize and relish the absurd that masquerades as "the all-serious." You can be relied on to charm a smile out of a sour-mouthed fishwife.

You who sustain the idea of an integrated national being have also been accused of being of the wrong ethnic group, which rendered you "unqualified" to take a job that your qualifications exceeded. So, daddy, even if a man's ethnic origin colors his being, how does this make you less of a human being, a minor citizen in a much yearned-for state?

I have a question. When ideals meet meaningless prejudice, how do you keep your soul from shattering? The droll gleam in your eye veils your deeply sensitive soul. (There are few humans I know who count the eyelashes on a butterfly.) When men choose to be their little tribes first – men who should have been your compatriots in nation-building – when those men judge you wanting, render you jobless, because your first language is different from theirs, why didn't you leave?

I have a picture of you when you were in Europe. You are what my friend would call a "pirate." Good-looking, like grandfather – dapper, slender and laughing. Mother says you were an excellent student *and* a king of the dance floor. I compare that with another picture of a man whom your country, the continent you love, has shuffled into low places. But because it is you, those low places became high.

In time you were asked to take up the job of architect of what must have been the most difficult work in our country at that time. We knew the nights you stayed up imagining and planning. You said: "Just a few men and women who love this land is all we need . . . if we could love this land . . ." Then one day, after everything, you quietly walked away when the unimaginative, seeing what you had done, jockeyed into position to take credit for your job well done.

You are the man who left his retirement party and walked to his car with his wife by his side, and the huge gap he had filled for half a century quickly closed behind him. The party continued. Daddy, after years of dedicated duty to an organization, behind your stoic gaze, what whispers to you? Does it shake your faith when those who used to swarm around you have lost your phone number? How about the unexpected battles, duels demanded by those you once nurtured? Simple matters turned into wars, so that you would . . . what? Stoop? (But time and age will give you that anyway.) Dear daddy, who stubbornly imagines light in that heartbreak space called our country, our continent. (You call it home, so I do. To deny it would be to deny you.)

But look! I also see, through this small memory-window, that you are the tall, greying man who roars a massive laugh. Around him, holding onto his coattails are his children, sons and daughters, dogs and cats and a woman, your wife of four decades, whose eyes still light up when you walk into the room. You are laughing because your granddaughter just gazed up at you, her head tilted back and eyes huge with the certainty of the innocent, and said, "*bes' ganpa in evywhere.*"

I know. Daddy, here, in this memory place, at the cusp of 40, I suddenly begin to see that the Southern star is a sentinel-warrior of profound integrity who loves even when the fickle world – whichever world that is – tumbles down. When the debris has settled and the night is at its darkest, the star gleams strongest, and its calm, knowing gaze encompasses the entire cosmos, asking little for itself.

Lighting anyway. Loving anyway.

ABOUT THE ORIGINAL CONTRIBUTORS

Ali Nobil Ahmad is conducting doctoral research on Pakistani migration at the Department of History of the European University Institute, Florence. He has worked as a journalist and a Research Officer at University College, London. His publications include articles in *Third Text, Wasafiri,* and *Metamute.* Email: ali.ahmad@iue.it

Mario I. Aguilar, Ph.D., is Director of the Centre for the Study of Religion and Politics at the University of St. Andrews, Scotland. He is the author of several books, including *A Social History of the Catholic Church in Chile, Vol. 1: The First Period of the Pinochet Government 1973–1980* (Edwin Mellen Press, 2004) and *Vol. 2: Cardinal Raul Silva Henriquez 1907–1999* (Edwin Mellen Press, 2005). Email: mia2@st-andrews.ac.uk

Tlahtoki Aguirre is a MacArthur Fellow and Ph.D. candidate in the Department of American Studies at the University of Minnesota, Twin Cities, where he currently teaches courses on cultural studies, indigenous movements, and critical theory in the Department of Chicano Studies. His teaching, research, and community activities revolve around social justice and healing among indigenous Mexican, Chicano, and related populations. Email: agui0017@umn.edu

George Olusola Ajibade is a Lecturer in the Department of African Languages and Literatures at the Obafemi Awolowo University, Ile-Ife, Nigeria. He is currently an Alexander von Humboldt Research Fellow at the University of Bayreuth, Germany. His research interests are African cultural studies, critical social and literary theories, and folklore. He is the author of a number of articles on Yorùbá culture. Email: solajibade@yahoo.com

Shyamal Bagchee, Ph.D., was born in Kolkata and lives in rural northern Alberta. He teaches poetry and poetics at the University of Alberta, and is the author of two volumes of poetry: *Gabardine* (Tsar Publications, 2004) and *A Scrupulous Meanness* (Buschek, 2004). A third volume, *Nightsoil, or the Book of the Lotus,* is currently in press. His poems have appeared in literary magazines worldwide. Email: shyamal.bagchee@ualberta.ca

Dixie Beadle is a Ph.D. candidate in the Department of Theater and Drama at the University of Wisconsin–Madison, specializing in North and sub-Saharan African performance, with an additional interest in Middle Eastern theater. Her articles about North African and Middle Eastern theater have appeared in the journal *Theatron,* for which she is now an Associate Editor. Her dissertation will examine the form and content of intellectual African theater in the post-independence era as an educational and activist tool. Email: dixie_beadle@yahoo.com

Amy Berson is a Master's student in Human Rights at Curtin University, Western Australia. She has lived in Uganda, where she worked on a sport-for-health project and spent a considerable period of time in the war-afflicted north. She now works with people with disabilities, refugees, migrants, and indigenous youth in Western Australia, and is involved in advocacy to end the war in northern Uganda by peaceful means. Email: amy_berson@yahoo.com.au

Mona Bhan is a Ph.D. candidate in the Department of Anthropology at Rutgers University, New Jersey. Her research is based on 17 months of ethnographic fieldwork in Kargil (Jammu and Kashmir) on issues of development, decentralization, militarization, and citizenship. She received her MA in Anthropology from Delhi University in 1999. Email: monabhan@yahoo.com

Monica Campbell is a freelance journalist based in Mexico City. As a contributor to *The Christian Science Monitor, The San Francisco Chronicle,* and *Newsweek,* she has covered topics ranging from a village's fight against a planned open-pit mine to staging areas for migrants preparing to cross the US–Mexico border. Formerly a deputy Latin America editor in New York for the Economist Intelligence Unit, part of *The Economist* magazine group, she has covered political and economic issues throughout Latin America and the Caribbean. Email: moni.campbell@gmail.com

Aje Carlbom holds a Ph.D. in Social Anthropology from the University of Lund, Sweden. He is currently working on a project related to psychological well-being among marginalized immigrant communities in the city of Malmö, Sweden, administered by Malmö University. He is also finishing a project on Islam in Europe and the ideological struggle to define "Euro-Islam." Email: aje.carlbom@djingis.se

Jungbong Choi, Ph.D., is Assistant Professor in the Department of Cinema Studies at New York University. He is co-editor of *Television, Japan, and Globalization* (University of Michigan Press, forthcoming), and is currently working on a book called *The Rise of East Asian Media Sphere.* Email: jbc7@nyu.edu

Mark Clifford has worked as a human rights advocate, outreach support coordinator, and program manager with Jamaican and international organizations, addressing topics related to citizenship, gender, and sexuality. He is exploring these issues further through a postgraduate degree in Cultural Studies at the University of the West Indies, Mona, and is currently co-editing a book on Caribbean intra-regional migration. Email: mark.clifford@uwimona.edu.jm

Peter Collins is an independent Western Australian journalist and writer. Over the past two decades, he has researched and documented a "final wave" of cultural dispossession of Australian aboriginal tribes, including the theft of sacred objects containing early human knowledge from remote tribal custodians. His recent work concerns the effects of land-settlement issues on the social and political stability of contemporary tribespeople. He lives and works in Perth. Email: peter.g.collins@bigpond.com

Daniel Conway, Ph.D., is a Postdoctoral Fellow in Politics at the University of Bristol. His research focuses on masculinities and war resistance in the South African apartheid state. He also has wider research and teaching interests in gender, development, and sexuality. Email: Daniel.Conway@Bristol.ac.uk

Don Conway-Long, Ph.D., is Assistant Professor in the Behavior and Social Sciences Department at Webster University in St. Louis, Missouri. He has worked on critical studies of men and masculinities since the late 1970s. Email: dconlong@webster.edu

Donald Cosentino, Ph.D., is Professor of World Arts and Cultures at the University of California, Los Angeles. Vodou and related religions of the Black Atlantic have been a central focus of his research. His publications include *The Sacred Arts of Haitian Vodou* (UCLA Fowler Museum of Cultural History, 1995); *Vodou Things: The Art of Pierrot Barra and Marie Cassaise* (University Press of Mississippi, 1998); and *Divine Revolution: The Art of Édouard Duval-Carrié* (UCLA Fowler Museum of Cultural History, 2004). He is currently writing a book about a Los Angeles *santero* and his Kongo spirit guide. Email: cosentin@arts.ucla.edu

Dina Dahbany-Miraglia, Ph.D., is a linguistic anthropologist and communication specialist who has published several articles and lectured on the subject of Yemenite Jews, including their languages, their performance art, and their emigration to Palestine, Israel, and the United States. She has just published a *muwashshah*, a form of Andalusian strophic poetry, and is the first Yemenite woman to do so. She is currently working on a book titled *Yemenites in America: The Invisible Jews*. Email: ddmqcc@att.net

Shukria Dini is a Canadian Consortium on Human Security Fellow who is currently conducting doctoral research on the roles of Somali women's organizations in peacebuilding and post-conflict reconstruction. She is a Ph.D. candidate at the School of Women's Studies, York University, Toronto. A former refugee from Somalia, she has lived in Canada since 1993. Email: sdini@hotmail.com

Alex Doniach is a freelance writer living in the United States. Email: alexdoniach@gmail.com

Jane Gilbert is a Consultant Clinical Psychologist based in the United Kingdom. After many years in the UK National Health Service, she is now a freelancer specializing in the design and facilitation of workshops and training on psychological and mental health issues in cross-cultural contexts, particularly in Africa. She is available for consultancy to NGOs and Mental Health Services. Email: janegilbert@janegilbert.entadsl.com

Iklim Göksel is a Ph.D. candidate in the Department of English at the University of Illinois, Chicago. Her dissertation project, *Rhetorics of Virginity in Turkish Modernity*, is an ethnographic study that looks at how virginity is articulated and manifested in Turkish daily life. She holds a BA in English Literature from Bilkent University in

Ankara, Turkey, and an MA in English from Eastern Michigan University, Ypsilanti, USA. Email: igoksel@msn.com

Nate Haken is a Master's candidate at the American University's School of International Service in Washington, DC. His fiction and *haiku* poetry have been published or are forthcoming in *The Massachusetts Review, Kaleidoscope, The Iconoclast, Modern Haiku,* and other publications. Selections from his work can be found at www.natehaken.blogspot.com. Email: natehaken@yahoo.com

Nicole Hallett has spent time researching human rights in Bangladesh, Korea, South Africa, and Denmark. She is Executive Director of the Bangladesh Children's Educational Endowment, an organization that gives educational opportunities to youth in rural Bangladesh. She received an M.Sc. in Refugee Studies from the University of Oxford, and is currently studying for her J.D. at Yale Law School. Email: nicole.hallett@gmail.com

Jan Jansen, Ph.D., is Lecturer in the Department of Cultural Anthropology and Development Sociology at Leiden University, Netherlands. His main areas of interest are Mande oral tradition and sociocultural change in West Africa. He is co-editor of the monograph series *African Sources for African History* (Brill Publishers). Email: JANSENJ@FSW.leidenuniv.nl

Smita Tewari Jassal, Ph.D., teaches Gender and Development in the Department of South Asian Studies at the Nitze School of Advanced International Studies, Johns Hopkins University, Washington, DC. She is author of *Daughters of the Earth: Women and Land in Uttar Pradesh* (Manohar, 2001), and co-editor, with Eyal Ben-Ari, of *The Partition Motif in Contemporary Conflicts* (Sage, forthcoming). Her articles have appeared in *The Journal of Peasant Studies, Contributions to Indian Sociology,* and the *Indian Journal of Gender Studies.* She is currently working on folk cultures and an ethnography of communities along the Ganges River. Email: stj89@yahoo.com

Adam Jones, Ph.D., is Associate Research Fellow for 2005–7 in the Genocide Studies Program at Yale University. His most recent book is *Genocide: A Comprehensive Introduction* (Routledge, 2006). He has edited two other books on genocide and authored two on mass media and political transition. His writings on gender and international politics have appeared in *Review of International Studies, Ethnic and Racial Studies, Journal of Human Rights,* and other publications. Website: http://adamjones.freeservers.com. Email: adamj_jones@hotmail.com

Abdul-Karim Khan, Ph.D., is Associate Professor of History in the University of Hawaii System. He is author of *Afghanistan: A Global Studies Handbook* (ABC-CLIO, 2006). Email: khana@hawaii.edu

Leslie Lewis, MPH, MA, is an advanced Ph.D. candidate in the Department of Anthropology at the University of California, San Diego. She is currently a Research Fellow at the Institute for Gender and Women's Studies at the American University in Cairo, where she is completing her field research. Email: lrlewis@hirecapital.com

Sabine Luning, Ph.D., is Lecturer in the Department of Cultural Anthropology and Development Sociology at Leiden University, Netherlands. She is an anthropologist by training, with primary research interests in the dynamics of ritual and the anthropology of money. She is the author of a book and several articles about ritual practices and politics in the Mossi chiefdom of Maane, Burkina Faso. Her recent fieldwork examines artisanal gold mining in Burkina Faso, with an emphasis on social practices of mapping, policing, and exploiting gold sites. Email: sluning@fsw.leidenuniv.nl

Susan P. Mains, Ph.D., is Lecturer in Human Geography at the University of the West Indies, Mona. Her research focuses on the themes of gender, diaspora, transnationalism, and postcolonialism in relation to Jamaican migration and tourism, Caribbean cities, and media representations of place. She is currently working on a documentary film titled *Ackee, Burgers, and Chips: An ABC of Jamaican Migration*, as well as an accompanying book. Her articles have appeared in *Social and Cultural Geography*, *Hagar: International Review of Social Science*, *GeoJournal*, and other journals. Email: susanroaming@yahoo.com

Douglas Midgett, Ph.D., is Associate Professor of Anthropology at the University of Iowa. He has conducted research for over three decades in the Eastern Caribbean on topics including language and expressive culture, electoral politics, trade union history, land tenure systems, and migration. Email: douglas-midgett@uiowa.edu

Naeem Mohaiemen is a filmmaker and visual artist. His essay "Islam and Hip-Hop" will be published in DJ Spooky, ed., *Sound Unbound* (MIT Press, forthcoming). He directs the Visible Collective, whose project *Disappeared In America* (disappearedinamerica.org) has been shown at various galleries, including the 2006 Whitney Biennial. His film on image politics in struggles between "radical" and "moderate" Muslims, *Muslims or Heretics?* (muslimsorheretics.org), was screened in the British House of Lords and other venues. Email: info@disappearedinamerica.org

Knolly Moses, a Trinidadian, lived in New York for over two decades. He has worked as a journalist for *Newsweek*, *Emerge*, and *Black Enterprise* magazines. His articles have also appeared in the *Washington Post*, *Elle*, *Essence*, and *Family Circle*. For the past 13 years, he has lived in Kingston, Jamaica, where he owns Panmedia, a new-media company. Email: kmoses@panmedia.com.jm

Nargis Nurullo-Khoja, Ph.D., is Senior Professor of History at the Technological University of Tajikistan. The author of many articles on gender and statehood, she is also Deputy Director of the Shahidi International Cultural Foundation, where she works to develop an international focus on intercultural relations. Email: nargis_fm@hotmail.com

Stella Nyanzi is a Ugandan medical anthropologist and a Ph.D. candidate at the London School of Hygiene and Tropical Medicine. Her doctoral thesis focuses on culture, sexuality, and health among Gambian youths. Since 1997, she has conducted qualitative research on sexuality and sexual behavior, reproductive health, breastfeeding practices, masculinities, and the idiom of HIV/AIDS in society, both in Uganda and in the Gambia. Email: snyanzi@yahoo.com

Tom Odhiambo is a Research Officer at the Wits Institute for Social and Economic Research, University of the Witwatersrand, Johannesburg. His main research area is African Studies, with a focus on African popular media, literature, and culture. He has published essays on Kenyan popular literature, and is currently conducting research on transnationalism in African popular media. Email: ongidio@yahoo.co.uk

Dean Peacock is co-director of Sonke Gender Justice (www.genderjustice.org.za) and an activist with the Men as Partners Network. The MAP Network consists of more than 50 civil society organizations working together to promote gender equality, end men's violence, and reduce the spread and impact of HIV and AIDS. Email: dean@genderjustice.org.za

Bob Pease, Ph.D., is Chair of Social Work in the School of Health and Social Development at Deakin University, Geelong, Australia. He is the author of *Men and Sexual Politics* (Dulwich Center Publications, 1997), *Recreating Men* (Sage, 2000), and *Men and Gender Relations* (Tertiary Press, 2002), and co-editor of *Transforming Social Work Practice* (Allen & Unwin, 1999), *Working with Men in the Human Services* (Allen & Unwin, 2001), *A Man's World? Changing Men's Practices in a Globalized World* (Zed, 2001), and *Critical Social Work* (Allen & Unwin, 2003). He is a founding member of Men Against Sexual Assault in Australia. Email: bob.pease@deakin.edu.au

Suren Pillay is Senior Lecturer in the Department of Political Studies at the University of the Western Cape, Cape Town, South Africa, where he teaches political theory and political philosophy. His research currently focuses on intersections of political violence and political identity in apartheid-era South Africa. Email: spillay@uwc.ac.za

Guy Podoler, Ph.D., teaches Korean history in the Department of East Asian Studies at Hebrew University, Jerusalem. His current field of research, on which he has published articles and book chapters, is nationalism and the relationship between history and memory in post-colonial South Korea. Email: gpodoler@gmail.com

Abel Polese is a Ph.D. candidate at L'École des Hautes Études en Sciences Sociales (EHESS) in Paris, and Visiting Lecturer at the Institute of Theology and Liberal Arts, Odessa, Ukraine. After focusing on the economic consequences of post-Soviet transition, he is now conducting research on changing identities in the Odessa region. He has also served as Coordinator of the SAVA Working Group in the postwar Balkans region. Email: abelpolese@yahoo.co.uk

Margaret Power, Ph.D., is Associate Professor of History at the Illinois Institute of Technology. She is the author of *Right-Wing Women in Chile* (Pennsylvania State University Press, 2002) and co-editor of *Right-Wing Women Around the World* (Routledge, 2002). She is also a political activist and active in the peace movement. Email: power@iit.edu

A. Sean Pue is a Ph.D. candidate in Middle East and Asian Languages and Cultures, as well as Comparative Literature and Society, at Columbia University in New York. Email: asp49@columbia.edu

Juan Carlos Ramírez Rodriguez, Ph.D., is Researcher and Lecturer in the Interdisciplinary Program for Gender Studies (PIEGE) at the Department of Regional Studies, University of Guadalajara, Mexico. Email: jucarlos@cucea.udg.mx

Ana Ruiz-Fodor is Assistant Professor of Humanities at Salem International University in West Virginia, specializing in language, communication, and history. She previously spent 15 years writing and editing for the Nicaraguan newspaper *La Prensa*. Her current work focuses on twentieth-century studies of phenomenology in mystical thought. Email: inky124@adelphia.net

Guy Saville is a writer. After graduating from London University he became a freelance correspondent working mainly in South America and the Middle East. His articles have appeared in the *Daily Telegraph, Guardian* and *Independent* (UK) as well as publications in the US, Canada and Asia. He spent two years in Rio de Janeiro researching the phenomenon of Funk Balls, as well as filming a documentary on the subject. Email: guysaville@hotmail.com

Magid Shihade is a Ph.D. candidate in Middle Eastern Studies at the University of Washington. His dissertation explores the link between government policies and inter-communal/ethnic violence in Israel. Email: mshihade@u.washington.edu

Jason E. Strakes is a Ph.D. candidate in the Department of Politics and Policy at Claremont Graduate University. His primary research interests are conflict and security, and the politics of the developing world. His articles have appeared in the *Journal of Central Asian Studies* and *Journal of Muslim Minority Affairs*. He is an affiliate of the Mindanao Research Agenda based at the Third World Studies Center, University of the Philippines, Diliman. Email: JNIGHT99@cs.com

Madia Thomson, Ph.D., is an ethnographic historian. Her published works include the translations *Serving the Master: Slavery and Society in Nineteenth-Century Morocco* (St. Martin's Press, 1999) and a selection from "Feuilles dHôpital" ("Hospital Notes," a Lorand Gaspar manuscript) in *Critical Moments: Doctor and Nurse Narratives and Reflections*. She recently completed a manuscript titled *The Historical Present: Modernization, Slavery, and the Transformation of Social Hierarchy in Southwestern Morocco, 1860–2000*. Email: madiat2000@yahoo.com

Irina Vainovski-Mihai is Lecturer in Arabic Literature at Spiru Haret University, Bucharest, Romania. She has spent several years in various Arabic countries and published travel notes, essays, and research on literature and cultural studies, as well as translations from Arabic, Hungarian, and French. In 2005, her poetry was awarded the Naji Naaman Literary Prize. Email: ivainovski@hotmail.com

Thomas Michael Walle, M.Phil., is Research Fellow at Norwegian Social Research (NOVA). He is currently conducting doctoral research on masculinities in the Norwegian Pakistani community in Oslo. His earlier research focused on masculinities and gender relations in Lahore, Pakistan. Email: tmwalle@broadpark.no

Emily Wentzell is a Ph.D. candidate in the Department of Anthropology at the University of Michigan, Ann Arbor. Her research focuses on the social, psychological, and economic consequences of Mexican and American men's use of medical treatments for erectile dysfunction. Email: wentzell@umich.edu

Metasebia Woldemariam, Ph.D., is Associate Professor in Communication Studies at Plymouth State University in New Hampshire. Her research focuses on media and African representations. Email: metty123@yahoo.com

Robert Wyrod is a Ph.D. candidate in the Department of Sociology at the University of Chicago. His dissertation examines how AIDS is implicated in changing conceptions of masculinity in urban Uganda. Email: rjwyrod@uchicago.edu

Metin Yüksel is a Ph.D. candidate in the Department of Near Eastern Languages and Civilizations at the University of Chicago. He is currently focusing on Kurdish oral tradition in Turkey. Email: metin@uchicago.edu

Get a different perspective

- **A global perspective**

- **Independent, uncompromising reporting**

- **In-depth coverage of key international issues**

New Internationalist brings together editors and writers from around the world, providing you with a rich mix of international insights and viewpoints.

What's more, we bring you stories and analysis that you won't find in corporate owned media.

Each month *New Internationalist* tackles one pressing global issue. The subject is taken apart and looked at from all angles. The arguments are presented and alternatives given, leaving you with a complete insight and a fresh perspective.

New Internationalist – try something different

FREE! For a 3 month free trial respond now!
www.newint.org/free2 01858 4388896 (quote 2333)